Mobil
Travel Guide®

South

2007

Alabama

Arkansas

Kentucky

Louisiana

Mississippi

Tennessee

ExxonMobil
Travel Publications

D1208395

Acknowledgements

We gratefully acknowledge the help of our representatives for their efficient and perceptive inspections of the lodging and dining establishments listed; the establishments' proprietors for their cooperation in showing their facilities and providing information about them; and the many users of previous editions who have taken the time to share their experiences. Mobil Travel Guide is also grateful to all the talented writers who contributed entries to this book.

www.mobiltravelguide.com

Front cover photo: Decatur Street, New Orleans and *Creole Queen* steam boat by Shutterstock, Horse race by iStockphoto

ISBN: 0-7627-4264-X or 978-0-7627-4264-6

ISSN: 1550-1930

Manufactured in the United States of America.

10 9 8 7 6 5 4 3 2 1

Contents

MAP SYMBOLS

TRANSPORTATION

CONTROLLED ACCESS HIGHWAYS

Freeway

Tollway

Under Construction

Interchange and Exit Number

OTHER HIGHWAYS

Primary Highway

Secondary Highway

Divided Highway

Other Paved Road

Unpaved Road
Check conditions locally

HIGHWAY MARKERS

Interstate Route

U.S. Route

State or Provincial Route

County or Other Route

Trans-Canada Highway

Canadian Provincial Autoroute

Mexican Federal Route

OTHER SYMBOLS

Distances along Major Highways
Miles in U.S.; kilometers in Canada and Mexico

Tunnel; Pass

Auto Ferry; Passenger Ferry

OTHER MAP FEATURES

Time Zone Boundary

Mt. Olympus
7,965   Mountain Peak; Elevation
in Feet

Perennial; Intermittent River

RECREATION

National Park

National Forest; National Grassland

Other Large Park or Recreation Area

Small State Park
with and without Camping

Military Lands

Indian Reservation

Trail

Ski Area

Point of Interest

CITIES AND TOWNS

National Capital

State or Provincial Capital

Cities, Towns, and Populated Places
Type size indicates relative importance

Urban Area
State and province maps only

Large Incorporated Cities
City maps only

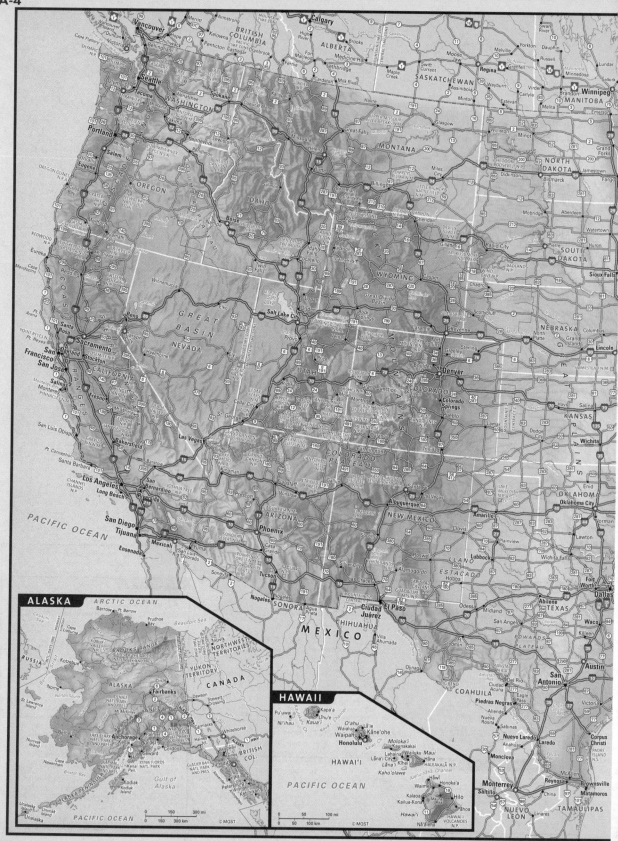

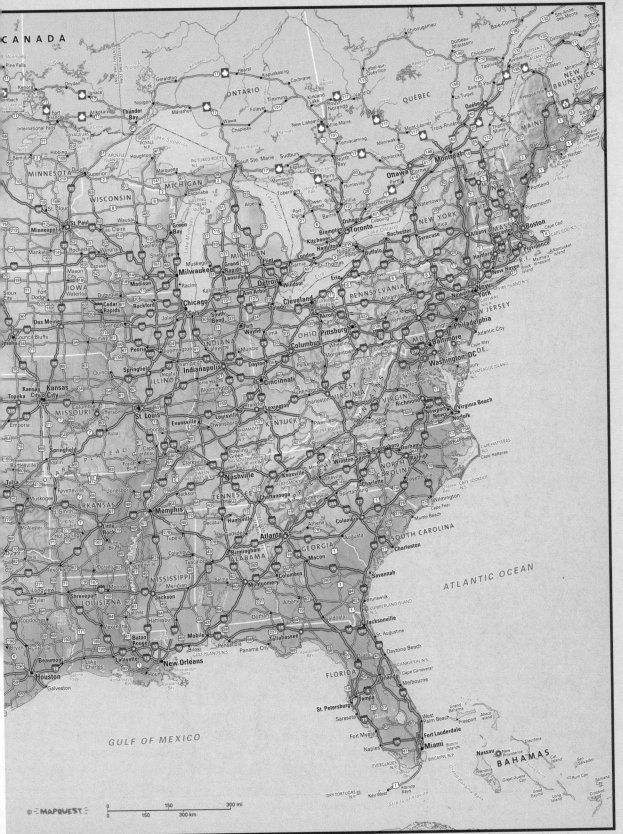

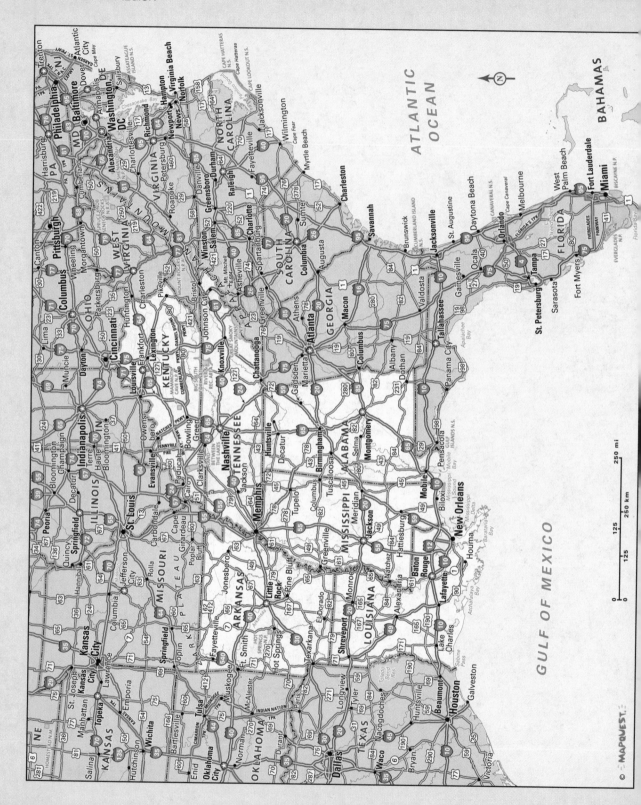

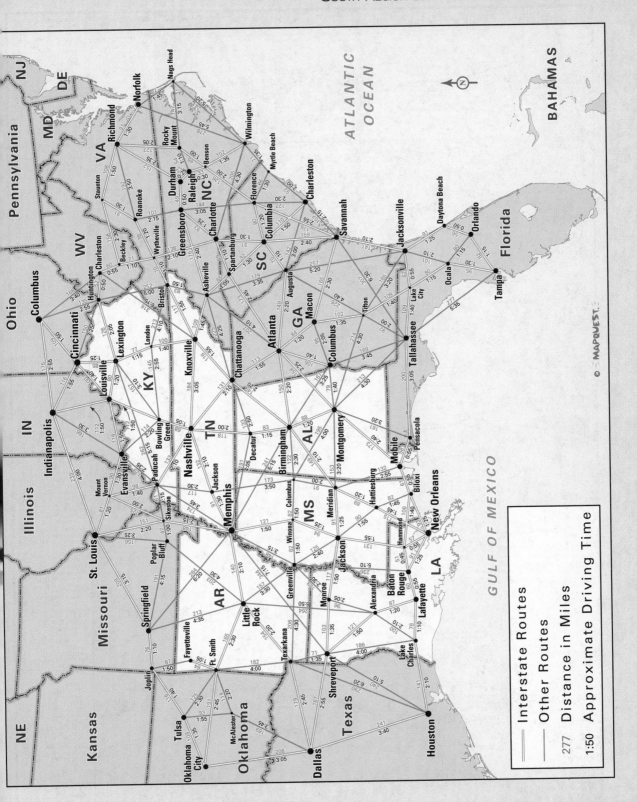

Alabama

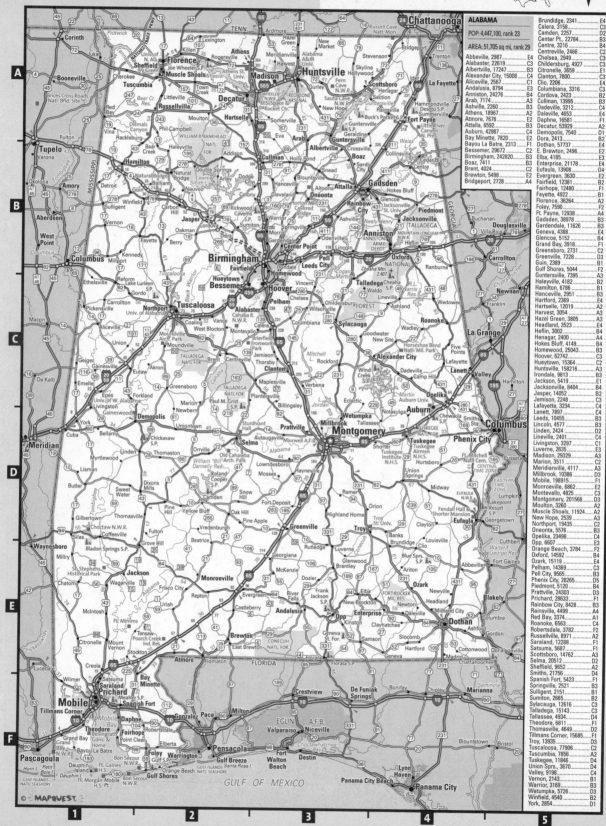

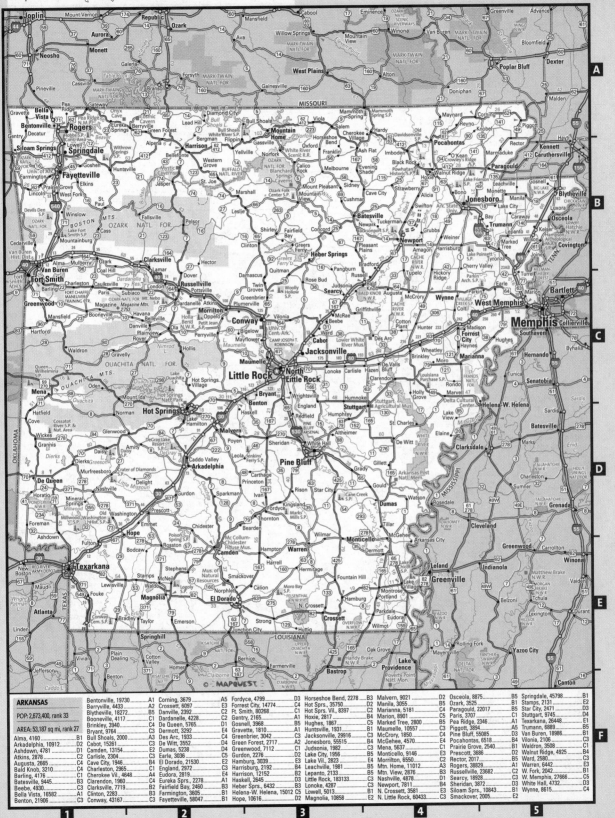

ARKANSAS

POP: 2,673,400, rank 33

AREA: 53,187 sq mi, rank 27

Kentucky & Tennessee

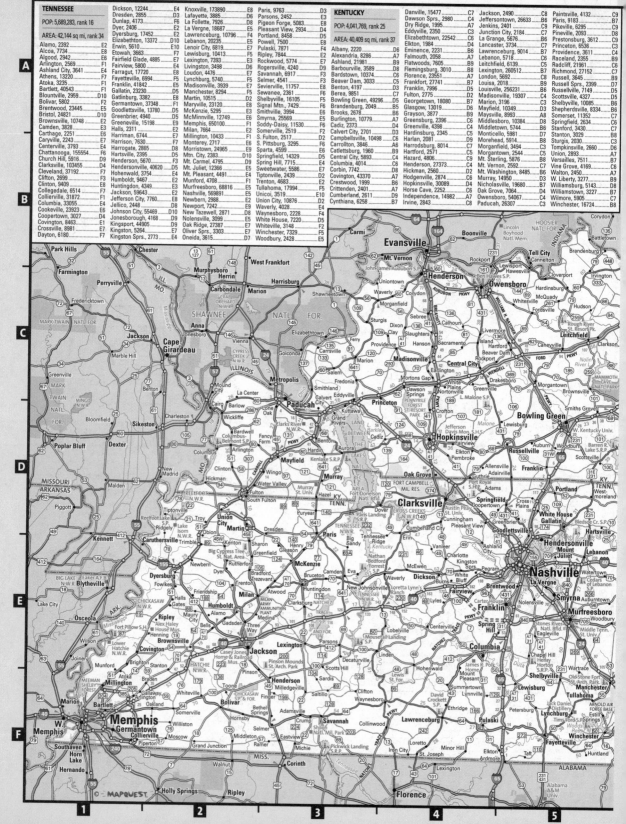

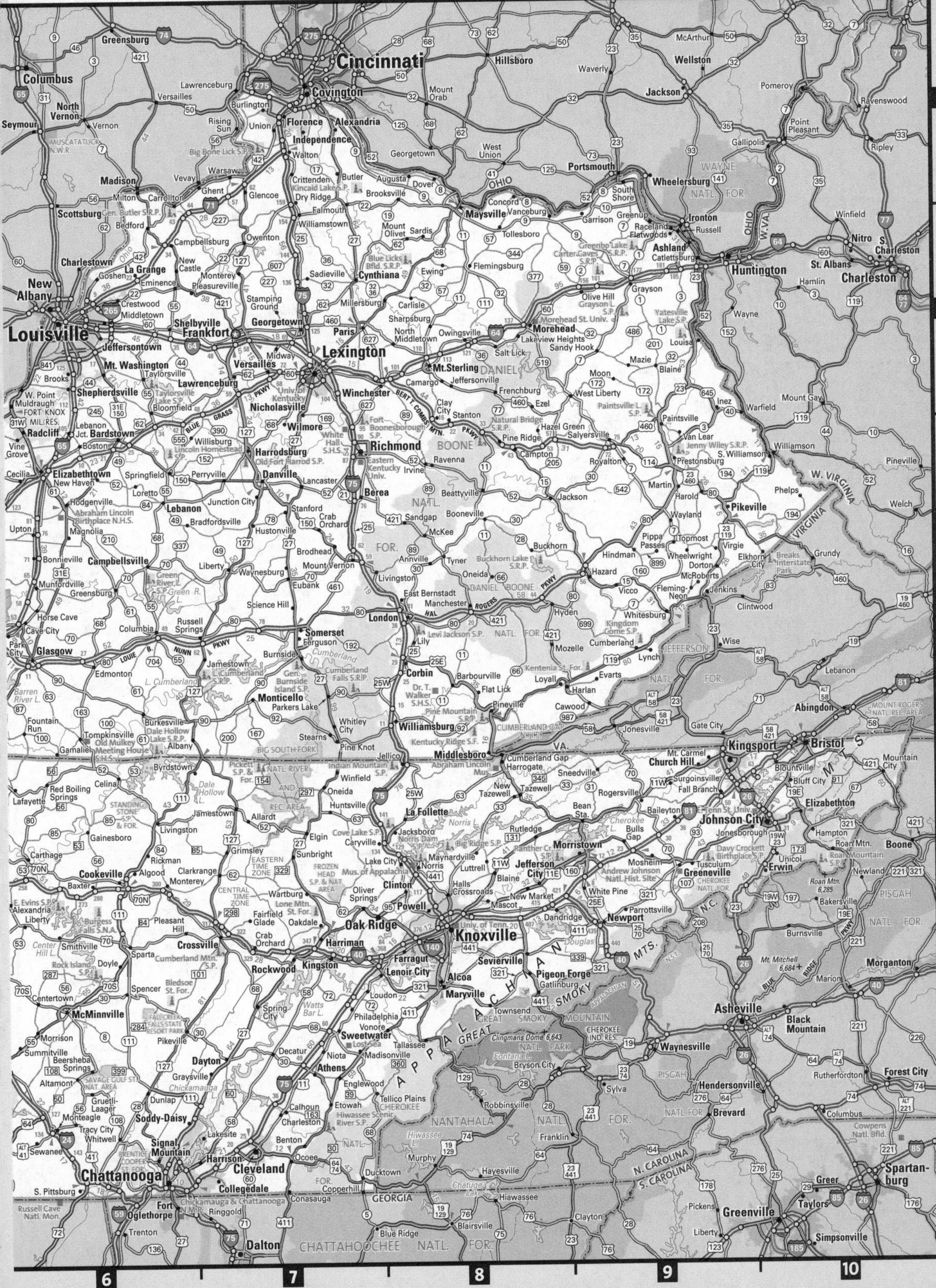
A
B
C
D
E
F
6
7
8
9
10
Cincinnati
Covington
Greensburg
Columbus
North Vernon
Seymour
Lawrenceburg
Versailles
Burlington
Rising Sun
Union
Florence
Alexandria
Independence
Hillsboro
Waverly
Jackson
McArthur
Wellston
Pomeroy
Ravenswood
Point Pleasant
Gallipolis
Ripley
Mount Orab
Georgetown
West Union
Portsmouth
Wheelersburg
South Shore
Madison
Vevay
Warsaw
Ghent
Carrollton
Milton
Scottsburg
Bedford
Glencoe
Crittenden
Dry Ridge
Butler
Falmouth
Williamstown
Augusta
Dover
Brooksville
Maysville
Vanceburg
Concord
Tollesboro
Garrison
Greenup
Raceland
Flatwoods
Ironton
Russell
Ashland
Catlettsburg
Huntington
Winfield
Nitro
St. Albans
Charleston
Hamlin
Mount Olivet
Sardis
Owenton
Campbellsburg
Charlestown
La Grange
New Castle
Goshen
Eminence
Monterey
Pleasureville
New Albany
Crestwood
Middletown
Louisville
Shelbyville
Frankfort
Georgetown
Stamping Ground
Cynthiana
Sadieville
Millersburg
Carlisle
Ewing
Flemingsburg
Sharpsburg
Paris
North Middletown
Owingsville
Morehead
Olive Hill
Grayson
Wayne
Lexington
Jeffersontown
Mt. Washington
Taylorsville
Versailles
Midway
Lawrenceburg
Nicholasville
Winchester
Mt. Sterling
Salt Lick
Lakeview Heights
Sandy Hook
Louisa
Mazie
Blaine
Moon
West Liberty
Inez
Warfield
Mount Gay
Brooks
Shepherdsville
W. Point
Muldraugh
Fort Knox
Radcliff
Lebanon Jct.
Bardstown
Boston
Bloomfield
Harrodsburg
Wilmore
Richmond
Camargo
Jeffersonville
Frenchburg
Ezel
Clay City
Stanton
Hazel Green
Salyersville
Paintsville
Van Lear
Prestonsburg
S. Williamson
Williamson
Pineville
Vine Grove
Cecilia
Elizabethtown
Springfield
Perryville
Danville
Lancaster
Berea
Ravenna
Irvine
Pine Ridge
Campton
Royalton
Martin
Harold
Pikeville
Phelps
Welch
New Haven
Hodgenville
Loretto
Lebanon
Junction City
Stanford
Crab Orchard
Beattyville
Booneville
Jackson
Wayland
Upton
Magnolia
Bradfordsville
Hustonville
Sandgap
McKee
Buckhorn
Hindman
Pippa Passes
Topmost
Virgie
Elkhorn City
Grundy
Bonnieville
Campbellsville
Liberty
Brodhead
Mount Vernon
Annville
Tyner
Hazard
Wheelwright
Dorton
Munfordville
Greensburg
Waynesburg
Eubank
Livingston
Oneida
Vicco
Fleming-Neon
McRoberts
Jenkins
Clintwood
East Bernstadt
Manchester
Hyden
Whitesburg
Horse Cave
Science Hill
London
Cave City
Columbia
Russell Springs
Somerset
Ferguson
Glasgow
Edmonton
Burnside
Jamestown
Lily
Corbin
Barbourville
Mozelle
Cumberland
Lynch
Wise
Lebanon
Flat Lick
Loyall
Harlan
Evarts
Fountain Run
Monticello
Parkers Lake
Williamsburg
Pineville
Cawood
Abingdon
Tompkinsville
Burkesville
Whitley City
Stearns
Pine Knot
Gate City
Kingsport
Bristol
Gamaliel
Albany
Jellico
Middlesboro
Cumberland Gap
Harrogate
Jonesville
Mt. Carmel
Church Hill
Mountain City
Byrdstown
Winfield
Sneedville
Surgoinsville
Blountville
Bluff City
Celina
Lafayette
Red Boiling Springs
Oneida
Huntsville
New Tazewell
Tazewell
Rogersville
Fall Branch
Elizabethton
Jamestown
Allardt
La Follette
Bean Sta.
Baileyton
Johnson City
Jonesborough
Hampton
Roan Mtn.
Boone
Livingston
Gainesboro
Elgin
Jacksboro
Caryville
Rutledge
Bulls Gap
Carthage
Rickman
Grimsley
Sunbright
Lake City
Norris
Maynardville
Luttrell
Morristown
Jefferson City
Mosheim
Greeneville
Tusculum
Erwin
Unicoi
Newland
Cookeville
Algood
Clarkrange
Monterey
Baxter
Halls Crossroads
Blaine
White Pine
Alexandria
Liberty
Wartburg
Oliver Springs
Clinton
New Market
Mascot
Dandridge
Newport
Parrottsville
Bakersville
Burnsville
Smithville
Pleasant Hill
Fairfield Glade
Crab Orchard
Crossville
Oak Ridge
Oakdale
Powell
Knoxville
Harriman
Kingston
Rockwood
Farragut
Lenoir City
Alcoa
Sevierville
Pigeon Forge
Gatlinburg
Maryville
Morganton
Sparta
Doyle
Marion
Centertown
Spencer
Spring City
Loudon
Philadelphia
Vonore
Townsend
Asheville
Black Mountain
McMinnville
Pikeville
Sweetwater
Madisonville
Tallassee
Waynesville
Morrison
Summitville
Dayton
Decatur
Niota
Athens
Bryson City
Sylva
Hendersonville
Rutherfordton
Forest City
Beersheba Springs
Altamont
Graysville
Englewood
Tellico Plains
Robbinsville
Brevard
Columbus
Gruetli-Laager
Monteagle
Tracy City
Whitwell
Dunlap
Soddy-Daisy
Calhoun
Etowah
Charleston
Franklin
Sewanee
Signal Mountain
Lakesite
Harrison
Cleveland
Benton
Ocoee
Murphy
Hayesville
Spartanburg
Greer
Taylors
Chattanooga
Collegedale
Ducktown
Copperhill
Hiawassee
Pickens
Greenville
S. Pittsburg
Fort Oglethorpe
Ringgold
Conasauga
Blairsville
Clayton
Trenton
Dalton
Blue Ridge
Liberty
Simpsonville
OHIO
W. VA.
W. VIRGINIA
VIRGINIA
VA.
N. CAROLINA
S. CAROLINA
GEORGIA
N.C.
GREAT SMOKY MOUNTAIN NATL. PARK
APPALACHIAN MTS.
DANIEL BOONE NATL. FOR.
JEFFERSON NATL. FOR.
CHATTAHOOCHEE NATL. FOR.
NANTAHALA NATL. FOR.
PISGAH NATL. FOR.
CHEROKEE NATL. FOR.
WAYNE NATL. FOR.
BIG SOUTH FORK NATL. RIVER AND REC. AREA
CUMBERLAND GAP N.H.P.
EASTERN TIME ZONE
CENTRAL TIME ZONE
Clingmans Dome 6,643
Mt. Mitchell 6,684
Roan Mtn. 6,285

Louisiana

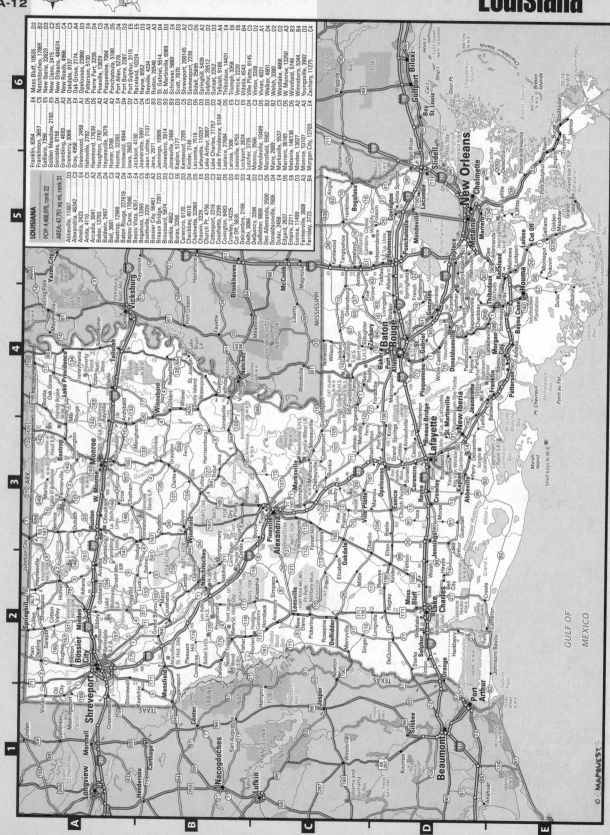

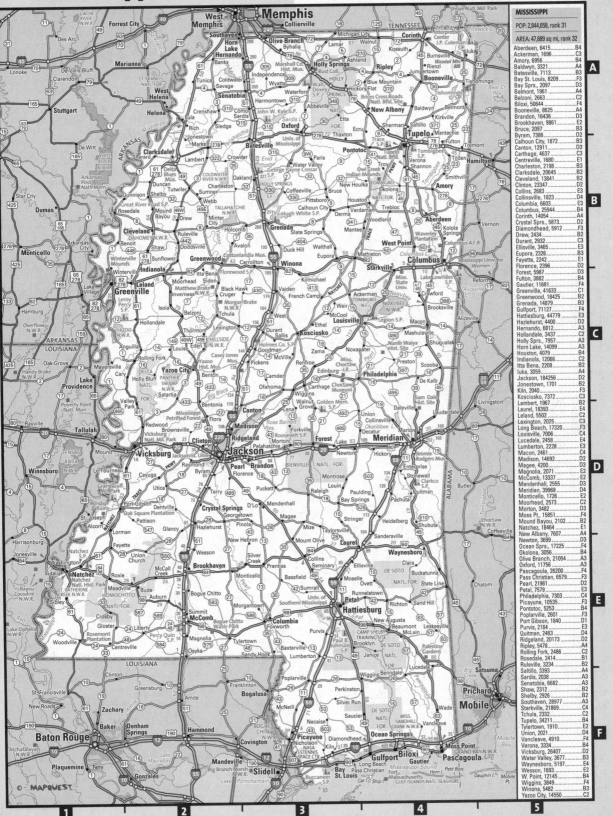

MISSISSIPPI

POP: 2,844,658, rank 31

AREA: 47,689 sq mi, rank 32

Aberdeen, 6415	B4
Ackerman, 1696	C3
Amory, 6956	B4
Baldwyn, 3321	A4
Batesville, 7113	B3
Bay St. Louis, 8209	F3
Bay Sprs., 2097	D3
Belmont, 1961	A4
Belzoni, 2663	C2
Biloxi, 50644	F4
Booneville, 8625	A4
Brandon, 16436	D3
Brookhaven, 9861	E2
Bruce, 2097	B3
Byram, 7386	D2
Calhoun City, 1872	B3
Canton, 12911	D3
Carthage, 4637	C3
Centreville, 1680	E1
Charleston, 2198	B3
Clarksdale, 20645	B2
Cleveland, 13841	B2
Clinton, 23347	D2
Collins, 2683	E3
Collinsville, 1823	D4
Columbia, 6603	E2
Columbus, 25944	C4
Corinth, 14054	A4
Crystal Sprs., 5873	D2
Diamondhead, 5912	F3
Drew, 2434	B2
Durant, 2932	C3
Ellisville, 3465	E3
Eupora, 2326	B3
Fayette, 2242	E1
Florence, 2396	D2
Forest, 5987	D3
Fulton, 3882	B4
Gautier, 11681	F4
Greenville, 41633	C1
Greenwood, 18425	B2
Grenada, 14879	B3
Gulfport, 71127	F4
Hattiesburg, 44779	E3
Hazlehurst, 4400	D2
Hernando, 6812	A3
Hollandale, 3437	C2
Holly Sprs., 7957	A3
Horn Lake, 14099	A3
Houston, 4079	B4
Indianola, 12066	C2
Itta Bena, 2208	B2
Iuka, 3059	A4
Jackson, 184256	D2
Jonestown, 1701	B2
Kiln, 2040	F3
Kosciusko, 7372	C3
Lambert, 1867	B2
Laurel, 18393	E3
Leland, 5502	C2
Lexington, 2025	C3
Long Beach, 17320	F3
Louisville, 7006	C4
Lucedale, 2458	E4
Lumberton, 2228	E3
Macon, 2461	C4
Madison, 14692	D2
Magee, 4200	D3
Magnolia, 2041	E2
McComb, 13337	E2
Mendenhall, 2555	D3
Meridian, 39968	D4
Monticello, 1726	E2
Moorhead, 2573	C2
Morton, 3482	D3
Moss Pt., 15851	F4
Mound Bayou, 2102	B2
Natchez, 18464	E1
New Albany, 7607	A4
Newton, 3699	D3
Ocean Sprs., 17225	F4
Okolona, 3056	B4
Olive Branch, 21054	A3
Oxford, 11756	A3
Pascagoula, 26200	F4
Pass Christian, 6579	F3
Pearl, 21961	D2
Petal, 7579	E3
Philadelphia, 7303	C4
Picayune, 10535	F3
Pontotoc, 5253	B4
Poplarville, 2601	F3
Port Gibson, 1840	D1
Purvis, 2164	E3
Quitman, 2463	D4
Ridgeland, 20173	D2
Ripley, 5478	A4
Rolling Fork, 2486	C2
Rosedale, 2414	B1
Ruleville, 3234	B2
Saltillo, 3393	A4
Sardis, 2038	A3
Senatobia, 6682	A3
Shaw, 2312	B2
Shelby, 2926	B2
Southaven, 28977	A3
Starkville, 21869	C4
Tchula, 2332	C2
Tupelo, 34211	B4
Tylertown, 1910	E2
Union, 2021	D4
Vancleave, 4910	F4
Verona, 3334	B4
Vicksburg, 26407	D1
Water Valley, 3677	B3
Waynesboro, 5197	E4
Wesson, 1693	E2
W. Point, 12145	B4
Wiggins, 3849	F4
Winona, 5482	B3
Yazoo City, 14550	C2

Distances in chart are in miles. To convert miles to kilometers, multiply the distance in miles by 1.609

Example:
New York, NY to Boston, MA = 215 miles or 346 kilometers (215 x 1.609)

	ALBUQUERQUE, NM	ATLANTA, GA	BALTIMORE, MD	BILLINGS, MT	BIRMINGHAM, AL	BISMARCK, ND	BOISE, ID	BOSTON, MA	BUFFALO, NY	BURLINGTON, VT	CHARLESTON, SC	CHARLESTON, WV	CHARLOTTE, NC	CHEYENNE, WY	CHICAGO, IL	CINCINNATI, OH	CLEVELAND, OH	DALLAS, TX	DENVER, CO	DES MOINES, IA	DETROIT, MI	EL PASO, TX	HOUSTON, TX	INDIANAPOLIS, IN	JACKSON, MS	KANSAS CITY, MO	LAS VEGAS, NV	LITTLE ROCK, AR	LOS ANGELES, CA	LOUISVILLE, KY	MEMPHIS, TN	MIAMI, FL
ALBUQUERQUE, NM		1490	1902	991	1274	1333	966	2240	1808	2178	1793	1568	1649	538	1352	1409	1619	754	438	1091	1608	263	994	1298	1157	894	578	900	806	1320	1033	2155
ATLANTA, GA	1490		679	1889	150	1559	2218	1100	910	1158	317	503	238	1482	717	476	726	792	1403	967	735	1437	800	531	386	801	2067	528	2237	419	389	661
BALTIMORE, MD	1902	679		1959	795	1551	2401	422	370	481	583	352	441	1665	708	521	377	1399	1690	1031	532	2045	1470	600	1032	1087	2445	1072	2705	602	933	1109
BILLINGS, MT	991	1889	1959		1839	413	626	2254	1796	2181	2157	1755	2012	455	1246	1552	1597	1433	554	1007	1534	1255	1673	1432	1836	1088	965	1530	1239	1547	1625	2554
BIRMINGHAM, AL	1274	150	795	1839		1509	2170	1215	909	1241	466	578	389	1434	667	475	725	647	1356	919	734	1292	678	481	241	753	1852	381	2092	369	241	812
BISMARCK, ND	1333	1559	1551	413	1509		1039	1846	1388	1773	1749	1347	1604	594	838	1144	1189	1342	693	675	1126	1597	1582	1024	1548	801	1378	1183	1702	1139	1337	2224
BOISE, ID	966	2218	2401	626	2170	1039		2697	2239	2624	2520	2182	2375	737	1708	1969	2040	1711	833	1369	1977	1206	1952	1852	2115	1376	760	1808	1033	1933	1954	2883
BOSTON, MA	2240	1100	422	2254	1215	1846	2697		462	214	1003	741	861	1961	1003	862	654	1819	2004	1326	741	2465	1890	940	1453	1427	2757	1493	3046	964	1353	1529
BUFFALO, NY	1808	910	370	1796	909	1388	2239	462		375	899	431	695	1502	545	442	197	1393	1546	868	277	2039	1513	508	1134	995	2299	1066	2572	545	927	1425
BURLINGTON, VT	2178	1158	481	2181	1241	1773	2624	214	375		1061	782	919	1887	930	817	567	1763	1931	1253	652	2409	1916	878	1479	1366	2684	1437	2957	915	1297	1587
CHARLESTON, SC	1793	317	583	2157	466	1749	2520	1003	899	1061		468	204	1783	907	622	724	1109	1705	1204	879	1754	1110	721	703	1102	2371	900	2554	610	760	583
CHARLESTON, WV	1568	503	352	1755	578	1347	2182	741	431	782	468		265	1445	506	209	255	1072	1367	802	410	1718	1192	320	816	764	2122	745	2374	251	606	994
CHARLOTTE, NC	1649	238	441	2012	389	1604	2375	861	695	919	204	265		1637	761	476	520	1031	1559	1057	675	1677	1041	575	625	956	2225	754	2453	464	614	730
CHEYENNE, WY	538	1482	1665	455	1434	594	737	1961	1502	1887	1783	1445	1637		972	1233	1304	979	100	633	1241	801	1220	1115	1382	640	843	1076	1116	1197	1217	2147
CHICAGO, IL	1352	717	708	1246	667	838	1708	1003	545	930	907	506	761	972		302	346	936	1015	337	283	1543	1108	184	750	532	1768	662	2042	299	539	1382
CINCINNATI, OH	1409	476	521	1552	475	1144	1969	862	442	817	622	209	476	1233	302		253	958	1200	599	261	1605	1079	116	700	597	1955	632	2215	106	493	1141
CLEVELAND, OH	1619	726	377	1597	725	1189	2040	654	197	567	724	255	520	1304	346	253		1208	1347	669	171	1854	1328	319	950	806	2100	882	2374	356	742	1250
DALLAS, TX	754	792	1399	1433	647	1342	1711	1819	1393	1763	1109	1072	1031	979	936	958	1208		887	752	1218	647	241	913	406	554	1331	327	1446	852	466	1367
DENVER, CO	438	1403	1690	554	1356	693	833	2004	1546	1931	1705	1367	1559	100	1015	1200	1347	887		676	1284	701	1127	1088	1290	603	756	984	1029	1118	1116	2069
DES MOINES, IA	1091	967	1031	1007	919	675	1369	1326	868	1253	1204	802	1057	633	337	599	669	752	676		606	1283	992	481	931	194	1429	567	1703	595	720	1632
DETROIT, MI	1608	735	532	1534	734	1126	1977	741	277	652	879	410	675	1241	283	261	171	1218	1284	606		1799	1338	318	960	795	2037	891	2310	366	752	1401
EL PASO, TX	263	1437	2045	1255	1292	1597	1206	2465	2039	2409	1754	1718	1677	801	1543	1605	1854	647	701	1283	1799		758	1489	1051	1085	717	974	801	1499	1112	1959
HOUSTON, TX	994	800	1470	1673	678	1582	1952	1890	1513	1916	1110	1192	1041	1220	1108	1079	1328	241	1127	992	1338	758		1033	445	795	1474	447	1558	972	586	1201
INDIANAPOLIS, IN	1298	531	600	1432	481	1024	1852	940	508	878	721	320	575	1115	184	116	319	913	1088	481	318	1489	1033		675	485	1843	587	2104	112	464	1196
JACKSON, MS	1157	386	1032	1836	241	1548	2115	1453	1134	1479	703	816	625	1382	750	700	950	406	1290	931	960	1051	445	675		747	1735	269	1851	594	211	915
KANSAS CITY, MO	894	801	1087	1088	753	801	1376	1427	995	1366	1102	764	956	640	532	597	806	554	603	194	795	1085	795	485	747		1358	382	1632	516	536	1466
LAS VEGAS, NV	578	2067	2445	965	1852	1378	760	2757	2299	2684	2371	2122	2225	843	1768	1955	2100	1331	756	1429	2037	717	1474	1843	1735	1358		1478	274	1874	1611	2733
LITTLE ROCK, AR	900	528	1072	1530	381	1183	1808	1493	1066	1437	900	745	754	1076	662	632	882	327	984	567	891	974	447	587	269	382	1478		1706	526	140	1190
LOS ANGELES, CA	806	2237	2705	1239	2092	1702	1033	3046	2572	2957	2554	2374	2453	1116	2042	2215	2374	1446	1029	1703	2310	801	1558	2104	1851	1632	274	1706		2126	1839	2759
LOUISVILLE, KY	1320	419	602	1547	369	1139	1933	964	545	915	610	251	464	1197	299	106	356	852	1118	595	366	1499	972	112	594	516	1874	526	2126		386	1084
MEMPHIS, TN	1033	389	933	1625	241	1337	1954	1353	927	1297	760	606	614	1217	539	493	742	466	1116	720	752	1112	586	464	211	536	1611	140	1839	386		1051
MIAMI, FL	2155	661	1109	2554	812	2224	2883	1529	1425	1587	583	994	730	2147	1382	1141	1250	1367	2069	1632	1401	1959	1201	1196	915	1466	2733	1190	2759	1084	1051	
MILWAUKEE, WI	1426	813	805	1175	763	767	1748	1100	642	1027	1003	601	857	1012	89	398	443	1010	1055	378	380	1617	1193	279	835	573	1808	747	2082	394	624	1478
MINNEAPOLIS, MN	1339	1129	1121	839	1079	431	1465	1417	958	1343	1319	918	1173	881	409	714	760	999	924	246	697	1530	1240	596	1151	441	1677	814	1951	711	940	1794
MONTRÉAL, QC	2172	1241	564	2093	1289	1685	2535	313	397	92	1145	822	1003	1799	841	815	588	1772	1843	1165	564	2363	1892	872	1514	1359	2596	1446	2869	920	1306	1671
NASHVILLE, TN	1248	242	716	1648	194	1315	1976	1136	716	1086	543	395	397	1240	474	281	531	681	1162	725	541	1328	801	287	423	559	1826	355	2054	175	215	907
NEW ORLEANS, LA	1276	473	1142	1955	351	1734	2234	1563	1254	1588	783	926	713	1502	935	820	1070	525	1409	1117	1079	1118	360	826	185	932	1854	455	1917	714	396	874
NEW YORK, NY	2015	869	192	2049	985	1641	2491	215	400	299	773	515	631	1755	797	636	466	1589	1799	1121	622	2235	1660	715	1223	1202	2552	1262	2820	739	1123	1299
OKLAHOMA CITY, OK	546	944	1354	1227	729	1136	1506	1694	1262	1632	1248	1022	1102	773	807	863	1073	209	681	546	1062	737	449	752	612	348	1124	355	1352	774	487	1609
OMAHA, NE	973	989	1168	904	941	616	1234	1463	1005	1390	1290	952	1144	497	474	736	806	669	541	136	743	1236	910	618	935	188	1294	570	1567	704	724	1654
ORLANDO, FL	1934	440	904	2333	591	2003	2662	1324	1221	1383	379	790	525	1926	1161	920	1045	1146	1847	1411	1180	1738	980	975	694	1245	2512	969	2538	863	830	232
PHILADELPHIA, PA	1954	782	104	2019	897	1611	2462	321	414	371	685	454	543	1725	768	576	437	1501	1744	1091	592	2147	1572	655	1135	1141	2500	1175	2760	678	1035	1211
PHOENIX, AZ	466	1868	2366	1199	1723	1662	993	2706	2274	2644	2184	2035	2107	1004	1819	1876	2085	1077	904	1558	2074	432	1188	1764	1482	1360	285	1367	369	1786	1500	2390
PITTSBURGH, PA	1670	676	246	1719	763	1311	2161	592	217	587	642	217	438	1425	467	292	136	1246	1460	791	292	1893	1366	370	988	857	2215	920	2476	394	780	1167
PORTLAND, ME	2338	1197	520	2352	1313	1944	2795	107	560	233	1101	839	959	2059	1101	960	751	1917	2102	1424	838	2563	1988	1038	1550	1525	2855	1590	3144	1062	1451	1627
PORTLAND, OR	1395	2647	2830	889	2599	1301	432	3126	2667	3052	2948	2610	2802	1166	2137	2398	2469	2140	1261	1798	2405	1767	2381	2280	2544	1805	1188	2237	971	2362	2382	3312
RAPID CITY, SD	841	1511	1626	379	1463	320	930	1921	1463	1848	1824	1422	1678	305	913	1219	1264	1077	404	629	1201	1105	1318	1101	1458	710	1035	1093	1309	1215	1247	2176
RENO, NV	1020	2440	2623	960	2392	1372	430	2919	2460	2845	2741	2403	2595	959	1930	2191	2262	1933	1054	1591	2198	1315	2072	2073	2337	1598	442	2030	519	2155	2175	3105
RICHMOND, VA	1876	527	152	2053	678	1645	2496	572	485	630	428	322	289	1760	802	530	471	1309	1688	1126	627	1955	1330	641	914	1085	2444	983	2682	572	843	954
ST. LOUIS, MO	1051	549	841	1341	501	1053	1628	1181	749	1119	850	512	704	892	294	350	560	635	855	436	549	1242	863	239	505	252	1610	416	1856	264	294	1214
SALT LAKE CITY, UT	624	1916	2100	548	1868	960	342	2395	1936	2322	2218	1880	2072	436	1406	1667	1738	1410	531	1067	1675	864	1650	1549	1813	1074	417	1507	691	1631	1652	2581
SAN ANTONIO, TX	818	1000	1671	1500	878	1599	1761	2092	1665	2036	1310	1344	1241	1046	1270	1231	1481	271	946	1009	1490	556	200	1186	644	812	1272	600	1356	1125	739	1401
SAN DIEGO, CA	825	2166	2724	1302	2021	1765	1096	3065	2632	3020	2483	2393	2405	1179	2105	2234	2437	1375	1092	1766	2373	730	1487	2122	1780	1695	337	1703	124	2144	1841	2688
SAN FRANCISCO, CA	1111	2618	2840	1176	2472	1749	646	3135	2677	3062	2934	2620	2759	1176	2146	2407	2478	1827	1271	1807	2415	1181	1938	2290	2232	1814	575	2012	385	2372	2144	3140
SEATTLE, WA	1463	2705	2775	816	2657	1229	500	3070	2612	2997	2973	2571	2827	1234	2062	2368	2413	2208	1329	1822	2350	1944	2449	2249	2612	1872	1256	2305	1148	2364	2440	3370
TAMPA, FL	1949	455	960	2348	606	2018	2677	1380	1276	1438	434	845	581	1941	1176	935	1101	1161	1862	1426	1194	1753	995	990	709	1259	2526	984	2553	878	845	274
TORONTO, ON	1841	958	565	1762	958	1354	2204	570	106	419	1006	537	802	1468	510	484	303	1441	1512	834	233	2032	1561	541	1183	1028	2265	1115	2538	589	975	1532
VANCOUVER, BC	1597	2838	2908	949	2791	1362	633	3204	2745	3130	3106	2705	2960	1368	2196	2501	2547	2342	1463	1956	2483	2087	2583	2383	2746	2007	1390	2439	1291	2497	2574	3504
WASHINGTON, DC	1896	636	38	1953	758	1545	2395	458	384	517	539	346	397	1659	701	517	370	1362	1686	1025	526	2008	1433	596	996	1083	2441	1036	2702	596	896	1065
WICHITA, KS	707	989	1276	1067	838	934	1346	1616	1184	1554	1291	953	1145	613	728	785	995	367	521	390	984	898	608	674	771	192	1276	464	1513	705	597	1655

	MILWAUKEE, WI	MINNEAPOLIS, MN	MONTRÉAL, QC	NASHVILLE, TN	NEW ORLEANS, LA	NEW YORK, NY	OKLAHOMA CITY, OK	OMAHA, NE	ORLANDO, FL	PHILADELPHIA, PA	PHOENIX, AZ	PITTSBURGH, PA	PORTLAND, ME	PORTLAND, OR	RAPID CITY, SD	RENO, NV	RICHMOND, VA	ST. LOUIS, MO	SALT LAKE CITY, UT	SAN ANTONIO, TX	SAN DIEGO, CA	SAN FRANCISCO, CA	SEATTLE, WA	TAMPA, FL	TORONTO, ON	VANCOUVER, BC	WASHINGTON, DC	WICHITA, KS
ALBUQUERQUE, NM	1426	1339	2172	1248	1276	2015	546	973	1934	1954	466	1670	2338	1395	841	1020	1876	1051	624	818	825	1111	1463	1949	1841	1597	1896	707
ATLANTA, GA	813	1129	1241	242	473	869	944	989	440	782	1868	676	1197	2647	1511	2440	527	549	1916	1000	2166	2618	2705	455	958	2838	636	989
BALTIMORE, MD	805	1121	564	716	1142	192	1354	1168	904	104	2366	246	520	2830	1626	2623	152	841	2100	1671	2724	2840	2775	960	565	2908	38	1276
BILLINGS, MT	1175	839	2093	1648	1955	2049	1227	904	2333	2019	1199	1719	2352	889	379	960	2053	1341	548	1500	1302	1176	816	2348	1762	949	1953	1067
BIRMINGHAM, AL	763	1079	1289	194	351	985	729	941	591	897	1723	763	1313	2599	1463	2392	678	501	1868	878	2021	2472	2657	606	958	2791	758	838
BISMARCK, ND	767	431	1685	1315	1734	1641	1136	616	2003	1611	1662	1311	1944	1301	320	1372	1645	1053	960	1599	1765	1749	1229	2018	1354	1362	1545	934
BOISE, ID	1748	1465	2535	1976	2234	2491	1506	1234	2662	2462	993	2161	2795	432	930	430	2496	1628	342	1761	1096	646	500	2677	2204	633	2395	1346
BOSTON, MA	1100	1417	313	1136	1563	215	1694	1463	1324	321	2706	592	107	3126	1921	2919	572	1181	2395	2092	3065	3135	3070	1380	570	3204	458	1616
BUFFALO, NY	642	958	397	716	1254	400	1262	1005	1221	414	2274	217	560	2667	1463	2460	485	749	1936	1665	2632	2677	2612	1276	106	2745	384	1184
BURLINGTON, VT	1027	1343	92	1086	1588	299	1632	1390	1383	371	2644	587	233	3052	1848	2845	630	1119	2322	2036	3020	3062	2997	1438	419	3130	517	1554
CHARLESTON, SC	1003	1319	1145	543	783	773	1248	1290	379	685	2184	642	1101	2948	1824	2741	428	850	2218	1310	2483	2934	2973	434	1006	3106	539	1291
CHARLESTON, WV	601	918	822	395	926	515	1022	952	790	454	2035	217	839	2610	1422	2403	322	512	1880	1344	2393	2620	2571	845	537	2705	346	953
CHARLOTTE, NC	857	1173	1003	397	713	631	1102	1144	525	543	2107	438	959	2802	1678	2595	289	704	2072	1241	2405	2759	2827	581	802	2960	397	1145
CHEYENNE, WY	1012	881	1799	1240	1502	1755	773	497	1926	1725	1004	1425	2059	1166	305	959	1760	892	436	1046	1179	1176	1234	1941	1468	1368	1659	613
CHICAGO, IL	89	409	841	474	935	797	807	474	1161	768	1819	467	1101	2137	913	1930	802	294	1406	1270	2105	2146	2062	1176	510	2196	701	728
CINCINNATI, OH	398	714	815	281	820	636	863	736	920	576	1876	292	960	2398	1219	2191	530	350	1667	1231	2234	2407	2368	935	484	2501	517	785
CLEVELAND, OH	443	760	588	531	1070	466	1073	806	1045	437	2085	136	751	2469	1264	2262	471	560	1738	1481	2437	2478	2413	1101	303	2547	370	995
DALLAS, TX	1010	999	1772	681	525	1589	209	669	1146	1501	1077	1246	1917	2140	1077	1933	1309	635	1410	271	1375	1827	2208	1161	1441	2342	1362	367
DENVER, CO	1055	924	1843	1162	1409	1799	681	541	1847	1744	904	1460	2102	1261	404	1054	1688	855	531	946	1092	1271	1329	1862	1512	1463	1686	521
DES MOINES, IA	378	246	1165	725	1117	1121	546	136	1411	1091	1558	791	1424	1798	629	1591	1126	436	1067	1009	1766	1807	1822	1426	834	1956	1025	390
DETROIT, MI	380	697	564	541	1079	622	1062	743	1180	592	2074	292	838	2405	1201	2198	627	549	1675	1490	2373	2415	2350	1194	233	2483	526	984
EL PASO, TX	1617	1530	2363	1328	1118	2235	737	1236	1738	2147	432	1893	2563	1767	1105	1315	1955	1242	864	556	730	1181	1944	1753	2032	2087	2008	898
HOUSTON, TX	1193	1240	1892	801	360	1660	449	910	980	1572	1188	1366	1988	2381	1318	2072	1330	863	1650	200	1487	1938	2449	995	1561	2583	1433	608
INDIANAPOLIS, IN	279	596	872	287	826	715	752	618	975	655	1764	370	1038	2280	1101	2073	641	239	1549	1186	2122	2290	2249	990	541	2383	596	674
JACKSON, MS	835	1151	1514	423	185	1223	612	935	694	1135	1482	988	1550	2544	1458	2337	914	505	1813	644	1780	2232	2612	709	1183	2746	996	771
KANSAS CITY, MO	573	441	1359	559	932	1202	348	188	1245	1141	1360	857	1525	1805	710	1598	1085	252	1074	812	1695	1814	1872	1259	1028	2007	1083	192
LAS VEGAS, NV	1808	1677	2596	1826	1854	2552	1124	1294	2512	2500	285	2215	2855	1188	1035	442	2444	1610	417	1272	337	575	1256	2526	2265	1390	2441	1276
LITTLE ROCK, AR	747	814	1446	355	455	1262	355	570	969	1175	1367	920	1590	2237	1093	2030	983	416	1507	600	1703	2012	2305	984	1115	2439	1036	464
LOS ANGELES, CA	2082	1951	2869	2054	1917	2820	1352	1567	2538	2760	369	2476	3144	971	1309	519	2682	1856	691	1356	124	385	1148	2553	2538	1291	2702	1513
LOUISVILLE, KY	394	711	920	175	714	739	774	704	863	678	1786	394	1062	2362	1215	2155	572	264	1631	1125	2144	2372	2364	878	589	2497	596	705
MEMPHIS, TN	624	940	1306	215	396	1123	487	724	830	1035	1500	780	1451	2382	1247	2175	843	294	1652	739	1841	2144	2440	845	975	2574	896	597
MIAMI, FL	1478	1794	1671	907	874	1299	1609	1654	232	1211	2390	1167	1627	3312	2176	3105	954	1214	2581	1401	2688	3140	3370	274	1532	3504	1065	1655
MILWAUKEE, WI		337	939	569	1020	894	880	514	1257	865	1892	564	1198	2063	842	1970	899	367	1446	1343	2145	2186	1991	1272	607	2124	799	769
MINNEAPOLIS, MN	337		1255	886	1337	1211	793	383	1573	1181	1805	881	1515	1727	606	1839	1216	621	1315	1257	2014	2055	1654	1588	924	1788	1115	637
MONTRÉAL, QC	939	1255		1094	1632	383	1625	1300	1466	454	2637	607	282	2963	1758	2756	714	1112	2232	2043	2931	2972	2907	1522	330	3041	600	1547
NASHVILLE, TN	569	886	1094		539	906	703	747	686	818	1715	569	1234	2405	1269	2198	626	307	1675	954	2056	2360	2463	701	764	2597	679	748
NEW ORLEANS, LA	1020	1337	1632	539		1332	731	1121	653	1245	1548	1108	1660	2663	1643	2431	1002	690	1932	560	1846	2298	2731	668	1302	2865	1106	890
NEW YORK, NY	894	1211	383	906	1332		1469	1258	1094	91	2481	367	313	2920	1716	2713	342	956	2189	1861	2839	2929	2864	1150	507	2998	228	1391
OKLAHOMA CITY, OK	880	793	1625	703	731	1469		463	1388	1408	1012	1124	1792	1934	871	1727	1331	505	1204	466	1370	1657	2002	1403	1295	2136	1350	161
OMAHA, NE	514	383	1300	747	1121	1258	463		1433	1228	1440	928	1561	1662	525	1455	1263	440	932	927	1630	1672	1719	1448	971	1853	1162	307
ORLANDO, FL	1257	1573	1466	686	653	1094	1388	1433		1006	2169	963	1422	3091	1955	2884	750	993	2360	1180	2467	2918	3149	82	1327	3283	860	1434
PHILADELPHIA, PA	865	1181	454	818	1245	91	1408	1228	1006		2420	306	419	2890	1686	2683	254	895	2160	1774	2779	2900	2835	1062	522	2968	140	1330
PHOENIX, AZ	1892	1805	2637	1715	1548	2481	1012	1440	2169	2420		2136	2804	1335	1308	883	2343	1517	651	987	358	750	1513	2184	2307	1655	2362	1173
PITTSBURGH, PA	564	881	607	569	1108	367	1124	928	963	306	2136		690	2590	1386	2383	341	611	1859	1519	2494	2599	2534	1019	321	2668	240	1046
PORTLAND, ME	1198	1515	282	1234	1660	313	1792	1561	1422	419	2804	690		3223	2019	3016	670	1279	2493	2189	3162	3233	3168	1478	668	3301	556	1714
PORTLAND, OR	2063	1727	2963	2405	2663	2920	1934	1662	3091	2890	1335	2590	3223		1268	578	2925	2057	771	2322	1093	638	170	3106	2633	313	2824	1775
RAPID CITY, SD	842	606	1758	1269	1643	1716	871	525	1955	1686	1308	1386	2019	1268		1151	1720	963	628	1335	1372	1368	1195	1970	1429	1328	1620	712
RENO, NV	1970	1839	2756	2198	2431	2713	1727	1455	2884	2683	883	2383	3016	578	1151		2718	1850	524	1870	642	217	755	2899	2426	898	2617	1568
RICHMOND, VA	899	1216	714	626	1002	342	1331	1263	750	254	2343	341	670	2925	1720	2718		834	2194	1530	2684	2934	2869	805	660	3003	108	1274
ST. LOUIS, MO	367	621	1112	307	690	956	505	440	993	895	1517	611	1279	2057	963	1850	834		1326	968	1875	2066	2125	1008	782	2259	837	441
SALT LAKE CITY, UT	1446	1315	2232	1675	1932	2189	1204	932	2360	2160	651	1859	2493	771	628	524	2194	1326		1419	754	740	839	2375	1902	973	2094	1044
SAN ANTONIO, TX	1343	1257	2043	954	560	1861	466	927	1180	1774	987	1519	2189	2322	1335	1870	1530	968	1419		1285	1737	2275	1195	1714	2410	1635	624
SAN DIEGO, CA	2145	2014	2931	2056	1846	2839	1370	1630	2467	2779	358	2494	3162	1093	1372	642	2684	1875	754	1285		508	1271	2481	2601	1414	2720	1531
SAN FRANCISCO, CA	2186	2055	2972	2360	2298	2929	1657	1672	2918	2900	750	2599	3233	638	1368	217	2934	2066	740	1737	508		816	2933	2643	958	2834	1784
SEATTLE, WA	1991	1654	2907	2463	2731	2864	2002	1719	3149	2835	1513	2534	3168	170	1195	755	2869	2125	839	2275	1271	816		3164	2577	140	2769	1843
TAMPA, FL	1272	1588	1522	701	668	1150	1403	1448	82	1062	2184	1019	1478	3106	1970	2899	805	1008	2375	1195	2481	2933	3164		1383	3297	916	1448
TORONTO, ON	607	924	330	764	1302	507	1295	971	1327	522	2307	321	668	2633	1429	2426	660	782	1902	1714	2601	2643	2577	1383		2711	563	1217
VANCOUVER, BC	2124	1788	3041	2597	2865	2998	2136	1853	3283	2968	1655	2668	3301	313	1328	898	3003	2259	973	2410	1414	958	140	3297	2711		2902	1977
WASHINGTON, DC	799	1115	600	679	1106	228	1350	1162	860	140	2362	240	556	2824	1620	2617	108	837	2094	1635	2720	2834	2769	916	563	2902		1272
WICHITA, KS	769	637	1547	748	890	1391	161	307	1434	1330	1173	1046	1714	1775	712	1568	1274	441	1044	624	1531	1784	1843	1448	1217	1977	1272	

A Word to Our Readers

Travelers are on the roads in great numbers these days. They're exploring the country on day trips, weekend getaways, business trips, and extended family vacations, visiting major cities and small towns along the way. Because time is precious and the travel industry is ever-changing, having accurate, reliable travel information at your fingertips is critical. Mobil Travel Guide has been providing invaluable insight to travelers for more than 45 years, and we are committed to continuing this service well into the future.

The Mobil Corporation (known as Exxon Mobil Corporation since a 1999 merger) began producing the Mobil Travel Guide books in 1958, following the introduction of the US interstate highway system in 1956. The first edition covered only five Southwestern states. Since then, our books have become the premier travel guides in North America, covering all 50 states and Canada.

Since its founding, Mobil Travel Guide has served as an advocate for travelers seeking knowledge about hotels, restaurants, and places to visit. Based on an objective process, we make recommendations to our customers that we believe will enhance the quality and value of their travel experiences. Our trusted Mobil One- to Five-Star rating system is the oldest and most respected lodging and restaurant inspection and rating program in North America. Most hoteliers, restaurateurs, and industry observers favorably regard the rigor of our inspection program and understand the prestige and benefits that come with receiving a Mobil Star rating.

The Mobil Travel Guide process of rating each establishment includes:

○ Unannounced facility inspections

○ Incognito service evaluations for Mobil Four-Star and Mobil Five-Star properties

○ A review of unsolicited comments from the general public

○ Senior management oversight

For each property, more than 450 attributes, including cleanliness, physical facilities, and employee attitude and courtesy, are measured and evaluated to produce a mathematically derived score, which is then blended with the other elements to form an overall score. These quantifiable scores allow comparative analysis among properties and form the basis that we use to assign our Mobil One- to Five-Star ratings.

This process focuses largely on guest expectations, guest experience, and consistency of service, not just physical facilities and amenities. It is fundamentally a relative rating system that rewards those properties that continually strive for and achieve excellence each year. Indeed, the very best properties are consistently raising the bar for those that wish to compete with them. These properties proactively respond to consumers' needs even in today's uncertain times.

Only facilities that meet Mobil Travel Guide's standards earn the privilege of being listed in the guide. Deteriorating, poorly managed establishments are deleted. A Mobil Travel Guide listing constitutes a positive quality recommendation; every listing is an accolade, a recognition of achievement. Our Mobil One- to Five-Star rating system highlights its level of service. Extensive in-house research is constantly underway to determine new additions to our lists.

○ The Mobil Five-Star Award indicates that a property is one of the very best in the country and consistently provides gracious and courteous service, superlative quality in its facility, and a unique ambience. The lodgings and restaurants at the Mobil Five-Star level consistently and proactively respond to consumers' needs and continue their commitment to excellence, doing so with grace and perseverance.

○ Also highly regarded is the Mobil Four-Star Award, which honors properties for outstanding achievement in overall facility and for providing very strong service levels in all areas. These award winners provide a distinctive experience for the ever-demanding and sophisticated consumer.

- The Mobil Three-Star Award recognizes an excellent property that provides full services and amenities. This category ranges from exceptional hotels with limited services to elegant restaurants with a less-formal atmosphere.

- A Mobil Two-Star property is a clean and comfortable establishment that has expanded amenities or a distinctive environment. A Mobil Two-Star property is an excellent place to stay or dine.

- A Mobil One-Star property is limited in its amenities and services but focuses on providing a value experience while meeting travelers' expectations. The property can be expected to be clean, comfortable, and convenient.

Allow us to emphasize that we do not charge establishments for inclusion in our guides. We have no relationship with any of the businesses and attractions we list and act only as a consumer advocate. In essence, we do the investigative legwork so that you won't have to.

Keep in mind, too, that the hospitality business is ever-changing. Restaurants and lodgings—particularly small chains and stand-alone establishments—change management or even go out of business with surprising quickness. Although we make every effort to double-check information during our annual updates, we nevertheless recommend that you call ahead to make sure the place you've selected is still open and offers all the amenities you're looking for. We've provided phone numbers; when available, we also list fax numbers and Web site addresses.

We hope that your travels are enjoyable and relaxing and that our books help you get the most out of every trip you take. If any aspect of your accommodation, dining, or sightseeing experience motivates you to comment, please drop us a line. We depend a great deal on our readers' remarks, so you can be assured that we will read your comments and assimilate them into our research. General comments about our books are also welcome. You can write to us at Mobil Travel Guide, 7373 N Cicero Ave, Lincolnwood, IL 60712, or send an e-mail to info@ mobiltravelguide.com.

Take your Mobil Travel Guide books along on every trip you take. We're confident that you'll be pleased with their convenience, ease of use, and breadth of dependable coverage.

Happy travels!

How to Use This Book

The Mobil Travel Guide Regional Travel Planners are designed for ease of use. Each state has its own chapter, beginning with a general introduction that provides a geographical and historical orientation to the state and gives basic statewide tourist information, from climate to calendar highlights to seatbelt laws. The remainder of each chapter is devoted to travel destinations within the state—mainly cities and towns, but also national parks and tourist areas—which, like the states, are arranged in alphabetical order.

The following sections explain the wealth of information you'll find about those travel destinations: information about the area, things to see and do there, and where to stay and eat.

Maps and Map Coordinates

At the front of this book in the full-color section, we have provided state maps as well as maps of selected larger cities to help you find your way around once you leave the highway. You'll find a key to the map symbols on the Contents page at the beginning of the map section.

Next to most cities and towns throughout the book, you'll find a set of map coordinates, such as C-2. These coordinates reference the maps at the front of this book and help you find the location you're looking for quickly and easily.

Destination Information

Because many travel destinations are close to other cities and towns where travelers might find additional attractions, accommodations, and restaurants, we've included cross-references to those cities and towns when it makes sense to do so. We also list addresses, phone numbers, and Web sites for travel information resources—usually the local chamber of commerce or office of tourism—as well as pertinent statistics and, in many cases, a brief introduction to the area.

Information about airports, ground transportation, and suburbs is included for large cities.

Driving Tours and Walking Tours

The driving tours that we include for many states are usually day trips that make for interesting side excursions, although they can be longer. They offer you a way to get off the beaten path and visit an area that travelers often overlook. These trips frequently cover areas of natural beauty or historical significance.

Each walking tour focuses on a particularly interesting area of a city or town. Again, these tours can provide a break from everyday tourist attractions. The tours often include places to stop for meals or snacks.

What to See and Do

Mobil Travel Guide offers information about nearly 20,000 museums, art galleries, amusement parks, historic sites, national and state parks, ski areas, and many other types of attractions. A white star on a black background ★ signals that the attraction is a must-see—one of the best in the area. Because municipal parks, public tennis courts, swimming pools, and small educational institutions are common to most towns, they generally are not mentioned.

Following an attraction's description, you'll find the months, days, and, in some cases, hours of operation; the address/directions, telephone number, and Web site (if there is one); and the admission price category. The following are the ranges we use for admission fees, based on one adult:

- ✪ **FREE**
- ✪ **$** = Up to $5
- ✪ **$$** = $5.01-$10
- ✪ **$$$** = $10.01-$15
- ✪ **$$$$** = Over $15

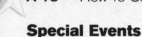

Special Events

Special events are either annual events that last only a short time, such as festivals and fairs, or longer, seasonal events such as horse racing, theater, and summer concerts. Our Special Events listings also include infrequently occurring occasions that mark certain dates or events, such as a centennial or other commemorative celebration.

Listings

Lodgings, spas, and restaurants are usually listed under the city or town in which they're located. Make sure to check the related cities and towns that appear right beneath a city's heading for additional options, especially if you're traveling to a major metropolitan area that includes many suburbs. If a property is located in a town that doesn't have its own heading, the listing appears under the town nearest it, with the address and town given immediately after the establishment's name. In large cities, lodgings located within 5 miles of major commercial airports may be listed under a separate "Airport Area" heading that follows the city section.

LODGINGS

Travelers have different wants and needs when it comes to accommodations. To help you pinpoint properties that meet your particular needs, Mobil Travel Guide classifies each lodging by type according to the following characteristics.

Mobil Rated Lodgings

○ **Limited-Service Hotel.** A limited-service hotel is traditionally a Mobil One-Star or Mobil Two-Star property. At a Mobil One-Star hotel, guests can expect to find a clean, comfortable property that commonly serves a complimentary continental breakfast. A Mobil Two-Star hotel is also clean and comfortable but has expanded amenities, such as a full-service restaurant, business center, and fitness center. These services may have limited staffing and/or restricted hours of use.

○ **Full-Service Hotel.** A full-service hotel traditionally enjoys a Mobil Three-Star, Mobil Four-Star, or Mobil Five-Star rating. Guests can expect these hotels to offer at least one full-service restaurant in addition to amenities such as valet parking, luggage assistance, 24-hour room service, concierge service, laundry and/or dry-cleaning services, and turndown service.

○ **Full-Service Resort.** A resort is traditionally a full-service hotel that is geared toward recreation and represents a vacation and holiday destination. A resort's guest rooms are typically furnished to accommodate longer stays. The property may offer a full-service spa, golf, tennis, and fitness facilities or other leisure activities. Resorts are expected to offer a full-service restaurant and expanded amenities, such as luggage assistance, room service, meal plans, concierge service, and turndown service.

○ **Full-Service Inn.** An inn is traditionally a Mobil Three-Star, Mobil Four-Star, or Mobil Five-Star property. Inns are similar to bed-and-breakfasts (see below) but offer a wider range of services, most significantly a full-service restaurant that serves at least breakfast and dinner.

Specialty Lodgings

Mobil Travel Guide recognizes the unique and individualized nature of many different types of lodging establishments, including bed-and-breakfasts, limited-service inns, and guest ranches. For that reason, we have chosen to place our stamp of approval on the properties that fall into these two categories in lieu of applying our traditional Mobil Star ratings.

○ **B&B/Limited-Service Inn.** A bed-and-breakfast (B&B) or limited-service inn is traditionally an owner-occupied home or residence found in a residential area or vacation destination. It may be a structure of historic significance. Rooms are often individually decorated, but telephones, televisions, and private bathrooms may not be available in every room. A B&B typically serves only breakfast to its overnight guests, which is included in the room rate. Cocktails and refreshments may be served in the late afternoon or evening.

○ **Guest Ranch.** A guest ranch is traditionally a rustic, Western-themed property that specializes in stays of three or more days. Horseback riding is often a feature, with stables and trails found on the property. Facilities can range from clean, comfortable establishments to more luxurious facilities.

Mobil Star Rating Definitions for Lodgings

○ ★ ★ ★ ★ ★ : A Mobil Five-Star lodging provides consistently superlative service in an exceptionally distinctive luxury environment, with expanded services. Attention to detail is evident throughout the hotel, resort, or inn, from bed linens to staff uniforms.

○ ★ ★ ★ ★ : A Mobil Four-Star lodging provides a luxury experience with expanded amenities in a distinctive environment. Services may include, but are not limited to, automatic turndown service, 24-hour room service, and valet parking.

○ ★ ★ ★ : A Mobil Three-Star lodging is well appointed, with a full-service restaurant and expanded amenities, such as a fitness center, golf course, tennis courts, 24-hour room service, and optional turndown service.

○ ★ ★ : A Mobil Two-Star lodging is considered a clean, comfortable, and reliable establishment that has expanded amenities, such as a full-service restaurant on the premises.

○ ★ : A Mobil One-Star lodging is a limited-service hotel, motel, or inn that is considered a clean, comfortable, and reliable establishment.

Information Found in the Lodging Listings

Each lodging listing gives the name, address/location (when no street address is available), neighborhood and/or directions from downtown (in major cities), phone number(s), fax number, total number of guest rooms, and seasons open (if not year-round). Also included are details on business, luxury, recreational, and dining facilities at the property or nearby. A key to the symbols at the end of each listing can be found on the page following the "A Word to Our Readers" section.

For every property, we also provide pricing information. Because lodging rates change frequently, we list a pricing category rather than specific prices. The pricing categories break down as follows:

○ **$** = Up to $150

○ **$$** = $151-$250

○ **$$$** = $251-$350

○ **$$$$** = $351 and up

All prices quoted are in effect at the time of publication; however, prices cannot be guaranteed. In some locations, short-term price variations may exist because of special events, holidays, or seasonality. Certain resorts have complicated rate structures that vary with the time of year; always confirm rates when making your plans.

Because most lodgings offer the following features and services, information about them does not appear in the listings:

○ Year-round operation

○ Bathroom with tub and/or shower in each room

○ Cable television in each room

○ In-room telephones

○ Cots and cribs available

○ Daily maid service

○ Elevators

○ Major credit cards accepted

SPAS

Mobil Travel Guide is pleased to announce its newest category: hotel and resort spas. Until now, hotel and resort spas have not been formally rated or inspected by any organization. Every spa selected for inclusion in this book underwent a rigorous inspection process similar to the one Mobil Travel Guide has been applying to lodgings and restaurants for more than four decades. After spending a year and a half researching more than 300 spas and performing exhaustive incognito inspections of more than 200 properties, we narrowed our list to the 48 best spas in the United States and Canada.

Mobil Travel Guide's spa ratings are based on objective evaluations of more than 450 attributes. Approximately half of these criteria assess basic expectations, such as staff courtesy, the technical proficiency and skill of the employees, and whether the facility is maintained properly and hygienically. Several standards address issues that impact a guest's physical comfort and convenience, as well as the staff's ability to impart a sense of personalized service and anticipate clients' needs. Additional criteria measure the spa's ability to create a completely calming ambience.

The Mobil Star ratings focus on much more than the facilities available at a spa and the treatments it offers. Each Mobil Star rating is a cumulative score achieved from multiple inspections that reflects the spa management's attention to detail and commitment to consumers' needs.

Mobil Star Rating Definitions for Spas

✪ ★ ★ ★ ★ ★ : A Mobil Five-Star spa provides consistently superlative service in an exceptionally distinctive luxury environment with extensive amenities. The staff at a Mobil Five-Star spa provides extraordinary service above and beyond the traditional spa experience, allowing guests to achieve the highest level of relaxation and pampering. A Mobil Five-Star spa offers an extensive array of treatments, often incorporating international themes and products. Attention to detail is evident throughout the spa, from arrival to departure.

✪ ★ ★ ★ ★ : A Mobil Four-Star spa provides a luxurious experience with expanded amenities in an elegant and serene environment. Throughout the spa facility, guests experience personalized service. Amenities might include, but are not limited to, single-sex relaxation rooms where guests wait for their treatments, plunge pools and whirlpools in both men's and women's locker rooms, and an array of treatments, including at a minimum a selection of massages, body therapies, facials, and a variety of salon services.

✪ ★ ★ ★ : A Mobil Three-Star spa is physically well appointed and has a full complement of staff to ensure that guests' needs are met. It has some expanded amenities, such as, but not limited to, a well-equipped fitness center, separate men's and women's locker rooms, a sauna or steam room, and a designated relaxation area. It also offers a menu of services that at a minimum includes massages, facial treatments, and at least one other type of body treatment, such as scrubs or wraps.

RESTAURANTS

All Mobil Star rated dining establishments listed in this book have a full kitchen and offer seating at tables; most offer table service.

Mobil Star Rating Definitions for Restaurants

✪ ★ ★ ★ ★ ★ : A Mobil Five-Star restaurant offers one of few flawless dining experiences in the country. These establishments consistently provide their guests with exceptional food, superlative service, elegant décor, and exquisite presentations of each detail surrounding a meal.

✪ ★ ★ ★ ★ : A Mobil Four-Star restaurant provides professional service, distinctive presentations, and wonderful food.

✪ ★ ★ ★ : A Mobil Three-Star restaurant has good food, warm and skillful service, and enjoyable décor.

✪ ★ ★ : A Mobil Two-Star restaurant serves fresh food in a clean setting with efficient service. Value is considered in this category, as is family friendliness.

✪ ★ : A Mobil One-Star restaurant provides a distinctive experience through culinary specialty, local flair, or individual atmosphere.

Information Found in the Restaurant Listings

Each restaurant listing gives the cuisine type, street address (or directions if no address is available), phone and fax numbers, Web site (if available), meals served, days of operation (if not open daily year-round), and pricing category. Information about appropriate attire is provided, although it's always a good idea to call ahead and ask if you're unsure; the meaning of "casual" or "business casual" varies widely in different parts of the country. We also indicate whether the restaurant has a bar, whether a children's menu is offered, and whether outdoor seating is available. If reservations are recommended, we note that fact in the listing. When valet parking is available, it is noted in the description. In many cases, self-parking is available at the restaurant or nearby.

Because menu prices can fluctuate, we list a pricing category rather than specific prices. The pricing categories are defined as follows, per diner, and assume that you order an appetizer or dessert, an entrée, and one drink:

✪ **$** = $15 and under

✪ **$$** = $16-$35

✪ **$$$** = $36-$85

✪ **$$$$** = $86 and up

Again, all prices quoted are in effect at the time of publication, but prices cannot be guaranteed.

SPECIAL INFORMATION FOR TRAVELERS WITH DISABILITIES

The Mobil Travel Guide ▣ symbol indicates that an establishment is not at least partially accessible to people with mobility problems. When the ▣ symbol follows a listing, the establishment is not equipped with facilities to accommodate people using wheelchairs or crutches or otherwise needing easy access to doorways and rest rooms. Travelers with severe mobility problems or with hearing or visual impairments may or may not find the facilities they need. Always phone ahead to make sure hat an establishment can meet your needs.

Understanding the Symbols

What to See and Do

⭐	=	One of the top attractions in the area
$	=	Up to $5
$$	=	$5.01 to $10
$$$	=	$10.01 to $15
$$$$	=	Over $15

Lodgings

$	=	Up to $150
$$	=	$151 to $250
$$$	=	$251 to $350
$$$$	=	Over $350

Restaurants

$	=	Up to $15
$$	=	$16 to $35
$$$	=	$36 to $85
$$$$	=	Over $85

Lodging Star Definitions

★★★★★   A Mobil Five-Star lodging establishment provides consistently superlative service in an exceptionally distinctive luxury environment with expanded services. Attention to detail is evident throughout the hotel/resort/inn from the bed linens to the staff uniforms.

★★★★   A Mobil Four-Star lodging establishment is a hotel/resort/inn that provides a luxury experience with expanded amenities in a distinctive environment. Services may include, but are not limited to, automatic turndown service, 24-hour room service, and valet parking.

★★★   A Mobil Three-Star lodging establishment is a hotel/resort/inn that is well appointed, with a full-service restaurant and expanded amenities, such as, but not limited to, a fitness center, golf course, tennis courts, 24-hour room service, and optional turndown service.

★★   A Mobil Two-Star lodging establishment is a hotel/resort/inn that is considered a clean, comfortable, and reliable establishment, but also has expanded amenities, such as a full-service restaurant on the premises.

★   A Mobil One-Star lodging establishment is a limited-service hotel or inn that is considered a clean, comfortable, and reliable establishment.

Restaurant Star Definitions

★★★★★   A Mobil Five-Star restaurant is one of few flawless dining experiences in the country. These restaurants consistently provide their guests with exceptional food, superlative service, elegant décor, and exquisite presentations of each detail surrounding the meal.

★★★★   A Mobil Four-Star restaurant provides professional service, distinctive presentations, and wonderful food.

★★★   A Mobil Three-Star restaurant has good food, warm and skillful service, and enjoyable décor.

★★   A Mobil Two-Star restaurant serves fresh food in a clean setting with efficient service. Value is considered in this category, as is family friendliness.

★   A Mobil One-Star restaurant provides a distinctive experience through culinary specialty, local flair, or individual atmosphere.

Symbols at End of Listings

🚫 Facilities for people with disabilities not available

🐾 Pets allowed

⛷ Ski in/ski out access

⛳ Golf on premises

🎾 Tennis court(s) on premises

🏊 Indoor or outdoor pool

🏋 Fitness room

✈ Major commercial airport within 5 miles

🏃 Business center

Making the Most of Your Trip

A few hardy souls might look back with fondness on a trip during which the car broke down, leaving them stranded for three days, or a vacation that cost twice what it was supposed to. For most travelers, though, the best trips are those that are safe, smooth, and within budget. To help you make your trip the best it can be, we've assembled a few tips and resources.

Saving Money

ON LODGING

Many hotels and motels offer discounts—for senior citizens, business travelers, families, you name it. It never hurts to ask—politely, that is. Sometimes, especially in the late afternoon, desk clerks are instructed to fill beds, and you might be offered a lower rate or a nicer room to entice you to stay. Simply ask the reservation agent for the best rate available. Also, make sure to try both the toll-free number and the local number. You may be able to get a lower rate from one than from the other.

Timing your trip right can cut your lodging costs as well. Look for bargains on stays over multiple nights, in the off-season, and on weekdays or weekends, depending on the location. Many hotels in major metropolitan areas, for example, have special weekend packages that offer leisure travelers considerable savings on rooms; they may include breakfast, cocktails, and/or dinner discounts.

Another way to save money is to choose accommodations that give you more than just a standard room. Rooms with kitchen facilities enable you to cook some meals yourself, reducing your restaurant costs. A suite might save money for two couples traveling together. Even hotel luxury levels can provide good value, as many include breakfast or cocktails in the price of a room.

State and city taxes, as well as special room taxes, can increase your room rate by as much as 25 percent per day. We are unable to include information about taxes in our listings, but we strongly urge you to ask about taxes when making reservations so that you understand the total cost of your lodgings before you book them.

Watch out for telephone-usage charges that hotels frequently impose on long-distance, credit-card, and other calls. Before phoning from your room, read the information given to you at check-in, and then be sure to review your bill carefully when checking out. You won't be expected to pay for charges that the hotel didn't spell out. Consider using your cell phone if you have one; or, if public telephones are available in the hotel lobby, your cost savings may outweigh the inconvenience of using them.

Here are some additional ways to save on lodgings:

○ Stay in B&B accommodations. They're generally less expensive than standard hotel rooms, and the complimentary breakfast cuts down on food costs.

○ If you're traveling with children, find lodgings at which kids stay free.

○ When visiting a major city, stay just outside the city limits; these rooms are usually less expensive than those in downtown locations.

○ Consider visiting national parks during the low season, when prices of lodgings near the parks drop by 25 percent or more.

○ When calling a hotel, ask whether it is running any special promotions or if any discounts are available; many times reservationists are told not to volunteer these deals unless they're specifically asked about them.

○ Check for hotel packages; some offer nightly rates that include a rental car or discounts on major attractions.

ON DINING

There are several ways to get a less expensive meal at an expensive restaurant. Early-bird dinners are popular in many parts of the country and offer considerable savings. If you're interested in visiting a Mobil Four- or Five-Star establishment, consider going at lunchtime. Although the prices are probably still relatively high at midday, they may be half of those at dinner, and you'll experience the same ambience, service, and cuisine.

ON ENTERTAINMENT

Although many national parks, monuments, seashores, historic sites, and recreation areas may be visited free of charge, others charge an entrance fee and/or a usage fee for special services and facilities. If you plan to make several visits to national recreation areas, consider one of the following money-saving programs offered by the National Park Service:

○ **National Parks Pass.** This annual pass is good for entrance to any national park that charges an entrance fee. If the park charges a per-vehicle fee, the pass holder and any accompanying passengers in a private noncommercial vehicle may enter. If the park charges a per-person fee, the pass applies to the holder's spouse, children, and parents as well as the holder. It is valid for entrance fees only; it does not cover parking, camping, or other fees. You can purchase a National Parks Pass in person at any national park where an entrance fee is charged; by mail from the National Park Foundation, PO Box 34108, Washington, DC 20043-4108; by calling toll-free 888/467-2757; or at www.nationalparks .org. The cost is $50.

○ **Golden Eagle Sticker.** When affixed to a National Parks Pass, this hologram sticker, available to people who are between 17 and 61 years of age, extends coverage to sites managed by the US Fish and Wildlife Service, the US Forest Service, and the Bureau of Land Management. It is good until the National Parks Pass to which it is affixed expires and does not cover usage fees. You can purchase one at the National Park Service, the Fish and Wildlife Service, or the Bureau of Land Management fee stations. The cost is $15.

○ **Golden Age Passport.** Available to citizens and permanent US residents 62 and older, this passport is a lifetime entrance permit to fee-charging national recreation areas. The fee exemption extends to those accompanying the permit holder in a private noncommercial vehicle or, in the case of walk-in facilities, to the holder's spouse and children. The passport also entitles the holder to a 50 percent discount on federal usage fees charged in park areas, but not on concessions. Golden Age Passports must be obtained in person and are available at most National Park Service units that charge an entrance fee. The applicant must show proof of age, such as a driver's license or birth certificate (Medicare cards are not acceptable proof). The cost is $10.

○ **Golden Access Passport.** Issued to citizens and permanent US residents who are physically disabled or visually impaired, this passport is a free lifetime entrance permit to fee-charging national recreation areas. The fee exemption extends to those accompanying the permit holder in a private noncommercial vehicle or, in the case of walk-in facilities, to the holder's spouse and children. The passport also entitles the holder to a 50 percent discount on usage fees charged in park areas, but not on concessions. Golden Access Passports must be obtained in person and are available at most National Park Service units that charge an entrance fee. Proof of eligibility to receive federal benefits (under programs such as Disability Retirement, Compensation for Military Service-Connected Disability, and the Coal Mine Safety and Health Act) is required, or an affidavit must be signed attesting to eligibility.

A money-saving move in several large cities is to purchase a **CityPass.** If you plan to visit several museums and other major attractions, CityPass is a terrific option because it gets you into several sites for one substantially reduced price. Currently, CityPass is available in Boston, Chicago, Hollywood, New York, Philadelphia, San Francisco, Seattle, southern California (which includes Disneyland, SeaWorld, and the San Diego Zoo), and Toronto. For more information or to buy one, call toll-free 888/330-5008 or visit www. citypass.net. You can also buy a CityPass from any participating CityPass attraction.

Here are some additional ways to save on entertainment and shopping:

○ Check with your hotel's concierge for various coupons and special offers; they often have two-for-one tickets for area attractions and coupons for discounts at area stores and restaurants.

○ Purchase same-day concert or theater tickets for half-price through the local cheap-tickets outlet, such as TKTS in New York or Hot Tix in Chicago.

- Visit museums on their free or "by donation" days, when you can pay what you wish rather than a specific admission fee.

- Save receipts from purchases in Canada; visitors to Canada can get a rebate on federal taxes and some provincial sales taxes.

ON TRANSPORTATION

Transportation is a big part of any vacation budget. Here are some ways to reduce your costs:

- If you're renting a car, shop early over the Internet; you can book a car during the low season for less, even if you'll be using it in the high season.

- Rental car discounts are often available if you rent for one week or longer and reserve in advance.

- Get the best gas mileage out of your vehicle by making sure that it's properly tuned up and keeping your tires properly inflated.

- Travel at moderate speeds on the open road; higher speeds require more gasoline.

- Fill the tank before you return your rental car; rental companies charge to refill the tank and do so at prices of up to 50 percent more than at local gas stations.

- Make a checklist of travel essentials and purchase them before you leave; don't get stuck buying expensive sunscreen at your hotel or overpriced film at the airport.

FOR SENIOR CITIZENS

Always call ahead to ask if a discount is being offered, and be sure to carry proof of age. Additional information for mature travelers is available from the American Association of Retired Persons (AARP), 601 E St NW, Washington, DC 20049; phone 202/434-2277; www.aarp.org.

Tipping

Tips are expressions of appreciation for good service. However, you are never obligated to tip if you receive poor service.

IN HOTELS

- Door attendants usually get $1 for hailing a cab.

- Bell staff expect $2 per bag.

- Concierges are tipped according to the service they perform. Tipping is not mandatory when you've asked for suggestions on sightseeing or restaurants or for help in making dining reservations. However, a tip of $5 is appropriate when a concierge books you a table at a restaurant known to be difficult to get into. For obtaining theater or sporting event tickets, $5 to $10 is expected.

- Maids should be tipped $1 to $2 per day. Hand your tip directly to the maid, or leave it with a note saying that the money has been left expressly for the maid.

IN RESTAURANTS

Before tipping, carefully review your check for any gratuity or service charge that is already included in your bill. If you're in doubt, ask your server.

- Coffee shop and counter service waitstaff usually receive 15 percent of the bill, before sales tax.

- In full-service restaurants, tip 18 percent of the bill, before sales tax.

- In fine restaurants, where gratuities are shared among a larger staff, 18 to 20 percent is appropriate.

- In most cases, the maitre d' is tipped only if the service has been extraordinary, and only on the way out. At upscale properties in major metropolitan areas, $20 is the minimum.

- If there is a wine steward, tip $20 for exemplary service and beyond, or more if the wine was decanted or the bottle was very expensive.

- Tip $1 to $2 per coat at the coat check.

AT AIRPORTS

Curbside luggage handlers expect $1 per bag. Car-rental shuttle drivers who help with your luggage appreciate a $1 or $2 tip.

Staying Safe

The best way to deal with emergencies is to avoid them in the first place. However, unforeseen situations do happen, so you should be prepared for them.

IN YOUR CAR

Before you head out on a road trip, make sure that your car has been serviced and is in good working order. Change the oil, check the battery and belts, make sure that your windshield washer fluid is full and your tires are properly inflated (which can also improve your gas mileage). Other inspections recommended by the vehicle's manufacturer should also be made.

Next, be sure you have the tools and equipment needed to deal with a routine breakdown:

- Jack
- Spare tire
- Lug wrench
- Repair kit
- Emergency tools
- Jumper cables
- Spare fan belt
- Fuses
- Flares and/or reflectors
- Flashlight
- First-aid kit
- In winter, a windshield scraper and snow shovel

Many emergency supplies are sold in special packages that include the essentials you need to stay safe in the event of a breakdown.

Also bring all appropriate and up-to-date documentation—licenses, registration, and insurance cards—and know what your insurance covers. Bring an extra set of keys, too, just in case.

En route, always buckle up! In most states, wearing a seatbelt is required by law.

If your car does break down, do the following:

- Get out of traffic as soon as possible—pull well off the road.
- Raise the hood and turn on your emergency flashers or tie a white cloth to the roadside door handle or antenna.
- Stay in your car.
- Use flares or reflectors to keep your vehicle from being hit.

IN YOUR HOTEL

Chances are slim that you will encounter a hotel or motel fire, but you can protect yourself by doing the following:

- Once you've checked in, make sure that the smoke detector in your room is working properly.
- Find the property's fire safety instructions, usually posted on the inside of the room door.
- Locate the fire extinguishers and at least two fire exits.
- Never use an elevator in a fire.

For personal security, use the peephole in your room door and make sure that anyone claiming to be a hotel employee can show proper identification. Call the front desk if you feel threatened at any time.

PROTECTING AGAINST THEFT

To guard against theft wherever you go:

- Don't bring anything of more value than you need.
- If you do bring valuables, leave them at your hotel rather than in your car.
- If you bring something very expensive, lock it in a safe. Many hotels put one in each room; others will store your valuables in the hotel's safe.
- Don't carry more money than you need. Use traveler's checks and credit cards or visit cash machines to withdraw more cash when you run out.

For Travelers with Disabilities

To get the kind of service you need and have a right to expect, don't hesitate when making a reservation to question the management about the availability of accessible rooms, parking, entrances, restaurants, lounges, or any other facilities that are important to you, and confirm what is meant by "accessible."

The Mobil Travel Guide 🅳 symbol indicates establishments that are not at least partially accessible to people with special mobility needs (people using wheelchairs or crutches or otherwise needing easy access to buildings and rooms). Further information about these criteria can be found in the earlier section "How to Use This Book."

A thorough listing of published material for travelers with disabilities is available from the Disability Bookshop, Twin Peaks Press, Box 129, Vancouver, WA 98666; phone 360/694-2462; disabilitybookshop.virtualave.net. Another reliable organization is the Society for Accessible Travel & Hospitality (SATH), 347 Fifth Ave, Suite 610, New York, NY 10016; phone 212/447-7284; www.sath.org.

Important Toll-Free Numbers and Online Information

Hotels

Adams Mark 800/444-2326
www.adamsmark.com

America's Best Value Inn 888/315-2378
www.americasbestvalueinn.com

AmericInn 800/634-3444
www.americinn.com

AmeriHost Inn 800/434-5800
www.amerihostinn.com

Amerisuites 800/833-1516
www.amerisuites.com

Baymont Inns 800/621-1429
www.baymontinns.com

Best Inns & Suites 800/237-8466
www.bestinn.com

Best Western 800/780-7234
www.bestwestern.com

Budget Host Inn 800/283-4678
www.budgethost.com

Candlewood Suites 888/226-3539
www.candlewoodsuites.com

Clarion Hotels 800/252-7466
www.choicehotels.com

Comfort Inns and Suites 800/252-7466
www.comfortinn.com

Country Hearth Inns 800/848-5767
www.countryhearth.com

Country Inns & Suites 800/456-4000
www.countryinns.com

Courtyard by Marriott 800/321-2211
www.courtyard.com

Crowne Plaza Hotels and Resorts 800/227-6963
www.crowneplaza.com

Days Inn 800/544-8313
www.daysinn.com

Delta Hotels 800/268-1133
www.deltahotels.com

Destination Hotels & Resorts 800/434-7347
www.destinationhotels.com

Doubletree Hotels 800/222-8733
www.doubletree.com

Drury Inn 800/378-7946
www.druryhotels.com

Econolodge 800/553-2666
www.econolodge.com

Embassy Suites 800/362-2779
www.embassysuites.com

ExelInns of America 800/367-3935
www.exelinns.com

Extended StayAmerica 800/398-7829
www.extendedstayhotels.com

Fairfield Inn by Marriott 800/228-2800
www.fairfieldinn.com

Fairmont Hotels 800/441-1414
www.fairmont.com

Four Points by Sheraton 888/625-5144
www.fourpoints.com

Four Seasons 800/819-5053
www.fourseasons.com

Hampton Inn 800/426-7866
www.hamptoninn.com

Hard Rock Hotels, Resorts, and Casinos 800/473-7625
www.hardrockhotel.com

Harrah's Entertainment 800/427-7247
www.harrahs.com

Hawthorn Suites 800/527-1133
www.hawthorn.com

Hilton Hotels and Resorts (US) 800/774-1500
www.hilton.com

Holiday Inn Express 800/465-4329
www.hiexpress.com

Holiday Inn Hotels and Resorts 800/465-4329
www.holiday-inn.com

Homestead Studio Suites 888/782-9473
www.extendedstayhotels.com

Homewood Suites 800/225-5466
www.homewoodsuites.com

Howard Johnson 800/406-1411
www.hojo.com

Hyatt 800/633-7313
www.hyatt.com

Inns of America 800/826-0778
www.innsofamerica.com

InterContinental 888/424-6835
www.intercontinental.com

Joie de Vivre 800/738-7477
www.jdvhospitality.com

Kimpton Hotels 888/546-7866
www.kimptonhotels.com

Knights Inn 800/843-5644
www.knightsinn.com

La Quinta 800/531-5900
www.lq.com

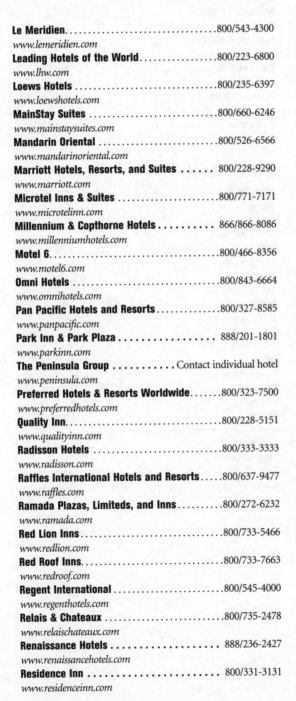

Le Meridien. 800/543-4300
www.lemeridien.com

Leading Hotels of the World. 800/223-6800
www.lhw.com

Loews Hotels 800/235-6397
www.loewshotels.com

MainStay Suites 800/660-6246
www.mainstaysuites.com

Mandarin Oriental 800/526-6566
www.mandarinoriental.com

Marriott Hotels, Resorts, and Suites 800/228-9290
www.marriott.com

Microtel Inns & Suites 800/771-7171
www.microtelinn.com

Millennium & Copthorne Hotels 866/866-8086
www.millenniumhotels.com

Motel 6. . . . . .800/466-8356
www.motel6.com

Omni Hotels 800/843-6664
www.omnihotels.com

Pan Pacific Hotels and Resorts. 800/327-8585
www.panpacific.com

Park Inn & Park Plaza 888/201-1801
www.parkinn.com

The Peninsula Group . . . . Contact individual hotel
www.peninsula.com

Preferred Hotels & Resorts Worldwide. 800/323-7500
www.preferredhotels.com

Quality Inn. 800/228-5151
www.qualityinn.com

Radisson Hotels 800/333-3333
www.radisson.com

Raffles International Hotels and Resorts. 800/637-9477
www.raffles.com

Ramada Plazas, Limiteds, and Inns. 800/272-6232
www.ramada.com

Red Lion Inns. 800/733-5466
www.redlion.com

Red Roof Inns. 800/733-7663
www.redroof.com

Regent International 800/545-4000
www.regenthotels.com

Relais & Chateaux 800/735-2478
www.relaischateaux.com

Renaissance Hotels 888/236-2427
www.renaissancehotels.com

Residence Inn 800/331-3131
www.residenceinn.com

Ritz-Carlton. 800/241-3333
www.ritzcarlton.com

RockResorts. 888/367-7625
www.rockresorts.com

Rodeway Inn. 800/228-2000
www.rodeway.com

Rosewood Hotels & Resorts 888/767-3966
www.rosewoodhotels.com

Select Inn 800/641-1000
www.selectinn.com

Sheraton 888/625-5144
www.sheraton.com

Shilo Inns 800/222-2244
www.shiloinns.com

Shoney's Inn. 800/552-4667
www.shoneysinn.com

Signature/Jameson Inns. 800/822-5252
www.jamesoninns.com

Sleep Inn 877/424-6423
www.sleepinn.com

Small Luxury Hotels of the World. 800/525-4800
www.slh.com

Sofitel 800/763-4835
www.sofitel.com

SpringHill Suites 888/236-2427
www.springhillsuites.com

St. Regis Luxury Collection. 888/625-5144
www.stregis.com

Staybridge Suites 800/238-8000
www.staybridge.com

Summit International 800/457-4000
www.summithotelsandresorts.com

Super 8 Motels 800/800-8000
www.super8.com

The Sutton Place Hotels. 866/378-8866
www.suttonplace.com

Swissôtel 800/637-9477
www.swissotels.com

TownePlace Suites. 888/236-2427
www.towneplace.com

Travelodge 800/578-7878
www.travelodge.com

Vagabond Inns. 800/522-1555
www.vagabondinn.com

W Hotels 888/625-5144
www.whotels.com

Wellesley Inn and Suites. 800/444-8888
www.wellesleyinnandsuites.com

WestCoast Hotels............................800/325-4000
www.westcoasthotels.com
Westin Hotels & Resorts....................800/937-8461
www.westinhotels.com
Wingate Inns..............................800/228-1000
www.thewingateinns.com
Woodfin Suite Hotels........................800/966-3346
www.woodfinsuitehotels.com
WorldHotels..............................800/223-5652
www.worldhotels.com
Wyndham Hotels & Resorts.................800/996-3426
www.wyndham.com

Airlines

Air Canada.........................888/247-2262
www.aircanada.com
AirTran..................................800/247-8726
www.airtran.com
Alaska Airlines............................800/252-7522
www.alaskaair.com
American Airlines...........................800/433-7300
www.aa.com
ATA......................................800/435-9282
www.ata.com
Continental Airlines.........................800/523-3273
www.continental.com
Delta Air Lines.............................800/221-1212
www.delta.com
Frontier Airlines...........................800/432-1359
www.frontierairlines.com
Hawaiian Airlines...........................800/367-5320
www.hawaiianairlines.com
Jet Blue Airlines...........................800/538-2583
www.jetblue.com

Midwest Airlines............................800/452-2022
www.midwestairlines.com
Northwest Airlines..........................800/225-2525
www.nwa.com
Southwest Airlines..........................800/435-9792
www.southwest.com
Spirit Airlines.............................800/772-7117
www.spiritair.com
United Airlines.............................800/241-6522
www.united.com
US Airways.................................800/428-4322
www.usairways.com

Car Rentals

Advantage.................................800/777-5500
www.arac.com
Alamo....................................800/327-9633
www.alamo.com
Avis.....................................800/831-2847
www.avis.com
Budget...................................800/527-0700
www.budget.com
Dollar...................................800/800-4000
www.dollar.com
Enterprise................................800/325-8007
www.enterprise.com
Hertz....................................800/654-3131
www.hertz.com
National..................................800/227-7368
www.nationalcar.com
Payless..................................800/729-5377
www.paylesscarrental.com
Rent-A-Wreck.com..........................800/535-1391
www.rentawreck.com
Thrifty...................................800/847-4389
www.thrifty.com

Meet The Stars

Mobil Travel Guide 2007 *Five-Star* Award Winners

CALIFORNIA
Lodgings
The Beverly Hills Hotel, *Beverly Hills*
Chateau du Sureau, *Oakhurst*
Four Seasons Hotel San Francisco,
  San Francisco
Hotel Bel-Air, *Los Angeles*
The Peninsula Beverly Hills, *Beverly Hills*
Raffles L'Ermitage Beverly Hills, *Beverly Hills*
St. Regis Monarch Beach Resort & Spa, *Dana
  Point*
St. Regis San Francisco, *San Francisco*
The Ritz-Carlton, San Francisco, *San Francisco*

Restaurants
The Dining Room, *San Francisco*
The French Laundry, *Yountville*

COLORADO
Lodgings
The Broadmoor, *Colorado Springs*
The Little Nell, *Aspen*

CONNECTICUT
Lodging
The Mayflower Inn, *Washington*

DISTRICT OF COLUMBIA
Lodging
Four Seasons Hotel Washington, DC
  Washington

FLORIDA
Lodgings
Four Seasons Resort Palm Beach, *Palm Beach*
The Ritz-Carlton Naples, *Naples*
The Ritz-Carlton, Palm Beach, *Manalapan*

GEORGIA
Lodgings
Four Seasons Hotel Atlanta, *Atlanta*

The Lodge at Sea Island Golf Club,
  St. Simons Island

Restaurants
The Dining Room, *Atlanta*
Seeger's, *Atlanta*

HAWAII
Lodging
Four Seasons Resort Maui, *Wailea, Maui*

ILLINOIS
Lodgings
Four Seasons Hotel Chicago, *Chicago*
The Peninsula Chicago, *Chicago*
The Ritz-Carlton, A Four Seasons Hotel, *Chicago*

Restaurants
Alinea, *Chicago*
Charlie Trotter's, *Chicago*

MAINE
Restaurant
The White Barn Inn, *Kennebunkport*

MASSACHUSETTS
Lodgings
Blantyre, *Lenox*
Four Seasons Hotel Boston, *Boston*

NEVADA
Lodging
Tower Suites at Wynn, *Las Vegas*

Restaurants
Alex, *Las Vegas*
Joel Robuchon at the Mansion, *Las Vegas*

NEW YORK
Lodgings
Four Seasons, Hotel New York, *New York*
Mandarin Oriental, *New York*
The Point, *Saranac Lake*

The Ritz-Carlton New York, Central Park,
  New York
The St. Regis, *New York*

Restaurants
Alain Ducasse, *New York*
Jean Georges, *New York*
Masa, *New York*
per se, *New York*

NORTH CAROLINA
Lodging
The Fearrington House Country Inn, *Pittsboro*

PENNSYLVANIA
Restaurant
Le Bec-Fin, *Philadelphia*

SOUTH CAROLINA
Lodging
Woodlands Resort & Inn, *Summerville*

Restaurant
Dining Room at the Woodlands, *Summerville*

TENNESSEE
Lodging
The Hermitage, *Nashville*

TEXAS
Lodging
The Mansion on Turtle Creek, *Dallas*

VERMONT
Lodging
Twin Farms, *Barnard*

VIRGINIA
Lodgings
The Inn at Little Washington, *Washington*
The Jefferson Hotel, *Richmond*

Restaurant
The Inn at Little Washington, *Washington*

Mobil Travel Guide has been rating establishments with its Mobil One- to Five-Star system since 1958. Each establishment awarded the Mobil Five-Star rating is one of the best in the country. Detailed information on each award winner can be found in the corresponding regional edition listed on the back cover of this book.

Four- and Five-Star Establishments in the South

Louisiana

★★★★ Lodging
Windsor Court Hotel, *New Orleans*

★★★★ Restaurants
Bayona, *New Orleans*
Emeril's Restaurant, *New Orleans*
The Grill Room, *New Orleans*
La Provence, *Lacombe*

Tennessee

★★★★★ Lodging
The Hermitage Hotel, *Nashville*

★★★★ Lodging
Blackberry Farm, *Maryville*

★★★★ Restaurants
The Capitol Grille, *Nashville*
Chez Philippe, *Memphis*

Alabama

From the Confederacy's first capital at Montgomery to America's first "space capital" at Huntsville, Alabama has successfully spanned a century that began in sectional conflict but ended in a dedication to man's quest to bridge the universe. The drive from the business center of Birmingham to the heart of the Cotton Kingdom surrounding Montgomery and Selma is less than 100 miles, but these miles mark one of the transitions between the 19th and 20th centuries.

Harnessing the Tennessee River made it possible to control floods and turn the eroded soil into bountiful crop land. The river became the South's most important waterway, and giant Tennessee Valley Authority (TVA) dams brought electric power and industrialization to once bypassed cities. They also gave northern Alabama nationally renowned water recreation areas.

Cotton, the traditional wealth of Alabama's rich Black Belt, fed the busy port of Mobile until the 1870s, when Birmingham grew into an industrial center. TVA brought the other great shift in the 1930s, culminating in new hydroelectric and steam plant power production in the 1960s.

Cotton and river waterways were the combination on which the Old South was built. The Cotton State supreme by the 1850s, Alabama built river towns like Selma, the old capital of "Cahawba," and Montgomery, the new capital and "cradle of the Confederacy." The red iron ore in the northern mountains was neglected, except for isolated forges operated by individuals, until just before the Civil War.

On January 11, 1861, Alabama became the fourth state to secede from the Union. Jefferson Davis was

Population: 4,447,100

Area: 50,750 square miles

Elevation: 0-2,407 feet

Peak: Cheaha Mountain (Cleburne County)

Entered Union: December 14, 1819 (22nd state)

Capital: Montgomery

Motto: We Dare Defend Our Rights

Nickname: Heart of Dixie

Flower: Camellia

Bird: Yellowhammer

Tree: Southern Pine

Time Zone: Central

Web Site: www.touralabama.org

Fun Fact:

- Alabama is the only state with all major natural resources needed to make iron and steel. It is also the largest supplier of cast-iron and steel pipe products.

inaugurated as president of the Confederacy in Montgomery the following month, and on April 12 he ordered General P. G. T. Beauregard to fire on Fort Sumter. The Confederate capital was moved to Richmond on May 21, 1861.

Alabama's troops fought with every active Southern force, the state contributing between 65,000 and 100,000 men from a white population of 500,000. At least 2,500 white soldiers and 10,000 black soldiers went north to support the Union. When Huntsville, Decatur, and Tuscumbia fell to Union forces in 1862, every male from 16 to 60 was ordered to the state's defense. Little fighting took place on Alabama's soil and water again until Admiral Farragut's Union fleet won the Battle of Mobile Bay in 1864, though the city of Mobile did not fall. Full-scale invasions by Wilson's Raiders occupied several important cities in the spring of 1865.

Reconstruction days were made bitter by carpet-baggers who supported the Republican Party. The

Calendar Highlights

MARCH

Historic Mobile Tours *(Mobile). Phone toll-free 800/566-2453.* Houses, buildings open to visitors.

MAY

Alabama Jubilee *(Decatur). Point Mallard Park. Phone 800/524-6181.* Highlight of festivities are the hot-air balloon races.

City Stages *(Birmingham). Phone toll-free 205/251-1272.* Music festival of national artists. Food, dancing, children's activities, and regional craftsmen.

SEPTEMBER

Big Spring Jam *(Huntsville). Phone 256/551-2230.* Music festival, including pop, rock, jazz, country, and other genres. Foods from local restaurants, shows for kids.

OCTOBER

Alabama Renaissance Faire *(Florence). Phone 256/740-4141.* Renaissance-era arts and crafts, music, food, entertainment. Fair workers in period costumes.

Greater Gulf State Fair *(Mobile). Phone 334/344-4573.* Commercial, industrial, military, and educational exhibits; entertainment.

State Fair *(Birmingham). Phone 205/786-8100.*

DECEMBER

Blue-Gray All-Star Classic *(Montgomery). Contact Lion's Club/Blue-Gray Association, phone 334/265-1266.*

state refused to ratify the Fourteenth Amendment, and military law was reinstated. But by the 1880s, recovery was beginning. Birmingham had weathered the national panic of 1873 successfully and was producing steel in earnest.

Historic attractions are plentiful. There is the birthplace of Helen Keller at Tuscumbia (see SHEFFIELD); the unusual Ave Maria Grotto in Cullman (see), an inspiring work of faith by one Benedictine monk who built scores of miniature religious buildings; and the museum and laboratory of the great black educator and scientist, George Washington Carver, at the Tuskegee Institute (see TUSKEGEE).

On Alabama's Gulf Coast, the port city of Mobile makes a splendid entry to the whole Gulf strip between Florida and New Orleans. Mobile is famous for the Bellingrath Gardens and Home, the annual Azalea Trail and Festival, and its own Mardi Gras celebration.

For golf enthusiasts, the Robert Trent Jones Golf Trail has 18 championship golf courses offering a total of 324 holes located at 7 sites: Anniston/Gadsden, Auburn/Opelika, Birmingham, Dothan, Greenville, Huntsville, and Mobile (phone toll-free 800/949-4444 for more information).

When to Go/Climate

Alabama's climate is mild almost year-round, although the extreme northern part of the state can experience cold weather and even some snow in winter. The southern part of the state can be extremely hot beginning as early as March. Fall is usually comfortable throughout the state and is generally a good time to visit.

AVERAGE HIGH/LOW TEMPERATURES (°F)

Birmingham

Jan 52/31	**May** 81/58	**Sept** 84/63
Feb 57/35	**June** 87/65	**Oct** 75/50
Mar 66/42	**July** 90/70	**Nov** 65/42
Apr 75/49	**Aug** 89/69	**Dec** 56/35

Mobile

Jan 60/40	**May** 85/64	**Sept** 87/69
Feb 64/43	**June** 90/71	**Oct** 80/57
Mar 71/50	**July** 91/73	**Nov** 70/49
Apr 79/57	**Aug** 91/73	**Dec** 63/43

Parks and Recreation

Water-related activities, hiking, riding, various sports, picnicking, camping, and visitor centers are available in many of Alabama's state parks. Nominal entrance fees are collected at some parks. The state parks accept telephone reservations for motel rooms, cabins, and improved campsites; primitive campsites are on a no-reservation basis. Fees for improved campsites are $10- $25/site per night. No pets at motels and cabins; pets on leash only at campgrounds. There are many state park fishing lakes and 12 parks that offer boat rentals and water-recreational equipment. Bait, tackle, and freshwater fishing permits are $2/day; under 13, 75/day. For details, contact the Alabama Department of Conservation and Natural Resources, Alabama State Parks Division, 64 N Union St, Montgomery 36130; phone 334/242-3334. For reservations, call 800/252-7275 or 334/242-3333.

FISHING AND HUNTING

More than 50,000 small ponds and lakes, including 22 public lakes and more than half a million acres of public impounded waters, provide ample freshwater fishing. Crappie, striped and white bass, bluegill, and redear sunfish can be caught statewide. State and national forests and state parks cater to anglers. White sandy beaches of the Gulf Coast are good for surf casting; trolling farther out in Gulf waters can net tarpon, snapper, king mackerel, and other game fish. Largemouth bass abound from the Tennessee River to Mobile Bay. The Lewis Smith and Martin reservoirs have both largemouth and spotted bass; the Wilson and Wheeler Dam tailwaters have smallmouth bass; the east central Alabama streams have redeye bass. Alabama has no closed season on freshwater game fish. Sport fishing licenses, nonresident: annual, $31; 7-day, $11 (includes issuance fee). The fees for reciprocal licenses for the residents of adjoining states and Louisiana vary.

Waterfowl, small game, turkey, and deer are found in the state, with state-managed and national forest wildlife areas providing hunting in season. Deer and turkey hunting require an all-game hunting license for nonresidents. Federal and State Waterfowl Stamps are required in addition to a regular hunting license when hunting waterfowl. Because nearly all lands in

Alabama are under private ownership and state law requires written permission from the owner before hunting, persons desiring to hunt should make arrangements accordingly. Hunting licenses, nonresident: annual all-game, $252; annual small game, $77; 10-day all-game, $127; 7-day small game, $47; 3-day all-game, $77; 3-day small game, $32. Management area deer and turkey licenses ($4) are required in the management areas in addition to the regular hunting license. A reciprocal agreement among Alabama and the state of Florida may alter the license fees charged residents of Florida. License costs for nonresident hunting licenses include a $2 issuance fee. For detailed information about seasons and other regulations, contact the Alabama Department of Conservation and Natural Resources, Game and Fish Division, 64 N Union St, Montgomery 36130; phone 334/242-3467. For information about fishing and hunting licenses, call 334/242-3829.

Driving Information

All passengers in the front seat of a vehicle must wear safety belts. Children under 6 years must be in approved passenger restraints anywhere in the vehicle; ages 4 and 5 may use regulation safety belts or child seats; age 3 and under must use federally approved safety seats. For further information, phone 334/242-4445.

INTERSTATE HIGHWAY SYSTEM

The following alphabetical listing of Alabama towns in this book shows that these cities are within 10 miles of the indicated interstate highways. Check a highway map for the nearest exit.

Highway Number	Cities/Towns within 10 Miles
Interstate 10	Mobile.
Interstate 20	Anniston, Bessemer, Birmingham, Tuscaloosa.
Interstate 59	Bessemer, Birmingham, Fort Payne, Gadsden, Tuscaloosa.
Interstate 65	Athens, Atmore, Birmingham, Clanton, Cullman, Decatur, Evergreen, Greenville, Mobile, Montgomery.
Interstate 85	Auburn, Motgomery, Opelika, Tuskegee.

AROUND MOBILE BAY TO THE GULF COAST

French colonists founded Mobile at the head of Mobile Bay. The bay remains southwest Alabama's most compelling feature. An 80-mile loop trip clockwise around the bay from Mobile takes visitors to old waterfront resort towns, state parks, Civil War forts, and across a ferry to Dauphin Island beaches before looping back up the west side of the bay.

From Mobile, head east on I-10 to the edge of the bay, where Meaher State Park offers a quiet marshland refuge for picnicking and bird-watching. From here, drop south on Highway 98. Take the split to Alt 98 north of the old resort town of Fairhope. Take this alternative seaside route to Fairhope's beachfront park, where there's a seafood restaurant, fishing pier, and a nice view of Mobile. Alt 98 continues along the shore 5 miles south to Point Clear, another small resort town, then rejoins Highway 98 at the north side of Weeks Bay. Here, the Weeks Bay National Estuarine Research Station has a nature museum and an elevated boardwalk over the waterfront, providing a close look at coastal ecology. Continue following Highway 98 East to Foley, where drivers pick up Highway 59 South to the Gulf of Mexico. The 6,150-acre Gulf State Park (phone 334/948-7275) lies directly along the east shore and has 2 1/2 miles of beaches, a beachfront hotel, buffet restaurant, golf course, pool, and tennis courts, in addition to hiking and biking trails, campgrounds, and lakefront cabins.

From Gulf Shores, Highway 180 leads west 22 miles across Pleasure Island, then past many more miles of beautiful beaches to Fort Morgan State Park (note that it's slow going with summer crowds). The brick fort here was built in 1834 to stand guard over the narrow entrance to Mobile Bay. The park also maintains a popular beach. The fort saw action in the Battle of Mobile Bay in 1864, when Confederate forces were overtaken by the Union navy.

A car ferry from Fort Morgan crosses the tiny mouth of the Bay over to Dauphin Island. Another Civil War fort, Fort Gaines, stands at the western entrance. Dauphin Island, with its high bluffs and low dunes, is a favorite spot for swimming, sunbathing, fishing, biking, and camping. There's also a small residential community with rental vacation cabins and a commercial district with motels, restaurants, and cafs. A freshwater lake near the ferry landing provides a bird sanctuary and trails through the marsh and sand dunes. You can also see the estuary up close at the Dauphin Island Sea Lab (phone 334/861-2141), which is located a block from the ferry dock. The exhibit hall explains different native habitats, and outside there's an interpretive boardwalk trail.

Highway 193 leads north back to the mainland and along the western shore of Mobile Bay. Near the town of Theodore, Bellingrath Gardens (phone 334/973-2217) features tours of the Bellingrath house, but the highlight of a visit is its 65-acre landscaped Southern garden at the water's edge, most popular when the azaleas bloom in spring. Continue up Highway 193 to I-10 to return to Mobile. **(Approximately 80 miles)**

Additional Visitor Information

Travel and vacation information is offered toll-free, phone 800/ALABAMA (Mon-Fri). For additional information, travelers may contact the Alabama Bureau of Tourism & Travel, 401 Adams Ave, PO Box 4927, Montgomery 36103; phone 334/242-4169.

There are eight welcome centers in Alabama; there visitors will find information and brochures that will help plan stops at points of interest: Alabama (I-59 S), Ardmore (I-65 S), Baldwin (I-10 W), Grand Bay (I-10 E), Hardy (I-20 W, near Heflin), Houston (Hwy 231 N), Lanett (I-85 S), and Sumter (I-59 N/20 E). Inquire locally for further information about these centers.

Alexander City (C-4)

See also Horseshoe Bend National Military Park, Sylacauga

Settled 1836
Population 15,008
Elevation 707 ft
Area Code 256
Zip 35010
Information Chamber of Commerce, 120 Tallapoosa St, Box 926, 35011; phone 256/234-3461
Web Site www.alexandercity.com

Martin Dam at Cherokee Bluffs not only supplies power but also creates Lake Martin on the Tallapoosa

River. Lake Martin, with a 760-mile shoreline, was the largest of its kind when it was formed in 1926. Today, it is one of the South's finest inland recreation areas.

What to See and Do

Wind Creek State Park. *4325 Hwy 128, Alexander City (35010). 7 miles SE off Hwy 63.Phone 256/329-0845. www.dcnr.state.al.us/parks/wind_creek_1a.html.* A 1,445-acre wooded park on Lake Martin. Swimming beach, bathhouses, waterskiing, fishing, boating (marina, ramps); hiking, bicycling, picnic area, concessions, improved campsites ($$$$). Observation tower. (Daily)

Limited-Service Hotels

★ **BEST WESTERN HORSESHOE INN.** *3146 Hwy 280, Alexander City (35010). Phone 256/234-6311; toll-free 800/780-7234; fax 256/234-6314. www.bestwestern.com.* 90 rooms. Check-out 11 am. Bar. Outdoor pool. **$**
🏊

★ **JAMESON INN ALEXANDER CITY.** *4335 Hwy 280, Alexander City (35010). Phone 256/234-7099; toll-free 800/526-3766; fax 256/234-9807. www.jamesoninns.com.* 60 rooms, 2 story. Pets accepted. Complimentary continental breakfast. Check-out 11 am. Fitness room. Outdoor pool. **$**
🐾🏋🏊

Restaurant

★ **CECIL'S PUBLIC HOUSE.** *243 Green St, Alexander City (35010). Phone 256/329-0732.* Set in a restored turn-of-the-century home, this local favorite features country standbys like chicken-fried steak and an array of sandwiches, but surprises diners with dishes like a cranberry-citrus vinaigrette for salads, chicken margoux and lobster ravioli. American menu. Lunch, dinner. Closed Sun; holidays. Bar. Children's menu. **$**

Anniston (B-4)

See also Gadsden, Talladega

Settled 1872
Population 24,276
Elevation 710 ft
Area Code 205
Zip 36202
Information Convention & Visitors Bureau, 14th St and Quintard Ave, PO Box 1087; phone 256/237-3536 or toll-free 800/489-1087
Web Site www.calhounchamber.com

Anniston was founded by Samuel Noble, an Englishman who headed the ironworks in Rome, Georgia, and Daniel Tyler, a Connecticut capitalist. They established textile mills and blast furnaces designed to help launch the South into the industrial revolution after the devastation of the Civil War. In 1879, the owners hired accomplished Eastern architects, including the renowned Stanford White, to design and build a modern company town. The town was named after Mrs. Anne Scott Taylor (Annie's Town), wife of one of the local iron magnates. Anniston remained a private company town until 1883, when it was opened to the public. Today, Anniston retains many historic structures and much of its original character.

What to See and Do

Anniston Museum of Natural History. *Lagarde Park, 800 Museum Dr, Anniston (36207). Phone 256/237-6766. www.annistonmuseum.org.* Museum featuring Regar-Werner bird exhibit with more than 400 specimens including endangered and extinct; full-scale model of an Albertosaurus and a meteorite; Egyptian mummies; and changing exhibition gallery. Situated in 185-acre John B. Lagarde Environmental Interpretive Park; nature trails, picnic facilities. (Tues-Sat 10 am-5 pm, Sun 1-5 pm; also open Mon in summer; closed holidays) **$**

Berman Museum. *Lagarde Park, 840 Museum Dr, Anniston (36206). Phone 205/237-6261. www.berman-museum.org.* Collection of unique artifacts amassed by a real spy on his worldly missions. Treasures from the American West and World War II eras are featured, including a Royal Persian Scimitar encrusted with 1,295 rose-cut diamonds, 60 carats of rubies, and a single 40-carat emerald set in three pounds of gold. (Sept-May: Tues-Sat 10 am-5 pm, Sun 1-5 pm; June-Aug: Mon-Sat 10 am-5 pm, Sun 1-5 pm; closed holidays) **$**

Church of St. Michael and All Angels. *W 18th St and Cobb Ave, Anniston. Phone 205/237-4011.* (1888) (Episcopal) Gothic church, parish house, assembly room, and bell tower of native stone are connected by cloisters. Twelve-foot Carrara marble altar with alabaster reredos surmounted by seven statues of angels. Stained-glass memorial windows. Lithographs of Christian history are in assembly room. (Daily)

Coldwater Covered Bridge. *Coldwater. 3 miles S via Hwy 431, 5 miles W on Hwy 78 in Coldwater at Oxford Lake and Civic Center.* Built before 1850; one of 13 restored covered bridges in Alabama.

Limited-Service Hotels

★ ★ **AMERICAS BEST VALUE INN.** *11900 Hwy 78, Riverside (35135). Phone 205/338-3381; fax 205/338-3183. www.bestvalueinn.com.* 70 rooms, 2 story. Pets accepted, some restrictions. Check-in 1 pm, check-out 11 am. Restaurant. Outdoor pool, children's pool. **$**

★ **HAMPTON INN.** *1600 Hwy 21 S, Oxford (36203). Phone 256/835-1492; toll-free 800/426-7866; fax 256/835-0636. www.hamptoninn.com.* 129 rooms, 2 story. Complimentary continental breakfast. Check-out noon. Outdoor pool. **$**

Full-Service Inn

★ ★ ★ **THE VICTORIA COUNTRY INN.** *1604 Quintard Ave, Anniston (36202). Phone 256/236-0503; fax 256/236-1138. www.thevictoria.com.* For a quiet and memorable getaway, this beautifully restored country inn, built in 1888, is a wonderful example of early Victorian architecture. Much thought was given to design and comfort with stylish guest rooms, fine dining, and a piano lounge. 60 rooms, 3 story. Check-in 3 pm, check-out noon. Restaurant. Outdoor pool. **$**

Restaurants

★ **BETTY'S BAR-B-Q.** *401 S Quintard Ave, Anniston (36201). Phone 256/237-1411.* American menu. Lunch, dinner. Closed Sun; holidays; also week of July 4. Children's menu. **$**

★ ★ **THE VICTORIA.** *1604 Quintard Ave, Anniston (36201). Phone 256/236-0503; fax 256/236-1138. www.thevictoria.com.* Romantic dining in a Victorian house. American menu. Dinner. Closed Sun; holidays. Bar. Outdoor seating. **$$$**

Athens (E-3)

See also Decatur, Huntsville

Founded 1818
Population 18,967

Elevation 720 ft
Area Code 256
Zip 35611
Information Athens-Limestone County Chamber of Commerce, PO Box 150, 35612; phone 256/232-2600 or 256/232-2609
Web Site www.ci.athens.al.us

The quiet, tree-lined streets and Greek Revival houses lend an air of the old antebellum South to Athens. This was the first major Alabama town to be occupied by Union troops in the Civil War (1862). It was also the first Alabama city to get electricity (1934) from the Tennessee Valley Authority. Electrification soon spread to the surrounding area, aiding in the development of light manufacturing.

What to See and Do

Athens State University. *300 N Beaty St, Athens (35611). Between Beaty and Hobbs sts. Phone 256/233-8100. www.athens.edu.* (1822) (2,600 students) On campus is Founders Hall (1843), as well as many examples of Greek Revival architecture. On the second floor of Founders Hall is the Pi Tau Chi Chapel, housing a hand-carved altar depicting scenes from the New Testament. Tours of campus (academic year, Mon-Fri).

Houston Memorial Library and Museum. *101 N Houston St, Athens (35611). Market and Houston sts. Phone 256/233-8770.* Built in 1835, this house was once owned by George S. Houston, governor of Alabama and US senator. It is now maintained by the city of Athens. Meeting rooms display Houston coat of arms, family portraits, and drawing-room furniture. (Mon-Fri, also Sat mornings; closed holidays) **FREE**

Special Events

Homespun. *507 Hoffman St, Athens (35611). Phone 256/232-3525.* Craft show featuring woodworking, quilting, basketmaking; also buggy rides. Early May.

Musical Explosion. *Athens Bible School, 507 Hoffman St, Athens (35611). Phone 256/232-3525.* Mostly country music, some contemporary. Two weekends in late Mar.

Tennessee Valley Old Time Fiddler's Convention. *Athens State University, 300 N Beaty St, Athens (35611). Phone 256/233-8100. www.athens.edu/fiddlers.* A weekend of traditional American music. Fiddle, mandolin, guitar, banjo, and old-time singing; also buck dancing. National and international musicians perform; ends with the naming of the Tennessee Valley Fiddle King. Fri, Sat of first full weekend in Oct.

Limited-Service Hotels

★ **BEST WESTERN ATHENS INN.** *1329 Hwy 72, Athens (35612). Phone 256/233-4030; toll-free 800/780-7234; fax 256/233-4554. www.bestwestern.com.* 88 rooms, 2 story. Pets accepted, some restrictions; fee. Complimentary continental breakfast. Check-out noon. Outdoor pool. **$**

★ **HAMPTON INN.** *1488 Thrasher Blvd, Athens (35611). Phone 256/232-0030; toll-free 800/426-7866; fax 256/233-7006. www.hamptoninn.com.* 56 rooms, 2 story. Complimentary continental breakfast. Check-out 11 am. Outdoor pool, whirlpool. **$**

Auburn (C-4)

See also Opelika, Tuskegee

Settled 1836
Population 42,987
Elevation 709 ft
Area Code 334
Zip 36831
Information Auburn/Opelika Convention & Visitors Bureau, 714 E Glenn Ave, PO Box 2216; phone 334/887-8747 or toll-free 800/321-8880
Web Site www.auburn-opelika.com

Auburn took its name from the opening line in Oliver Goldsmith's poem, "The Deserted Village," which reads "Sweet Auburn, the loveliest village of the plain." Located on the southeastern slope of the Piedmont plateau, this trading and university community is graced with Greek Revival, Victorian, and early 20th-century architecture.

What to See and Do

Auburn University. *202 Mary Martin Hall, Auburn (36849). SW section of town off I-85, Hwys 14, 29, 147. Phone 334/844-4000. www.auburn.edu.* (1856) (22,000 students) One of the nation's earliest land-grant colleges and the first four-year educational institution in Alabama to admit women on an equal basis with men. A golden eagle, the university mascot, is housed on campus. Tours of campus. Adjacent is

The Tiger Trail of Auburn. *College St and Magnolia Ave, Auburn.* Granite plaques bearing the names of athletes and coaches that have brought recognition to Auburn.

Chewacla State Park. *124 Shell Toomer Pkwy, Auburn (36830). 4 miles S off Hwy 29; 2 miles off I-85, exit 51. Phone toll-free 800/252-7275. www.dncr.state.al.us.* This 696-acre park, on the fall line separating the Piedmont plateau from the coastal plain, includes a 26-acre lake. Swimming, bathhouse, fishing, boating (rentals); hiking, nature, and mountain bike trails, picnicking, playground, concession, improved camping, cabins.

Lovelace Athletic Museum. *Donahue Dr and Stamford Ave, Auburn. Phone 334/844-0764. www.lovelacemuseum.com.* Orange-and-blue shrine to such famous Auburn University athletes as Bo Jackson and Charles Barkley. Interactive exhibits. (Mon-Fri 8 am-4:30 pm, Sat 9 am-4 pm) **FREE**

Limited-Service Hotel

★ ★ **BEST WESTERN UNIVERSITY CONVENTION CENTER.** *1577 S College St, Auburn (36830). Phone 334/821-7001; toll-free 800/282-8763; fax 334/821-7008. www.bestwestern.com.* 122 rooms, 3 story. Pets accepted. Complimentary continental breakfast. Check-out 11 am. Restaurant, bar. Fitness room. Outdoor pool. **$**

Full-Service Hotel

★ ★ ★ **AUBURN UNIVERSITY HOTEL.** *241 S College St, Auburn (36830). Phone 334/821-8200; toll-free 800/228-2876; fax 334/826-8746. www.auhcc.com.* This hotel and conference center, with elegantly furnished rooms, is located near Auburn University. 248 rooms, 6 story. Pets accepted. Check-out noon. Restaurant, bar. Fitness room. Outdoor pool. **$**

Specialty Lodging

CRENSHAW HOUSE BED & BREAKFAST. *371 N College St, Auburn (36830). Phone 334/821-1131; toll-free 800/950-1131; fax 334/826-8123. www.bbonline.com/al/crenshaw/.* 6 rooms, 2 story. Complimentary continental breakfast. Check-in 2 pm, check-out 11 am. Restored house built in 1890. **$**

Bessemer (E-3)

See also Birmingham, Tuscaloosa

Founded 1887
Population 29,672
Elevation 513 ft
Area Code 205
Information Bessemer Area Chamber of Commerce, PO Box 648, 35021; phone 205/425-3253 or toll-free 888/423-7736
Web Site www.bessemerchamber.com

The city of Bessemer was founded on April 12, 1887, by Henry F. DeBardeleben. It was named after Sir Henry Bessemer, inventor of the steel-making process that bears his name. As additional furnaces were built in Bessemer, the population grew. By the 1930s, the town ranked second only to Birmingham as a state center for heavy industry. The factories turned out iron and steel, cast-iron pipe, steel railway cars, explosives, fertilizer, and building materials. Today, various industries dominate Bessemer's economy; the medical community is among the city's largest employers.

What to See and Do

Hall of History Museum. *1905 Alabama Ave, Bessemer (35020). In Southern Railway Depot. Phone 205/426-1633.* Displays of pioneer life in Jefferson County, Mound Indians, the Civil War, and Bessemer city history. (Tues-Sat; closed holidays)

Tannehill State Historical Park. *12632 Confederate Pkwy, McCalla (35111). 12 miles SW off I-59, exit 100 at Bucksville. Phone 205/477-5711. www.tannehill.org.* Restored ironworks that once produced 20 tons of pig iron a day for the Confederacy. Iron & Steel Museum (daily). Park features bathhouses, fishing; nature trails, picnicking, concession, camping (hookups, dump station; fee). Park (daily). **$**

VisionLand Amusement Park. *5051 Prince St, Bessemer (35023). 1 mile N of Hwy 459 on I-20/59 W at exit 108. Phone 205/481-4750. www.visionland.com.* Theme park features four separate themed areas—Main Street, a replica of an old-fashioned town with shops and carousel; Marvel City, a giant playground for kids; Celebration City, featuring a wooden roller coaster and other thrill rides; and Steel Waters, a water park with slides and tubing. (May-Sept, daily) **$$$$**

Special Event

Christmas Parade. *Bessemer. Downtown. Phone 205/425-3253.www.bessemerchamber.com.* Bessemer residents decorate their cars for the holiday season (fee for participants). Pre-parade activities take place in Debardeleben Park. Early Dec. **FREE**

Limited-Service Hotel

★ ★ **DAYS INN.** *1121 A 9th Ave SW, Bessemer (35022). Phone 205/424-9780; fax 205/424-9780. www.daysinn.com.* 156 rooms, 2 story. Check-out noon. Restaurant, bar. Outdoor pool, children's pool. **$**

Restaurant

★ **BOB SYKES BAR-B-QUE.** *1724 9th Ave N, Bessemer (35020). Phone 205/426-1400; fax 205/428-5751. www.bobsykes.com.* Lunch, dinner. Closed Sun; Jan 1, Thanksgiving, Dec 25. **$**

Birmingham (B-3)

See also Bessemer, Cullman, Jasper, Talladega

Founded 1871
Population 242,820
Elevation 601 ft
Area Code 205
Information Convention & Visitors Bureau, 2200 9th Ave N, 35203; phone 205/458-8000 or toll-free 800/458-8085
Web Site www.birminghamal.org

A city of great industrial strength, Birmingham once proudly called itself the "Pittsburgh of the South." Today Birmingham is equally proud of its reputation as an international medical center. Advances in medical science through research at the University of Alabama medical complex attract patients worldwide.

At the turn of the 19th century, Native Americans who painted their faces and weapons red were known by early settlers as "Red Sticks." Even when the red paint was found to be hematite iron ore, it was still considered worthless, and many years passed before Red Mountain ore became the foundation for Birmingham's steel industry. The Confederacy's lack of iron in 1863 led to the building of a small blast furnace which produced cannonballs and rifles until Wilson's Raiders destroyed it in 1865.

Birmingham was born in 1871 when two railroads intersected. A year later, the Elyton Land Company had sold most of its 4,150 acres at fabulous prices. (It had bought the land for $25 an acre.) But in 1873, a double disaster struck. First, cholera drove hundreds from the new city; then, the nationwide financial panic nearly doomed Birmingham to extinction. Refusing to give in, Charles Linn, a former Civil War blockade runner who had opened a small bank in 1871, built a grand three-story brick bank for the huge (at that time) sum of $36,000. He then sent out 500 invitations to a "Calico Ball," as he called it, to celebrate its opening. Guests came from all over the state, women in ball gowns and men in formal dress all cut from calico. "Linn's folly" paid off—Birmingham was saved.

Today Birmingham is a modern, progressive city— one of culture as well as steel, and of education as well as the social life that began with the Calico Ball. To visitors, it offers much in recreational and sightseeing opportunities. Birmingham Green, a major renaissance of the downtown area, added walkways, plantings, benches, and the DART trolley. The Five Points South area, featuring clubs with many styles of quality entertainment, plays a major role in Birmingham's nightlife. This is indeed the heart of the New South.

Additional Information

Contact the Greater Birmingham Convention & Visitors Bureau, 2200 9th Ave N, Birmingham (35203). Phone 205/458-8000; or the Birmingham/Jefferson Visitor Information Center, 1201 University Blvd; phone 205/458-8001

Public Transportation

Buses (Birmingham/Jefferson County Transit Authority); phone 205/521-0101

Airport Birmingham International Airport. Weather phone 205/945-7000

Information Phone 205/599-0500

Lost and Found Phone 205/599-0500

What to See and Do

Alabama Sports Hall of Fame Museum. *2150 Civic Center Blvd, Birmingham (35203). Phone 205/323-6665. www.alasports.org.* Showcase for memorabilia of Alabama sports figures; sound-sensored displays; theater. (Mon-Sat 9 am-5 pm, Sun 1-5 pm; closed holidays) **$$**

Arlington Antebellum Home and Gardens. *331 Cotton Ave SW, Birmingham (35211). Phone 205/780-5656.* (Circa 1850) Birmingham's last remaining antebellum house in the Greek Revival style features a diverse collection of 19th-century decorative art. Located on a sloping hill in Elyton, the house is surrounded by oak and magnolia trees, and seasonal plantings. (Tues-Sat 10 am-4 pm, Sun 1-4 pm; closed holidays) **$**

Birmingham Botanical Gardens. *2612 Lane Park Rd, Birmingham (35223). Phone 205/414-3950. www. bbgardens.org.* Includes orchids, lilies, dogwood, wildflowers, azaleas; 26-foot floral clock, conservatory, and arboretum of rare plants, shrubs, and trees. (Daily, dawn-dusk) Restaurant on grounds. **FREE** Includes

Japanese Gardens. *2616 Lane Park Rd, Birmingham (35223). Phone 205/414-3950.* Gardens landscaped with Asian plants, waterfalls. Also here is a bonsai complex, Asian statuary, and a Zen garden. Gravel paths. (Daily)

Birmingham Civil Rights Institute. *520 16th St N, Birmingham (35203). Phone 205/328-9696; toll-free 866/328-9696. www.bcri.org.* Exhibits portray the struggle for civil rights in Birmingham and across the nation from the 1920s to the present; multimedia presentations. Free admission on Martin Luther King, Jr. holiday (Tues-Sat 10 am-5 pm, Sun 1-5 pm; closed Mon and holidays) **$$**

Birmingham Museum of Art. *2000 8th Ave N, Birmingham (35203). Across from Linn Park. Phone 205/254-2565. www.artsbma.org.* Features collections of Renaissance, Asian, and American art, including Remington bronzes; 20th-century collection; 17th- through 19th-century American and European paintings and decorative arts. Also featured are pre-Columbian art and artifacts, Native American art, and the largest collection of Wedgwood outside of England. Changing exhibits. Multilevel sculpture garden with two reflecting pools and a waterfall. (Tues-Sat 10 am-5 pm, Sun noon-5 pm; closed holidays) **FREE**

Birmingham Zoo. *2630 Cahaba Rd, Birmingham (35223). Phone 205/879-0409. www.birminghamzoo. com.* Nearly 1,000 animals on display. Highlights include sea lions, Endochinese tiger, and the predator building. (Daily 9 am-5 pm; extended hours Memorial Day-Labor Day: Tues, Fri-Sat to 7 pm) **$$**

Birmingham-Jefferson Convention Complex. *Birmingham. Between 9th and 11th aves N, 19th and 21st sts. Phone 205/458-8400. www.bjcc.org.* The entire complex covers seven square blocks. The center contains

Downtown Birmingham

Birmingham, the home of the Civil Rights Institute, is an important stop on any African-American history tour itinerary. While the city is most notorious for turbulence during the civil rights era, the cultural contributions of African Americans to Birmingham are less well known.

Start at the Historical Fourth Avenue Visitor Center (319 17th St N; phone 205/328-1850), where you can pick up a map or take a guided tour of the historic African-American business district.

Across the street from the visitor center is the Alabama Jazz Hall of Fame, located within the historic Carver Theater (1631 Fourth Ave N; phone 205/254-2731). Exhibits cover the history of jazz and celebrate such artists as Dinah Washington, Nat King Cole, Duke Ellington, and W. C. Handy, among others. The theater also plays host to live performances. On the other side of the visitor center, the Alabama Theater (1817 Third Ave N) has been restored to its 1920s splendor and is now a cinema.

Head west along Third Avenue one block to another beloved local landmark: La Vase (328 16th St N), a restaurant that serves hearty home-style soul food. After your meal, proceed north up 16th Street three blocks to Kelly Ingram Park, the scene of civil rights clashes in the 1950s and 1960s. The inscription at its entrance reads A Place for Revolution and Reconciliation, and the park commemorates its role in civil rights history with statues and sculptures.

The Birmingham Civil Rights Institute (520 16th St; phone 205/328-9696), across the street from the park, is the city's premiere attraction. A short film introduces the city's history, and vintage footage illustrates the Jim Crow era and the development of the civil rights movement. Exhibits emphasize the events that took place in Birmingham, including, for example, the door from the city jail cell that housed Reverend Martin Luther King, Jr., the inspiration for Dr. Kings famous Letter from a Birmingham Jail. The bookshop has a good selection of African-American history and heritage titles.

Cross Sixth Avenue to reach the 16th Street Baptist Church (1530 Sixth Ave N; phone 205/251-9402), which was bombed in a 1963 attack that killed four girls. The rebuilt church hosts tens of thousands of visitors each year.

220,000 square feet of exhibition space; 3,000-seat concert hall; 1,100-seat theater; 18,000-seat coliseum.

Birmingham-Southern College. *900 Arkadelphia Rd, Birmingham (35254). Phone 205/226-4600. www.bsc. edu.* (1856) (1,500 students) A 200-acre campus on wooded rolling hills. Here is the state's first planetarium (for schedule, reservations, phone 205/226-4771; fee). Tours of campus.

McWane Center. *1421 22nd St S, Birmingham (35234). Phone 205/714-8300. www.mcwane.org.* Natural history museum located on the slopes of Red Mountain. Extensive collection of fossils including a 14-foot mosasaur (extinct marine lizard); geologic history displays and exhibits; hands-on exhibits. Walkway carved into the face of the mountain above expressway. More than 150 million years of geologic history are exposed for 1/3 mile. Picnicking. (Sept-May: Mon-Fri 9 am-5 pm, Sat 10 am-6 pm, Sun 1-5 pm; June-Aug: Mon-Sat 10 am-6 pm, Sun 1-6 pm; closed holidays) **$**

Miles College. *5500 Myron Massey Blvd, Fairfield (35064). Phone 205/929-1000. www.miles.edu.* (1905) (1,500 students) Extensive collection of African-American literature; exhibits of African art forms. Two historic landmark buildings. Tours.

Oak Mountain State Park. *200 Terrace Dr, Pelham (35124). 15 miles S on I-65, exit 246. Phone 205/620-2524. www.dcnr.state.al.us.* Peavine Falls and Gorge and two lakes sit amidst 9,940 acres of the state's most rugged mountains. Activities include swimming, fishing, boating (marina, ramp, rentals), hiking, backpacking, bridle trails, golf (18 holes; fee), tennis, picnicking (shelters, barbecue pits, fireplaces), concession, camping, cabins, and a demonstration farm. **$**

Rickwood Caverns State Park. *370 Rickwood Park Rd, Warrior (35180). 20 miles N on I-65 to exit 284 (just N of Warrior) then 4 miles W on Skyline Dr to Rickwood Rd, follow state signs. Phone 205/647-9692. www.dcnr. state.al.us.* This 380-acre park offers swimming pools;

hiking, carpet golf, miniature train ride, picnicking, concession, gift shop, primitive and improved camping (standard fees). One-hour tours of cave with 260 million-year-old limestone formations (Memorial Day-Labor Day, daily; rest of Sept-Oct and Mar-May, weekends). Park (all year); pool (seasonal). Fee for some activities. **$**

Ruffner Mountain Nature Center. *1214 81st St S, Birmingham (35206). Phone 205/833-8264. www. ruffnermountain.org.* Contains 1,011 acres of the last undeveloped section of this area's Appalachian Mountains. Displays focus on Ruffner Mountain's biology, geology, and history. Wildlife refuge with nature trails. Special programs (fee). (Tues-Sat 9 am-5 pm, Sun 1-5 pm; closed holidays, also Dec 24) **FREE**

Samford University. *800 Lakeshore Dr, Birmingham (35229). In Shades Mountain section. Phone 205/726-2011. www.samford.edu.* (1841) (4,600 students) A 172-acre campus with brick Georgian Colonial buildings. The Samford Murals are on view in Rotunda, Dwight and Lucille Beeson Center for the Healing Arts. Science Center has conservatory of medicinal plants and planetarium with shows (Mon evenings). Beeson Divinity Hall Chapel is topped by a copper-clad dome that has a detailed ceiling mural on the interior (tours available). Tours of campus.

Sloss Furnaces National Historic Landmark. *20 32nd St N, Birmingham (35222). Phone 205/324-1911. www. slossfurnaces.com.* An industrial museum and site for concerts and downtown festivals. (Tues-Sun) **FREE**

Southern Museum of Flight/Alabama Aviation Hall of Fame. *4343 73rd St N, Birmingham (35206). Phone 205/833-8226. www.southernmuseumofflight.org.* View a full-size Wright Flyer replica, a 1912 Curtiss Pusher replica, a Fokker VII, a VariEze experimental home-built, two US Air Force fighter jet cockpit simulators, and flight-related memorabilia. (Tues-Sat 9:30 am-4:30 pm, Sun 1-4:30 pm) **$**

University of Alabama at Birmingham. *1400 University Blvd, Birmingham (35233). Phone 205/934-4475. www.uab.edu.* (16,500 students) On 70-square-block area on south edge of downtown. **Reynolds Historical Library** in the Lister Hill Library of the Health Sciences, 1700 University Blvd, six blocks W of Hwy 31 and Hwy 280, has collections of ivory anatomical mannequins, original manuscripts, and rare medical and scientific books; **Alabama Museum of Health Sciences** has memorabilia of Alabama doctors, surgeons, optometrists, and other medical practitioners; repro-

ductions of doctor and dentist turn-of-the-century offices (Mon-Fri). **FREE**

Vulcan. *20th St and 19th Ave, Birmingham. On Valley Ave off Hwy 31 at top of Red Mountain in Vulcan Park. Phone 205/328-2863.* (1904) The figure of Vulcan, designed for the Louisiana Purchase Exposition in St. Louis, is one of the largest iron figures ever cast, standing 55 feet tall and weighing 60 tons. It surveys the city from a pedestal 124 feet high. Made of Birmingham iron and cast locally, Vulcan, Roman god of fire and forge, legendary inventor of smithing and metalworking, stands as a monument to the city's iron industry atop Red Mountain; and since 1939, he holds a lighted torch aloft over the city. A glass-enclosed elevator takes passengers to observation deck. Vulcan's torch shines bright red when there's been a traffic fatality in the city in the previous 24 hours. Park (daily; closed Thanksgiving, Dec 25). **$**

Special Events

City Stages. *1929 3rd Ave N, Birmingham. Phone 205/251-1272.* Billed as "Birmingham's World-Class Music Festival," City Stages features approximately 160 musical performances on 11 stages. Artists include both local and nationally known musicians (George Clinton, Al Green, and Kid rock have been past performers). Third weekend in June.

Greater Alabama Fall Fair & Festival. *Alabama State Fairgrounds, 2331 Bessemer Rd, Birmingham (35208). Phone 205/786-8100.* Features food, games, agricultural exhibitions, contests, livestock demonstrations, and arts and crafts vendors. Ten days in late Oct-early Nov.

International Festival. *205 20th St N, Birmingham. Phone 205/252-7652.* Each year, the Birmingham International Festival highlights the culture of a different country to promote education as well as business and trade relationships between Alabama and the selected country. A party early in the year kicks off a series of events to take place in the months to follow, which includes a trade expo, conferences, art exhibits, lectures, and a black-tie dinner. The free educational programs bring musicians, performers, and storytellers to Alabama schools, and includes a student art exhibition. Feb-May.

Limited-Service Hotels

★ ★ **BEST WESTERN RIME GARDEN INN & SUITES.** *5320 Beacon Dr, Birmingham (35210). Phone 205/951-1200; toll-free 888/828-1768; fax*

205/951-1692. www.bestwestern.com. 290 rooms, 3 story. Complimentary continental breakfast. Check-out noon. Restaurant, bar. Outdoor pool. Airport transportation available. **$**

★ ★ **COURTYARD BY MARRIOTT.** *500 Shades Creek Pkwy, Homewood (35209).Phone 205/879-0400; toll-free 800/321-2211; fax 205/879-6324.www.courtyard.com.* Conveniently located, this hotel is a short drive from Birmingham's airport. Great for the traveler on the go, guests should check out nearby Oak Mountain State Park or Birmingham Zoo.140 rooms, 3 story. Check-out noon. Restaurant, bar. Fitness room. Outdoor pool, whirlpool. **$**

★ ★ **CROWNE PLAZA HOTEL BIRMING-HAM.** *2101 5th Ave, Birmingham (35203). Phone 205/324-2101; toll-free 800/227-6963; fax 205/324-0610. www.crowneplaza.com/cpbhmdowntown.* As Birmingham's oldest operating hotel, this downtown location was originally The Redmont Hotel, and has since been meticulously renovated. Guests here are in the heart of the city's business and historical district, and are within walking distance of the Civil Rights Institute, the Alabama Theater, and the Alabama Sports Hall of Fame, among many other attractions. 114 rooms, 12 story. Check-in 3 pm, check-out noon. High-speed Internet access. Restaurant, bar. Fitness room. Airport transportation available. Business center. **$**

★ ★ **EMBASSY SUITES.** *2300 Woodcrest Pl, Birmingham (35051). Phone 205/879-7400; toll-free 800/362-2779; fax 205/870-4523. www.embassy-suites.com.* This hotel is situated in Corporate Business Park, Southbridge, and is only 3 miles from the University of Alabama. Spacious suites have a full array of amenities. 243 rooms, 8 story, all suites. Complimentary full breakfast. Check-out noon. Restaurant, bar. Indoor pool, whirlpool. Airport transportation available. **$**

★ ★ **FOUR POINTS BY SHERATON BIRMINGHAM AIRPORT.** *5216 Airport Hwy, Birmingham (35212). Phone 205/591-7900; fax 205/591-6004.* 193 rooms, 4 story. Check-out noon. Restaurant, bar. Fitness room. Outdoor pool. Airport transportation available. **$**

★ **HAMPTON INN BIRMINGHAM-COLONNADE.** *3400 Colonnade Pkwy, Birmingham (35243). Phone 205/967-0002; toll-free 800/861-7168; fax 205/969-0901. www.hamptoninn.com.* With a close proximity to area attractions such as botanical gardens, bowling, a zoo, and shopping, and a staff that exemplifies traditional Southern hospitality, this conveniently located hotel also features mountain views. 133 rooms, 5 story. Pets accepted, some restrictions. Complimentary continental breakfast. Check-in 3 pm, check-out noon. High-speed Internet access. Fitness room. Outdoor pool. Business center. **$**

★ **LA QUINTA INN.** *513 Cahaba Park Cir, Birmingham (35242). Phone 205/995-9990; fax 205/995-0563. www.laquinta.com.* 99 rooms, 3 story. Pets accepted. Complimentary continental breakfast. Check-out noon. **$**

★ ★ **QUALITY INN ON THE LAKE.** *1548 Montgomery Hwy, Birmingham (35216). Phone 205/822-4350; toll-free 800/228-5151; fax 205/822-0350. www.qualityinn.com.* 166 rooms, 3 story. Check-out noon. Restaurant, bar. Outdoor pool, whirlpool. **$**

★ ★ **RADISSON HOTEL BIRMINGHAM.** *808 S 20th St, Birmingham (35205). Phone 205/933-9000; toll-free 800/333-3333; fax 205/933-0920.www.radisson.com.*In the heart of downtown and two blocks from the University and UAB Medical Center. It is just a short walk to the Five Points entertainment and restaurant district. 298 rooms, 14 story. Check-out noon. Restaurant, bar. Outdoor pool. Airport transportation available. **$**

Full-Service Hotels

★ ★ ★ **HILTON BIRMINGHAM PERIMETER PARK.** *8 Perimeter Park S, Birmingham (35243). Phone 205/967-2700; toll-free 800/774-1500; fax 205/972-8603. www.hilton.com.* Set in an up-and-coming business and entertainment area, this large hotel is in close proximity to the downtown area, with its cultural and corporate destinations. Among the amenities in the attractive rooms are work desks and dual-line phones. 205 rooms, 8 story. Check-in 3 pm, check-out noon. Wireless Internet access. Restaurant, bar. Fitness room. Outdoor pool. Airport transportation available. Business center. **$**

★ ★ ★ **MARRIOTT BIRMINGHAM.** *3590 Grandview Pkwy, Birmingham (35243). Phone 205/968-3775; toll-free 800/228-9290; fax 205/968-3742. www.marriott.com.* A mix of cozy and contemporary furnishings gives this hotel, just off Highway 280, an inviting and comfortable feel. Friendly staff, a huge array of amenities, and a location close to many business headquarters and entertainment options make this a prime option. 295 rooms, 7 story. Check-in 3 pm, check-out noon. High-speed Internet access, wireless Internet access. Restaurant, bar. Fitness room. Indoor pool. Business center. **$$**

★ ★ ★ **SHERATON BIRMINGHAM.** *2101 Richard Arrington Jr. Blvd N, Birmingham (35203). Phone 205/324-5000; toll-free 800/325-3535; fax 205/307-3085. www.sheraton.com.* Located in downtown Birmingham, this hotel is a short stroll on the skywalk to the convention center. Explore the zoo, art museum, and Five Points South historical district nearby. 770 rooms, 17 story. Check-in 3 pm, check-out noon. Restaurant, bar. Fitness room. Indoor pool, whirlpool. Business center. **$$**

★ ★ ★ **WYNDHAM TUTWILER HOTEL.** *2021 Park Pl N, Birmingham (35203). Phone 205/322-2100; toll-free 877/999-3223; fax 205/325-1198. www.wyndham.com.* This American classic built in the 1920s has been restored to its original grandeur and now is an elegant experience with gracious service and amenities. Nearby is the McWane Center and the Birmingham Museum of Art. 147 rooms, 8 story. Pets accepted, some restrictions; fee. Complimentary full breakfast. Check-in 3 pm, check-out noon. High-speed Internet access. Restaurant, bar. Airport transportation available. Business center. **$$$**

★ ★ ★ **THE WYNFREY HOTEL.** *1000 Riverchase Galleria, Birmingham (35244). Phone 205/987-1600; toll-free 800/996-3739; fax 205/988-4597. www.wynfrey.com.* The Wynfrey Hotel is Birmingham's best lodging. Located just on the edge of the city, this gracious hotel combines Southern hospitality with European panache. The rooms and suites are tastefully appointed with stylish furnishings and plentiful amenities. This hotel is a favorite destination of shoppers, with special access to the city's renowned Riverchase Galleria. After a tiring day of bargain hunting, guests retire to the Spa Japonika to recharge and relax. Two restaurants and in-room dining ensure that all moods and tastes are satisfied at this sophisticated urban retreat. 329 rooms, 16 story. Check-in 4 pm, check-out 11 am. High-speed Internet access, wireless Internet access. Two restaurants, two bars. Fitness room. Outdoor pool. Airport transportation available. Business center. **$$**

Restaurants

★ **GOLDEN CITY CHINESE RESTAURANT.** *4647 Hwy 280, Birmingham (35242). Phone 205/991-3197.* Chinese menu. Lunch, dinner. Closed holidays. Bar. **$$**

★ ★ ★ **HIGHLANDS.** *2011 11th Ave S, Birmingham (35205). Phone 205/939-1400; fax 205/939-1405. www.highlandsbarandgrill.com.* This has been one of Birmingham's premiere restaurants for many years. The food has a Southern emphasis, the chef's signature style. French menu. Dinner. Closed Sun-Mon; holidays. Bar. Valet parking. **$$$**

★ ★ **NIKI'S WEST.** *233 Finley Ave W, Birmingham (35204). Phone 205/252-5751; fax 205/252-8163.* Steak and seafood are on the menu, but you are welcome to go through the busy cafeteria line as well. Niki's is known for its "meat and three" options. Come hungry. American menu. Lunch, dinner. Closed Sun; holidays. **$$**

Clanton (E-3)

See also Montgomery

Founded 1873
Population 7,800
Elevation 599 ft
Area Code 205
Zip 35045
Information Chamber of Commerce, PO Box 66; phone 205/755-2400 or toll-free 800/553-0493
Web Site www.clanton.al.us

A peach and truck farming area, Clanton also caters to fishermen along the Coosa River and its tributaries. Lay and Mitchell dams, to the north and east, respectively, are backed by lakes and furnish power to the region. Clanton is the seat of Chilton County.

What to See and Do

Confederate Memorial Park. *437 Country Rd 63, Marbury (36051). 10 miles S via Hwy 31. Phone 205/755-*

1990. *confmemparkinc.tripod.com.* Two Confederate cemeteries are located on 100 acres that once were the grounds of the Confederate Soldiers Home of Alabama. Museum contains mementos of Alabama's role in the Civil War as well as artifacts, records, documents, and photographs. Also hiking trails, picnicking (shelters). (Daily; closed Jan 1, Dec 25) **FREE**

Lay Dam. *626 County Rd 794, Clanton (35046). 12 miles NE via Hwy 145, County 55.* Phone 205/755-4520. Hydroelectric generating plant offers 30-minute guided tours (Mon-Fri afternoons). Plant (daily). **FREE**

Cullman (B-3)

See also Birmingham, Decatur, Jasper

Founded 1873
Population 13,995
Elevation 799 ft
Area Code 256
Information Cullman Area Chamber of Commerce, 211 Second Ave NE, PO Box 1104, 35056; phone 256/734-0454
Web Site www.cullmanchamber.org

Cullman was founded by Colonel John G. Cullmann, an immigrant whose dream was to build a self-sustaining colony of other German refugees and immigrants. In 1873, five German families settled on the 5,400 square miles of land he purchased from the Louisville & Nashville Railroad. He also laid out the town. Cullman's residents still enjoy the 100-foot-wide streets. In 1880, there were 6,300 people, many of them Germans, in the county that had already been named for Cullmann by the legislature. Located on the Cumberland Plateau, the area is rich in timber and coal. Today, Cullman is one of the main centers for agriculture and poultry production.

What to See and Do

✪ **Ave Maria Grotto.** *1600 E St Bernard Dr SE, Cullman (35055). I-65, exit 308.* Phone 256/734-4110. *www.avemariagrotto.com.* Brother Joseph Zoettl, a Benedictine monk, spent nearly 50 years building some 150 miniature replicas of famous churches, buildings, and shrines, including Bethlehem, Nazareth, Jerusalem, the Basilica of St. Peter's, and the California missions, using such materials as cement, stone, bits of jewelry, and marble. The miniatures cover 4 acres of a terraced, landscaped garden. Free picnic grounds adjacent to parking lot. (Apr-Sept: daily 7 am-7 pm;

Oct-Mar: daily 7 am-5 pm; closed Dec 25) **$**

Clarkson Covered Bridge. *Cullman. 9 miles W via Hwy 278 W.* Phone 256/739-3530. *www.cullmancountyparks.com/pages/clarkson.shtml.* (1904) One of the largest covered bridges in Alabama, the truss-styled Clarkson is 270 feet long and 50 feet high. Also here are a dogtrot cabin and gristmill. Nature trail. Picnic facilities. **FREE**

Cullman County Museum. *211 2nd Ave NE, Cullman (35055).* Phone 256/739-1258. *www.cullman.com/museum.* Large eight-room museum features items related to the origin and history of Cullman. (Mon-Wed, Fri 9 am-noon, 1-4 pm, Thurs 9 am-noon, Sat by appointment, Sun 1:30-4:30 pm; closed holidays) **$**

Hurricane Creek Park. *Cullman. 6 miles N on Hwy 31, near Vinemont.* Phone 256/734-2125. Gorge with observation platform; trail over swinging bridge; unusual rock formations, earthquake fault, and waterfalls. Picnic tables. (Daily) **$$**

Sportsman Lake Park. *1536 Sportsman Lake Rd NW, Cullman (35055). N off Hwy 31.* Phone 256/734-3052. *www.cullmancountyparks.com/pages/sportsmanlake.shtml.* Stocked with bream, bass, catfish, and other fish. Miniature golf; kiddie rides (Thurs-Sun), picnicking, concession, primitive camping. (Apr-Sept, daily) Fee for some activities. **FREE**

William B. Bankhead National Forest. *Double Springs. 25 miles W on Hwy 278.* Contact District Ranger, PO Box 278, Double Springs 35553. Phone 205/489-5111. This 180,684-acre forest includes the Sipsey Wilderness Area, which contains the last remaining stand of old-growth hardwood in the state. Swimming, fishing (bass, bream), boating; hunting (deer, turkey, squirrel), hiking, horseback riding. Fee for some activities.

Restaurant

★ ★ **ALL STEAK.** *314 2nd Ave SW, Cullman (35055).* Phone 256/734-4322; fax 205/734-4389. Seafood, steak menu. Breakfast, lunch, dinner. Closed holidays. Children's menu. **$$**

Dauphin Island (F-1)

See also Mobile

Population 1,371
Elevation 10 ft
Area Code 251
Zip 36528
Web Site www.dauphinisland.org

Dauphin Island is rich in history. Spaniards visited and mapped it in the 16th century. Pierre le Moyne, Sieur d'Iberville, used the island as his base for a short time in 1699. Native Americans left a bit of their past with the "Shell Mound," an ancient monument. Today, the island is part of Mobile County and a playground for Mobile's citizens. It is also a haven for birds; a 60-acre sanctuary is home to many local and migratory species.

The Battle of Mobile Bay began on the island on August 5, 1864. Admiral David G. Farragut assembled a fleet of Union warships near the mouth of the bay and faced crossfire from Fort Morgan to his east and Fort Gaines, on Dauphin Island, to his west. He proved successful; both forts were captured, and the port of Mobile was blocked.

Dauphin Island is reached from the north on Highway 193, via a 4-mile-long, high-rise bridge and causeway, which crosses Grants Pass. The island also has a 3,000-foot paved airstrip. A ferry service to Fort Morgan operates year-round.

What to See and Do

Fort Gaines. *109 Bienville Blvd, Dauphin Island (36528). At E end of island. Phone 251/861-6992.* This five-sided fort was begun in 1821 and completed in the 1850s. It was held by Confederate forces from 1861 until its capture by Union land troops on Aug 23, 1864. Museum. (Daily; closed Thanksgiving, Dec 25) **$$** Nearby is

> **Dauphin Island Campground.** *Dauphin Island (36528). Phone 251/861-2742.* Private path to secluded Gulf beaches, fishing piers, boat launches; hiking trail to Audubon Bird Sanctuary, recreation areas, camping, tent and trailer sites.

Decatur (A-2)

See also Athens, Cullman, Huntsville

Founded 1820
Population 53,929
Elevation 590 ft
Area Code 256
Information Convention & Visitors Bureau, 719 6th Ave SE, PO Box 2349, 35602; phone 256/350-2028 or toll-free 800/524-6181
Web Site www.decaturcvb.org

Decatur, center of northern Alabama's mountain lakes recreation area, is a thriving manufacturing and market city with historic districts and sprawling public parks.

The town site was selected by President Monroe in 1820. The Surveyor General was instructed to reserve the area near an old Tennessee River crossing. The place was already a settlement called Rhodes Ferry, named for pioneer Dr. Henry Rhodes' ferry business; the new town was named for Commodore Stephen Decatur.

The Civil War placed Decatur in a constant seesaw between invasion and resistance. It was continually attacked and abandoned; in fact, only five buildings were left standing at war's end.

The TVA brought industry to Decatur by creating a nine-foot-deep channel in the Tennessee River, making it a port for vessels from as far away as Minneapolis. Wheeler Lake, formed by the TVA's Wheeler Dam (see FLORENCE) downstream, offers fishing, boating, and other recreational activities.

What to See and Do

Cook's Natural Science Museum. *412 13th St SE, Decatur (35601). Phone 256/350-9347.* Extensive collection of insects; rocks, minerals, coral, sea shells. Mounted wildlife. (Daily; closed holidays) **FREE**

Mooresville. *Decatur. 6 miles E on Hwy 20.* State's oldest incorporated town is preserved as a living record of 19th-century life. Features the house of Andrew Johnson, who was a tailor's apprentice here; community brick church (circa 1840); frame Church of Christ (1854) in which James Garfield is said to have preached during the Civil War; antebellum houses (private); also the oldest stagecoach tavern in the state (1825). Details at Mooresville Post Office, which has original wooden call boxes (1830), mail hand-stamped. (Mon-Sat; closed holidays) **FREE**

Old Decatur & Albany historic districts. *719 6th Ave SE, Decatur (35601). Phone 256/350-2028.* Walking tour of Victorian neighborhood begins at restored Old Bank on historic Bank St; includes three antebellum and 194 Victorian structures. Contact Convention & Visitors Bureau.

Point Mallard Park. *1800 Point Mallard Dr SE, Decatur (35601). Phone toll-free 800/350-3000. www.pointmallardpark.com.* A 749-acre park on the Tennessee River. Includes swimming pool, wave pool, water slide, beach (mid-May-Labor Day); hiking, bicycle trails, 18-hole golf course, tennis courts, indoor ice rink, camping (hookups), recreation center. Fee for activities.

Princess Theatre. *112 2nd Ave NE, Decatur (35601). Phone 256/340-1778.* Renovated Art Deco-style theater featuring children's theater, dramatic and musical groups.

Wheeler National Wildlife Refuge. *2700 Refuge Headquarters Rd, Decatur (35603). 2 miles E via Hwy 67. Phone 256/350-6639. wheeler.fws.gov.* Alabama's oldest and largest (34,500 acres) wildlife refuge. Wintering ground for waterfowl and home to numerous species of animal and plant life. Fishing, boating; hunting (limited, permit required), picnicking. Bird study and photography. Wildlife Visitor Center and Waterfowl Observation Building. (Mar-Sept: Tues-Sat; rest of year, daily) **FREE**

Special Events

Alabama Jubilee Hot Air Balloon Classic. *Point Mallard Park, 1800 Point Mallard Dr SE, Decatur (35601). Phone toll-free 800/524-6181.* Since its beginnings in 1977, the Alabama Jubilee has become one of the most popular events in the state. Over the three-day Memorial Day weekend, more than 50,000 spectators gather to watch 60 pilots compete in five hot air balloon races. In addition to the races, there is also a fireworks display, antique tractor and classic car shows, entertainment, and arts and crafts. Memorial Day weekend. **FREE**

Civil War Reenactment/September Skirmish. *Point Mallard Park, 1800 Point Mallard Dr SE, Decatur (35601). Phone toll-free 800/524-6181.* This historical reenactment is held in honor of Confederate Generals "Fighting Joe" Wheeler and John Hunt. Events include craft fairs, displays of Civil War relics, living history of daily camp life, and battles between Confederate and Union "troops" dressed in authentic Civil War uniforms. Labor Day weekend. **FREE**

Racking Horse World Celebration. *Celebration Arena, 67 Horse Center Rd, Decatur (35603). Phone 256/353-7225.* Well-known event features gaited horses. Last full week in Sept.

Southern Wildlife Festival. *6250 Hwy 31, Decatur (35603). Phone toll-free 800/524-6181.* Competition and exhibits of wildlife carvings, artwork, photography, and duck calling. Third weekend in Oct.

Spirit of America Festival. *Point Mallard Park, 1800 Point Mallard Dr SE, Decatur (35601). Phone toll-free*

800/524-6181. Games, contests, beauty pageant, concerts, exhibits, fireworks. Early July.

Limited-Service Hotel

★ ★ COUNTRY INN & SUITES BY CARLSON DECATUR. *807 Bank St NE, Decatur (35601). Phone 256/355-6800; toll-free 800/456-4000; fax 256/350-0965. www.countryinns.com.* Located in historic Decatur, guests will appreciate the homey feel to this hotel with convenient amenities in each guest room. 110 rooms, 3 story, all suites. Check-out noon. Restaurant, bar. Fitness room. Outdoor pool, whirlpool. Airport transportation available. **$**
🏃 ⛵

Restaurants

★ ★ SIMP MCGHEE'S. *725 Bank St, Decatur (35601). Phone 256/353-6284; fax 256/353-6285.* Cajun/Creole, seafood menu. Dinner. Closed Sun; holidays. Bar. Children's menu. In 1890s dry goods building; many antiques. **$$**

★ ★ WATERSHED. *406 W Ponce De Leon Ave, Decatur (30030). Phone 404/378-4900; fax 404/378-8461. www.watershedrestaurant.com.* Soft wood tones and light green colors, wine displays, and fresh flowers on the tables make for a pleasant setting at this casual, comfortable restaurant located two and a half blocks west of downtown Decatur. Popular dishes such as fried catfish with hush puppies and Country Captain stew are served with Southern hospitality. American, Southern menu. Lunch, dinner, brunch. Closed holidays. Bar. Children's menu. Casual attire. Reservations recommended. Credit cards accepted. **$$**

Demopolis (D-1)

See also Athens, Cullman, Huntsville

Founded 1817
Population 7,540
Elevation 125 ft
Area Code 334
Zip 36732
Information Demopolis Area Chamber of Commerce, 102 E Washington, PO Box 667; phone 334/289-0270
Web Site www.demopolischamber.com

Visions of French-made wines and olive oil prompted the first European settlements in this region. The name, meaning "city of the people," is all that remains of the first settlers, a group of French exiles who were, for the most part, habitues of the French court and officers of Napoleon's armies. In July 1817, they were granted four townships by Congress as the "French Emigrants for the Cultivation of the Vine and Olive." In the end, the colonists failed to cope with the wilderness, and by the mid-1820s, they had scattered.

Americans came afterward to settle on the banks of the Tombigbee River. They established flourishing cotton plantations in this Black Belt area, and many of their fine Greek Revival mansions still can be seen. Agriculture and beef and dairy cattle, as well as a diversified industry, support Demopolis today.

What to See and Do

Bluff Hall. *405 N Commissioners St, Demopolis (36732). Phone 334/289-9644.* (1832) Restored antebellum mansion built by the slaves of Allen Glover, a planter and merchant, as a wedding gift for his daughter. The interior has Corinthian columns in drawing room, period furniture, many marble mantels. Also clothing museum and craft shop. (Tues-Sun; closed holidays) **$$**

Forkland Park.. *12 miles N on Hwy 43, 1 mile W of Forkland on River Rd. Phone 334/289-5530.* This park is on 10,000-acre Lake Demopolis, which was formed by a 40-foot-high dam on the Tombigbee River. Waterskiing, fishing, boating (ramp); camping (hookups, dump station; fees). (Daily)

Foscue Creek Park. *384 Rescue Management Dr, Demopolis (36732). 2 miles W via Hwy 80 W, exit Maria St, on Lock & Dam Rd. Phone 334/289-3540.* On Lake Demopolis. Boating (ramps); trails, picnic area, pavilion, playground, ballfields, camping (hookups, dump station; fees). (Daily)

Gaineswood. *805 S Cedar Ave, Demopolis (36732). Phone 334/289-4846.* (1860) Restored 20-room Greek Revival mansion furnished with many original pieces. (Daily; closed holidays) **$$**

Magnolia Grove. *1002 Hobson St, Greensboro (36744). 2 miles S on Hwy 43, 3 miles E on I-80, then 15 miles NE on Hwy 69. Phone 334/624-8618.* (1840) Built for wealthy planter Colonel Isaac Croom, Magnolia Grove was also the home of the builder's nephew, Richmond Pearson Hobson, congressman and admiral who was responsible for sinking the *Merrimac* and for blockading the Spanish fleet in Santiago Harbor in June 1898. Greek Revival house features an unsupported winding stairway; original furnishings. (Tues-Sun) **$$**

Special Event

Christmas on the River. *102 E Washington, Demopolis (36732). Phone 334/289-0270.* Christmas on the River has been a tradition in this Alabama town since 1972. The weeklong celebration kicks off with the lighting of the Love Light Tree and continues with live entertainment, a candlelight antebellum home tour, a barbecue cook-off, the Jingle Bells Run/Walk, parades, and a free screening of a family-friendly, Christmas-themed movie. Thousands of spectators gather along the river on the festival's final night to watch the nautical parade, where floats decorated with a dazzling array of lights glide down the water accompanied by a brilliant fireworks display. Late Nov-early Dec.

Dothan (E-4)

See also Blakely, Ozark

Settled 1858
Population 57,737
Elevation 326 ft
Area Code 334
Information Dothan Area Convention & Visitors Bureau, 3311 Ross Clark Circle NW, PO Box 8765, 36304; phone 334/794-6622
Web Site www.dothanalcvb.com

This marketing center in the "wiregrass" section of Alabama's southeastern corner is the seat of Houston County. Local agricultural products include peanuts, soybeans, corn, and cattle. Dothan is also a retail center.

The town had a lusty start. It was a rough pioneer settlement full of lumberjacks and turpentine workers in 1889 when the first railroad reached it. As the railroads developed, Dothan's population grew rapidly. The city owes a large part of its growth to its strategic location—almost equidistant from Atlanta, Birmingham, Jacksonville, and Mobile.

What to See and Do

Adventureland Theme Park. *3738 W Main St, Dothan (36305). Phone 334/793-9100. www.adventurelandthemepark.com.* Park includes two 18-hole miniature golf courses, a go-cart track, bumper boats, batting cages, and a game room. Snack bar. (Nov-Mar: Mon-Fri noon-10 pm, Sat 10 am-midnight, Sun noon-10 pm; rest of year: Mon-Sat 10 am-midnight, Sun noon-midnight) **FREE**

Landmark Park. *430 Landmark Dr, Dothan (36303). Hwy 431 N. Phone 334/794-3452. www.landmarkpark. com.* This 60-acre park features an 1890s living-history farm, natural science and history center, planetarium; nature trails, picnic area. (Mon-Sat 9 am-5 pm, Sun noon-6 pm; closed Jan 1, Thanksgiving, Dec 25) **$**

Opera House. *115 N St. Andrews St, Dothan (36303). Phone 334/793-0127.* (1915) Refurbished historical theater; 590 seats. (Daily by appointment). **FREE**

Westgate Park. *501 Recreation Rd, Dothan. Choctaw St and Westgate Pkwy off Ross Clark Cir. Phone 334/793-0297.* Recreation facility includes Water World, with children's pool, wave pool, triple flume slide, and giant slide (early May-Labor Day, daily; fee); recreation center with indoor pool, tennis, racquetball, basketball courts, and ballfields. (Daily; fee for various activities)

Special Events

Azalea Dogwood Festival. *Dothan's garden district. Phone 334/794-6622.* Marked route through residential areas at peak of bloom. Late Mar.

National Peanut Festival. *National Peanut Festival Fairgrounds, 5620 Hwy 231 S, Dothan (36301). Phone 334/793-4323.* Livestock exhibits, sports events, arts and crafts, midway, pageants, parade. Late Oct-early Nov.

Limited-Service Hotels

★ ★ **COMFORT INN.** *3593 Ross Clark Cir NW, Dothan (36304). Phone 334/793-9090; toll-free 800/474-7298; fax 334/793-4367. www.choicehotels.com.* Just 5 miles from Dothan Airport, this hotel is conveniently located. Within a short distance are area amusement parks, trails, and gardens. 122 rooms, 5 story. Pets accepted, some restrictions; fee. Complimentary continental breakfast. Check-in 2 pm, check-out 1 pm. Restaurant. Fitness room. Outdoor pool. **$**

★ ★ **HOLIDAY INN.** *2195 Ross Clark Cir SE, Dothan (36301). Phone 334/794-8711; toll-free 800/777-6611; fax 334/671-3781. www.holiday-inn.com.* 144 rooms, 2 story. Pets accepted; fee. Complimentary full breakfast. Check-out noon. Restaurant, bar. Outdoor pool. **$**

★ ★ **QUALITY INN.** *3053 Ross Clark Cir, Dothan (36301). Phone 334/794-6601; toll-free 800/228-5151; fax 334/794-9032. www.qualityinn.com.* 102 rooms, 2

story. Pets accepted; fee. Check-out noon. Restaurant, bar. Outdoor pool, children's pool. Business center. **$**

Eufaula (D-4)

See also Lumpkin

Settled 1823
Population 13,908
Elevation 257 ft
Area Code 334
Zip 36027
Information Chamber of Commerce, 102 N Orange St, PO Box 697, 36072-0697; phone 334/687-6664 or 334/687-6665
Web Site www.eufaulaalabama.com

This city stands on a bluff rising 200 feet above Lake Eufaula, a 45,000-acre impoundment of the Chattahoochee River known throughout the area for its excellent bass fishing.

What to See and Do

Eufaula National Wildlife Refuge. *509 Old Hwy 165, Eufaula (36027). 10 miles N on Hwy 431, Hwy 165. Phone 334/687-4065. eufaula.fws.gov.* Partially located in Georgia and superimposed on the Walter F. George Reservoir, the refuge was established to provide a feeding and resting area for waterfowl migrating between the Tennessee Valley and the Gulf Coast. Ducks, geese, egrets, and herons are among the 281 species of birds found at the refuge; beaver, fox, bobcat, and deer are among the 16 species of mammals. Observation tower, nature trail; hunting; photography. (Daily) **FREE**

Hart House. *211 N Eufaula Ave, Eufaula (36027). Phone 334/687-6631.* (Circa 1850) Single-story Greek Revival white frame structure with fluted Doric columns on porch serves as headquarters for the Historic Chattahoochee Commission and visitor information center for the Chattahoochee Trace of Alabama and Georgia. (Mon-Fri) **FREE**

Lakepoint Resort State Park. *104 Lakepoint Dr, Eufaula (36027). 7 miles N off Hwy 431. Phone 334/687-6676. www.dcnr.state.al.us.* A 1,220-acre picturesque park on the shores of the 45,200-acre Lake Eufaula. Swimming, fishing, boating (marina); hiking, 18-hole golf (fee), tennis, picnicking, concession, restaurant, resort inn. Camping, cottages. **$**

Shorter Mansion. *340 N Eufaula Ave, Eufaula (36027). Phone 334/687-3793.* Neoclassical mansion built in 1906; two floors contain antique furnishings, Confederate relics and memorabilia of six state governors from Barbour County. (Daily; closed holidays) Mini-tour by appointment (fee). **$$** Mansion is the headquarters for the Eufaula Heritage Association and is part of the

Seth Lore and Irwinton Historic District. *211 N Eufaula Ave, Eufaula (36027).* Second-largest historic district in Alabama, with approximately 582 registered landmarks. Mixture of Greek Revival, Italianate, and Victorian houses, churches, and commercial structures built between 1834-1911. Many are private. Obtain driving tour brochure from the Chamber of Commerce or Eufaula Heritage Association, PO Box 486.

Special Events

Eufaula Pilgrimage. *917 W Barbour St, Eufaula (36027). Phone 334/687-3793. www.eufaulapilgrimage.com.* Daytime and candlelight tours of antebellum houses and churches, antique show and sales, historic reenactments, and Civil War displays. First weekend in Apr.

Indian Summer Days. *N Randolph Ave, Eufaula. Historic District. Phone 334/687-6664.* Festival includes arts and crafts, music, food, children's activities. First or second weekend in Oct.

Evergreen (E-2)

Population 3,630
Elevation 367 ft
Area Code 334
Zip 36401
Information Chamber of Commerce, 100 Depot Sq, 36401; phone 334/578-1000
Web Site www.evergreenal.com

The seat of Conecuh County, this town is appropriately named for its abundance of evergreens. Each year carloads of Christmas trees and other evergreen products for use as decoration are shipped from the town.

What to See and Do

Conecuh National Forest. *Hwy 29 S, Andalusia. 25 miles E on Hwy 84, then 11 miles S on Hwy 29. Contact District Ranger, US Forest Service, Hwy 5, Box 157, Andalusia 36420. Phone 334/222-2555.* This 84,400-acre forest, mostly of southern pine, offers swimming (at Blue Pond, fee per vehicle), fishing, boating; hunting, hiking including 20 miles of the Conecuh Trail, campsites at Open Pond only (fee for overnight).

Limited-Service Hotel

★ **COMFORT INN.** *83 Ted Bates Rd, Evergreen (36401). Phone 251/578-4701; toll-free 800/228-5150; fax 251/578-3180. www.comfortinn.com.* 58 rooms, 2 story. Pets accepted; fee. Check-out 11 am. Outdoor pool. **$**
🐾 ⊵

Florence (A-2)

See also Russellville, Sheffield

Settled 1779
Population 36,264
Elevation 541 ft
Area Code 256
Zip 35630
Information Florence/Lauderdale Tourism, One Hightower Pl; phone 256/740-4141 or toll-free 888/356-8687
Web Site www.flo-tour.org

First settled as a trading post, Florence is still the trading center of a large area. With Sheffield, Tuscumbia, and Muscle Shoals, Florence lies along the Tennessee River's famous shoals area near Wilson Dam. Inexpensive TVA power helped to bring a number of industries to the town.

What to See and Do

Colbert Ferry. George Colbert, a leading Chickasaw of the area, operated a stand and ferry here and reportedly charged Andrew Jackson $75,000 to ferry his army across the river. (Open daily dawn-dusk)

Freedom Hills Overlook. A steep, 1/4-mile trail leads to Alabama's highest point on the parkway, at 800 feet. (Open daily dawn-dusk) **FREE**

Indian Mound and Museum. *1028 S Court St, Florence (35630). Phone 256/760-6427.* Largest ceremonial mound in the Tennessee Valley. Museum has large collection of Native American artifacts. (Tues-Sat; closed holidays) **$**

Ivy Green. *300 W North Commons, Tuscumbia (35630). Phone 256/383-4066. www.helenkellerbirthplace.org.* Helen Keller was born here in 1880. Deaf and blind from the age of 19 months, she learned to sign her first words at the water pump out back from her teacher Annie Sullivan, events recounted in the play *The Miracle Worker.* (Mon-Sat 8:30 am-4 pm, Sun 1-4 pm; closed holidays) **$$**

Joe Wheeler State Park. *201 Mclean Dr, Rogersville (35652). 2 miles W of Rogersville, off I-72. Phone toll-free 800/544-5629. www.joewheelerstatepark.com.* Named for Confederate General Joseph Wheeler of the Army of Tennessee, the 2,550-acre park is divided into three parts: Elk River, First Creek, and Wheeler Dam.

   Elk River. *15 miles W of Athens (see).Phone toll-free 800/544-5629.* Fishing, boating (launch), picnic facilities, playground, concession. Group lodge. (Daily) Standard fees. **$**

   First Creek. *Florence (35652). 2 miles W of Rogersville via Hwy 72. Phone toll-free 800/544-5629.* Beachfront swimming, boating (marina); nature and hiking trails, 18-hole golf, tennis, picnicking. Resort lodge overlooking the Tennessee River. Camping (primitive and improved).

   Wheeler Dam. *18 miles E on Hwy 72, then 4 miles S on 101.Phone 256/685-3306.* Part of the Muscle Shoals complex, this is a multipurpose TVA dam, chiefly built for navigation. It is 72 feet high and 6,342 feet long, impounding a lake 74 miles long. Lobby (daily). Swimming, fishing (daily), boat liveries and harbor; tennis, picnic facilities. Cabins.

Pope's Tavern. *203 Hermitage Dr, Florence (35630). Phone 256/760-6439.* (1830) General Andrew Jackson stayed in this stage stop, which served as a hospital for both Union and Confederate soldiers during the Civil War. (Tues-Sat 10 am-4 pm; closed holidays) **$**

Rock Spring Trail. *Florence.* This self-guided trail along Colbert Creek takes 20 minutes to walk. Interpretive trail markers are located at points of special interest. (Open daily) **FREE**

University of North Alabama. *600 Wesleyan Ave, Florence (35632). Phone 256/765-4100. www.una.edu.* (1830) (5,600 students) Tours. University Art Gallery (Mon-Fri), Planetarium-Observatory (open by appointment, phone 256/760-4284).

W. C. Handy Home, Museum, and Library. *620 W College St, Florence (35630). Phone 256/760-6434.* Restored birthplace of famous composer and "father of the blues" contains handwritten sheet music, personal papers, trumpet, and piano on which he composed "St. Louis Blues." (Tues-Sat; closed holidays)

Wilson Dam. *704 S Wilson Dam Rd, Florence (35630). 5 miles E on Hwy 72, then 2 miles S on Hwy 133. Phone 256/386-2327.* This dam is the foundation stone of the Tennessee Valley Authority. For many years, the Muscle Shoals area of the Tennessee River had been discussed as a source of power, and in 1918 the War Department began construction of Wilson Dam as a source of power for making munitions. The dam was completed in 1924, but little use was made of its generating capacity until the TVA took over in 1933. Today, it has the largest generating capacity (630,000 kilowatts) of any TVA dam; its main lock (completed Nov 1959) is 110 feet by 600 feet and lifts vessels 100 feet, one of the world's highest single lift locks. The treacherous Muscle Shoals are no longer a bottleneck to shipping. The dam, 4,541 feet long and 137 feet high, is one of the many TVA dams that prevents floods, provides 650 miles of navigable channel, and produces electricity for the area's residents, farms, and industry. **FREE** Also here is

   Wilson Lake. *719 Hwy 72 W, Tuscumbia (35674). Phone 256/383-0783.* Extends more than 15 miles upstream to Wheeler Dam. Swimming, fishing, boating.

Special Events

Alabama Renaissance Faire. *Wilson Park, 541 Riverview Dr, Florence (35630). Phone 256/740-4141.* Renaissance-era arts and crafts, music, food, entertainment. Fair workers in period costumes. Oct.

Festival of the Singing River. *McFarland Park, 2500 Chisholm Rd, Florence (35630). Phone 256/760-6416; toll-free 888/356-8687.* Honors the history and culture of Native Americans. Traditional dance competition, arts and crafts. Oct.

Helen Keller Festival. *Spring Park, 719 Hwy 72 W, Florence (35674). Phone 256/383-0783.* Three-day celebration with music, arts and crafts, and parade. Last full weekend in June. **FREE**

W. C. Handy Music Festival. *115 1/2 E Mobile, Florence (35630). Phone 256/766-7642. www.wchandyfest.com.* Week-long celebration of the musical contribution of the "father of the blues." Jazz, blues, gospel concerts, street celebration, running events, bike rides. First full week in Aug.

Foley (F-2)

See also Russellville, Sheffield

Restaurant

★ **GIFT HORSE.** *209 W Laurel, Foley (36535). Phone 251/943-3663; fax 251/949-6300.* American menu. Lunch, dinner, Sun brunch. Closed Dec 25. Children's menu. Restored building (1912); antique tables. **$$**

Fort Payne (A-4)

See also Gadsden

Population 12,938
Elevation 899 ft
Area Code 256
Zip 35968
Information DeKalb County Tourist Association, 2201-J Gault Ave N, PO Box 681165; phone 256/845-3957
Web Site www.fortpayne.com

The county seat and market town of DeKalb County, Fort Payne is in an area famed for natural wonders and Native American history. Sequoyah, who invented the Cherokee alphabet, lived in Will's Town, a Cherokee settlement located near Fort Payne.

What to See and Do

Cloudmont Ski Resort. *721 County Rd 614, Mentone (35984). 5 miles NE via I-59, exit 231 off Hwy 117. Phone 256/634-4344. www.cloudmont.com.* Two pony lifts; patrol, school, rentals, 100 percent snowmaking; concession area, snack bar. Chalets. Longest run 1,000 feet; vertical drop 150 feet. (Mid-Dec-early-Mar, daily) Summer activities include swimming, horseback riding, fishing; hiking, 9-hole golf. **$$$$**

DeSoto State Park. *13883 County Rd 89, Fort Payne (35967). 8 miles NE on County 89. Phone 256/845-5380. www.desotostatepark.com.* This 5,067-acre park includes Lookout Mountain, Little River Canyon, and DeSoto Falls and Lake. The area, rich in Cherokee lore, was a base of military operations before the Trail of Tears. The park is noted for its variety of plant life, including spring-blooming rhododendrons, wild azaleas, and mountain laurel. Songbirds abound. A scenic drive skirts the canyon, and 20 miles of hiking trail crosses the mountain top. Swimming pool, bathhouse, fishing; hiking trail, tennis, picnicking, playground, restaurant, country store, resort inn. Nature center. Camping (all year), cabins (reservations required for both). Standard fees. **$**

Fort Payne Opera House. *510 Gault Ave N, Fort Payne (35967). Phone 256/845-2741.* (1889) Alabama's oldest opera house still in use today. It was restored and reopened in 1970 as a cultural arts center. Tours of the theater include historic murals (by appointment).

Landmarks of DeKalb Museum. *105 5th St NE, Fort Payne (35968). Phone 256/845-5714. www.fortpaynedepotmuseum.com.* (1891) The museum, Richardsonian Romanesque in style, features Native American artifacts from several different tribes; turn-of-the-century house and farm items; railroad memorabilia; photographs and artwork of local historical significance. Special rotating exhibits. (Mon, Wed, Fri 10 am-4 pm, Sun 2-4 pm; closed holidays) **DONATION**

Sequoyah Caverns. *1438 County Rd 731, Fort Payne. 16 miles N off Hwy 11, I-59. Phone 256/635-0024.* Thousands of formations, reflecting lakes, and rainbow falls with indirect lighting; level walkways. Cave temperature 60° F all year. Rainbow trout pools, deer, buffalo. Swimming pool; picnic area, camping. Guided tours. (Mar-Nov: daily; rest of year: weekends) **$$$**

Special Event

DeKalb County VFW Agricultural Fair. *VFW Fairgrounds, 600 Golf Ave, Fort Payne (35967). Phone 256/845-4752. www.fortpayne.com.* The fair attracts nearly 45,000 visitors annually and features live music, a beauty pageant for ladies 65 years and older, and special events for kids. Late Sept-early Oct.

Gadsden (B-3)

See also Anniston, Fort Payne, Guntersville

Founded 1840
Population 38,978
Area Code 256
Information Gadsden-Etowah Tourism Board, PO Box 8267, 35902; phone 256/549-0351
Web Site www.ci.gadsden.al.us

The town was named for James Gadsden, the man who negotiated the purchase of Arizona and New Mexico in 1853. Today, it is one of the largest industrial centers in the state. Iron, manganese, coal, and limestone are found nearby. Steel, rubber, fabricated metal, electrical equipment, and electronic devices are among its chief products. It is the seat of Etowah County, a diversified agricultural area.

Union troops sacked Gadsden in 1863 and rode on toward Rome, Georgia. Two heroes were born of this action. Fifteen-year-old Emma Sansom bravely guided General Nathan Bedford Forrest and his men across a ford on Black Creek after the bridge was destroyed. John Wisdom made a night ride of 67 miles to warn the defenders of Rome that the Yankees were coming, a ride the people of Alabama celebrate more than Paul Revere's.

In 1887, electricity came to Gadsden when William P. Lay built an electrical plant, the result of years of effort to interest investors in the industrial future of the region. In 1902, it was replaced with a hydroelectric plant on Big Wills Creek. Eventually, Lay's dream of developing the water resources of the Coosa-Alabama river system led to the organization of the Alabama Power Company in 1906.

What to See and Do

Center for Cultural Arts. *501 Broad St, Gadsden (35901). Phone 256/543-2787. www.culturalarts.com.* Center features a wide variety of cultural and artistic traveling exhibits from the US and Europe; children's museum with hands-on exhibits features a miniature "walk-through" city. (Mon, Wed-Fri 9 am-6 pm, Tues to 9 pm, Sat 10 am-6 pm, Sun 1-5 pm; closed holidays) **$$**

Gadsden Museum of Art. *2829 W Meighan Blvd, Gadsden (35904). Phone 256/546-7365.* Features works by local, national, and international artists. Antique china and crystal collection, historical memorabilia. (Mon-Fri; closed holidays) **FREE**

Horton Mill Covered Bridge. *Hendrix. 18 miles W on Hwy 278, then 11 miles S on Hwy 75.* This 220-foot-long structure is one of the highest covered bridges in the US, 70 feet above the Calvert Prong of the Locust Fork of the Black Warrior River. Trails. (Daily) **FREE**

Noccalula Falls Park. *1500 Noccalula Rd, Gadsden (35902). Phone 256/549-4663.* Black Creek drops 90 feet over a limestone ledge on Lookout Mountain; according to legend, these falls were named for an Indian chief's daughter who leaped to her death after being disappointed in love. A 65-mile trail ending at

DeSoto Falls in DeSoto State Park in Fort Payne (see) includes four waterfalls and many Native American sites. Also originating in the park is the Lookout Mountain Pkwy, a scenic drive extending 100 miles to Chattanooga, Tennessee. Swimming pool, bathhouse; nature and hiking trails, miniature golf, picnic area, playground, camping, hookups (fee). Petting zoo and animal habitat house. Pioneer homestead and museum; train. Botanical gardens. (Daily)

Weiss Dam and Lake. *590 E Main St, Centre (35960). 18 miles NE off Hwy 411. Phone 256/526-8467.* An Alabama Power Company project impounds a 30,200-acre lake. Swimming, fishing, boating (daily); picnicking. Tours of power plant (daily, by appointment).

Greenville (D-3)

See also Montgomery

Settled 1819
Population 7,228
Elevation 422 ft
Area Code 334
Zip 36037
Web Site www.greenville-alabama.com

What to See and Do

Hank Williams, Sr., Boyhood Home & Museum. *127 Rose St, Georgiana (36033). Approximately 20 miles S on Hwy 31. Phone 334/376-2396. www.hankmuseum. com.* Restored house where Hank Williams, Sr., country music legend, lived as a young boy. Large collection of memorabilia including recordings, posters, and sheet music. (Mon-Sat, Sun afternoons) **$$**

Gulf Shores (F-2)

See also Gift Horse, Mobile

Population 5,044
Elevation 6 ft
Area Code 251
Zip 36542
Information Alabama Gulf Coast Convention & Visitors Bureau, 3150 Gulf Shores Pkwy, PO Box 457, 36547; phone 251/968-7511 or toll-free 800/745-7263
Web Site www.gulfshores.com

Located on Pleasure Island, southeast of Mobile, Gulf Shores is separated from the mainland by the Intracoastal Waterway. Between Alabama Point on the east and Mobile Point on the west is a 32-mile stretch of white sand beach that includes Orange Beach. Swimming and fishing in the Gulf are excellent, and charter boats are available. The island also has a number of freshwater lakes. At the eastern end, a bridge across Perdido Bay connects Orange Beach with Pensacola, Florida.

What to See and Do

Alabama Gulf Coast Zoo. *1204 Gulf Shores Pkwy, Gulf Shores (36542). Hwy 59 S to 12th Ave. Phone 251/968-5731. www.alabamagulfcoastzoo.com.* A 15-acre park with native and exotic animals; petting zoo; concession. (Daily 9 am-4 pm; closed Thanksgiving, Dec 25) **$$**

Bon Secour National Wildlife Refuge. *12295 State Hwy 180, Gulf Shores (36542). Phone 251/540-7720. bonsecour.fws.gov.* Consists of 6,000 acres of coastal lands ranging from sand dunes to woodlands; native and migratory birds, small mammals, and reptiles including the endangered loggerhead sea turtle. Swimming, fishing (fresh and salt water), foot trails, hiking. Visitor center (daily; closed holidays). **FREE**

Fort Morgan Park. *51 Hwy 180, Gulf Shores. 22 miles W on Hwy 180 (Fort Morgan Pkwy).* This area on the western tip of Mobile Point was explored by the Spanish in 1519. Between that time and 1813, Spain, France, England, and finally, the US, held this strategic point. It was the site of two engagements during the War of 1812. Fishing pier; picnicking, concessions. **$** Park admission includes

Fort Morgan. *Gulf Shores. Phone 251/540-7125.* This star-shaped brick fort was begun in 1819 and replaced a sand and log fort that figured in two battles during the War of 1812. Fort Morgan's most famous moment occurred during the Battle of Mobile Bay (Aug 1864). The Confederates' use of mines, then known as torpedoes, was the source of Union Admiral Farragut's legendary command, "Damn the torpedoes, full speed ahead!" Following the battle, the fort withstood a two-week siege before surrendering to Union forces. The fort was in active use during the Spanish-American War, World War I, and World War II. (Daily; closed Jan 1, Thanksgiving, Dec 25) **$**

Fort Morgan Museum. *Gulf Shores. Phone 251/540-7127.* (1967) Patterned after the ten-sided citadel damaged in 1864, the museum displays military artifacts from the War of 1812 through World War II; local history. (Daily; closed Jan 1, Thanksgiving, Dec 25) **FREE**

Gulf State Park. *20115 State Hwy 135, Gulf Shores. 2 miles E on Hwy 182 from junction Hwy 59. Phone 251/948-7275. www.dcnr.state.al.us.* The 6,000-acre park includes more than 2 miles of white sand beaches on the Gulf and freshwater lakes. Swimming, bathhouse, waterskiing, surfing, fishing in Gulf of Mexico (825-foot pier) and in lakes, marina, boathouse, rentals; hiking, bicycling, tennis, 18-hole golf (fee). Picnic area, pavilion, grills, restaurant, resort inn. Cabins (for reservations contact Cabin Reservations, 20115 Hwy 135, phone 251/948-7275). Camping (14-day maximum in season; phone 251/948-6353 Mon-Fri for reservations). (Daily) Standard fees. **$**

Special Events

Mardi Gras Celebration. *3150 Gulf Shores Pkwy, Gulf Shores (36542). Phone 251/968-6904.* Festively decorated boats and rock bands on flatbed trailers parade along the waters and roads of the Gulf Coast. Late Feb.

National Shrimp Festival. *Hwys 59 and 182, Gulf Shores. Phone 251/968-6904. www.nationalshrimpfestival.com.* While fabulous seafood is the main draw at this annual festival, visitors will also enjoy live music, a kids art show, and a sandcastle contest. Second full weekend of Oct. **FREE**

Pleasure Island Festival of Art. *1009 E Canal Dr, Gulf Shores (36542). Phone 251/981-1852.* More than 50 artists display their creations on the shores of Lake Shelby. Early Mar.

Limited-Service Hotels

★ ★ **BEST WESTERN ON THE BEACH.** *337 E Beach Blvd, Gulf Shores (36542). Phone 251/948-2711; toll-free 800/788-4557; fax 251/948-7339. www.bestwestern.com.* 111 rooms, 6 story. Check-out 11 am. Restaurant. Indoor pool, outdoor pool, whirlpool. **$**
⌷

★ ★ **HILTON GARDEN INN ORANGE BEACH BEACHFRONT.** *23092 Perdido Beach Blvd, Orange Beach (36561). Phone 251/974-1600; fax 251/974-1012.* White sandy beaches are the setting for this hotel on Alabama's gulf coast. With well-appointed guest rooms, an indoor/outdoor pool, and on-site laundry facilities, guests can relax in the sun or enjoy nearby championship golf courses and fishing. 137 rooms, 6 story. Check-out noon. Indoor/outdoor pool, whirl-pool. Business center. Beach. **$**

★ **SUPER 8.** *1517 S McKenzie St, Foley (36535). Phone 251/943-3297; toll-free 888/800-8000; fax 251/943-7548. www.super8.com.* 90 rooms, 2 story. Complimentary continental breakfast. Check-out 11 am. Fitness room. Outdoor pool. **$**

Full-Service Resort

★ ★ ★ **PERDIDO BEACH RESORT.** *27200 Per-dido Beach Blvd, Orange Beach (36561). Phone 251/981-9811; toll-free 800/634-8001; fax 251/981-5670. www. perdidobeachresort.com.* Directly on the Gulf of Mexico, this wonderful Mediterranean-style resort offers everything one could want, whether it be for business or vacation pleasure. Enjoy the sugar white sand beaches, boating, deep sea fishing, parasailing, and scuba diving. 345 rooms, 10 story. Check-out noon. Restaurant, bar. Children's activity center. Fitness room. Beach. Indoor pool, outdoor pool, whirlpool. Tennis. **$$**

Restaurants

★ **MIKEE'S SEAFOOD.** *1st St and 2nd Ave, Gulf Shores (36547). Phone 251/948-6452; fax 251/968-6276.* Lunch, dinner. Bar. Children's menu. **$$**

★ **ORIGINAL OYSTER HOUSE.** *701 Gulf Shores Pkwy, Gulf Shores (36542). Phone 251/948-2445. www. theoysterhouse.com.* Seafood menu. Lunch, dinner. Closed Dec 24-25. Bar. Children's menu. On Bayou. **$$**

★ **SEA-N-SUDS.** *405 E Beach Blvd, Gulf Shores (36542). Phone 251/948-7894. www.sea-n-suds.com.* Lunch, dinner. Closed Sun (off-season); Thanksgiving; also Dec. Bar. **$$**

Guntersville (A-3)

See also Gadsden, Huntsville

Population 7,395
Elevation 800 ft
Area Code 256
Zip 35976
Information Chamber of Commerce, 200 Gunter Ave, PO Box 577; phone 205/582-3612 or toll-free 800/869-5253
Web Site www.lakeguntersville.org

A thriving port and power-producing center of the Tennessee Valley Authority, this town was once the site of a Cherokee village. In the 1820s, steamboats plying the river turned Guntersville into a boomtown; still the Cherokees and settlers continued to live alongside each other peacefully. "Boat Day," it was said, was a great occasion for the settlers and Cherokees alike.

The Cumberland River Trail, the route Andrew Jackson took on his way to the Creek War in 1813, passed through Guntersville, and Cherokees from this area joined and fought bravely with Jackson's troops against the Creeks. But in 1837, just 24 years later, General Winfield Scott, under the direction of Andrew Jackson, rounded up the area's Cherokees and moved them westward.

Today, Guntersville receives and distributes river freight. South of town is the plateau of Sand Mountain, one of the great food-producing sections of the state. Part of the growing resort area of north Alabama's TVA lake country, Guntersville's municipal parks have numerous boat docks and launches.

What to See and Do

Buck's Pocket State Park. *393 County Rd 174, Guntersville (35975). 16 miles N and E via Hwy 227, County 50 to Groveoak. Phone 256/659-2000. www. dcnr.state.al.us.* Natural pocket of the Appalachian mountain chain on 2,000 acres. Fishing, boat launch; hiking trails, picnic facilities, playground, concession, primitive and improved camping. Visitor center.

Guntersville Dam and Lake. *1155 Lodge Dr, Guntersville (35976). 12 miles W and N via Hwy 69 and County 240, 50. Phone 256/582-3263.* (1939) Fifth of the nine TVA dams on the Tennessee River, it impounds a 67,900-acre lake that is 76 miles long. It is a favorite recreation area for swimming, fishing, and boating. Lobby (daily). **FREE**

Lake Guntersville State Park. *Guntersville. 6 miles NE off Hwy 227 on Guntersville Reservoir. Phone 256/571-5444; toll-free 800/548-4553. www.dcnr.state.al.us.* A 5,909-acre park with ridge tops and meadows. Swimming beach, waterskiing, fishing center, boating; hiking, bicycling, golf (18 holes, fee), tennis, nature programs, picnicking, playground, concession, restaurant, chalets, lakeside cottages, resort inn on Taylor Mountain (see Limited-Service Hotels). Camping (hookups).

Limited-Service Hotels

★ **COVENANT COVE LODGE AND MARINA.**
7001 Val Monte Dr, Guntersville (35976). Phone 256/582-1000; fax 256/582-1385. www.covenantcove.com. 53 rooms, 2 story. Pets accepted, some restrictions; fee. Complimentary continental breakfast. Check-out 11 am. Bar. Outdoor pool, children's pool. **$**

★ ★ **HOLIDAY INN.** *2140 Gunter Ave, Guntersville (35976). Phone 256/582-2220; toll-free 888/882-1160; fax 256/582-2059. www.holiday-inn.com.* 100 rooms, 3 story. Check-out 11 am. Restaurant, bar. Outdoor pool. **$**

Hamilton (B-1)

See also Montgomery, Russellville

Population 6,786
Elevation 498 ft
Area Code 205
Zip 35570
Web Site www.cityofhamilton.org

What to See and Do

Natural Bridge of Alabama. *Hwy 278 W, Natural Bridge. 1 mile W of AL 5. Phone 205/486-5330.* Two spans of sandstone, longest 148 feet, created by natural erosion of a tributary stream more than 200 million years ago. Picnicking. (Daily) **$**

Limited-Service Hotel

★ ★ **ECONO LODGE INN & SUITES.** *2031 Military St S, Hamilton (35806). Phone 205/921-7831; toll-free 800/553-2666; fax 205/921-7831. www.econolodge.com.* 80 rooms, 2 story. Check-out noon. Restaurant. Outdoor pool. **$**

Horseshoe Bend National Military Park (C-4)

See also Alexander City

Web Site www.nps.gov/hobe/

12 miles N of Dadeville on Hwy 49.

Early Spanish explorations led by de Soto found the Creeks in Alabama and Georgia living in a settled communal-agricultural society governed by complex rituals and customs. Following the American Revolution, a horde of settlers moved south and west of the Appalachians. Despite territorial guarantees in the Treaty of 1790, the United States repeatedly forced land and road concessions from the Creeks. The Creek Indian Agency was ordered to oversee trade and to reestablish the Native Americans' prehistoric agricultural economy.

The Lower Creeks of Georgia adjusted to life with the settlers. The Upper Creeks living in Alabama did not and vowed to defend their land and their customs after heeding the preachings of Tecumseh in 1811. When a few Upper Creeks, called Red Sticks, killed settlers near the Tennessee border, the Indian Agency ordered the Lower Creeks to execute the offending warriors. The order produced civil war within the Creek Nation by the spring of 1813. By summer, settlers became involved in the fray, attacking an Upper Creek munitions convoy at Burnt Corn Creek, fearing the Creeks' intentions. The Upper Creeks retaliated on August 30, 1813, attacking Fort Mims and killing an estimated 250 people. Soon after, the militias of Georgia, Tennessee, and the Mississippi Territory were brought in to combat the uprising of the "Red Sticks." Georgia troops defeated the Creeks in two battles at Autosee and Calabee Creek, but the Tennessee Militia, under Andrew Jackson, was the most effective force; battles were fought by Jackson's army at Talladega, Emuckfaw, and Enitachopco. In March of 1814, they struck and routed the Creeks at Horseshoe Bend of the Tallapoosa River, the bloodiest battle of the Creek War. The peace treaty that followed soon after cost the Creeks more than 20 million acres of land, opening a vast and rich domain to settlement, and eventually led to the statehood of Alabama in 1819.

For Jackson, Horseshoe Bend was the beginning; for the Creek Nation, the beginning of the end. In the 1830s, during Jackson's presidency, they were forced to leave Alabama and move to "Indian Territory" (Oklahoma).

A museum at the visitor center depicts the battle with a slide presentation and an electric map exhibit. The park contains 2,040 acres of forested hills and is situated on the banks of the Tallapoosa River. A 3-mile loop road tour with seven interpretive markers traverses the battle area. There are nature trails, picnic areas, and a boat ramp. (Daily; closed Jan 1, Thanksgiving, Dec 25) **FREE**

Huntsville (A-3)

See also Athens, Decatur, Guntersville, Scottsboro

Settled 1805
Population 158,216
Elevation 641 ft
Area Code 256
Information Convention & Visitors Bureau, 700 Monroe St, 35801; phone 256/551-2230 or toll-free 800/772-2348
Web Site www.huntsville.org

In Huntsville, the old and the new in Alabama meet. Now the seat of Madison County, the constitutional convention of Alabama Territory met here in 1819 and set up the state legislature. Many stately houses of that era may be seen. Today, Huntsville is deeply involved in space exploration. The NASA-Marshall Space Flight Center is NASA's rocketry headquarters and is where the space station was built.

Situated in a curving valley, Huntsville was an early textile town processing cotton raised in the surrounding country. Six Alabama governors called it home; so did the Confederate Secretary of War. The University of Alabama-Huntsville is located here.

What to See and Do

Alabama Constitution Village. *109 Gates Ave, Huntsville (35801). Phone 256/564-8100. www.earlyworks. com/village.html.* Re-created complex of buildings commemorating Alabama's entry into the Union at the 1819 Constitutional Convention; period craft demonstrations and activities; guides in period dress. (Sat 9 am-4 pm; June-Aug: Sat 10 am-5 pm; closed

Jan-Feb, holidays) **$$$**

Big Spring International Park. *700 Monroe, Huntsville (35801). Phone 256/533-5723.* The town's water supply, this natural spring produces 24 million gallons daily. The first homesteader was John Hunt, and it was this spring around which the town's nucleus grew.

Burritt Museum & Park. *3101 Burritt Dr, Huntsville (35801). Just off Monte Sano Blvd. Phone 256/536-2882. www.burrittmuseum.com.* Unusual 11-room house built in the shape of a cross. Exhibitions on gems and minerals, archaeology, antiques, historical items. On the grounds of this 167-acre park are four authentically furnished cabins, a blacksmith shop, a smokehouse, and a church. Nature trails, gardens. Picnicking. Panoramic view of city. Museum (Apr-Oct: Tues-Sat 9 am-5 pm, Sun from noon; Nov-Mar: Tues-Sat 10 am-4 pm, Sun from noon; closed Mon, holidays). Grounds (daily). **$**

Historic Huntsville Depot. *320 Church St, Huntsville (35801). Phone 256/564-8100; toll-free 800/678-1819. www.earlyworks.com/depot.html.* Opened in 1860 as a "passenger house" and eastern division headquarters for the Memphis & Charleston Railroad Company, the Huntsville depot was captured by Union troops and used as a prison; Civil War graffiti survives. Transportation, Civil War, and cotton exhibits. (Tues-Fri 10 am-4 pm, Sat 10 am-5 pm; closed Jan-Feb, holidays) **$$$**

Huntsville Museum of Art. *300 Church St, Huntsville (35801). Off I-565 at Big Spring International Park. Phone 256/535-4350. www.hsvmuseum.org.* Five galleries featuring traditional and contemporary work by regional and national artists; permanent collection and changing exhibits. Tours, lectures, concerts, films. (Mon-Wed, Fri-Sat 10 am-5 pm, Sun 1-5 pm; closed holidays) **$$**

Madison County Nature Trail. *12 miles SE on S Shawdee Rd, Green Mountain. Phone 256/883-9501.* Original house on first homestead. Chapel; covered bridge; 16-acre lake, waterfall; spring houses; wooded hiking trails. Braille trail. (Daily)

Monte Sano State Park. *5105 Nolan Ave, Huntsville (35801). 4 miles E, off Hwy 431. Phone 256/534-3757. www.dcnr.state.al.us.* A 2,340-acre scenic recreation area on top of 1,650-foot Monte Sano ("Mountain of Health"). Hiking trails, picnicking (tables, shelters, barbecue pits, fireplaces), playground, concession. Camping, cabins. Amphitheater. Park open all year. **$**

Twickenham Historic District. *700 Monroe St SW, Huntsville (35801). Downtown, S and E of Courthouse Sq. Phone 256/551-2230.* A living museum of antebellum architecture, the district contains Alabama's largest concentration of antebellum houses. Several of the houses are occupied by descendants of original builders/owners. Tours can be self-guided; guided tours available for groups. Contact the Convention and Visitors Bureau.

⭐ **US Space and Rocket Center.** *One Tranquility Base, Huntsville (35805). 5 miles W on Hwy 20 just off I-565 at exit 15. Phone 256/837-3400; toll-free 800/637-7223. www.spacecamp.com.* Space exhibits including Apollo capsule and space shuttle objects returned from orbit. Rocket Park displays development of Apollo-Saturn V moon rocket and life-size space shuttle model. Omnimax Theater with tilt dome screen seats 280 and shows 45-minute space shuttle and science films photographed by astronauts. NASA bus tours are escorted one- or two-hour bus trips through Marshall Space Flight Center, featuring mission control, space station construction, and tank where astronauts simulate weightlessness. US Space Camp offers one-week programs for children grades four and up. Campground. (Daily 9 am-5 pm; closed Jan 1, Thanksgiving, Dec 24-25, 31) **$$$$**

Von Braun Center. *700 Monroe St, Huntsville (35801). Downtown. Phone 256/533-1953. www.vonbrauncenter. com.* Largest multipurpose complex in northern Alabama, named for noted space pioneer, Dr. Wernher von Braun. Center has 9,000-seat arena, 2,171-seat concert hall, 502-seat theater-playhouse; 100,000-square-foot exhibit space, 25,000-square-foot meeting rooms; the city Tourist Information Center (24-hour phone 256/533-5723).

Special Events

Big Spring Jam. *Big Spring International Park, 700 Monroe St, Huntsville (35801). Phone 256/551-2359. www.bigspringjam.org.* More than 70 musical acts of all kinds perform at this three-day music festival. Past artists have included Wynonna Judd, Lynyrd Skynyrd, and Jewel. Late Sept. **$$$$**

Panoply Arts Festival. *Big Spring International Park, 700 Monroe St, Huntsville (35801). Phone 256/519-2787. www.panoply.org.* Enjoy dance performances at the choreography competition, interactive art activities at Artrageous, and the final round of excitement at Panoply Idol. Last full weekend of Apr. **$$**

Limited-Service Hotels

★ **COMFORT INN.** *3788 University Dr, Huntsville (35816). Phone 256/533-3291; toll-free 800/228-5150; fax 256/536-7389. www.choicehotels.com.* 67 rooms, 2 story. Complimentary continental breakfast. Check-out 11 am. Outdoor pool. **$**

★ ★ **COURTYARD BY MARRIOTT.** *4804 University Dr, Huntsville (35816). Phone 256/837-1400; toll-free 800/321-2211; fax 256/837-3582. www.courtyard. com.* This affordable and comfortable hotel in Huntsville welcomes visitors traveling for both business and pleasure. Guests can enjoy a day touring the US Space and Rocket Center or NASA Space Center. 149 rooms, 3 story. Check-out noon. Restaurant, bar. Fitness room. Outdoor pool, whirlpool. **$**

★ ★ **FOUR POINTS BY SHERATON.** *1000 Glenn Hearn Blvd, Huntsville (35824). Phone 256/772-9661; toll-free 888/625-5144; fax 256/464-9116. www. fourpoints.com.* This hotel is located on the 2nd level of the Huntsville International Airport. The Marshall Space Center is nearby. 148 rooms, 6 story. Check-out noon. Restaurant, bar. Fitness room. Outdoor pool. Golf. Tennis. Business center. **$**

★ **GUESTHOUSE INTERNATIONAL.** *4020 Independence Dr NW, Huntsville (35816). Phone 256/837-8907; toll-free 800/331-3131; fax 256/837-5435. www. guesthouseintl.com.* 112 rooms, 2 story. Pets accepted; fee. Complimentary continental breakfast. Check-out noon. Outdoor pool, whirlpool. Airport transportation available. **$**

★ ★ **HOLIDAY INN EXPRESS.** *3808 University Dr, Huntsville (35816). Phone 256/721-1000; toll-free 800/345-7720; fax 256/722-2016. www.hiexpress.com.* 112 rooms, 2 story. Pets accepted, some restrictions; fee. Check-out noon. Restaurant, bar. Outdoor pool. Airport transportation available. **$**

★ **LA QUINTA INN.** *3141 University Dr NW, Huntsville (35816). Phone 256/533-0756; toll-free 800/687-6667; fax 256/539-5414. www.laquinta.com.* 130 rooms, 2 story. Pets accepted. Complimentary continental breakfast. Check-out noon. Outdoor pool. **$**

★ ★ RADISSON SUITE HOTEL HUNTSVILLE.

6000 Memorial Pkwy S, Huntsville (35802). Phone 256/882-9400; toll-free 800/333-3333; fax 256/882-9684. www.radisson.com. This charming hotel features spacious, stretch-out comfortable suites. A Robert Trent Jones golf course is only 8 miles away. 153 rooms, 3 story, all suites. Check-out noon. Restaurant, bar. Fitness room. Outdoor pool, whirlpool. Airport transportation available. Business center. **$**

Full-Service Hotels

★ ★ ★ HOLIDAY INN SELECT HUNTSVILLE DOWNTOWN.

401 Williams Ave, Huntsville (35801). Phone 256/533-1400; fax 256/534-7787. www.holiday-inn.com. Located adjacent to the Big Springs International Park and a short walk from the Von Braun Civic Center, the Museum of Art, and the Historical District. 279 rooms, 4 story. Pets accepted, some restrictions. Check-out noon. Restaurant, bar. Fitness room. Outdoor pool, whirlpool. Airport transportation available. Business center. **$**

★ ★ ★ MARRIOTT HUNTSVILLE.

5 Tranquility Base, Huntsville (35805). Phone 256/830-2222; fax 256/895-0904. www.marriott.com. Enjoy the comfort of this fine hotel, which has rooms specifically designed for the business traveler. The Space and Rocket Museum is adjacent. 290 rooms, 7 story. Check-out noon. Restaurant, bar. Fitness room. Indoor pool, outdoor pool, whirlpool. Airport transportation available. Business center. **$**

Restaurant

★ ★ OL' HEIDELBERG.

6125 University Dr NW # E-14, Huntsville (35806). Phone 256/922-0556; fax 256/922-0514. American, German menu. Dinner. Closed holidays. **$$**

Mobile (F-1)

See also Atmore, Dauphin Island, Gulf Shores; also see Pascagoula, MS

Founded 1702
Population 198,915
Elevation 7 ft
Area Code 251

Information Convention & Visitors Corporation, 1 S Water St, PO Box 204, 36601; phone 251/208-2000 or toll-free 800/566-2453
Web Site www.mobile.org

Mobile, Alabama's largest port city, blends old Southern grace with new Southern enterprise. The city began in 1702 when Jean Baptiste le Moyne, Sieur de Bienville, moved his colony from Twenty-Seven Mile Bluff to the present site of Mobile.

Shipping, shipbuilding, and a variety of manufacturers make Mobile a great industrial center. Today, many millions of tons of cargo annually clear this international port. Paper, petroleum products, textiles, food processing, and woodworking are among the principal industries.

While remaining very much the vibrant industrial seaport, Mobile has still managed to retain its air of antebellum graciousness and preserve its past in the Church Street, DeTonti Square, Oakleigh Garden, and Old Dauphinway historical districts. These areas are famous for azaleas, oak-lined streets, and an extraordinary variety of architectural styles.

What to See and Do

Alabama State Docks. *Port of Mobile, 250 N Water St, Mobile (36602). Phone 251/441-7001.* Berths for 35 ocean-going vessels of up to 45-feet draft; 1,000-foot-wide turning basin. (Mon-Fri; closed holidays)

Battleship Memorial Park, USS *Alabama*. *2703 Battleship Pkwy, Mobile (36602). 1 mile E via Bankhead and Wallace tunnels on Battleship Pkwy, I-90. Phone 251/433-2703. www.ussalabama.com.* Visitors may tour the 35,000-ton USS *Alabama,* which serves as a memorial to the state's men and women who served in World War II, the Korean conflict, Vietnam, and Desert Storm. Also, submarine USS *Drum,* World War II aircraft, a B-52 bomber, and an A-12 Blackbird spy plane. (Oct-Mar: daily 8 am-4 pm; Apr-Sept: daily 8 am-6 pm; closed Dec 25) Parking fee. **$$**

Bay City tours. *PO Box 304, Mobile (36601). Phone 251/479-9970.*

Bellingrath Gardens and Home. *12401 Bellingrath Gardens Rd, Mobile. 20 miles SW via Hwy 90 or I-10 and Bellingrath Hwy, near Theodore. Phone 251/973-2217; toll-free 800/247-8420. www.bellingrath.org.* This 905-acre estate comprises natural woodland and some 65 acres of planted gardens on the Isle-aux-Oises (Fowl)

River. It is also a bird sanctuary. Many varieties of native and other trees are background for the innumerable flowers and flowering plants that are in bloom all year. Each season has its own special flowers but many bloom for more than one. There are approximately 250,000 azalea plants of 200 varieties, camellias, roses, water lilies, dogwood, and hydrangeas. Travels to world-famed gardens abroad inspired the Bellingraths to create their gardens in the 1920s. Visitors receive a pictorial map showing gardens' walks and principal features. Included in the gardens' admission is the world's largest public display of Boehm porcelain. There is a restaurant, a video display at the entrance, and a free "pet motel" near the exit. The Bellingrath house, in the center of the gardens, is furnished with antiques, fine china, and rare porcelain; it is open to a few people at a time (daily tours). Since the home is located within the gardens, it is not possible to visit the house without visiting the gardens. The riverboat *Southern Belle* provides 45-minute cruises along the Fowl River. House, gardens, and river cruise (daily). (Daily 8 am-5 pm; closed Dec 25) **$$$**

Bragg-Mitchell Mansion. *1906 Springhill Ave, Mobile (36607). Phone 251/471-6364. www.braggmitchellmansion.com.* (1855) Greek Revival 20-room mansion sits amidst 12 acres of landscaped grounds. Restored interior includes extensive faux-grained woodwork and stenciled moldings; period furnishings. Tours (Tues-Fri 10 am-4 pm). **$**

Cathedral of the Immaculate Conception. *2 S Claiborne, Mobile (36602). Phone 251/434-1565.* (1835) Greek Revival minor basilica with German art glass windows, bronze canopy over altar, and hand-carved stations of the cross. (Daily; limited hours Mon-Fri)

Claude D. Kelley State Park. *580 H. Kyle, Atmore (36502). 12 miles N of I-65, on Hwy 21 at Atmore exit. Contact Rte 2, Box 77. Phone 251/862-2511. www.dcnr. state.al.us.* A 25-acre lake is located beneath the towering pines of this 960-acre park. Swimming, fishing, boating (ramps, rentals); picnicking, primitive camping, RV hookups, cabins.

Conde-Charlotte Museum House. *104 Theatre St, Mobile (36602). Adjacent to Fort Cond. Phone 251/432-4722.* (1822-1824) Originally a jail, the museum house is now furnished with period antiques and artifacts; period kitchen and Spanish garden. (Tues-Sat 10 am-4 pm; closed holidays) **$**

Fort Conde Museum and Welcome Center. *150 S Royal St at Church St, Mobile (36602). Phone 334/208-7304.*

This reconstructed 1724-1735 French fort features workable reproductions of a 1740s naval cannon, muskets, and other arms. It's staffed by soldiers dressed in period French uniforms. (Daily 8 am-5 pm; closed Dec 25) **FREE**

Greyhound racing. *Mobile Greyhound Park, 7101 Old Pascagoula Rd, Mobile (36582). W via I-10, Theodore-Dawes exit (#13). Phone 251/653-5000. www.mobilegreyhoundpark.com.* Pari-mutuel betting; restaurant. Minimum age 18. (Nightly Mon, Wed-Sat 7:30 pm, matinees Mon, Wed, Sat 1 pm, Sun 11 am; closed mid-late Dec)

Malbis Greek Orthodox Church. *9865 Hwy 90, Daphne (36526). 13 miles E off I-10, exit 38 or Hwy 90. Phone 251/626-3050.* (1965) Impressive Byzantine church copied from a similar one in Athens, Greece. Pentelic marble is from the same quarries that supplied the Parthenon; skilled artists from Greece created the authentic paintings; hand-carved figures and ornaments were brought from Greece. Stained-glass windows, dome with murals, icons, and many works of art depicting the life of Christ. Guided tours by appointment. (Daily, closed Dec 25) **FREE**

Mobile Medical Museum. *1664 Springhill Ave, Mobile (36604). Phone 251/415-1109.* In the historic Vincet Down House. Named in honor of Dr. James Heustis and Dr. Samuel Eichold, this museum is the largest of its kind in the Southeast. It contains displays of medical artifacts and photographs. An extensive Civil War gallery of documents and rare artifacts, photographs and apothecary. (Mon-Fri 9 am-4 pm)

Mobile Museum of Art. *4850 Museum Dr, Mobile (36608). On S shore of lake in Langan Park.Phone 251/208-5200. www.mobilemuseumofart.com.* Permanent collection includes furniture, decorative arts; American and European 19th-century paintings and prints; contemporary arts and crafts; changing exhibits. (Mon-Sat 10 am-5 pm, Sun 1-5 pm) **$$**

Museum of Mobile. *111 S Royal St, Mobile (36602). Phone 251/208-7569. www.museumofmobile.com.* Paintings, documents, and artifacts of Mobile's French, British, Spanish, and Confederate periods; Mobile's maritime history, ship models, antique carriages, arms collection, Mardi Gras and other costumes. World's second-largest collection of Edward Marshall Boehm porcelains. Guided tours by appointment. Located in Bernstein-Bush House (1872), an Italianate town house. Free admission first Sun of each month. (Mon-Sat 9 am-5 pm, Sun 1-5 pm; closed holidays) **$**

Oakleigh Period House Museum. *350 Oakleigh Pl, Mobile. Phone 251/432-1281. www.historicmobile.org.* This 1833 antebellum house stands on the highest point of Simon Favre's old Spanish land grant, surrounded by azaleas and the live oaks for which it was named. Bricks for the first story were made on the site; the main upper portion is of hand-hewn timber. The Historic Mobile Preservation Society has furnished the house in the pre-1850 period; 1850s Cox-Deasy Creole cottage (fee). Museum collection of local items. (Tues-Sat 9 am-3 pm; closed holidays; also Mardi Gras) **$**

Phoenix Fire Museum. *203 S Claiborne St, Mobile (36602). Phone 251/208-7569. www.museumofmobile. com.* Firefighting equipment; memorabilia dating from first Mobile volunteer company (1819); steam fire engines; collection of silver trumpets and helmets. Housed in restored fire station (1859). Guided tours by appointment. (Tues-Sat 10 am-5 pm, Sun from 1 pm; closed holidays) **FREE**

Richards-DAR House. *256 N Joachim St, Mobile (36603). Phone 251/208-7320.* (Circa 1860) Restored Italianate town house features elaborate ironwork, curved suspended staircase, period furniture. (Mon-Fri 11 am-3:30 pm, Sat 10 am-4 pm, Sun 1-4 pm; closed Thanksgiving, late Dec) **$$**

University of South Alabama. *307 University Blvd, Mobile (36608). Phone 251/460-6211. www.southalabama. edu.* (1964) (12,000 students) Theater productions presented during the school year at Laidlaw Performing Arts Center (phone 334/460-6305) and at Saenger Theatre (phone 334/438-5686). Of architectural interest on campus are Seaman's Bethel Theater (1860); the Plantation Creole House (1828), a reconstructed Creole cottage; and Mobile town house (1870), a Federal-style building showing Italianate and Greek Revival influences that also houses the USA campus art gallery. Tours of campus.

Special Events

Azalea Trail Run Festival and Festival of Flowers. *Broad and Church sts, Mobile. Phone toll-free 800/566-2453.* During the period when the azaleas are usually at full bloom, many events are scheduled to entertain visitors in the city. A 35-mile-long driving tour winds through the floral streets in and around Mobile; printed guides available. Azaleas were first introduced to Mobile in the early 18th century and today they grow throughout the city. The Convention & Visitors Corporation has further details and maps for self-guided tours of Azalea Trail route and local historic sites. Late Mar.

Bay Fest. *2900 Dauphin St, Mobile (36606). Downtown, in the historic district. Phone 251/470-7730.* Various musical performers provide entertainment on five stages. First full weekend in Oct.

Blessing of the Fleet. *13790 S Wintzell, Bayou La Batre (36509). 25 miles SW. Phone 251/824-2415. www. fleetblessing.org.* A special mass, a live crab race, and a parade are just some of the activities at this annual church festival. Early May.

Greater Gulf State Fair. *1035 Cody Rd, Mobile (36608). Phone 251/344-4573. www.mobilefair.com.* Commercial, industrial, military, and educational exhibits; entertainment. Late Oct. **$**

Mobile Historic Homes Tours. *150 S Royal St, Mobile (36602). Phone 251/433-0259.* The Historic Mobile Preservation Society offers tours of the city's most beautiful private historic homes. Early Apr. **$$$**

Senior Bowl Football Game. *Ladd-Peebles Stadium, 1621 Virginia St, Mobile (36604). Phone 251/438-2276; toll-free 888/736-2695. www.seniorbowl.com.* This unique annual football game stars all the nation's leading NFL draft prospects on teams coached by NFL coaches. Late Jan.

Limited-Service Hotels

★ ★ **BEST WESTERN.** *600 S Beltline Hwy, Mobile (36608). Phone 251/344-8030; fax 251/344-8055. www. bestwestern.com.* Catering to the corporate traveler, this hotel is located in the heart of Mobile's business district. Guests will find comfort and convenience here. 236 rooms, 4 story. Check-out 1 pm. Restaurant, bar. Fitness room. Indoor pool, outdoor pool, children's pool, whirlpool. Tennis. Airport transportation available. **$**
🅳 🏋 ⚊ ⚐

★ **DAYS INN AND SUITES MOBILE.** *5472-A Inn Rd, Mobile (36619). Phone 251/660-1520; fax 251/666-4240. www.daysinn.com.* 118 rooms, 3 story. Pets accepted; fee. Check-out noon. Outdoor pool. **$**
🐾 ⚊

★ ★ **HOLIDAY INN.** *5465 Hwy 90 W, Mobile (36619). Phone 251/666-5600; toll-free 800/465-4329; fax 251/666-2773. www.holiday-inn.com.* 160 rooms, 5 story. Check-out noon. Restaurant, bar. Outdoor pool, children's pool, whirlpool. Airport transportation available. **$**
⚊

★ **LA QUINTA INN.** *816 S Beltline Hwy, Mobile (36609). Phone 251/343-4051; toll-free 800/531-5900; fax 251/343-2897. www.laquinta.com.* 122 rooms, 2 story. Pets accepted, some restrictions. Complimentary continental breakfast. Check-out noon. Outdoor pool. **$**

★ ★ **RADISSON ADMIRAL SEMMES HOTEL.** *251 Government St, Mobile (36602). Phone 251/432-8000; toll-free 800/333-3333; fax 251/405-5942. www.radisson.com.* Opened in 1940 and beautifully renovated in 1985, this hotel is on the list of Historic Hotels of America. Rooms are luxuriously appointed with Chippendale furnishings from the Queen Ann era. 170 rooms, 12 story. Check-out 11 am. Restaurant, bar. Outdoor pool, whirlpool. Business center. **$**

★ ★ **RIVERVIEW PLAZA.** *64 S Water St, Mobile (36602). Phone 251/438-4000; fax 251/415-0123.* Located in the heart of downtown's historic, business, and entertainment districts, this hotel is connected to the convention center. Don't miss a visit to the USS *Alabama* battleship, which is only 2 miles away. 375 rooms, 8 story. Check-out noon. Restaurant, bar. Outdoor pool. Business center. **$$**

★ **WESTMONT INN.** *930 S Beltline Hwy, Mobile (36609). Phone 251/344-4942; fax 251/341-4520. www. westmontinn.com.* 118 rooms, 2 story. Complimentary continental breakfast. Check-out 11 am. Outdoor pool. **$**

Full-Service Resort

★ ★ **MARRIOTT GRAND HOTEL.** *One Grand Blvd, Point Clear (36564). Phone 251/928-9201; toll-free 800/544-9933; fax 251/928-1149. www.marriott. com.* Guests can indulge in fun and relaxation at this hotel on 550 landscaped acres on Mobile Bay. A historic Civil War cemetery is on site. 306 rooms, 4 story. Check-in 4 pm, check-out noon. Restaurant, bar. Children's activity center. Fitness room. Indoor pool, outdoor pool, whirlpool. Golf. Tennis. Airport transportation available. Business center. **$**

Restaurants

★ ★ **THE PILLARS.** *1757 Government St, Mobile (36604). Phone 251/471-3411; fax 251/478-6348.* Respected as one of the best restaurants in Mobile, this special occasion destination draws a prominent crowd for classic, continental dining in a restored plantation house. Owner Filippo Milone is the perfect host, warmly greeting guests and watching over his excellent staff. American menu. Dinner. Closed Sun; holidays. Children's menu. **$$**

★ ★ ★ **RUTH'S CHRIS STEAK HOUSE.** *271 Glenwood St, Mobile (36606). Phone 251/476-0516; fax 251/476-0518. www.ruthschrissteakhouse.com.* In keeping with the style of New Orleans, where this restaurant originated, portions are generous. The custom-aged Midwestern beef is never frozen and cooked in a 1800° F broiler to customers' tastes. Dinner. Closed Thanksgiving, Dec 25. Bar. **$$$**

Montgomery (D-3)

See also Clanton, Greenville, Hamilton, Selma, Troy, Tuskegee

Settled 1819
Population 201,568
Elevation 287 ft
Area Code 334
Information Montgomery Area Chamber of Commerce, 41 Commerce St, 36101; phone 334/834-5200
Web Site www.montgomerychamber.com

Between tall, stately columns on the portico of the state capitol, a bronze star marks the spot where Jefferson Davis was inaugurated President of the Confederate States of America on February 18, 1861. At that moment, Montgomery became the Confederacy's first capital. From this city went the telegram "Fire on Fort Sumter" that began the Civil War. Approximately 100 years later, Montgomery became embroiled in another kind of "war," the battle for civil rights.

Today, Montgomery is home to the nation's first Civil Rights Memorial. The memorial chronicles key events and lists the names of approximately 40 people who died in the struggle for racial equality from 1955-1968.

Montgomery is a city of considerable distinction, with many historic houses and buildings. Although Montgomery's most important business is government, it is also a livestock market and a center of manufacturing. As an educational center, it offers many cultural activities.

What to See and Do

Alabama Shakespeare Festival. *1 Festival Dr, Montgomery (36117). Phone toll-free 800/841-8273. www. asf.net.* Professional repertory company performs classic and contemporary comedy and drama. Musical performances as well. Two theaters: 750-seat Festival Stage and 225-seat Octagon. (Nov-Sept, Wed-Sun; weekend matinees) Hotel/play packages available. Inquire about facilities for the disabled and hearing impaired.

Alabama State University. *915 S Jackson St, Montgomery (36104). Phone 334/229-4100. www.alasu.edu.* (1867) (5,500 students) Authorized by the legislature in 1873 as the Lincoln Normal School, this university was moved from Marion to Montgomery in 1887. On campus are an art gallery, African-American collection, and Tullibody Fine Arts Center (daily during academic year; closed holidays). Tours.

⭐ **Civil Rights Memorial.** *400 Washington Ave, Montgomery (36104). Washington Ave and Hull St at the Southern Poverty Law Center.* Designed by Vietnam Veterans Memorial artist Maya Lin.

⭐ **Dexter Avenue King Memorial Baptist Church.** *454 Dexter Ave, Montgomery (36104). Phone 334/263-3970. www.dexterkingmemorial.org.* (1877) The Reverend Dr. Martin Luther King, Jr., was a pastor from 1954 to 1960; from the church he directed the Montgomery bus boycott, which sparked the modern civil rights movement. In the church is the mural and original painting "The Beginning of a Dream." Guided tours (Mon-Thurs 10 am and 2 pm), walk through (Fri 10 am), and by appointment (Sat 10:30 am-1:30 pm). Sun worship 10:30 am.

F. Scott and Zelda Fitzgerald Museum. *919 Felder Ave, Montgomery (36106). Phone 334/264-4222. www. fitzgerald-museum.org.* The famous author and his wife lived in this house from 1931-1932. Museum contains personal artifacts detailing the couple's public and private lives. Paintings by Zelda, letters, and photographs; 25-minute video presentation. (Wed-Fri, Sat-Sun afternoons; closed holidays) **FREE**

Fort Toulouse/Jackson Park National Historic Landmark. *2521 W Fort Toulouse Rd, Montgomery (36093). 12 miles NE, 3 miles W off Hwy 231 near Wetumpka. Phone 334/567-3002.* At the confluence of the Coosa and Tallapoosa rivers, Fort Toulouse was opened by Bienville in 1717 to establish trade in the heart of Creek territory. Abandoned in 1763, Andrew Jackson built a fort on the same site in 1814 after the Battle of Horseshoe Bend. Fort Toulouse has been reconstructed, and Fort Jackson has been partially reconstructed. This is also the site of mounds dating from approximately AD 1100. The park features a boat ramp, nature walks, picnicking, improved camping, and a museum. A living history program can be seen the third weekend of each month. Visitor center. (Daily; closed Jan 1, Dec 25) **$**

Greyhound racing. *VictoryLand Track, 8680 County Rd 40, Shorter (36075). 20 miles E via I-85, exit 22. Phone 334/269-6087. www.victoryland.com.* Clubhouse, restaurant. Over 19 years only. (Nightly; Mon-Wed, Sat-Sun afternoons; closed Thanksgiving, late Dec) **$**

Hank Williams's grave. *Hank Williams Memorial, Oakwood Cemetery, 1305 Upper Wetumpka Rd, Montgomery (36107).* Gravesite memorial to country music legend.

Huntingdon College. *1500 Fairview Ave, Montgomery (36106). 2 miles SE. Phone 334/833-4497. www. huntingdon.edu.* (1854) (700 students) Founded in Tuskegee to provide higher education for women, the liberal arts school became coeducational after World War II; 58-acre campus of woods and hills; Gothic buildings. Tours (by appointment).

Lower Commerce Street Historic District. *100 block of Commerce St, Montgomery.* Wholesale and railroad district along the Alabama River. Buildings, primarily Victorian in style, date from the 1880s to turn of the century. Riverfront tunnel to Riverfront Park dates to cotton days.

Maxwell Air Force Base. *55 S LeMay Plz, Montgomery (36112). 2 miles S, off I-65. Phone 334/953-1110. www. au.af.mil.* This has been an airfield since 1910, when Wilbur Wright began the world's first flying school on this site. Orville Wright made his first flight in Montgomery on March 26, 1910, four years before the Aviation Section of the Signal Corps was created. Maxwell Field was named on November 8, 1922, for Lieutenant William C. Maxwell of Atmore, Alabama, killed while serving with the Third Aero Squadron in the Philippines. It is now the site of Air University. Tours by appointment. (Daily; closed holidays) **FREE**

Montgomery Museum of Fine Arts. *1 Museum Dr, Montgomery (36117). Phone 334/244-5700. www. fineartsmuseum.com.* Collections of 19th- and 20th-century American art; European works on paper; regional and decorative arts. Hands-on children's exhibits. Lectures, concerts. (Tues, Fri-Sat 10 am-5 pm, Thurs to 9 pm, Sat noon-5 pm; closed holidays) **FREE**

Montgomery Zoo. *2301 Colosseum Pkwy, Montgomery (36110). Phone 334/240-4900. zoo.ci.montgomery.al.us.* Forty-acre zoo housing, mammals, birds, and reptiles in geographical groupings. (Daily 9 am-5 pm; closed Jan 1, Thanksgiving, Dec 25) **$$**

Murphy House. *22 Bibb St, Montgomery (36104). Bibb and Coosa sts. Phone 334/206-1600.* (1851) Fine example of Greek Revival architecture with fluted Corinthian columns and wrought-iron balcony is now headquarters of the Montgomery Water Works. (Mon-Fri; closed holidays)

Old Alabama Town. *301 Columbus St, Montgomery (36104). Phone 334/240-4500. www.oldalabamatown. com.* Includes the Ordeman-Shaw House, an Italianate town house (circa 1850) with period furnishings; service buildings with household items; reconstructed 1840 barn; carriage house; 1820s log cabin depicting pioneer life; shotgun cottage depicting black urban life; urban church (circa 1890); country doctor's office; drugstore museum and cotton gin museum; blacksmith shop; print shop; corner grocery from the late 1890s; one-room schoolhouse; exhibition (Grange) hall. Taped driving tour of historic Montgomery also available. Films, tours, information center.(Mon-Sat 9 am-3 pm; closed holidays) **$$**

St. John's Episcopal Church. *113 Madison Ave, Montgomery (36104). At N Perry St. Phone 334/262-1937. www.stjohnsmontgomery.org.* (1855) Stained-glass windows, Gothic pipe organ, Jefferson Davis' pew. (Sun-Fri)

State Capitol. *Bainbridge and Dexter aves, Montgomery. Phone 334/242-3935.* (1851) Seat of Alabama's government for more than 100 years. Opposite the capitol are

> **Alabama Department of Archives and History.** *624 Washington Ave, Montgomery (36130). Phone 334/242-4363.* Houses historical museum and genealogical research facilities. Artifact collections include exhibits on the 19th century, the military, and early Alabama Native Americans. Also an interactive children's gallery. (Mon-Fri 8:30 am-4:30 pm, first Sat of the month 8:30 am-4:30 pm; closed holidays) **FREE**

> **First White House of the Confederacy.** *644 Washington Ave, Montgomery (36130). Phone 334/242-1861.* (1835) This two-story, white frame house was the residence of Jefferson Davis and his family while Montgomery was the Confederate capital. Moved from its original location at Bibb

and Lee streets in 1920, it is now a Confederate museum containing period furnishings, personal belongings, and paintings of the Davis family and Confederate mementos. (Mon-Fri 8 am-4:30 pm; closed holidays) **FREE**

Special Events

Alabama National Fair. *Garrett Coliseum, 1555 Federal Dr, Montgomery (36107). NE on Federal Dr. Phone 334/272-6831. www.alnationalfair.org.* This weeklong fair includes concerts, a circus, children's rides, and pig races. Oct. **$$**

Blue-Gray All-Star Classic. *Movie Gallery Stadium at Troy State University, 100 University Ave, Montgomery. www.bluegrayfootball.com.* This classic football game between North and South college senior all-stars was first played in 1939. The game was the brainchild of Champ Pickens, an Alabama football manager and promoter, but was acquired by the Montgomery Lions Club in 1955. Since then, the proceeds of each game are donated to Lions Club charities. Dec 25. **$$$$**

Jubilee City Fest. *640 S McDonough St, Montgomery (36104). Downtown. www.jubileecityfest.org.* This festival features national musical acts as well as cultural events and children's activities. Memorial Day weekend.

Southeastern Livestock Exposition and Rodeo. *Garrett Coliseum, 1555 Federal Dr, Montgomery (36107). Phone 334/265-1867.* Some of the nation's best cowboys and cowgirls compete in this PRCA event, the largest rodeo east of the Mississippi. Mid-Mar.

Limited-Service Hotels

★ **ECONO LODGE & SUITES.** *5924 Monticello Dr, Montgomery (36117). Phone 334/272-1013; fax 334/260-0425. www.choicehotels.com.* 49 rooms, 3 story, all suites. Complimentary continental breakfast. Check-out noon. Fitness room. Outdoor pool. **$**
🧍 🏊

★ **FAIRFIELD INN.** *5601 Carmichael Rd, Montgomery (36117). Phone 205/270-0007; toll-free 800/228-2800; fax 205/270-0007. www.fairfieldinn.com.* 133 rooms, 3 story. Complimentary continental breakfast. Check-out noon. Outdoor pool. **$**
🏊

★ ★ **HOLIDAY INN.** *1185 Eastern Bypass, Montgomery (36117). Phone 334/272-0370; toll-free 800/465-4329; fax 334/270-1046. www.holiday-inn. com.* 211 rooms, 2 story. Pets accepted, some restrictions; fee. Check-out noon. Restaurant, bar. Fitness room. Indoor pool, whirlpool. **$**

★ **LA QUINTA INN.** *1280 Eastern Blvd, Montgomery (36117). Phone 334/271-1620; toll-free 800/531-5980; fax 334/244-7919. www.laquinta.com.* 130 rooms, 2 story. Pets accepted. Complimentary continental breakfast. Check-out noon. Outdoor pool. **$**

★ ★ **RAMADA.** *1100 W South Blvd, Montgomery (36105). Phone 334/281-1660; toll-free 800/272-6232; fax 334/281-1667. www.ramada.com.* 150 rooms, 4 story. Pets accepted, some restrictions; fee. Check-out noon. Restaurant, bar. Outdoor pool. Airport transportation available. **$**

★ **ROADWAY INN.** *1355 East Blvd, Montgomery (36117). Phone 334/277-2200; fax 334/277-9874.* 152 rooms, 2 story. Complimentary full breakfast. Check-out noon. Bar. Outdoor pool. **$**

Specialty Lodgings

LATTICE INN. *1414 S Hull St, Montgomery (36104). Phone 334/832-9931.* Located in historic Garden District this home was built in 1906 and is furnished with antiques and family pieces. A large Southern breakfast is served each morning. 4 rooms, 2 story. **$**

RED BLUFF COTTAGE BED. *551 Clay St, Montgomery (36101). Phone 334/264-0056. www.redbluff-cottage.com.* 19th century Victorian cottage located in downtown Montgomery featuring a large Southern breakfast. 6 rooms, 3 story. **$**

Restaurants

★ ★ **ALA THAI.** *1361 Federal Dr, Montgomery (36114). Phone 334/262-5830.* Authentic cuisine with an emphasis on noodle dishes in a romantic environment. Thai menu. Lunch, dinner. **$**

★ **MARTHA'S PLACE.** *458 Sayre St, Montgomery (36104). Phone 334/263-9135.* Classic soul food restaurant in a homelike setting. Famous for fried chicken. American menu. Breakfast, lunch. Closed Sat-Sun. **$**

★ ★ **VINTAGE YEAR.** *405 Cloverdale Rd, Montgomery (36106). Phone 334/264-8463; fax 334/269-5700.* Located in Montgomery's historic Cloverdale

District, this restaurant serves unique appetizers and desserts. Modern décor with intimate lighting makes it a great spot for a romantic dinner. Seafood menu. Dinner. Closed Sun-Mon; holidays. Bar. **$$**

Orange Beach

Restaurants

★ **HAZEL'S FAMILY RESTAURANT.** *25311 Perdido Beach Blvd, Orange Beach (36561). Phone 251/981-4628; fax 251/981-2650.* American menu. Breakfast, lunch, dinner. Bar. Children's menu. **$ $**

★ ★ **ZEKE'S LANDING.** *26619 Perdido Beach Blvd, Orange Beach (36561). Phone 251/981-4001; fax 251/981-2651. www.zekeslandingrestaurant.com.* Seafood menu. Dinner, Sun brunch. Bar. Children's menu. **$$**

Ozark (E-4)

See also Dothan, Troy

Population 15,119
Elevation 409 ft
Area Code 334
Zip 36360
Information Ozark Area Chamber of Commerce, 308 Painter Ave; phone 334/774-9321 or toll-free 800/582-8497
Web Site www.ozarkalabama.org

What to See and Do

Blue Springs State Park. *2595 Hwy 10, Clio (36017). 20 miles NE via Hwy 105, County Rd 33, Hwy 10. Phone 334/397-4875. www.dcnr.state.al.us.* This 103-acre park features a spring-fed pool, swimming pool, bathhouse; tennis, picnic facilities, playground, softball field. Primitive and improved campsites. **$**

Point Clear

Restaurant

★ ★ ★ **THE GRAND DINING ROOM.** *One Grand Blvd, Point Clear (36564). Phone 251/928-9201; fax 251/928-1149.* Located on the 550-acre property of Marriott's Grand Hotel Resort & Golf Club, this signature restaurant with a view offers generous buffet dining during breakfast and lunch and romantic, festive dinners. Dinner. Closed Sun-Mon. Bar. Children's menu. **$$**

Russell Cave National Monument (A-4)

See also Scottsboro; also see Chattanooga, TN

Web Site www.nps.gov/ruca/

3729 County Rd 98, Bridgeport (35740). 8 miles W of Bridgeport off Hwy 72 via County 91, then County 98. Phone 256/495-2672.

This cave shelter is located on the edge of the Tennessee River Valley. Stone Age man made his home here in a giant room 210 feet long, 107 feet wide and averaging 26 feet in height. Excavation of refuse and debris deposited in the cave has dated the site to approximately 7000 BC. Archaeological exploration has revealed a record of almost continuous habitation to AD 1650. Paleo, Archaic, Woodland, and Mississippian cultures are represented. The 310-acre site, given to the United States by the National Geographic Society, is administered by the National Park Service and is preserved in its natural state.

The visitor center has displays detailing the daily life of the cave's prehistoric occupants, including exhibitions of weapons, tools, and cooking processes. Audiovisual programs. Area and visitor center (Daily; closed Jan 1, Thanksgiving, Dec 25). Contact 3729 County Rd 98, Bridgeport 35740. **FREE**

Russellville (A-2)

See also Florence, Hamilton, Sheffield

Population 8,971
Area Code 256
Zip 35653
Information Franklin County Area Chamber of Commerce, PO Box 44; phone 256/332-1760
Web Site www.russellvillegov.com

What to See and Do

Reservoirs. *11 County Rd 88, Russellville. Phone*

256/332-4392. Bear Creek Development Authority has built four dams in the area and, with the assistance of the TVA, has developed recreational facilities at several of the resulting reservoirs. For information and camping fees contact PO Box 670. **$**

Cedar Creek. *Russellville. 10 miles W via Hwy 24 and County 41. Phone 256/332-9809.* A 4,300-acre reservoir with five recreation areas. Swimming, bathhouses (Slick Rock Ford), boat launches (at dam, Slick Rock Ford, Lost Creek, Hellums Mill, Britton Bridge); picnicking, camping, hookups (Slick Rock Ford).

Little Bear Creek. *Hwy 88, Russellville. 12 miles W via Hwy 24. Phone 256/332-9804.* A 1,560-acre reservoir. Boat launch (Williams Hollow, Elliott Branch, McAfee Springs); picnicking, camping; tables, grills, electricity (Willams Hollow, Elliott Branch).

Upper Bear Creek. *I-43, Russellville. 16 miles S via Hwy 43 near Phil Campbell. Phone toll-free 800/264-3023.* A 1,850-acre reservoir. Boat launch (Twin Forks, Quarter Creek, Batestown, Mon Dye); picnicking, camping; tables, grills (Twin Forks). Float stream 28 miles below dam.

Selma (D-2)

See also Montogomery

Settled 1815
Population 20,512
Elevation 139 ft
Information Chamber of Commerce, 513 Lauderdale St, PO Drawer D, 36702; phone 334/875-7241 or toll-free 800/457-3562
Web Site www.selmaalabama.com

High on a bluff above the Alabama River, Selma is a marketing, agricultural, and manufacturing center. William Rufus King, vice president under Franklin Pierce, named the town after a poem by the Gaelic poet Ossian. The classic lines of Greek Revival and elegance of Georgian Colonial architecture blend with Early American cottages, Victorian mansions, and modern houses to lend the city an air of the antebellum South. Once an arsenal of the Confederacy—second only to Richmond—Selma was a leading target for Union armies in 1865.

Selma fell on April 2, 1865, when 2,000 soldiers were captured, ending the city's role as the Confederacy's supply depot. The naval foundry (where the warships

Tennessee, Huntsville, Tuscaloosa, and others were built), a rolling mill, powder works, and an arsenal were all destroyed. With defeat came an end to the era of wealthy plantation owners and a leisurely living in which horse racing and cockfighting were gentlemanly diversions.

Selma was also the scene of civil rights activity in the mid-1960s, with a march on the Edmund Pettus bridge. Spiritual leadership was provided by Dr. Martin Luther King, Jr., and Andrew Young at the Brown Chapel A. M. E. Church.

County farmers raise cattle, pecan trees, cotton, soybeans, hay, corn, and grain. Selma is also the headquarters of a number of industries. The town became an inland port city in 1969 when a nine-foot-deep channel on the Alabama River was completed.

What to See and Do

Black Heritage Tour. *Chamber of Commerce, 513 Lauderdale St, Selma (36701). Phone 334/875-7241.* Selma was a leading city in the march toward civil rights. Visit Brown Chapel A. M. E. Church (also a part of the Martin Luther King, Jr. self-guided Street Walking Tour), the Edmund Pettus Bridge, the National Voting Rights Museum, Selma University, the Dallas County Courthouse, and the Wilson Building.

Cahawba. *9518 Cahaba Rd, Selma. 9 miles W on Hwy 22, then 4 miles S on county road. Phone 334/872-8058.* Alabama's first permanent capital was a flourishing town from 1820 to 1860. By 1822, 184 town lots were sold for $120,000. Nearly swept away by floods in 1825, the capital was moved to Tuscaloosa in 1826; Cahawba was close to being abandoned by 1828 but rose again. By 1830, it had become the most important shipping point on the Alabama River. Despite another flood in 1833 and subsequent rebuilding in 1836, the city reached a peak population of approximately 5,000 by 1850. However, the Civil War and a third flood finally finished the town. Today, only a few of the original buildings remain intact. Ruins include the brick columns of a mansion on the river, old cemeteries, and walls enclosing artesian wells. Site currently under development as a historical park; in-progress archeological projects may be viewed by visitors. Welcome center. (Daily; closed Thanksgiving, Dec 25) **FREE**

Joseph T. Smitherman Historic Building. *109 Union St, Selma (36701). Phone 334/874-2174. www.selmaalabama.com/smithermn.htm.* (1847) The building has been restored and furnished with artifacts and an-

tiques; art pavilion. (Tues-Fri 9 am-4 pm, Sat 8 am-4 pm, also by appointment; closed holidays) **$$**

National Voting Rights Museum and Institute. *1012 Water Ave, Selma (36702). Phone 334/418-0800. www.voterights.org.* Located near the foot of Edmund Pettus Bridge, this museum offers a pictorial history of the voting rights struggle. It displays an exceptional record of events and participants, including Viola Liuzzo and Marie Foster, who made voting rights history. (Open 24 hours) **FREE**

Old Depot Museum. *4 Martin Luther King Jr. St, Selma (36703). Water Ave at Martin Luther King, Jr. St. Phone 334/874-2197.* (1891) Interpretive history museum with artifacts of Selma and Alabama's "black belt" region. (Mon-Sat 10 am-4 pm; other times by appointment; closed holidays) **$$**

Old Town Historic District. *Chamber of Commerce, 513 Lauderdale St, Selma (36701).* District includes more than 1,200 structures. Museums, specialty shops, restaurants. Self-guided tours (cassette, deposit required).

Paul M. Grist State Park. *1546 Grist Rd, Selma (36701). 15 miles N on County 37. Phone 334/872-5846. www.dcnr.state.al.us.* This 1,080-acre park has a 100-acre lake. Swimming, bathhouse, fishing, boating (launch rentals); hiking, picnic facilities (grills, shelters), playground. Primitive camping. **$**

Sturdivant Hall. *713 Mabry St, Selma (36701). Phone 334/872-5626. www.sturdivanthall.com.* (1853) Fine example of Greek Revival architecture designed by Thomas Helm Lee, cousin of Robert E. Lee, features massive Corinthian columns, original wrought iron on balconies, and belvedere on roof. Fully restored with period furnishings; kitchen with slave quarters above; smokehouse; wine cellar; carriage house; garden. Guided tour (one hour). (Tues-Sat 10 am-4 pm; closed holidays) **$$**

Special Events

Historic Selma Pilgrimage. *109 Union St, Selma (36701). Phone toll-free 800/457-3562. pilgrimage.selmaalabama.com.* Guides conduct daylight tours of historic houses; antique show. Contact Chamber of Commerce. Mid-Mar.

Reenactment of the Battle of Selma. *Battlefield Park. Phone 205/755-1990. www.members.aol.com/wwhitby/selma.html.* Battles take place on a Saturday and Sunday. Other activities during the weekend include a ladies home tour and the Grand Military Ball. Late Apr.

Tale Tellin' Festival. *Pickard Auditorium, 400 Wash-ington St, Selma (36703). Phone 334/875-7241; toll-free 800/457-3562. www.taletellin.selmaalabama.com.* Each year, three featured storytellers present tales from ghost stories to historical happenings to traditional fables. Early Oct. **$$**

Limited-Service Hotel

★ ★ **RAMADA INN.** *Hwy 80 W, Selma (36701). Phone 334/872-0461; fax 334/872-0461. www.ramada. com.* 165 rooms, 2 story. Pets accepted, some restrictions. Check-out noon. Restaurant, bar. Outdoor pool, children's pool. **$**

Specialty Lodging

BRIDGE TENDERS HOUSE. *2 Lafayette Park, Selma (36701). Phone 334/875-5517.* This small cottage sits in the shadow of Pettus Bridge on the Alabama River. Each suite is private with a full kitchen, living room, bedroom, and bath. 2 rooms, 2 story. **$**

Restaurants

★ **MAC'S FISH CAMP.** *4407 County Rd 17, Selma (36701). Phone 334/874-4087. www.outdoorusa.com/ macs/index.htm.* Famous for Southern fried catfish and very popular locally. American menu. Dinner. Closed Mon-Thurs. **$**

★ ★ **TALLY-HO.** *509 Mangum Ave, Selma (36701). Phone 334/872-1390.* Seafood, steak menu. Dinner. Closed Sun; holidays. Bar. Children's menu. Entrance and waiting area in old log cabin. **$$**

Sheffield (A-2)

See also Florence, Russellville

Settled 1815
Population 9,652
Elevation 502 ft
Area Code 256
Zip 35660
Information Colbert County Tourism and Convention Bureau, PO Box 440, Tuscumbia 35674; phone 256/383-0783

One of the Quad Cities, along with Florence (see), Tuscumbia, and Muscle Shoals, Sheffield was named for the industrial city in England. Andrew Jackson is said to be the first white man to foresee the potential of this stretch of the river. Deposits of iron ore spurred the building of five huge iron-making furnaces by 1888, giving Sheffield its start as a part of the major industrial center of the South.

What to See and Do

Alabama Music Hall of Fame. *617 Hwy 72 W, Tuscumbia (35674). 5 miles S on Hwy 43, W on Hwy 72. Phone 256/381-4417. www.alamhof.org.* Honors the contributions made to music by Alabamians. Exhibits on accomplishments of a variety of performers such as Hank Williams, Nat King Cole, and Lionel Richie. Recording stars of rock, rhythm and blues, gospel, contemporary, and country music are all included. A recording studio is available to record personal cassettes or videos. (Mon-Sat 9 am-5 pm, Sun from 1 pm) **$$**

★ **Ivy Green.** *300 N Commons St W, Tuscumbia (35674). Phone 256/383-4066. www.helenkellerbirth-place.org.* (1820) Birthplace and early home of Helen Keller. Anne Sullivan, of Boston's Perkins Institute, was hired to come to Tuscumbia and help Helen Keller, who was left blind and deaf at the age of 19 months following an illness. Miss Sullivan and Helen lived together in a small cottage, which had once been the plantation office. The cottage area includes the pump at which Helen learned her first word, "water"; the Whistle Path between the house and outdoor kitchen; and many personal items. (Mon-Sat 8:30 am-4 pm, Sun from 1 pm; closed holidays) **$$**

Special Events

Helen Keller Festival. *Ivy Green, 300 N Commons St W, Tuscumbia (35674). Phone 256/383-4066. www. helenkellerfestival.com.* First held in 1979, this festival includes Braille and sign language lessons as well as performances of "The Miracle Worker." Late June.

The Miracle Worker. *300 N Commons St W, Tuscumbia (35674). Ivy Green (see). Phone 256/383-4066.* Outdoor performance of William Gibson's prize-winning play based on Helen Keller's life. Limited number of tickets available at gate; advance purchase recommended. Price includes tour of Ivy Green preceding play. Mid-June-July, Fri-Sat. **$$**

Limited-Service Hotel

★ ★ **HOLIDAY INN.** *4900 Hatch Blvd, Sheffield (35660). Phone 256/381-4710; toll-free 800/465-4329; fax 256/381-7313. www.holiday-inn.com.* Located just

2 miles from downtown Huntsville, this modern and comfortable hotel has large guest rooms. Guests can take a beautiful drive along nearby Natchez Trace Parkway. 204 rooms, 3 story. Check-out noon. Restaurant, bar. Fitness room. Outdoor pool, whirlpool. Airport transportation available. **$**

Restaurants

★ ★ **GEORGE'S STEAK PIT.** *1206 Jackson Hwy, Sheffield (35660). Phone 256/381-1531. www.georgessteakpit.com.* American menu. Dinner. Closed Sun-Mon; holidays. Bar. **$$$**

★ **SOUTHLAND.** *1309 Jackson Hwy, Sheffield (35660). Phone 256/383-8236; fax 256/383-8236.* Lunch, dinner. Closed Mon. **$$**

Spanish Fort (F-1)

Restaurant

★ **PIER 4.** *1420 Battleship Pkwy, Spanish Fort (36527). Phone 251/626-6710; fax 251/626-6794.* Seafood menu. Dinner. Closed Thanksgiving, Dec 25. Children's menu. **$$**

Sylacauga (C-3)

See also Alexander City, Talladega

Population 12,616
Area Code 256
Zip 35150
Information Sylacauga Chamber of Commerce, 17 W Fort Williams St, PO Box 185; phone 256/249-0308
Web Site www.sylacauga.net

The city's fortune is literally its foundation—a bed of prized translucent white marble estimated to be 32 miles long, 1 1/2 miles wide, and about 400 feet deep. The bed is, in many places, only 12 feet below ground level. Marble from Sylacauga (said to mean "meeting place of the Chalaka Indians") has been used in the US Supreme Court Building and many other famous buildings in the United States and abroad. Sylacauga stone is also crushed and ground for use in products such as paint, putty, plastics, asphalt tile, and rubber.

What to See and Do

DeSoto Caverns Park. *5181 DeSoto Caverns Pkwy, Childersburg (35044). 12 miles NW via Hwy 21 and County 36; on Hwy 76, 5 miles E of junction Hwy 280. Phone 256/378-7252. www.cavern.com/desoto.* Scenic 80-acre wooded park, famous for its historic mammoth, onyx caverns. Visited by Hernando de Soto in 1540, the onyx caverns are the historic birthplace of the Creek Nation and one of the first officially recorded caves in the US—reported to President Washington in 1796. On display in the caverns is a 2,000-year-old "Copena" burial ground, Civil War gunpowder mining center, and a moonshine still from prohibition days when the caverns were known as "the bloody bucket." The main cavern, the Great Onyx Cathedral, is larger than a football field and higher than a 12-story building; a sound, laser, and water show is presented here. Featured at the park is DeSoto's Lost Trail, a 3/4-acre maze ($). Visitors also may view a water-powered rock-cutting saw in operation, pan for gold and gemstones($$), or visit the Bow and Arrow Arcade ($). Other facilities include picnic areas; shipboard playground and RV campground. Guided tours. (Apr-Oct: Mon-Sat 9 am-5:30 pm, Sun 1-5:30 pm; Nov-Mar: Mon-Sat 9 am-4:30 pm, Sun 1-4:30 pm; closed Thanksgiving, Dec 25) **$$$**

Isabel Anderson Comer Museum & Arts Center. *711 N Broadway Ave, Sylacauga (35150). Phone 256/245-4016. comermuseum.freeservers.com.* Permanent exhibits of local and Native American artifacts; special visiting exhibitions. (Tues-Fri 10 am-5 pm) **FREE**

Talladega (C-3)

See also Anniston, Birmingham, Sylacauga

Founded 1834
Population 15,143
Elevation 555 ft
Area Code 256
Zip 35161
Information Chamber of Commerce, 210 East St S, PO Drawer A, 35161; phone 256/362-9075
Web Site www.talladegachamber.com

Andrew Jackson defeated the Creeks in this area on November 9, 1813; it was the first of the battles in which he defeated the Creek Confederacy. Today, Talladega is both a center of diverse manufacturing and a center of preservation, with many fine old buildings. It is the home of Talladega College, founded by two former slaves, and the Alabama Institute for the Deaf and Blind. Logan Martin Lake, to the northwest, offers excellent water and outdoor recreation activities, and a large section of the Talladega National Forest is to the east. A Ranger District office is located in Talladega as well.

What to See and Do

Cheaha State Park. *19 Bunker Loop, Delta (36258). 7 miles NE on Hwy 21, then 15 miles E on County 398. Phone 256/488-5111. www.dcnr.state.al.us.* This park includes Mount Cheaha (2,407 feet), the state's highest point with an observation tower on top, and 2,719 acres of rugged forest country in the surrounding foothills. The area is mentioned in Hernando DeSoto's journal of his 1540 expedition. (During the expedition, the Spanish introduced hogs and horses to local Native Americans.) Swimming in Lake Cheaha, sand beach, wading area, swimming pool, bathhouse, fishing, boating; hiking, picnicking, motel, restaurant. Park (daily). Camping, cabins. **$**

Pinhoti Hiking Trail. *Talladega. Phone 256/463-2272.* Alabama's premier long-distance recreational trail, spanning 102 miles and through the Talladega Mountains. It starts at the southern end of the Talladega National Forest and extends through Calhoun County to the Georgia line. (Daily) **FREE**

Silk Stocking District. *25 W 11th St, Anniston (36201). Phone 256/761-2108.* This district includes much of East St S, Court St S, and South St E; many antebellum and turn-of-the-century houses along tree-lined streets. **Talladega Square** (1834), in the heart of town, includes the renovated Talladega County Courthouse, the oldest courthouse in continuous use in the state.

Talladega National Forest. *Forest Supervisor, 2946 Chestnut, Montgomery (36107). SE on Hwy 77. Phone 256/362-2909.* This 364,428-acre forest offers high ridges with spectacular views of valleys heavily wooded with Southern pine and hardwood. Divided into two sections, the park includes the Talladega and the beautiful Oakmulgee, southwest of Birmingham. The Talladega division has lake swimming (fee), fishing; hiking trails, including the 100-mile Pinhoti National Recreation Trail, a national byway extending from Hwy 78 to Cheaha State Park. Camping (no electric hookup; fee).

Talladega Superspeedway. *5200 Speedway Blvd, Eastaboga (36260). 10 miles N on Hwy 77, then 6 miles E on I-20. Phone 256/362-5002. www.talladegasuper-* *speedway.com.* Said to be one of the world's fastest speedways, with 33-degree banks in the turns. Stock car races include the EA Sports 500, Aaron's 499, and Aaron's 312. Also here is

International Motorsports Hall of Fame. *3198 Speedway Blvd, Talladega. Phone 256/362-5002.* Official hall of fame of motor sports, with memorabilia and displays of more than 100 vehicles. Race car simulator. Gift shop. Annual hall of fame induction ceremony (late Apr). (Daily 8 am-5 pm; closed Easter morning, Thanksgiving, Dec 25) **$$**

Talladega-Texaco Walk of Fame. *Talladega. Downtown. Phone 256/362-9075. www.talladegawalk.com.* An outdoor tribute to stock car racers, including a memorial for Davey Allison, one of NASCAR's greatest champions.

Troy (D-3)

See also Montgomery, Ozark

Settled 1824
Population 13,935
Elevation 543 ft
Information Pike County Chamber of Commerce, 246 US 231 North; phone 334/566-2294
Web Site www.pikecountychamber.com

What to See and Do

Pioneer Museum of Alabama. *248 Hwy 231 N, Troy (36081). Phone 334/566-3597. www.pioneer-museum. org.* Antique farm and household implements; reconstructed log house, country store, and other buildings re-create 19th-century life. (Mon-Sat 9 am-5 pm, Sun from 1 pm; closed Jan 1, Thanksgiving, Dec 25) **$**

Troy State University. *University Ave, Troy. 1 1/2 miles SE. Phone 334/670-3000. www.troyst.edu.* (1887) (5,200 students) Guided tours of campus. Home of the National Hall of Fame of Distinguished Band Conductors and the Malone Art Gallery.

Limited-Service Hotel

★ **SUPER 8.** *1013 Hwy 231, Troy (36081). Phone 334/566-4960; toll-free 800/800-8000; fax 334/566-5858. www.super8.com.* 69 rooms, 2 story. Pets accepted, some restrictions. Complimentary continental breakfast. Check-out 11 am. Outdoor pool. **$**

Restaurant

★ **MOSSY GROVE SCHOOLHOUSE.** *1902 Elba Hwy, Troy (36079). Phone 334/566-4921.* Restored schoolhouse (1857); original fireplace, blackboard; antiques. American menu. Dinner. Closed Sun-Mon; holidays. Children's menu. **$$**

Tuscaloosa (C-2)

See also Montgomery, Ozark

Founded 1818
Population 77,906
Elevation 227 ft
Area Code 205
Information Convention & Visitors Bureau, PO Box 32167, 35403; phone 205/391-9200 or toll-free 800/538-8696
Web Site www.tcvb.org

Located on the Black Warrior River, Tuscaloosa (Choctaw for "Black Warrior") was the capital of Alabama from 1826-1846. It was an exciting capital; cotton was a highly profitable crop, and the planters gave extravagant parties. But an increase in cotton production toppled prices, and the capital was moved to Montgomery. Although the Civil War ravaged the university and most of the town, some antebellum houses do remain. After the war, industry and farm trading grew, making Tuscaloosa the busy, pleasant metropolis it is today. It is also the home of the University of Alabama.

What to See and Do

Battle-Friedman House. *1010 Greensboro Ave, Tuscaloosa (35401). Phone 205/758-6138.* (Circa 1835) This house was built by Alfred Battle and was acquired by the Friedman family in 1875. It contains fine antiques; period gardens occupy 1/2 block. (Tues-Sat 10 am-noon and 1-4 pm, Sun 1-4 pm) **$**

Children's Hands-On Museum. *2213 University Blvd, Tuscaloosa (35401). Phone 205/349-4235. www.chomonline.org.* Participatory exhibits for children include a Choctaw Indian Village, a bank, a drugstore, an art studio, and general store, as well as a hospital, a beaver's den, and TV studio. Also available is a computer and science lab resource center. (Mon-Thurs, Sat 10 am-5 pm, Fri to 9 pm, Sun noon 5 pm) **$$**

Lake Lurleen State Park. *13226 Lake Lurleen Rd, Coker (35452). 12 miles NW off Hwy 82. Phone 205/339-1558.* www.dcnr.state.al.us. This 1,625-acre park has a 250-acre lake. Swimming, bathhouses, fishing (piers), bait and tackle shop, boating (ramps, rentals); hiking, picnic shelters, playgrounds, concession. Camping (**$$$**). **$**

Moundville Archaeological Park. *100 Mound Pkwy, Moundville. 16 miles S on Hwy 69 in Moundville, part of the University of Alabama Museum of Natural History.Phone 205/371-2234. moundville.ua.edu.* Group of more than 20 Native American ceremonial mounds (AD 1000-1450). The Jones Archaeological Museum (daily 9 am-5 pm) traces prehistory of southeastern Native Americans and exhibits products of this aboriginal culture. Nature trails along river. Picnic facilities. Tent and trailer sites (fee). (Daily 8 am-8 pm; closed holidays) **$**

Old Tavern. *500 28th Ave, Tuscaloosa (35401). University Blvd and 28th Ave, on Historic Capitol Park. Phone 205/758-2238.* (1827) Frequented by Governor Gayle (1831-1835) and members of the Alabama legislature when Tuscaloosa was capital. (Tues-Fri 10 am-noon, 1-4pm; closed Jan 1, Thanksgiving, Dec 25) **FREE**

University of Alabama. *801 University Blvd E, Tuscaloosa (35401). University Blvd (Hwy 11) between Thomas St and 5th Ave E. Phone 205/348-6010. www.ua.edu.* (1831) (21,000 students) Tours of the 850-acre campus may be arranged in the Students Services Center, Room 203 (Mon-Sat). The information desk is located in Ferguson Student Union. On the campus is an art gallery in Garland Hall with changing exhibits, a museum of natural history, a 60-acre arboretum on Loop Rd, and the Paul W. Bryant Museum. The Frank Moody Music Building holds concerts and is the home of the largest pipe organ in the Southeast. Four antebellum buildings remain, the only ones on campus spared from burning by Union troops. Other buildings on campus are

Denny Chimes. *Tuscaloosa. Opposite President's Mansion. Phone 205/348-6010.* A 115-foot-high tower erected in honor of former university president Dr. George H. Denny. On the quarter-hour, the Westminster Chimes are struck, and selections are played each afternoon on the campanile (carillon).

Gorgas House. *Tuscaloosa. 9th Ave and Capstone Dr. Phone 205/348-6010.* (1829) A three-story brick structure named for General Josiah Gorgas, former university president. One of the school's original structures, Gorgas now houses a museum with historical exhibits; Spanish Colonial silver display. (Tues-Sat 10 am-4 pm; closed school holidays) **$**

Little Round House. *Tuscaloosa. Adjacent to Gorgas Library. Phone 205/348-6010.* (Sentry Box circa 1860) Once used by students on guard duty, it was fired on but not destroyed by Union troops.

The Old Observatory. *Tuscaloosa. Phone 205/348-6010.* (1844) The only pre-Civil War classroom building still standing.

Westervelt Warner Museum of American Art. *1400 Jack Warner Pkwy NE, Tuscaloosa (35404). Phone 205/553-6200. www.warnermuseum.org.* Four Asian buildings house an outstanding collection of sculpture and art, including primitive artifacts from Africa and the South Pacific; Asian art; large collection of paintings including works by Georgia O'Keeffe, Mary Cassatt, and James A. M. Whistler. Guided tours. (Mon-Fri 5:30 & 6:30 pm, Sat 10 am-4 pm, Sun 1-4 pm) **FREE**

Will T. Murphy African American Museum. *2601 Paul W Bryant Dr, Tuscaloosa (35401). Phone 205/758-2861.* (Circa 1925) House features two rooms with changing exhibits relating to culture and heritage of African Americans; antique doll collection; rare books; some period furnishings. (By appointment only) **$$**

Special Event

Moundville Native American Festival. *Moundville Archaeological Park (see), 100 Mound Pkwy, Tuscaloosa. Phone 205/371-2572. moundville.ua.edu/festival.html.* Celebrates the culture of the southeastern Native Americans with craft demonstrations, songs, dances, and folktales. Final day (Sat) is Indian Market Day, when artisans exhibit their wares. Phone 205/371-2234 or 205/371-2572. Early Oct.

Limited-Service Hotels

★ **BEST WESTERN PARK PLAZA MOTOR INN.** *3801 McFarland Blvd, Tuscaloosa (35405). Phone 205/556-9690; toll-free 800/235-7282; fax 205/561-0184. www.bestwestern.com.* 120 rooms, 2 story. Complimentary continental breakfast. Check-out noon. Outdoor pool, whirlpool. **$**

★ ★ **FOUR POINTS BY SHERATON.** *320 Paul Bryant Dr, Tuscaloosa (35401). Phone 205/752-3200; toll-free 888/625-5144; fax 205/759-9314. www.fourpoints.com.* Located on the University of Alabama's campus, this hotel has spacious guest rooms. For those in town to see Bama play, it's within walking distance of the game. 152 rooms, 3 story. Check-out

noon. Restaurant, bar. Outdoor pool. Tennis. Airport transportation available. **$**

★ **HAMPTON INN.** *600 Harper Lee Dr, Tuscaloosa (35404). Phone 205/553-9800; toll-free 800/426-7866; fax 205/553-0082. www.hamptoninn.com.* 102 rooms, 3 story. Complimentary continental breakfast. Check-out noon. Outdoor pool. **$**

Restaurant

★ ★ **HENSON'S CYPRESS INN.** *501 Rice Mine Rd N, Tuscaloosa (35406). Phone 205/345-6963; fax 205/345-6997. www.cypressinnrestaurant.com.* Steak menu. Lunch, dinner. Closed holidays. Bar. Children's menu. **$$**

Tuskegee (D-4)

See also Auburn, Montgomery, Opelika

Settled circa 1763
Population 11,846
Elevation 468 ft
Area Code 334
Zip 36083
Information Office of the Mayor, City Hall, 101 Fonville St; phone 334/727-2180

An important part of Tuskegee's history lies in the story of Tuskegee Institute and two well-known men in African Amerian history, Booker T. Washington and George Washington Carver. But it was Lewis Adams, a former slave, who was largely responsible for gathering financial support from northern and southern whites to launch Tuskegee Normal and Industrial Institute. It began on July 4, 1881, with 30 students housed in an old frame building; Booker T. Washington was its president. Tuskegee also has a number of antebellum houses and a Ranger District office of the Tuskegee National Forest.

What to See and Do

Tuskegee Institute National Historic Site. *1212 W Montgomery Rd, Tuskegee (36088). Phone 334/727-6390. www.nps.gov/tuin.* (1881) Booker T. Washington is generally given credit for having founded Tuskegee Institute. In 1965, the college was designated a National Historical Landmark in recognition of the outstanding role it has played in the educational, economic, and social advancement of African Americans in our nation's history. In 1974, Congress established Tuskegee Institute National Historic Site to include "The Oaks," home of Booker T. Washington, the George Washington Carver Museum, and the Historic Campus District. The 5,000-acre campus consists of more than 160 buildings. (Daily 9 am-4:30 pm; closed Jan 1, Thanksgiving, Dec 25) **FREE**

Booker T. Washington Monument. Larger-than-life bronze figure of the man who advocated "lifting the veil of ignorance" from the heads of freed slaves.

Chapel. (1969) Paul Rudolph designed this unusual structure with saw-toothed ceilings and deep beams. Adjacent are the graves of George Washington Carver and Booker T. Washington.

George Washington Carver Museum. *Phone 334/727-3200.* The museum includes Dr. Carver's original laboratory, his extensive collection of native plants, minerals, needlework, paintings, drawings, personal belongings, and the array of products he developed. (Daily 9 am-4:40 pm; closed Jan 1, Thanksgiving, Dec 25) **FREE**

Tuskegee National Forest. *125 National Forest Rd 949, Tuskegee (36083). E via Hwy 80. Phone 334/727-2652.* An 11,077-acre forest with fishing; hunting and hiking on Bartram National Recreation Trail. Atasi and Taska picnic sites. Primitive camping. Tsinia Wildlife Viewing Area. Contact District Ranger. (Daily)

Full-Service Hotel

★ ★ **KELLOGG CONFERENCE CENTER.**
Tuskegee University, Tuskegee Institute (36088). Phone 334/727-3000; toll-free 800/949-6161. This guest tower hotel is located in the historic campus district and is a comprehensive meeting center facility. 110 rooms, 4 story. Check-out noon. Restaurant, bar. Fitness room. Indoor pool. Airport transportation available. Business center. **$**
🖾 🛌 🖾

Arkansas

Arkansas' areas of forested wilderness are much the same as those de Soto discovered in 1541. In the lovely Ozark and Ouachita mountain ranges, separated by the Arkansas River, there are splendid forests. Pine and hardwood trees shade streams filled with enough black bass, bream, and trout to restore any angler's faith. There are deer, geese, ducks, and quail to hunt and feast on in season. Ducks fly over eastern Arkansas, and such towns as Stuttgart make a big event of hunting them. The White River National Wildlife Refuge east of here is a wilderness area. Caves, springs, meadows, valleys, bayous, rice and cotton fields, and magnificent lakes and rivers dot the state. For an enjoyable backwoods vacation, the visitor can hardly do better than a choice of either a quiet rustic resort or cosmopolitan Hot Springs National Park the renowned spa dedicated to sophisticated pleasures as well as therapeutic treatment.

Population: 2,673,400

Area: 53,182 square miles

Elevation: 54-2,753 feet

Peak: Magazine Mountain (Logan County)

Entered Union: June 15, 1836 (25th state)

Capital: Little Rock

Motto: The People Rule

Nickname: The Natural State

Flower: Apple Blossom

Bird: Mockingbird

Tree: Pine

Time Zone: Central

Web Site: www.arkansas.com

Fun Fact:

- Arkansas contains six national park sites, 2 1/2 million acres of national forests, seven national scenic byways, three state scenic byways, and 50 state parks.

Arkansas is one of the major producers of bromine brine in the United States. In addition, a large amount of crude oil and bauxite (aluminum ore) comes from Arkansas every year. Sixty useful tree varieties grow here, and timber is big business. In fact, practically every crop except citrus fruit is cultivated on its acres, including rice, strawberries, peaches, grapes, apples, cotton, soybeans, sorghum, and wheat. Arkansas is also a state plentiful in raw materials and has the only diamond field in North America open to the public. Preserved as Crater of Diamonds State Park (see MURFREESBORO), visitors may dig for diamonds on a "finders, keepers" basis.

Because Arkansas was remote, of rugged terrain, and slightly off-track of the western surge of frontier expansion, the area was slow to develop. After the Spaniards came the French Marquette and Joliet visited the territory in 1673, and La Salle took possession for France in 1682. The first permanent settlement was made by Henri de Tonty in 1686 at Arkansas Post (see), which today is a national memorial. It was not until 1804, a year after Arkansas and the rest of the Louisiana Purchase had become US property, that the government paid any attention to the area. A United States headquarters was established at Arkansas Post; in 1819 the Arkansas Territory was organized and two years later the capital was moved to Little Rock.

When to Go/Climate

Arkansas enjoys a generally moderate climate, punctuated by hot, humid summers and mild winters. Early spring can be rainy and damp. Mild winter temperatures (daytime highs in the 50s) make this a comfortable time as well.

Calendar Highlights

APRIL

Arkansas Folk Festival *(Mountain View)*. *Phone 870/269-3851*. Arts and crafts, parade, rodeo, traditional music of the Ozarks, games, food.

MAY

Riverfest *(Little Rock)*. *Phone 501/255-3378*. Visual and performing arts festival. Food, crafts, entertainment, fireworks.

JULY

National Invitational Explorer Canoe Race *(Batesville)*. *Phone 870/793-2378*. Races on the White River.

Old Fort River Festival *(Fort Smith)*. *Phone 501/783-6363*. Arts and crafts festival, entertainment, sporting events.

Rodeo of the Ozarks *(Springdale)*. *Parsons Stadium. Phone 501/927-4530*.

AUGUST

Hope Watermelon Festival *(Hope)*. *Phone 870/777-3640*. Seed-spitting, melon-eating contests; arts and crafts, music.

OCTOBER

Arkansas State Fair & Livestock Show *(Little Rock)*. *State Fairgrounds. Phone 501/372-8341*. Rodeo shows and more.

Frontier Days *(Hope)*. *Old Washington Historic State Park. Phone 870/983-2684*. Period activities and demonstrations.

AVERAGE HIGH/LOW TEMPERATURES (°F)

Fort Smith

Jan 48/26	**May** 81/58	**Sept** 85/62
Feb 54/30	**June** 88/66	**Oct** 76/49
Mar 64/39	**July** 93/70	**Nov** 63/38
Apr 74/49	**Aug** 92/69	**Dec** 51/29

Parks and Recreation

Water-related activities, hiking, various other sports, picnicking and visitor centers, camping, as well as cabins and lodges are available in many of Arkansas' state parks. Camping: $7.50-$28.50/day. Swimming: $3-$6.75; under 6 free. Pets on leash only. Campers must register at the park office before occupying a site; all sites assigned, reservations available. Parks open all year; some facilities closed Dec-Feb or Mar. Brochures on state parks may be obtained from the Department of Parks and Tourism, Parks Division, One Capitol Mall, Little Rock 72201; phone 501/682-7777 or 800/628-8725.

FISHING AND HUNTING

Nonresident fishing license: annual, $40; 14-day, $22; seven-day, $17; three-day, $11. Trout permit, $12. Largemouth bass can be found in all big lakes; trout in the White, Little Red, Spring, and Little Missouri rivers; bluegill and crappie in most Arkansas lakes and rivers. Annual nonresident hunting license: basic (for small game), $80; annual nonresident all game hunting license: $300. Nonresident short trip license (five days for small game) for anything in season except deer, turkey, and bear, $55. Nonresident all game license five days, $150; 3 days, $100. State duck stamp: $20 (non-resident). Licenses may be ordered by phone, 800/364-GAME (credit card only). Arkansas fishing and hunting regulations are available from the Game and Fish Commission, #2 Natural Resources Dr, Little Rock 72205; phone 501/223-6300 or 800/364-4263.

Driving Information

Safety belts are mandatory for all persons in the front seat of a vehicle. Every driver who regularly transports a child under the age of 5 years in a motor vehicle registered in this state, except one operated for hire, shall provide for the protection of such child by properly placing, maintaining, and securing such child in a child passenger safety seat meeting federal standards. For any child 3-5 years of age, a safety belt is sufficient. For further information, phone 501/569-2000.

INTERSTATE HIGHWAY SYSTEM
The following alphabetical listing of Arkansas towns in this book shows that these cities are within 10 miles of the indicated interstate highways. Check a highway map for the nearest exit.

Highway Number Cities/Towns Within 10 Miles

Highway Number	Cities/Towns Within 10 Miles
Interstate 30	Arkadelphia, Benton, Hop Little Rock, Malvern.
Interstate 40	Alma, Conway, Forrest City, Fort Smith, Little Rock, Morrilton, Russellville.
Interstate 55	Blytheville.

Additional Visitor Information

A variety of pamphlets and maps are distributed by the Arkansas Department of Parks and Tourism, One Capitol Mall, Little Rock 72201; phone 501/682-7777 or 800/628-8725.

Tourist information centers can be found at several points of entry into Arkansas; travel consultants provide suggested tour routes, a state tour guide, and literature on places of interest. The centers are open daily and are located in the following cities: Bentonville, Hwy 71 S; Blytheville, I-55 S; Corning, Hwy 67 S; Fort Smith/Van Buren (Dora), I-40 E; El Dorado, Hwy 167 N; Harrison, Hwy 65 S; Helena, Hwy 49 E; Lake Village, junction Hwy 65, 82 and Hwy 144; Mammoth Spring, Hwy 63; Red River, Hwy 71 N; Siloam Springs, hwy 412 E; Texarkana, I-30 E; and West Memphis, I-40 W. Inquire locally for exact locations.

A CLINTON DRIVING TOUR

Take a tour that follows part of the life of former President Bill Clinton. Little Rock is a good starting place to learn about Mr. Clinton's years as governor, but to explore his early years, you'll want to continue on to Hot Springs, stopping along the way to visit sites of natural beauty and historical significance. From Little Rock, take I-30 west to Hot Springs, and then go north along Highway 278 to downtown. Bill Clinton lived here from age eight through high school. Hot Springs is also the site of a national park marking the mountain spring resort that had its heyday here in the early 20th century. To get to Hot Springs National Park, jog east on Highway 70 for 1/2 mile, then north on Highway 7. A scenic drive further north leads to the summit of Hot Springs Mountain, where a 216-foot observation tower provides a panoramic overlook.

The headquarters of 4,700-acre Hot Springs National Park is located in the 1915 Fordyce Bathhouse along Bathhouse Row at the entrance to the park off Highway 7. The visitor center heads up a row of restored bathhouses from the town's days as a spa resort. The Buckstaff remains the only operating public bathhouse, offering thermal baths and Swedish massage. At the top of the row, the Arlington Resort Hotel offers spa facilities to its overnight guests only. A promenade behind Bathhouse Row overlooks the springs.

At the south end of Bathhouse Row, a city visitor center distributes maps of 16 Clinton-related sites, including his church, local bowling alley, and favorite hamburger joint. The 1914 Hot Springs High School, where Bill Clinton graduated in 1964, is being transformed into the William Jefferson Clinton Cultural Campus, a residential community art center that will also include a restored theater and presidential museum with exhibits from Clinton's high school days.

From Hot Springs, return to I-30, travel west 80 miles to Hope, and follow the signs to the visitor center at the train depot on Main and Division streets. The small depot with the large green sign of HOPE may be recognizable to many as a familiar image from presidential campaign videos. From here, the birthplace of Bill Clinton is just four blocks away. The modest home on Hervey Street where Clinton lived until age eight is now open to the public as a historic site and museum. Hervey Street now forms the central commercial artery of Hope, where many quaint shops are located. North of town lies the Old Washington State Historic Park, which contains pioneer exhibits from the mid-1800s. Back onto I-30, Little Rock is a 100-mile drive away. **(Approximately 230 miles)**

Altus

What to See and Do

Wiederkehr Wine Cellars. *3324 Swiss Family Dr, Altus (72821). 4 miles S of I-40 exit 41, near Altus. Phone 479/468-9463; toll-free 800/622-9463. www.wiederkeh-rwines.com.* Guided wine-tasting tour (gourmet and nonalcoholic beverage tasting for persons under 21); self-guided tour of the vineyards; observation tower; restaurant; gift shop. (Daily 9 am-4:30 pm; closed holidays) **FREE**

Restaurant

★ ★ ★ **WEINKELLER RESTAURANT.** *3324 Swiss Family Dr, Altus (72821). Phone 479/468-3551; fax 479/468-4791. www.wiederkehrwines.com.* This restaurant is listed in the National Register of Historical Places; it is located on the site where the first Wiederkehr wine cellar was dug in 1880. The menu is not very extensive, featuring old-world cuisine. European menu. Lunch, dinner. Closed holidays. Children's menu. **$$**

Arkadelphia (D-2)

See also Hot Springs and Hot Springs National Park, Malvern

Settled 1809
Population 10,912
Elevation 245 ft
Area Code 870
Zip 71923
Information Chamber of Commerce, 770 Clay St, PO Box 38; phone 870/246-5542 or toll-free 800/874-4289
Web Site www.arkadelphia.org

On a bluff overlooking the Ouachita River and once an important landing for steamboats, this community is now an agricultural and industrial center producing boats, wood products, jeans, commercial roofing, brake shoes, and fiberglass vaults. It is the home of Henderson State University (1890) and Ouachita Baptist University.

What to See and Do

DeGray Lake. *2027 State Park Entrance Rd, Bismark (71929). 1 mile NW off Hwy 7. Phone 501/865-2801.*

www.degray.com. DeGray Dam impounds the waters of the Caddo River to form this 13,000-acre lake with 207 miles of shoreline. Water-skiing, fishing, boating, swimming beach; picnicking. Visitor center. Camping (fee). (Daily) **$$** On the northeast shore is

DeGray Lake Resort State Park. *Arkadelphia (71929). 6 miles N of I-30, on Hwy 7. Phone 501/865-2851.* A 938-acre resort park. Swimming, fishing, boating (houseboat and sailboat rentals, marina, launch); nature trail, 18-hole golf and pro shop, tennis. Picnicking, playground, store, laundry, restaurant, lodge. Camping (many water, electric hookups; dump station; reservations available Apr-Oct). Visitor center; interpretive programs. Guided hikes, lake cruises, square dances, hay rides, live animal demonstrations, evening slides and films.

Hot Springs National Park. *101 Reserve St, Hot Springs (71901). 32 miles N via Hwy 7. Phone 501/624-3383. www.nps.gov/hosp.* (see)

Ouachita Baptist University. *410 Ouachita St, Arkadelphia (71998). Phone 870/245-5206.* (1886) (1,350 students.) On the banks of the Ouachita River, surrounded by the foothills of the Ouachita Mountains. McClellan Hall contains the official papers and memorabilia of US Senator John L. McClellan. Campus tours.

Special Events

Clark County Fair. *Clark County Fairgrounds, Arkadelphia. Phone 870/246-5542.* Sept.

Festival of the Two Rivers. *Clay and 4th sts, Arkadelphia (71923). Phone 870/246-5542.* Arts and crafts, juried art show, contests, games, food. Mid-Apr.

Limited-Service Hotel

★ ★ **BEST WESTERN CONTINENTAL INN.** *136 Valley St, Arkadelphia (71923). Phone 870/246-5592; toll-free 800/780-7234; fax 870/246-3583. www. bestwestern.com.* 59 rooms, 2 story. Pets accepted. Check-out 11 am. Restaurant. Outdoor pool. **$**

Arkansas Post National Memorial (D-4)

See also Dumas, Pine Bluff

Web Site www.nps.gov/arpo/

Arkansas Post was established at a Quapaw Indian village in 1686 as a trading post by Henri de Tonty, lieutenant to La Salle during the latter's pioneer explorations. Although the post was never a major French settlement, by 1759 it had grown to an impressive 40-man garrison. Ownership abruptly changed hands following the British victory in the French and Indian War. France ceded Louisiana, including the Arkansas territory, to Spain in 1762. Spanish interests, however, were not long served. The Spaniards joined the American patriots during the American Revolution, not out of sympathy but as a matter of self-interest. The resulting skirmishes between Spain and Britain over the territory came to an end less than two years after Yorktown. Unable to cope with raids and aggressive frontiersmen, Spain ceded the territory back to France.

The Post was bought by the United States as part of the Louisiana Purchase in 1803. In 1819, it became the capital of the new Arkansas Territory and the home of Arkansas' first newspaper, the Arkansas *Gazette*. In 1821 the capital and the *Gazette* both moved to Little Rock. The Post continued as a river port until the Civil War, when battles and numerous floods finally destroyed the little town.

Arkansas Post was made a state park in 1929 and a national memorial in 1964. Fishing, hiking, and picnicking are enjoyed on the 389 acres of this wildlife sanctuary. Personnel and exhibits, including a partial replica of a 1783 Spanish fort, tell the story of the post. Visitor center (daily; closed Jan 1, Dec 25). Contact Superintendent, 1741 Old Post Rd, Gillett 72055; phone 870/548-2207.

What to See and Do

Arkansas Post Museum. *5530 Hwy 165 S, Gillett (72055). 5 miles S . Phone 870/548-2634.* Museum and five buildings housing artifacts of early settlers on the grand prairie of Arkansas; colonial kitchen; 1877 log house with period furnishings; Civil War memorabilia; child's three-room furnished playhouse. (Daily; closed holidays) **$**

Ashdown (D-1)

See also Texarkana

Founded 1892
Population 4,781
Elevation 327 ft
Area Code 870
Zip 71822
Web Site www.ashdownar.org

What to See and Do

Millwood Dam and Reservoir. *1528 Hwy 32 E, Ashdown (71822). 9 miles E on Hwy 32. Phone 870/898-3343.* This dam impounds a 29,500-acre lake. Swimming, fishing. Playgrounds. Camping (electric hookups; fee). (Daily) Adjacent is

Millwood State Park. *Ashdown (71822). Phone 870/898-2800.* Approximately 800 acres. Fishing, boating (rentals, marina); hiking trails, picnicking, playground, rest rooms, store, camping (hookups, dump station).

Batesville (E-3)

See also Greers Ferry Lake Area, Mountain View, Newport

Population 9,445
Elevation 364 ft
Area Code 870
Zip 72501
Information Batesville Area Chamber of Commerce, 409 Vine St; phone 870/793-2378
Web Site batesville.dina.org

Special Events

National Invitational Explorer Canoe Race. *409 Vine St, Batesville (72501). White River, from Cotter to Batesville. Phone 870/793-2378.* Last day of Water Carnival.

Ozark Scottish Festival. *Lyon College, 2300 Highland Rd, Batesville (72501). Phone 870/793-9813.* Pipe bands, Highland dancing, Scottish feast, Parade of clans. Late Apr.

White River Water Carnival. *409 Vine St, Batesville (72501). Phone 870/793-2378. www.batesvillepromotions.com.* Parade, arts and crafts, beauty pageant. First weekend in Aug.

Limited-Service Hotel

★ ★ **RAMADA.** *1325 N St. Louis St, Batesville (71701). Phone 870/698-1800; fax 870/698-1800. www.ramada.com.* 124 rooms, 2 story. Pets accepted, some restrictions. Check-out noon. Restaurant. Pool, whirlpool. **$**

Benton (C-3)

See also Hot Springs and Hot Springs National Park, Little Rock, Malvern

Founded 1836
Population 21,906
Elevation 416 ft
Area Code 501
Zip 72015
Information Chamber of Commerce, 607 N Market St; phone 501/315-8272 or 501/315-8290

Benton is the seat of Saline County. A large amount of bauxite mined in the United States comes from this area. The city also has important wood products factories.

What to See and Do

Gann Museum. *218 S Market St, Benton. Phone 501/778-5513.* This is the only known building made of bauxite; dug from a nearby farm, hand-sawed into blocks, and allowed to harden. It originally was a medical office built in 1893 by patients who could not afford to pay the doctor. Contains furniture and artifacts reflecting local pioneer, Native American, and church history. (Tues-Thurs 10 am-4 pm; tours by appointment; closed Jan 1, Thanksgiving, Dec 25) **FREE**

Hot Springs National Park. (see). *101 Reserve St, Hot Springs (71901). 27 miles W via Hwy 70. Phone 501/624-3383. www.nps.gov/hosp.*

Restaurant

★ **BROWN'S.** *18718 I-30, Benton (72015). Phone 501/778-5033; fax 501/315-1715.* Breakfast, lunch, dinner. Closed Thanksgiving, Dec 25. Children's menu. **$**

Bentonville (A-1)

See also Fayetteville, Rogers, Springdale

Founded 1837
Population 19,730
Elevation 1,305 ft
Area Code 479
Zip 72712
Information Bentonville-Bella Vista Chamber of Commerce, 202 E. Central St; phone 479/273-2841
Web Site www.bbvchamber.com

Bentonville was named for Thomas Hart Benton, the first senator from Missouri and a militant champion of pioneers. Benton was also the great-uncle of the painter by the same name. The town square maintains a turn-of-the-century character.

What to See and Do

Peel Mansion & Heritage Gardens. *400 S Walton Blvd, Bentonville (72712). Phone 479/273-9664. www.peelmansion.org.* Villa tower Italianate mansion (1875) built by Colonel Samuel West Peel, the first native-born Arkansan to serve in the US Congress, has been restored and refurnished in Victorian style. The 180-acre site also has an outdoor museum of historic roses, perennials, and native plants. The pre-Civil War Andy Lynch log cabin serves as gatehouse and gift shop. (Tues-Sat 10 am-4 pm; closed two weeks in late Dec-early Jan)**$**

Special Event

Sugar Creek Arts & Crafts Fair. *805 S Main St, Bentonville (72712). Phone 479/273-3270.* Nearly 200 exhibitors come to display their works. Third weekend in Oct. **FREE**

Limited-Service Hotels

★ **BEST WESTERN BENTONVILLE INN.** *2307 SE Walton, Bentonville (72712). Phone 479/273-9727; toll-free 800/780-7234; fax 479/273-1763. www.bestwestern.com.* 54 rooms, 2 story. Check-out 11 am. Outdoor pool. **$**

★ **HOLIDAY INN EXPRESS.** *2205 SE Walton Blvd, Bentonville (72712). Phone 479/271-2222; fax 479/271-2227. www.holiday-inn.com.* 84 rooms, 4 story. Complimentary continental breakfast. Check-in 3 pm, check-out 11 am. High-speed Internet access, wireless Internet access. Fitness room. Business center. **$**

Restaurant

★ ★ **FRED'S HICKORY INN.** *1502 N Walton Blvd, Bentonville (72712). Phone 479/273-3303; fax 479/271-8319.* Steak menu. Lunch, dinner. Closed holidays. Bar. Children's menu. **$$**

Berryville (A-2)

See also Eureka Springs, Harrison

Founded 1850
Population 4,433
Area Code 870
Zip 72616
Information Chamber of Commerce, Hwy 62 E, PO Box 402; phone 870/423-3704
Web Site www.cswnet.com/~berryvil/

This area is known for poultry raising and dairy farming. There is also good fishing. Berryville is the southern gateway to the Table Rock Lake Area in Missouri (see).

What to See and Do

Carroll County Heritage Center. *403 Public Sq, Berryville (72616). Phone 870/423-6312.* Local historical exhibits and genealogical material housed in an old courthouse (1880). (Apr-Oct: Mon-Fri 9 am-4 pm; closed Mon from Nov-Mar; also holidays) **$**

Cosmic Cavern. *6386 Hwy 21, Berryville (72616). 7 miles N on Hwy 21. Phone 870/749-2298. www.cosmiccavern.com.* Cavern below a mountain features Ozark's largest underground lake; electrically lighted; constant 62 F. Visitor center, picnic area. One-hour guided tours. (Schedule varies; call or visit the Web site for more information) **$$**

Saunders Memorial Museum. *115 E Madison, Berryville (72616). On Hwy 21.Phone 870/423-2563.* Revolvers, pistols, and small arms, some originally owned by Pancho Villa, Jesse James, and Wild Bill Hickok; antiques, handcrafts; silver, china; rugs and furniture. (Apr-Oct: Mon-Sat) **$**

Special Events

Carroll County Fair. *Hwy 21 N, Berryville (72616). Carroll County Fairgrounds. Phone 870/423-3704.*

www.berryvillear.com. A parade and the Miss Carroll County competition are highlights of the week of events. Week of Labor Day.

Ice Cream Social. *Public Square,Hwys 62 E and 21 S, Berryville (72616). Phone 870/423-3704.www.berryvillear.com.* Browse the arts and crafts booths, purchase some baked goods, or join the 5K fun run. Second weekend in June.

Saunders Memorial Muzzleloading and Frontier Gun Shoot & Handcrafters' Show. *Luther Owens Muzzleloading Range and Park, Berryville.* Costumed contestants; gun show. Last full weekend in Sept.

Blytheville (B-5)

Settled 1880
Population 18,272
Area Code 870
Zip 72315
Information Chamber of Commerce, PO Box 485, 72316; phone 870/762-2012
Web Site Blytheville.dina.org

Blytheville is one of two seats of Mississippi County. It is a leading industrial and retail trade center for northeast Arkansas and maintains its agricultural heritage. Duck hunting is good here, especially on the Mississippi Flyway. Mallard Lake, 12 miles W on Hwy 18, has good bass, bream, and crappie fishing. Big Lake Wildlife Refuge, 12 miles west on Hwy 18, is a winter nesting area for migratory waterfowl.

Limited-Service Hotels

★ **HAMPTON INN.** *301 N Access Rd, Blytheville (72315). Phone 870/763-5220; fax 870/762-1397. www.hamptoninn.com.* 87 rooms, 2 story. Pets accepted, some restrictions; fee. Complimentary continental breakfast. Check-out noon. Restaurant, Pool. **$**

★ **HOLIDAY INN.** *1121 E Main, Blytheville (72315). Phone 870/763-8500; fax 870/763-1326. www.holidayinn.com.* 153 rooms, 2 story. Pets accepted; fee. Check-out noon. Restaurant, bar. Indoor pool, outdoor pool, whirlpool. **$**

Buffalo National River

Web Site www.nps.gov/buff/

(Buffalo Point Contact Station, 17 miles S of Yellville via Hwy 14, 268; Tyler Bend Visitor Center, 11 miles N of Marshall via Hwy 65)

Buffalo National River, preserving 135 miles of the free-flowing river in the scenic Ozarks of northwestern Arkansas, is known for its diversity. In the spring, whitewater enthusiasts float the upper river from Ponca to Pruitt, stopping at primitive campgrounds at Steel Creek, Kyles Landing, Erbie, and Ozark. These areas also provide river access. Springs, waterfalls, streams, and woods along the river attract hikers; Lost Valley features self-guided hikes. River levels fluctuate; contact park headquarters for information on floatable areas. Primitive campgrounds on lower and middle stretches include Hasty, Carver, Mount Hersey, Woolum, Maumee, and Rush.

Visitor information is available at Buffalo Point Contact Station, at Tyler Bend Visitor Center, and at Pruitt Ranger Station. They offer swimming, fishiing; canoe rentals; self-guided trails and hikes, picnicking, camping (fee). Programs and demonstrations led by interpreters. Evening programs blend natural and historic interpretation. The interpreters also lead float trips for novices and for those desiring a guided trip.

Housekeeping cabins are available from April through November. For information concerning cabin reservations, contact the Buffalo Point Concessioner, HCR #66, Box 388, Yellville 72687; phone 870/449-6206. For general information contact the Superintendent, Buffalo National River, Box 1173, Harrison 72602; phone 870/741-5443.

Bull Shoals Lake Area (E-3)

See also Harrison, Mountain Home

Web Site www.bullshoals.com

Bull Shoals Lake, on the White River in the Ozarks, was created by the US Army Corps of Engineers as a flood control and hydroelectric project in 1952. The lake has a 1,000-mile shoreline with recreation areas and boat docks at many points. Fishing is excellent both in the lake and in the White River below the dam, and other recreational activities abound. Fees are charged at most recreation areas.

What to See and Do

Bull Shoals State Park. *129 Bull Shoals Park, Lakeview (72642). 6 miles N of Mountain Home on Hwy 5, then 7 miles W on Hwy 178.* Phone 870/431-5521. *www.bullshoals.com.* More than 680 acres at southeast corner of lake below dam. Fishing for trout, boating (ramp, rentals, dock); hiking trails, picnicking, playground, store, camping (hookups, dump station; daily). Visitor center; interpretive programs (Apr-Oct). Golden Age Passport (see MAKING THE MOST OF YOUR TRIP).

Camden (E-2)

See also El Dorado, Magnolia

Founded 1824
Population 13,154
Elevation 198 ft
Area Code 870
Zip 71701
Information Camden Area Chamber of Commerce, 141 Jackson SW, PO Box 99; phone 870/836-6426
Web Site www.growingcamden.org

Camden, home to many large industries, is situated on the Ouachita River, which is navigable throughout the year.

What to See and Do

Confederate Cemetery. *Adams Ave and Pearl St, Camden.* More than 200 veterans of the Civil War and many unknown soldiers are buried here.

Fort Lookout. *800 N Monroe, Camden (71701). End of Monroe St.* Rifle trenches and cannon pits are still evident on the site of the old fort overlooking the Ouachita River. It was one of several forts constructed to guard the town.

McCollum-Chidester House. *926 Washington St NW, Camden (71701). Phone 870/836-9243.* (1847) Once a stage coach headquarters, this historic house was used as headquarters at various times by Confederate General Sterling Price and Union General Frederick Steele. Contains original furnishings; mementos of the Civil War period. Setting for segments of the TV miniseries *North and South.* **$$** Also includes

> **Leake-Ingham Building.** *Phone 870/836-6426.* (1850) Used as a law office before the Civil War and as a freedmen's bureau during Reconstruction; now houses books and other memorabilia of the antebellum South.

Poison Spring Battleground Historical Monument. *Hwy 76, Bluff City (71722). 7 miles NW on Hwy 24, then 2 miles W on Hwy 76. Phone 870/836-6426.* Site of Union defeat during Steele's Red River Campaign into southwest Arkansas. Exhibits and diorama tracing troop movement; trail to small spring; picnic area. **FREE**

White Oak Lake State Park. *563 Hwy 387, Bluff City (71722). 20 miles NW on Hwy 24, then 3 miles SE on Hwy 387. Phone 870/685-2748.* Swimming; fishing for bass, crappie and bream on 2,765-acre lake; boating (rentals). Hiking trails. Picnicking, store. Camping (hookups, dump station). Visitor center; interpretive programs (summer only). (Daily) **FREE**

Special Event

Ouachita County Fair and Livestock Show. Includes carnival rides, food, and live music. Sept. **$**

Conway (C-3)

See also Morrilton

Founded 1871
Population 43,167
Elevation 316 ft
Area Code 501
Zip 72033
Information Chamber of Commerce, 900 Oak St; phone 501/327-7788 or -7789
Web Site www.conwayarkcc.org

Among the many products manufactured here are school furniture and buses, automotive testing equipment, vending machines, agricultural machinery, shoes, folding cartons, bolts, and pianos. Conway also is home to the University of Central Arkansas, Central Baptist College, and Hendrix College.

What to See and Do

Cadron Settlement Park. *6298 Hwy 60 W, Conway (72032). About 5 miles W via Hwy 64, then S on Hwy 319. Phone 501/329-2986.* Replica of blockhouse built by early settlers in the 1770s. Also within this day-use park is Tollantusky Trail, which contains much historical information and beautiful scenery. (Daily) **FREE**

Hendrix College. *1600 Washington Ave, Conway (72032). Front and Washington sts, north side of town on Hwy 64, 65. Phone toll-free 800/277-9017. www.hendrix.edu.* (1876) (1,034 students) The Mills Center houses Congressional office contents and some personal papers of former Congressman Wilbur D. Mills, chairman of the House Ways and Means Committee and graduate of Hendrix College (Mon-Fri; closed holidays and week of Dec 25).

Toad Suck Ferry Lock and Dam. *6298 Hwy 60 W, Conway (72032). 5 miles W on Hwy 60, on the Arkansas River. Phone 501/329-2986.* Site of 1820 river crossing; public viewing platform; historical markers. Adjacent park offers fishing, boating; picnicking, camping (fee; electricity and water available). (All year) **FREE**

Woolly Hollow State Park. *82 Woolly Hollow Rd, Greenbrier (72058). 12 miles N on Hwy 65, 6 miles E on Hwy 285. Phone 501/679-2098. www.arkansasstateparks.com/parks.* Within this 400-acre wooded park surrounding 40-acre Lake Bennett is the Woolly Cabin, a restored one-room log structure built in 1882, and many historical markers. Swimming beach, fishing, boating (rentals); hiking trails. Picnicking, playground, snack bar. Camping (hookups). Interpretive programs (Memorial Day-Labor Day, daily).

Special Events

Faulkner County Fair. Mid-Sept.

Toad Suck Daze. *1234 Main St, Conway (72034). Phone 501/327-7788.* Regional celebration featuring toad jumping; bluegrass, country, and gospel music; carnival rides; arts and crafts. First weekend in May.

Limited-Service Hotels

★ ★ **BEST WESTERN CONWAY.** *PO Box 1619, Conway (72032). Phone 501/329-9855; toll-free 800/780-7234; fax 501/327-6110. www.bestwestern.com.* 70 rooms, 2 story. Pets accepted, some restrictions. Check-out noon. Wireless Internet access. Restaurant. Outdoor pool. **$**

★ **QUALITY INN.** *150 Hwy 65 N, Conway (72032). Phone 501/329-0300; toll-free 800/228-5150; fax 501/329-8367. www.choicehotels.com.* 60 rooms, 2 story. Pets accepted; fee. Complimentary continental breakfast. Check-in 3 pm, check-out 11 am. Outdoor pool. **$**

Restaurant

★ **FU LIN.** *195 Farris Rd, Conway (72032). Phone 501/329-1415; fax 501/329-5150.* Chinese menu. Lunch, dinner. Closed holidays. **$$**

Dumas (D-4)

See also El Dorado, Magnolia

Population 5,238
Elevation 163 ft
Area Code 870
Zip 71639
Information Chamber of Commerce, 165 S Main, PO Box 431

What to See and Do

Desha County Museum. *Hwy 54 E, Dumas (71639). 1 mile on Hwy 165 E. Phone 870/382-4222.* Artifacts depicting history of area; agricultural display, arrowhead collection. Log house farmstead. (Mon, Thurs-Fri, Sun; closed holidays) **FREE**

Lake Chicot State Park. *2542 Hwy 257, Lake Village (71653). Phone 870/265-5480.* Surrounding Arkansas' largest natural lake (formed centuries ago when the Mississippi changed its course); famous for its bream, crappie, catfish, and bass fishing. Swimming pool, lifeguard, boating (rentals, ramp, marina); picnicking, playground. Camping (hookups, dump station), cabins, store, coin laundry. Visitor center; exhibits; interpretive programs. Archery lessons (summer).**$**

Norrell and No. 2 Locks and Dams. *628 Wild Goose Ln, Tichnor (71639). About 11 miles E and N via Hwys 165, 1; E on 44, then S on unnumbered roads before crossing the river.Phone 870/548-2291.*Major recreation areas: **Wild Goose Bayou,** north of Norrell Lock; **Merrisach Lake,** west of Lock No. 2; **Pendleton Bend,** west of Dam No. 2; **Moore Bayou,** south of Gillet on Hwy 165; **Notrebes Bend,** east of Dam No. 2. All areas offer fishing, boating; picnicking, playground. Camping

only at Merrisach Lake, Notrebes Bend, and Pendleton Bend (electric hookups, dump stations) and Moore Bayou. Fees charged at some areas. (Daily) **FREE**

El Dorado (E-2)

See also Camden, Magnolia

Population 21,530
Elevation 286 ft
Zip 71730
Information Chamber of Commerce, 111 W Main; phone 870/863-6113
Web Site www.goeldorado.com

Legend has it that when Matthew F. Rainey's wagon broke down one day in a forest of hardwood and pine, he was so discouraged he offered all his worldly goods for sale. The farmers in the area were such eager customers that Rainey decided to open a store on the spot and call the place El Dorado. The town led a quiet existence until oil was discovered in 1921. Soon it was inundated with drillers, speculators, engineers, and merchants. Before the year was out, there were 460 oil-producing wells, and the name El Dorado had a significant ring. Today this flourishing community is the location of an oil refinery, chemical plants, and many other industries.

What to See and Do

Arkansas Museum of Natural Resources. *3853 Smackover Hwy, Smackover (71762). 15 miles N via Hwy 7. Phone 870/725-2877.* Ten-acre outdoor exhibit depicts working examples of oil production from 1920s-present. Museum exhibits; research center. Gift shop. Picnic area. (Mon-Sat 8 am-5 pm, Sun from 1 pm; closed holidays) **FREE**

Moro Bay State Park. *6071 Hwy 600, Jersey (71651). 25 miles NE via Hwy 15, at the confluence of Moro Bay, Raymond Lake, and the Ouachita River. Phone 870/463-8555.* Fishing, boating; hiking. Picnicking, playground, store. Camping (hookups, dump station). Visitor center. Standard fees. (Daily) **FREE**

South Arkansas Arboretum. *South Arkansas Community College, 501 Timberlane, El Dorado (71730). Phone 870/862-8131.* Seventeen-acre arboretum featuring indigenous trees and plants. Nature trails, wooden bridges. (Daily 8 am-5 pm; closed holidays) **FREE**

Special Event

Union County Fair. *3853 Smackover Hwy, Smackover (71762). Phone 870/725-2877.* A carnival, various food boths, and a livestock auction are just some of the things that this fair has to offer. Mid-Sept.

Limited-Service Hotel

★ ★ **BEST WESTERN KING'S INN CONFERENCE CENTER.** *1920 Junction City Rd, El Dorado (71730). Phone 870/862-5191; fax 870/863-7511. www.bestwestern.com.* 131 rooms, 2 story. Pets accepted, some restrictions; fee. Check-out noon. Restaurant. Indoor pool, outdoor pool, children's pool, whirlpool. Tennis. Airport transportation available. **$**

Eureka Springs (A-1)

See also Berryville, Harrison, Rogers

Founded 1879
Population 2,278
Elevation 1,329 ft
Area Code 479
Zip 72632
Information Chamber of Commerce, 516 Village Circle, PO Box 551; phone 479/253-8737 or toll-free 800/638-7352
Web Site www.eurekasprings.org

Eureka Springs is a lovely Victorian city. In the 19th century this was a well-known health spa; its springs, which gushed from limestone crevices, gained a reputation for having curative powers. Thousands of people with every possible affliction flocked to the city. Visitors continue to come to this community, drawn by the charm of the area, the scenery, and the fishing.

What to See and Do

Eureka Springs & North Arkansas Railway. *299 N Main St (Hwy 23), Eureka Springs. Phone 479/253-9623. www.esnrailway.com.* Powered by restored diesel engines; dining car. (Apr-Oct, Mon-Sat) **$$**

Eureka Springs Gardens. *1537 Carroll, #210, Eureka Springs (72632). 5 miles W off Hwy 62. www.eureka-gardens.com.* Specialty gardens and natural garden settings project changing panorama of color, form, and shadow from sunrise to sunset. (Apr-Oct: daily 9 am-6 pm; Nov-Mar: to 5 pm) **$$$**

Eureka Springs Historical Museum. *95 S Main St, Eureka Springs (72632). Phone 479/253-9417.* Nineteenth-century area artifacts including household items, tools, and photographs. (Mon-Sat 9:30 am-4 pm, Sun 11 am-3:30 pm; closed Mon from Jan-Feb) **$**

Eureka Springs Trolley. *137 W Van Buren, Eureka Springs (72632). Phone 479/253-9572.* Regularly scheduled trips through the city, historic district, and many points of interest. (Apr-Nov) **$$**

Frog Fantasies. *151 Spring St, Eureka Springs (72632). Phone 479/253-7227.* Museum display featuring thousands of man-made frogs. Gift shop. (Daily) **$**

Onyx Cave Park. *338 Onyx Cave Rd, Eureka Springs (72632). 3 miles E on Hwy 62, 3 1/2 miles N on Onyx Cave Rd. Phone 479/253-9321.* Unusual onyx formations in 57° F cave; blind cave fish display; museum of Gay `90s costumes, dolls; antique button collection; gift shop, picnicking. Continuous tours (daily). **$**

Pivot Rock and Natural Bridge. *1708 Pivot Rock Rd, Eureka Springs (72632). 1/2 mile W on Hwy 62, 2 1/2 miles N on Pivot Rock Rd. Phone 479/253-8982.* The top of Pivot Rock is 15 times as wide as the bottom; yet it is perfectly balanced. A natural bridge and caves believed to be hiding places of Jesse James are nearby. (Apr-mid-Nov) **$**

Rosalie House. *282 Spring St, Eureka Springs (72632). Phone 479/253-7377. www.estc.net/rosalie/wedding. phtm.* (1883). Built of handmade brick with gingerbread trim; original interior, gold leaf molding, ceiling frescoes, handmade woodwork; period furnishings. Guided tours (Thurs-Mon 11 am-5 pm). **$$**

Sacred Arts Center. *935 Passion Play Rd, Eureka Springs (72632). Off Hwy 62 E. Phone 479/253-9200.* More than 1,000 works of Christian art. (Tues-Sun) **$$$$** Also here are

Bible Museum. Rare bibles, artifacts, and more than 6,000 volumes in 625 languages, including works on papyrus, parchment, and clay cylinders and cones dating from 2000 BC (Tues-Sun)

Christ of the Ozarks. A 7-story-tall statue of Jesus, more than 1 million pounds in weight and with an arm spread of 65 feet.

New Holy Land. Contains old and new testament exhibits with costumed guides, features full-size replica of Moses's tabernacle; Dead Sea; Jordan River; Sea of Galilee; Nativity scene; Last Supper re-creation. (Mon-Sat)

Thorncrown Chapel. *12968 Hwy 62 W, Eureka Springs (72632). Phone 479/253-7401. www.thorncrown.com.* Sensational glass chapel structure tucked in to the woods in the Ozarks, designed by Arkansas' noted architect E. Fay Jones.

Withrow Springs State Park. *Hwy 23 N, Huntsville (72740). 20 miles S on Hwy 23. Phone 479/559-2593. www.arkansasstateparks.com.* This 700-acre recreation area stretches across mountains and valleys along the bluffs of War Eagle River. The waters of a large spring gush from a shallow cave at the foot of a towering bluff. Swimming pool (Memorial Day-mid-Aug, daily; also Labor Day weekend), lifeguard, canoeing (rentals); hiking, tennis, picnicking, snack bar, playground, camping (hookups; dump station). Visitor center.(Daily) **FREE**

Special Events

Candlelight Tour of Homes. *137 W Van Buren, Eureka Springs (72632). Historic district. Phone 479/253-9417. www.eurekasprings.com.* The Eureka Springs Preservation Society annually sponsors this tour of historic Victorian homes. Sun in mid-Dec.

Country Music Shows. *137 W Van Buren, Eureka Springs (72632). Phone 479/253-8737.* Various productions with country music, comedy skits, and other family entertainment. Contact Chamber of Commerce. Most shows Mar.

The Great Passion Play. *Mount Oberammergau, Passion Play Rd, Eureka Springs (72632). Phone 479/253-9200; toll-free 800/882-7529.* Portrayal of the life of Jesus from Palm Sunday through the Ascension; evening performances. Late Apr-late Oct, Mon-Tues and Thurs-Sat.

Ozark Folk Festival. *36 S Main St, Eureka Springs (72632). Phone toll-free 888/855-7823.* National headliners and other musical acts, beauty pageant, Gay `90s costume parade, other events. Early Oct.

Limited-Service Hotels

★ ★ **BEST WESTERN INN OF THE OZARKS.** *207 W Van Buren St, Eureka Springs (72632). Phone 479/253-9768; toll-free 800/780-7234; fax 479/253-9768. www.innoftheozarks.com.* Because of its many kids' activities, this rustic hotel is a great choice for families. There is a recreation center under a pavillion which includes air hockey, mini golf, a play area for small children, shuffleboard, and table tennis. Tennis courts, swings and a climbing bar, and a pool are located outside. 122 rooms, 2 story. Pets accepted, some restrictions. Check-in, check-out 11 am. Restaurant. Children's activity center. Outdoor pool, whirlpool. Tennis. **$**

★ **DAYS INN.** *120 W Van Buren St, Eureka Springs (72632). Phone 479/253-8863; toll-free 800/329-7466; fax 479/253-7885. www.daysinn.com.* 24 rooms, 2 story. Pets accepted, some restrictions; fee. Complimentary continental breakfast. Check-in 2 pm, check-out 11 am. Wireless Internet access. Outdoor pool. **$**

★ ★ **NEW ORLEANS HOTEL & SPA.** *63 Spring St, Eureka Springs (72632). Phone 479/253-8630; toll-free 800/243-8630; fax 479/253-5949. www.neworleanshotelandspa.net.* Located in the historic downtown district, which is listed on the National Register of Historic Places, this restored hotel (built in 1892) features antique furnishings and Victorian décor. At night, relax on the balcony that overlooks town or take a leisurely stroll. Shopping, cafes, and galleries are just a few steps away so there's always plenty to do. But if you feel like just relaxing, head down to the lobby level and indulge in some spa services. The menu includes massages, facials, body wraps, and much more. 20 rooms, 6 story. Check-in 3 pm, check-out noon. High-speed Internet access. Restaurant, bar. Spa. Business center. **$**

Full-Service Hotel

★ ★ ★ **1886 CRESCENT HOTEL & SPA.** *75 Prospect Ave, Eureka Springs (72632). Phone 479/253-9766; toll-free 800/342-9766; fax 479/253-5296. www.crescent-hotel.com.* 72 rooms. Pets accepted; fee. Check-in 3 pm, check-out 11 am. Two restaurants. Spa. Outdoor pool. Airport transportation available. **$**

Specialty Lodgings

1881 CRESCENT COTTAGE INN. *211 Spring St, Eureka Springs (72632). Phone 479/253-6022; toll-free 800/223-3246; fax 479/253-6234. www.1881crescent cottageinn.com.* Built in 1881; antiques. 4 rooms, 3 story. Children over 16 years only. Complimentary full breakfast. Check-in 2:30 pm, check-out 11 am. **$**

ARSENIC & OLD LACE BED AND BREAKFAST INN. *60 Hillside Ave, Eureka Springs (72632). Phone 479/253-5454; toll-free 800/243-5223; fax*

479/253-2246. *www.eurekaspringsromancebb.com.* This elegant Queen Anne mansion (built in 1992) has old-fashioned bed-and-breakfast charm with modern conveniences. Located just a ten-minute walk from the downtown area, it is set back from the road in a quiet neighborhood. The large, welcoming porch invites you to stay awhile, and each room has a whirlpool tub. The complimentary breakfast will start each day off right. 5 rooms, 2 story. Pets accepted. Children over 12 years only. Complimentary full breakfast. Check-in 2 pm, check-out 11 am. **$$**

BRIDGEFORD HOUSE. *263 Spring St, Eureka Springs (72632). Phone 479/253-7853; toll-free 888/567-2422; fax 479/253-5497. www.bridgefordhouse. com.* This 1884 Victorian mansion (listed on the National Register of Historic places) is located in a quaint historic neighborhood. Downtown shops and cafes are located within walking distance. The exterior of the home features a peach-colored frame and dark turquoise trim, a large porch with white wicker furniture, and a small garden area. The interior is filled with antiques and period furniture. And the comfortable rooms feature fireplaces and whirlpool tubs. This is a perfect destination for a weekend escape. 5 rooms, 2 story. Children over 8 years only. Complimentary full breakfast. Check-in 3 pm, check-out 11 am. **$**

HEARTSTONE INN AND COTTAGES. *35 Kings Hwy, Eureka Springs (72632). Phone 479/253-8916; toll-free 800/494-4921; fax 479/253-5361. www. heartstoneinn.com.* Set amidst the tranquillity of the Ozarks, this Victorian inn has visitors coming back time and time again. With its quiet beauty, charming service, and delectable breakfast, guests will be delighted that they found this magnificent place. And its location can't be beat—in the Historic Loop, on the trolley route, and four blocks from downtown. 11 rooms, 2 story. Closed a few weeks in Jan. Children over 10 years only. Complimentary full breakfast. Check-in 3 pm, check-out 11 am. Spa. **$**

THE INN AT ROSE HALL. *56 Hillside Ave, Eureka Springs (72632). Phone 479/253-8313; toll-free 800/544-7734. www.innatrosehall.com.* Located on a quiet, tree-lined street, this reproduction Victorian house is the perfect romantic escape. Stained-glass windows and elegant Victorian furniture are featured throughout the house, and there is a tin-style ceiling in the dining room. The spacious rooms are decorated in soothing colors and have fireplaces and whirlpool tubs for guests to kick back and relax. 5 rooms, 2 story.

No children allowed. Complimentary full breakfast. Check-in 2 pm, check-out 11 am. **$$**

PALACE HOTEL & BATH HOUSE. *135 Spring St, Eureka Springs (72632). Phone 479/253-7474. www. palacehotelbathhouse.com.* Built in 1901, this historic Victorian-era property was fully restored to its original beauty. Large guest suites are beautifully decorated and include whirlpool tubs, wet bars, and refrigerators. The bath house has been in operation for more than 100 years and offers services such as natural clay masks and Swedish massage therapy. 8 rooms, 2 story. No children allowed. Complimentary continental breakfast. Check-in 3:30 pm, check-out noon. Spa. **$$**

Restaurants

★ **BUBBA'S BARBECUE.** *166 W Van Buren, Eureka Springs (72632). Phone 479/253-7706.* For a "come as you are" dining experience, locals, tourists, and families head to this charming spot just outside the downtown area for traditional barbecue favorites. It doesn't get much more casual than Bubba's Barbecue, where wooden benches, old-style chairs, and pictures of pigs decorate the room. If you're on the go, pick up your order at the take-out window. Barbecue menu. Lunch, dinner. Closed Sun; also mid-Dec-late Feb. Casual attire. No credit cards accepted. **$$**

★ **CENTER STREET PUB.** *10 Center St, Eureka Springs (72632). Phone 479/253-7147.* A broad menu of American favorites are served at this small, cozy pub located in the heart of downtown Eureka Springs. American menu. Lunch, dinner. Bar. Casual attire. No credit cards accepted. **$$**

★★★ **THE CRYSTAL DINING ROOM.** *75 Prospect Ave, Eureka Springs (72632). Phone 479/253-9766; toll-free 800/342-9766; fax 479/253-5296. www. crescent-hotel.com/dining.* American menu. Breakfast, lunch, dinner, brunch. Children's menu. Business casual attire. Reservations recommended. **$$$**

Fayetteville (B-1)

See also Bentonville, Rogers, Springdale

Population 58,047
Elevation 1,400 ft
Area Code 479
Information Chamber of Commerce, 123 W Mountain St, PO Box 4216, 72702; phone 479/521-1710 or toll-free 800/766-4626

Web Site www.fayettevillear.com

This is a resort center in the Ozark Mountains. The countryside is famous for its scenery during spring and fall. There are many lakes and streams nearby for fishing. Fayetteville is the home of the University of Arkansas.

What to See and Do

Arkansas Air Museum. *4290 S School St, Fayetteville (72701). 5 miles S on Hwy 71, at Drake Field. Phone 479/521-4947. www.arkairmuseum.org.* Exhibit spanning the history of manned flight; features collection of antique and World War II aircraft. (Sun-Fri 11 am-4:30 pm, Sat from 10 am; closed Jan 1, Thanksgiving, Dec 25) **$**

Devil's Den State Park. *11333 Hwy 74 W, West Fork (72774). 8 miles S on Hwy 71, then 18 miles SW of West Fork on Hwy 170. Phone 479/761-3325. www.arkansasstateparks.com.* Situated in a scenic valley in the Boston Mountains, this 2,000-acre park in the heart of rugged Ozark terrain includes unusual sandstone formations; Devil's Den Cave; and the Devil's Icebox, where the temperature never goes above 60° F. Swimming pool (summer; lifeguard), fishing, canoeing (rentals); nature, hiking, bridle, mountain biking trails, picnicking, playground, restaurant (summer), snack bar, store, camping (electric hookups, dump station; standard fees); horse camp; cabins, coin laundry. Visitor center has exhibits, camping and backpack equipment rentals. Interpretive programs. (Daily)

Headquarters House. *118 E Dickson St, Fayetteville (72701). Phone 479/521-2970.* (1853) Greek Revival house, residence of wealthy Union sympathizer Judge Jonas Tebbetts, was used as headquarters for both Union and Confederate forces during the Civil War; period furnishings, local historical artifacts, Civil War relics. (By appointment) **DONATION**

Prairie Grove Battlefield State Park. *506 E Douglas, Prairie Grove (72753). 10 miles W on Hwy 62. Phone 479/846-2990.* The park covers approximately 750 acres of the 3.5-square-mile site where more than 22,000 Union and Confederate forces fought on Dec 7, 1862; the armies suffered a combined loss of 2,700 dead, wounded, or missing. Hindman Hall Museum houses a visitor center with exhibits, battle diorama, artifacts, and an audiovisual presentation. Historic structures in the park include Battle Monument, a chimney from Rhea's Mill; Borden House, the scene of the heaviest fighting of the battle; and a spring house,

smokehouse, detached kitchen, schoolhouse, church, blacksmith shop, and sorghum mill. Guided tours (daily). Picnicking, playground. For more information, contact the Superintendent, PO Box 306, Prairie Grove 72753. **FREE**

University of Arkansas. *1125 W Maple St, Fayetteville (72701). In center of town. Phone 479/575-2000. www.uark.edu.* (1871) (15,800 students) On campus are

> **Fine Arts Center.** *Garland St, Fayetteville . Phone 479/575-4752.* Includes a theater, concert hall, library, and exhibition gallery. (Daily; closed holidays).

> **University Museum.** *Garland Ave Museum Bldg # 202, Fayetteville . Phone 479/575-3466.* Houses science, natural history, and ethnological exhibits; films. (Mon-Sat closed holidays, also Dec 24-Jan 1)

Walton Arts Center. *495 W Dickson St, Fayetteville (72701). Dickson and Springs sts. Phone 479/443-5600.* Musicals, opera, plays, symphonies.

Special Event

Battle Reenactment. *Prairie Grove Battlefield State Park, 506 E Douglas, Prairie Grove (72753). Phone 479/846-2990.* Costumed volunteers reenact historic battle and demonstrate war tactics and life of a Civil War soldier. First full weekend in Dec.

Limited-Service Hotels

★ **BEST WESTERN WINDSOR SUITES.** *1122 S Futrall, Fayetteville (72701). Phone 479/587-1400; toll-free 800/780-7234; fax 479/587-8630. www.bestwestern. com.* Located just off Interstate 540 and 1-mile from the University of Arkansas, this traditional property is a great choice for budget-minded travelers and families. Some of its amenities include an indoor pool and whirlpool, a fitness room, and complimentary continental breakfast. 68 rooms, 2 story. Pets accepted, some restrictions; fee. Complimentary continental breakfast. Check-in 2 pm, check-out 11 am. High-speed Internet access. Fitness room. Indoor pool, whirlpool. Business center. **$**

★ ★ **CLARION CARRIAGE HOUSE INN AT THE MILL.** *3906 Great House Springs Rd, Johnson (72741). Phone 479/443-1800; fax 479/444-6274. www. innatthemill.com.* Set on 7 acres of land in the Pisgah National Forest, this inn's property offers a historic dam, a private orchard, and many trails. Guests will enjoy the piano, library, and solarium with a goldfish pond. 48 rooms, 2 story. Complimentary continental breakfast. Check-out noon. Restaurant. Historic water mill built 1835. **$**

★ **DAYS INN.** *2402 N College Ave, Fayetteville (72703). Phone 479/443-4323; toll-free 800/329-7466; fax 479/444-7409. www.daysinn.com.* A favorite with families, this traditional hotel is located 2 mile from the University of Arkansas and just over a mile from the Northwest Arkansas Mall. The complimentary continental breakfast is served in a large breakfast area which is separated from the lobby by a full door and etched glass windows. 149 rooms, 2 story. Complimentary continental breakfast. Check-in 3 pm, check-out noon. Outdoor pool. **$**

★ ★ **RADISSON HOTEL FAYETTEVILLE.** *70 N East Ave, Fayetteville (72701). Phone 479/442-5555; toll-free 800/333-3333; fax 479/442-2105. www.radisson.com/fayettevillear.* Located in the beautiful setting of the Ozarks, excellent accommodations await guests at this property. Explore the nearby Civil War Battlefields and Eureka Springs. 235 rooms, 15 story. Pets accepted, some restrictions; fee. Check-in 3 pm, check-out 11 am. High-speed Internet access, wireless Internet access. Restaurant, bar. Fitness room. Indoor pool, outdoor pool. Business center. **$**

Forrest City (C-4)

See also Helena

Founded 1866
Population 14,774
Elevation 276 ft
Area Code 870
Zip 72335
Information Chamber of Commerce, 203 N Izard; phone 870/633-1651
Web Site www.forrestcitychamber.com

This town is named for Confederate General Nathan Bedford Forrest, who contracted to put a railroad across Crowley's Ridge, on which the city stands. The ridge, 100 feet high and composed of loess (wind-blown, fine, yellowish loam that generally stands in vertical cliffs), roughly parallels the Mississippi from Missouri to Helena, Arkansas.

What to See and Do

Village Creek State Park. *201 CR 754, Wynne (72396). E on I-40 exit 242, then 13 miles N on Hwy 284. Phone 870/238-9406.* Approximately 7,000-acre park with two lakes situated entirely upon the unusual geologic formation of Crowley's Ridge. Swimming, fishing, boating (rentals); hiking trails, tennis, picnicking, playground, store, camping (hookups, dump station); ten fully-equipped cabins. Visitor center with history, geology, and botany exhibits; audiovisual presentations; interpretive programs (summer). Contact Superintendent, 201 CR 754, Wynne 72396. (Daily) **FREE**

Limited-Service Hotel

★ ★ **DAYS INN.** *350 Barrow Hill Rd, Forrest City (72335). Phone 870/633-0777; toll-free 800/329-7466; fax 870/633-0770. www.daysinn.com.* 53 rooms, 2 story. Complimentary full breakfast. Check-out 11 am. Wireless Internet access. Restaurant. Outdoor pool. **$**

Fort Smith (C-1)

See also Alma, Paris

Population 80,268
Elevation 450 ft
Area Code 479
Information Chamber of Commerce, 612 Garrison Ave, PO Box 1668, 72902; phone 479/783-6118
Web Site www.fortsmithchamber.com

The original fort was built on the Arkansas River in 1817 to stand between the Osages upstream and the Cherokees downstream. It also gave protection to traders, trappers, and explorers and encouraged settlement in the area. Captain John Rogers became the first settler in 1821; by 1842 the town had a population of nearly 500.

In 1848, when gold was discovered in California, Fort Smith immediately became a thriving supply center and starting point for gold rush wagons heading south across the plains. Bandits, robbers, gamblers, and cut-throats moved in. Without peace officers, the territory was wild and tough until 1875, when Judge Isaac C. Parker—known later as "the hanging judge"—was sent in to clean it up. He was judge of the Federal District Court at Fort Smith for 21 years; during his first 14 years, there were no appeals of his decisions. Under Parker's rule, 151 men were sentenced to die and about 79 hanged, sometimes as many as six at a time. Parker was a strict judge with a reputation for knowing and respecting the rules of evidence.

Today Fort Smith is a leading manufacturing center in Arkansas, with more than 200 manufacturing plants and major corporations. Boston Mountain to the north is a good hunting area.

What to See and Do

Fort Smith Art Center. *423 N 6th St, Fort Smith (72901). Phone 479/782-1156. www.ftsartcenter. com.* Built in 1879 as a residence. Changing exhibits monthly; guided tours, by appointment. (Tues-Sat 9:30 am-4:30 pm, Sun 1-4 pm; closed holidays) **FREE**

Fort Smith Museum of History. *320 Rogers Ave, Fort Smith (72901). Phone 479/783-7841. www.fortsmith-museum.com.* Regional history, period pharmacy with working soda fountain, transportation exhibit with 1899 steam fire pumper. Changing exhibits. (Tues-Sat 10 am-5 pm; from 9 am June-Aug; Sun noon-5 pm; closed Jan 1, Thanksgiving, Dec 24-25) **$**

Fort Smith National Historic Site. *301 Parker Ave, Fort Smith (72901). Rogers Ave and 3rd St. Phone 479/783-3961. www.nps.gov/fosm.* Park contains foundations of the first Fort Smith; the original commissary from the second Fort Smith; the famous Judge Parker's court-room, jail, and reconstructed gallows. (Daily 9 am-5 pm; closed Jan 1, Thanksgiving, Dec 25) **$**

White Rock Mountain Recreation Area. *Alma. 13 miles NE on Hwy 215, forest roads, in the Boston Mountain range of the Ozark National Forest.Phone 479/369-4128.* A 94-acre primitive area at the summit of 2,287-foot White Rock peak with panoramic views. Nature trails. Picnicking, camping. Six miles from the summit on Forest Service Rd 1505 is the 82-acre Shores Lake with water sports; picnicking, camping (fee). Fees charged at recreation sites. (Daily)

Special Events

Arkansas-Oklahoma State Fair. *Kay Rodgers Park, 4400 Midland Blvd, Fort Smith (72904). Phone 479/783-6176; toll-free 800/364-1080. www.kayrodgerspark.com/ fair_index.html.* Kay Rodgers Park is home to a number of events throughout the year, including the Arkansas-Oklahoma State Fair, held nine days in September and October. The fair features live musical entertainment, a youth talent contest, a circus, a demolition derby, mon-ster truck racing, a carnival, and livestock, poultry, and horticulture exhibits. Late Sept-early Oct. **$$**

Old Fort Days Rodeo. *Kay Rodgers Park, 4400 Midland Blvd, Fort Smith (72904). Phone 479/783-6176; toll-free 800/364-1080. www.oldfortdaysrodeo.com.* Calf roping, wild horse racing, steer wrestling, and rodeo clown bullfighting acts mark this fast-paced rodeo. Late May-early June. **$$**

Limited-Service Hotels

★ **ASPEN HOTEL & SUITES.** *2900 S 68th, Fort Smith (72903). Phone 479/452-9000; toll-free 800/627-9417; fax 479/484-0551. www.aspenhotelandsuites. com.* 49 rooms, 2 story. Complimentary continental breakfast. Check-out 11 am. Fitness room. Outdoor pool. Airport transportation available. **$**

★ ★ **HOLIDAY INN.** *700 Rogers Ave, Fort Smith (72901). Phone 479/783-1000; toll-free 800/465-4329; fax 479/783-0312. www.holiday-inn.com.* 255 rooms, 9 story. Pets accepted; fee. Check-out noon. Wireless In-ternet access. Restaurant. Fitness room. Indoor pool, whirlpool. Airport transportation available. **$**

Restaurants

★ **CALICO COUNTY.** *2409 S 56th St, Fort Smith (72903). Phone 479/452-3299; fax 479/452-4286. www. calicocounty.net.* Breakfast, lunch, dinner. Closed Thanksgiving, Dec 25. Children's menu. **$$**

★ **THE LIGHTHOUSE INN.** *6000 Midland, Fort Smith (72904). Phone 479/783-9420.* Seafood, steak menu. Lunch, dinner. Closed Sun; holidays. Bar. Children's menu. Old lighthouse on river. **$$$**

Greers Ferry Lake Area (B-3)

See also Batesville, Mountain View, Searcy

Web Site greers-ferry.com

This 50-mile-long lake, impounded by a dam built by the US Army Corps of Engineers, was dedicated by President John F. Kennedy shortly before his assassina-tion in November 1963. Since then, the area has devel-oped rapidly, now offering 15 public recreation areas on more than 31,000 acres. Swimming, water-skiing, scuba diving; boating (rentals, marina, ramps); hunting, nature trail up Sugar Loaf Mountain. Picnicking. Camping. Fees are charged for some recreation areas. For further information, contact Heber Springs Chamber of Commerce, 1001 W Main, Heber Springs 72543; phone 501/362-2444 or toll-free 800/774-3237.

What to See and Do

Little Red River. *Greers Ferry Lake Area.* One of the finest trout streams in the area is stocked weekly. Trout weighing more than 15 pounds have been caught. Five commercial docks.

William Carl Gardner Visitor Center. *700 Heber Springs Rd N, Heber Springs (72543). Phone 501/362-9067.* Provides tourist information and houses exhibits interpreting history and culture of the southern Ozark region; displays relate history of the Corps of Engineers and their projects in Arkansas; interpretive slide/tape programs; guided tours of Greers Ferry Dam and Powerhouse depart from visitor center (Memorial Day-Labor Day, Mon-Fri). Nature trail with access for the disabled (guided tours in summer by appointment). Visitor center (Mar-Oct, daily; Feb, Nov-Dec, weekends; closed Jan, Thanksgiving, Dec 25). **FREE**

Limited-Service Hotel

★ ★ **RED APPLE INN.** *1000 Club Rd, Heber Springs (72543). Phone 501/362-3111; toll-free 800/733-2775; fax 501/362-8900. www.redappleinn. com.* Set on 60 acres of natural Ozark land, this Mediterranean-style inn is known as a beautiful "Garden of Eden." 59 rooms, 2 story. Check-out noon. Restaurant, bar. Two outdoor pools, children's pool. Golf. Tennis. Airport transportation available. **$**

🅿 🏊 🍴 🎿

Harrison (B-2)

See also Berryville, Bull Shoals Lake Area, Eureka Springs

Population 12,152
Elevation 1,182 ft
Area Code 870
Zip 72601
Information Chamber of Commerce, 621 E Rush; phone 870/741-2659 or toll-free 800/880-6265
Web Site www.harrison-chamber.com

Harrison, headquarters for a rustic resort area in the wild and beautiful Ozarks, is excellent for vacationing. The entire region is scenic, especially along Highway 7.

What to See and Do

Boone County Heritage Museum. *124 S Cherry, Harrison (72601). Phone 870/741-3312.* History and antiques from the Civil War and the Missouri & North Arkansas Railroad Co. Native American artifacts, old clocks, medical and domestic tools from the 1800s. (Mar-Nov, Mon-Fri; Jan-Feb, Dec, Thurs) **$**

Float trips. *Walnut and Erie, Harrison . Phone 870/741-5443.* Excursions down the Buffalo River through the Ozark Mountains and the forested hill country. Contact Buffalo National River (Float Trips), National Park Service, Department of the Interior, 402 N Walnut, Suite 136, 72601.

Mystic Caverns. *Hwy 7 S, Dogpatch. 8 miles S on Hwy 7. Phone 870/743-1739. www.mysticcaverns.com.* Two caves with large formations; 35-foot pipe organ, eight-story crystal dome. One-hour guided tours cover 3/8 mile of lighted walks (may be strenuous). (Mar-Dec, Mon-Sat 9 am-6 pm; Wed-Sat 10 am-5 pm in Feb; closed Thanksgiving, Dec 25) **$$$**

Special Events

Coca-Cola Airshow of the Ozarks. *Walnut Ridge Regional Airport, 10 Skywatch, Walnut Ridge (72476).* Sept.

Crooked Creek Crawdad Days. Spring festival. Arts, crafts, music. May.

Harvest Homecoming. *Phone 870/741-1789.* During the first weekend in October, the people of Harrison flock to the downtown area to take part in the city's largest festival. The Harvest Homecoming celebrates Harrison's history with fun and activities the whole family can enjoy. In addition to autumn food and live entertainment, the festival features a farmers' market, working craftsmen, children's activities, sports-related activities, a car show, tractor races, and a scarecrow decorating contest. Oct. **FREE**

Northwest Arkansas Bluegrass Music Festival. *Northwest Arkansas Fairgrounds, 1400 Fairgrounds Rd, Harrison (72601). 5 miles N of Harrison on Hwy 65. Phone 870/427-3342. www.southshore.com.* Festival-goers can camp out and enjoy impromptu "jam sessions" throughout the weekend in addition to catching the scheduled stage acts. Aug. **$$**

Northwest Arkansas District Fair. *1400 Fair Ground Rd, Harrison (72601). 2 miles S off Hwy 65. Phone 870/743-1011.* Includes a livestock show and rodeo. Sept.

Limited-Service Hotels

★ **COMFORT INN.** *1210 Hwy 62-65 N, Harrison (72601). Phone 870/741-7676; toll-free 800/228-5150; fax 870/741-0827. www.choicehotels.com.* 93 rooms, 2 story. Complimentary continental breakfast. Outdoor pool. **$**

★ **DAYS INN.** *1425 Hwy 62/65 N, Harrison (72601). Phone 870/391-3297; toll-free 800/329-7466; fax 870/365-7378. www.daysinn.com.* 82 rooms, 3 story. Complimentary continental breakfast. Check-in 3 pm, check-out 11 am. Bar. Outdoor pool, whirlpool. **$**

Restaurant

★ ★ **OL' ROCKHOUSE.** *416 S Pine St, Harrison (72601). Phone 870/741-8047; fax 870/741-8170.* Lunch, dinner. Closed Thanksgiving, Dec 25. Children's menu. Casual attire. Outdoor seating. **$$**

Heber Springs

Limited-Service Hotel

★ ★ **RED APPLE INN.** *1000 Club Rd, Heber Springs (72543). Phone 501/362-3111; toll-free 800/733-2775; fax 501/362-8900. www.redappleinn. com.* Set on 60 acres of natural Ozark land, this Mediterranean-style inn is known as a beautiful "Garden of Eden." 59 rooms, 2 story. Check-out noon. Restaurant, bar. Two outdoor pools, children's pool. Golf. Tennis. Airport transportation available. **$**

Restaurants

★ ★ **CAFE KLASER.** *600 W Main St, Heber Springs (72543). Phone 501/206-0688.* French, German menu. Lunch, dinner. Closed Sun-Mon. Children's menu. Outdoor seating. **$$**

★ ★ **RED APPLE DINING ROOM.** *1000 Club Rd, Heber Springs (72543). Phone 501/362-3111. www. redappleinn.com.* American menu. Breakfast, lunch,

dinner, Sun brunch. Children's menu. Jacket required. **$$**

Helena (C-5)

See also Forrest City

Population 6,323
Elevation 195 ft
Area Code 870
Zip 72342
Information Phillips County Chamber of Commerce, 111 Hickory Hill Dr, PO Box 447; phone 870/338-8327

Helena, a river barge port of call since 1880, was once described by Samuel Clemens as occupying "one of the prettiest situations on the Mississippi." This broad, flat section of the Mississippi River Valley is part of the cotton country known as "the Delta" and is the southern end of Crowley's Ridge, a stretch of wind-deposited yellowish loess hills that runs north to the Missouri border.

What to See and Do

Delta Cultural Center. *141 Cherry St, Helena (72342). Phone 870/338-4350. www.deltaculturalcenter.com.* Housed in a 1912 Missouri Pacific rail depot, the center has exhibits on the history of "the Delta." (Tues-Sun; closed Jan 1, Thanksgiving, Dec 25) **FREE**

Ozark-St. Francis National Forests. *2675 Hwy 44, Helena (72801). 2 miles N on Hwy 44. Phone 870/295-5278. www.fs.fed.us/oonf/ozark.* Almost 21,000 acres, including the 510-acre Storm Creek Lake and the 520-acre Bear Creek Lake. The park offers opportunities for swimming, fishing, boating, hunting for small game, and picnicking, as well as overnight camping. Fees may be charged at recreation sites. (Daily)

Phillips County Museum. *623 Pecan St, Helena (72342). Adjacent to public library. Phone 870/338-7790.* Native American artifacts, Civil War relics; local history collection; glass, china; paintings, costumes. (Tues-Sat; closed holidays) **FREE**

Special Events

King Biscuit Blues Festival. *Cherry St, Helena (72342). Phone 870/338-8798. www.kingbiscuitfest.org.* Nearly 100,000 people come from all around each year for three full days of blues music and culture. Columbus

The Heart of the Mississippi River Delta

Helena is in the heart of the Mississippi River Delta, 120 miles east of Little Rock. For a cultural adventure, take I-40 east of Little Rock and Highway 49 south to Helena. On the west riverbank a mile north of the Highway 49 bridge, the near ghost town of Helena stands behind a high levee. The town comes alive every October, when tens of thousands of people come to this isolated Delta outpost to commemorate the towns greatest claim to fame. It was here in the early 1940s that a local radio station started broadcasting a program hosted by blues musicians Sonny Boy Williamson and Robert Junior Lockwood. A local biscuit company sponsored the show, *King Biscuit Time*, which brought the blues sound to the attention of a wide audience. Now the King Biscuit Blues Festival, held the second weekend in October, draws internationally known artists in an annual pilgrimage.

The Delta Cultural Center, located inside a converted 1913 train depot downtown at 95 Missouri Street, tells the story. Host Sunshine Sonny Payne continues to broadcast *King Biscuit Time*—the longest-running blues program in the United States—from the KFFA-AM studio within the depot (weekdays only). One exhibit, with a vintage jukebox and historical photographs of famous Delta musicians and couples jitterbugging, tells the story of the Delta blues. Other exhibits explain the rise and fall of the local industries, the ethnic and frontier heritage, and the vicissitudes of life in the Mississippi River floodplain.

The depot sits high up against the levee, overlooking the town plaza where the festival is held and the commercial length of Cherry Street, the towns main drag. From the depot, hop up first to the top of the levee for a river view of what remains of the once-busy port. Then walk down Missouri Street past the depot to the first block of Cherry Street. Here, among the abandoned storefronts across from the plaza, you might be surprised to find a valet opening doors for what turns out to be the fanciest restaurant for nearly 50 miles. The candlelit Bells Ducks by the Levee (phone 870/338-6655), serves steak, catfish, and surf-and-turf combos to what remains of the towns aristocracy.

Amid the wig shops and discount clothing stores in the four-block stretch of Cherry Street downtown, the Sonny Boy Blues Society across from the music store occasionally hosts live performances by local artists. A half-block off Cherry Street from here, Eddie Maes is a popular old dive.

Day weekend. **FREE**

Warfield Concert Series. *1000 Campus Dr, Helena (72342). Phone 877/338-8327. www.warfieldconcerts. com.* A series of productions by internationally known artists. Tickets at Chamber of Commerce. Fall shows.

Limited-Service Hotel

★ **DELTA INN.** *1207 Hwy 49 W, West Helena (72390). Phone 870/572-7915; fax 870/572-3757.* 94 rooms. Pets accepted, some restrictions. Complimentary continental breakfast. Check-out 11 am. Outdoor pool. **$**

Specialty Lodgings

EDWARDIAN INN. *317 Biscoe St, Helena (72342). Phone 870/338-9155; toll-free 800/598-4749; fax 870/338-4215. www.edwardianinn.com.* This restored historic mansion, built in 1904, is located near the Mississippi River. 12 rooms, 3 story. Complimentary full breakfast. Check-in 2 pm. Check-out 11 am. **$**

MAGNOLIA HILL B&B. *608 Perry St, Helena (72342). Phone 870/338-6874; fax 870/338-7938. www. magnoliahillbnb.com.* 8 rooms, 3 story. Complimentary full breakfast. Check-in 1 pm, check-out noon. Queen Anne Victorian house built in 1895. **$**

Hope (D-2)

See also Murfreesboro, Texarkana

Founded 1852
Population 10,616
Elevation 348 ft
Area Code 870
Zip 71801
Information Chamber of Commerce, 200 E Division, PO Box 250, 71802-0250; phone 870/777-3640
Web Site www.hopeusa.com

Hope is the birthplace of the 42nd President of the United States, William Jefferson Clinton, who lived here until age eight. It is also the home of the annual Watermelon Festival, which regularly has winners in the 150-200 pound range. The all-time winner weighed in at 260 pounds.

What to See and Do

Clinton Birthplace Home. *117 S Hervey, Hope (71802). Phone 870/777-4455. www.clintonbirthplace.com.* The first home of President Bill Clinton; he lived here from the time of his birth in 1946 until his mother married Roger Clinton in 1950. A National Register Historic Site. Visitor center; gift shop. (Mon-Sat 10 am-5 pm)**$**

Old Washington Historic State Park. *Hwys 195 and 278, Washington (71862). 9 miles NW on Hwy 278. Phone 870/983-2684. www.oldwashingtonstatepark. com.* During the early 19th century, Washington was a convenient stop on the Southwest Trail, visited by such men as Stephen Austin, Sam Houston, and Davy Crockett. Washington became the Confederate capital for the state after Little Rock was captured in 1863. The park preserves and interprets the town's past from 1824 to 1875. (Daily 8 am-5 pm; closed Jan 1, Thanksgiving, Dec 25) Many historic structures remain, including

Guided tours of park and historical buildings. *Hwys 195 and 278, Hope. Phone 870/983-2684.* Guided tours of park include historical buildings (daily; closed Jan 1, Thanksgiving, Dec 24-25). Contact the Park Superintentent, PO Box 98, Washington 71862.

Old Tavern. *Hwys 195 and 278, Hope . Phone 870/983-2733.* (Circa 1840) With detached kitchen, taproom; blacksmith shop where, between 1826-1831, James Black designed the bowie knife

for James Bowie; **1874 Courthouse** now serving as park information center; **Confederate state capitol** from 1863-1865; **Royston House,** restored residence of Arkansas Militia General Grandison D. Royston, president of Arkansas Constitutional Convention of 1874; **Sanders House** (1845), restored Greek Revival house; **Purdom House,** which served as the medical offices of Dr. James Purdom; **gun museum** with more than 600 antique weapons; and the **Goodlett Cotton Gin.**

Special Events

Frontier Days. *Hwy 195 and Hwy 278, Washington (71862). Phone 870/983-2684.* Old Washington Historic State Park. Pioneer activity demonstrations: knife-making and throwing, lye soap-making, lard rendering, turkey shoot. Third weekend in Oct.

Hope Watermelon Festival. *108 W 3rd St, Hope (71801). Phone 870/777-3640. www.hopemelonfest.com.* The festival harkens back to the 1920s, when many trains went through this small town and local watermelon growers would sell their wares to parched travelers. These days, the festival sees a Watermelon Queen crowned and sometimes a world-record watermelon grown, like one that weighed in at 260 pounds in 1985. There are also more than 300 booths selling arts and crafts from a six-state area, as well as an antique car show and the Watermelon Olympics, with events like a seed-spitting contest and a melon toss. Early Aug.

Jonquil Festival. *Old Washington Historic State Park, Hwy 195 and Hwy 278, Washington (71862). Phone 870/983-2684.* Coincides with blooming of jonquils planted by early settlers. Craft demonstrations, bluegrass music. Mid-Mar.

Limited-Service Hotel

★ **BEST WESTERN OF HOPE.** *I-30 and Hwy 278, Hope (71801). Phone 870/777-9222; toll-free 800/429-4494; fax 870/777-9077. www.bestwestern. com.* 75 rooms, 2 story. Pets accepted. Check-out noon. Outdoor pool. **$**

Hot Springs and Hot Springs National Park (C-2)

See also Arkadelphia, Benton, Malvern

Settled Town of Hot Springs: 1807
Population 35,750
Elevation 632 ft
Area Code 501
Information Convention & Visitors Bureau, 134 Convention Blvd, PO Box 6000, 71902; phone 501/321-2277 or toll-free 800/772-2489
Web Site www.nps.gov/hosp and www.hotsprings.org

One of the most popular spas and resorts in the United States, the colorful city of Hot Springs surrounds portions of the nearly 4,700-acre Hot Springs National Park. Approximately 1 million gallons of thermal water flow daily from the 47 springs within the park. The springs have been administered by the federal government since 1832.

At an average temperature of 143° F, the water flows to a reservoir under the headquarters building; here it is distributed to bathhouses through insulated pipes. Some of it is cooled to 90° F without being exposed to air or mixed with other water. Bathhouses mix cooled and hot thermal water to regulate bath temperatures. The only differences among bathhouses are in the appointments and service.

The Libbey Memorial Physical Medicine Center specializes in hydrotherapy treatments given under the supervision of a registered physical therapist. Patients may be referred to this center by registered physicians or may get a standard bath without a referral.

Hot Springs, however, is more than a spa. It is a cosmopolitan city visited by travelers from all over the world; it is also a delightful vacation spot in the midst of beautiful wooded hills, valleys, and lakes of the Ouachita region. Swimming, boating, and water sports are available at nearby Catherine, Hamilton, and Ouachita lakes. All three offer good year-round fishing for bream, crappie, bass, and rainbow trout. The 42nd President of the United States, William Jefferson Clinton, grew up

here. A Ranger District office of the Ouachita National Forests is located in Hot Springs.

What to See and Do

Arkansas Alligator Farm & Petting Zoo. *847 Whittington Ave, Hot Springs (71901). Phone 501/623-6172. www.hotspringsusa.com/gatorfarm.* Houses alligators, rhesus monkeys, mountain lions, llamas, pygmy goats, ducks, and other animals. (Daily) **$$**

Auto tours. *Fountain St and Hot Springs Mountain Dr, Hot Springs. Phone 501/321-2277.* Just north of Bathhouse Row, drive from the end of Fountain Street up Hot Springs Mountain Drive to scenic overlooks at Hot Springs Mountain Tower and a picnic area on the mountaintop. West Mountain Drive, starting from either Prospect Avenue (on the south) or from Whittington Avenue (on the north) also provides excellent vistas of the city and surrounding countryside.

Bath House Show. *701 Central Ave, Hot Springs (71901). Phone 501/623-1415. www.thebathhouse-show.com.* Two-hour show of music and comedy acts derivative of 1930s-present; musical anthologies, re-enactments of radio shows. (Feb-Dec, schedule varies; closed Jan) **$$$$**

Belle of Hot Springs. *5200 Central Ave (Hwy 7 S), Hot Springs (71913). Phone 501/525-4438. www.belleriver-boat.com.* Sightseeing, lunch, and dinner cruises along Lake Hamilton on the 400-passenger vessel (Feb-Nov, daily). Charter cruises available.

Coleman's Crystal Mine. *5837 N Hwy 7, Jesseville (71909). 16 miles N on Hwy 7 N. Phone 501/984-5328.* Visitors may dig for quartz crystals; tools supplied. Shop. (Daily; closed Dec 25) **$$$**

Dryden Potteries. *341 Whittington Ave, Hot Springs (71901). Phone 501/623-4201. www.drydenpottery.com.* Pottery-making demonstrations. (Mon-Fri 9 am-3:30 pm, Sat from 10 am; closed Jan 1, Thanksgiving, Dec 25) **FREE**

Hot Springs Mountain Tower. *401 Hot Springs Mountain Dr, Hot Springs (71902). Atop Hot Springs Mountain. Phone 501/623-6035.* Tower rises 216 feet above Hot Springs National Park; glass-enclosed elevator rides 1,256 feet above sea level for spectacular view of Ouachita Mountains; fully enclosed viewing area and higher up there's an open-air deck. (Daily; closed Jan 1, Thanksgiving, Dec 24-25) **$$$**

Josephine Tussaud Wax Museum. *250 Central Ave, Hot Springs (71901). Phone 501/623-5836. www.rideaduck.com.* Set in the former Southern Club, which was the city's largest casino and supper club until the late 1960s, this museum displays more than 100 wax figures. (Summer: Sun-Thurs 9 am-8 pm, Fri-Sat 9 am-9 pm; winter: Sun-Thurs 9:30 am-5 pm, Fri-Sat 9:30 am-8 pm; closed Jan 1, Thanksgiving, Dec 25) **$$**

Lake Catherine State Park. *5386 N Hwy 7, Hot Springs Village (71909). S and E via Hwy 128, 171. Phone 501/844-4176. www.arkansasstateparks.com.*

Mid-America Science Museum. *500 Mid-America Blvd, Hot Springs (71913). Phone 501/767-3461. www.midamericamuseum.org.* Exhibits focus on life, energy, matter, perception, state of Arkansas. Museum features 35,000-gallon freshwater aquarium; erosion table; laser theater. Snack bar (seasonal), gift shop. (Memorial Day-Labor Day: daily 9:30 am-6 pm; rest of year: Tues-Sun 10 am-5 pm; closed Jan 1, Thanksgiving, Dec 24-25) **$$$**

National Park & Hot Springs Duck Tours. *418 Central Ave, Hot Springs (71901). Phone 501/321-2911; toll-free 800/682-7044. www.rideaduck.com.* The "Amphibious Duck" travels on both land and water. Board in the heart of Hot Springs and proceed onto Lake Hamilton around St. John's Island. (Mar-Oct: daily; Nov-Feb: weather permitting) **$$$**

Ouachita National Forest. *100 Reserve St, Hot Springs (71901). 12 miles W on Hwy 270 or 20 miles N on Hwy 7. Phone 501/321-5202. www.fs.fed.us.oonf/ouachita. htm.* The Ouachita (WASH-i-taw), located in 15 counties in west-central Arkansas and southeast Oklahoma, covers approximately 1.7 million acres and includes 7 wilderness areas, 35 developed recreation areas, 7 equestrian trails, 9 navigable rivers, and 8 lakes suitable for boating. Some recreation areas charge fees. For more information, contact the Forest Supervisor, PO Box 1270, 71902. (Daily)On Lake Ouachita is

Lake Ouachita State Park. *5451 Mountain Pine Rd, Mountain Pine (71956). 3 miles W on Hwy 270, 12 miles N on Hwy 227. Phone 501/767-9366.* Approximately 400 acres. Swimming, fishing, boating (rentals, marina); hiking trails, picnicking, camping (hookups, dump station), cabins. Interpretive programs, exhibits. Standard fees. (Daily)

Tiny Town. *374 Whittington Ave, Hot Springs (71901). Phone 501/624-4742.* Indoor train town with trains across America; mechanical display; handmade miniatures. (Apr-Nov, Mon-Sat) **$$**

⭐ **Walking tour.** Start at

Bathhouse Row. *Central Ave, Hot Springs (71902). Phone 501/624-3383.* Self-guided tours of the Fordyce Bathhouse are offered. (Daily; closed July 4, Thanksgiving, Dec 25)

Grand Promenade. *Grand Promenade and Fountain sts, Hot Springs (71902). Phone 501/624-3383.* Leads through a landscaped park above and behind Bathhouse Row, offering pleasant vistas of the city.

Park Headquarters and Visitor Center. *101 Reserve St, Hot Springs (71901). Phone 501/624-3383.* Exhibit on workings and origin of the hot springs. A self-guided nature trail starts here and follows the Grand Promenade. Visitor center is located in the Hill Wheatley Plaza at the park entrance (daily; closed Jan 1, Dec 25). Gulpha Gorge Campground is available for stays limited to 14 days April-October, and to 30 days in a calendar year (fee). Inquire at National Park Fordyce Visitor Center on Bathhouse Row.

Two Open Hot Springs. *Hot Springs. At the S end of Bathouse Row. Phone 501/623-6172.*

Special Event

Thoroughbred racing. *Oaklawn Jockey Club, 2705 Central Ave, Hot Springs (71902). Phone 501/623-4411; toll-free 800/625-5296. www.oaklawn.com.* While watching and wagering on live races at Oaklawn, fans can also follow simulcast races or dine on a variety of tasty treats. Daily, Jan-Apr.

Limited-Service Hotels

⭐ **DAYS INN.** *106 Lookout Pt, Hot Springs (71913). Phone 501/525-5666; toll-free 800/995-9559; fax 501/525-5666. www.daysinn.com.* 58 rooms, 2 story. Check-out 11 am. Outdoor pool, whirlpool. **$**
▨

⭐ **HAMPTON INN.** *151 Temperance Hill Rd, Hot Springs (71913). Phone 501/525-7000; toll-free 800/426-7866; fax 501/525-7626. www.hamptoninn. com.* 82 rooms, 4 story. Complimentary continental breakfast. Check-out 11 am. Outdoor pool. **$**
▨

Full-Service Hotels

⭐⭐⭐ **ARLINGTON RESORT HOTEL AND SPA.** *239 Central Ave, Hot Springs (71901). Phone*

501/623-7771; toll-free 800/643-1502; fax 501/623-2243. www.arlingtonhotel.com. Guests will find total relaxation and enjoyment at this resort in the beautiful Ouachita Mountains of the Hot Springs National Park. Guests can unwind in twin cascading pools or in the refreshing outdoor mountainside hot tub. 484 rooms, 11 story. Check-out 11 am. Restaurant, bar. Fitness room. Two outdoor pools, whirlpool. Tennis. Grand old hotel (circa 1925); overlooks park. **$**

★ ★ ★ **THE AUSTIN HOTEL & CONVENTION CENTER.** 305 Malvern Ave, Hot Springs (71901). Phone 501/623-6600; toll-free 877/623-6697; fax 501/624-7160. www.theaustinhotel.com. This wonderful getaway is located in the Hot Springs Park with a spectacular view of the Ouachita Mountains. It is a unique setting for guests to rejuvenate themselves with a visit to the famous spa in the park. Art galleries and music shows are just a few miles away; also connected to the Hot Springs Convention Center via covered walkway. 200 rooms, 14 story. Check-out 11 am. High-speed Internet access. Restaurant, bar. Spa. Indoor, outdoor pool; whirlpool. **$$**

Restaurants

★ ★ **BOHEMIA.** 517 Park Ave, Hot Springs (71901). Phone 501/623-9661; fax 501/623-9661. Czech, German menu. Lunch, dinner. Closed Sun; holidays; also part of Dec, Jan. Children's menu. **$**

★ **CAJUN BOILERS.** 2806 Albert Pike Hwy, Hot Springs (71913). Phone 501/767-5695; fax 501/767-0952. Cajun menu. Lunch, dinner. Closed Sun-Mon; Thanksgiving, Dec 25. Children's menu. Dock for boat dining. **$$**

★ ★ **COY'S STEAK HOUSE.** 300 Coy St, Hot Springs (71901). Phone 501/321-1414; fax 501/321-1497. Seafood, steak menu. Dinner. Closed Thanksgiving, Dec 24-25, 31. Bar. Children's menu. Valet parking. **$$$**

★ ★ ★ **HAMILTON HOUSE.** 130 Van Lyell Trail, Hot Springs (71913). Phone 501/520-4040; fax 501/525-1717. This is the most appropriate choice in town for a dress-up, fine-dining occasion. The restaurant occupies four stories of an old estate home with seating in several cozy dining rooms. The quiet, peninsula setting is on beautiful Lake Hamilton. American menu. Dinner, Sun brunch. Closed holidays. Bar. Children's menu. Outdoor seating. **$$$**

★ ★ **HOT SPRINGS BRAU-HOUSE.** 801 Central Ave, Hot Springs (71901). Phone 501/624-7866. German menu. Dinner. Closed Mon; holidays. Bar. Children's menu. Outdoor seating. In cellar of 110-year-old building. **$**

★ **MCCLARD'S BAR-B-Q.** 505 Albert Pike, Hot Springs (71913). Phone 501/624-9586. Lunch, dinner. Closed Sun-Mon; Thanksgiving, Dec 25. Children's menu. Casual attire. **$**

★ **MOLLIE'S.** 538 W Grand Ave, Hot Springs (71901). Phone 501/623-6582. American menu. Lunch, dinner. Closed Sun; Jan 1, Thanksgiving, Dec 25. Bar. Children's menu. Outdoor seating. **$$**

Jonesboro (B-4)

See also Pocahontas, Walnut Ridge

Founded 1859
Population 55,515
Elevation 320 ft
Area Code 870
Zip 72401
Information Greater Jonesboro Chamber of Commerce, 1709 E Nettleton, PO Box 789, 72403; phone 870/932-6691
Web Site www.jonesborochamber.org

The largest city in northeast Arkansas, Jonesboro is on Crowley's Ridge, the long, narrow ridge of loess (fine, windblown, yellowish loam) that stretches 150 miles from the Missouri line to Helena, more or less parallel to the Mississippi River. Rice, cotton, soybean, wheat, and livestock processing, manufacturing, and shipping are the principal businesses of this community; education and medicine are also important. Hunting and fishing are popular in this area.

What to See and Do

Arkansas State University. 106 N Caraway, Jonesboro (72401). NE edge of city on Hwy 49. Phone 870/972-2100. www.astate.edu. (1909) (10,568 students) Nine colleges and a graduate school on 941-acre campus. Tours of campus. Also here is

> **Ellis Library, Convocation Center and Museum.** Jonesboro. Houses natural and state history displays. (Daily)

Craighead Forest Park. 4910 S Culberhouse, Jonesboro (72401). 2 miles S on Hwy 141. Phone 870/933-4604.

Approximately 600 acres with swimming, fishing, paddleboats; picnicking, playground, camping (hookups, showers, dump station). Fee for most activities. (Daily; closed Jan 1, Thanksgiving, Dec 25) **FREE**

Crowley's Ridge State Park. *2092 Hwy 168, Walcott (72474). 15 miles N on Hwy 141. Phone 870/573-6751. www.arkansasstateparks.com.* This 271-acre area, once a campground for the Quapaw, has two lakes, miles of wooded hills, and is colorful with dogwood in season. The ridge is named for Benjamin Crowley, whose homestead and burial place are here. Swimming (lifeguard), fishing, boating (paddleboat rentals); hiking trails. Picnicking, playground, snack bar (summer), store. Camping (many hookups, dump station), cabins. Interpretive programs (summer). (Daily)

Lake Frierson State Park. *7904 Hwy 141, Jonesboro (72401). 10 miles N on Hwy 141. Phone 870/932-2615. www.arkansasstateparks.com.* Famous for its brilliant array of dogwood blossoms in spring, this 135-acre park is located on the eastern shore of 350-acre Lake Frierson, which fronts the western edge of Crowley's Ridge. Fishing, boating (rentals, ramp); hiking trails. Picnicking, playground. Camping. (Daily)

Limited-Service Hotels

★ ★ **HOLIDAY INN.** *3006 S Caraway Rd, Jonesboro (72401). Phone 870/935-2030; fax 870/935-3440. www. holiday-inn.com.* 179 rooms, 2 story. Pets accepted, some restrictions. Check-out noon. Restaurant, bar. Fitness room. Indoor pool, whirlpool. Airport transportation available. **$**

★ **HOLIDAY INN EXPRESS.** *2407 Phillips Dr, Jonesboro (72401). Phone 870/932-5554; toll-free 800/465-4329; fax 870/932-2586. www.hiexpress.com.* 103 rooms, 4 story. Pets accepted. Complimentary continental breakfast. Check-in, check-out noon. High-speed Internet access, wireless Internet access. Fitness room. Outdoor pool. Airport transportation available. Business center. **$**

Restaurant

★ **FRONT PAGE CAFE.** *2117 E Parker, Jonesboro (72404). Phone 870/932-6343.* Breakfast, lunch, dinner. Closed July 4, Thanksgiving, Dec 25. Casual attire. **$**

Little Rock (C-3)

See also Benton, Searcy

Settled Little Rock: 1812
Population 183,133
Elevation 286 ft
Area Code 501
Information Little Rock Convention & Visitors Bureau, Robinson Center, Markham & Broadway, PO Box 3232, Little Rock 72203; phone 501/376-4781 or toll-free 800/844-4781
Web Site www.littlerock.com

These two separate cities on opposite sides of the Arkansas River are closely allied in every way and, from the standpoint of the tourist, are one community. Little Rock, the state capital, is a regional center for transportation, entertainment, culture, medicine, education, commerce, and industry. More than a "city of roses," it is known for its warm hospitality and recreational facilities. Little Rock is a modern, forward-looking capital.

Little Rock apparently got its name from French explorers who called this site on the Arkansas River "La Petite Roche" to distinguish it from larger rock outcroppings up the river. The first shack probably was built on the site in 1812, and by 1819, a town site had been staked. The community became the territorial capital in 1821 when the seat of government was moved here from Arkansas Post (see). The first steamboat, the *Eagle*, came up the Arkansas River in 1822.

Additional Information

Travelers may stop at the visitor information centers (daily) at the Statehouse Convention Center, and Little Rock National Airport to get more information. Telefun, 501/372-3399, is a 24-hour prerecorded entertainment hotline with a bi-weekly update on events in the Little Rock area. For any additional information, contact the Little Rock Convention & Visitors Bureau, Statehouse Plaza, PO Box 3232, Little Rock 72203; 501/376-4781 or 800/844-4781.

What to See and Do

Arkansas Arts Center. *MacArthur Park, 501 E 9th St, Little Rock (72202). Phone 501/372-4000. www.arkarts. com.* Exhibits include paintings, drawings, prints, sculpture, and ceramics; public classes in visual and performing arts; library, restaurant, theater. Performances by the Arkansas Arts Center Children's Theater; community events. (Tues-Sat 10 am-5 pm, Sun from 11 am; closed Dec 25) **FREE**

Arkansas Repertory Theatre. *601 Main St, Little Rock (72203). Phone toll-free 866/684-3737. www.therep.org.* Professional theatrical productions.

Arkansas Symphony Orchestra. *Robinson Center Music Hall, 2417 N Tyler St, Little Rock (72207). Phone 501/666-1761. www.arkansassymphony.org.* For schedule, contact Arkansas Symphony Orchestra Society, PO Box 7328, Little Rock 72217. (Sept-May)

Burns Park. *1 Eldor Johnson Dr, North Little Rock (72119). Off I-40 at exit 150. Phone 501/791-8537.* More than 1,500 acres with fishing, boating; wildlife trail; 27-hole golf, miniature golf, tennis. Camping (10-day maximum). Amusement rides; 9-hole Frisbee golf course. Fee for some activities. (Daily) **FREE**

Decorative Arts Museum. *501 E 9th St, Little Rock (72202). Phone 501/372-4000.* Restored Greek Revival mansion (1839) houses decorative art objects ranging from Greek and Roman period to contemporary American; ceramics, glass, textiles, crafts, Asian works of art. (Tues-Sat) **FREE**

Museum of Discovery. *500 President Clinton Ave, Little Rock (72201). In River Market Entertainment District. Phone 501/396-7050; toll-free 800/880-6475. www. amod.org.* Exhibits on the sciences, social sciences, and technology. (Mon-Sat; closed holidays) **$$$**

Old Mill. *Lakeshore and Fairway Ave, North Little Rock (72116). Phone 501/791-8537.* (1828) Old waterwheel gristmill. Two stones on the road to the mill are original milestones laid out by Jefferson Davis. This scenic city park is famous for its appearance in the opening scene of *Gone with the Wind.* (Daily) **FREE**

Pinnacle Mountain State Park. *11901 Pinnacle Valley Rd, Little Rock (72223). 7 miles W via Hwy 10, 2 miles N via Hwy 300. Phone 501/868-5806. www. arkansasstateparks.com.* A cone-shaped mountain juts 1,000 feet above this heavily forested, 1,800-acre park; bordered on the west by 9,000-acre Lake Maumelle. Fishing; boating (ramps); hiking, backpacking, picnicking, playground. Gift shop. Visitor center with natural history exhibits; interpretive programs. (Daily; closed Thanksgiving, Dec 25)

⭐ **Quapaw Quarter Historic Neighborhoods.** *1315 Scott St, Little Rock and North Little Rock. Phone 501/371-0075.* Encompassing the original town of Little Rock and its early additions through the turn of the century, this area contains three National Register historic districts and well over 150 buildings listed on the National Register of Historic Places. Named for Arkansas' native Quapaw, the area includes sites and structures associated with the history of Arkansas' capital city from the 1820s to the present. A tour of historic houses in the area is held the first weekend of May. Contact the Quapaw Quarter Association, PO Box 165023, 72216. Restored sites in the area include

Historic Arkansas Museum. *200 E 3rd St, Little Rock (72201). Phone 501/324-9351.* Built in the 1820s-1850s, the restoration includes four houses, outbuildings, and a log house arranged to give a realistic picture of pre-Civil War Arkansas. The museum houses Arkansas-made exhibits and a crafts shop. Guided tours. (Mon-Sat 9 am-5 pm, Sun 1-5 pm; closed holidays) **$**

The Old State House. *300 W Markham St, Little Rock (72201). Phone 501/324-9685.* Originally designed by Kentucky architect Gideon Shryock, this beautiful Greek Revival building was the capitol from 1836 to 1911; it now houses a museum of Arkansas history. Features include: restored governor's office and legislative chambers; Granny's Attic, a hands-on exhibit; President William J. Clinton exhibit; interpretive display of Arkansas' First Ladies' gowns. Self-guided tours.(Mon-Sat 9 am-5 pm, Sun 1-5 pm) **FREE**

Villa Marre. *1321 Scott St, Little Rock (72202). Phone 501/371-0075.* (1881) Restored Italianate mansion reflects the exuberance of the period with ornate parquet floors, walnut woodwork, and highly decorated stenciled ceilings; antique furnishings are mainly Victorian with some American empire and Edwardian pieces. The house is featured in the opening credits of TV series *Designing Women.* Tours (Mon-Fri mornings, also Sun afternoons). **$$**

State Capitol. *1 State Capitol, Little Rock (72201). W end of Capitol Ave. Phone 501/682-5080.* A reduced-scale replica of the nation's capitol, the building is constructed of Batesville (AR) limestone. On the south lawn is a 1,600-bush rose garden comprising 150 varieties. The legislature meets the second Mon in Jan of odd-numbered years for 60 days. Self-guided and guided tours (Mon-Fri). **FREE**

Toltec Mounds Archeological State Park. *490 Toltec Mounds Rd, Scott (72142). 15 miles SE of North Little*

Rock, off Hwy 165 on Hwy 386. *Phone 501/961-9442. www.arkansasstateparks.com.* This 182-acre park is the site of one of the largest and most complex prehistoric Native American settlements in the Lower Mississippi Valley; several mounds and a remnant of the embankment are visible. Guided on-site tours (by appointment; fee); a paved trail is accessible to the disabled. Tours depart from the visitor center, which has exhibits explaining how archaeologists work and the history of the site, as well as audiovisual programs and an archaeological laboratory. (Tues-Sat, also Sun afternoons; closed holidays) **$$**

War Memorial Park. *300 S Monroe, Little Rock (72205). Phone 501/664-6976.* On approximately 202 acres are rides and amusements. Golf, tennis, fitness center. Picnicking. (Daily) Also here is

    Little Rock Zoo. *, Little Rock (72205). Phone 501/666-2406.* More than 500 animals on 40 acres. (Nov-Mar daily, 9:30 am-4:30 pm, rest of year to 5 pm; closed Jan 1, Thanksgiving, Dec 25) **$$$**

Wild River Country. *6820 Crystal Hill Rd, North Little Rock (72118). Jct I-40 and I-430, Crystal Hill Rd. Phone 501/753-8600. www.wildrivercountry.com.* A 23-acre themed water park with nine different water attractions. (June-Labor Day: daily; May: weekends) **$$$$**

Special Events

Arkansas All-Arabian Horse Show. *Barton Coliseum, 2600 Howard St, Little Rock (72206). Phone 501/372-8341.* Second full weekend in Apr.

Arkansas State Fair and Livestock Show. *2300 W Roosevelt Rd, Little Rock (72206). Phone 501/372-8341. www.arkfairgrounds.com.* Enjoy some down-home fun at this popular fair, which attracts more than 400,000 people over its ten-day run. Live music, motor sports, rodeos, and children's shows, as well as a 10-acre Midway with carnival rides, food, and games will surely please every member of the family. Early-mid Oct.**$$**

Riverfest. *Riverfront Park, Little Rock. Phone 501/255-3378. www.riverfestarkansas.com.* Visual and performing arts festival includes exhibits by 60 artists; ballet, symphony, opera, theater, jazz, bluegrass, and rock groups; children's area; bike race, 5-mile run; concessions. Memorial Day weekend.

Wildwood Festival. *20919 Denny Rd, Little Rock (72223). Phone 501/821-7275; toll-free 888/278-7727.* Series of musical programs, exhibits, lectures, and events centered on the performing arts. Late May-June.

Limited-Service Hotels

★ **BEST WESTERN GOVERNORS SUITES.** *1501 Merrill Dr, Little Rock (72211). Phone 501/224-8051; toll-free 800/422-8051; fax 501/224-8051. www.bestwestern.com.* 49 rooms, 3 story, all suites. Complimentary full breakfast. Check-out noon. Outdoor pool, whirlpool. **$**
🏊

★ ★ **COURTYARD BY MARRIOTT.** *10900 Financial Centre Pkwy, Little Rock (72211). Phone 501/227-6000; toll-free 800/321-2211; fax 501/227-6912. www.courtyard.com.* 149 rooms, 3 story. Check-out noon. Restaurant, bar. Fitness room. Outdoor pool, whirlpool. **$**
🏃 🏊

★ **HAMPTON INN.** *6100 Mitchell Dr, Little Rock (72209). Phone 501/562-6667; toll-free 800/426-7866; fax 501/568-6832. www.hamptoninn.com.* 122 rooms, 4 story. Complimentary continental breakfast. Check-out noon. Outdoor pool. **$**
🏊

★ ★ **LA QUINTA INN.** *11701 I-30, Little Rock (72209). Phone 501/455-2300; toll-free 800/687-6667; fax 501/455-5876. www.laquinta.com.* 145 rooms, 3 story. Pets accepted, some restrictions. Complimentary continental breakfast. Check-out noon. Restaurant, bar. Outdoor pool, whirlpool. **$**
🐾 🏊

Full-Service Hotels

★ ★ ★ **THE CAPITAL HOTEL.** *111 W Markham St, Little Rock (72201). Phone 501/374-7474; toll-free 800/766-7666; fax 501/370-7091. www.thecapitalhotel.com.* Built in 1876, this hotel is at home amidst Little Rock's historical district. Turn-of-the-century ambiance and attentive service will be found throughout the hotel. 125 rooms, 4 story. Check-out 1 pm. Restaurant, bar. **$$**

★ ★ ★ **THE PEABODY LITTLE ROCK.** *3 Statehouse Plz, Little Rock (72201). Phone 501/375-5000; fax 501/375-4721.* Travelers to historic Little Rock would be hard-pressed to find a place more heartwarming than The Peabody, located on the banks of the Arkansas River. Special memories are made here, where twice daily the hotels five North American mallards, four hens, and one drake march to the tune of John Philip Sousa's *King Cotton March* to take a splash in the fountain. The ducks aren't the only ones treated with kid gloves here; guests can expect to be cosseted in this thoroughly modern hotel. Whether traveling for business or pleasure, visitors appreciate the plentiful guest services and sophisticated accommodations. Gourmet dining at Capriccio rounds out the unique experience at this cherished hotel. 417 rooms, 19 story. Check-out 11 am. Three restaurants, bar. Fitness room. Airport transportation available. Business center. **$$**

Full-Service Inn

★ ★ ★ **EMPRESS OF LITTLE ROCK.** *2120 S Louisiana, Little Rock (72206). Phone 501/374-7966; toll-free 877/374-7966. www.theempress.com.* Step back in time to the 19th century at this fully restored Queen Anne-style mansion built in 1888. With ornate architecture and unique antique-filled suites, guests will feel like royalty as they experience a high dose of southern hospitality here. All rooms are named after historic Arkansas figures. 5 rooms. Complimentary full breakfast. Check-in 3 pm. Check-out 11 am. **$$**

Restaurants

★ ★ **1620.** *1620 Market St, Little Rock (72211). Phone 501/221-1620; fax 501/221-1921.* American menu. Dinner. Closed Sun; holidays. Bar. **$$**

★ **BROWNING'S.** *5805 Kavanaugh Blvd, Little Rock (72207). Phone 501/663-9956.* Mexican, American menu. Lunch, dinner. Closed Sun-Mon; holidays. Children's menu. **$$**

★ **BRUNO'S LITTLE ITALY.** *315 N Bowman Rd #15, Little Rock (72211). Phone 501/224-4700. www. brunoslittleitaly.com.* Italian menu. Dinner. Closed Sun; holidays. Children's menu. **$$**

★ **BUFFALO GRILL.** *1611 Rebsamen Park Rd, Little Rock (72202). Phone 501/663-2158; fax 501/663-7698.* Lunch, dinner. Closed Sun; Thanksgiving, Dec 25. Children's menu. **$**

★ **CHIP'S BARBECUE.** *9801 W Markham St, Little Rock (72205). Phone 501/225-4346; fax 501/225-1056.* Lunch, dinner. Closed Mon. Children's menu. **$**

★ **FADED ROSE.** *1619 Rebsamen Park Rd, Little Rock (72207). Phone 501/663-9734.* American, Cajun menu. Lunch, dinner. Closed Thanksgiving, Dec 25. Bar. Children's menu. Casual attire. **$$**

★ ★ **GRAFFITI'S.** *7811 Cantrell Rd, Little Rock (72207). Phone 501/224-9079; fax 501/224-9161.* Italian menu. Dinner. Closed Sun; holidays. Bar. **$$**

★ ★ **SIR LOIN'S INN.** *801 W 29th St, North Little Rock (72115). Phone 501/753-1361; fax 501/753-3379.* Dinner. Closed Sun; holidays. Bar. **$$$**

Magnolia (E-2)

See also Camden, El Dorado

Founded 1852
Population 10,858
Elevation 325 ft
Area Code 870
Information Magnolia-Columbia County Chamber of Commerce, 202 N Pine, PO Box 866, 71754; phone 870/234-4352

Created to serve as the seat of Columbia County, Magnolia was largely dependent on cotton for many years. The town boomed with the discovery of oil in 1937. Today there are many wells in the vicinity, as well as chemical, aluminum, plastic, steel, lumber, and structural wood plants.

What to See and Do

Logoly State Park. *31 Columbia 459, Mc Neil (71752). 6 miles N on Hwy 79, on County 47 (Logoly Rd). Phone 870/695-3561. www.arkansasstateparks.com.* Situated on 368 acres of forested coastal plain, this park is the first in Arkansas' system to be set aside for environmental education. Formerly a Boy Scout camp, Logoly represents southern Arkansas before commercial logging operations began. Most of the park has been designated a Natural Area because of its unique plant life and 11 natural springs. Well-marked hiking trails, observation stands, and photo blinds. Picnicking. Tent camping. Visitor center displays flora, fauna, and history of the area; interpretive programs, exhibits. (Daily; closed Jan 1, Dec 25) **FREE**

Southern Arkansas University. *100 E University St, Magnolia (71753). N on N Jackson St, off Hwy 79. Phone 870/235-4000. www.saumag.edu.* (1909) (2,700 students) On a 781-acre campus are a Greek theater and model farm; Ozmer House, an original dog-trot style farmhouse; Carl White Caddo Native American Collection is on permanent display in the Magale Library. Campus tours.

Limited-Service Hotel

★ ★ **BEST WESTERN COACHMAN'S INN.** *420 E Main St, Magnolia (71753). Phone 870/234-6122; toll-free 800/237-6122; fax 870/234-1254. www.best-western.com.* 84 rooms, 2 story. Pets accepted, some restrictions; fee. Complimentary continental breakfast. Check-out noon. Restaurant. Outdoor pool. **$**

Malvern (D-2)

See also Arkadelphia, Benton, Hot Springs and Hot Springs National Park

Population 9,021
Elevation 312 ft
Area Code 501
Zip 72104
Information Chamber of Commerce, 213 W 3rd St, PO Box 266; phone 501/332-2721
Web Site www.malvernchamber.com

Although dubbed "the brick capital of the world," Malvern also manufactures lumber and aluminum. The city also has small mining operations, mostly in barium and rare minerals.

What to See and Do

Hot Springs National Park. *101 Reserve St, Hot Springs (71901). 20 miles NW via Hwy 270. www.nps.gov/hosp.* (see).

Jenkins' Ferry State Historic Monument. *16 miles E on Hwy 270, 6 miles S on Hwy 291, 2 miles SW on Hwy 46.* Civil War battleground site. Exhibits.

Special Events

Brickfest. *Courthouse grounds, 305 Locust St, Malvern (72104). Phone 501/332-2721.* Town festival with bands, singing groups, arts and crafts, contests, concession stands. Last weekend in June.

Hot Spring County Fair and Rodeo. *Fairgrounds. Phone 501/332-5267.* Weekend after Labor Day.

Limited-Service Hotel

★ **SUPER 8.** *Hwy 270 W; RR 8 Box 719-6, Malvern (72104). Phone 501/332-5755; toll-free 800/800-8000; fax 501/332-3401. www.super8.com.* 74 rooms, 2 story. Complimentary continental breakfast. Check-out 11 am. **$**

Marion

What to See and Do

America's Best Campground Memphis. *7037 I-55, Marion (72364). Phone 870/739-4801; toll-free 888/857-4890. www.tldirectory.com.* 100 sites, 68 full hook-ups, 34 with water and electricity. Laundry services, convenience store, ice. Pool, playground, volleyball and basketball courts.

Mena (C-1)

Founded 1896
Population 5,637
Elevation 1,150 ft
Area Code 479
Zip 71953
Information Mena/Polk County Chamber of Commerce, 524 Sherwood St; phone 479/394-2912
Web Site www.mena-ark.com

This town was named after the wife of a Dutch coffee broker who provided financial assistance for the construction of the Kansas City, Pittsburg, and Gulf Railroad (now Kansas City Southern Railroad). A Ranger District office of the Ouachita National Forests (see HOT SPRINGS and HOT SPRINGS NATIONAL PARK) is located here.

What to See and Do

Janssen Park. *Janssen and 7th sts, Mena (71953). Opposite post office. Phone 479/394-2382.* Historic park contains a log cabin built in 1851; two small lakes, a spring, and picnic areas.

Queen Wilhelmina State Park. *3877 Hwy 88 W, Mena (71953). 13 miles NW on Hwy 88. Phone 479/394-2863; toll-free 800/264-2477.* This 640-acre park atop Rich Mountain boasts magnificent scenery and more than 100 species of flowers, mosses, and ferns. A miniature railroad takes visitors on a 1 1/2-mile circuit of the mountaintop in the summer (fee). The original inn (1898) was built by the Kansas City Railroad as a luxury retreat; financed by Dutch investors, the inn was named for the reigning queen of the Netherlands. The current building is a reconstruction of the original. The park also offers hiking trails, miniature golf; picnicking, playground; store, restaurant. Camping (electric and water hookups), shower facilities. Interpretive programs, exhibits (summer). (Daily) Also here is

Talimena Scenic Drive. *524 Sherwood Ave, Mena (71953). Follow Hwy 88 N and W, Hwy 1. Phone 479/394-2912.* This 55-mile "roller-coaster" drive through the Ouachita National Forests to Talihina, OK, passes through the park and other areas rich in botanical and geological interest. In addition to campgrounds in the park, there are other camping locations along the drive (fees may be charged). Drive may be difficult in winter.

Special Event

Ouachita Hertiage Days. *Downtown. Phone 479/394-2912.* Festival in honor of famed radio personalities features arts and crafts, fiddlers' contest, entertainment. First weekend in June.

Specialty Lodging

QUEEN WILHELMINA LODGE. *3877 Hwy 88 W, Mena (71953). Phone 479/394-2863; fax 479/394-0061.* 38 rooms, 2 story. Check-out 11 am. Restaurant. Children's activity center. Airport transportation available. **$**

Morrilton (C-2)

See also Conway, Petit Jean State Park, Russellville

Founded 1870
Population 6,550
Area Code 501
Zip 72110
Information Chamber of Commerce, 120 N Division; phone 501/354-2393

What to See and Do

Museum of Automobiles. *8 Jones Ln, Morrilton (72110). 15 miles SW of Morrilton. Phone 501/727-5427.* Founded by former Arkansas governor Winthrop Rockefeller, the museum features an attractive display of antique and classic cars. There are autos from Rockefeller's personal collection as well as changing exhibits of privately owned cars. (Daily; closed Dec 25) **$$**

Special Event

Great Arkansas PigOut Festival. *120 N Division St, Morrilton (72110). Phone 501/354-2393.* Food, family fun. Softball, volleyball, bike rides, tennis, 3-on-3 basketball tournaments. Children's activities; hog calling, pig chase. Local and nationally known entertainment. First full weekend in Aug.

Mountain Home (A-3)

See also Bull Shoals Lake Area

Population 11,012
Elevation 820 ft
Area Code 870
Zip 72653
Information Chamber of Commerce, PO Box 488; phone 870/425-5111 or toll-free 800/822-3536
Web Site www.enjoymountainhome.com

This is a vacation town situated midway between Arkansas' two big Ozark lakes: Bull Shoals (see) and Norfork. Fishing in lakes and rivers is good; all varieties of water sports are available on both lakes. There are many resorts and marinas in this popular area.

What to See and Do

Norfork Lake. *324 W 7th St, Mountain Home (72653). 9 miles NE on Hwy 62. Phone 870/425-2700. www.norfork.com.* This 40-mile lake, impounded by a dam on the North Fork of the White River, is one of Arkansas' most attractive water vacation areas. It offers water sports and boating (ramps, rentals, ten marinas); fishing for largemouth, striped, and white bass, plus walleye, crappie, bream, bluegill, and catfish; rainbow and brown trout are found in the North Fork River below the dam. Also hunting. Camping (seasonal, some electric hookups; fee); lodges. Toll-free state bridges cross the lake. Fees are charged at some areas. (Daily)

Norfork National Fish Hatchery. *1414 Hwy 177 S, Mountain Home (72653). 12 miles SE on Hwy 5, E on Hwy 177. Phone 870/499-5255.* One of the largest federal trout hatcheries in the country; annually distributes more than two million rainbow, brown, cutthroat, and brook trout. (Daily) **FREE**

Special Events

Baxter County Fair. *Baxter County Fairgrounds. Phone 870/425-6828. www.baxtercountyfair.com.* Families will enjoy the Horse Fun Show, carnival, and live bands; children can participate in a hula hoop contest, treasure hunt, and pogo jump. Mid-Sept.

Red, White and Blues Festival. *Fairgrounds. Phone 870/425-5111.* Blues music, food, beer. Late June

Limited-Service Hotel

★ ★ **BEST WESTERN CARRIAGE INN.** *963 Hwy 62 E, Mountain Home (72653). Phone 870/425-6001; toll-free 800/780-7234; fax 870/425-6001. www.bestwestern.com.* 82 rooms, 2 story. Pets accepted, some restrictions. Check-out noon. Restaurant. Outdoor pool. **$**

Restaurant

★ **FRED'S FISH HOUSE.** *Hwy 62 E, Mountain Home (72653). Phone 870/492-5958.* Seafood, steak menu. Lunch, dinner. Closed Sun; Thanksgiving, Dec 25. Children's menu. Outdoor seating. **$$**

Mountain View (B-3)

See also Batesville, Greers Ferry Lake Area

Population 2,876
Elevation 768 ft
Area Code 870
Zip 72560
Information Mountain View Area Chamber of Commerce, PO Box 133; phone 870/269-8068
Web Site www.ozarkgetaways.com

The folk music heritage brought to these mountains by the early settlers is still an important part of the community today. Each Saturday night, if the weather is nice, folks head for the courthouse square with chairs and instruments to hear and play music. A Ranger District office of the Ozark National Forest (see RUSSELLVILLE) also is here.

What to See and Do

Blanchard Springs Caverns. *Mountain View. 15 miles NW on Hwy 14, in Ozark National Forest. Phone 870/757-2211; toll-free 888/757-2246.* Spectacular "living" caverns feature crystalline formations, an underground river, and huge chambers. Guided tours depart from visitor information center, which has an exhibit hall and free movie; one-hour tour of the 1/2-mile Dripstone Trail (year-round) and 1 3/4-hour tour of more strenuous 1 1/4-mile Discovery Trail (summer only). (Apr-Oct, daily; Nov-Mar, Wed-Sun; closed Jan 1, Thanksgiving, Dec 25). **$$$**

Ozark Folk Center State Park. *Mountain View. 2 miles N on Hwy 382. Phone 870/269-3851; toll-free 800/264-3655. www.ozarkfolkcenter.com.* This 915-acre site has an 80-acre, 50-building living museum complex dedicated to Ozark folk heritage, crafts, and music. Using skills, tools, and materials of the period 1820-1920, artisans demonstrate basketry, quilt-making, and woodcarving and re-create informal gatherings. Lodge, restaurant, 1,000-seat music auditorium, outdoor stage with 300 covered seats; special events all year (see SPECIAL EVENTS). Crafts area (daily); music shows (Mon-Sat evenings). (Mid-Apr-Oct, daily)

Special Events

Arkansas Folk Festival. *Citywide. Phone 870/269-8068. www.ozarkgetaways.com/folk_festival.html.* Relax in the shade of blooming dogwood trees, browse the arts and crafts, and delight in local fare, all the while taking in enjoyable acoustic music. Third weekend in Apr.

Arkansas State Old-Time Fiddle Contest. *Ozark Folk Center, Hwy 382, Mountain View (72560). Phone 870/269-3851; toll-free 800/264-3655. www.ozarkfolkcenter.com.* This annual event celebrates the talent of fiddlers from the state of Arkansas. Early Oct.

Bean Fest and Great Arkansas Championship Outhouse Race. *Courthouse Sq, Mountain View (72560). Phone 870/269-8068.* Homemade "outhouses" race around Courthouse Square. Music, bean cook-off, games. Last Sat in Oct.

Herb Harvest Fall Festival. *Ozark Folk Center, Hwy 382, Mountain View (72560). Phone 870/269-3851.* Concerts, crafts demonstrations, races, fiddlers' jamboree, contests. Early Oct.

Tribute to Merle Travis: National Thumbpicking Guitar Contest. *Ozark Folk Center, Hwy 382, Mountain View (72560). Phone 870/269-3851. www.ozarkfolkcenter.com.* This two-day event and contest honors the guitarist, singer, and composer Merle Travis who mastered the thumb and finger guitar technique. Mid-May.

Limited-Service Hotel

★ **BEST WESTERN FIDDLERS INN.** *601 Sylamore Ave, Mountain View (72560). Phone 870/269-2828; toll-free 800/780-7234; fax 870/269-2570. www.bestwestern.com.* 48 rooms, 2 story. Check-out 11 am. Outdoor pool. **$**

Specialty Lodging

INN AT MOUNTAIN VIEW. *307 W Washington, Mountain View (72560). Phone 870/269-4200; toll-free 800/535-1301; fax 870/269-2956. www.innatmounta-inview.com.* 10 rooms, 2 story. No children allowed. Complimentary full breakfast. Check-in 2 pm, check-out 11 am. Built in 1886. **$**

Murfreesboro (D-1)

See also Hope

Population 1,764
Elevation 340 ft
Area Code 870
Zip 71958
Information Chamber of Commerce, PO Box 166; phone 870/285-3131
Web Site www.murfreesboroarkansas.info

What to See and Do

Crater of Diamonds State Park. *RR 1, Box 364, Murfreesboro . 2 miles SE on Hwy 301. Phone 870/285-3113. www.craterofdiamondsstatepark.com.* This 888-acre pine-covered area along the banks of the Little Missouri River contains the only North American diamond mine open to the public (fee; assessment and certification free). Worked commercially from 1906-1949, this rare 36 1/2-acre field is open to amateur diamond hunters. More than 70,000 diamonds have been found here, including such notables as Uncle Sam (40.23 carats), Amarillo Starlight (16.37 carats), and Star of Arkansas (15.33 carats). Other stones found here include amethyst, agate, jasper, quartz. Hiking trail. Picnicking, playground, coin laundry, restaurant (seasonal). Camping (hookups, dump station; standard fees). Visitor center; exhibits; interpretive programs. (Daily; closed Jan 1, Thanksgiving, Dec 25) **$$**

The Ka-Do-Ha Indian Village. *1010 Caddo Dr, Murfreesboro (71958). Off Hwy 27, follow signs.Phone 870/285-3736.* Excavated ancient Native American ceremonial site; prehistoric mound builder village; trading post; museum; arrowhead hunting; tours of excavations. (Daily; closed Thanksgiving, Dec 25) **$$** Opposite is

> **Arkansas Horse Park.** *Murfreesboro.* Features the Peruvian Paso, "the world's smoothest-riding horse." Video history of breed. Self-guided stable tours. (Daily) **FREE**

Newport (B-4)

See also Batesville

Founded 1875
Population 7,811
Elevation 224 ft
Area Code 870
Zip 72112
Information Newport Area Chamber of Commerce, 201 Hazel St, PO Box 518; phone 870/523-3618
Web Site www.newportar.org

The town was named Newport because in 1873, it was a new port on the White River. The seat of Jackson County, it is in an agricultural area with farming as the basic industry. Hunting, boating, and fishing are major recreational activities. The White River, Black River, and 35 lakes are nearby.

What to See and Do

Jacksonport State Park. *205 Avenue St, Jacksonport (72112). 3 miles NW on Hwy 69 in Jacksonport.Phone 870/523-2143. www.arkansasstateparks.com.* Swimming, fishing. Picnicking. Camping (hookups, dump station). (Daily) Also here are

> **Courthouse Museum.** Restored courthouse (1869); furniture represents various periods of Delta life. Indian Room; War Memorial Room with uniforms and relics; original papers. (Tues-Sun; closed Jan 1, Thanksgiving, Dec 24-25) **$$**

> **Mary Woods II.** Refurbished White River steamboat, berthed at Jacksonport Landing, houses maritime museum. (May-early Sept: Tues-Sun; Sept and Oct: weekends)

Special Event

Portfest & State Catfish Cooking Contest. *205 Avenue St, Newport (72075). Phone 870/523-2143.* In Jacksonport State Park (see). Catfish dinners, arts and crafts show, footraces, concerts, stage entertainment, waterski show. First weekend in June.

Limited-Service Hotel

★ ★ **FORTUNE INN AND SUITES.** *907 Hwy 367 N, Newport (72112). Phone 870/523-5851; fax 870/523-9890.* 58 rooms. Pets accepted. Check-out noon. Restaurant, bar. Outdoor pool. **$**

Restaurant

★ ★ ★ **LE BISTRO.** *41 Bowen's Wharf, Newport (02840). Phone 401/849-7778. www.lebistronewport. com.* This casually elegant bistro on Bowmen's Wharf has been serving fresh, flavorful New England specialties and classic French food for decades. French menu. Lunch, dinner. Closed Super Bowl Sun, Thanksgiving. Bar. Business casual attire. Reservations recommended. **$$$**

Paris (C-1)

See also Fort Smith, Russellville

Population 3,707
Elevation 432 ft
Area Code 479
Zip 72855
Information Paris Area Chamber of Commerce, 301 W Walnut; phone 479/963-2244 or toll-free 800/980-8660
Web Site www.paris-ar.com

A Ranger District office of the Ozark National Forest (see RUSSELLVILLE) is located here.

What to See and Do

Blue Mountain Lake. *Waveland. 15 miles S on Hwy 109 to Magazine, then 11 miles E on Hwy 10 to Waveland. Phone 479/947-2372.* Swimming, waterskiing, fishing, boating; hunting. Picnicking. Camping. Fees charged at some areas. (Daily) **FREE**

Cove Lake Recreation Area. *3001 E Walnut St, Paris (72855). 9 miles S via Hwy 309. Phone 479/963-3076.* Near Magazine Mountain, the highest point in the state, with a 160-acre lake. Swimming (fee), fishing, boating (ramps); picnicking, camping (fee). (Year-round, daily) **$$**

Logan County Museum. *202 N Vine, Paris (72855). Phone 479/963-3936.* Historical information and artifacts regarding Paris and Logan County. (Mon-Sat afternoons; closed holidays) **FREE**

Petit Jean State Park (C-2)

See also Morrilton, Russellville

Web Site www.petitjeanstatepark.com

This nearly 3,000-acre rugged area is the oldest, and one of the most beautiful, of the Arkansas parks. Both the park and forested Petit Jean Mountain, 1,100 feet high, are named for a French girl who is said to have disguised herself as a boy to accompany her sailor sweetheart to America. While in the New World, the girl contracted an unknown disease and died, never having returned to France. Legend has it that she was buried on the mountain by friendly Native Americans.

Adjoining the park is the Museum of Automobiles (see MORRILTON) and Winrock Farm, former governor Winthrop Rockefeller's experimental demonstration farm, where he raised Santa Gertrudis cattle. The park also offers a swimming pool (lifeguard); boating (paddleboat, fishing boat rentals). Hiking trails, tennis. Picnicking, playgrounds, restaurant, snack bar (Memorial Day-Labor Day). Camping (hookups, rent-a-camp, dump station), trailer sites, cabins, lodge. Interpretive programs. Visitor center (phone 501/727-5441). Contact the Superintendent, 1285 Petit Jean Mountain Rd, Morrilton 72110.

Pine Bluff (D-3)

See also Arkansas Post National Memorial, Stuttgart

Founded 1819
Population 55,085
Elevation 230 ft
Area Code 870
Information Convention Center & Visitors Bureau, 1 Convention Center Plaza, 71601; phone 870/536-7600 or toll-free 800/536-7660
Web Site www.pinebluffonline.com

Any loyal citizen of Pine Bluff will tell you that, contrary to rumors, the Civil War began right here. In April 1861, several days before Fort Sumter, a musket shot was fired across the bow of a federal gunboat in the Arkansas River. The vessel hove to and its supplies were confiscated. On October 25, 1863, Pine Bluff was occupied by Union troops who held it against a

Confederate attack. It remained in Union hands until the end of the Civil War.

This is an old town founded as a trading post by Joseph Bonne, who dealt with the Quapaw with unusual success—partly because he was half Quapaw.

Today cotton, rice, soybeans, wood processing, transformers, chemicals, and paper manufacturing are the main industries. The "Murals on Main" project features 22 murals on downtown buildings. The surrounding area offers excellent hunting and fishing. North of town on Highway 79 is the local branch of the University of Arkansas.

What to See and Do

Arkansas Entertainers Hall of Fame. *One Convention Center Plz, Pine Bluff (71601). Phone 870/536-7600; toll-free 800/536-7600.* Programs and displays trace the careers of featured Arkansas entertainers. Included are Johnny Cash, Glenn Campbell, Billy Bob Thornton, and Mary Steenburgen. Personal memorabilia belonging to the stars is also on display. (Mon-Fri; Sat-Sun, seasonal) **FREE**

Arts & Science Center for Southeast Arkansas. *701 Main St, Pine Bluff (71601). Phone 870/536-3375.* Houses visual arts and science exhibits. Educational workshops for children; performance arts. (Daily; closed holidays) **FREE**

Dexter Harding House. *110 N Pine St, Pine Bluff (71601). Hwy 65 and Pine St. Phone 870/536-8742.* A tourist information center is located in this 1850s house. (Daily)

Jefferson County Historical Museum. *201 E 4th St, Pine Bluff (71601). Phone 870/541-5402.* Features exhibits on history of Pine Bluff and Jefferson County, development of area transportation, including river, roads, and rail; displays of Victorian artifacts and clothing used by early settlers. Gift shop. (Mon-Sat; closed holidays) **DONATION**

Navigation Pool (Lock) No. 3. *Altheimer. 15 miles SE via Hwy 65, Hwy 11. Phone 870/534-0451.* Part of the Arkansas River multiple purpose project; Huffs Island, Rising Star (fee), and Trulock. Fishing; boat launching facilities. Picnicking (fee for group picnicking in Rising Star and Trulock). Camping (Rising Star has electrical hookups, showers, and dump station; fee). Some facilities closed during winter months. (Daily) **FREE**

Navigation Pool (Lock) No. 4. *Altheimer. 5 miles E on Hwy 81 at junction of Hwy 425 and Hwy 65. Phone 870/534-0451.* Ste. Marie and Sheppard Island have fishing, boat launching facilities; picnicking. Ste. Marie also has a fishing dock designed for use by the disabled. Some facilities closed during winter months. **FREE**

Limited-Service Hotel

★ ★ **RAMADA.** *Two Convention Center Dr, Pine Bluff (71601). Phone 870/535-3111; fax 870/534-5083.* 84 rooms, 5 story. Pets accepted; fee. Check-out 11 am. Restaurant, bar. Fitness room. Indoor pool, whirlpool. **$**

Specialty Lodging

MARGLAND BED AND BREAKFAST. *703 W 2nd St, Pine Bluff (71601). Phone 870/536-6000; toll-free 800/545-5383; fax 870/536-7941. www.margland. net.* 22 rooms, 2 story. Complimentary continental breakfast. Check-in noon, check-out noon. Fitness room. Outdoor pool. Four turn-of-the-century houses, porches, leaded glass; Victorian décor, antiques, old wicker. **$**

Pocahontas (B-4)

See also Jonesboro, Walnut Ridge

Population 6,518
Elevation 310 ft
Area Code 870
Zip 72455
Information Randolph County Chamber of Commerce, 107 E Everett St, PO Box 466; phone 870/892-3956

What to See and Do

Maynard Pioneer Museum & Park. *516 Spring St at Hwy 328 W, Maynard (72444). 13 miles N via Hwy 115. Phone 870/647-2701.* Log cabin museum; displays of antique farm equipment. Park; picnic areas. (June-Sept, Tues-Sun)

Old Davidsonville State Park. *7953 Hwy 166 S, Pocahontas (72455). 2 miles W on Hwy 62, 9 miles S on Hwy 166. Phone 870/892-4708. www.arkansasstateparks. com.* This 163-acre park on the Black River was the site of historic Davidsonville, a small town established by French settlers in 1815; the first post office and courthouse in the state were located here. Fishing, canoeing, and boating (no motors; rentals); hiking trails. Picnicking, playground; snack bar, coin laundry nearby. Camping (tent sites, hookups, dump station; fee). Visitor center (exhibits of local artifacts). Standard fees. (Daily)

Special Event

Randolph County Fair. *Fairgrounds, Hwy 90 and Thomasville Ave, Pocahontas (72455). Phone 870/892-8346.* The fair begins with a parade, and other events throughout the week include gospel and country music, Friday night rodeo, and a pet show. Late Aug-early Sept. **FREE**

Rogers (A-1)

See also Bentonville, Eureka Springs, Fayetteville, Springdale

Founded 1881
Population 38,829
Elevation 1,371 ft
Area Code 479
Information Chamber of Commerce, 317 W Walnut, 72756; phone 479/636-1240 or toll-free 800/364-1240
Web Site www.rogerslowell.com

This pleasant town in the Ozark area has diversified industries including the manufacture of air rifles, electric motors, pumps, tools, stereo speakers, office furniture, and the processing of poultry.

What to See and Do

Beaver Lake. *2260 N 2nd St, Rogers (72756). 4 miles E on Hwy 12. Phone 501/636-1210.* A 30,000-acre reservoir with a 483-mile shoreline. Swimming, water-skiing, fishing, boating (ramp, marine station, rental boats, motors); hunting. Picnicking, playground. Camping (hookups, dump station). Fee for some activities. (Daily) **$$**

Daisy International Airgun Museum. *202 W Walnut, Rogers (72756). Phone 479/986-6873. www.daisymuseum.com.* Large display of nonpowdered guns, some dating to late 18th century. (Tues-Sat; closed holidays) **$**

Pea Ridge National Military Park. *15930 Hwy 62, Garfield (72732). 10 miles NE on Hwy 62. Phone 479/451-8122. www.nps.gov/peri.* A decisive battle was fought here Mar 7-8, 1862, saving Missouri for the Union and

resulting in the deaths of three Confederate generals: McCulloch, McIntosh, and Slack. Auto tour through historic area; the Elkhorn Tavern has been restored. 30-minute DVD video about the battle. Visitor center (daily; closed Jan 1, Thanksgiving, Dec 25). **$$**

Rogers Historical Museum (Hawkins House). *322 S 2nd St, Rogers (72756). Phone 479/621-1154. www.rogersarkansas.com/museum.* Exhibits on local history; re-created turn-of-the-century businesses; Victorian-era furnishings; hands-on children's discovery room. (Tues-Sat; closed holidays) **FREE**

War Eagle Mill. *11045 War Eagle Rd, Rogers (72756). Hwy 12 E.Phone 479/789-5343. www.wareaglemill.com.* This picturesque little community is the site of one of the state's largest and most popular arts and crafts shows (May and Oct). Tours of working, water-powered gristmill (all year). Nearby is

> **War Eagle Cavern.** *21494 Cavern Rd, Rogers (72756). Hwy 12 E.Phone 479/789-2909.* Spectacular natural entrance. Guided tours. (Mid-Mar-Nov: daily)

Restaurant

★ ★ **THE BEAN PALACE.** *11045 War Eagle Rd, Rogers (72756). Phone 479/789-5343; fax 479/789-2972. www.wareaglemill.com.* Breakfast, lunch. Closed Thanksgiving, Dec 25; weekdays Jan-Feb. Children's menu. Reproduction of 1873 mill. **$**

Russellville (C-2)

See also Morrilton, Paris, Petit Jean State Park

Founded 1842
Population 23,682
Area Code 479
Information Chamber of Commerce, 708 W Main St; phone 479/968-2530

Russellville is the seat of Pope County, a region producing soybeans, peaches, and truck crops. The town has several types of manufacturing industries including chemicals, rubber products, frozen foods, aluminum foil, and paper containers. This is also the home of Arkansas Tech University and the headquarters for the Ozark and St. Francis National Forests.

What to See and Do

Holla Bend National Wildlife Refuge. *Rte 1, Box 59, Dardanelle (72834). 14 miles SE via Hwy 7, 155. Phone 479/229-4300.* Late Nov-Feb is the best time for viewing ducks and geese; other species including golden and bald eagles, herons, egrets, sandpipers, and scissor-tailed flycatchers. Fishing (Mar-Oct). Self-guided auto tour. (Daily) **$$**

Lake Dardanelle. *100 State Park Dr, Russellville (72802). NW edge of town on Hwy 326. Phone 479/967-5516.* More than 300 miles of shoreline on the lake formed by Dardanelle Dam. On the lake is

Lake Dardanelle State Park. *Russellville (72802).* Swimming, fishing, boating (rentals); bicycling, hiking, and nature trails, miniature golf. Picnicking. Camping (hookups, dump station). Seasonal interpretive programs. Standard fees. (Daily)

Mount Nebo State Park. *1 State Park Dr, Dardanelle (72834). 4 miles S on Hwy 7, 7 miles W on Hwy 155.; toll-free 800/264-2458. www.arkansasstateparks.com.* Approximately 3,400 acres atop 1,800-foot Mount Nebo, with a panoramic view of the Arkansas River Valley. The approach to the summit winds up the eastern side of the mountain with several scenic overlooks along the road. From base to top are a series of tight hairpin turns; not recommended for trailers over 15 feet. Swimming pool, fishing (nearby); bicycling (rentals), hiking trails, tennis. Picnicking, playground, store. Camping (electric hookups), cabins. Visitor center; exhibits; interpretive programs. Standard fees. (Daily)

Nimrod Lake. *Hwy 60 E, Plainview . 28 miles S on Hwy 7 at Fourche junction. Phone 479/272-4324.* A reservoir formed by a dam on the Fourche LaFave River. Swimming, water-skiing, fishing, boating; hunting, picnicking, tent and trailer camping (electric hookups, dump station; fee). Quarry Cove, County Line, and Sunlight Bay parks have showers; free camping at Carden Point Park (all year). (Daily) **FREE**

Ozark National Forest. *605 W Main, Russellville (72801). 20 miles N on Hwy 7. Phone 479/964-7200.* Sparkling waterfalls, lakes, underground caverns, unusual rock formations, oak forests, natural bridges, and 500-1,400-foot-deep gorges are features of this 1.1 million-acre forest. Mount Magazine, the highest point in the state at 2,753 feet, is in the southern part of the forest. Swimming, fishing, boating; hunting for deer, turkey, and small game. Fees may be charged at recreation sites. (Daily) **FREE**

Potts Tavern/Museum. *Russellville. 6 miles SE via I-40, exit 88. Phone 479/968-2530.* (1850) Former stagecoach stop on the Butterfield Overland mail route between Memphis and Fort Smith. Restored; museum, ladies' hats display. (Sat and Sun) **$**

Special Events

Pope County Fair. *Pope County Fairgrounds. Phone 479/967-0320. www.pcfg.org.* The fair features a youth horse show; arts, crafts, and horticulture exhibits; a carnival; and a talent show. Mid-Sept. **$**

Valley Fest. *300 E Third St, Russellville (72801). Phone 479/968-7819.* At Valley Fest, you can enjoy a fun-filled weekend while helping a worthy cause. The fun includes a barbecue cook-off, 3-on-3 basketball, volleyball, a fishing derby, rides, live music, and games like horseshoes and hoop shooting (entry fees for most). Proceeds from the event benefit the Boys and Girls Clubs of the Arkansas River Valley. Note that there is a fee for parking ($). Late Aug.

Limited-Service Hotel

★ ★ **HOLIDAY INN.** *2407 N Arkansas, Russellville (72811). Phone 479/968-4300; toll-free 800/465-4329; fax 479/968-4300. www.holiday-inn.com.* 149 rooms, 2 story. Pets accepted. Complimentary continental breakfast. Check-out noon. Restaurant. Outdoor pool. Airport transportation available. **$**

Searcy (C-3)

See also Little Rock, Greers Ferry Lake Area

Founded 1860
Population 18,928
Elevation 264 ft
Area Code 501
Zip 72143
Web Site searcy.dina.org

Limited-Service Hotel

★ ★ **HAMPTON INN.** *3204 E Race St, Searcy (72143). Phone 501/268-0654; fax 501/278-5546. www. hamptoninn.com.* 106 rooms, 2 story. Complimentary continental breakfast. Check-out noon. Restaurant. Fitness room. Indoor, outdoor pool; whirlpool. Business center. **$**

Springdale (B-1)

See also Bentonville, Fayetteville, Rogers

Population 45,798
Elevation 1,329 ft
Area Code 479
Information Chamber of Commerce, 202 W Emma Ave, PO Box 166, 72765; phone 479/872-2222 or toll-free 800/972-7261
Web Site www.springdale.com

Poultry processing is the main industry, but there are colorful and interesting vineyards in the area around this Ozark town. The best are a few miles west on Highway 68 near Tontitown, a community settled by Italian immigrants in 1897.

What to See and Do

Arts Center of the Ozarks. *214 S Main, Springdale (72764). Phone 479/751-5441. www.artscenteroftheozarks.com.* Visual and performing arts center. Art gallery (Mon-Sat; closed two weeks around Dec 25); concerts; theater productions (fee).

Shiloh Historic District. *118 W Johnson Ave, Springdale (72764). Johnson and Spring sts. Phone 479/750-8165.* Here are the Shiloh Museum, Shiloh Church (1871), Shiloh Memorial Park, and early residences. Markers in the park show locations of historic Springdale buildings, streets, and sites.

Shiloh Museum. *118 W Johnson Ave, Springdale (72764). Phone 479/750-8165.* The name is derived from the original name of the settlement and church established in 1840. Native American artifacts, antique photographic equipment, photographs, and historic items of northwest Arkansas; log cabin (circa 1855); post office/general store (1871); country doctor's office (circa 1870); farm machinery. (Mon-Sat; closed holidays) **FREE**

Special Event

Rodeo of the Ozarks. *Parsons Stadium, 1433 E Emma Ave, Springdale (72764). At Old Missouri Rd. Phone toll-free 877/927-6336. www.rodeooftheozarks.org.* The four-day event begins and ends with a parade—the time in between is filled with exciting calf roping, steer wrestling, and bull riding events. Early July. **$$**

Limited-Service Hotels

★ **HAMPTON INN.** *1700 S 48th St, Springdale (72762). Phone 479/756-3500; toll-free 800/426-7866; fax 479/927-3500. www.hamptoninnspringdale.com.* Corporate travelers and families visiting for sporting events at the University of Arkansas and Tyson's Sports Complex are the main clients at this hotel. Located in a business area, this property is near the corporate headquarters for Tyson, J. B. Hunt, and Wal-Mart. Guests staying here also have access to amenities, including room service, at the neighboring Holiday Inn. 102 rooms, 3 story. Pets accepted, some restrictions; fee. Complimentary full breakfast. Check-in 3 pm, check-out noon. High-speed Internet access, wireless Internet access. Fitness room. Outdoor pool. Airport transportation available. Business center. **$**

★ ★ **HOLIDAY INN.** *1500 S 48th St, Springdale (72762). Phone 479/751-8300; toll-free 800/465-4329; fax 479/751-4640. www.holiday-inn.com.* Located near Interstate 540, this convenient hotel is just a short drive to the University of Arkansas, and the corporate headquarters of Tyson, J. B. Hunt, and Wal-Mart. Although it caters to mostly business people, it does host quite a few families (and kids eat free). Business travelers will appreciate the fitness room, business center, and Internet access, while families will enjoy the pool and bicycles. 206 rooms, 8 story. Pets accepted; fee. Check-in 2 pm, check-out noon. High-speed Internet access, wireless Internet access. Two restaurants, two bars. Fitness room. Indoor pool, whirlpool. Airport transportation available. Business center. **$**

Restaurant

★ **A. Q. CHICKEN HOUSE.** *1207 N Thompson, Springdale (72765). Phone 479/751-4633; fax 479/751-9515. www.aqchickenhouse.com.* The owners of this country-casual restaurant have been raising chickens since 1947, so it's no surprise that chicken is the specialty here. Every day, A. Q. Chicken House offers all-you-can-eat chicken done three ways—pan friend, barbecue, and over the coals. American menu. Lunch, dinner. Children's menu. Casual attire. **$$**

Stuttgart (D-4)

See also Pine Bluff

Settled 1878
Population 9,745
Elevation 217 ft
Area Code 870
Zip 72160
Information Chamber of Commerce, 507 S Main, PO Box 932; phone 870/673-1602
Web Site www.stuttgartarkansas.com

Founded by German immigrants led by Reverend Adam Buerkle, Stuttgart is situated on the Mississippi Flyway. Stuttgart is a lively town from November through January, when it is invaded by duck hunters.

What to See and Do

Agricultural Museum of Stuttgart. *921 E 4th St, Stuttgart (72160). Phone 870/673-7001.* Displays depict pioneer life and prairie farming; wildlife exhibit; farm equipment, including a 25,000-pound steam engine; replica prairie village; scale model of early newspaper office with working printing press; toy collection; scale model of first church in Stuttgart; simulated duck hunt. Agricultural aviation presentation; rice milling exhibit. Video presentation on modern rice, soybean, and fish farming. (Tues-Sat; closed holidays) Under 16 only with adult.

White River National Wildlife Refuge. *57 S CC Camp Rd, St. Charles (72140). 25 miles SE on Hwy 165 to De Witt, then 16 miles NE on Hwy 1 to St. Charles. Inquire locally for road conditions. Phone 870/282-8200. whitriver.fws.gov.* A more than 113,000-acre bottomland with 165 small lakes. Fishing, boat access; hunting for duck, deer, turkey, squirrel, raccoon. Picnicking. Primitive camping. (Mar-Oct, daily) **FREE**

Special Event

Wings Over The Prairie Festival. *Downtown. Phone 870/673-1602.* Includes championship duck calling contest, midway, exhibits, other contests. Thanksgiving week.

Limited-Service Hotel

★ **BEST WESTERN DUCK INN.** *704 W Michigan St, Stuttgart (72160). Phone 870/673-2575; fax 870/673-2575. www.bestwestern.com.* 72 rooms, 2 story. Pets accepted. Check-out noon. Indoor pool. **$**

Texarkana (E-1)

See also Ashdown, Hope

Limited-Service Hotel

★ ★ **BEST WESTERN KINGS ROW INN & SUITES.** *4200 State Line Ave, Texarkana (71854). Phone 870/774-3851; fax 870/772-8440. www.bestwestern.com.* 116 rooms, 2 story. Pets accepted, some restrictions; fee. Check-out noon. Restaurant. Pool. Airport transportation available. **$**

Walnut Ridge (B-4)

See also Jonesboro, Pocahontas

Population 4,925
Elevation 270 ft
Area Code 870
Zip 72476
Information Walnut Ridge Area Chamber of Commerce, 109 SW Front, PO Box 842; phone 870/886-3232

What to See and Do

Lake Charles State Park. *3705 Hwy 25, Powhatan (72458). 2 miles S on Hwy 67, 8 miles W on Hwy 63, 4 miles SW on Hwy 25. Phone 870/878-6595.* In the northeastern foothills of the Arkansas Ozarks, this 645-acre lake offers swimming beach; bass, crappie, catfish, and bream fishing; nature trail. Camping (hookups, bathhouse, dump station). Visitor center; interpretive programs (Year-round, daily). Standard fees.

Special Event

Coca-Cola Airshow of the Ozarks. *Walnut Ridge Regional Airport, 10 Skywatch, Walnut Ridge (72476).* Sept.

West Memphis

What to See and Do

Tom Sawyer's Mississippi River RV Park. *1286 S Eighth St, West Memphis (72301). Phone 870/735-9770.* 80 sites, full hook-ups. Laundry services, ice. Pavilion.

Kentucky

The spirits of native sons Abraham Lincoln, Daniel Boone, and Henry Clay are still present in many aspects of modern-day Kentucky. Known for such traditions as mountain music, mint juleps, and the Derby, Kentucky's rich heritage has not faded over time. Although the bluegrass is blue only for a short time in the spring, and few self-respecting Kentuckians will dilute a good bourbon with sugar and mint leaves, Kentucky has not sought to distance itself from its history. To many, this is still the land where Lincoln was born, where Zachary Taylor spent his youth, and where Harriet Beecher Stowe witnessed the auctioning of slaves and found the inspiration to write *Uncle Tom's Cabin.* Such pioneers and visionaries continue to be revered today, perhaps more so in Kentucky than anywhere else. The state itself has been assured immortality through the words of Stephen Foster's song, "My Old Kentucky Home."

Population: 3,685,296
Area: 40,409 square miles
Elevation: 257-4,145 feet
Peak: Black Mountain (Harlan County)
Entered Union: June 1, 1792 (15th state)
Capital: Frankfort
Motto: United We Stand, Divided We Fall
Nickname: Bluegrass State
Flower: Goldenrod
Bird: Kentucky Cardinal
Time Zone: Eastern and Central
Web Site: www.kentuckytourism.com
Fun Fact:
- Mammoth Cave is the world's longest cave and was first promoted in 1816, making it the second oldest tourist attraction in the United States. Niagara Falls, New York, is first.

Kentucky stretches from Virginia to Missouri, a geographic and historic bridge in the westward flow of American settlement. The state can be divided into four sections: the Bluegrass, the south central cave country, the eastern mountains, and the western lakes. Each differs drastically in geography, culture, and economics. A circular area in the north-central portion of the state, the Lexington plain is bluegrass country, home of great horses and gentlemen farmers. A predominantly rural nature has remained even though a patina of industry has been imposed, thanks to generous tax laws that have added industrial muscle to almost every major community. The great dams of the Tennessee Valley Authority have harnessed floods, generated cheap power, lured chemical plants, and created new vacation resources.

More than 450 million pounds of burley and dark tobacco are typically grown in Kentucky each year.

This principal crop is followed by corn, soybeans, and wheat. Cattle, hogs, sheep, and poultry round out the farm family. Not all of Kentucky's corn is served on the cob; much of it winds up as bourbon whiskey, respected and treasured in much of the world. Kentucky is a major mining state as well, with rich deposits of bituminous coal, petroleum, natural gas, fluorspar, natural cement, and clay. Tobacco and food products, electronic equipment, transportation equipment, chemicals, and machinery are the principal factory products.

The Cumberland Gap, a natural passageway through the mountains that sealed the Kentucky wilderness off from Virginia, was the gateway of the pioneers. Dr. Thomas Walker, the first recorded explorer to make a thorough land expedition into the state, arrived in 1750. Daniel Boone and a company of axmen hacked the Wilderness Road through the Cumberland Gap and far into the wilds. The first permanent settlement was at Harrodsburg in 1774, followed quickly by Boonesborough in 1775. Richard Henderson, founder of the Transylvania Com-

Calendar Highlights

MARCH

Spiral Stakes *(Covington). Turfway Park Race Track in Florence. Phone 859/371-0200.* One of the largest pursed thoroughbred races for 3-year-olds. The race culminates a weeklong festival.

APRIL

Kentucky Derby Festival *(Louisville). Phone 502/584-6383 or toll-free 800/928-FEST.* Two-week celebration with Pegasus Parade, Great Steamboat Race, Great Balloon Race, mini-marathon, concerts, and sports tournaments.

Rolex Kentucky Three-Day Event *(Lexington). Phone 859/233-2362.* Three-day endurance test for horse and rider in dressage, cross-country, and stadium jumping. Fair features boutiques.

MAY

Governor's Derby Breakfast *(Frankfort). Phone 502/564-2611.* Breakfast, entertainment, and Kentucky crafts.

JUNE

Capital Expo Festival *(Frankfort). Capital Plaza Complex. Phone 502/875-3524.* Traditional music, country music, fiddling; workshops, demonstrations, arts and crafts; balloon race, dancing, games, contests, puppets, museum exhibitions, ethnic and regional foods, entertainment.

Festival of the Bluegrass *(Lexington). Kentucky Horse Park. Phone 859/846-4995.* Top names in Bluegrass music, with more than 20 bands appearing. Includes special shows for children;

crafts; and workshops with the musicians. The 600-acre park has more than 750 electric hook-ups for campers.

AUGUST

Kentucky Heartland Festival *(Elizabethtown). Freeman Lake Park. Phone 270/765-4334 or 270/769-2391.* Antique auto show, arts and crafts, races, hot-air balloon, bluegrass music, games, and food.

Kentucky State Fair *(Louisville). Kentucky Fair & Expo Center. Phone 502/367-5000.* Livestock shows; championship horse show; home and fine arts exhibits; midway and entertainment.

SEPTEMBER

Riverfest *(Covington). Phone 513/621-9326.* One of the largest fireworks displays in the country; shot from barges moored on the Ohio River.

OCTOBER

Big River Arts & Crafts Festival *(Henderson). Audubon State Park. Phone 270/926-4433.* More than 250 exhibitors.

Daniel Boone Festival *(Barbourville). Phone 606/546-4300.* Celebrates Boone's search for a route through Kentucky. Square dancing, musket shooting, reenactment of Native American treaty signing, horse show, parade, old-time fiddling, long rifle shoot between neighboring states, exhibits, antique displays, arts and crafts, parade, entertainment, and homemade candies and cakes. The Cherokee make annual pilgrimage to the city.

pany, asked Congress to recognize Transylvania as the 14th state; instead, Virginia claimed Kentucky as one of its counties, and Transylvania passed into history. Finally, in 1792, Congress admitted Kentucky as a state. The Civil War found Kentucky for the Union but against abolition. It remained officially with the North but fought on both sides.

When to Go/Climate

Kentucky enjoys a temperate climate with four distinct seasons. Winter snowfall ranges from five to ten inches in the southwestern part of the state, to as much as 40 inches in the highest elevations. Thunderstorms are common in the Ohio River Valley in spring and summer.

AVERAGE HIGH/LOW TEMPERATURES (°F)

Louisville

Jan 40/32	**May** 76/55	**Sept** 80/59
Feb 45/27	**June** 84/63	**Oct** 69/46
Mar 56/36	**July** 87/67	**Nov** 57/37
Apr 67/45	**Aug** 86/66	**Dec** 45/29

Parks and Recreation

Water-related activities, hiking, riding, and various other sports; picnicking, and camping are available in many of Kentucky's state parks. Eighteen areas have lodges and/or cottages (rates vary; phone 800/255-7275 for information); 30 have tent and trailer sites (Apr-Oct: $17-$27 for two people; $3 for each additional person over 16 years; senior citizens rate; electricity and water included; primitive camping $12; rates subject to change). Thirteen state parks have campgrounds open year-round. Campsites are rented on a first-come, first-served basis; pets on leash only. No entrance fee is charged at state parks. For further information about state parks or camping, contact the Kentucky Department of Parks, 500 Mero St, Frankfort 40601. Phone 502/564-2172 or toll-free 800/255-7275.

FISHING AND HUNTING

Mountain streams, giant lakes, and major rivers invite anglers and are productive throughout the year. Both largemouth bass and crappie can be found throughout the state. Lake Cumberland (see SOMERSET) has walleye; Laurel River Lake (see CORBIN), Lake Cumberland tailwaters, and Paintsville Lake have trout; Buckhorn, Cave Run (see MOREHEAD), and Green River lakes have muskie; Lake Barkley, Kentucky Lake (see GILBERTSVILLE), and tailwaters have sauger; and Lake Cumberland has striped bass. Statewide nonresident fishing license: $35; trout stamp $10; nonresident three-day fishing license $21; 15-day license $25; no fishing license required for children under age 16. Annual nonresident hunting license: $115; deer permit with two tags, gun or archery $25; turkey permit $20; five-day small game license $32.50. For open season dates and other details, contact the Department of Fish and Wildlife Resources, #1 Game Farm Rd, Frankfort 40601; phone 502/564-4336 or toll-free 800/858-1549.

Driving Information

All persons anywhere in a vehicle are required to use safety belts. Children under 40 inches in height must be in approved safety seats anywhere in the vehicle. Phone 502/695-6356.

Highway Number Cities/Towns within 10 Miles

Interstate 24	Cadiz, Gilbertsville, Hopkinsville, Paducah.
Interstate 64	Ashland, Frankfort, Georgetown, Lexington, Louisville, Morehead, Olive Hill, Winchester.
Interstate 65	Bowling Green, Cave City, Elizabethtown, Glasgow, Hodgenville, Horse Cave, Louisville, Mammoth Cave National Park, Park City, Shepherdsville.
Interstate 71	Carrollton, Covington, Louisville, Walton.
Interstate 75	Berea, Corbin, Covington, Georgetown, Lexington, London, Mount Vernon, Richmond, Walton, Williamsburg, Williamstown.

Additional Visitor Information

The Department of Travel, Department MR, PO Box 2011, Frankfort 40602, phone 800/225-8747, distributes literature and information, including a list of the state's many interesting festivals and fairs. The *Kentucky Official Vacation Guide* is informative, comprehensive, and revised annually.

There are eight welcome centers in Kentucky; visitors who stop by will find information and brochures helpful in planning stops at points of interest. Their locations are: Florence Welcome Center, I-75 southbound exit 180, Walton; Franklin Welcome Center, I-65 northbound exit 2, Franklin; Hopkinsville Welcome Center, I-24 westbound exit 89, Hopkinsville; Grayson Welcome Center, I-64 westbound exit 181, Grayson; Shelby County Welcome Center, I-64 eastbound exit 28, Shelbyville; Bullitt County Welcome Center, I-65 southbound exit 116, Shepherdsville; Whitehaven Welcome Center, I-24 eastbound and Hwy 45, Paducah; and Williamsburg Welcome Center, I-75 northbound exit 11, Williamsburg.

THE COUNTRY MUSIC HIGHWAY

Highway 23, the preinterstate thoroughfare that runs north-south along a narrow longitudinal line from Canada to Florida, rides through a 150-mile section of Kentucky up along its riverine border with West Virginia. Highway 23 is distinguished as the "Country Music Highway" for the region's contribution to popular culture. Here in the Southern Highlands that stretch across Kentucky, West Virginia, Virginia and Tennessee, bluegrass music originated from religious and musical traditions dating back to the Appalachian frontier days. As it mixed with musical strains from Nashville after World War II, the sound evolved into country music.

Begin at the Ohio River where Kentucky, West Virginia, and Ohio come together near Huntington, WV; pick up Highway 23 in Ashland, approximately 8 miles north of I-64. Settled on the banks of the Ohio River in 1786, Ashland heads up a driving tour of the Country Music Highway with a country music exhibit at its Highlands Museum and Discovery Center, downtown at 1620 Winchester Avenue (Highway 23; phone 606/329-8888). The museum also highlights the region's Appalachian heritage and industry.

But perhaps the most illustrative exhibit is Highway 23 itself, which runs 55 miles south through the isolated Tug River valley to Paintsville. Outside of Paintsville is Butcher Hollow, the remote mining town where Loretta Lynn was born. The acclaimed country singer describes these backwoods in her autobiographical song "Coal Miner's Daughter," which was made into a film starring Sissy Spacek in 1980. Twelve miles south of Paintsville, Jenny Wiley State Resort Park outside Prestonville is set along Dewey Lake and offers camping, lodging, dining, boating, and other recreation for folks passing through.

Twenty-five miles farther south on Highway 23, Pikeville is notorious as the setting of the legendary feud between the Hatfields and McCoys in the late 1800s. The feud between the two families originated as a dispute over a razorback hog and a failed romance and escalated from there. A public hanging for one perpetrator and long prison sentences for several others ended the feud in 1897.

Veering off Highway 23 9 miles south of Pikeville, Highway 460 leads east to Belcher, where a 3-mile turnoff takes you to Breaks Interstate Park (phone 540/865-4413), at the Virginia border. The centerpiece of this 4,600-acre park is the deepest canyon east of the Mississippia 5-mile-long, 1,600-foot-deep gorge dubbed "the Grand Canyon of the South." Whitewater rafting and kayaking are popular activities on the Russell Fork River below, which has carved out the deep gorge. At the thickly forested rim, hiking trails lead through story-high rhododendron dells.

Returning to Highway 23, crosses into Virginia in another 25 miles. Continuing the route another hundred miles leads drivers to attractions in Virginia that shed more light on the heritage of the Highland region.

Off Highway 23 approximately 20 miles south of the border, Big Stone Gap has two museums downtown that relate more stories of the boom and bust of the coal industry and its subsequent impact on this remote Appalachian region: the Southwest Virginia Museum (phone 540/523-1322) and the Harry Meador Coal Museum (phone 540/523-4950). Sixty miles from Big Stone Gap, Highway 23 south and a jog east on Highway 58 lands drivers at Bristol on the Tennessee-Virginia border. Here, the first recordings of country music were made in 1927 by the Victor Talking Machine Company, earning the town the designation "the birthplace of country music."
(Approximately 150 miles)

Abraham Lincoln Birthplace National Historic Site (C-6)

See also Elizabethtown, Hodgenville

Web Site www.nps.gov/abli/

3 miles S of Hodgenville on Hwy 31 E/Hwy 61.

On Feb 12, 1809, the Sinking Spring Farm, named after a small limestone spring, became the birthplace of Abraham Lincoln, the 16th President of the United States. Less than three years later, in 1811, Thomas Lincoln, the President's father, moved the family to Knob Creek Farm, located about 10 miles northeast.

Later moves eventually took the Lincoln family to Indiana and Illinois.

The Lincoln Farm Association purchased the farm in 1905. In 1916, the Lincoln Farm Association deeded the farm to the War Department and it was later transferred to the National Park Service in 1933. Today 110 acres of the original Lincoln Farm are contained within the 116-acre park.

⭐ Visitor Center Audiovisual program (18 minutes) and exhibits explore Lincoln's background and environment. Thomas Lincoln's Bible is on display.

More than 100,000 citizens contributed funds to construct the granite and marble Memorial Building in 1911. Inside is the log cabin originally believed to be the Lincoln birthplace; research has revealed that this is most likely not the case. The cabin was disassembled, moved, exhibited, and stored many times before being reconstructed permanently inside the Memorial Building. (Daily; closed Jan 1, Thanksgiving, December 25) For specific and possible holiday closures contact Superintendent, 2995 Lincoln Farm Rd, Hogdenville 42748. Phone 270/358-3137. **FREE**

Special Events

Lincoln's Birthday. *2995 Lincoln Farm Rd, Hodgenville (42748). Phone 270/358-3137.* Wreath-laying ceremony. Afternoon of Feb 12.

Martin Luther King's Birthday. *2995 Lincoln Farm Rd, Hodgenville (42748). Phone 270/358-3137.* Sun, mid-Jan.

Ashland (B-9)

See also Olive Hill

Settled 1815
Population 21,981
Elevation 548 ft
Area Code 606
Information Ashland Area Convention & Visitors Bureau, 1509 Winchester Ave, PO Box 987, 41105; phone 606/329-1007 or toll-free 800/377-6249
Web Site www.visitashlandky.com

Set in the highlands of northeastern Kentucky, on the Ohio River, Ashland is an industrial city that produces oil, steel, and chemicals.

What to See and Do

Bennett's Mill Bridge. *8 miles W on Hwy 125 off Hwy 7.* Built in 1855 to service mill customers, the bridge spans Tygarts Creek. At 195 feet, this is one of Kentucky's longest single-span covered bridges; original footings and frame intact. Closed to traffic.

Central Park. *Phone 606/327-2046.* A 47-acre park with prehistoric Native American mounds. Sport facilities; playgrounds, picnicking.

Discovery Center Highlands Museum. *1620 Winchester, Ashland (41101). Phone 606/329-8888.* Displays trace history and cultural heritage of the region. Period clothing; Native American artifacts; WWII memorabilia; industrial exhibits. Gift shop. (Tues-Sat; Mon by appointment; closed holidays) **$**

Greenbo Lake State Resort Park. *18 miles W via Hwy 23 to Hwy 1. Phone 606/473-7324. www.state.ky.us/agencies/parks.* This 3,330-acre park with a 225-acre lake, has an early buffalo (pig-iron) furnace. Swimming pool (Memorial Day-Labor Day), fishing, boating (marina); hiking, bicycle rentals, tennis, picnicking, playground, lodge, tent and trailer sites (Apr-Oct). Recreation program for children.

Oldtown Bridge. *14 miles W via Hwy 23, then 9 miles S on Hwy 1. Phone toll-free 800/377-6249.* Built in 1880 to Burr's design; 194-foot, dual-span bridge crosses Little Sandy River. Closed to traffic.

Paramount Arts Center. *1300 Winchester Ave, Ashland (41101). Phone 606/324-3175.* Historical 1930s Art Deco theater. Hosts children's events, concerts. Tours. (Daily)

Special Event

Poage Landing Days Festival. *Central Park, Winchester Ave, Ashland (41101). Phone 606/329-1007; toll-free 800/377-6249.* Fiddle festival, national and local entertainers, arts and crafts, children's activities. Third weekend in Sept.

Limited-Service Hotels

★ **DAYS INN.** *12700 Hwy 180, Ashland (41102). Phone 606/928-3600; toll-free 800/329-7466; fax 606/928-6515. www.daysinn.com.* 63 rooms, 2 story. Pets accepted; fee. Complimentary continental breakfast. Check-out noon. Fitness room. Outdoor pool. Business center. **$**

★ **FAIRFIELD INN.** *10945 Hwy 60, Ashland (41102). Phone 606/928-1222; toll-free 800/228-2800; fax 606/928-1222. www.fairfieldinn.com.* 63 rooms, 3 story. Complimentary continental breakfast. Checkout noon. Wireless Internet access. Indoor pool, whirlpool. **$**

★ ★ **GREENBO LAKE STATE RESORT.** *HC 60, Box 562, Ashland (41144). Phone 606/473-7324; toll-free 800/325-0083; fax 606/473-7741.parks.ky.gov/greenbo2.htm.* 36 rooms, 3 story. Restaurant. Children's activity center. Outdoor pool, children's pool. **$**

Barbourville (D-8)

See also Corbin, Pineville

Founded 1800
Population 3,589
Elevation 986 ft
Area Code 606
Zip 40906
Information Knox County Chamber of Commerce, 196 Daniel Boone Dr, Suite 205; phone 606/546-4300
Web Site www.barbourville.com

In the valley of the scenic Cumberland River, Barbourville is protected by a $2.5-million flood wall built around the city. Tobacco, coal mining, and timber are the area's major industries. The city has also produced two Kentucky governors, a lieutenant governor, three US congressmen, and many other statesmen who served outside Kentucky.

What to See and Do

Dr. Thomas Walker State Historic Site. *Hwy 459, Barbourville (40906). 5 miles SW on Hwy 459. Phone 606/546-4400. www.state.ky.us/agencies/pars/drwalker. htm.* Replica of original log cabin built in 1750 by Dr. Thomas Walker; surrounded by 12 acres of parkland. Miniature golf (fee). Picnic area, shelter, playground. Grounds (daily). **FREE**

Special Event

Daniel Boone Festival. *Knox and Daniel Boone Dr, Barbourville (40906). Phone 606/546-4300.* Celebrates Boone's search for a route through Kentucky. Square dancing, musket shooting, reenactment of Native American treaty signing, horse show, parade, old time fiddling, long rifle shoot between neighboring states, exhibits, antique displays, arts and crafts, parade, entertainment, homemade candies and cakes. The Cherokee make an annual pilgrimage to city. Seven days in early Oct.

Bardstown (C-6)

See also Elizabethtown

Settled 1775
Population 10,374
Elevation 647 ft
Area Code 502
Zip 40004
Information Bardstown-Nelson County Tourist & Convention Commission, 1 Court Square, PO Box 867; phone 502/348-4877 or toll-free 800/638-4877
Web Site www.bardstowntourism.com

One of Kentucky's oldest settlements, Bardstown includes many historic sites. It is the seat of Nelson County, home of four bourbon distilleries. Today, the chief agricultural product is tobacco.

What to See and Do

Bernheim Forest (see). *State Hwy 245, Shepherdsville (40110). 14 miles NW on Hwy 245. Phone 502/955-8512. www.bernheim.org.*

Jim Beam American Outpost. *Hwy 245, Clermont (40110). 15 miles NW on Hwy 245. Phone 502/543-9877.* Visitors can tour the historic Beam family home and stroll the grounds. Craft shop. (Daily; closed holidays) **FREE**

Lincoln Homestead State Park. *5079 Lincoln Park Rd, Bardstown (40069). 20 miles SE on Hwy 150 to Hwy 528. Phone 859/336-7461. www.state.ky.us/agencies/parks/linchome.htm.* In a compound framed by split rail fences is a replica of the cabin built on this land, which was originally settled in 1782 by Abraham Lincoln, Sr., grandfather of the President. This was the home of Thomas Lincoln until he was 25. Furnished in pioneer style, it includes several pieces made by Thomas Lincoln. Also, the Berry House, home of Nancy Hanks during her courtship by Thomas Lincoln; pioneer relics, photostatic copies of the Thomas and Nancy Lincoln marriage bonds. A replica of the blacksmith and carpenter shop where Thomas Lincoln worked is also in the compound. Houses (May-Sept, daily). The 150-acre park offers 18-hole golf (daily, fee). Picnic facilities, playground. **$**

My Old Kentucky Dinner Train. *602 N 3rd St, Bardstown (40004). Departs from 602 N 3rd St. Phone 502/348-7300. www.kydinnertrain.com.* Scenic dining excursions aboard elegant, restored dining cars from the 1940s. Round trip through the countryside, includes three-course lunch or four-course dinner. (Feb-Dec, Tues-Sat) **$$$$**

My Old Kentucky Home State Park. *501 E Stephen Foster Ave, Bardstown (40004). 1 mile E on Hwy 150. Phone 502/348-3502. www.state.ky.us/agencies/parks/kyhome.htm.* The composer Stephen Foster occasionally visited his cousin, Judge John Rowan, at the stately house, Federal Hill (1795). These visits may have inspired him to write "My Old Kentucky Home," a melody that is a lasting favorite. The house and its 290 acres of grounds are now a state park. Attendants wear period costumes; period furnishings. Golf course. Picnic area, playground. Tent and trailer sites (standard fees). Guided tour (fee). Gardens; amphitheater (see SPECIAL EVENT). (Daily; closed Jan 1, Thanksgiving, week of Dec 25) **FREE**

Spalding Hall. *114 N 5th St, Bardstown (40004). Just off N 5th St. Phone 502/348-2999.* (circa 1825) Once part of St. Joseph College; used as a hospital in the Civil War. Former dormitory; now houses art. (May-Oct: daily; rest of year: Tues-Sun) Also here are

> **Bardstown Historical Museum.** *114 N 5th St, Bardstown (40004). Phone 502/348-2999.* Features items covering 200 years of local history. Exhibits include Native American artifacts, Lincoln papers concerning Lincoln-Reed suit, John Fitch papers and a replica of the first steamboat, Stephen Foster memorabilia, tools and utensils of Trappist Monks, Civil War artifacts, gifts of King Louis Phillipe and King Charles X of France, pioneer items, period costumes (1850s-1890s), natural science display. (May-Oct: daily; rest of year: Tues-Sun)

> **Oscar Getz Museum of Whiskey History.** *114 N 5th St, Bardstown (40004). Phone 502/348-2999.* Copper stills, manuscripts, documents, bottles, and advertising art chronicle the history of whiskey from pre-colonial days to Prohibition era. (May-Oct: daily; rest of year: Tues-Sun) **FREE**

St. Joseph Proto-Cathedral. *310 W Stephen Foster Ave, Bardstown (40004). At junction Hwy 31 E, 62. Phone 502/348-3126.* (1816) First Catholic cathedral west of the Allegheny Mountains. Paintings donated by Pope Leo XII. (Daily)

Special Event

Stephen Foster, *The Musical.* *Bardstown. J. Dan Talbott Amphitheater, in My Old Kentucky Home State Park. Phone 502/348-5971; toll-free 800/626-1563.* Musical with 50 Foster melodies, tracing composer's triumphs and romance. (Nightly Tues-Sun; Sat also matinee. In the event of rain, indoor theater is used.) Early June-late Aug.

Limited-Service Hotels

★ **BEST WESTERN GENERAL NELSON.** *411 W Stephen Foster Ave, Bardstown (40004). Phone 502/348-3977; toll-free 800/225-3977; fax 502/348-7596. www.generalnelson.com.* 52 rooms, 2 story. Check-out 11 am. Outdoor pool. **$**

★ ★ **DAYS INN.** *1875 New Haven Rd, Bardstown (40004). Phone 502/348-9253; toll-free 800/329-7466; fax 502/348-5478. www.daysinn.com.* 102 rooms, 2 story. Pets accepted; fee. Check-out 11 am. Restaurant, bar. Fitness room. Outdoor pool. Golf. **$**

★ **HAMPTON INN.** *985 Chambers Blvd, Bardstown (40004). Phone 502/349-0100; fax 502/349-1191. www.hamptoninn.com.* 106 rooms, 2 story. Pets accepted. Complimentary continental breakfast. Check-out noon. Fitness room. Indoor pool. **$**

Specialty Lodging

JAILER'S INN BED AND BREAKFAST. *111 W Stephen Foster Ave, Bardstown (40004). Phone 502/348-5551; toll-free 800/948-5551; fax 502/349-1837. www.jailersinn.com.* 6 rooms. Closed Jan. Complimentary full breakfast. Check-in 2 pm, check-out 11 am.

Restaurant

★ ★ **KURTZ.** *418 E Stephen Foster Ave, Bardstown (40004). Phone 502/348-8964; toll-free 800/732-2384; fax 502/349-6973.* American menu. Lunch, dinner. Closed Dec 25. Bar. State park adjacent. **$$**

Berea (C-7)

See also Mount Vernon, Richmond

Settled 1855
Population 9,851
Elevation 1,034 ft
Area Code 859
Zip 40403
Information Welcome Center, 3 Artist Circle; phone 859/986-2540 or toll-free 800/598-5263
Web Site www.berea.com

Berea College and diverse industry provide the income for this community in the foothills of the Cumberland Mountains and the Daniel Boone National Forest. Designated the "Folk Arts and Crafts Capital of Kentucky" by the state legislature, Berea boasts more than 155 antique shops, 40 craft shops, and working studios. Indian Fort Mountain nearby is the site of prehistoric fortifications. A Ranger District office of the Daniel Boone National Forest (see) is located here.

What to See and Do

Churchill Weavers. *100 Churchill Ct, Berea (40403). I-75 to Hwy 25 N. Phone 859/986-3127. www.churchill-weavers.com.* Established in 1922, Churchill is one of the nation's oldest producers of handwoven goods. Self-guided tours through loomhouse (Mon-Thurs; closed Jan 1, Dec 25). Gift shop and outlet shop. **FREE**

Studio Craftspeople of Berea. *Berea. Phone 859/986-2540.* An organization of craftspeople working in various media invite visitors to their studios. The Tourist and Convention Commission has a list of studios that are open to the public.

Special Events

Berea Craft Festival. *Indian Fort Theater at Berea College, Berea. Phone 859/986-2258; toll-free 800/598-5263.* This more-than-20-year-old festival features the works of 120 craftspeople from around the US, along with entertainment, regional food, and demonstrations. Three days in mid-July.

Celebration of Traditional Music Festival. *Berea.* Features traditional music, dancers, concerts. Last weekend in Oct.

Kentucky Guild of Artists and Craftsmen's Fair. *Indian Fort Theater, Hwy 21 E, Berea (40403). Phone 859/986-* 2540; toll-free 800/598-5263. Crafts, art, folk dances, singing. Third weekend in May and second weekend in Oct.

Limited-Service Hotel

★ ★ **BOONE TAVERN HOTEL.** *Main and Prospect sts, Berea (40403). Phone 859/986-9358; toll-free 800/366-9358; fax 859/986-7711.* Stay in one of the guest rooms and enjoy the historic grace of this property. The rooms feature handmade furnishings along with all of the modern conveniences expected in a hotel. The dining room serves fine regional cuisine. 59 rooms. Check-out 11 am. Restaurant. **$**

Restaurants

★ **DINNER BELL.** *I-75 Plaza, Berea (40403). Phone 859/986-2777.* American menu. Breakfast, lunch, dinner. Children's menu. **$**

★ **PAPALENO'S.** *108 Center St, Berea (40403). Phone 859/986-4497.* Italian menu. Lunch, dinner. Closed Thanksgiving, Dec 25. Children's menu. **$$**

Bowling Green (D-5)

See also Park City, South Union

Founded 1780
Population 49,296
Elevation 496 ft
Area Code 270
Information Bowling Green Area Chamber of Commerce, 812 State St, PO Box 51, 42102; phone 270/781-3200
Web Site www.bgchamber.com

In the early days of the community, county court was held in the house of Robert Moore, a founder of the town, and visiting lawyers would idle away their time bowling on the lawn—hence the name. A cultural center for southern Kentucky with a variety of industries, Bowling Green is also sustained by Warren County's dairy cattle, livestock, and tobacco farms. For a short time, it was the Confederate capital of Kentucky.

What to See and Do

Beech Bend Park. *798 Beech Bend Rd, Bowling Green (42101). Phone 270/781-7634. www.beechbend.com.* Water park includes a swimming pool, water slide, paddleboats, 42 rides; miniature golf, picnic area, camping. Separate fee for each activity. (Late May-early Sept, Sun-Fri 10 am-7 pm, Sat to 8 pm) **$$**

Capitol Arts Center. *416 E Main, Bowling Green (42101). Phone 270/782-2787.* Restored Art Deco building; national and local live presentations, gallery exhibits. (Mon-Fri; closed holidays) Admission varies with event.

Historic Riverview at Hobson Grove. *1100 W Main Ave, Bowling Green (42101). In Hobson Grove Park. Phone 270/843-5565.* (1857) House in Italianate style, furnished with a collection of Victorian furniture from 1860-1890. (Feb-mid-Dec, Tues-Sun; closed holidays) **$$**

⭐ **National Corvette Museum.** *350 Corvette Dr, Bowling Green (42101). I-65 exit 28. Phone 270/781-7973. www.corvettemuseum.com.* Hands-on educational exhibits and displays on the history of this classic American car. More than 50 vintage cars. (Daily 8 am-5 pm; closed Jan 1, Thanksgiving, Dec 24-25) **$$$**

Western Kentucky University. *1 Big Red Way St, Bowling Green (42101). Phone 270/745-0111. www.wku. edu.* (1906) (16,500 students) High on a hill, Western Kentucky University was built around the site of a Civil War fort. On campus are

> **Hardin Planetarium.** *Phone 270/745-4044.* Varying programs year-round. **FREE**
>
> **Kentucky Library.** *Phone 270/745-2592.* Contains 30,000 books, manuscripts, maps, broadsides, photographs, sheet music, scrapbooks, materials relating to Kentucky and to genealogical research of Kentucky families. (Tues-Sat; closed university holidays) **FREE**
>
> **Kentucky Museum.** *Kentucky Building. Phone 270/745-2592.* Collections include costumes, implements, art works, and textiles relating to the cultural history of Kentucky and the region. Exhibits, tours, special programs. Gift shop. (Tues-Sat 9:30 am-4 pm, Sun from 1 pm; closed university holidays) **$**

Limited-Service Hotels

⭐⭐ **BEST WESTERN MOTOR INN.** *166 Cumberland Trace Rd, Bowling Green (42102). Phone 270/782-3800; toll-free 800/780-7234; fax 270/782-2384. www.bestwestern.com.* 179 rooms, 3 story. Check-out noon. Restaurant. Indoor pool, outdoor pool, children's pool, whirlpool. Tennis. **$**

⭐ **FAIRFIELD INN.** *1940 Mel Browning St, Bowling Green (42104). Phone 270/782-6933; toll-free 800/228-2800; fax 270/782-6967. www.fairfieldinn.com.* 105 rooms, 3 story. Complimentary continental breakfast. Check-out noon. Fitness room. Outdoor pool. **$**

⭐ **HAMPTON INN.** *233 Three Springs Rd, Bowling Green (42104). Phone 270/842-4100; toll-free 800/426-7866; fax 270/782-3377. www.hamptoninn.com.* 131 rooms, 4 story. Complimentary continental breakfast. Check-out noon. Outdoor pool. **$**

Restaurant

⭐⭐ **MARIAH'S.** *801 State St, Bowling Green (42102). Phone 270/842-6878; fax 270/842-2426. www. mariahs.com.* American menu. Lunch, dinner. Closed Memorial Day, Labor Day, Dec 25. Bar. Children's menu. Historic home from the 1800s; large mural of downtown in the early 1940s. **$$**

Breaks Interstate Park (C-10)

See also Pikeville

(7 miles SE of Elkhorn City, KY and 8 miles N of Haysi, VA on KY-VA80)

Where the Russell Fork of the Big Sandy River plunges through the mountains is called the "Grand Canyon of the South," the major focus of this 4,600-acre park on the Kentucky-Virginia border. From the entrance, a paved road winds through an evergreen forest and then skirts the canyon rim. Overlooks provide a spectacular view of the "Towers," a huge pyramid of rocks. Within the park are extraordinary rock formations, caves, springs, a profusion of rhododendron and, of course, the 5-mile-long, 1,600-foot-deep gorge.

The visitor center houses historical and natural exhibits, including a coal exhibit (Apr-Oct, daily). Laurel Lake is stocked with bass and bluegill. Swimming pool, pedal boats; hiking, bridle, and mountain bike trails, picnicking, playground, camping (Apr-Oct, fee); motor lodge, cottages (year-round), restaurant, gift shop. Park (daily); facilities (Apr-late Dec, daily). Contact Breaks Interstate Park, PO Box 100, Breaks, VA 24607. Phone 276/865-4413 or toll-free 800/982-5122.

Limited-Service Hotel

★ ★ **BREAKS INTERSTATE.** *Hwy 1, Breaks (24607). Phone 540/865-4414; toll-free 800/982-5122; fax 540/865-5561. www.breakspark.com.* Woodland setting; overlooks Breaks Canyon. 34 rooms, 2 story. Closed late Dec-Mar. Check-out 11 am. Restaurant. Outdoor pool, children's pool. **$**

Cadiz (D-4)

See also Gilbertsville, Hopkinsville, Kenlake State Resort Park, Land Between the Lakes

Population 2,373
Elevation 423 ft
Area Code 270
Zip 42211
Information Cadiz-Trigg County Chamber of Commerce, 22 Main St, PO Box 647; phone 270/522-3892
Web Site www.gocadiz.com

With the development of "Land Between the Lakes," a 170,000-acre wooded peninsula between the Tennessee Valley Authority's Kentucky Lake and the Army Corps of Engineers' Lake Barkley on the Cumberland River, Cadiz became a staging area for the major recreation project. The area covers much of Trigg County, of which Cadiz is the seat.

What to See and Do

Barkley Dam, Lock, and Lake. (see). *35 miles NW in Gilbertsville.* On the lakeshore is

> **Lake Barkley State Resort Park.** *2711 Blue Springs Rd, Canton (42211). 7 miles W on Hwy 80 to Hwy 1489. Phone 270/924-1131; toll-free 800/325-1708.* A 3,700-acre park on a 57,920-acre lake. Swimming beach, pool, bathhouse (seasonal), fishing, boating, canoeing (ramps, rentals, marina); hiking, backpacking, horseback riding (seasonal), 18-hole golf course (year-round), tennis, trapshooting, shuffleboard, basketball, picnicking, restaurant, cottages, lodge (see FULL-SERVICE). Camping (fee). Children's programs. Lighted airstrip. Standard fees.

Cadiz Public Use Area. *Hwy 68 On W side of town.* Fishing, launching ramp; playground, picnic area. **FREE**

Hurricane Creek Public Use Area. *12 miles NW via Hwy 274. Phone 270/522-8821.* Swimming, launching ramp; playground, improved campsites (fee). (Apr-mid-Oct, daily) Golden Age Passport accepted (see MAKING THE MOST OF YOUR TRIP).

Original Log Cabin. *22 Main St, Cadiz (42211). Phone 270/522-3892.* Four-room log cabin, furnished with 18th- and 19th-century artifacts, was occupied by a single family for more than a century. (Mon-Fri; closed holidays) **FREE**

Limited-Service Hotel

★ **HOLIDAY INN EXPRESS.** *153 Broadbent Blvd, Cadiz (42211). Phone 270/522-3700; toll-free 800/456-4000; fax 270/522-0636. www.holiday-inn.com.* 48 rooms, 2 story. Pets accepted; fee. Complimentary continental breakfast. Check-out noon. Wireless Internet access. Indoor pool. **$**

Full-Service Resort

★ ★ **LAKE BARKLEY STATE RESORT PARK.** *3500 State Park Rd, Cadiz (42211). Phone 270/924-1131; toll-free 800/325-1708; fax 270/924-0013. parks.ky.gov/lakebark.htm.* Located on the shores, this lake resort offers a plethora of outdoor activities. Explore the hiking trails or relax with a quiet picnic. No matter what guests like, there is something fun for everyone here. 124 rooms, 2 story. Check-in 4 pm, check-out noon (cottages 11 am). Restaurant. Fitness room. Beach. Outdoor pool, children's pool, whirlpool. Golf. Tennis. Airport transportation available. **$**

Campbellsville (C-6)

See also Jamestown

Population 10,498
Elevation 813 ft
Area Code 270
Zip 42718
Information Taylor County Tourism Commision, 107 W Broadway, PO Box 4021, 42719; phone 270/465-3786 or toll-free 800/738-4719
Web Site www.campbellsvilleky.com

Located geographically in the heart of Kentucky, Campbellsville is near the junction of the Pennyrile, Bluegrass, and Knobs regions of the state. Nearby, at

Tebbs Bend, the Battle of Green River was fought on July 4, 1863. Also in the vicinity is the town of Greensburg, with its interesting historic district dating to the 18th century.

What to See and Do

Green River Lake State Park. *179 Park Office Rd, Campbellsville (42718). 6 miles S on Hwy 55. Phone 270/465-8255. www.state.ky.us/agencies/parks/green-riv.htm.* Beach, fishing, marina (rentals); picnicking, camping. (Daily) Standard fees.

Limited-Service Hotel

★ **BEST WESTERN CAMPBELLSVILLE LODGE.** *1400 E Broadway, Campbellsville (42718). Phone 270/465-7001; toll-free 800/770-0430; fax 270/465-4949. www.bestwesternlodge.com.* 60 rooms. Complimentary continental breakfast. Check-out 11 am. Outdoor pool, whirlpool. **$**

Carrollton (A-6)

Founded 1794
Population 3,846
Elevation 469 ft
Area Code 502
Zip 41008
Information Carroll County Tourism Commission, 515 Highland Ave, PO Box 293; phone 502/732-7036 or toll-free 800/325-4290
Web Site www.carrolltontourism.com

At the confluence of the Ohio and Kentucky rivers, this tree-shaded residential town is named in honor of Charles Carroll. Originally from Carrollton, Maryland, Carroll was one of the signers of the Declaration of Independence.

What to See and Do

Edge of Speedway Campground. *4125 Hwy 1130, Sparta (41083). Phone 859/576-2161.* This well-manicured campground overlooks the Kentucky Speedway and has space for 200 campers. Gravel roads and large sites set it apart from other camping spots in the area. Its about a half-mile walk to track shuttle buses, or a 1 1/2-mile drive to the track parking area. Water stations, showers (fee).

General Butler State Resort Park. *1608 Hwy 227, Carrollton (41008). 2 miles S on Hwy 227, exit 44. Phone 502/732-4384. www.parks.ky.gov/resortparks/gb.* A 795-acre memorial to William O. Butler, native of Carrollton and hero of the Battle of New Orleans. Swim, fish, and boat (rentals available) at the 30-acre lake, or play nine-hole golf (fee) or tennis. Picnic sites, playground, cottages, lodge, dining room, tent and trailer camping also available (daily, fees).

Historic District. *Highland and Court sts, Carrollton.* Self-guided auto tour of historic sites and houses begins at Old Stone Jail. Tourist center on the second floor houses a small museum on local history. **FREE**

Special Events

Blues to the Point—Two Rivers Blues Festival. *Point Park Pavillion in downtown Carrollton. Phone 502/732-7036.* Two-day event with regional and national blues music performances. Early Sept.

Kentucky Scottish Weekend. *Phone 502/239-2665. www.kyscottishweeekend.org.* Celebration of Scottish heritage including pipe bands, bagpipers; Scottish athletic competition, Celtic music; British auto show. Second weekend in May.

Limited-Service Hotels

★ ★ **GENERAL BUTLER STATE RESORT PARK.** *1608 Hwy 227, Carrollton (41008). Phone 502/732-4384; toll-free 800/325-0078; fax 502/732-4270.* Open year-round, this resort features beach games, golf, tennis, hiking trails, and large recreational areas. Plan a conference in one of the many meeting rooms. 77 rooms, 3 story. Check-in 4 pm, check-out noon (cottages 11 am). Restaurant. Children's activity center. Outdoor pool, children's pool. Golf, 9 holes. Tennis. Business center. **$**

★ **HOLIDAY INN EXPRESS.** *141 Inn Rd, Carrollton (41008). Phone 502/732-6661; toll-free 800/465-4329; fax 502/732-6661. www.holiday-inn.com.* 62 rooms, 2 story. Complimentary continental breakfast. Check-in 3 pm, check-out noon. Wireless Internet access. **$**

Cave City (C-6)

See also Glasgow, Horse Cave, Mammoth Cave National Park, Park City

Population 1,880
Elevation 636 ft
Area Code 270
Zip 42127
Information Cave City Convention Center, PO Box 518; phone 270/773-3131 or toll-free 800/346-8908
Web Site www.cavecity.com

Located in the heart of Cave Country, this village primarily serves tourists passing through the region en route to Mammoth Cave and other commercially operated caves nearby.

What to See and Do

Crystal Onyx Cave. *8709 Happy Valley Rd, Cave City (42127). 2 miles SE on Hwy 90, off I-65. Phone 270/773-2359. www.crystalonyxcave.com.* Helectites, stalagmites, stalactites, onyx columns, rare crystal onyx rimstone formations; pre-historic burial site. Temperature in cave is 54° F. Guided tours every 45 minutes. Improved and primitive camping adjacent (fee). (June-Aug: 8 am-6 pm; early Aug-late May: 9 am-5 pm; closed Thanksgiving, Dec 25) **$$$**

Kentucky Action Park. *3057 Mammoth Cave Rd, Cave City (42127). 1 1/2 miles W on Hwy 70. Phone 270/773-2636. www.mammothcave.com/kyaction. htm.* Chairlift to top of mountain, slide downhill in individual alpine sleds with braking system. Go-carts, bumper boats, bumper cars (fees); horseback riding (fee). (Memorial Day-Labor Day: daily; Easter-Memorial Day: Labor Day-Oct, weekends) **$$**

Mammoth Cave Chair Lift and Guntown Mountain. *101 Mammoth Cave Rd, Cave City (42127). At junction Hwy 70, I-65. Phone 270/773-3530.* Lift ascends 1,350 feet to Guntown Mountain. On grounds is authentic reproduction of 1880s frontier town; museums, saloon, entertainment. Onyx Cave tours (Apr-Nov, daily). (Memorial Day-Labor Day: daily; May-Memorial Day and Labor Day-mid-Oct: Sat, Sun only) **$$$**

Limited-Service Hotels

★ **BEST WESTERN KENTUCKY INN.** *1009 Doyle Ave, Cave City (42127). Phone 270/773-3161; toll-free 800/780-7234; fax 270/773-5494. www.best-*

western.com. 50 rooms. Check-out 11 am. Outdoor pool, children's pool. **$**

★ ★ **QUALITY INN.** *Mammoth Cave Rd, Cave City (42127). Phone 270/773-2181; toll-free 800/321-4245; fax 270/773-3200. www.qualityinn.com.* 100 rooms, 2 story. Pets accepted; fee. Check-out 11 am. Restaurant. Outdoor pool. **$**

Restaurant

★ **SAHARA STEAK HOUSE.** *413 E Happy Valley St, Cave City (42127). Phone 270/773-3450.* Steak menu. Lunch, dinner. Closed Thanksgiving, Dec 25. Children's menu. **$$**

Corbin (D-8)

See also Barbourville, Cumberland Falls State Resort Park, London, Williamsburg

Settled 1883
Population 7,742
Elevation 1,080 ft
Area Code 606
Zip 40701
Information Tourist & Convention Commission, 222 Corbin Center Dr; phone 606/528-8860
Web Site www.corbinkycityguide.com

What to See and Do

Colonel Harland Sanders' Original Restaurant. *2 miles N on Hwy 25. Phone 606/528-2163.* (1940) Authentic restoration of the first Kentucky Fried Chicken restaurant. Displays include original kitchen, artifacts, motel room. Original dining area is still in use. (Daily 10 am-10 pm; closed Dec 25) **FREE**

Laurel River Lake. *1433 Laurel Lake Rd, London (40744).* Approximately 10 miles W, in Daniel Boone National Forest (see); access from I-75, Hwy 25 W, Hwy 312, and Hwy 192. Phone 606/864-6412. A 5,600-acre lake with fishing, boating (launch, rentals); hiking, recreation areas, picnicking, camping (fee). **FREE**

Special Event

Nibroc Festival. *Depot St, Corbin (40701). Phone 606/528-8860.* Mountain arts and crafts, parade, square dancing, beauty pageant, midway, entertainment, food booths. Early Aug.

Limited-Service Hotels

★ **BEST WESTERN CORBIN INN.** *2630 Cumberland Falls Hwy, Corbin (40701). Phone 606/528-2100; toll-free 800/780-7234; fax 606/523-1704. www. bestwestern.com.* 63 rooms, 2 story. Complimentary continental breakfast. Check-out 11 am. Outdoor pool. **$**

★ ★ **CUMBERLAND FALLS STATE PARK.** *7351 Hwy 90, Corbin (40701). Phone 606/528-4121; toll-free 800/325-0063; fax 606/528-0704. parks. ky.gov/cumbfal2.htm.* 78 rooms, 3 story. Check-in 4 pm, check-out noon (cottages 11 am). Restaurant. Outdoor pool, children's pool. Tennis. **$**

★ **HAMPTON INN.** *125 Adams Rd, Corbin (40701). Phone 606/523-5696; toll-free 800/426-7866; fax 606/523-1130. www.hamptoninn.com.* 82 rooms, 2 story. Complimentary continental breakfast. Check-out noon. Fitness room. Outdoor pool, whirlpool. **$**

Covington (Cincinnati Airport Area) (A-7)

See also Maysville, Walton, Williamstown

Founded 1815
Population 43,370
Elevation 531 ft
Area Code 859
Information Northern Kentucky Convention and Visitors Bureau, 50 E River Center Blvd, Suite 200, 41011; phone 859/261-4677 or toll-free 800/782-9659
Web Site www.staynky.com

This town is linked to Cincinnati, Ohio, by five broad bridges spanning the Ohio River. Named for a hero of the War of 1812, Covington in its early days had many German settlers who left their mark on the city. East of the city, the Licking River meets the Ohio. The 1867 suspension bridge that crosses from Third and Greenup streets to Cincinnati is the prototype of the Brooklyn Bridge in New York City. The adjacent riverfront area includes Covington Landing, a floating restaurant and entertainment complex.

What to See and Do

Cathedral Basilica of the Assumption. *Madison Ave and 12th St, Covington (Cincinnati Airport Area). Phone 859/431-2060.* (1901) Patterned after the Abbey of St. Denis and the Cathedral of Notre Dame, France, the basilica has massive doors, classic stained-glass windows (including one of the largest in the world), murals and mosaics by local and foreign artists. (Daily; closed holidays) Guided tours (Sun, after 10 am mass; also by appointment). **$**

Devou Park. *Park Dr and Montague Rd, Covington. Phone 859/292-2151.* A 550-acre park with a lake overlooking the Ohio River. Golf (fee), tennis. Picnic grounds. Lookout point, outdoor concerts (mid-June-mid-Aug). (Daily) **FREE** In the park is

> **Behringer-Crawford Museum.** *1600 Montague Rd, Covington (41011). Phone 859/491-4003.* Exhibits on local archaeology, paleontology, history, fine art, and wildlife. (Tues-Sun) **$**

Jillian's. *1200 Jillians Way, Covington (41011). Phone 859/491-5388.* A former brewery converted into a massive entertainment and dining complex, Jillians features restaurants, video and arcade games, a billiards lounge, bowling, dancing, live music, and plenty of TVs to catch the game. (Sun-Tues 11 am-midnight, Wed-Sat 11-2 am)

MainStrasse Village. *W 5th and Main sts, Covington (41011). Phone 859/491-0458. www.mainstrasse.org.* Approximately five square blocks in Covington's old German area offer a historic district of residences, shops, and restaurants in more than 20 restored buildings dating from the mid- to late 1800s. (Mon-Sat 11 am-5 pm, Sun noon-5 pm) Also featured is the

> **Carroll Chimes Bell Tower.** *W end of Village.* Completed in 1979, this 100-foot tower has a 43-bell carillon and mechanical figures that portray the legend of the Pied Piper of Hamelin.

Newport on the Levee. *1 Levee Way, Suite 1113, Newport (41071). Phone toll-free 866/538-3359. www. newportonthelevee.com.* This 10-acre entertainment district on the river includes a trendy shopping center; 12 stylish restaurants; a state-of-the-art, 20-screen movie theater; and the highly acclaimed Newport Aquarium. (June-Aug: Mon-Thurs 10 am-9 pm, Fri-Sat 10 am-10 pm, Sun noon-6 pm; Sept-May: Mon-Thurs 11 am-9 pm, Fri-Sat 11 am-10 pm, Sun noon-6 pm; closed Easter, Thanksgiving, Dec 25)

Vent Haven Museum. *33 W Maple Ave, Fort Mitchell (41011). Phone 859/341-0461; fax 859/341-0461. www. venthavenmuseum.net.* This unique museum features more than 500 ventriloquist figures from 20 countries, and pictures and collectibles related to ventriloquism. (By appointment only, May-Sept) **$**

World of Sports. *7400 Woodspoint Dr, Florence (41042). Phone 859/371-8255. www.landrumgolf.com.* This family entertainment complex includes an 18-hole golf course (daily 7 am-dark), 25-station lighted practice range and nine covered tees, miniature golf course, billiard hall, snack bar, and video arcade. (Sun-Thurs 9 am-11 pm, Fri-Sat 9-1 am)

Special Events

Horse racing. *Turfway Park Race Course. 7500 Turfway Rd, Florence (41042). Phone 859/371-0200; toll-free 800/733-0200. www.turfway.com.* Thoroughbred racing Wed-Sun. Early Sept-early Oct and late Nov-early Apr.

Lanes End Spiral Stakes Race. *Turfway Park Race Track, 7500 Turfway Rd, Florence (41042). Phone 859/371-0200. www.spiralstakes.com.* One of the largest pursed thoroughbred races for 3-year-olds. Race culminates week-long festival. Late Mar.

Maifest. *MainStrasse Village, 605 Philadelphia St, Covington (41011). Phone 859/491-0458.* Traditional German spring festival with entertainment, arts and crafts, food, games, and rides. Third weekend in May.

Oktoberfest. *MainStrasse Village, 605 Philadelphia St, Covington (41011).* Entertainment, arts and crafts, food. Early Sept.

Riverfest. *Banks of Ohio River. Phone 859/261-4677.* One of the largest fireworks displays in the country; shot from barges moored on the river. Labor Day weekend.

Limited-Service Hotels

★ **ASHLEY QUARTERS.** *4880 Houston Rd, Florence (41042). Phone 859/525-9997; toll-free 888/525-9997; fax 859/525-9980. www.ashleyquarters.com.* 70 rooms, 2 story. Pets accepted; fee. Check-out noon. Wireless Internet access. Outdoor pool. Business center. **$**

★ ★ **BEST WESTERN FT. MITCHELL INN.** *2100 Dixie Hwy, Fort Mitchell (41011). Phone 859/331-1500; toll-free 800/780-7234; fax 859/331-5265. www. bestwestern.com.* This hotel, close to both downtown and the airport, features many services with families

and children in mind. 214 rooms, 2 story. Check-out 11 am. Bar. Fitness room. Indoor pool, whirlpool. Airport transportation available. **$**

★ **BEST WESTERN INN FLORENCE.** *7871 Commerce Dr, Florence (41042). Phone 859/525-0090; toll-free 800/780-7234; fax 859/525-6743. www. bestwestern.com.* 51 rooms, 3 story. Complimentary continental breakfast. Check-out 11 am. Fitness room. Outdoor pool. **$**

★ ★ **DRAWBRIDGE INN.** *2477 Royal Dr, Fort Mitchell (41017). Phone 859/341-2800; toll-free 800/354-9793; fax 859/341-5644. www.drawbridgeinn. com.* 505 rooms, 4 story. Check-out noon. Restaurant, bar. Fitness room. Indoor pool, two outdoor pools, whirlpool. Tennis. Airport transportation available. The Oldenberg brewery is adjacent. **$**

★ **HAMPTON INN.** *200 Crescent Ave, Covington (41011). Phone 859/581-7800; fax 859/581-8282. www. hamptoninn.com.* 151 rooms, 6 story. Complimentary continental breakfast. Check-in 3 pm, check-out noon. High-speed Internet access. Fitness room. Indoor pool. **$**

★ ★ **RESIDENCE INN BY MARRIOTT.** *2811 Circleport Dr, Erlanger (41018). Phone 859/282-7400; toll-free 800/331-3131; fax 859/282-1790. www. residenceinn.com.* 96 rooms, 3 story. Pets accepted; fee. Complimentary continental breakfast. Check-out noon. Fitness room. Outdoor pool, whirlpool. Airport transportation available. **$**

Full-Service Hotels

★ ★ **EMBASSY SUITES.** *10 E River Center Blvd, Covington (41011). Phone 859/261-8400; toll-free 800/362-2779; fax 859/261-8486. www.cincinnatiriver-suites.embsuites.com.* Located on the Ohio River, just 1/2 mile from Cincinnati, this hotel offers a complimentary full breakfast, an indoor pool, a fitness center, and meeting facilities. Guest suites feature data ports, hair dryers, satellite television, and kitchenettes. 226 rooms, 8 story, all suites. Pets accepted, some restrictions. Complimentary full breakfast. Check-in 3 pm, check-out noon. High-speed Internet access, wireless Internet access. Restaurant, bar. Fitness room. Indoor pool, whirlpool. Business center. **$**

★ ★ ★ **HILTON GREATER CINCINNATI AIRPORT.** *7373 Turfway Rd, Florence (41042). Phone 859/371-4400; toll-free 800/932-3322; fax 859/371-3361. www.hilton.com.* 206 rooms, 5 story. Check-in 3 pm, check-out noon. Restaurant, bar. Fitness room. Outdoor pool. Tennis. Airport transportation available. **$**
🚶 🏊 ⛷

★ ★ ★ **MARRIOTT AT RIVERCENTER.** *10 W RiverCenter Blvd, Covington (41011). Phone 859/261-2900; toll-free 800/228-9290; fax 859/261-0900. www.marriott.com.* 326 rooms, 14 story. Check-in 4 pm, check-out 11 am. High-speed Internet access, wireless Internet access. Restaurant, bar. Fitness room. Indoor pool, whirlpool. Airport transportation available. Business center. **$**
🚶 🏊 🏃

★ ★ ★ **RADISSON HOTEL CINCINNATI RIVERFRONT.** *668 W 5th St, Covington (41011). Phone 859/491-1200; fax 859/491-0326. www.radisson.com.* The guest rooms are handsomely appointed, offering views of the beautiful Ohio River, the lush wooded hills of northern Kentucky, or the scenic area of downtown Cincinnati. Nearby attractions include the Cincinnati Reds and Bengals, the Newport Aquarium, and Cincinnati Zoo. 236 rooms, 18 story. Check-out 11 am. Restaurant, bar. Fitness room. Indoor, outdoor pool; whirlpool. Airport transportation available. **$**
🚶 🏊

Restaurants

★ ★ **DEE FELICE CAFE.** *529 Main St, Covington (41011). Phone 859/261-2365; fax 859/261-6253. www.deefelice.com.* This is a neighborhood spot featuring Cajun classics such as shrimp creole and jambalaya; large portions, reasonable prices. Cajun/Creole menu. Dinner, Sun brunch. Casual attire. Reservations recommended. Outdoor seating. **$$**

★ ★ **MIKE FINK.** *1 Ben Bernstein Pl, Covington (41011). Phone 859/261-4212; fax 859/261-3941. www.mikefink.com.* Old paddlewheel steamer, permanently moored. Seafood menu. Lunch, dinner, Sun brunch. Bar. Children's menu. Casual attire. Reservations recommended. **$$**

★ ★ **RIVERVIEW.** *668 W 5th St, Covington (41011). Phone 859/491-5300; fax 859/491-8668.* Located on the 18th floor of the Radisson Hotel Cincinnati Riverfront, this revolving eatery offers a panoramic view of downtown Cincinnati and northern Kentucky. Ameri-can menu. Breakfast, lunch, dinner. Bar. Children's menu. Business casual attire. Reservations recommended. **$$**

★ ★ ★ **WATERFRONT.** *14 Pete Rose Pier, Covington (41011). Phone 859/581-1414; fax 859/392-2774. www.jeffruby.com.* This bustling steak and lobster house has a stunning view of the Cincinnati skyline and a sit-down sushi bar. Steak menu. Dinner. Closed Sun. Business casual attire. Reservations recommended. Valet parking. Outdoor seating. **$$$**

Cumberland Falls State Resort Park (D-7)

See also Corbin, Williamsburg; also see Harrogate, TN

Web Site www.cumberlandfallspark.com

7351 Hwy 90, Corbin (40701). 19 miles SW of Corbin via Hwy 25 W, Hwy 90. Phone 606-528-4121.

In this 1,657-acre park on the Cumberland River is a magnificent waterfall, 65 feet high and 125 feet wide, amid beautiful scenery. Surrounded by Daniel Boone National Forest (see), this awesome waterfall is the second largest east of the Rockies. By night, when the moon is full and the sky clear, a mysterious moonbow appears in the mist. This is the only place in the Western Hemisphere where this phenomenon can be seen. Swimming pool (seasonal), fishing, nature trails, nature center, riding (seasonal), tennis, picnicking, playground, lodge, cottages, tent and trailer campsites (standard fees).

What to See and Do

Blue Heron Mining Community. *In Big South Fork National River/Recreation Area (KY side); S via Hwy 27 and Hwy 92 to Stearns, then 9 miles W on Hwy 742 (Mine 18 Rd). Phone 606/376-3787. www.nps.gov/biso/bheron.htm.* Re-created mid-20th century mining town where 300 miners were once employed. Depot has exhibits on the history of the town with scale models, photographs. Town features giant coal tipple built in 1937 and metal frame representations of miners' houses, church, school, company store. Snack bar and gift shop (Apr-Oct). A scenic railway line connects Blue Heron with the town of Stearns (see SOMERSET). **FREE**

Sheltowee Trace Outfitters. *117 Hawkins Ave, Somerset. Phone 606/376-5567; toll-free 800/541-7238. www. ky-rafting.com.* River rafting, canoeing, and "funyak" trips in the scenic Cumberland River below the falls; Big South Fork Gorge. five- to seven-hour trips, appointments required. (Memorial Day-Sept: daily; mid-Mar-mid-May and Oct: Sat-Sun). **$$$$**

Limited-Service Hotel

★ ★ **CUMBERLAND FALLS STATE PARK.** *7351 Hwy 90, Corbin (40701). Phone 606/528-4121; toll-free 800/325-0063; fax 606/528-0704. parks. ky.gov/cumbfal2.htm.* 78 rooms, 3 story. Check-in 4 pm, check-out noon (cottages 11 am). Restaurant. Outdoor pool, children's pool. Tennis. **$**
🛏️ 🎿

Cumberland Gap National Historical Park (D-8)

See also Pineville, Williamsburg; also see Harrogate, TN

Information Park Superintendent, Hwy 25E, Box 1848, Middlesboro 40965; phone 606/248-2817
Web Site www.nps.gov/cuga/

Cumberland Gap, a natural passage through the mountain barrier that effectively sealed off the infant American coastal colonies, was the open door to western development. Through this pass first came Dr. Thomas Walker in 1750, followed by Daniel Boone in 1769. In 1775, Boone and 30 axmen cut a 208-mile swath through the forests from Kingsport, Tennessee, to the Kentucky River, passing through the Cumberland Gap. Settlers poured through the pass and along Boone's "Wilderness Road," and in 1777 Kentucky became Virginia's westernmost county. Although pioneers were harassed by Native Americans during the Revolution, travel over the Wilderness Road continued to increase and became heavier than ever. After the Revolution, the main stream of western settlement poured through Cumberland Gap and slowed only when more direct northerly routes were opened. During the Civil War, the gap was a strategic point, changing hands several times.

Nearly 22,300 acres of this historic and dramatically beautiful countryside in Kentucky, Tennessee, and Virginia have been set aside as a national historical park. More than 50 miles of hiking trails provide a variety of walks, long and short. Park (daily; closed Jan 1, Dec 25).

What to See and Do

Camping. *Off Hwy 58, Cumberland Gap.* Tables, fireplaces, water, and bathhouse. 14-day limit. **$$$**

Civil War fortifications. *Corbin.* Throughout the Gap area.

Hensley Settlement. An isolated mountain community, now a restored historic site that is accessible by hiking 3 1/2 miles up the Chadwell Gap trail or by driving up a Jeep road.

Pinnacle Overlook. Broad vistas of mountains and forests viewed from a high peak jutting above the Cumberland valley. Vehicles over 20 feet in length and all trailers are prohibited.

Tri-State Peak. View of meeting point of Kentucky, Virginia, and Tennessee.

Visitor center. Historical exhibits, audiovisual program. (Closed holidays). At west end of park (near Middlesboro).

Daniel Boone National Forest (C-8)

See also Hazard, London, Morehead, Williamsburg

Web Site www.southernregion.fs.fed.us/boone/

Stretches roughly north-south from Morehead on Hwy 60 to Whitley City on Hwy 27.

Within these 692,164 acres is some of the most spectacular scenery in Kentucky, from the Cave Run and Laurel River lakes to the Natural Arch Scenic Area. The forest includes the Red River Gorge Geological Area, known for its natural arches. The gorge has colorful rock formations and cliffs that average 100 to 300 feet high. A scenic loop drive of the gorge begins north of Natural Bridge State Resort Park (see) on Hwy 77. The nearest camping facilities (fee) are located at Koomer Ridge, on Hwy 15 between the Slade (33) and Beattyville (40) exits of Mount Parkway.

The Sheltowee Trace National Recreation Trail runs generally north to south, begininning near Morehead (see) and continuing to Pickett State Rustic Park, Tennessee (see JAMESTOWN, TN), a total distance of more than 260 miles. Forest Development Road 918, the main road into the Zilpo Recreation Area, has been designated a National Scenic Byway. The 11.2-mile road features a pleasant, winding trip through Kentucky hardwood forest, with interpretive signs and pull-overs with views of Cave Run Lake.

Cave Run Lake (see MOREHEAD) has swimming beaches, boat ramps, and camping at Twin Knobs and Zilpo recreation areas. Laurel River Lake (see CORBIN) has boat ramps and camping areas at Holly Bay and Grove (vehicle access). Clay Lick (Cave Run Lake), Grove, and White Oak (Laurel River Lake) have boat-in camping. Hunting and fishing are permitted in most parts of the forest under Kentucky regulations; backpacking is permitted on forest trails. For further information contact the Forest Supervisor, 1700 Bypass Rd, Winchester 40391; phone 859/745-3100 or toll-free 800/255-7275.

Danville (C-7)

See also Harrodsburg

Founded 1775
Population 15,477
Elevation 989 ft
Area Code 859
Zip 40422
Information Danville-Boyle County Convention & Visitors Bureau, 105 E Walnut; phone 859/236-7794 or toll-free 800/755-0076
Web Site www.danvillekentucky.com

The birthplace of Kentucky government, Danville is near the geographical center of the state. Ten years after the city was founded, it became the first capital of the Kentucky district of Virginia. Later, nine conventions were held leading to admission of the state to the Union. From 1775-1792, Danville was the most important center in Kentucky, the major settlement on the Wilderness Road. "Firsts" seem to come naturally to Danville, which claims the state's first college, first log courthouse, first post office, first brick courthouse, first school for the deaf, and first law school.

One of the largest tobacco markets in the state, Danville has also attracted several industrial plants.

What to See and Do

Constitution Square State Shrine. *134 S 2nd St, Danville (40422). On Hwy 127 in the center of town.* Phone 859/239-7089. Authentic reproduction of Kentucky's first courthouse square stands at the exact site where the first state constitution was framed and adopted in 1792. Original post office; replicas of jail, courthouse, meetinghouse; restored row house, Dr. Goldsmith House, and Grayson Tavern. Governor's Circle has a bronze plaque of each Kentucky governor. Museum store, art gallery. (Daily) **FREE**

Herrington Lake. *1200 Gwinn Island Rd, Danville (40422). 3 miles N off Hwy 33.* Phone 859/236-4286. Formed by Dix Dam, one of the world's largest rock-filled dams, Herrington has 333 miles of shoreline. Balanced fish population maintained through conservation program. Fishing (fee), boat launch (fee; rentals); camping (hookups), cabins. **FREE**

Kids Farm Education Center. *636 Quirks Run Rd, Danville (40422).* Phone 859/236-1414. A working farm open to the public to experience wildlife management techniques, exotic animals, and wild game in a natural setting. (Daily) **$$**

McDowell House and Apothecary Shop. *125 S 2nd St, Danville (40422).* Phone 859/236-2804. www.mcdowellhouse.com. Residence and shop of Dr. Ephraim McDowell, noted surgeon of the early 19th century. Restored and refurbished with period pieces. Large apothecary-ware collection. Gardens include trees, wildflowers, and herbs of the period. (Mon-Sat 10 am-noon, 1-4 pm, Sun 2-4 pm; closed Mon from Nov-Mar; also holidays) **$**

Perryville Battlefield State Historic Site. *1825 Battlefield Rd, Perryville (40468). 10 miles W on Hwy 150, 4 miles N on Hwy 68.* Phone 859/332-8631. www.state.ky.us/agencies/parks/perryvil.htm. A 300-acre park, once a field, appears much as it did Oct 8, 1862, when Confederate forces under General Braxton Bragg and Union troops under General Don Carlos Buell clashed. A total of 4,241 Union soldiers and 1,822 Confederate troops were killed, wounded, or missing. Still standing are the Crawford House, used by Bragg as headquarters, and Bottom House, center of some of the heaviest fighting. Mock battle is staged each year (weekend nearest Oct 8). A 30-acre area at the north end of what was the battle line includes a memorial erected in 1902 to the Confederate dead and one raised in 1931 to the Union dead. Museum with artifacts from battle; 9-by-9-foot, detailed battle map;

battle dioramas (fee). Hiking, picnicking, playground. Self-guided tours. (Apr-Oct: daily; rest of year: by appointment) **$**

Pioneer Playhouse Village-of-the-Arts. *840 Stanford Rd, Danville (40422). 1 mile S on Stanford Ave, Hwy 150. Phone 859/236-2747.* Reproduction of an 18th-century Kentucky village on a 200-acre site; drama school, museum. Camping (fee). (See SPECIAL EVENT) (May-mid-Oct, daily) **FREE**

Special Event

Pioneer Playhouse. *Pioneer Playhouse Village-of-the-Arts, 840 Stanford Rd, Danville (40422). Phone 859/236-2747.* Summer stock; Broadway comedies, musicals. Tues-Sat evenings. June-Aug.

Limited-Service Hotels

★ ★ **COUNTRY HEARTH INN - DANVILLE.** *Hwy 127, Danville (40422). Phone 859/236-8601; fax 859/236-0314. www.countryhearth.com.* 81 rooms, 2 story. Pets accepted. Check-out noon. Restaurant. Outdoor pool. **$**

★ **HOLIDAY INN EXPRESS.** *96 Daniel Dr, Danville (40422). Phone 859/236-8600; fax 859/236-4299. www.hiexpress.com.* 63 rooms. Complimentary continental breakfast. Check-out noon. Outdoor pool, whirlpool. **$**

Elizabethtown (C-6)

See also Abraham Lincoln Birthplace National Historic Site, Bardstown, Fort Knox, Hodgenville, Shepherdsville

Founded 1797
Population 22,542
Elevation 731 ft
Area Code 270
Zip 42701
Information Elizabethtown Tourism & Convention Bureau, 1030 N Mulberry St; phone 270/765-2175 or toll-free 800/437-0092
Web Site www.touretown.com

The Lincoln story has deep roots in this town. Thomas Lincoln, the President's father, owned property and worked in Elizabethtown; it is the town to which Thomas Lincoln brought his bride, Nancy Hanks, immediately after their marriage. Abe's older sister Sarah was born in Elizabethtown. After his first wife's death, Thomas Lincoln returned to marry Sarah Bush Johnston.

What to See and Do

Brown-Pusey Community House. *128 N Main St, Elizabethtown. Phone 270/765-2515.* (1825) This former stagecoach inn is an excellent example of Georgian Colonial architecture; General George Custer lived here from 1871 to 1873. Restored as a historical genealogy library (fee) and community house; garden. (Mon-Sat 10 am-4 pm; closed holidays) **FREE**

Lincoln Heritage House. *1 mile N on Hwy 31 W in Freeman Lake Park. Phone 270/765-2175; toll-free 800/437-0092. www.touretown.com/heritagehouse. html.* Double log cabin (1789, 1805) was the home of Hardin Thomas. Unusual trim work done by Thomas Lincoln. Pioneer implements, early surveying equipment, period furniture. Park facilities include pavilions, paddle and row boats, canoes. (June-Sept, Tues-Sun 10 am-5 pm) **FREE**

Schmidt Museum of Coca-Cola Memorabilia. *109 Buffalo Creek Dr, Elizabethtown (42701). Just off I-65, exit 94, in the Elizabethtown Visitor's Center. Phone 270/234-1100. www.schmidtmuseum.com.* The world's largest private collection of Coca-Cola memorabilia includes more than 80,000 items dating back to 1886. More than 1,100 pieces are on display at this museum at a given time. Expect to see artifacts like old Coca-Cola toys, bottles, Santas, trays, and vending machines. (Mon-Fri 9 am-5 pm; also Sat 10 am-2 pm May-Sept; closed holidays) **$**

Special Events

Hardin County Fair. *Hardin County Fairgrounds, Elizabethtown (42701). S on Hwy 31 W Phone 270/765-2175.* Hardin County Fairgrounds. Mid-July.

Kentucky Heartland Festival. *Freeman Lake Park, 111 W Dixie, Elizabethtown (42701). Phone 270/765-4334.* Antique auto show, arts and crafts, canoe race, running event, hot air balloon, bluegrass music, games, food. Last full weekend in Aug.

Limited-Service Hotels

★ **BEST WESTERN ATRIUM GARDENS.** *1043 Executive Dr, Elizabethtown (42701). Phone 270/769-3030; fax 270/769-2516.www.bestwestern.com.*133 rooms, 2 story. Pets accepted. Complimentary continental breakfast. Check-out 11:30 am. Indoor pool. **$**

★ **KENTUCKY CARDINAL INN.** *642 E Dixie Ave, Elizabethtown (42701). Phone 270/765-6139; toll-free 800/528-1234; fax 270/765-7208. www.bestwestern. com.* 54 rooms, 2 story. Pets accepted, some restrictions; fee. Complimentary continental breakfast. Check-out 11:30 am. Outdoor pool. **$**

Restaurants

★ **JERRY'S.** *612 E Dixie Ave, Elizabethtown (42701). Phone 270/769-2336; fax 270/769-6596.* American menu. Breakfast, lunch, dinner. Closed Dec 25. Children's menu. **$$**

★ ★ **STONE HEARTH.** *1001 N Mulberry, Elizabethtown (42701). Phone 270/765-4898.* Lunch, dinner. Closed Jan 1, Dec 25. **$$**

Fort Knox (B-6)

See also Elizabethtown, Louisville, Shepherdsville

Population 12,377
Elevation 740 ft
Area Code 270
Zip 40121
Information Public Affairs Office, US Army Armor Center & Fort Knox, PO Box 995
Web Site www.knox.army.mil

This military post, established in 1918, is home for the US Army Armor Center and School and the Army's home of Mounted Warfare. Named for Major General Henry Knox, first Secretary of War, the post has been a major installation since 1932, when mechanization of the Army began.

What to See and Do

Patton Museum of Cavalry and Armor. *4554 Fayette Ave, Fort Knox (40121). Phone 502/624-3812. www.generalpatton.org.* The Armor Branch Museum was named in honor of General George S. Patton, Jr. The collection includes US and foreign armored equipment, weapons, art, and uniforms; mementos of General Patton's military career, including the sedan in which he was riding when he was fatally injured in 1945. Also on display are a 10-by-12-foot section of the Berlin Wall and foreign armored equipment from Operation Desert Storm.

(Mon-Fri 9 am-4:30 pm; Sat-Sun, holidays from 10 am; Jan 1, Dec 24-25, 31) **FREE**

United States Bullion Depository. *Gold Vault Rd. www. usmint.gov.* Two-story granite, steel, and concrete building. Opened in 1937, the building houses part of the nation's gold reserves. The depository and the surrounding grounds are not open to the public.

Special Event

Armored Vehicle Presentation. *Patton Museum, 4554 Fayette Ave, Fort Knox (40121). Phone 502/624-3812.* Operational armored vehicle demonstration features restored World War II tanks and authentically uniformed troops. July 4.

Limited-Service Hotel

★ **RADCLIFF INN.** *438 S Dixie Blvd, Radcliff (40160). Phone 270/351-8211; toll-free 800/421-2030; fax 270/351-3227. www.radcliffinn.com.* 83 rooms, 3 story. Complimentary continental breakfast. Check-out noon. Fitness room. Outdoor pool. **$**

Frankfort (B-7)

See also Georgetown, Lexington

Founded 1786
Population 27,741
Elevation 510 ft
Area Code 502
Zip 40601
Information Frankfort/Franklin County Tourist and Convention Commisssion, 100 Capital Ave; phone 502/875-8687 or toll-free 800/960-7200
Web Site www.visitfrankfort.com

Frankfort is split by the Kentucky River, which meanders through the city. Although rich farmlands funnel burley tobacco and corn through Frankfort, the chief crop is politics, especially when the legislature is in session. Frankfort was chosen as the state capital in 1792 as a compromise to settle the rival claims of Lexington and Louisville. Frankfort was briefly held by the Confederates during the Civil War. Later, the "corn liquor" industry blossomed in this area, utilizing water from flowing limestone springs. Bourbon distilleries carry on this tradition.

What to See and Do

Daniel Boone's Grave. *215 E Main St, Frankfort (40601). In Frankfort Cemetery.* Monument to Boone and his wife. Boone died in Missouri but his remains were brought here in 1845.

Kentucky Military History Museum. *Main St and Capital Ave, Frankfort.* Phone 502/564-3265. *www.history.ky.gov/Museums/Kentucky_Military_History_Museum.htm.* Exhibits trace Kentucky's involvement in military conflicts through two centuries. Weapons, flags, uniforms. (Tues-Sat 10 am-5 pm; closed Sun, holidays) **$**

Kentucky State University. *400 E Main St, Frankfort (40601).* Phone 502/597-6000. *www.kysu.edu.* (1886) (2,300 students) Liberal studies institution. Jackson Hall (1887) has art and photo gallery exhibits (Sept-mid-May); King Farouk butterfly collection in Carver Hall. Jackson Hall and Hume Hall (1909) are on the historic register.

Kentucky Vietnam Veterans Memorial. *300 Coffee Tree Rd, Frankfort (40601). Adjacent to State Library and Archives. www.kyvietnammemorial.com.* Unique memorial is a 14-foot sundial that casts a shadow across veterans' names on the anniversaries of their deaths. Memorial contains more than 1,000 names.

Liberty Hall. *218 Wilkinson St, Frankfort. At W Main St.* Phone 502/227-2560. *www.libertyhall.org.* (Circa 1796) Fine example of Georgian architecture, built by the first US senator from Kentucky, John Brown, is completely restored to its original state and furnished with family heirlooms. Period gardens. (Mar-mid-Dec, tours given Tues-Sun at 10:30 am, noon, 1:30 pm, 3 pm, Sun noon, 1:30 pm and 3 pm; closed holidays) **$** On the same block is

Orlando Brown House. *202 Wilkinson St, Frankfort (40601).* Phone 502/227-2560. (1835) Early Greek Revival house built for Orlando Brown, son of Senator John Brown; original furnishings and artifacts. (Mar-Dec, Tues-Sun; closed holidays) **$$**

Old State Capitol Building. *Broadway and Lewis sts, Frankfort. www.history.ky.gov/Museums/Old_State_Capitol.htm.* Kentucky's third capitol building, erected in 1827-1829, was used as the capitol from 1829-1909 and was the first Greek Revival statehouse west of the Alleghenies. Completely restored and furnished in period style, the building features an unusual self-balanced double stairway. (Tues-Fri 10 am-5 pm; closed Sat-Sun) **FREE** In the Old Capitol Annex are

Kentucky History Center. *100 W Broadway St, Frankfort (40601).* Phone 502/564-3016. Exhibits pertaining to the history and development of the state and the culture of its people. (Tues-Sat 10 am-5 pm also Sun afternoons; closed Sun-Mon, holidays) **$**

Library. *100 W Broadway St, Frankfort (40601).* Phone 502/564-3016. Manuscripts, maps, photographs, and special collections cover Kentucky's history; genealogy section. (Tues-Sat 8 am-4 pm; closed Sun-Mon, holidays) **FREE**

State Capitol. *700 Capitol Ave, Frankfort (40601).* Phone 502/564-3449. *www.state.ky.us/agencies/finance/attract/capitol2.htm.* (1910) The building is noted for Ionic columns and the high central dome on an Ionic peristyle, topped with a lantern cupola. In the rotunda are statues of Abraham Lincoln, Jefferson Davis, Henry Clay, Dr. Ephraim McDowell, and Alben Barkley, vice president under Harry S. Truman. Guided tours. (Mon-Fri 8:30 am-3:30 pm, Sat 10 am-2 pm, Sun 1-4 pm; closed holidays). **FREE** On the grounds are

Floral Clock. *300 Capitol Ave, Frankfort (40601).* Phone 502/564-3449. Functioning outdoor timepiece is adorned with thousands of plants and elevated above a reflecting pool. Mechanism moves a 530-pound minute hand and a 420-pound hour hand. Visitors toss thousands of dollars in coins into the pool, all of which are turned over to state child-care agencies.

Old Governor's Mansion. *420 High St, Frankfort (40601).* Phone 502/564-3449. (1914) Official residence of the Governor is styled after the Petit Trianon, Marie Antoinette's villa at Versailles. Guided tours (Tues and Thurs 1:30-3:30 pm). **FREE**

Special Events

Capital Expo Festival. *405 Mero St, Capital Plaza Complex, Frankfort (40601).* Phone 502/695-7452. *www.capitalexpofestival.com.* Traditional music, country music, fiddling; workshops, demonstrations, arts and crafts; balloon race, dancing, games, contests, puppets, museum exhibitions, ethnic and regional foods, entertainment. First full weekend in June.

Governor's Derby Breakfast. *700 Capitol Ave, Frankfort (40601).* Phone 502/564-2611. Breakfast, entertainment, and Kentucky crafts. First Sat in May.

Limited-Service Hotel

★ **BEST WESTERN PARKSIDE INN.** *80 Chenault Rd, Frankfort (40601). Phone 502/695-6111; toll-free 800/938-8376; fax 502/695-6112. www.best-western.com.* 99 rooms, 2 story. Complimentary continental breakfast. Check-in 3 pm, check-out noon. Fitness room. Indoor pool, outdoor pool. Airport transportation available. **$**

Full-Service Hotel

★ ★ **CAPITAL PLAZA HOTEL.** *405 Wilkinson Blvd, Frankfort (40601). Phone 502/227-5100; fax 502/875-7147.* Located only two blocks from downtown, shopping, restaurants, and historic attractions, this hotel is perfect for business and leisure travelers. 189 rooms, 8 story. Pets accepted, some restrictions; fee. Check-in 3 pm, check-out noon. Restaurant, bar. Fitness room. Indoor pool. **$**

Restaurant

★ **JIM'S SEAFOOD.** *950 Wilkinson Blvd, Frankfort (40601). Phone 502/223-7448; fax 502/227-7419.* Seafood menu. Lunch, dinner. Closed Sun; holidays. Children's menu. **$$**

Georgetown (B-7)

See also Frankfort, Lexington, Paris

Settled 1776
Population 18,080
Elevation 871 ft
Information Georgetown/Scott County Chamber of Commerce, 399 Outlet Center Dr, PO Box 825; phone 502/863-2547 or toll-free 888/863-8600
Web Site www.georgetownky.com

Royal Spring's crystal-clear water flows in the center of this city. This spring attracted pioneer settlers, who established an outpost at Georgetown and rebuffed frequent Native American attacks. The town was named for George Washington and was incorporated in 1790 by the Virginia legislature. Today it remains a quiet college town, with a large portion of the business area designated as a historic district.

What to See and Do

Cardome Centre. *800 Cincinnati Pike, Georgetown (40324). I-75 exit 125/126, on Hwy 25 N. Phone 502/863-1575.* Former house of Civil War Governor J. F. Robinson and later home of the Academy of the Sisters of the Visitation. Serves as a community center. (Mon-Fri, also by appointment; closed holidays) **FREE**

Royal Spring Park. *W Main and S Water sts, Georgetown (40324). Phone 502/863-2547.* Location of Royal Spring, largest in Kentucky and source of city water since 1775. Former site of McClelland's Fort (1776), first paper mill in the West, pioneer classical music school, and state's first ropewalk. Reputed site of first bourbon distillation in 1789. Cabin of former slave relocated and restored here for use as an information center (mid-May-mid-Oct, Tues-Sun). Picnicking. (Daily)

Scott County Courthouse. *101 E Main St, Georgetown (40324). At Broadway. Phone 502/863-7850.* (1877) Designed in Second Empire style by Thomas Boyd of Pittsburgh. Part of the historic business district. (Mon-Fri; closed holidays) **FREE**

Toyota Motor Manufacturing, Kentucky, Inc. *1001 Cherry Blossom Way, Georgetown (40324). Phone 502/868-3027; toll-free 800/866-4485. www.toyotageorge-town.com.* About 400,000 cars and 350,000 engines are made here annually. The visitor center has interactive exhibits. One-hour tours of the plant (ages six and up) include a video presentation and tram ride through different levels of production. Visitor center (Mon-Fri). Tours (reservations required; Mon-Fri). **FREE**

Gilbertsville (C-6)

See also Cadiz, Land Between the Lakes, Paducah

Population 500
Area Code 270
Zip 42044
Information Marshall County Chamber of Commerce, Inc, 17 Hwy 68 W, Benton 42025; phone 270/527-7665

Fishing parties heading for Kentucky Lake stop in Gilbertsville for last-minute provisions. The area also caters to tourists bound for the resorts and state parks. Chemical plants have been built nearby, utilizing Kentucky Dam's hydroelectric power.

What to See and Do

Barkley Lock and Dam. *Hwy 62 and Hwy 641, Gilberts-*

ville (42044). Phone 270/362-4236. A 1,004-mile shoreline created by the damming of the Cumberland River; information and visitor center. Contact the Resource Manager, PO Box 218, Grand Rivers 42045. **FREE**

Kentucky Dam. *Phone 270/362-4221.* Longest dam in the TVA system, 22 miles upstream from Paducah; 206 feet high, 8,422 feet long, costing $118 million, created a lake 184 miles long with 2,380 miles of shoreline. Regulates flow of water from the Tennessee River into the Ohio River. Carries Hwy 62/641 across northern end of Kentucky Lake. Viewing balcony (daily); tours of powerhouse (by appointment). **FREE**

Kentucky Dam Village State Resort Park. *Just S of town off Hwy 62/641 on Kentucky Lake. Phone 270/362-4271.* A 1,352-acre park on a 160,300-acre lake. Fishing, swimming beach, pool, bathhouse (seasonal), waterskiing, boating (rentals, launching ramps, docks); hiking, 18-hole and miniature golf (seasonal fee), tennis, picnicking, playground, shops, grocery, camping, lodge, cottages. Supervised recreation. Lighted 4,000-foot airstrip.

Limited-Service Hotel

★ ★ **KENTUCKY DAM STATE RESORT.** *113 Administration Drive, Gilbertsville (42044). Phone 270/362-4271; toll-free 800/325-0146; fax 270/362-2951.* 156 rooms, 2 story. Check-in 4 pm, check-out noon (cottages 11 am). Restaurant. Outdoor pool, children's pool. Golf. Tennis. Airport transportation available. **$**

Glasgow (D-6)

See also Cave City, Horse Cave, Mammoth Cave National Park, Park City

Settled 1799
Population 12,351
Elevation 790 ft
Area Code 270
Zip 42141
Information Glasgow-Barren County Chamber of Commerce, 118 E Public Sq; phone 270/651-3161
Web Site www.glasgowbarrenchamber.com

Glasgow was one of the first towns to be settled in the "barrens," then an almost treeless plateau west of the bluegrass section of Kentucky. Today, lumber products are important in Glasgow, although tobacco is the leading money crop, followed by dairy products.

What to See and Do

Barren River Dam and Lake. *11088 Finney Rd, Glasgow (42141). 12 miles SW on Hwy 31 E. Phone 270/646-2055.* Impounds the waters of the Barren River and its tributaries. There is good bass fishing, boating (ramps), water sports; picnic areas, camping, lodge, cabins (most have fee). Other recreation areas and campsites include Baileys Point, Beaver Creek, Browns Ford. Also here is

> **Barren River Lake State Resort Park.** *1149 State Park Rd, Lucas (42156). Phone 270/646-2151.* Approximately 2,100 acres with a 10,000-acre lake. Swimming beach, pool, fishing, boating (rentals); hiking, horseback riding, bicycle trails, 18-hole golf course, tennis, picnicking, playground, tent and trailer sites (Apr-Oct, standard fees), cottages, lodge. Some fees.

Special Event

Highland Games and Gathering of Scottish Clans. *1149 St Park Rd, Lucas (42156). Phone 270/651-3161.* 14 miles S via Hwy 31 E in Barren River Lake State Resort Park (see). Six-day festival. Weekend following Memorial Day.

Limited-Service Hotel

★ **DAYS INN.** *105 Days Inn Blvd, Glasgow (42141). Phone 270/651-1757; fax 270/651-1755. www.daysinn.com.* 59 rooms, 2 story. Check-out noon. Indoor pool, whirlpool. **$**

Full-Service Resort

★ ★ **BARREN RIVER LAKE STATE RESORT PARK.** *1149 State Park Rd, Lucas (42156). Phone 270/646-2151; fax 270/646-3645.* A water lover's resort on 2,187 acres. Enjoy boat rentals, a golf course, lodge, marina with nature program and swimming, a beautiful 4-mile nature trail, and a 2-mile paved trail for bikes and wheelchairs. 51 rooms, 3 story. Closed five days the week of Dec 25. Check-in 4 pm, check-out noon (cottages 11 am). Restaurant. Children's activity center. Outdoor pool, children's pool. Golf. Tennis. **$**

Specialty Lodging

FOUR SEASONS COUNTRY INN. *4107 Scottsville Rd, Glasgow (42141). Phone 270/678-1000; fax 270/678-1017.* This quaint Victorian-style bed-and-breakfast features many rooms furnished with four-poster beds and fireplaces, set within a comfortable, homestyle atmosphere. 21 rooms, 3 story. Complimentary continental breakfast. Check-in 2 pm, check-out 11 am. Outdoor pool. **$**

Restaurant

★ ★ **BOLTON'S LANDING.** *2433 Scottsville Rd, Glasgow (42141). Phone 270/651-8008; fax 270/651-1576. www.mammothcave.com.* Lunch, dinner. Closed Sun; holidays. Children's menu. **$$**

Greenville (C-4)

See also Hopkinsville, Madisonville

Settled 1799
Population 4,689
Elevation 538 ft
Area Code 270
Zip 42345
Information Chamber of Commerce, 200 Court St; phone 270/338-5422

Located in the heart of the western Kentucky coal, oil, and natural gas fields, Greenville is the seat of Muhlenberg County. There is good hunting and fishing in the area.

What to See and Do

Lake Malone State Park. *331 Hwy 8001, Dunmor. 8 miles S on Hwy 973, between Hwy 431 and Hwy 181. Phone 270/657-2111. www.state.ky.us/agencies/parks/lmalone.htm.* A 325-acre park on 788-acre Lake Malone; located in a hardwood tree forest, with tall pines on scenic cliffs. A natural rock bridge, steep sandstone bluffs, and a wooded shoreline can be seen from a ride on the lake. Swimming beach, fishing for bass, bluegill, crappie, boating (ramp, rentals, motors); hiking trail, picnicking, playground, tent and trailer camping (Apr-mid-Nov). (Daily) Standard fees.

Harrodsburg (C-7)

See also Danville

Founded 1774
Population 7,335
Elevation 886 ft
Area Code 859
Zip 40330
Information Harrodsburg/Mercer County Tourist Commission, 488 Price Ave, PO Box 283; phone 859/734-2364 or toll-free 800/355-9192
Web Site www.harrodsburgky.com

When James Harrod and a troop of surveyors came here early in 1774 and established a township, they were creating Kentucky's first permanent white settlement. Here, the first corn in Kentucky was grown, the first English school was established, and the first gristmill in the area was operated. Today the state's oldest city, its sulphur springs and historical sites make it a busy tourist town. Tobacco, cattle, and horse-breeding are important to the economy.

What to See and Do

Morgan Row. *220-222 S Chiles St, Harrodsburg (40330). Behind the courthouse. Phone 859/734-5985.* (1807-1845) Probably the oldest standing row house west of the Alleghenies; once a stagecoach stop and tavern. Houses the Harrodsburg Historical Society Museum (Tues-Sat). **FREE**

Old Fort Harrod State Park. *100 S College, Harrodsburg (40330). On Hwy 68/127, in town. Phone 859/734-3314. www.state.ky.us/agencies/parks/ftharrd2.htm.* This 28-acre park includes a reproduction of Old Fort Harrod in an area known as Old Fort Hill, site of the original fort (1774). The stockade shelters Ann McGinty Block House, George Rogers Clark Block House, James Harrod Block House, and the first school, complete with hand-hewn benches. Authentic cooking utensils, tools, and furniture are displayed in the cabins. The Mansion Museum includes Lincoln Room, Confederate Room, gun collection, Native American artifacts. Lincoln Marriage Temple shelters the log cabin in which Abraham Lincoln's parents were married on June 12, 1806 (moved from its original site in Beech Fork). Pioneer Cemetery. Picnic facilities, playground, gift shop. Living history crafts program in fort (mid-Apr-late Oct). Museum (mid-Mar-Nov, daily); fort (mid-Mar-Oct: Mon-Fri 8 am-5 pm; Nov-mid-Mar: Mon-Fri to 4:30 pm; closed Thanksgiving, the week of Dec 25). **$**

Old Mud Meeting House. *4 miles S off Hwy 68. Phone 859/734-5985.* (1800) First Dutch Reformed Church west of the Alleghenies. The original mud-thatch walls have been restored. (By appointment only) **FREE**

Shaker Village of Pleasant Hill. *3501 Lexington Rd, Harrodsburg (40330). 7 miles NE on Hwy 68. Phone 859/734-5411. www.shakervillageky.org.* (1805-1910) Thirty-three buildings (1805-1859) including frame, brick, and stone houses. Center Family House has exhibits; Trustees' House (see RESTAURANT) has twin spiral staircases. Craft shops with reproductions of Shaker furniture, Kentucky craft items; craft demonstrations; lodging in 15 restored buildings. Year-round calendar of special events includes music, dance, and Sept weekend big events. (Daily; closed Dec 24-25) Sternwheeler offers one-hour excursions on the Kentucky River (late Apr-Oct; fee). **$$$**

Special Event

The Legend of Daniel Boone. *Harrodsburg. Phone 859/734-3346; toll-free 800/852-6663.* James Harrod Amphitheater, in Old Fort Harrod State Park (see). Outdoor drama traces the story of Boone. Tues-Sun. Mid-June-Aug.

Limited-Service Hotel

★ **DAYS INN OF DANVILLE.** *1680 Danville Rd, Harrodsburg (40330). Phone 859/734-9431; fax 859/734-5559. www.daysinn.com.* 69 rooms, 3 story. Complimentary continental breakfast. Check-out 11 am. Outdoor pool. **$**

Full-Service Inn

★ ★ **BEAUMONT INN.** *638 Beaumont, Harrodsburg (40330). Phone 859/734-3381; toll-free 800/352-3992; fax 859/734-6897. www.beaumontinn. com.* Maintaining the style and tradition of the past, this property offers unique accomodations with the rich heritage of the area. Guests experience the meaning of "Southern Decadence" when they treat themselves to dinner here. 33 rooms. Closed late Dec-Feb. Check-out noon. Restaurant. Outdoor pool, children's pool. Rooms are in four buildings; the main building is furnished with antiques. **$**

Specialty Lodging

SHAKER VILLAGE OF PLEASANT HILL. *3501 Lexington Rd, Harrodsburg (40330). Phone 859/734-5411; fax 859/734-7278. www.shakervillageky.org.* 81 rooms, 4 story. Closed Dec 24-25. Check-out 11 am. Restaurant. Thirty restored buildings (circa 1800) furnished with Shaker reproductions, hand-woven rugs and curtains; some trundle beds. **$**

Restaurant

★ ★ **TRUSTEES' HOUSE AT PLEASANT HILL.** *3501 Lexington Rd, Harrodsburg (40330). Phone 859/734-5411. www.shakervillageky.org.* Breakfast, lunch, dinner. Closed Dec 24-25. **$$**

Hazard (C-9)

See also Daniel Boone National Forest

Population 4,086
Elevation 867 ft
Area Code 606
Zip 41701
Information Hazard-Perry County Chamber of Commerce & Tourism Commission, 601 Main St, Suite 3; phone 606/439-2659

In rugged mountain country, Hazard is a coal mining town, a trading center and the seat of Perry County. Both town and county were named for Commodore Oliver Hazard Perry, naval hero of the War of 1812.

What to See and Do

Bobby Davis Memorial Park. *Walnut St, Hazard (41701).* Picnic area, reflecting pool, World War II Memorial, 400 varieties of shrubs and plants. (Daily) In the park is

> **Bobby Davis Park Museum.** *234 Walnut St, Hazard (41701). Phone 606/439-4325.* Community museum housing local historical artifacts and photographs relating to life on Kentucky River waterways. (Mon-Fri; closed holidays) **FREE**

Buckhorn Lake State Resort Park. *4441 Hwy 1833, Hazard (41721). 25 miles NW via Hwy 15/28. Phone 606/398-7510. www.kystateparks.com/buckhorn.htm.* This 856-acre park encompasses a 1,200-acre lake. Swimming beach, pool, bathhouse (seasonal), fishing, boating (ramp, motors, rentals); hiking, bicycle rentals, miniature golf, tennis, picnicking, playground. Lodge, cottages.

Carr Fork Lake. *843 Sassafras Creek Rd, Sassafras (41759). 15 miles SE. Phone 606/642-3308.* A 710-acre lake. Beach, fishing, boating (ramps, marina); picnic shelters, camping (hookups, dump station; fee). Observation points. Some facilities are seasonal.

Special Event

Black Gold Festival. *Main St, Hazard (41701). Phone 606/436-0161. www.blackgoldfestival.com.* Celebrates local coal resources. Food and craft booths, games, entertainment, carnival, parade. Third full weekend in Sept.

Limited-Service Hotels

★ ★ **BUCKHORN LAKE STATE RESORT PARK.** *4441 Hwy 1833, Buckhorn (41721). Phone 606/398-7510; toll-free 800/325-0058; fax 606/398-7077. parks.ky.gov/buckhorn.htm.* 36 rooms, 2 story. Check-out noon. Restaurant. Children's activity center. Outdoor pool, children's pool. Tennis. **$**

★ **SUPER 8.** *125 Village Ln, Hazard (41701). Phone 606/436-8888; toll-free 800/800-8000; fax 606/439-0768. www.super8.com.* 86 rooms, 2 story. Complimentary continental breakfast. Check-out 11 am. **$**

Henderson (C-4)

See also Owensboro

Founded 1797
Population 27,373
Elevation 409 ft
Area Code 270
Zip 42420
Information Tourist Commission, 101 Water St, Suite B; phone 270/826-3128 or toll-free 800/648-3128
Web Site www.go-henderson.com

Henderson was developed by the Transylvania Company and named for its chief executive, Colonel Richard Henderson. This town along the banks of the Ohio River has long attracted residents, most notably naturalist John James Audubon, W. C. Handy, well-known "father of the Blues," and A. B. "Happy" Chandler, former governor and commissioner of baseball.

What to See and Do

John James Audubon State Park. *3100 I-41 N, Henderson (42420). 2 miles N on Hwy 41. Phone 270/826-2247. www.state.ky.us/agencies/parks/audubon2.htm.* Here stand 692 acres of massive hardwood trees, woodland plants, nature preserve, densely forested tracts, and two lakes favored by migratory birds and described in Audubon's writings. Bathhouse (seasonal), fishing, paddleboat rentals (seasonal); 9-hole golf (year-round; fee), picnicking, playground, tent and trailer camping (standard fees), cottages (year-round). Supervised recreation (seasonal); guided nature walks (by appointment). Some fees. **FREE**

Special Events

Big River Arts & Crafts Festival. *Audubon State Park (see). 2910 Hwy 41 N, Henderson (42420).* More than 250 exhibitors. Early Oct.

Bluegrass in the Park. *Audubon Mill Park, Henderson. Phone 270/826-3128. www.go-henderson.com/bluegrass.* First weekend in Aug.

Horse racing. *Ellis Park, 3300 Hwy 41 N, Henderson (42419). 5 miles N on Hwy 41. Phone 812/425-1456; toll-free 800/333-8110. www.ellisparkracing.com.* Thoroughbred racing. Tues-Sun. Early July-Labor Day.

W. C. Handy Blues & Barbecue Festival. *Atkinson Park, Elm St, Henderson (42420). Phone 270/826-3128. www.handyblues.org.* Mid-June.

Limited-Service Hotel

★ **COMFORT INN.** *2820 Hwy 41 N, Henderson (42420). Phone 270/827-8191; fax 270/827-3424. www.choicehotels.com.* 60 rooms, 2 story. Check-out 11 am. Outdoor pool, children's pool. **$**

Hodgenville (C-6)

See also Abraham Lincoln Birthplace National Historic Site, Elizabethtown

Founded 1789
Population 2,874
Elevation 730 ft
Area Code 270
Zip 42748
Information LaRue County Chamber of Commerce, 60 Lincoln Sq, PO Box 176; phone 270/358-3411

Web Site www.laruecountychamber.org

Robert Hodgen built a mill and tavern here and entertained many prominent people. Young Abraham Lincoln often came to the mill with corn to be ground from his father's farm 7 miles away. Soon after Hodgen's death in 1810, the settlement surrounding his tavern adopted his name and was known thereafter as Hodgenville. In 1909, a bronze statue of Lincoln was erected on the town square.

What to See and Do

⭐ **Lincoln's Boyhood Home.** *7120 Bardstown Rd, Hodgenville (42748). 7 miles NE on Hwy 31 E, on Knob Creek Farm. www.nps.gov/libo.* Replica of the log cabin where Lincoln lived for five years (1811-1816) during his childhood; contains historic items and antiques. (Apr-Oct, daily) **$**

Lincoln Jamboree. *2579 Lincoln Farm Rd, Hodgenville (42748). 2 miles S on Hwy 31 E. Phone 270/358-3545.* Family entertainment featuring traditional and modern country music. (Sat evenings; reservations recommended in summer) **$$$**

Lincoln Museum. *66 Lincoln Sq, Hodgenville (42748). Phone 270/358-3163.* Dioramas depicting events in Lincoln's life; memorabilia; special and permanent exhibits. (Daily; closed holidays) **$$**

Special Events

Lincoln Days Celebration. *Lincoln Sq, Hodgenville (42748). Phone 270/358-3411.* Railsplitting competition; pioneer games; classic car show; arts and crafts exhibits; parade. Second weekend in Oct.

Lincoln's Birthday. *2995 Lincoln Farm Rd, Hodgenville (42748). Phone 270/358-3137.* Wreath-laying ceremony. Afternoon of Feb 12.

Martin Luther King's Birthday. *2995 Lincoln Farm Rd, Hodgenville (42748). Phone 270/358-3137.* Sun, mid-Jan.

Hopkinsville (D-4)

See also Cadiz, Greenville, Jefferson Davis Monument State Shrine; also see Clarksville

Founded 1797
Population 30,089
Elevation 548 ft

Area Code 270
Zip 42240
Information Hopkinsville-Christian County Convention & Visitors Bureau, 2800 Ft. Campbell Blvd, PO Box 1382; phone 270/885-9096 or toll-free 800/842-9959
Web Site www.ci.hopkinsville.ky.us

The tobacco auctioneers' chant has long been the theme song of Hopkinsville. Industry has moved in, and Hopkinsville now manufactures precision springs, magnetic wire, lighting fixtures, bowling balls, hardwood, plastic and cement products, non-woven textiles, wearing apparel, and hydraulic motors. Tobacco redrying and flour and cornmeal milling are also done here. Fort Campbell military post has played an important role in the city's growth.

Hopkinsville was the site of the Night Rider War, brought on by farmers' discontent at the low prices they received for their dark tobacco. They raided the town in December 1907, burning several warehouses. In 1911, the culprits were tried and their group disbanded.

Hopkinsville was also a stop on the "Trail of Tears." The site of the Cherokee encampment is now a park with a museum and memorial dedicated to those who lost their lives. Famous sons of the town include Adlai Stevenson, Vice President of the United States 1892-1897; Edgar Cayce, famous clairvoyant, who is buried here; Colonel Wil Starling, Chief of the White House Secret Service 1914-1944; and Ned Breathitt, Governor of Kentucky 1963-1967.

What to See and Do

Fort Campbell. *2334 19th St, Hopkinsville (42223). 16 miles S on Hwy 41A in both KY and TN. Phone 270/798-2151. www.campbell.army.mil/campbell. htm.* One of the nation's largest military installations (105,000 acres); home of 101st Airborne Division (Air Assault). Wickham Hall houses Don F. Pratt Museum, which displays historic military items (daily; closed Jan 1, Dec 25). **FREE**

Pennyrile Forest State Resort Park. *20781 Pennyrile Lodge Rd, Dawson Springs (42408). Approximately 17 miles NW on Hwy 109. Phone 270/797-3421. www. state.ky.us/agencies/parks/pennyril.htm.* (see MADISONVILLE)

Pennyroyal Area Museum. *217 E 9th St, Hopkinsville (42240). Phone 270/887-4270.* Exhibits feature area's agriculture and industries, miniature circus, old railroad items. Civil War items; 1898 law office furniture; Edgar Cayce exhibit, books. (Mon-Sat; closed holidays) **$**

Special Events

Little River Days. *1209 S Virginia St, Hopkinsville (42240). Phone 270/885-9096.* Downtown. Festival consists of road races, canoe races; arts and crafts; entertainment; children's events. Early May.

Western Kentucky State Fair. *Phone 270/885-9096.* Midway, rides, concerts, local exhibits, and events. First week in Aug.

Limited-Service Hotels

★ **BEST WESTERN HOPKINSVILLE.** *4101 Ft Campbell Blvd, Hopkinsville (42240). Phone 270/886-9000; fax 270/886-9000. www.bestwestern.com.* 111 rooms, 3 story. Pets accepted, some restrictions; fee. Complimentary continental breakfast. Check-out noon. Bar. Fitness room. Outdoor pool. **$**
🖥🏃🏊

★ ★ **HOLIDAY INN.** *2910 Fort Campbell Blvd, Hopkinsville (42240). Phone 270/886-4413; fax 270/886-4413. www.holiday-inn.com.* 101 rooms, 5 story. Pets accepted. Check-out noon. Restaurant, bar. Fitness room. Indoor pool. **$**
🖥🏃🏊

Horse Cave (D-6)

See also Cave City, Glasgow, Mammoth Cave National Park

Population 2,252
Elevation 132 ft
Area Code 270
Zip 42749

Tobacco, livestock, and caves are important sources of local income. The town took its name from a nearby cave, which provided water for the area's first settlers ("horse" meant large).

What to See and Do

⭐ **Kentucky Down Under/Kentucky Caverns.** *3700 Land Turnpike Rd N, Horse Cave (42749). 2 miles NW on Hwy 218, just E of I-65, exit 58. Phone 270/786-2634; toll-free 800/762-2869. www.kdu.com.* This Australian-themed animal park features free-roaming kangaroos, wallabies, emus, and other animals native to Australia. Walk into the exotic bird garden and feed colorful lorikeets while they sit on your head and shoulders. Learn about sheep hearding firsthand in the sheep station area, or learn about Australia's aborigines and their way of life at Camp Corroboree. View bison from the Overlook Deck and then try not to feel guilty as you munch on a bison burger at the Outback Cafe. (Mid-Mar-Oct, daily 8 am-5 pm) Included in the price of admission to Kentucky Down under, Kentucky Caverns (formerly Mammoth Onyx Cave) lets visitors get up close and personal with the beautiful onyx formations found underground here in Kentucky's "Cave Country." The 45-minute guided cave tour includes colorful stalactites and stalagmites, flowstone, and hanging bridges and is leisurely enough to accommodate most people (though not those in wheelchairs). Best of all, the cave stays at a comfortable temperature of approximately 60 F year-round, so it stays open through the winter (closed Jan 1, Thanksgiving, Dec 25). **$$$$**

Kentucky Repertory Theatre. *107 E Main St, Horse Cave (42749). Phone toll-free 800/342-2177. www.horsecave-theatre.org.* Southern Kentucky's resident professional festival theater. Six of the season's plays run in rotating repertory in summer. Concessions. (June-Nov, Tues-Sun evenings; matinees Sat-Sun) **$$$$**

Jamestown (D-7)

See also Campbellsville, Somerset

Population 1,624
Elevation 1,024 ft
Information Russell County Tourist Commission, 650 S Hwy 127, PO Box 64, Russell Springs 42642; phone 270/866-4333

What to See and Do

Wolf Creek Dam. *855 Boat Dock Rd, Jamestown (42501). 12 miles S via Hwy 127. Phone 270/679-6337.* United States Army Corps of Engineers dam; 258 feet high, 5,736 feet long, draining a 5,789-square-mile area and creating 101-mile-long Lake Cumberland (see SOMERSET). Camping (mid-Mar-Nov; fee). Visitor center. On the north shore of the lake is

Lake Cumberland State Resort Park. *5465 State Park Rd, Jamestown (42629). 14 miles S on Hwy 127. Phone 270/343-3111; toll-free 800/325-1709.*

www.state.ky.us/agencies/parks/lakecumb.htm. More than 3,000 acres on a 50,250-acre lake. Swimming pools, fishing, boating (ramps, rentals, dock), hiking, riding (seasonal), nine-hole par-3 and miniature golf (seasonal), tennis, shuffleboard, bicycling, picnicking, playground, lodge, rental houseboats, cottages, tent and trailer camping (Apr-Nov; standard fees). Nature center, supervised recreation.

Limited-Service Hotel

★ ★ **LAKE CUMBERLAND STATE RESORT PARK.** *5465 State Park Rd, Jamestown (42629). Phone 270/343-3111; toll-free 800/325-1709; fax 270/343-5510. www.lakecumberlandpark.com.* This Kentucky lake resort is a water sportsmen's dream, with boating rental available, and an abundance of fish waiting to be caught. Riding trails, spa and exercise facilities are also offered on site. 106 rooms. Check-in 4 pm, check-out noon. Restaurant. Children's activity center. Two outdoor pools, children's pool. Golf. Tennis. **$**
⌛ 🎿 📶

Jefferson Davis Monument State Shrine (D-4)

See also Hopkinsville

10 miles E of Hopkinsville on Hwy 68 in Fairview. Phone 270/886-1765.

The monument, a cast-concrete obelisk 351 feet tall, ranks as the fourth-tallest obelisk in the country and the tallest of such material. It marks the birthplace of Jefferson Davis, the only President of the Confederate States of America. Overlooking a 19-acre park, the monument, built at a cost of $200,000 and raised by public subscription, was dedicated in 1924. Visitors may take an elevator to the top (fee).

The son of a Revolutionary War officer, Jefferson Davis was born here in 1808, less than 100 miles from Abraham Lincoln's birthplace. Davis graduated from West Point, became a successful cotton planter in Mississippi, was elected to the US Senate, and was Secretary of War in President Franklin Pierce's Cabinet. Elected President of the Confederacy, he served for the duration of the war, was captured in Georgia, and imprisoned for two years. Picnic area; playground. (May-Oct, daily)

Kenlake State Resort Park (D-3)

See also Cadiz, Land Between the Lakes

Web Site www.kentuckylake.com/kenlake.htm

16 miles NE of Murray on Hwy 94. Phone 270/474-2211; toll-free 800/325-0143.

Located 16 miles northeast of Murray (see), Kenlake State Resort Park lies on 1,800 acres with a 4-mile shoreline on 160,300-acre Kentucky Lake. Pool, bathhouse (seasonal), waterskiing, fishing, boating (ramps, rentals, marina); hiking trail, 9-hole golf (rentals), shuffleboard, tennis (indoor, outdoor, shop), picnicking, playgrounds, cottages, dining room, lodge, tent and trailer sites (Apr-Oct, standard fees).

Limited-Service Hotel

★ ★ **KENLAKE STATE RESORT PARK.** *542 Kenlake Rd, Hardin (42048). Phone 270/474-2211; toll-free 800/425-0143; fax 270/474-2018. www.kenlake. com.* 82 rooms, 1 story. Closed week of Dec 25. Check-in 4 pm, check-out noon, cottages 11 am; Restaurant. Outdoor pool, children's pool. Golf. Tennis. **$**
⌛ 🎿 📶

Restaurant

★ ★ **BRASS LANTERN.** *16593 Hwy 68 E, Aurora (42048). Phone 270/474-2773. www.brasslanternrestaurant.com.* American menu. Dinner. Closed Mon; also Jan. Children's menu. Casual attire. Reservations recommended. **$$**

Land Between the Lakes (D-3)

See also Cadiz, Gilbertsville, Murray, Paris, Kenlake State Resort Park

Web Site www.lbl.org

100 Van Morgan Dr, Murray (42211). 20 miles NE off Hwy 94. Phone 270/924-5897.

This 170,000-acre wooded peninsula, running 40 miles from north to south and located between Kentucky Lake and Lake Barkley in western Kentucky and Tennessee, is one of the largest outdoor recreation areas in the country.

There are four major family campgrounds: **Hillman Ferry, Piney, Energy Lake** (year-round; electric hookups; fee), and **Wranglers Campground**, which is equipped for horseback riders. Eleven other lake access areas offer more primitive camping (fee). All areas offer swimming, fishing, boating, ramps; picnic facilities. Family campgrounds have planned recreation programs (summer).

There is a 5,000-acre wooded Environmental Education Area that includes the Nature Station, which presents interpretive displays of native plant and animal life. Within this area are several nature trails. Elk and Bison Prairie is a drive-through wildlife viewing area featuring native plants and wildlife (daily; fee). Nature center (Mar-Nov, daily; fee).

What to See and Do

Golden Pond Visitor Center. *Golden Pond.* Main orientation center for Land Between the Lakes visitors. Planetarium presentation (Mar-Dec, fee). Seasonal programs. Visitor center (daily).

The Homeplace-1850. *745 Hwy 2275, Land Between the Lakes. 17 miles SE of Aurora via Hwy 68, Land Between the Lakes exit.* Living history farm. (Apr-Nov, daily) **$$**

The Nature Station. *Golden Pond. 14 miles NE of Aurora via Hwy 68, Land Between the Lakes exit.* Interpretive displays of native animals and plants. (Mar-Nov, daily 9 am-5 pm) **$$**

Lexington (B-7)

See also Frankfort, Georgetown, Maysville, Paris, Richmond, Winchester

Founded 1779
Population 260,512
Elevation 983 ft
Area Code 859
Information Lexington Convention & Visitors Bureau, 301 E Vine St, 40507; phone 859/233-7299 or toll-free 800/845-3959
Web Site www.visitlex.com

A midland metropolis rooted in the production of tobacco and thoroughbreds, Lexington is a gracious city decorated with rich bluegrass and dotted with aristocratic old houses. The legendary steel-blue tint of the bluegrass is perceptible only in May's early morning sunshine, but throughout spring, summer, and fall it is unrivaled for turf and pasture.

An exploring party camping here in 1775 got news of the Battle of Lexington and so named the spot. The city was established four years later, rapidly becoming a center for barter and a major producer of hemp (used by New England's clipper ships). Lexington cashed in on its tobacco crop when smoking became popular during the Civil War. Pioneers who settled here brought their best horses with them from Maryland and Virginia; as they grew wealthy, they imported bloodlines from abroad to improve the breed. The first races were held in Lexington in 1780, and the first jockey club was organized in 1797.

Lexington is the world's largest burley tobacco market with well over 100 million pounds sold each year. Precious bluegrass seed, beef cattle, and sheep are also merchandised in Lexington. More than 50 major industries, manufacturing everything from peanut butter and bourbon to air brakes and ink jet printers, are located here.

What to See and Do☆

Ashland. *Richmond and Sycamore rds, Lexington. Phone 859/266-8581. www.henryclay.org.* (1806) Estate on 20 acres of woodland was the home of Henry Clay, statesman, orator, senator, and would-be president. Occupied by the Clay family for five generations, Ashland is furnished with family possessions. The estate was named for the ash trees that surround it. A number of outbuildings still stand. (Mon-Sat 10 am-4 pm, Sun from 1 pm; closed Jan, Mon from Nov-Mar, holidays) **$$$**

Headley-Whitney Museum. *4435 Old Frankfort Pike, Lexington (40510). 4 1/2 miles NW of New Circle Rd. Phone 859/255-6653. www.headley-whitney.org.* Unusual buildings house display of bibelots (small decorative objects) executed in precious metals and jewels; Oriental porcelains, paintings, decorative arts, shell grotto, special exhibits; library. (Tues-Fri 10 am-5 pm, Sat-Sun from noon; closed Mon, holidays) **$$**

Horse farms. More than 400 in area, most concentrated in Lexington-Fayette County. Although the majority are thoroughbred farms, other varieties such as standardbreds, American saddle horses, Arabians, Morgans, and quarter horses are bred and raised here as well. Farms may be seen by taking one of the many tours offered by tour companies in Lexington.

Hunt-Morgan House. *201 N Mill St, Lexington (40507). At W 2nd St. Phone 859/253-0362. www.bluegrasstrust. org/hunt-morgan.* (Circa 1812-1814) In Gratz Park area, a historic district with antebellum residences. Federal-period mansion with a cantilevered elliptical staircase and fanlight doorway. Built for John Wesley Hunt, Kentucky's first millionaire. Later occupied by his grandson, General John Hunt Morgan, known as the "Thunderbolt of the Confederacy." Nobel Prize-winning geneticist Thomas Hunt Morgan was also born in this house. Family furniture, portraits, and porcelain. Walled courtyard garden. Gift shop. (Mar-mid-Dec; tours Tues-Sun 10:15 am-3:15 pm, Sun 2:15-4:15 pm; closed rest of year; also holidays) **$$**

⭐ **Kentucky Horse Park.** *4089 Iron Works Pkwy, Lexington (40511). 6 miles N via I-75, Kentucky Horse Park exit 120. Phone 859/233-4303; toll-free 800/568-8813. www.kyhorsepark.com.* More than 1,000 acres of beautiful bluegrass fill the park; features Man O' War grave and memorial, visitors' information center with wide-screen film presentation, *Thou Shalt Fly Without Wings.* Also located within the park are the International Museum of the Horse, Parade of Breeds (seasonal), Calumet Trophy Collection, Sears Collection of hand-carved miniatures; Hall of Champions stable that houses famous thoroughbreds and standardbreds; walking farm tour, antique carriage display. Swimming. Tennis, ball courts. Picnic area, playgrounds. Campground (fee). Special events (see SPECIAL EVENTS); horsedrawn rides (fee). (Mid-Mar-Oct: daily 9 am-5 pm; rest of year: Wed-Sun 9

am-5 pm; closed Jan 1, Thanksgiving, late Dec) Parking fee (seasonal). **$$$** Also on grounds is

American Saddlebred Museum. *4093 Iron Works Pkwy, Lexington (40511). Phone 859/259-2746.* Museum dedicated to the American Saddlebred horse, Kentucky's only native breed. Contemporary exhibits on the development and current uses of the American Saddlebred. Multimedia presentation. Gift shop. (Memorial Day-Labor Day, daily 9 am-6 pm; rest of year to 5 pm; closed Mon-Tues Nov-mid-Mar, also Jan 1, Thanksgiving Eve and Day, Dec 24-25) **$$**

Lexington Cemetery. *833 W Main St, Lexington (40508). On Hwy 421. Phone 859/255-5522. www.lexcem.org.* Buried on these 170 acres are Henry Clay, John C. Breckinridge, General John Hunt Morgan, the Todds (Mrs. Abraham Lincoln's family), coach Adolph Rupp, and many other notable persons. Also interred are 500 Confederate and 1,110 Union veterans. Sunken gardens, lily pools, 4-acre flower garden, extensive plantings of spring-flowering trees and shrubs. (Daily)

Mary Todd Lincoln House. *578 W Main St, Lexington (40507). Phone 859/233-9999. www.mtlhouse. org.* Childhood residence of Mary Todd Lincoln is authentically restored; period furnishings, personal items. (Mid-Mar-Nov, Mon-Sat 10 am-4 pm; closed holidays) **$$**

Opera House. *401 W Short St, Lexington (40507). Phone 859/233-4567. www.lexingtonoperahouse.com.* (1886) Restored and reconstructed opera house is a regional performing arts center; performances include Broadway shows and special events. (Sept-June) Contact Lexington Center Corp, Performing Arts, 430 W Vine St, 40507.

Sightseeing tours. Many tour companies offer tours of working horse farms in the Lexington area. Many of these companies also offer historic sightseeing tours. For more information, contact the Convention & Visitors Bureau.

Transylvania University. *300 N Broadway, Lexington (40508). Phone 859/233-8120. www.transy.edu.* (1780) (926 students) The oldest institution of higher learning west of the Allegheny Mountains, it has educated two US vice presidents, 36 state and territorial governors, 34 ambassadors, 50 senators, 112 members of the US House of Representatives, and Confederate President Jefferson Davis. Thomas Jefferson was one of Transylvania's early supporters. Henry Clay taught law courses and was a member of the university's governing board. Administration Building, "Old Morrison" (1833), Greek Revival architecture, was used as a hospital during the Civil War. Tours of campus (by appointment).

University of Kentucky. *104 Administration Bldg, Lexington (40506). Area of S Limestone St and Euclid Ave. Phone 859/257-9000. www.uky.edu.* (1865) (24,000 students) **FREE** On campus is

> **Art Museum.** *Singletary Center for the Arts, Euclid Ave and Rose St, Lexington. Phone 859/257-5716.* Permanent collections; special exhibitions. (Tues-Thurs, Sat-Sun noon-5 pm, Fri to 8 pm; closed Mon: also holidays and Dec 26-Jan 2) **FREE**

Victorian Square. *401 W Main St, Lexington (40507). Phone 859/252-7575.* Shopping area located in downtown restoration project. Specialty stores; restaurants; children's museum (phone 859/258-3253); parking in 400-car garage with covered walkway into mall.

Waveland State Historic Site. *225 Waveland Museum Ln, Lexington (40514). Phone 859/272-3611. www.state. ky.us/agencies/parks/wavelan2.htm.* Greek Revival mansion (1847) with three original outbuildings. Exhibits depict plantation life of 1840s. Playground. (Apr-mid-Dec, Mon-Sat 10 am-5 pm, Sun from 1 pm) **$$**

Special Events

Blue Grass Stakes. *4201 Versailles Rd, Lexington (40510). Phone 859/254-3412.* Keeneland Race Course. Three-year-olds; one of the last major prep races before Kentucky Derby. Mid-Apr.

Egyptian Event. *Kentucky Horse Park, 4089 Iron Works Pkwy, Lexington (40511). Phone 859/231-0771. www. pyramidsociety.org/event.html.* Activities highlighting rare Egyptian Arabian horses. Show classes, Walk of Stallions, Breeder's Sale, native costumes, seminars, art auction, and Egyptian Bazaar. Early June.

Festival of the Bluegrass. *Kentucky Horse Park, 4089 Iron Works Pkwy, Lexington (40511). Campground. Phone 859/846-4995. www.festivalofthebluegrass.com.* Top names in Bluegrass music, with more than 20 bands appearing. Includes special shows for children; crafts; workshops with the musicians. The 600-acre park has more than 750 electric hookups for campers. Second full weekend in June.

Grand Circuit Meet. *The Red Mile Track, 1200 Red Mile Rd, Lexington (40585). Phone 859/255-0752. www. redmile.com.* Features Kentucky Futurity race, the final leg of trotting's Triple Crown. Two weeks, late Sept-early Oct.

Harness racing. *The Red Mile Harness Track, 1200 Red Mile Rd, Lexington (40585). 1 1/2 miles S on Hwy 68. Phone 859/255-0752. www.tattersallsredmile.com.* Also the site of Grand Circuit racing. Night racing (May-June: Thurs-Sat; Sept-Oct: Mon-Tues, Fri-Sat).

High Hope Steeplechase. *Kentucky Horse Park, 4089 Iron Works Pkwy, Lexington (40511). www.high-hopesteeplechase.com.* Mid-May.

Junior League Horse Show. *The Red Mile Harness Track, 1200 Red Mile Rd, Lexington (40588). Phone 859/252-8014.* Outdoor Saddlebred horse show. Six days in early-mid-July.

Rolex Kentucky Three-Day Event. *Kentucky Horse Park, 4080 Iron Works Pkwy, Lexington (40511). Phone 859/254-8123.* Kentucky Horse Park. Three-day endurance test for horse and rider in dressage, cross-country, and stadium jumping. Fair features boutiques. Late Apr.

Thoroughbred racing. *Keeneland Race Course, 4201 Versailles Rd, Lexington (40510). 6 miles W on Hwy 60. Phone 859/254-3412. www.keeneland.com.* Three weeks in Apr and three weeks in Oct.

Limited-Service Hotels

★ **BEST WESTERN REGENCY/LEXINGTON.** *2241 Elkhorn Rd, Lexington (40505). Phone 859/293-2202; fax 859/293-1821. www.bestwestern.com.* 110 rooms, 2 story. Complimentary continental breakfast. Check-out 11 am. Wireless Internet access. Outdoor pool, whirlpool. **$**

★ **COMFORT INN.** *2381 Buena Vista Dr, Lexington (40505). Phone 859/299-0302; fax 859/299-2306. www. choicehotels.com.* 123 rooms, 3 story. Complimentary continental breakfast. Check-out noon. Fitness room. Indoor pool, whirlpool. **$**

★ ★ **CROWNE PLAZA HOTEL LEXINGTON-THE CAMPBELL HOUSE.** *1375 Harrodsburg Rd, Lexington (40504). Phone 859/255-4281; fax 859/254-4368.* 370 rooms, 3 story. Check-out noon. Restaurant, bar. Fitness room. Indoor pool. Golf. Tennis. Airport transportation available. Business center. **$**

★ **HAMPTON INN.** *2251 Elkhorn Rd, Lexington (40505). Phone 859/299-2613; toll-free 800/426-7866;*

fax 859/299-9664. www.hamptoninn.com. 125 rooms, 5 story. Pets accepted. Complimentary continental breakfast. Check-in 3 pm, check-out noon. High-speed Internet access, wireless Internet access. Fitness room. Indoor pool. **$**

★ ★ **HOLIDAY INN.** *5532 Athens Boonesboro Rd, Lexington (40509). Phone 859/263-5241; toll-free 800/465-4329; fax 859/263-4333. www.holiday-inn. com.* 150 rooms, 2 story. Pets accepted, some restrictions; fee. Check-in 3 pm, check-out noon. High-speed Internet access. Restaurant, bar. Children's activity center. Fitness room. Indoor pool, outdoor pool, whirlpool. **$**

★ ★ **RADISSON PLAZA HOTEL LEXINGTON.** *369 W Vine St, Lexington (40507). Phone 859/231-9000; fax 859/281-3737. www.radisson.com.* Located on Lexington's Triangle Park, this hotel is in the middle of the Bluegrass region. It is connected by skyway to the Rupp Arena, the Lexington Civic Center and the Victorian Square Shopping Center. 367 rooms, 22 story. Pets accepted, some restrictions; fee. Check-out noon. Restaurant, bar. Fitness room. Indoor pool, whirlpool. Airport transportation available. Business center. **$$**

Full-Service Hotels

★ ★ ★ **HILTON SUITES.** *245 Lexington Green Cir, Lexington (40503). Phone 859/271-4000; toll-free 800/774-1500; fax 859/273-2975. www.hilton.com.* This hotel features deluxe two-room suites. Near restaurants and a shopping mall, it is also less than 7 miles from Bluegrass Airport. 174 rooms, 6 story, all suites. Check-out noon. Restaurant, bar. Fitness room. Outdoor pool. Airport transportation available. Business center. **$**

★ ★ ★ **HYATT REGENCY LEXINGTON.** *401 W High St, Lexington (40588). Phone 859/253-1234; fax 859/233-7974. www.hyatt.com.* This hotel is perfectly situated in the downtown business district at Triangle Park and Lexington Center, near shopping, restaurants, a convention center, sports, and entertainment. 365 rooms, 16 story. Check-out noon. Restaurant, bar. Fitness room. Indoor pool. Airport transportation available. Business center. **$$**

★ ★ ★ **SHERATON SUITES LEXINGTON.** *2601 Richmond Rd, Lexington (40509). Phone 859/268-*

0060; toll-free 800/262-3774; fax 859/268-6209. www. sheraton.com. 155 rooms, 5 story, all suites. Pets accepted, some restrictions. Check-in 3 pm, check-out noon. High-speed Internet access, wireless Internet access. Restaurant, bar. Fitness room. Outdoor pool. Airport transportation available. **$**

Full-Service Resort

★ ★ ★ **MARRIOTT'S GRIFFIN GATE RESORT.** *1800 Newtown Pike, Lexington (40511). Phone 859/231-5100; toll-free 888/236-2427; fax 859/255-9944. www.marriott.com.* This resort sits in the heart of Kentucky Bluegrass Country. Recreational facilities, such as a championship golf course, tennis courts, and an indoor and outdoor pool, please leisure guests, while dataport and voice mail-equipped rooms, a business center, and corporate-team-challenge programs attract business clientele. Four restaurants offer both casual and fine dining. 409 rooms, 7 story. Pets accepted; fee. Check-out noon. Restaurant, bar. Children's activity center. Fitness room. Indoor pool, outdoor pool, whirlpool. Golf. Tennis. Airport transportation available. Business center. **$**

Full-Service Inn

★ ★ ★ **GRATZ PARK INN.** *120 W 2nd St, Lexington (40507). Phone 606/231-1777; toll-free 800/752-4166; fax 606/233-7593. www.gratzparkinn.com.* Once you've stayed at Gratz Park, just steps away from many of Lexington's attractions, you'll wonder why you ever stayed anywhere else. The rooms are beautiful and Chef Lundy's cuisine is mouthwatering. 44 rooms, 3 story. Check-in 3 pm, check-out noon. Restaurant. Fitness room. Airport transportation available. Elegantly restored building (1916). **$$**

Specialty Lodgings

1823 HISTORIC ROSE HILL INN. *233 Rose Hill Ave, Versailles (40383). Phone 859/873-5957; toll-free 800/307-0460; fax 859/873-1813. www.rosehillinn.com.* 4 rooms, 2 story. Pets accepted, some restrictions; fee. Complimentary full breakfast. Check-in 3 pm. Check-out noon. Built in 1823; 3 acres. **$$**

MONTGOMERY INN. *270 Montgomery Ave, Versailles (40383). Phone 859/873-4478; toll-free*

800/526-9801; fax 859/873-7099. www.montgomeryin-nbnb.com. Restored Victorian elegance sits on this quaint property in the center of bluegrass-horse-farm country. Built in 1911, the inn is filled with Kentucky antiques and is only a ten minute drive from Lexington and Frankfort. 12 rooms, 3 story. Complimentary full breakfast. Check-out 11 am. Airport transportation available. Business center. **$**

🔲 🚶 ✈️

Restaurants

★ ★ **A-LA LUCIE.** *159 N Limestone St, Lexington (40507). Phone 859/252-5277; fax 859/225-5027. www.alalucie.com.* American menu. Lunch, dinner. Closed Sun; holidays. Bar. **$$**

★ ★ **DE SHA'S GRILLE AND BAR.** *101 N Broadway, Lexington (40509). Phone 859/259-3771; fax 859/254-1602. www.deshas.com.* Lunch, dinner. Closed Jan 1, Thanksgiving, Dec 25. Bar. Children's menu. In Victorian Square. **$$**

★ ★ **DUDLEY'S.** *380 S Mill St, Lexington (40508). Phone 859/252-1010; fax 859/253-9383. www.dudleysrestaurant.com.* Mediterranean menu. Lunch, dinner. Closed holidays. Bar. Restored school (1851); paintings. Outdoor seating. **$$**

★ ★ **MALONE'S.** *3347 Tates Creek Rd, Lexington (40502). Phone 859/335-6500; fax 859/335-1815. www.malonesrestaurant.com.* American menu. Lunch, dinner. Closed holidays. Service bar. Children's menu. **$$$**

★ ★ ★ **MANSION AT GRIFFIN GATE.** *1800 Newtown Pike, Lexington (40511). Phone 859/288-6142; fax 859/288-6216. www.mansionrestaurant.com.* This elegant restaurant is housed in a Southern antebellum mansion that was the original home of Griffin Gate Farm. The traditional, seasonal food and extensive wine list are matched in quality by the sophisticated décor and professional service. American menu. Dinner. Bar. Valet parking. **$$$**

★ ★ **MERRICK INN.** *3380 Tates Creek Rd, Lexington (40502). Phone 859/269-5417.* American menu. Lunch, dinner. Closed Sun. Bar. Casual attire. Reservations recommended. Valet parking. Outdoor seating. **$$**

★ ★ **MURRAY'S.** *3955 Harrodsburg Rd, Lexington (40513). Phone 859/219-9922.* American menu. Dinner. Closed Sun. Bar. Casual attire. Reservations recommended. Valet parking. Outdoor seating. **$$$**

★ ★ **REGATTA SEAFOOD GRILLE.** *161 Lexington Green Cir, Lexington (40503). Phone 859/273-7875; fax 859/273-7859. www.regattaseafood.com.* Seafood menu. Lunch, dinner. Closed Dec 25. Bar. Children's menu. Outdoor seating overlooking lake. **$$**

London (C-8)

See also Corbin, Daniel Boone National Forest, Somerset

Founded 1825
Population 5,692
Elevation 1,255 ft
Area Code 606
Information London-Laurel County Tourist Commission, 140 W Daniel Boone Parkway, 40741; phone 606/878-6900 or toll-free 800/348-0095
Web Site www.laurelkytourism.com

London is a county seat of Daniel Boone National Forest (see). A Ranger District office of the forest is located in London.

What to See and Do

Canoe trips. *Phone 606/864-9407.* Canoe trips on the Rockcastle River ranging from three hours to three days; rentals. Contact Rockcastle Adventures, PO Box 662. **$$$$**

Levi Jackson Wilderness Road State Park. *998 Levi Jackson Mill Rd, London (40744). 3 miles S on Hwy 25, exit 38 off I-75. Phone 606/878-8000. www.state.ky.us/agencies/parks/levijack.htm.* An 896-acre park. Descendants of pioneer farmer Levi Jackson deeded some of this land to the state as a historical shrine to those who carved homes out of the wilderness. Boone's Trace and Wilderness Road pioneer trails converge within the park. Recreational facilities include swimming pool (fee), bathhouse; hiking, archery range, miniature golf (Apr-Oct, fee), picnicking, playgrounds, camping (tent and trailer sites). Supervised recreation (Memorial Day-Labor Day). Standard fees. Here are

  McHargue's Mill. One of the largest collections of millstones in the world. Mill built in 1812, reconstructed on present site in 1939. Tours and demonstrations. (Memorial Day-Labor Day, daily) **FREE**

  Mountain Life Museum. Split-rail fences enclose rustic cabins with household furnishings, pioneer relics, farm tools, Native American artifacts;

smokehouse, blacksmith shop, barn with prairie schooner. (Apr-Oct, daily) **$**

Limited-Service Hotel

★ **COMFORT INN.** *1918 W Hwy 192, London (40741). Phone 606/877-7848; fax 606/877-7907.* 62 rooms, 3 story. Complimentary continental breakfast. Check-out noon. Indoor pool. **$**
🏊

Louisville (B-6)

See also Fort Knox, Shepherdsville

Founded 1778
Population 256,231
Elevation 462 ft
Area Code 502
Information Convention and Visitors Bureau, 400 S First St, 40202; phone 502/584-2121 or toll-free 800/792-5595
Web Site www.gotolouisville.com

Louisville is a unique city. It has southern graces and a determined dedication to music and the arts, but to the world, Louisville is "Derby City" for at least two weeks of every year. Since its first running on May 17, 1875, the Kentucky Derby has generated tremendous excitement. Modeled after England's Epsom Derby, it is the oldest race in continuous existence in the United States. The first Saturday in May each year, world attention focuses on Churchill Downs as the classic "run for the roses" is played out against its backdrop of Edwardian towers and antique grandstands.

The social highlight of a very social city, Derby festivities are a glamorous mlange of carnival, fashion show, spectacle, and celebration of the horse. From the opening strains of "My Old Kentucky Home," played before the big race, until the final toast of bourbon is made, Louisville takes on a uniquely festive character. Afterward, the center of thoroughbred racing quickly returns to normalcy—a city southern in manner, midwestern in pace.

Situated at the falls of the Ohio River, Louisville is a city long nurtured by river traffic. The Spanish, French, English, Scottish, Irish, and Germans all had roles in its exploration, settlement, and development. George Rogers Clark established the first real settlement, a base for military operations against the

British, on a spit of land above the falls, now entirely erased by the river. Named after Louis XVI of France, the settlement became an important portage point around the falls; later a canal bypassed them. Today, the McAlpine Locks and Dam provide modern navigation around the falls of the Ohio.

Louisville is a top producer of bourbon and a leader in synthetic rubber, paint and varnish, cigarettes, home appliances, and aluminum for home use.

Louisville Fun Fact

• The Kentucky Derby is the oldest continuously held horse race in the country. It is held at Churchill Downs in Louisville on the first Saturday in May.

This is a community that takes its culture seriously, with a public subscription Fund for the Arts subsidizing the Tony Award-winning Actors Theater. The city also boasts the Kentucky Center for the Arts, home of ballet, opera, art and music groups, and other cultural organizations.

Additional Visitor Information

The Louisville Convention & Visitors Bureau, 400 S First St, 40202, phone 502/582-3732 or toll-free 800/792-5595, provides literature and information. Also available is information about several unique areas of special interest, such as Old Louisville, Butchertown, Phoenix Hill, Cherokee Triangle, and the Main Street Preservation District.

The Convention & Visitors Bureau also operates three visitor information centers that can be found on westbound I-64, in the central lobby of Louisville International Airport and downtown at First and Liberty streets.

For information on parks and courses in the area, phone the Metropolitan Park and Recreation Board, 502/222-2154.

What to See and Do

American Printing House for the Blind. *1839 Frankfort Ave, Louisville (40206). Phone 502/895-2405. www. aph.org.* The largest and oldest (1858) publishing house for the blind. In addition to books and music in Braille, it issues talking books, magazines, large-type

A Slugger of a Tour

Louisville was founded at the falls of the Ohio River in 1788. Today, the city's waterfront around Main Street at Fourth Avenue is a great place to start exploring the old downtown area. From the banks you'll see a view of the river and of the floating Louisville Falls Fountain, which periodically lets loose a geyser 375 feet into the air. At night the display is dramatically lit.

Glance upriver and you'll see the *Belle of Louisville* (See RIVERBOAT EXCURSION), docked at the end of Fourth Street (phone 502/574-2355). This 1914 steamboat continues to ply the waters for sightseeing cruises. The *Star of Louisville* (phone 502/589-7827) is another sightseeing boat docked a few blocks farther up on the far side of the Highway 31 bridge.

Surrounding the riverfront park is the city's historic district (see) of old warehouses and cast iron buildings—now restored as restaurants, galleries, and shops. Start exploring around West Main Street at the southwest corner of Riverfront Park. The city's main attractions are conveniently lined up here in a compact row. Proceed west.

At the head of Sixth Street, the Kentucky Center for the Arts, 5 Riverfront Plaza, is home to the city's resident opera, ballet, orchestra, and children's theater. They also have an impressive collection of 20th-century sculpture throughout the dramatic glass-walled center. Free audiotape tours are available. The Kentucky's Art and Craft Center at 609 West Main Street displays contemporary pieces by native artists (phone 502/589-0102). Down at Seventh and Main streets is the site of Fort Nelson, where the towns original settlement was built in 1782.

Louisville Science Center (see) (727 West Main St; phone 502/561-6100) contains five stories of hands-on exhibits in a transformed warehouse. Children particularly enjoy the Egyptian mummy and space exhibits, not to mention the IMAX theater.

At the corner of West Main and Eighth streets, the landmark 120-foot-high Louisville Sluggerthe worlds largest baseball batmarks the site of the Louisville Slugger Museum (see) (phone 502/528-7728). Not only does the museum hold beloved baseball artifacts and memorabilia, but visitors can also watch the bats being made during the factory tour.

textbooks, and educational aids. Tours (Mon-Fri 10 am-2 pm; closed holidays). **FREE**

Bellarmine University. *2001 Newburg Rd, Louisville (40205). Phone 502/452-8000. www.bellarmine.edu.* (1950) (2,300 students) A 115-acre campus. Liberal arts and sciences. The campus houses the Thomas Merton Studies Center, with his manuscripts, drawings, tapes, and published works (Tues-Fri, by appointment; closed holidays). Guided campus tours (by appointment).

Cave Hill Cemetery. *701 Baxter Ave, Louisville (40204). At E end of Broadway. Phone 502/451-5630. www.cavehillcemetery.com.* Burial ground of George Rogers Clark. Colonel Harland Sanders, of fried chicken fame, is also buried here. Rare trees, shrubs, and plants; swans, geese, ducks. (Daily)

★ **Churchill Downs.** *700 Central Ave, Louisville (40208). Phone 502/636-4400. www.churchilldowns.com.* Founded in 1875, this historic and world-famous thoroughbred race track is the home of the Kentucky Derby, "the most exciting two minutes in sports." (See SPECIAL EVENTS) (Spring race meet, late Apr-June; fall race meet, late Oct-late Nov; Kentucky Derby, first Sat in May.) Adjacent is

★ **Kentucky Derby Museum.** *704 Central Ave, Louisville (40208). Phone 502/637-1111.* Features exhibits on thoroughbred racing and the Kentucky Derby. High definition 360 show, hands-on exhibits, artifacts, educational programs, tours, and special events. Outdoor paddock area with thoroughbreds. Tours of Churchill Downs (weather permitting). Gift shop; café serving lunch (weekdays). (Mon-Sat 8 am-5 pm, Sun from noon; closed Oaks and Derby Days, Dec 25) **$$**

E. P. "Tom" Sawyer State Park. *3000 Freys Hill Rd, Louisville (40241). Phone 502/426-8950. http://parks.ky.gov/tomsawyr.htm.* Approximately 370 acres with swimming pool. Tennis; archery range; BMX track; ballfields; gymnasium, games area. Picnicking. Some fees.

Farmington Historic Home. *3033 Bardstown Rd N, Louisville (40205). At junction Watterson Expy (I-264), 6 miles SE on Hwy 31 E. Phone 502/452-9920. www.historicfarmington.org.* (1815) Federal-style house built from plans drawn by Thomas Jefferson. Abraham Lincoln visited here in 1841. Furnished with pre-1820 antiques; hidden stairway, octagonal rooms; museum room; blacksmith shop, stone barn, 19th-century garden. (Tues-Sat 10 am-4:30 pm, Sun from 1:30 pm; closed holidays) **$$**

Filson Historical Society. *1310 S 3rd St, Louisville (40208). Phone 502/635-5083. www.filsonhistorical. org.* Historical library (fee); manuscript collection, photographs and prints collection. (Mon-Sat 10 am-2 pm; closed holidays) **FREE**

Historic districts. *Old Louisville, between Breckinridge and 9th sts, near Central Park.* Features renovated Victorian housing; **West Main Street Historic District** is a concentration of cast iron buildings being renovated on Main St between 1st and 8th sts; **Butchertown** is a renovated 19th-century German community between Market St and Story Ave; **Cherokee Triangle** is a well-preserved Victorian neighborhood with diverse architectural details; and **Portland** is an early settlement and commercial port with Irish and French heritage.

Kentucky Center for the Arts. *501 W Main St, Louisville (40202). Phone 502/584-7777; toll-free 800/775-7777. www.kentuckycenter.org.* Three stages present national and international performers showcasing a wide range of music, dance, and drama. Distinctive glass-arched lobby features a collection of 20th-century sculpture and provides a panoramic view of Ohio River and Falls Fountain. Restaurant, gift shop, parking garage.

Kentucky Fair and Exposition Center. *937 Phillips Ln, Louisville (40209). I-65 S at I-264 W. Phone 502/367-5000. www.kentuckycenter.org.* More than 1 million-square-foot complex includes coliseum, exposition halls, stadium, amusement park. More than 1,500 events take place throughout the year, including basketball and Milwaukee Brewers minor league affiliate team.

Locust Grove. *561 Blankenbaker Ln, Louisville (40207). 6 miles NE on River Rd, then 1 mile SW. Phone 502/897-9845. www.locustgrove.org.* (Circa 1790) Home of General George Rogers Clark from 1809-1818. Handsome Georgian mansion on 55 acres; original paneling, staircase; authentic furnishings; garden; eight restored outbuildings. Visitors center features audiovisual program. (Mon-Sat 10 am-4:30 pm, Sun 1:30-4:30 pm; closed holidays, Derby Day) **$$**

Louisville Presbyterian Theological Seminary. *1044 Alta Vista Rd, Louisville (40205). 1/2 mile off Hwy 60 Business, adjacent to Cherokee Park. Phone 502/895-3411. www.lpts.edu.* (1853) (250 students) On 52-acre campus is Gardencourt and a renovated turn-of-the-century mansion. **FREE**

Louisville Science Center & IMAX Theatre. *727 W Main St, Louisville (40202). Phone 502/561-6100. www. louisvillescience.org.* Hands-on scientific exhibits; aerospace hall; IMAX four-story screen film theater (fee); World We Create interactive exhibit. (Mon-Thurs 9:30 am-5 pm, Fri-Sat to 9 pm, Sun noon-6 pm; closed Thanksgiving, Dec 24-25) **$$**

Louisville Slugger Museum & Bat Factory. *800 W Main St, Louisville (40202). Phone 502/588-7228. www. sluggermuseum.org.* Manufacturers of Louisville Slugger baseball bats and Power-bilt golf clubs. No cameras. Children over 8 years only; must be accompanied by adult. Tours. (Mon-Sat 9 am-5 pm, also Apr-Nov: Sun noon-5 pm; closed holidays) **$$**

Louisville Zoo. *1100 Trevilian Way, Louisville (40213). 7 miles SE via I-65, I-264 to Poplar Level Rd N. Phone 502/459-2181. www.louisvillezoo.org.* Modern zoo exhibits more than 1,600 animals in naturalistic settings. In HerpAquarium are simulated water, desert, and rain forest ecosystems. Islands exhibit highlights endangered species and habitats. Camel and elephant rides (summer). (Sept-Mar: daily 10 am-4 pm, rest of year: to 5 pm; closed Jan 1, Thanksgiving, Dec 25). **$$**

Riverboat excursion. *Riverfront Plaza, 4th St and River Rd, Louisville (40202). Phone 502/574-2355.* Two-hour afternoon trips on sternwheeler *Belle of Louisville* and *Spirit of Jefferson* (Memorial Day-Labor Day, Tues-Sun); sunset cruise (Tues and Thurs); dance cruise (Sat).

Six Flags Kentucky Kingdom. *937 Phillips Ln, Louisville (40209). Adjacent to Kentucky Fair and Exposition Center. Phone 502/366-7508. www.sixflags.com.* Amusement and water park with more than 110 rides and attractions, including five roller coasters. (Memorial Day-Labor Day: daily; early Apr-Memorial Day: Fri evenings, Sat-Sun; Labor Day-Oct: Sat-Sun) **$$$$**

Spalding University. *851 S 4th St, Louisville (40203). Phone 502/585-9911. www.spalding.edu.* (1814) (1,400 students) Liberal arts college. On campus is Whitestone Mansion (1871), a Renaissance Revival house with period furniture (Mon-Fri; closed holidays), art gallery. **FREE**

Thomas Edison House. *729-731 E Washington, Louisville (40202). Phone 502/585-5247. www.edisonhouse.org.* The restored 1850 cottage where Edison lived while working for Western Union after the Civil War. The bedroom is furnished in the period; four display rooms with Edison memorabilia and inventions: phonographs, records and cylinders, and an early bulb collection. (Tues-Sat 10 am-2 pm; also by appointment) **$**

University of Louisville. *2301 S 3rd St, Louisville (40292). 3 miles S at 3rd St and Eastern Pkwy. Information centers at 3rd St entrance or at corner of 1st and Brandeis sts. Phone 502/852-5555. www.louisville.edu.* (1798)(23,000 students) On Belknap Campus is the Ekstrom Library with the John Patterson rare book collection; original town charter signed by Thomas Jefferson; and the Photo Archives, one of the largest collections of photographs in the country. Also here is an enlarged cast of Rodin's sculpture *The Thinker;* a Foucault pendulum more than 73 feet high, demonstrating the Earth's rotation; and the largest concert organ in the Midwest. Two art galleries feature works by students and locals as well as national and international artists (Mon-Fri, Sun). The grave of Supreme Court Justice Louis D. Brandeis is located under the School of Law portico. Also on campus is

> **Rauch Memorial Planetarium.** *1st and Brandeis sts, Louisville. Phone 502/852-6665.* Planetarium shows (Sat afternoons). **$$**

Speed Art Museum. *2035 S 3rd St, Louisville (40292). Phone 502/634-2700.* Oldest and largest in state. Traditional and modern art, English Renaissance Room, sculpture collection, Kentucky artists; special exhibits. Caf, shop, and bookstore; tours on request. (Tues-Wed, Fri 10:30 am-4 pm, Thurs to 8 pm, Sun noon-5 pm; closed holidays) **FREE**

Water Tower. *Zorn Ave and River Rd, Louisville (40207). Phone 502/896-2146.* Restored tower and pumping station built in the classic style in 1860. Tower houses Louisville Visual Art Association, Center for Contemporary Art. Exhibits vary. (Daily; closed holidays) **FREE**

Zachary Taylor National Cemetery. *4701 Brownsboro Rd, Louisville (40207). 7 miles E on Hwy 42. Phone 502/893-3852.* The 12th President of the United States is buried here, near the site where he lived from infancy to adulthood. The Taylor family plot is surrounded by this national cemetery, established in 1928. (Daily)

Special Events

Corn Island Storytelling Festival. *12019 Donohue Ave, Louisville (40243). Phone 502/245-0643. www.cornislandstorytellingfestival.org. Citywide.* Recaptures bygone days of yarn spinning. Events held at various sites in the city. Programs include ghost stories at night in Long Run Park and storytelling cruises. Third weekend in Sept.

Horse racing. *Churchill Downs, 700 Central St, Louisville (40208).* (see)

Kentucky Derby. *Churchill Downs, 700 Central Ave, Louisville (40208). Phone 502/636-4400. www.kentuckyderby.com.* The first jewel in the Triple Crown. First Sat in May.

Kentucky Derby Festival. *1001 S 3rd St, Louisville (40203). Phone 502/584-6383; toll-free 800/928-3378.* Two-week celebration with Pegasus Parade, Great Steamboat Race (between *Belle of Louisville* and *Delta Queen*), Great Balloon Race, mini-marathon, concerts, sports tournaments. Held two weeks prior to Kentucky Derby.

Kentucky State Fair. *Kentucky Fair and Exposition Center, 937 Phillips Ln, Louisville (40209). Phone 502/367-5002. www.kystatefair.org.* Livestock shows; championship horse show; home and fine arts exhibits; midway, entertainment. Aug.

Performing arts. *300 W Main St, Louisville (40202). Phone 502/637-4933.* Louisville Orchestra (phone 502/587-8681), Kentucky Opera (phone 502/584-4500), Broadway Series (phone 502/561-1003), Louisville Ballet (phone 502/583-2623), Stage One: Louisville's Family Theatre; all at Kentucky Center for the Arts; phone 502/584-7777. Actors Theatre, 316 W Main St, phone 502/584-1265. Kentucky Shakespeare Festival, free plays in Central Park, Mon-Sat, mid-June-late July.

Limited-Service Hotels

★ **AMERISUITES.** *701 S Hurstbourne Pkwy, Louisville (40222). Phone 502/426-0119; toll-free 800/833-1516; fax 502/426-3013. www.amerisuites.com.* 123 rooms, 5 story. Complimentary continental breakfast. Check-out noon. Fitness room. Outdoor pool. Airport transportation available. Business center. **$**
🏃 🏊 🏋

★ **BAYMONT INN.** *9400 Blairwood Rd, Louisville (40222). Phone 502/339-1900; fax 502/339-2494.*

105 rooms, 3 story. Check-out noon. Fitness room. Outdoor pool. High-speed Internet acceess. Business center. **$**

★ ★ BEST WESTERN BROWNSBORO INN. *4805 Brownsboro Rd, Louisville (40207). Phone 502/893-2551; toll-free 800/528-1234; fax 502/895-2417. www. bestwestern.com.* 144 rooms, 2 story. Check-out 11 am. Bar. Fitness room. Indoor pool, outdoor pool, whirlpool. Airport transportation available. **$**

★ ★ COURTYARD BY MARRIOTT. *9608 Blairwood Rd, Louisville (40222). Phone 502/429-0006; fax 502/429-5926. www.courtyard.com.* 151 rooms, 4 story. Check-out noon. Restaurant, bar. Fitness room. Outdoor pool, whirlpool. **$**

★ ★ ★ EXECUTIVE INN. *978 Phillips Ln, Louisville (40209). Phone 502/367-6161; toll-free 800/626-2706; fax 502/366-2613. www.executiveinnhotel.com.* This property has an interesting Tudor-style design with all the charm and warmth of a European hotel. It has richly crafted woodwork and spacious comfortable rooms overlooking a beautiful courtyard and heated pool; surrounded with magnolia trees and water wheels. 465 rooms, 6 story. Pets accepted; fee. Check-out 1 pm. Restaurant, bar. Fitness room. Indoor pool, outdoor pool, children's pool. Airport transportation available. **$**

★ ★ THE GALT HOUSE HOTEL. *140 N 4th Ave, Louisville (40202). Phone 502/589-5200; toll-free 800/626-1814; fax 502/589-3444. www.galthouse.com.* Overlooks Ohio River. 700 rooms, 25 story. Check-out noon. Restaurant, bar. Fitness room. Outdoor pool. **$$**

★ HAMPTON INN. *800 Phillips Ln, Louisville (40209). Phone 502/366-8100; fax 502/366-0700. www. hamptoninn.com.* 130 rooms, 4 story. Complimentary continental breakfast. Check-out noon. Fitness room. Outdoor pool. Airport transportation available. Business center. **$**

★ ★ HOLIDAY INN. *1325 S Hurstbourne Pkwy, Louisville (40222). Phone 502/426-2600; toll-free 800/465-4329; fax 502/423-1605. www.holiday-innhurstbourne.com.* 267 rooms, 7 story. Pets accepted; fee. Check-out noon. Restaurant, bar. Fitness room.

Indoor pool. Airport transportation available. **$**

★ ★ HOLIDAY INN. *120 W Broadway, Louisville (40202). Phone 502/582-2241; toll-free 800/626-1558; fax 502/584-8591. www.holiday-inn.com.* 289 rooms, 12 story. Pets accepted, some restrictions. Check-out noon. Restaurant, bar. Fitness room. Indoor pool. Airport transportation available. **$**

★ JAMESON INN. *6515 Signature Dr, Louisville (40213). Phone 502/968-4100; toll-free 800/822-5252; fax 502/968-6375. www.jamesoninn.com.* 123 rooms, 2 story. Complimentary continental breakfast. Check-out noon. Fitness room. Outdoor pool. Airport transportation available. Business center. **$**

★ RAMADA INN. *1902 Embassy Square Blvd, Louisville (40299). Phone 502/491-2577; fax 502/491-1325. www.ramadainneast.com.* 118 rooms, 2 story. Complimentary continental breakfast. Check-out noon. Wireless Internet access. Outdoor pool. **$**

Full-Service Hotels

★ ★ ★ THE BROWN HOTEL. *335 W Broadway, Louisville (40202). Phone 502/583-1234; toll-free 888/888-5252; fax 502/587-7006. www.camberleyhotels.com.* The beautifully restored lobby of this hotel exudes Southern elegance, with intricate plaster moldings, polished woodwork, stained glass, and crystal chandeliers. Built by philanthropist J. Graham Brown in 1923, the property's Georgian Revival-style building remains a cornerstone of Louisville social life. The elegance of the public spaces continues through the magnificent mirrored Crystal Ballroom. 292 rooms, 16 story. Check-out 11 am. Restaurant, bar. Fitness room. Airport transportation available. Business center. **$$**

★ ★ EXECUTIVE WEST HOTEL. *830 Phillips Ln, Louisville (40209). Phone 502/367-2251; toll-free 800/626-2708; fax 502/366-2499. www.executivewest. com.* Just 6 miles from downtown, this hotel is adjacent to Louisville International Airport and opposite Kentucky Kingdom Amusement Park. 611 rooms, 8 story. Pets accepted; fee. Check-out noon. Restaurant, bar. Fitness room. Indoor pool, outdoor pool. Airport transportation available. **$**

★ ★ ★ **HYATT REGENCY LOUISVILLE.** *320 W Jefferson, Louisville (40202). Phone 502/587-3434; fax 502/581-0133. www.hyatt.com.* From this hotel, guests will find views that overlook the Ohio River and the downtown area. The hotel is connected to both the Commonwealth Convention Center and the Louisville Galleria shopping mall. 392 rooms, 18 story. Check-out noon. Restaurant, bar. Fitness room. Indoor pool, whirlpool. Tennis. Business center. **$**

★ ★ ★ **THE SEELBACH HILTON LOUISVILLE.** *500 4th Ave, Louisville (40202). Phone 502/585-3200; toll-free 800/333-3399; fax 502/585-9239. www.hilton. com.* Turn-of-the-century glamour is the calling card of The Seelbach Hilton Louisville. Built in 1905 by brothers Otto and Louis Seelbach, this historic landmark in the heart of downtown Louisville makes visitors feel like characters in a novel. Indeed, this hotel was the setting for Tom and Daisy Buchanan's wedding in *The Great Gatsby.* Magnificent Belle Epoque architecture and glittering interiors transport guests to a bygone era, yet this hotel is well equipped to handle the contemporary traveler. Elegant and historic, the rooms and suites are infused with an inimitable charm and enhanced with period reproductions and rich fabrics. In addition to providing a luxurious home-away-from-home, this hotel is also a gourmet destination, thanks to its sensational Oak Room. Reminiscent of a gentlemans club, this restaurant is on the must-visit list of every lover of good food. 321 rooms, 11 story. Pets accepted; fee. Check-out 1 pm. Restaurant, bar. Airport transportation available. Indoor pool, outdoor pool. Business center. **$$**

Specialty Lodging

COLUMBINE BED AND BREAKFAST. *1707 S 3rd St, Louisville (40208). Phone 502/635-5000; toll-free 800/635-5010. www.thecolumbine.com.* House built in 1900 with full-length porch. 6 rooms, 3 story. Children over 12 years only. Complimentary full breakfast. Check-in 3 pm, check-out 11 am. **$**

WOODHAVEN BED AND BREAKFAST. *401 S Hubbards Ln, Louisville (40207). Phone 502/895-1011. www.innatwoodhaven.com.* Gothic Revival house built in 1853. 8 rooms, 2 story. Pets accepted, some restrictions. Complimentary full breakfast. Check-in 3 pm, check-out 11:30 am. **$**

Restaurants

★ ★ **CAFE METRO.** *1700 Bardstown Rd, Louisville (40205). Phone 502/458-4830; fax 502/458-4252.* American menu. Dinner. Closed Sun; holidays. Bar. **$$**

★ **CAFE MIMOSA.** *1216 Bardstown Rd, Louisville (40204). Phone 502/458-2233; fax 502/451-8887.* Chinese, Vietnamese menu. Lunch, dinner, Sun brunch. Children's menu. **$$**

★ ★ **ENGLISH GRILL.** *335 W Broadway, Louisville (40202). Phone 502/583-1234; fax 502/587-7006. www.camberleyhotels.com.* This ornate dining room in the Brown Hotel has a decidedly uppercrust English feel and a menu by Joe Castro to match. The sophisticated service and a wine list heavy on Bordeaux complete the experience, considered by many to be the best in town. American menu. Dinner. Closed Sun. Bar. **$$$**

★ ★ **EQUUS.** *122 Sears Ave, Louisville (40207). Phone 502/897-9721; fax 502/897-0535. www.equus-restaurant.com.* American menu. Dinner. Closed Sun. Bar. Casual attire. **$$$**

★ ★ **FERD GRISANTI.** *10212 Taylorsville Rd, Louisville (40299). Phone 502/267-0050; fax 502/267-0119. www.ferdgrisanti.com.* This restaurant, in historic Jeffersontown, has been serving up traditional Italian fare on white linen covered tables since 1972. The atmosphere is dressy but not stuffy, and the service is warm and professional. The seafood, eggplant parmesan, and pasta dishes are sure to please, so don't fill up on the great bread sticks before the entrées arrive. Italian menu. Dinner. Closed Sun. Bar. Children's menu. **$$**

★ ★ **FIFTH QUARTER STEAKHOUSE.** *1241 Durrett Ln, Louisville (40213). Phone 502/361-2363; fax 502/361-3135.* American menu. Lunch, dinner. Bar. Children's menu. Casual attire. Reservations recommended. **$$**

★ ★ **JACK FRY'S.** *1007 Bardstown, Louisville (40204). Phone 502/452-9244; fax 502/452-9289.* American menu. Lunch, dinner. Bar. Casual attire. **$$$**

★ **JESSIE'S FAMILY RESTAURANT.** *9609 Dixie Hwy, Louisville (40272). Phone 502/937-6332.* American menu. Breakfast, lunch, dinner. Closed Thanksgiving, Dec 24-26; also week of July 4. **$$**

★ ★ ★ **KUNZ'S FOURTH AND MARKET.** *115 S 4th St, Louisville (40202). Phone 502/585-5555; fax 502/585-5567.* This Louisville institution has been owned and operated by the same family since 1892. Although the original burned down in 1987 and the new building has a little less charm, you can still get great steaks, seafood, and raw bar treats. Steak menu. Lunch, dinner, brunch. Closed Sun. Bar. Children's menu. Business casual attire. Reservations recommended. **$$**

★ ★ ★ **LE RELAIS.** *2817 Taylorsville Rd, Louisville (40205). Phone 502/451-9020; fax 502/459-3112. www. lerelaisrestaurant.com.* French menu. Dinner. Closed Mon; holidays. Business casual attire. Reservations recommended. Outdoor seating. **$$$**

★ ★ ★ **LILLY'S.** *1147 Bardstown Rd, Louisville (40204). Phone 502/451-0447; fax 502/458-7546. www. lillyslapeche.com.* A brightly colored neon sign marks the window of chef Kathy Cary's innovative dining room, a hint to the Art Deco interior that lies beyond the red-brick entrance. Her seasonally changing menu, which in its early days showed more of a Kentucky accent, has an eclectic, urban edge with dishes such as seared scallops in mango-tarragon beurre blanc. International menu. Lunch, dinner. Closed Sun-Mon. Bar. Casual attire. Reservations recommended. Outdoor seating. **$$$**

★ ★ **LIMESTONE.** *10001 Forest Green Blvd, Louisville (40223). Phone 502/426-7477.* American menu. Lunch, dinner, Sun brunch. Bar. Children's menu. Casual attire. Reservations recommended. Outdoor seating. **$$**

★ **LYNN'S PARADISE CAFE.** *984 Barret Ave, Louisville (40204). Phone 502/583-3447; fax 502/583-0211. www.lynnsparadisecafe.com.* American menu. Breakfast, lunch, dinner. Bar. Casual attire. Reservations recommended. Outdoor seating. **$$**

★ ★ **SICHUAN GARDEN.** *9850 Linn Station Rd, Louisville (40223). Phone 502/426-6767.* Frosted glass room dividers. Chinese menu. Lunch, dinner. Bar. Casual attire. Reservations recommended. **$$**

★ **THAI SIAM.** *3002 1/2 Bardstown Rd, Louisville (40205). (502)www.thaisiamky.com.* Thai menu. Lunch, dinner. Closed Mon; holidays. **$$**

★ ★ **UPTOWN CAFE.** *1624 Bardstown Rd, Louisville (40205). Phone 502/458-4212; fax 502/458-4252. www. louisvillediner.com.* Converted storefront. American menu. Lunch, dinner. Closed Sun; holidays. Bar. **$$**

★ ★ ★ **VINCENZO'S.** *150 S 5th St, Louisville (40202). Phone 502/580-1350; fax 502/580-1355.* This restaurant is situated in downtown Louisville. Italian menu. Lunch, dinner. Closed Sun; holidays. Valet parking (dinner). **$$$**

★ ★ **WINSTON'S.** *3101 Bardstown Rd, Louisville (40205). Phone 502/456-0980; fax 502/454-4880. www. sullivan.edu.* Operated by senior culinary students. Lunch, dinner, Sun brunch. Closed Mon-Thurs; also Dec 25-mid-Jan. Bar. Business casual attire. Reservations recommended. **$$$**

Madisonville (C-4)

See also Greenville

Founded 1807
Population 19,307
Elevation 470 ft
Area Code 270
Zip 42431
Information Madisonville-Hopkins County Chamber of Commerce, 15 E Center St; phone 270/821-3435 or toll-free 877/243-5280
Web Site www.hopkinschamber.com

In a region of hills, rivers, and creek bottoms, and in the center of a coal mining area, Madisonville is a growing industrial center and a marketplace for loose-leaf tobacco. Between the Tradewater and the Pond rivers, the town is named for President James Madison.

What to See and Do

Historical Library. *107 Union St, Madisonville (42431). Phone 270/821-3986.* More than 4,000 items are on display, including Civil War material, old maps and photos, and a 150-gallon whiskey still confiscated in Hopkins County. Special events. (Mon-Fri afternoons) **$**

Pennyrile Forest State Resort Park. *20781 Pennyrile Lodge Rd, Madisonville (42408). 10 miles S on Hwy 41, then 14 miles W on Western Kentucky Pkwy, then 7 miles S on Hwy 109. Phone 270/797-3421; toll-free 800/325-1711. www.state.ky.us/agencies/parks/pennyril.htm.* An 863-acre park surrounding a 55-acre lake. Swimming beach, pool, bathhouse (seasonal), fishing, boating (no motors), rentals; hiking, riding, 9-hole and miniature golf (seasonal, rentals), tennis, picnicking, playground, grocery, cottages, and lodge, tent and trailer sites (Apr-Oct, standard fees), cottages. Supervised recreation.

Special Event

Hopkins County Fair. *Hopkins County Fairgrounds, Arch St, Madisonville (42431). Phone 270/821-0950.* Last week in July-first week in Aug.

Limited-Service Hotels

★ ★ **BEST WESTERN PENNYRILE INN.** *Pennyrile Pkwy, Mortons Gap (42440). Phone 270/258-5201; fax 270/258-9072. www.bestwestern.com.* 60 rooms, 2 story. Pets accepted; fee. Complimentary full breakfast. Check-out noon. Restaurant. Outdoor pool. **$**

★ ★ **PENNYRILE FOREST STATE RESORT PARK.** *20781 Pennyrile Lodge Rd, Madisonville (42408). Phone 270/797-3421; toll-free 800/325-1711; fax 270/797-3413.* 24 rooms, 2 story. Check-in 4 pm, check-out noon, cottages 11 am. Restaurant. Outdoor pool. Golf. Tennis. **$**

Restaurant

★ ★ **BARTHOLOMEW'S FINE FOODS.** *51 S Main St, Madisonville (42431). Phone 270/821-1061; fax 270/821-5518.* American menu. Lunch, dinner. Closed Sun; holidays. Bar. Children's menu. Casual attire. **$$**

Mammoth Cave National Park (C-5)

See also Cave City, Glasgow, Horse Cave, Park City

Web Site www.nps.gov/maca

On Hwy 70, 10 miles W of Cave City or 8 miles NW of Park City on Hwy 255.

This enormous underground complex of intertwining passages, totaling more than 350 miles in length, was carved by mildly acidic water trickling for thousands of years through limestone. Species of colorless, eyeless fish, crayfish, and other creatures make their home within. Visible are the remains of a crude system used to mine 400,000 pounds of nitrate to make gunpowder for use in the War of 1812. The cave was the scene of an experiment aimed at the cure of tuberculosis. Mushroom growing was also attempted within the cave.

Above ground, the park consists of 52,830 acres with sinkholes, rivers, and 70 miles of hiking trails. Picnicking; lodging. Camping (Mar-Dec, daily; some fees). An orientation movie is offered at the visitor center (daily; closed Dec 25). Evening programs are conducted by park interpreters (summer, daily; spring and fall, weekends).

Ranger-led tours of Mammoth Cave vary greatly in distance and length. Trails are solid and fairly smooth, and require stooping or bending in places. Most tours involve steps and extensive walking; many are considered strenuous; proper footwear is recommended (no sandals). A sweater or wrap is also advised, even though it may be a hot day above ground. Tours are conducted by experienced National Park Service interpreters. Contact the Superintendent, PO Box 7, Mammoth Cave 42259; phone 270/758-2328.

What to See and Do

☆ **Cave tours.** *Mammoth Cave National Park. Phone 270/758-2328; toll-free 800/967-2283.* Depart from the visitor center (schedules vary with season; no tours Dec 25). Advance reservations highly recommended. Tickets may be purchased in advance through Destinet Outlets. The following is a partial list of available cave tours:

Frozen Niagara. *Park City. Phone toll-free 800/967-2283.* This moderately strenuous tour (two hours) explores huge pits, domes, and decorative dripstone formations. **$$$**

Travertine. *Park City. Phone toll-free 800/967-2283.* Quarter-mile Travertine (one hour) is considered an easy tour through Drapery Room, Frozen Niagara, and Crystal Lake. Designed for those unable to take many steps. **$$$**

Violet City. *Park City. Phone toll-free 800/967-2283.* A 3-mile lantern-light tour (three hours) of historic features, including tuberculosis hospital huts and some of the cave's largest rooms and passageways. **$$$$**

***Miss Green* Riverboat Trip.** *511 Grinstead Mill Rd, Mammoth Cave (42259). Phone 270/758-2243.* Round-trip cruise (60 minutes) through scenic and wildlife areas of the park. Advance tickets may be purchased at the visitor center. (Apr-Oct, daily) **$$$**

Limited-Service Hotel

★ **MAMMOTH CAVE HOTEL.** *Hwy 70, Mammoth Cave (42259). Phone 270/758-2225; fax 270/258-2301. www.mammothcavehotel.com.* 62 rooms, 2 story. Check-out noon. Restaurant. Tennis. **$**

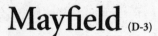

Mayfield (D-3)

See also Murray

Settled 1823
Population 10,349
Area Code 270
Zip 42066
Information Mayfield-Graves County Chamber of Commerce, 201 E College St; phone 270/247-6101
Web Site www.mayfieldchamber.com

Rich clay fields in Mayfield provide resources for all parts of the country. Tobacco is an important crop in this area.

What to See and Do

Wooldridge Monuments. *In Maplewood Cemetery, N end of town on Hwy 45.* Eccentric horse trader and breeder Henry C. Wooldridge is buried here. Near the stone vault, in which he is interred, are life-size statues of his parents, his brothers, five girls, his favorite dogs, a deer, a fox, and a statue of himself mounted on a favorite horse—all facing east. (Daily)

Maysville (A-8)

See also Covington (Cincinnati Airport Area), Lexington

Founded 1787
Population 8,993
Elevation 514 ft
Area Code 606
Zip 41056
Information Tourism Commission, 216 Bridge St; phone 606/564-9419
Web Site www.cityofmaysville.com

This Ohio River town, first known as Limestone, was established by the Virginia Legislature. By 1792, it had become a leading port of entry for Kentucky settlers. Daniel Boone and his wife maintained a tavern in the town for several years. Maysville is now an important burley tobacco market. Many buildings and sites in the eight-block historic district are included on the National Historic Register.

What to See and Do

Blue Licks Battlefield State Park. *Hwy 68 Maysville Rd, Maysville (41064). 26 miles SW on Hwy 68. www.* state.ky.us/agencies/parks/bluelick.htm. Approximately 150 acres on the site of one of the bloodiest battles of the frontier and the last Kentucky battle of the Revolutionary War (Aug 19, 1782, one year after Cornwallis' surrender). A monument in the park honors pioneers killed in an ambush. Also here is a museum with exhibits and displays depicting the history of the area from the Ice Age through the Revolution. Recreational facilities include swimming pool, fishing; miniature golf, picnic shelters, playground, camping (standard fees). (Apr-Oct, daily) **$**

Historic Washington. *2215 Old Main St, Washington (41906). 4 miles S on Hwy 68. Phone 606/759-7411. www.washingtonky.com.* The original seat of Mason County, Washington was founded in 1786 and soon was the second-largest town in Kentucky, with 119 cabins. Restored buildings include Paxton Inn (1810), Albert Sidney Johnston House (1797), Old Church Museum (1848), Mefford Fort, Simon Kenton Trading store, and the Cane Brake, thought to be one of the original cabins of 1790. Guided tours (mid-Mar-Dec, daily). (See SPECIAL EVENTS) **$$**

Mason County Museum. *215 Sutton St, Maysville (41056). Phone 606/564-5865. www.masoncountymuseum.org.* Restored building (1876) houses art gallery, local historical exhibits, genealogical library. (Apr-Dec,: Mon-Sat 10 am-4 pm; rest of year: Tues-Sat 10 am-4 pm; closed Jan, holidays) **$**

Special Events

Simon Kenton Festival. *Old Main St-Historic District, Maysville (41096). Phone 606/564-9411.* Third weekend in Sept.

Sternwheeler Annual Regatta. *Riverside Dr, Augusta (41002). 16 miles NE. Phone 606/756-2183.* Last weekend in June.

Monticello (D-7)

Population 5,981
Elevation 923 ft
Area Code 270
Zip 42633
Information Monticello-Wayne County Chamber of Commerce, 157 S Main St, PO Box 566
Web Site www.monticellokychamber.com

What to See and Do

Dale Hollow Lake State Resort Park. *6371 State Park Rd, Burkesville (42717). SE via Hwys 90, 449. Phone 270/433-7431.* A 3,398-acre park on a 27,700-acre lake. Swimming pool, boat rentals, marina (fee); playground, camping (hookups, dump station). Standard fees.

Limited-Service Hotel

★ ★ **GRIDER HILL DOCK AND INDIAN CREEK LODGE.** *Hwy 1266, Albany (42602). Phone toll-free 866/387-7656; fax 270/387-7023. www.griderhilldock.com.* 34 rooms, 2 story. Closed Nov-Mar. Check-out noon. Restaurant. **$**
🅱

Morehead (B-8)

See also Daniel Boone National Forest, Olive Hill

Population 5,914
Elevation 748 ft
Area Code 606
Zip 40351
Information Chamber of Commerce, 150 E 1st St; phone 606/784-6221 or toll-free 800/654-1944
Web Site www.moreheadrowan.com

The seat of Rowan County, Morehead is a university town and a provisioning point for lumbermen and tourists visiting the northern portions of Daniel Boone National Forest (see). A Ranger District office for the forest is located in Morehead.

What to See and Do

Cave Run Lake. *2375 Hwy 801 S, Morehead (40351). In Daniel Boone National Forest (see), 10 miles SW via Hwy 60 then S on Hwy 801; or S on Hwy 211. Phone 606/784-5624. www.lrl.usace.army.mil/crl.* An 8,270-acre lake created by the impoundment of the Licking River. Beach, bathhouse, and seasonal interpretive programs at Twin Knobs and Zilpo campgrounds, fishing for bass and muskie, 12 boat ramps, two marinas with boat rentals; hiking, picnicking, camping at Twin Knobs and Zilpo campgrounds, boat-in camping at Clay Lick campground. Morehead Visitor Center, on Hwy 801, has exhibits, information. Scenic roads and views, including Forest Development Rd 918, designated a National Scenic Byway. (Mid-Apr-Oct, daily) Some fees. **$$**

Minor Clark State Fish Hatchery. *120 Fish Hatchery Rd, Morehead (40351). 10 miles SW on Hwy 60, then 2 miles S on Hwy 801. Phone 606/784-6872.* Largemouth bass, smallmouth bass, walleye, muskellunge, and rockfish are reared here; on display in exhibition pool. (May-Sept, Mon-Fri; closed holidays) **FREE**

Morehead State University. *150 University Blvd, Morehead (40351). Just off I-64, in center of town. Phone 606/783-2221. www.morehead-st.edu.* (1922) (7,800 students) One-room schoolhouse (by appointment); Folk Art Museum, first floor of Claypool-Young Art Building (Mon-Fri). Also on campus is

> **MSU Appalachian Collection.** Fifth floor of Camden Carroll Library Tower. Collection includes books, periodicals, geneaological materials, government documents. Special holdings devoted to authors James Still and Jesse Stuart, displays of regional art. (Daily)**FREE**

Special Event

Appalachian Celebration. *150 University Blvd, Morehead (40351). Phone 606/784-6221.* Week devoted to history and heritage of Appalachia in Kentucky; dances, concerts, arts and crafts, exhibitions. Late June.

Mount Vernon (C-7)

See also Berea

Population 2,592
Elevation 1,156 ft
Area Code 606
Zip 40456

What to See and Do

William Whitley House Historic Site. *625 William Whitley Rd, Mount Vernon (40484). 15 miles NW on Hwy 150. Phone 606/355-2881. www.state.ky.us/agencies/parks/wmwhitly.htm.* (1785-1792) First brick house west of the Alleghenies, building was used as a protective fort from Native Americans and as a haven for travelers on the Wilderness Road. Was called Sportsman's Hill because of the circular racetrack built nearby (first in US), which ran counter-clockwise, unlike those in England. Panels symbolizing each of the 13 original states are over the mantel in the parlor. Restored and furnished with period pieces. (Memorial Day-Labor Day: daily; rest of year: Tues-Sun) Picnicking, playground. **$$**

Murray (D-3)

See also Land Between the Lakes, Mayfield

Population 14,950
Elevation 515 ft
Area Code 270
Zip 42071
Information Murray Tourism Commission, 805 N 12th St, PO Box 190; phone 270/759-2199 or toll-free 800/651-1603
Web Site www.murraylink.com

Here in 1892, Nathan B. Stubblefield made the first radio broadcast in history. Rainey T. Wells, attorney for the Woodmen of the World, was about 1 mile away when he heard Stubblefield's voice saying "Hello Rainey! Hello Rainey!" Wells was astounded and urged Stubblefield to patent his invention. Because of delays and ill-advised deals while perfecting his invention, Stubblefield was not the first to obtain the patent. He finally received one in 1908, but died in poverty in 1928. This is the home of Murray State University (1922), of which Rainey Wells was the second president.

What to See and Do

Boy Scouts of America National Museum. *N 16th St, Murray. On Murray State University campus. Phone 270/762-3383.* Houses the 54 original Norman Rockwell paintings of the scouting movement; several thousand items of scouting memorabilia and artifacts. (Mar-Nov, Tues-Sun; closed Easter, Thanksgiving) **$$**

Special Events

Calloway County Fair. *County Fairgrounds, Hwy 121, Murray (42071). Phone 270/759-2199.* June.

Freedom Fest. *805 N 12th St, Murray (42071). Phone 270/759-2199.* July 4th.

Limited-Service Hotel

★ **DAYS INN.** *517 S 12th St, Murray (42071). Phone 270/753-6706; fax 270/767-9816. www.daysinn.com.* 41 rooms. Pets accepted; fee. Complimentary continental breakfast. Check-out 11 am. Outdoor pool. **$**

Natural Bridge State Resort Park (C-8)

See also Winchester

Web Site www.state.ky.us/agencies/parks/natbridg. htm

2135 Natural Bridge Rd, Winchester. On Hwy 11 near Slade.

Surrounded by 1,899 acres and a 54-acre lake in Daniel Boone National Forest (see), the natural bridge is 78 feet long and 65 feet high. The park has a balanced rock and native hemlocks. Swimming pool (seasonal), fishing, boating; nature trails and center (no pets are allowed on the trails), picnicking, playground, dining room, cottages, lodge, tent and trailer sites (Apr-Oct; standard fees), central service buildings. Skylift (mid-Apr-Oct, daily; fee); square dance pavilion; festivals. 2135 Natural Bridge Rd, Slade, 40376; phone 606/663-2214 or 800/325-1710.

Full-Service Resort

★★ **NATURAL BRIDGE STATE PARK.** *2135 Natural Bridge Rd, Slade (40376). Phone 606/663-2214; toll-free 800/325-1710; fax 606/663-5037.* 35 rooms, 2 story. Closed week of Dec 25. Check-in 4 pm, check-out noon. Restaurant. Children's activity center. Outdoor pool, children's pool. **$**

Olive Hill (B-9)

See also Ashland, Morehead

Population 1,813
Elevation 160 ft
Area Code 606
Zip 41164

What to See and Do

Carter Caves State Resort Park. *344 Caveland Dr, Olive Hill (41164). 7 miles NE via Hwy 60, Hwy 182. Phone 606/286-4411. www.state.ky.us/agencies/parks/cartcave.htm.* This 1,350-acre park lies in a region of cliffs, streams, and many caves. Swimming pool (seasonal); boating (rentals), fishing, canoe trips, 9-hole and miniature golf, tennis, shuffleboard, picnicking, playground, cottages, lodge, tent and trailer sites (fees); central service building. Planned recreation, films, dances, festivals. Several guided cave tours. (Daily; closed late Dec)

Grayson Lake State Park. *314 Grayson Lake Park Rd, Olive Hill (41164). 15 miles E via Hwy 60, then 10 miles S on Hwy 7. Phone 606/474-9727. www.state. ky.us/agencies/parks/graysonl.htm.* A 1,500-acre park and 1,512-acre lake. Fishing, boating (boat launch); hiking, picnicking, playground, camping (hookups, dump station).

Limited-Service Hotel

★ ★ **CARTER CAVES STATE RESORT PARK.** *344 Caveland Dr, Olive Hill (41164). Phone 606/286-4411; toll-free 800/325-0059; fax 606/286-8165.* 43 rooms, 2 story. Check-in 4 pm, check-out noon, cottages 11 am. Outdoor pool, children's pool. Golf. Tennis. **$**

Owensboro (C-4)

See also Henderson

Settled 1800
Population 54,057
Elevation 401 ft
Area Code 270
Zip 42303
Information Owensboro-Daviess County Tourist Commission, 215 E 2nd St; phone 270/926-1100 or toll-free 800/489-1131
Web Site www.visitowensboro.com

The third-largest city in the state, Owensboro serves as the major industrial, commercial, and agricultural hub of western Kentucky. A progressive arts program has provided Owensboro with a symphony orchestra, fine art museum, dance theater, science museum, and theater workshop. In spring the many historic houses along tree-arched Griffith Avenue are brightened by dogwood and azalea blossoms.

Once known as Yellow Banks from the color of the clay on the Ohio River's high banks, the town saw clashes between Union and Confederate troops during the Civil War. An earlier clash between the values of the North and South occured when Harriet Beecher

Stowe found inspiration for her novel *Uncle Tom's Cabin* after a visit to a local plantation.

What to See and Do

Ben Hawes State Park. *400 Boothfield Rd, Owensboro (42301). 4 miles W off Hwy 60. Phone 270/684-9808. www.kystateparks.com/benhawes.htm.* Approximately 300 acres with hiking, 9-hole and 18-hole golf (fee, rentals), picnicking, playground.

Owensboro Area Museum of Science & History. *220 Daviess St, Owensboro (42303). Phone 270/687-2732.* Live reptiles, insects; archaeological, geological, and ornithological displays; historic items. Gift shop. (Mon-Sat; closed holidays) **$**

Owensboro Museum of Fine Art. *901 Frederica St, Owensboro (42303). Phone 270/685-3181.* Permanent collection includes 16th-20th-century American, French, and English paintings, drawings, sculpture, graphic and decorative arts. Special collection of 19th- and 20th-century regional art; Appalachian folk art. (Tues-Sun; closed holidays) **$**

Windy Hollow Recreation Area. *10874 Hwy81, Owensboro (42376). 10 miles SW off Hwy 81. Phone 270/785-4150.* Area of 214 acres offers swimming, 240-foot water slide (Memorial Day-Labor Day, fee), fishing; miniature golf (fee). Grocery. Tent and trailer camping (fee). Park (Apr-Oct, daily).

Special Events

Daviess County Fair. *Hwy 54 and Philpot, Owensboro (42303). Phone 270/281-9424; toll-free 800/489-1139. www.daviesscountyfair.com.* Four days in late July-early Aug.

International Bar-B-Q Festival. *2nd St, Owensboro (42303). Phone 270/926-6938.* Cooks compete with recipes for mutton, chicken, burgoo. Also tobacco-spitting, pie-eating, fiddling contests. Arts and crafts, music, dancing. Early May.

Owensboro Symphony Orchestra. *RiverPark Center, 122 E 18th St, Owensboro (42303). Phone 270/684-0661. www.owensborosymphony.org.* Includes guest appearances by renowned artists, ballet companies. Oct-Apr.

Limited-Service Hotel

★ ★ **EXECUTIVE INN RIVERMONT.** *1 Executive Blvd, Owensboro (42301). Phone 270/926-8000; toll-*

free 800/626-1936; fax 270/926-8000. www.executivein-nrivermont.com. Spacious rooms with microwaves, refrigerators, and cable television are offered here. After a day of shopping, relax in the heated indoor/outdoor pool, or re-energize in the modern fitness center, complete with racquetball, whirlpool and sauna. 550 rooms, 7 story. Check-out 11 am. Restaurant, bar. Fitness room. Indoor pool, outdoor pool. Tennis. Airport transportation available. Business center. **$**

Restaurant

★ ★ **COLBY'S.** 202 W 3rd St, Owensboro (42303). Phone 270/685-4239; fax 270/685-1399. Lunch, dinner. Closed holidays. Bar. Children's menu. Historic house (1895); restored. **$$**

Paducah (C-3)

See also Gilbertsville, Wickliffe

Founded 1827
Population 26,307
Elevation 339 ft
Area Code 270
Information Paducah-McCracken County Convention and Visitors Bureau, 128 Broadway, PO Box 90, 42001; phone 270/443-8784 or toll-free 800/723-8224
Web Site www.paducah-tourism.org

Historic gateway to western Kentucky, Paducah has been shaped and influenced by its location at the convergence of the Ohio and Tennessee rivers. The waters have brought both prosperity and ruin in the form of disastrous floods; the worst occurred in 1937.

Explorer William Clark laid out the town site and named it after his Chickasaw friend, Chief Paduke. Paducah quickly developed as a shipping center and was a strategic point hotly contested during the Civil War. TVA dams have tamed the rivers and created the recreation areas of the Land Between the Lakes (see). Timber, tobacco, soybeans, coal, and livestock flow through Paducah as they have for more than a century.

Paducah is perhaps most famous as the birthplace of author and actor Irvin S. Cobb, known for his witty humor and beloved "Old Judge Priest" stories.

What to See and Do

Alben W. Barkley Monument. *28th and Jefferson sts, Paducah.* The senator and vice president was one of Paducah's most famous citizens.

Chief Paduke Statue. *19th and Jefferson sts, Paducah.* Memorial to the Chickasaw chief by Lorado Taft.

Irvin S. Cobb Memorial. *Oak Grove Cemetery, 1613 Park Ave, Paducah (42001). Phone 270/444-8532.*

Market House. *S 2nd St and Broadway, Paducah (42001). Phone 270/443-7759.* (1905) This cultural center now houses

> **Market House Museum.** *101 S 2nd St, Paducah. Phone 270/443-7759.* Early Americana, including complete interior of a drugstore more than 100 years old. River lore, Alben Barkley and Irvin S. Cobb memorabilia, Native American artifacts, Civil War exhibits. (Mar-Dec, Mon-Sat; closed holidays) **$**

> **Market House Theatre.** *132 Market House Sq, Paducah (42001). Phone 270/444-6828.* A 250-seat professionally directed community playhouse. (All year) **$$$**

> **Yeiser Arts Center.** *200 Broadway, Paducah (42001). Phone 270/442-2453.* Monthly changing exhibits; collection ranges from European masters to regional artists. Gift shop. Tours. (Tues-Sun; closed holidays). **$$**

Museum of the American Quilter's Society. *215 Jefferson St, Paducah (42001). Phone 270/442-8856. www.quiltmuseum.org.* More than 200 quilts exhibited. Special exhibits scheduled regularly. Gift shop. (Mon-Sat 10 am-5 pm; also Sun 1-5 pm from Apr-Oct; closed Jan 1, Easter, Thanksgiving, Dec 24-25) **$$**

Red Line Scenic Tour. *128 Broadway, Paducah (42001). Phone 270/443-8783.* Self-guided driving tour (with map) of city points of interest, including Market House and City Hall, designed by Edward Durell Stone.

Whitehaven. *1845 Lone Oak Rd, Paducah (42003). I-24, exit 7. Phone 270/554-2077.* Antebellum mansion remodeled in Classical Revival style in 1903; elaborate plasterwork, stained glass, 1860s furnishings. State uses a portion of the house as a tourist welcome center and rest area. Tours (afternoons). (Daily; closed Jan 1, Thanksgiving, Dec 24, 25) **FREE**

Special Events

Kiwanis West Kentucky-McCracken County Fair. *301*

Joe Clifton Dr, Carson Park, Paducah (42001). Society and Western horse shows; harness racing; motorcycle racing; gospel singing. Last full week in June.

Players Bluegrass Downs. *150 Downs St, Paducah (42001). Phone 270/444-7117. www.playersbluegrass-downs.casinocity.com.* Pari-mutuel horse racing. Thurs-Sun. Oct.

Summer Festival. *Riverfront, foot of Broadway, Paducah (42001). Phone 270/443-8783; toll-free 800/789-8224.* Hot air balloons, symphony and fireworks, free entertainment nightly. Events along riverfront and throughout city. Last week in July.

Limited-Service Hotels

★ ★ **COURTYARD BY MARRIOTT.** *3835 Technology Dr, Paducah (42001). Phone 270/442-3600; fax 270/442-3619. www.marriott.com.* 100 rooms, 3 story. Check-out noon. Bar. Fitness room. Indoor pool, whirlpool. **$**

★ **DRURY INN.** *3975 Hinkleville Rd, Paducah (42001). Phone 270/443-3313; fax 270/443-3313. www.druryinn.com.* 118 rooms, 5 story. Pets accepted, some restrictions. Complimentary full breakfast. Check-out 11 am. Indoor pool, whirlpool. **$**

★ **HOLIDAY INN EXPRESS.** *3994 Hinkleville Rd, Paducah (42001). Phone 270/442-8874; fax 270/443-3367. www.hiexpress.com.* 76 rooms, 3 story. Pets accepted, some restrictions. Complimentary continental breakfast. Check-out 11 am. Indoor pool, whirlpool. **$**

Restaurants

★ **C. C. COHEN.** *103 S 2nd St, Paducah (42001). Phone 270/442-6391; fax 270/442-5314.* American menu. Lunch, dinner. Closed Sun; Thanksgiving, Dec 25. Bar. Children's menu. Casual attire. Reservations recommended. **$$**

★ **JEREMIAH'S.** *225 Broadway, Paducah (42001). Phone 270/443-3991; fax 270/443-3997.* Dinner. Closed Sun; Dec 25. Bar. Former bank (1800s); rustic décor. **$$**

★ ★ **WHALER'S CATCH.** *123 N 2nd St, Paducah (42001). Phone 270/444-7701; fax 270/444-0708.* Specializes in Southern-style seafood. Lunch, dinner. Closed Sun; holidays. Bar. Children's menu. Outdoor seating. **$$$**

Paris (B-7)

See also Georgetown, Lexington, Land Between the Lakes

Founded 1789
Population 9,183
Elevation 845 ft
Area Code 859
Zip 40361
Information Paris-Bourbon County Tourism Commission, Courthouse-301 Main St, Suite 114; phone toll-free 888/987-3205
Web Site www.parisky.com

Both Paris and Bourbon County were named in appreciation of France's aid to the colonies during the Revolution. While the French dynasty is long gone, the whiskey made in this county is a lasting tribute to the royal name. In early days, the limited herds of livestock could not consume all the corn produced and the surplus grain was used to make corn liquor. Corn liquor made in Paris in 1790 had such respected qualities that soon all Kentucky corn whiskey came to be called bourbon. Fine tobacco and thoroughbred horse farms are also important to the economy of this town in the Bluegrass region.

What to See and Do

Duncan Tavern Historic Shrine. *323 High St, Paris (40361). Phone 859/987-1788.* Includes Duncan Tavern (1788) and adjoining Anne Duncan House (1800). Daniel Boone and many leading figures of the day were entertained in this tavern. The Anne Duncan House was built flush to the wall of the tavern by the innkeeper's widow, who ran the tavern for many years after his death. Both the tavern, which is made of local limestone, and the old clapboard house of log construction have been restored and furnished with period pieces. (Tues-Sat; closed holidays) **$**

Old Cane Ridge Meeting House. *1655 Cane Ridge Rd, Paris (40361). 8 miles E on Hwy 537. Phone 859/987-5350.* (1791) Birthplace of the Christian Church (Disciples of Christ). Original log meetinghouse has been restored within an outer building of stone. In the early 1800s, revival meetings outside Old Cane Ridge attracted 20,000 to 30,000 persons at a time. Tours (by appointment). (Daily) **FREE**

Special Events

Bourbon County Fair. *Bourbon County Park, Legion Rd, Paris (40361).* Phone 859/987-1895. Carnival; farm and craft exhibits. Late June-early July.

Central Kentucky Steam and Gas Engine Show. *Bourbon County Park, Legion Rd, Paris (40361). Phone 859/987-3205.* Old operating farm machinery; steam traction engines; old gasoline tractors; threshing grain; flea market; country music. July.

Limited-Service Hotel

★ **BEST WESTERN PARIS INN.** *2011 Alverson Dr, Paris (40361). Phone 859/987-0779; toll-free 800/528-1234; fax 859/987-6566. www.bestwestern.com.* 49 rooms, 2 story. Complimentary continental breakfast. Check-in 3 pm, check-out noon. Outdoor pool. **$**

Park City (D-6)

See also Bowling Green, Cave City, Glasgow, Mammoth Cave National Park

Population 517
Elevation 650 ft
Area Code 270
Zip 42160

What to See and Do

Kentucky Diamond Caverns. *660 Doyle Rd, Park City (42160). 1 mile NW on Hwy 255.* Phone 270/749-2891. *www.diamondcaverns.com.* Guided tours of projecting peaks, rock palaces, and some of the world's largest stalactites and stalagmites. Constant 54° F, smooth walks, handrails. (Mar 15-June 14, after Labor Day-Oct 31: daily 8 am-5 pm; June 15-Labor Day: daily 9 am-6 pm; Nov 1-March 14: daily 10 am-4 pm; closed Thanksgiving, Dec 25) **$$$**

Pikeville (C-9)

See also Prestonsburg, Breaks Interstate Park

Founded 1824
Population 6,295
Area Code 606
Zip 41501
Information Pike County Chamber of Commerce, 225 College St, Suite 2; phone toll-free 800/844-7453

Location of the notorious Hatfield-McCoy feud, Pikeville sits astride the Levisa Fork of the Big Sandy River and is the seat of Pike County, a leading producer of deep-mined coal. The town was named for Zebulon M. Pike, the explorer.

What to See and Do

Fishtrap Lake. *2204 Fishtrap Rd, Pikeville (41501). 15 miles SE via Hwy 460 on Hwy 1789.* Phone 606/437-7496. Created by the US Army Corps of Engineers dam on the Levisa Fork of the Big Sandy River, this lake offers fishing and boating (marina). In the area are opportunities for picnicking and camping, as well as a playground and ballfields. (Mon-Fri) **FREE**

Grapevine Recreation Area. *Fish Trap Lake Rd and Hwy 194, Pikeville (41501). In Phyllis, S via Hwy 194.* Phone 606/437-7496. Boating; picnicking, playground, camping (May-Sept; fee).

Special Event

Hillbilly Days Spring Festival. *Main St, Pikeville (41501).* Phone 606/432-5504. *www.hillbillydays.com.* Antique car show, music, arts and crafts. Third weekend in Apr.

Limited-Service Hotel

★ ★ **LANDMARK INN.** *190 S Mayo Trail, Pikeville (41502).* Phone 606/432-2545; toll-free 800/831-1469. 103 rooms, 4 story. Check-out noon. Restaurant, bar. Outdoor pool. **$**

Pineville (D-8)

See also Barbourville, Cumberland Gap National Historical Park

Settled 1799
Population 2,093
Elevation 1,015 ft
Area Code 606
Zip 40977

In 1797, the Kentucky legislature authorized funds for the construction of a tollhouse on the Wilderness Road at a gap called the Narrows. Pineville grew around the tollhouse, which was abandoned in 1830.

What to See and Do

Bell Theatre. *114 W Kentucky Ave, Pineville (40977). Phone 606/337-3806.* (1939) Restored Art Deco movie house. **$**

Pine Mountain State Resort Park. *1050 State Park Rd, Pineville (40977). 1 mile S on Hwy 25 E. Phone 606/337-3066; toll-free 800/325-1712. www.state. ky.us/agencies/parks/pinemtn2.htm.* Approximately 1,500-acre park, surrounded by 12,000-acre Kentucky Ridge State Forest, has nature center, supervised recreation, and Laurel Cove Amphitheater. Swimming pool (seasonal); 9-hole and miniature golf, shuffleboard, picnicking, playgrounds, cottages, lodge, camping (Apr-Oct, standard fees), central service building. (See SPECIAL EVENT)

Special Event

Mountain Laurel Festival. *Pine Mountain State Resort Park, 1050 State Park Rd, Pineville (40977). Phone 606/337-3066.* College women from the entire state compete for Festival Queen title. Parade, art exhibits, contests, sporting events, concerts. Memorial Day weekend.

Limited-Service Hotel

★ ★ **PINE MOUNTAIN STATE RESORT PARK.** *1050 State Park Rd, Pineville (40977). Phone 606/337-3066; toll-free 800/325-1712; fax 606/337-7250. www. kystateparks.com.* 49 rooms, 2 story. Check-in 4 pm. Check-out noon, cottages 11 am. Restaurant. Children's activity center. Outdoor pool. Golf. **$**
🏊 🛠️

Prestonsburg (C-9)

See also Pikeville

Settled 1791
Population 3,612
Elevation 642 ft
Area Code 606
Zip 41653
Information Floyd County Chamber of Commerce, 113 S Central Ave, Suite 204, PO Box 1508; phone 606/886-0364
Web Site www.floydcountykentucky.com

Prestonsburg, located between the Big Sandy River and forested hills, is surrounded by coal, oil, and natural gas fields. In 1862, Colonel James A. Garfield achieved a decisive Union victory nearby; the first major triumph for the Union cause in the Civil War. This victory elevated Garfield to the rank of general and started him on the road to the presidency.

What to See and Do

Jenny Wiley State Resort Park. *75 Theatre Ct, Prestonsburg (41653). 2 miles S on Hwy 23, then 3 miles N on Hwy 3. Phone 606/886-2711; toll-free 800/325-0142. www.state.ky.us/agencies/parks/jwiley2.htm.* Mountainous terrain spanning more than 1,600 acres. Swimming pool (seasonal), fishing in 1,150-acre Dewey Lake, boating (rentals, ramp, dock); 9-hole golf (seasonal, fee), shuffleboard, picnicking, playground, cottages, lodge, tent and trailer sites (Apr-Oct, standard fees). Skylift (Memorial Day-Labor Day, daily; rest of year, weekends only, weather permitting; fee); amphitheater (see SPECIAL EVENT); recreational programs.

Mountain Arts Center. *1 Hal Rogers Dr, Prestonsburg (41653). Phone 606/886-2623. www.macarts.com.* Performance theater seats 1,060. Home of the Kentucky Opry; variety of entertainment scheduled year-round. **$$$$**

Special Events

Jenny Wiley Theatre. *Jenny Wiley State Resort Park (see), 75 Theatre Ct, Prestonsburg (41653). Phone 606/886-9274. www.jwtheatre.com.* Broadway musicals. Mid-June-late Aug.

Kentucky Apple Festival. *Paintsville. 11 miles N via Hwy 23/460. Phone 606/789-4355. www.kyapplefest. org.* Parade, amusement rides, antique car show, arts and crafts, flea market, 5K run, square dancing, music, and entertainment. First Sat in Oct.

Limited-Service Hotels

★ ★ **BEST WESTERN.** *1887 Hwy 23 N, Prestonsburg (41653). Phone 606/886-0001; fax 606/886-9850.* 117 rooms, 3 story. Check-out noon. Restaurant, bar. Fitness room. Outdoor pool, whirlpool. **$**
🛠️ 🏊

★ ★ **JENNY WILEY STATE RESORT PARK.** *75 Theater Ct, Prestonsburg (41653). Phone 606/886-2711; fax 606/889-0462.* 49 rooms, 2 story. Check-in 4 pm, check-out noon. Restaurant. Children's activity center. Two outdoor pools, children's pool. Golf. **$**
🏊 🛠️

Richmond (C-7)

See also Berea, Lexington, Winchester

Founded 1798
Population 27,152
Elevation 975 ft
Area Code 859
Zip 40475
Information Tourism & Visitor Center, 345 Lancaster Ave; phone 859/626-8474 or toll-free 800/866-3705.
Web Site www.richmond-ky.com

Scene of a major Civil War battle—the first Confederate victory in Kentucky—Richmond is an industrial and agricultural center and the home of Eastern Kentucky University (1906).

What to See and Do

Courthouse. *Courthouse Sq, N 1st and Main sts, Richmond (40475).* (1849) Greek Revival courthouse in downtown historic district was used as a hospital by Union and Confederate forces during Civil War. In the lobby is

> **Squire Boone Rock.** One of the Wilderness Road markers.

Hummel Planetarium and Space Theater. *521 Lancaster Avenue, Richmond (40475). On Eastern Kentucky University campus. Phone 859/622-1547. www. planetarium.eku.edu.* One of the largest and most sophisticated planetariums in the US; state-of-the-art projection and audio systems; large-format film system. Public programs (Mon-Sat). **$$**

White Hall State Historic House. *500 White Hall Shrine Rd, Richmond (40475). 9 miles N; I-75 exit 95. Phone 859/623-9178. www.state.ky.us/agencies/parks/ whthall.htm.* Restored 44-room house of Cassius M. Clay (1810-1903), emancipationist, diplomat, and publisher of *The True American*, an antislavery newspaper. The 1799 Georgian house incorporates an Italianate addition from the 1860s. Period furnishings, some original; personal mementos. Picnicking. (Daily) **$$**

Special Event

Madison County Fair & Horse Show. *Hwy 52 (Irving Rd), Richmond (40475). Phone 859/623-7542.* Last week in July.

Limited-Service Hotels

★ **DAYS INN.** *2109 Belmont Dr, Richmond (40475). Phone 859/624-5769; toll-free 800/329-7466; fax 859/625-1690. www.daysinn.com.* 70 rooms, 2 story. Pets accepted, some restrictions; fee. Check-out 11 am. Outdoor pool. **$**

★ **LA QUINTA INN.** *1751 Lexington Rd, Richmond (40475). Phone 859/623-9121; toll-free 800/575-5339; fax 859/623-3160. www.laquinta.com.* 95 rooms, 2 story. Pets accepted, some restrictions; fee. Complimentary continental breakfast. Check-out noon. Outdoor pool. **$**

Rough River Dam State Resort Park (C-5)

See also Berea, Lexington, Winchester

Web Site www.state.ky.us/agencies/parks/roughrv2. htm

On Hwy 79 at NE end of Rough River Lake. Phone 270/257-2311.

This 637-acre park is at the northeast end of 4,860-acre Rough River Lake, on Hwy 79. Beach with bathhouse, pool (seasonal), fishing, boat dock (ramps, rentals); hiking, fitness trail, 9-hole golf, pro shop, driving range, miniature golf; tennis, shuffleboard, picnicking, playgrounds, lodge, dining room, cottages, tent and trailer camping (Apr-Oct, standard fees); central service building.

Limited-Service Hotel

★ ★ **ROUGH RIVER DAM STATE PARK RESORT.** *450 Lodge Rd, Falls of Rough (40019). Phone 270/257-2311; toll-free 800/325-1713; fax 270/257-8682.* 40 rooms, 2 story. Closed week of Dec 25. Check-in 4 pm, check-out noon, cottages 11 am. Restaurant. Outdoor pool. Golf. Tennis. **$**

Shepherdsville (B-6)

See also Elizabethtown, Fort Knox, Louisville

Population 8,334

Elevation 449 ft
Area Code 502
Zip 40165

Shepherdsville is the seat of Bulitt County, which was named for Thomas Bullitt, who established Bullitt's Lick in 1773. Salt was produced from this site of prehistoric animal licks. A state information center is located here.

What to See and Do

Bernheim Arboretum and Research Forest. *Shepherdsville (40110). 6 miles S on I-65, exit 112, then 1 mile E on Hwy 245. Phone 502/543-2451. www.bernheim.org.* This 2,000-acre arboretum offers a nature center with trails, a nature museum (daily), waterfowl lakes, and a 12,000-acre research forest. The 200-acre landscape arboretum features 1,800 species of plants. (Daily 7 am-sunset; closed Jan 1, Dec 25) **$**

Limited-Service Hotel

★ ★ **BEST WESTERN SOUTH.** *211 S Lakeview Dr, Shepherdsville (40165). Phone 502/543-7097; toll-free 877/543-5080; fax 502/543-2407. www.bestwestern. com.* 85 rooms, 2 story. Check-out noon. Restaurant, bar. Outdoor pool, children's pool. **$**
🖼

Somerset (C-7)

See also Jamestown, London

Founded 1801
Population 11,352
Elevation 975 ft
Area Code 606
Zip 42501
Information Somerset/Pulaski Convention & Visitors Bureau, 522 Ogden St; phone 606/679-6394 or toll-free 800/642-6287
Web Site www.lakecumberlandtourism.com

Centrally located, Somerset is only 4 miles from Lake Cumberland. Many of the state's most popular attractions are within an hour's drive. A Ranger District office of the Daniel Boone National Forest (see) is located in Somerset.

What to See and Do

Beaver Creek Wilderness. *15 miles S on Hwy 27.*

Phone 606/376-5323. On 4,791 acres below the cliff lines of the Beaver Creek Drainage within the Daniel Boone National Forest (see). Vertical sandstone cliffs, rockhouses; streams, waterfalls; flowering trees, shrubs, and plants; variety of game and wildlife. Trail, compass hiking; backpacking; scenic overlooks. (Daily) **FREE**

General Burnside State Park. *S Hwy 27, Burnside. 10 miles S on Hwy 27. Phone 606/561-4104. www. state.ky.us/agencies/parks/genburns.htm.* On General Burnside Island in Lake Cumberland. Swimming pool, fishing, boating (ramps); 18-hole golf, picnicking, playground, tent and trailer sites (Apr-Oct, standard fees). Recreation program (June-Labor Day).

Lake Cumberland. *S Hwy 27, Somerset (42501). 10 miles S. Phone 606/679-6337.* This man-made lake with 1,255 miles of shoreline has five recreation areas with campsites (mid-Apr-Oct). Swimming, fishing, commercial docks, houseboats and other boats for rent; picnicking.

South Union (C-6)

See also Bowling Green

Founded 1807
Elevation 608 ft
Area Code 270
Zip 42283
Information Logan County Chamber of Commerce, 116 S Main St, Russellville 42276; phone 270/726-2206
Web Site www.loganchamber.com

The Shakers, officially the United Society of Believers in Christ's Second Appearing, settled this town as a religious community. Crafters and farmers of great skill and ingenuity, the Shakers were widely known both for the quality of their products and for their religious observances. When "moved by the spirit" they performed a dance that gave them the name "Shakers." Celibacy was part of the religious observance. By 1922, the community had dwindled to only nine members. The property was sold at auction, and the remaining members dispersed. Nearby are many historic buildings, including the **Red River Meeting House** in Adairville; the **Bibb House**; and the **Old Southern Bank** in Russellville, robbed by the James Gang in 1868.

What to See and Do

Shaker Museum. *850 Shaker Museum Rd, South Union (42283). On Hwy 68. Phone 270/542-4167.* Located in the original 1824 building, the museum houses Shaker crafts, furniture, textiles, and tools. (Daily; closed Thanksgiving) **$$**

Special Event

Tobacco Festival. *116 S Main St, Russellville (42276). Phone 270/726-2206.* 12 miles SW on Hwy 68 in Russellville. Parade; reenactment of the Jesse James bank robbery; house tours in historic district; tobacco displays; antiques; arts and crafts exhibits; bicycle rides; run (5 miles), 5k walk; entertainment. One week in early Oct.

Walton (A-7)

See also Covington (Cincinnati Airport Area)

Population 2,450
Elevation 930 ft
Area Code 859
Zip 41094
Web Site www.cityofwalton.org

What to See and Do

Big Bone Lick State Park. *3380 Beaver Road, Union (41091). 7 miles W on Hwy 338. Phone 859/384-3522. www.parks.ky.gov/stateparks/bb.* On the grounds of this 547-acre park are a museum and diorama explaining prehistoric mammal life preserved in the soft sulphur spring earth around the salt lick (daily) and displays of Ice Age formations. Swimming pool is open for campers only (fee for camping). Tennis (free) and picnicking available. **FREE**

Oak Creek Campground. *Hwy 16 and Oak Creek Rd, Walton (41094). Phone 859/485-9131; toll-free 877/604-3503. www.oakcreekcampground.com.* This highly regarded, family-run campground has 99 sites with water and electric hook-ups. Four primitive tent areas. Restrooms, showers, laundry services, pool.

Wickliffe (D-2)

See also Paducah

Population 794
Elevation 330 ft

Area Code 270
Zip 42087

On high ground, Wickliffe is near the confluence of the Ohio and the Mississippi rivers. The Lewis and Clark Expedition's Fort Jefferson (1789) was at a nearby site, now marked, 1 mile south on Hwy 51.

What to See and Do

Wickliffe Mounds. *94 Green St, Wickliffe (42087). On Hwy 51/60/62 in NW area of city. Phone 270/335-3681.* Remnants of a Mississippian culture of 1,000 years ago. Museum exhibits, pottery, ongoing research. (Mar-mid Oct, daily; closed Thanksgiving) **$$**

Williamsburg (D-8)

See also Corbin, Cumberland Falls State Resort Park, Cumberland Gap National Historical Park, Daniel Boone National Forest

Founded 1817
Population 5,143
Elevation 951 ft
Area Code 606
Zip 40769
Information Tourist & Convention Commission, 650 S Tenth St, PO Box 2; phone 606/549-0530
Web Site www.williamsburgky.com

Shadowed by ridges that rise nearly 2,000 feet, Williamsburg is the seat of Whitley County. Both town and county are named in honor of William Whitley, pioneer.

What to See and Do

Cumberland River. *Cemetery Rd, Williamsburg.* Runs through Williamsburg and then 18 miles N to Cumberland Falls State Resort Park (see), offers one of the most remote and rustic float trips in the US.

Williamstown (B-7)

See also Covington (Cincinnati Airport Area)

Settled 1820
Population 3,227
Elevation 974 ft
Area Code 859
Zip 41097
Information Grant County Chamber of Commerce,

149 N Main St, PO Box 365; phone 859/824-3322
Web Site www.grantcommerce.com

What to See and Do

Kincaid Lake State Park. *17 miles NE via Hwy 22, then 3 miles N off Hwy 27. Phone 859/654-3531. www.state. ky.us/agencies/parks/kincaid2.htm.* An 850-acre park with 183-acre lake stocked with bass, bluegill, crappie, channel catfish, swimming pool (seasonal; fee), fishing, boating (dock, rentals, maximum 16-foot and 10-HP motor); hiking, miniature golf, camping (Apr-Oct). Amphitheater; planned recreation.

Lloyd Wildlife Management Area. *Williamstown. 10 miles N via Hwy 25, E at Gardnersville Rd (Hwy 491) exit. Phone 859/428-3193.* A 1,200-acre area with archery and shooting ranges (shooting allowed only during sponsored events). Five-acre lake with fishing for catfish, bass, and bluegill. Hunting. Forty acres of virgin timberland includes monument to founder Curtis Lloyd; hiking trails. (Daily) **FREE**

Limited-Service Hotel

★ **DAYS INN.** *211 Hwy 36 W, Williamstown (41097). Phone 859/824-5025; toll-free 800/329-7466; fax 859/824-5028. www.daysinn.com.* 51 rooms, 2 story. Pets accepted, some restrictions; fee. Complimentary continental breakfast. Check-in 2 pm, check-out 11 am. Outdoor pool. **$**

Winchester (B-8)

See also Lexington, Natural Bridge State Resort Park, Richmond

Population 16,724
Elevation 972 ft
Area Code 859
Zip 40391
Information Winchester-Clark County Tourism Commission, 2 S Maple St; phone 859/744-0556 or toll-free 800/298-9105
Web Site www.tourwinchester.com

Winchester is the location of several industrial plants. Nearby coal and gas fields and fertile farmland also contribute to the economy. Henry Clay made his first and last Kentucky speeches in the town. The Forest Supervisor's office of the Daniel Boone National Forest (see) is located in Winchester.

What to See and Do

★ **Fort Boonesborough State Park.** *4375 Boonsboro Rd, Winchester (40475). 9 miles SW via Hwy 627, located on the Kentucky River. Phone 859/527-3131.* Site of the settlement where Daniel Boone defended his fort against Native American sieges. The fort houses craft shops where costumed "pioneers" produce wares; a museum with Boone memorabilia and other historical items; and an audiovisual program (Apr-Labor Day: daily; after Labor Day-Oct: Wed-Sun). Exhibits in cabins and blockhouses re-create life at the fort. Sand beach, swimming pool, bathhouse, fishing, boating (ramp, dock); miniature golf, picnicking, playground, snack bar, tent and trailer sites (standard fees). Recreation director; special events all year. **$$**

Historic Main Street. Has a number of restored buildings, most of the Victorian era, and unique shops (Mon-Sat). Walking tour available.

Old Stone Church. *Old Stone Church Rd, Winchester. 6 miles S off Hwy 627.* Built in the late 1700s, this famous landmark in the Boonesboro section of Clark County is the oldest active church west of the Allegheny Mountains. Daniel Boone and his family worshiped here.

Special Event

Daniel Boone Pioneer Festival. *34 S Main St, College and Lynkins parks, Winchester (40391). Phone 859/744-0556.* Juried arts and crafts, antiques, street dance, 5K run, 2-mile walk, concerts, music, food, fireworks. Labor Day weekend.

Limited-Service Hotels

★ ★ **DAYS INN.** *1100 Interstate Dr, Winchester (40391). Phone 859/744-9111; fax 859/745-1369. www. daysinn.com.* 64 rooms, 2 story. Pets accepted, some restrictions; fee. Check-out 11 am. Restaurant. Outdoor pool. **$**

★ **HAMPTON INN.** *1025 Early Dr, Winchester (40391). Phone 859/745-2000; fax 859/745-2001. www. hamptoninn.com.* 60 rooms, 2 story. Complimentary continental breakfast. Check-out 11 am. Fitness room. Outdoor pool. **$**

Restaurant

★ **HALL'S ON THE RIVER.** *1225 Athens-Boonesborough Rd, Winchester (40391). Phone 859/527-6620; fax 859/527-9940. www.hallsontheriver.com.* Lunch, dinner. Closed Thanksgiving, Dec 25. Bar. Children's menu. Outdoor seating. **$$**

Louisiana

The soil of Louisiana was carried down from the central valley of the United States by the Ouachita, Mississippi, Red, Sabine, and Pearl rivers. Much of the state is a flat, moist, rich-soiled delta with a distinct historic and ethnic atmosphere.

The area was discovered by Spaniards, named by the French (for Louis XIV), and settled by both. People with the blood of those French Canadians driven from Acadia (Nova Scotia) by the British in 1755 are called Acadians ("Cajuns"). Americans of English, Irish, and German origin also helped settle Louisiana.

The land is semitropical, beautifully unusual, full of legend and tradition; a land of bayous with cypress and live oak overhung with Spanish moss. Some of its people live in isolation on the bayous and riverbanks, where they still fish, trap, and do a little farming. Southern and southwestern Louisiana are predominantly Roman Catholic; the northern section is largely Protestant. It is the only state whose divisions are called parishes rather than counties.

The northern and southern parts of the state are quite different topographically. In the southern area are fine old mansions and sugar cane plantation estates, many of which are open to the public. (See BATON ROUGE for a plantation tour.) The north is more rural, with beautiful rivers, hills, forests, and cotton plantation mansions. This is the area from which the colorful Huey Long came; he was born in Winnfield.

Petroleum and natural gas taken from far underground, shipped abroad, or processed in large plants, contribute to Louisiana's thriving industrial and manufacturing economy. As these businesses expand, the service sector continually grows to meet demands.

Hernando de Soto discovered the Mississippi in 1541. La Salle claimed Louisiana for France in 1682. Pierre le Moyne, Sieur d'Iberville, first came to the state in 1699. His brother Jean Baptiste le Moyne, Sieur de Bienville, founded New Orleans in 1718, three years after the founding of Natchitoches by Cavalier St. Denis.

To prevent Louisiana from falling into the hands of the English, Louis XV of France gave it to his cousin, Charles III of Spain. In 1801, Napoleon regained it for France, though no one in Louisiana knew of this until 1803, only 20 days before the Louisiana Purchase made it US territory.

This colorful history established it as the state it is—individual, different, exciting. It remains the old Deep South at its best—gracious, cultured, and hospitable.

Population: 4,468,976
Area: 44,520 square miles
Elevation: 0-535 feet
Peak: Driskill Mountain (Bienville Parish)
Entered Union: April 30, 1812 (18th state)
Capital: Baton Rouge
Motto: Union, Justice, Confidence
Nickname: Bayou State, Sportsman's Paradise, Pelican State
Flower: Magnolia
Bird: Eastern Brown Pelican
Tree: Bald Cypress
Time Zone: Central
Web Site: www.louisianatravel.com
Fun Fact:
• Louisiana was named in honor of King Louis XIV.

Calendar Highlights

JANUARY
Sugar Bowl College Football Classic *(New Orleans)*. Superdome. Phone 504/525-8573.

FEBRUARY
Mardi Gras *(New Orleans)*. Phone 504/566-5005. Perhaps the most famous celebration in the United States. Officially opens two weeks before Shrove Tuesday; includes torchlight parades, street dancing, costume balls, and masquerades.

APRIL
Festival International de Louisiane *(Lafayette)*. Phone 337/232-8086. Artists from Africa, Canada, the Caribbean, Europe, and the US celebrate Louisiana culture.

New Orleans Jazz & Heritage Festival *(New Orleans)*. Phone 504/522-4786. Eleven stages offer everything from rock-and-roll to jazz, blues, and Afro-Caribbean music. Evening concerts in various concert halls and clubs.

JULY
Natchitoches-Northwestern Folk Festival *(Natchitoches)*. Phone 318/357-4332. NSU Prather Coliseum. Festival spotlights a different industry or occupation each year and works to preserve Louisiana folk art forms; music, dance, crafts, storytelling, and food.

SEPTEMBER
Blues Festival *(Baton Rouge)*. Phone 225/383-0968. Three-day event featuring blues, Cajun, zydeco, and gospel music, plus traditional Louisiana cuisine.

Louisiana Shrimp and Petroleum Festival *(Morgan City)*. Phone 504/385-0703. Amusement rides, hands-on children's village, coronation and ball, blessing of the shrimp and petroleum fleets on Berwick Bay, parade, fireworks, and food.

OCTOBER
Louisiana State Fair *(Shreveport)*. Fairgrounds. Phone 318/635-1361. One of the largest fairs in the country; draws more than 300,000 people annually. Entertainment, agriculture and livestock competitions.

DECEMBER
Christmas Festival of Lights *(Natchitoches)*. Phone 318/352-8072 or toll-free 800/259-1714. More than 140,000 lights are turned on after a full day of celebration to welcome the Christmas season.

When to Go/Climate

Temperatures in Louisiana rarely dip below freezingeven in winter. Summers are hot, with oppressive humidity. Hurricane season runs from June 1 through November 1, and Gulf Coast towns are prime targets during this time of year. Annual rainfall can exceed 65 inches in the coastal areas.

AVERAGE HIGH/LOW TEMPERATURES (°F)

New Orleans

Jan 61/42	May 84/65	Sept 87/70
Feb 64/44	June 89/71	Oct 79/59
Mar 72/52	July 91/73	Nov 71/51
Apr 79/58	Aug 90/73	Dec 64/45

Shreveport

Jan 55/35	May 83/62	Sept 87/66
Feb 61/38	June 90/69	Oct 79/54
Mar 69/46	July 93/72	Nov 68/45
Apr 77/54	Aug 93/71	Dec 59/37

Parks and Recreation

Water-related activities, hiking, various other sports, picnicking, and camping, are available in many of Lousiana's state parks. An admission fee $1 per person is charged at most Louisiana state parks. Many parks have swimming, fishing, boating (rentals); camping (unimproved/improved sites, $16-18/site per night; two-week maximum). Swimming pools are operated Memorial Day-Labor Day. Some parks have cabins (two-week maximum reservations made at each park). Reservations

CAJUN COUNTRY

West of New Orleans is Cajun Country, the 22-parish region considered "French Louisiana." The name traces back to the 18th century, when French refugees forced out of Nova Scotia by the British sought refuge in the French colony of New Orleans. They built a distinct French-influenced life and culture among the bayous and swamps.

Although Lafayette, "the Capital of French Louisiana," can be reached in two hours from New Orleans by interstate, Highway 90 offers a leisurely backroads introduction to Cajun Country that could take 1/2 day or more. You can catch Highway 90 just west of the French Quarter, but you're better off bypassing suburban congestion by taking I-10 west to the I-310 spur south. Here the interstate bridge crosses a fierce bend of the Mississippi River barely contained by a high levee. West of the river, I-310 deposits you in the subtropical Cajun wetlands region onto Highway 90; follow this route west toward Gibson. At the industrial port of Morgan City, Highway 90 expands to four lanes.

In New Iberia, a detour south on Highway 329 leads to Avery Island, home of the world-famous McIlhenny Tabasco Sauce. Visit their factory for free. After your detour, cross 90 and follow Bayou Teche ("Tesh") toward downtown New Iberia, settled by the Spanish in 1779. Here Shadows-on-the-Teche, built in 1834, opens a stately plantation house museum with an extensive garden of magnolias, oaks, and Spanish moss on Highway 182 at 317 East Main Street (phone 337/369-6446).

Ten miles north of New Iberia on Highway 31, St. Martinville is famous for its live oak memorialized in Longfellow's epic poem "Evangeline." The 1847 poem tells the story of Acadian lovers reunited under the venerable oak. Today, a pair of local troubadours called the Romero Brothers croon Cajun standards beside the oak to re-create the romance. A statue of Evangeline stands outside the St. Martin de Tours Church in the small downtown square nearby; there's also a replica of the Grotto of Lourdes and a museum with carnival costumes on display. At the Longfellow Evangeline Commemorative Area a mile north of town, guides offer tours of the 19th-century sugar plantation house (phone 337/394-4284).

Farther up Bayou Teche via Highway 31, Breaux Bridge proclaims itself "Crawfish Capital of the World." The town's annual Crawfish Festival on the first full weekend in May features crawfish races, a crawfish-eating contest, the crowning of the Crawfish King and Queen, and continuous Cajun and zydeco music. But at any time, you can find people dancing away at Mulate's (MOO-lots), 1/4 mile west of Highway 31, practically spitting distance south of I-10. Follow signs (phone 337/332-4648).

In downtown Breaux Bridge, near the drawbridge over Bayou Teche, Cafe des Amis (phone 337/332-5273) operates out of an old general store built in 1925, retaining the stamped tin ceiling, ceiling fans, and brick walls. Stay overnight at the adjacent Maison des Amis. The visitor center at the drawbridge distributes local information (phone 337/332-8500 or toll-free 888/565-5939).

Founded as Vermilionville alongside the Bayou Vermilion in 1821, Lafayette was later renamed in honor of the Marquis de Lafayette. Today the historic attraction of Vermilionville re-creates a 19th-century village, with guides in period costume, craft demonstrations, and Cajun music in the barnhouse. It's open daily at 1600 Surrey Street (phone 337/233-4077). Across the bayou at Jean Lafitte National Historic Park (501 Fisher Road; phone 337/232-0789), a 30-minute film dramatizes the story of the British removal of the Acadians from Nova Scotia in 1755.

Two of the region's most famous restaurants are north of Lafayette off I-49. Find crawfish and blackened Cajun specialties at Prejean's ("PRAY-jhonz"; phone 337/896-3247) or farther north in Carenco at Enola Prudhomme's Cajun Cafe (phone 337/896-3646), named for the sister of internationally famous chef Paul. After a visit to Cajun Country, you can easily loop back to New Orleans along I-10 East.
(Approximately 350 miles)

for October-March are placed July 1-3 by phone only on a first-come, first-served basis annually. After July 3, reservations can be made by calling or writing the particular park. Reservations for

April-September are placed January 2-4 by phone only on first-come first-served basis annually. After January 4, reservations can be made by phoning or writing the particular park. *Note:* Reservations may be made Monday-Friday 8 am-5 pm. In the event that the above dates fall on a weekend or holiday, reservations may be made the following business day. Golden Age Passport accepted. Pets on leash only; not permitted within any state park building. For further information, contact the Office of State Parks, PO Box 44426, Baton Rouge 70804-4426; phone 225/342-8111 or toll-free 888/677-1400.

FISHING AND HUNTING

Nonresident fishing license: $60; three-day, $15. Nonresident saltwater fishing license: $60; four-days; $20, one day. Marine conservation stamp (required for saltwater fishing): $3. Fishing licenses are valid from the date of purchase until June 30. Nonresident basic season hunting license: $150; five-day, $100. Nonresident All Game Season: $150; five-day, $75. Nonresident migratory game bird license (three-day): $75; nonresident waterfowl (duck) stamp: $25. Nonresident archery license: $26. For details on hunting and fishing regulations, contact the Louisiana Department of Wildlife and Fisheries, PO Box 98000, Baton Rouge 70898; phone 225/765-2887 or toll-free 888/765-2602.

Driving Information

Safety belts are mandatory for all persons in the front seat of a vehicle. Children under 13 years must be in age- or size-appropriate restraint systems anywhere in a vehicle. For more information, phone 225/925-6991.

INTERSTATE HIGHWAY SYSTEM

The following alphabetical listing of Louisiana towns shows that these cities are within 10 miles of the indicated interstate highways. Check a highway map for the nearest exit.

Highway Number	Cities/Towns within 10 Miles
Interstate 10	Baton Rouge, Jennings, Kenner, Lafayette, Lake Charles, Metairie, New Orleans, Slidell.
Interstate 12	Baton Rouge, Covington, Hammond, Slidell.
Interstate 20	Bossier City, Minden, Monroe, Ruston, Shreveport, West Monroe.
Interstate 49	Alexandria, Lafayette, Natchitoches, Opelousas, Shreveport.
Interstate 55	Hammond, Kenner.
Interstate 59	Slidell.

Additional Visitor Information

For detailed information about Louisiana, contact the Office of Tourism, Inquiry Section, PO Box 94291, Baton Rouge 70804-9291; phone 225/342-8119 or toll-free 800/334-8626.

There are several tourist information centers in Louisiana; visitors will find information and brochures helpful in planning stops at points of interest. Some of the locations are as follows: in the northern part of the state on westbound I-20 at Tallulah and on eastbound I-20 at Greenwood; in the central part of the state on the eastern border on Hwy 84 at Vidalia; in the southern part of the state at Baton Rouge in Memorial Hall of the State Capitol, on St. Ann Street in the French Quarter in New Orleans, southbound on I-59 near Pearl River, westbound on I-10 near Slidell, southbound on I-55 at Kentwood, eastbound on I-10 near Sabine River and south of the Louisiana-Mississippi state line on Hwy 61 in St. Francisville. (Daily; hours may vary)

Abita Springs (D-5)

Restaurants

★ **ABITA BREW PUB.** *72011 Holly St, Abita Springs (70420). Phone 985/892-5837; fax 985/892-9565. www.abita.com.* American menu. Lunch, dinner. Closed holidays. Bar. **$$**

★ ★ ★ **ARTESIA.** *21516 Hwy 36, Abita Springs (70420). Phone 985/892-1662; fax 985/871-9952. www. artesiarestaurant.com.* Often referred to as the country sibling of owner Vicky Bayley's Mike's on the Avenue in New Orleans, this quaint restaurant is housed in a two-story 1885 Creole mansion listed on the National Register of Historic Places. The young chef, John Besh, creates a frequently changing country French menu focusing on vibrant, local ingredients with dishes such as spicy crab soup with garlic croutons. French menu. Lunch, dinner. Closed Mon-Wed. **$$$**

Alexandria (C-3)

Founded 1806
Population 46,342
Elevation 82 ft
Area Code 318
Information Alexandria/Pineville Area Visitors & Convention Bureau, 707 Main St, 71301; phone 318/443-7049
Web Site www.louisianafromhere.org

In the heart of Louisiana, Alexandria became the center of the 1864 Red River Campaign of the Civil War, which resulted in the burning of the town. During World War II camps Beauregard, Livingston, Claiborne, Polk, and Alexandria Air Force Base, all nearby, feverishly trained young Americans to fight. The largest maneuvers in US history, involving 472,000 servicemen, took place in this area.

Both Alexandria and Pineville, located on the Red River where it is joined by the Bayou Rapides, are centers for farming and livestock production, lumbering, and light manufacturing. Water sports are popular at Fort Buhlow Lake and other nearby lakes.

What to See and Do

Alexandria Museum of Art. *933 Main St, Alexandria (71301). Phone 318/443-3458.* National and regional changing exhibits. (Tues-Sat; closed holidays) **$$**

Bringhurst Park. *3016 Masonic Dr, Alexandria (71301). Phone 318/473-1385.* Tennis, 9-hole golf, picnicking, playground. (Daily) **FREE**

Cotile Recreation Area. *75 Cotile Lake Rd, Hot Wells, Boyce (71409). Phone 318/793-8995.* Swimming, bathhouse, water skiing, fishing, boating (ramp); picnicking, tent and trailer camping (fee). (Daily) Additional fee for boat, ski rig. **$$**

Kent House. *3601 Bayou Rapides Rd, Alexandria (71303). One block W of Hwy 165/71. Phone 318/487-5998. www.kenthouse.org.* (Circa 1800) Restored French colonial plantation house furnished with period pieces; outbuildings include a milkhouse, barn, cabins, detached kitchen, carriage house, sugar mill, and spinning and weaving cottage. Herb and formal gardens; open-hearth cooking demonstration (Oct-Apr, Wed). Guided tours. (Daily; closed Jan 1, Thanksgiving, Dec 25) **$**

Kisatchie National Forest. *2500 Shreveport Hwy, Pineville (71360). N, W, and S of town. Phone 318/473-7160. www.southernregion.fs.fed.us/kisatchie.* Louisiana's only national forest covers 600,000 acres. Dogwood and wild azalea bloom in the shadows of longleaf, loblolly, and slash pine. Wild Azalea National Recreation Trail, the state's longest hiking trail (31 miles), is in the Evangeline District. Swimming, water skiing, fishing; hunting, hiking, off-road vehicles, picnicking, camping (tent and trailer sites). Fees are charged at some recreation sites.

National Cemetery. *Shamrock St, Pineville (71360).* (1867) Also in Pineville is Rapides Cemetery (1772), at David St.

Limited-Service Hotels

★ **BEST WESTERN OF ALEXANDRIA INN & SUITES & CONFERENCE CENTER.** *2720 W MacArthur Dr, Alexandria (71303). Phone 318/445-5530; toll-free 888/338-2008; fax 318/445-8496. www. bestwestern.com.* 198 rooms, 2 story. Pets accepted, some restrictions. Complimentary continental breakfast. Check-out noon. Bar. Fitness room. Indoor pool, children's pool, outdoor pool, whirlpool. Airport transportation available. **$**

★ ★ **HOLIDAY INN.** *701 4th St, Alexandria (71301). Phone 318/442-9000; toll-free 800/465-4329;*

fax 318/442-9007. www.holiday-inn.com. 173 rooms, 7 story. Check-out 11 am. Restaurant, bar. Outdoor pool, whirlpool. Tennis. Airport transportation available. **$**

Avondale

Restaurant

★ ★ **MOSCA'S.** *4137 Hwy 90W, Avondale (70094). Phone 504/436-9942.* Italian menu. Dinner. Closed Sun-Mon; Dec 25; Aug. Bar. **$$$**

Bastrop (A-3)

See also Monroe, West Monroe

Founded 1846
Population 12,988
Elevation 126 ft
Area Code 318
Zip 71220
Information Bastrop-Morehouse Chamber of Commerce, 110 N Franklin, PO Box 1175, 71221; phone 318/281-3794

Bastrop is one of the few industrial cities in northern Louisiana. Wood pulp and wood products are the principal output. This is a center of the Monroe Gas Field, with its more than 1,700 producing wells. Bastrop is also a cattle and agricultural area with cotton, rice, and soybeans the staple crops. Seasonal hunting for dove, quail, duck, squirrel, and deer is popular.

What to See and Do

Bussey Brake Reservoir. *5373 Boat Dock Rd, Bastrop (71220). 7 miles N on Hwy 599. Phone 318/281-4507.* On 2,200 acres. Fishing, boating (fee); camping (fee). (Daily; closed Dec 25) **FREE**

Chemin-a-Haut State Park. *14656 State Park Rd, Bastrop (71220). 10 miles N on Hwy 425. Phone 318/283-0812; toll-free 888/677-2436.* More than 500 wooded acres at the intersection of bayous Chemin-a-Haut and Bartholomew. A portion of the "high road to the South" was originally a Native American trail. Swimming, bathhouse, fishing, boating (rentals); hiking, picnicking, tent and trailer sites (hookups, dump

station). All-year overnight cabins capacity of four, maximum of six. (Daily) **$**

Snyder Memorial Museum. *1620 E Madison Ave, Bastrop (71220). Phone 318/281-8760.* Museum covers 150 years of Morehouse Parish history; antique furniture, kitchen utensils, farm equipment, clothing, and Native American artifacts. Gallery features changing art and photographic exhibits. (Tues-Fri) **FREE**

Special Event

North Louisiana Cotton Festival and Fair. *Bastrop. Phone 318/281-3794.* Sept.

Baton Rouge (D-4)

See also Hammond, Jackson, St. Francisville

Founded 1719
Population 227,818
Elevation 58 ft
Area Code 225
Information Baton Rouge Area Convention & Visitors Bureau, 730 North Blvd, PO Box 4149, 70821; phone 225/383-1825 or toll-free 800/527-6843
Web Site www.bracvb.com

Named by its French founders for a red post that marked the boundary between the lands of two Native American tribes, Baton Rouge, the busy capital of Louisiana, is also a major Mississippi River port. Clinging to its gracious past, the area has restored antebellum mansions, gardens, tree-shaded campuses, splendid Cajun and Creole cuisine, and historic attractions that reflect the culture and struggle of living under ten flags over a period of three centuries. Institutions of higher education in Baton Rouge include Louisiana State University, Southern University, and Agricultural and Mechanical College.

What to See and Do

Brec's Baton Rouge Zoo. *3601 Thomas Rd, Baton Rouge (70704). 6 miles N off I-10, exit 8, then right on Thomas Rd. Phone 225/775-3877. www.brzoo.org.* Walkways overlook 140 acres of enclosed habitats for more than 900 animals and birds. Sidewalk trams and miniature train tour zoo (fee). Free admission Wed afternoon. (Daily; closed Jan 1, Thanksgiving, Dec 24-25)**$**

Brec's Magnolia Mound Plantation. *2161 Nicholson Dr, Baton Rouge (70802). Phone 225/343-4955. www.magnoliamound.org.* Early 19th-century, Creole-style building restored to emphasize the lifestyle of colonial Louisiana; period rooms; detached kitchen with garden; weekly demonstrations of open-hearth Creole cooking. Costumed docents. Visitor center; gift shop. (Mon-Sun; closed holidays) **$$$**

⭐ **Downtown riverfront.** Along the banks of the Mississippi in downtown Baton Rouge are the

Louisiana Art & Science Museum. *100 S River Rd, Baton Rouge (70802). Phone 225/344-5272.* Originally a railroad depot, this building houses fine art, sculpture, cultural and historical exhibits, an Egyptian exhibition, Discovery Depot (for children ages 6 months to 9 years), hands-on galleries, and science exhibits for children. The Irene W. Pennington Planetarium features large-format films and laser shows. Outside are a sculpture garden and a restored five-car train. Additional fees are charged for Space Theater shows. (Tues-Fri 10 am-5 pm, Sat 10 am- 8 pm; Sun 1-5 pm; planetarium also open Fri-Sat 7-10 pm; closed holidays) **$**

Old State Capitol. *100 North Blvd at River Rd, Baton Rouge (70801). Phone 225/342-0500.* Completed in 1849, Louisiana's old state capitol may be the country's most extravagant example of the Gothic Revival style popularized by the British Houses of Parliament. The richly ornamented building was enlarged in 1881 and abandoned as the capitol in 1932. Self-guided tours. (Tues-Sun; closed holidays)

USS *Kidd*. *305 S River Rd, Baton Rouge (70802). Phone 225/342-1942.* World War II *Fletcher*-class destroyer. Visitors may roam the decks and explore the interior compartments. A unique dock allows the ship to be exhibited completely out of water when the Mississippi River is in its low stages. The adjacent museum houses a ship model collection, maritime artifacts, and a restored P-40 Flying Tiger plane. Visitor center, observation tower overlooks the river; the Memorial Wall is dedicated to service personnel. (Daily; closed Thanksgiving, Dec 25) **$$**

Heritage Museum and Village. *1606 Main St, Baker (70714). 10 miles N on Hwy 19. Phone 225/774-1776.* Turn-of-the-century Victorian house with period rooms and exhibits. Also a rural village with replicas including a church, school, store, and town hall. (Mon-Fri; closed holidays) **FREE**

Houmas House. *40136 Hwy 92, Burnside (70725). 22 miles SE on I-10 to Gonzales, then right 4 miles S on Hwy 44 to River Rd. Phone 225/473-7841; toll-free 888/323-8314. www.houmashouse.com.* (1840) Large restored sugar plantation features a Greek Revival mansion with early Louisiana-crafted furnishings, spiral staircase, belvedere, and hexagonal garconnieres in gardens. Used in the filming of *Hush, Hush, Sweet Charlotte.* (Daily; closed Jan 1, Thanksgiving, Dec 25) **$$$**

Laurens Henry Cohn, Sr., Memorial Plant Arboretum. *12056 Foster Rd, Baton Rouge (70811). Phone 225/775-1006.* This unusual 16-acre tract of rolling terrain contains more than 120 species of native and adaptable trees and shrubs; several major plant collections; an herb/fragrance garden; and a tropical collection in a greenhouse. Tours are available by appointment. (Daily; closed Jan 1, Dec 25) **FREE**

Louisiana State University. *Highland Rd and Dalrymple Dr, Baton Rouge (70803). Phone 225/578-1175. www.lsu.edu.* (1860) (31,000 students.) On campus are

Indian Mounds. *Field House and Dalrymple drs, Baton Rouge (70803).* These mounds are believed to have served socio-religious purposes and date from 3300-2500 BC. **FREE**

LSU Tigers. *Nicholson Dr at N Stadium Dr, Baton Rouge (70894). Phone toll-free 800/960-8587.* Louisiana State University fields 20 athletic teams and draws some of the largest crowds in college athletics. The LSU mascots are Mike the Tiger, Mike VI (a live Bengal tiger that hosts daily feedings at the Tiger Cage), and Ellis Hugh (an inflatable acrobatic tiger). LSU adopted its Fighting Tigers nickname in 1896 from a Civil War volunteer company from New Orleans—the Tiger Rifles. Their snarling tiger image comes from the logo of New Orleans' famous Washington Artillery unit.

Memorial Tower. *Highland Rd and Dalrymple Dr, Baton Rouge (70803). Phone 225/578-1175.* Built in 1923 as a monument to Louisianians who died in World War I. Houses the LSU Museum of Art that features original 17th- through mid-19th-century rooms from England and America. Self-guided tours. (Daily; closed holidays) **FREE**

Museum of Natural Science. *Baton Rouge (70803). Foster Hall. Phone 225/578-3080.* Features an extensive collection of birds from around the world; wildlife scenes include Louisiana marshlands and swamps, the Arizona desert, alpine regions, and Honduran jungles. (Mon-Fri) **FREE**

Outdoor Greek Theater. *Baton Rouge .* This natural amphitheater seats 3,500.

Rural Life Museum. *4650 Essen Ln, Baton Rouge (70809). Entrance at junction I-10 and Essen Ln, at Burden Research Plantation. Phone 225/765-2437.* Three-acre museum complex of 25 buildings is divided into plantation, folk architecture, and exhibits building. The plantation includes a blacksmith shop, open-kettle sugar mill, commissary, and church. (Daily; closed holidays) **$$$**

Union Art Gallery. *Union Building., Highland Rd and Dalrymple Dr, Baton Rouge (70803). Phone 225/578-1175.* (Daily) **FREE**

Nottoway Plantation. *30970 Hwy 405, White Castle (70788). 18 miles S via Hwy 1. Phone 225/545-2730; toll-free 866/527-6884. www.nottoway.com.* (Circa 1860) One of the South's most imposing houses, Nottoway contains more than 50,000 square feet, including 64 rooms, 200 windows, and 165 doors. In a near-perfect state of "originality," the house is famous for its all-white ballroom. Restaurant; overnight accommodations available. Tours (daily; closed Dec 25). **$$$**

Old Governor's Mansion. *502 North Blvd, Baton Rouge (70802). Phone 225/387-2464. wwww.oldgovernors-mansion.org.* The mansion is restored to the period of the 1930s, when it was built for Governor Huey P. Long. Original furnishings, memorabilia of former governors. (Tues-Fri 10 am-4 pm; closed holidays) **$$**

Parlange Plantation. *8211 False River Rd, Baton Rouge (70760). 19 miles W on Hwy 190, then 8 miles N on Hwy 1. Phone 225/638-8410.* (1750) Owned by relatives of the builder, this working plantation is a National Historic Landmark. It includes a French colonial home with a rare example of "bousillage" construction. Doorways and ceiling moldings are of hand-carved cypress; two octagonal brick dovecotes flank the driveway. (By appointment; closed holidays) **$$$**

⭐ **Plantations and St. Francisville.** Driving tour (approximately 100 miles). Drive north from Baton Rouge on Hwy 61 approximately 23 miles, then turn east on Hwy 965 to

Butler Greenwood Plantation. *6838 Highland Rd, St. Francisville (70775). Phone 225/655-4475.* (1830) Original Greek Revival plantation house survived the Civil War and post-war economic recession only to burn in 1960. A working plantation producing cattle, hay, and pecans, Greenwood has been rebuilt and furnished with period antiques. (Daily 9 am-5 pm; closed holidays) **$**

Cottage Plantation. *10528 Cottage Ln, St. Francisville (70775). Phone 225/635-3674.* (1795-1850) The oldest part of the main house was begun during Spanish control of the area. Outbuildings include a smokehouse, a school, kitchens, and slave cabins. Accommodations and breakfast are available. Tours (daily; closed holidays). **$$**

Oakley House. *Audubon State Historic Site, Hwy 965, St. Francisville (70775). Phone 225/635-3739; toll-free 888/677-2838.* (1806) While living at Oakley and working as a tutor, John James Audubon painted 32 of his *Birds of America*. Spanish colonial Oakley is part of the **Audubon State Historic Site,** a 100-acre tract set aside as a wildlife sanctuary. House and park (daily; closed Jan 1, Thanksgiving, Dec 25). **$**

Rosedown Plantation and Gardens. *12501Hwy 10, St. Francisville (70775). Phone 225/635-3332; toll-free 888/376-1867.* (1835) Magnificently restored antebellum mansion with many original furnishings; 28 acres of formal gardens include century-old camellias and azaleas, fountains, gazebos, and an *allee* of century-old, moss-draped live oaks. (Daily; closed Jan 1, Thanksgiving, Dec 25) **$$$**

The Myrtles Plantation. *7747 Hwy 61, St. Francisville (70775). Phone 225/635-6277.* (1796) Known as one of America's most haunted mansions, this carefully restored house of French influence boasts outstanding examples of wrought iron and ornamental plasterwork; period furniture. (Daily; closed holidays) **$$**

Plaquemine Lock State Historic Site. *57730 Main St, Plaquemine (70764). 15 miles S on Hwy 1, across from Old City Hall. Phone 225/687-7158; toll-free 877/987-7158. www.crt.state.la.us/crt/parks/plaquemine_lock/plaqlock.htm.* The locks were built (1895-1909) to control the water level between the Bayou Plaquemine and the Mississippi. Larger locks built at Port Allen in 1961 caused the closing of these historic locks designed by George Goethals, who later designed the Panama Canal. When built, the Plaquemine Locks had the highest freshwater lift in the world, at 51 feet. The area features the original lockhouse and locks;

interpretive center with displays. (Daily; closed Jan 1, Thanksgiving, Dec 25) **$**

Port Hudson State Historic Site. *236 Hwy 61, Jackson (70748). 15 miles N via Hwy 61. Phone 225/654-3775; toll-free 888/677-3400. www.crt.state.la.us/crt/parks/porthud/pthudson.htm.* This 650-acre area encompasses part of a Civil War battlefield, site of the longest siege in American military history. It features viewing towers (40 feet), Civil War guns, trenches, and hiking trails. Interpretive programs tell the story of how in 1863, 6,800 Confederates held off a Union force of 30,000 to 40,000 men. (Daily; closed holidays) **$**

State Capitol. *N 3rd St and State Capitol Dr, Baton Rouge (70821). Phone 225/342-7317; toll-free 800/527-6843.* (1932) Built during Huey P. Long's administration, the 34-story, 450-foot *moderne* skyscraper capitol is decorated with 26 different varieties of marble. The Memorial Hall floor is laid with polished lava from Mount Vesuvius; the ceiling is leafed in gold. An observation tower offers views of the city; Lorado Taft sculpture groups on either side of the entrance symbolize the pioneer and patriotic spirit. Tour of the first floor on request at the information desk; observation tower (daily; closed holidays). **FREE** The Capitol complex includes the

> **Capitol Grounds.** *Phone 225/342-0401.* On the south side are formal gardens that focus on a sunken garden with a monumental statue erected over the grave of Huey P. Long, who was buried here in 1935 after being assassinated in the Capitol.

> **Governor's Mansion.** *1001 Capitol Access Rd, Baton Rouge (70802). Phone 225/342-5855.* Greek Revival/Louisiana style plantation, the mansion was built in 1963 to replace an earlier official residence. Tours (Mon-Fri, by appointment). **FREE**

> **Louisiana State Library.** *401 N 4th St, Baton Rouge (70802). Phone 225/342-4913.* Houses a collection of some 350,000 books, including an extensive section of Louisiana historical books, maps, and photographs. (Mon-Fri 8 am-4:30 pm; closed state holidays) **FREE**

> **Old Arsenal Museum.** *State Capitol grounds. Phone 225/342-0401.* One-time military garrison that dates to 1838.

> **Pentagon Barracks Museum.** *959 Third St, Baton Rouge (70802). Phone 225/387-2464.* Built in 1822 as part of a US military post, the columned, gal-

leried buildings later became the first permanent home of Louisiana State University.

West Baton Rouge Museum. *845 N Jefferson, Port Allen (70767). 2 miles W on I-10. Phone 225/336-2422. www.westbatonrougemuseum.com.* Exhibits include a large-scale 1904 model sugar mill; a bedroom featuring American Empire furniture; and a sugar plantation slave cabin (circa 1850) and French Creole house (circa 1830). Changing exhibits. (Tues-Sat, also Sun afternoons; closed holidays) **$**

Special Event

Blues Week. *730 North Blvd, Baton Rouge (70802). Phone 225/383-0968. www.louisianasmusic.com.* Event featuring blues, jazz, Cajun, zydeco, and gospel music. Traditional Louisiana cuisine. Late Apr-early May.

Limited-Service Hotels

★ **BEST WESTERN RICHMOND SUITES HOTEL.** *5668 Hilton Ave, Baton Rouge (70808). Phone 225/924-6500; toll-free 800/332-2582; fax 225/924-3074. www.bestwestern.com.* 121 rooms, 2 story. Complimentary full breakfast. Check-out noon. Fitness room. Outdoor pool, whirlpool. Tennis. Business center. **$**
🧍 ⛱ 🎿 🚶

★ ★ **EMBASSY SUITES.** *4914 Constitution Ave, Baton Rouge (70808). Phone 225/924-6566; toll-free 800/445-8667; fax 225/923-3712. www.embassybatonrouge.com.* This newly renovated hotel features an eight-story tropical garden atrium complete with waterfall and fish pond. 223 rooms, 8 story, all suites. Complimentary full breakfast. Check-out noon. Restaurant, bar. Fitness room. Indoor pool, whirlpool. Airport transportation available. **$$**
🧍 ⛱

★ ★ **HOLIDAY INN.** *9940 Airline Hwy, Baton Rouge (70816). Phone 225/924-7021; toll-free 888/814-9602; fax 225/924-9816. www.holiday-inn.com.* 333 rooms, 6 story. Check-out noon. Wireless Internet access. Restaurant, bar. Fitness room. Indoor pool, outdoor pool, children's pool, whirlpool. Business center. **$**
🧍 ⛱ 🚶

★ **QUALITY INN.** *9138 Bluebonnet Centre Blvd, Baton Rouge (70809). Phone 225/293-1199; toll-free 800/228-5151; fax 225/296-5014. www.qualitybatonrouge.com.* 120 rooms, 3 story. Complimentary full breakfast. Check-out 11 am. Restaurant, bar. Fitness room. Outdoor pool. **$**

Full-Service Hotels

★ ★ ★ **MARRIOTT BATON ROUGE.** *5500 Hilton Ave, Baton Rouge (70808). Phone 225/924-5000; fax 225/925-1330. www.marriott.com.* 300 rooms, 21 story. Check-out noon. Restaurant, bar. Fitness room. Outdoor pool. Business center. **$**

★ ★ ★ **SHERATON BATON ROUGE CONVENTION CENTER HOTEL.** *102 France St, Baton Rouge (70802). Phone 225/242-2600; fax 225/242-2601. www.sheraton.com.* 300 rooms, 10 story. Check-out noon. Restaurant, bar. Outdoor pool, whirlpool. Airport transportation available. Business center. **$$**

Full-Service Inn

★ ★ ★ **NOTTOWAY PLANTATION RESTAURANT & INN.** *30970 Great River Rd, White Castle (70788). Phone 225/545-2730; toll-free 866/527-6884; fax 225/545-8632. www.nottoway.com.* This Victorian-style inn was built in 1859. Today, the home retains its original hand-painted Dresden doorknobs, elaborate plaster friezework, and marble fireplaces. A lovely plantation-style restaurant serves Cajun and Southern cuisine. 13 rooms, 3 story. Complimentary full breakfast. Check-in 2:30 pm, check-out 11 am. Restaurant. Outdoor pool. **$**

Restaurants

★ ★ **DAJONEL'S.** *7327 Jefferson Hwy, Baton Rouge (70806). Phone 225/924-7537; fax 225/925-5692.* Seafood, steak menu. Lunch, dinner, Sun brunch. Closed Jan 1, July 4, Dec 25. Bar. Business casual attire. Reservations recommended. **$$$**

★ ★ **DON'S SEAFOOD & STEAK HOUSE.** *6823 Airline Hwy, Baton Rouge (70805). Phone 225/357-0601; fax 225/357-9543.* Seafood, steak menu. Lunch, dinner. Closed Thanksgiving, Dec 25. Bar. Children's menu. Casual attire. Outdoor seating. **$$**

★ ★ ★ **JUBAN'S.** *3739 Perkins Rd, Baton Rouge (70808). Phone 225/346-8422; fax 225/387-2601. www.jubans.com.* Diners will find fine southern Louisiana cuisine with a Creole-American blend. The chef never misses with his veal T-bone with shitake mushroom hash with a port wine demi-glace or the hallelujah crab topped with Creolaise sauce. Creole menu. Lunch, dinner. Closed Sun; holidays. Bar. Children's menu. **$$$**

★ ★ **MIKE ANDERSON'S.** *1031 W Lee Dr, Baton Rouge (70820). Phone 225/766-7823; fax 225/766-3205. www.mikeandersons.com.* Seafood menu. Lunch, dinner. Closed holidays. Bar. Casual attire. Outdoor seating. **$$**

★ ★ **PARRAIN'S SEAFOOD RESTAURANT.** *3225 Perkins Rd, Baton Rouge (70808). Phone 225/381-9922; fax 225/343-3275.* Seafood menu. Lunch, dinner. Bar. Children's menu. Casual attire. Outdoor seating. **$$**

★ ★ ★ **RUTH'S CHRIS STEAK HOUSE.** *4836 Constitution, Baton Rouge (70808). Phone 225/925-0163; fax 225/927-0368. www.ruthschris.com.* The excellent service and atmosphere are on par with the steaks at this upscale national chain. Steak menu. Lunch, dinner. Closed Sun; holidays. Bar. Business casual attire. Reservations recommended. **$$$**

Bayou Sauvage National Wildlife Refuge (D-5)

Web Site southeastlouisiana.fws.gov/bayousauvage.html

This 22,000-acre site offers ample opportunity for bird-watching, with brown pelicans, peregrine falcons, and bald eagles among the species sheltered here. A variety of habitats from marshes to forests protect the park's wildlife, which includes alligators, swamp rabbits, and other small mammals, reptiles, and amphibians. Visitors can also hike, bike, fish, and canoe. Guided tours are available on weekends, with reservations required. Contact the US Fish and Wildlife Service, Southeast Louisiana Refuges, 61389 Hwy 434, Lacomb, LA 70458.

Bossier City (A-2)

See also Minden, Shreveport

Population 56,461
Elevation 174 ft
Area Code 318
Information Shreveport-Bossier Convention & Tourist Bureau, 629 Spring St, PO Box 1761, Shreve-

port 71166; phone 318/222-9391 or toll-free 800/551-8682

Web Site www.shreveport-bossier.org

Barksdale Air Force Base, home of the 8th Air Force and the 2nd Bombardment Wing, is located near Bossier City.

What to See and Do

Eighth Air Force Museum. *Barksdale Air Force Base, North gate, 841 Fairchild Ave, Bossier City (71111). Barksdale Air Force Base, North gate. Phone 318/456-3067. www.8afmuseum.net.* Aircraft displayed include B-52D Stratofortress, P-51 Mustang, and F-84F Thunderstreak. Desert Storm memorabilia. Gift shop. (Daily) **DONATION**

Isle of Capri Casino. *711 Isle of Capri Blvd, Bossier City (71111). Phone 318/678-7777; toll-free 800/843-4753. www.isleofcapricasino.com.*

Touchstone Wildlife & Art Museum. *3386 Hwy 80, Bossier City (71037). 5 miles E on Hwy 80. Phone 318/949-2323.* Various dioramas depict animals and birds in their natural habitats. (Tues-Sat; closed holidays) **$**

Special Event

Thoroughbred racing. Louisiana Downs. *8000 E Texas Ave, Bossier City (71111). Phone 318/742-5555. www.ladowns.com.* 3 miles E on Hwy 80 at I-220. Thurs-Sun; also Memorial Day, July 4, Labor Day. Late June-mid-Nov.

Limited-Service Hotels

★ ★ **HOLIDAY INN.** *2015 Old Minden Rd, Bossier City (71111). Phone 318/742-9700; toll-free 800/465-4329; fax 318/747-4627. www.holiday-inn.com.* 212 rooms, 2 story. Check-out noon. Restaurant, bar. Fitness room. Outdoor pool, whirlpool. Airport transportation available. **$**

★ **ISLE OF CAPRI INN.** *711 Isle of Capri Blvd, Bossier City (71111). Phone 318/678-7777; toll-free 800/843-4753; fax 318/424-1470. www.isleofcapricasino.com.* 245 rooms, 2 story. Complimentary continental breakfast. Check-out noon. Bar. Fitness room. Outdoor pool. Airport transportation available. **$**

★ **LA QUINTA INN.** *309 Preston Blvd, Bossier City (71111). Phone 318/747-4400; toll-free 800/687-6667; fax 318/747-1516. www.laquinta.com.* 130 rooms, 2 story. Complimentary continental breakfast. Check-out noon. Outdoor pool. Airport transportation available. **$**

Restaurant

★ ★ **RALPH & KACOO'S.** *1700 Old Minden Rd, Suite 141, Bossier City (71111). Phone 318/747-6660; fax 318/747-9816. www.ralphandkacoos.com.* Cajun menu. Lunch, dinner, Sun brunch. Closed Thanksgiving, Dec 25. Bar. **$$**

Covington (D-5)

See also Hammond, Kenner, Metairie, New Orleans, Slidell

Founded 1813
Population 8,483
Elevation 25 ft
Area Code 985
Zip 70433
Information St. Tammany Parish Tourist & Convention Commission, 68099 Hwy 59, Mandeville 70471; phone 985/892-0520 or toll-free 800/634-9443
Web Site www.louisiananorthshore.com

Covington is situated in a wooded area north of Lake Pontchartrain, which is crossed via the 24-mile Lake Pontchartrain Causeway from New Orleans. With mild winters and semitropical summers, Covington is a town of pecan, pine, and oak woods; vacation houses; and recreational opportunities. A number of thoroughbred horse farms are also in the area.

What to See and Do

Fontainebleau State Park. *62883 Hwy 1089, Mandeville (70470). 12 miles SE on Hwy 190. Phone 985/624-4443; toll-free 888/677-3668. www.lastateparks.com/fontaine/fontaine.htm.* A live oak *allee* forms the entrance to this 2,700-acre park on the north shore of Lake Pontchartrain; on the grounds are the ruins of a plantation brickyard and sugar mill. Swimming, fishing, boating; picnicking, tent and trailer sites (hookups, dump station). (Daily)

Pontchartrain Vineyards & Winery. *81250 Hwy 1082 (Old Military Rd), Bush (70431). Phone 985/892-9742.*

www.pontchartrainvineyards.com. Located about an hour from New Orleans, the Pontchartrain Vineyards & Winery produces wines to complement the unique cuisine of southern Louisiana. To sample the wines, you can drive out to the winery for a tasting, buy a case at a local spirits shop, or order a bottle with your meal in any number of fine New Orleans restaurants. (Wed-Fri 10 am-5 pm, Sat to 4 pm, Sun noon-4 pm) **$**

St. Tammany Art Association. *320 N Columbia, Covington (70433). Phone 982/892-8650.* Gallery. (Mon-Sat, also Sun afternoons)

Tammany Trace. *Hwy 59, exit Koop Dr.Phone 985/867-9490. www.tammanytrace.org.* Follows the old Illinois Central Railroad corridor for 31 miles, ending in Slidell. Ten-foot-wide, paved hiking/biking trail; unpaved equestrian trail. (Daily; closed Dec 25) **FREE**

Limited-Service Hotel

★ ★ **HOLIDAY INN.** *501 N Hwy 190, Covington (70433). Phone 985/893-3580; toll-free 800/613-2012; fax 985/893-4807. www.holiday-inn.com.* 156 rooms, 2 story. Check-in 4 pm, check-out noon. Restaurant, bar. Fitness room. Indoor pool, outdoor pool, whirlpool. **$**

Franklin (E-4)

See also Morgan City, New Iberia

Founded 1808
Population 8,354
Elevation 15 ft
Area Code 337
Zip 70538
Information Tourism Department, City of Franklin, 15307 Hwy 90 W Frontage Road, PO Box 2332, Morgan City, 70381; phone 337/828-2555, 337/828-6326, or toll-free 800/962-6889

Said to be named by founder Guinea Lewis for Benjamin Franklin, this town on the Bayou Teche is a center of salt mining, sugar refining, sugarcane growing, and the manufacturing of carbon black, which is used in the production of rubber and ink.

What to See and Do

Chitimacha Cultural Center. *365 Canal St, Charenton (70130). Approximately 15 miles N on Hwy 87. Phone 318/923-4395.* Museum exhibits, crafts, and a ten-minute video focus on the history and culture of the Chitimacha tribe of Louisiana. Walking tours. A unit of Jean Lafitte National Historical Park (see). (Daily; closed Jan 1, Dec 25) **FREE**

Cypremort Point State Park. *306 Beach Ln, Franklin (70538). 5 miles N via Hwy 90, 16 miles W via Hwy 83, then 7 miles SW on Hwy 319. Phone 337/867-4510. www.lastateparks.com/cypremor/cyprempt.htm.* This 185-acre site offers access to the Gulf of Mexico. Man-made beach in the heart of a natural marsh affords fresh and saltwater fishing and other seashore recreation opportunities. (Daily) **$**

Grevemberg House. *407 Sterling Rd, Franklin (70538). St. Mary Parish Museum. Phone 337/828-2092.* (Circa 1850) Greek Revival house with fine collection of antique furnishings dating from the 1850s; children's toys; paintings and Civil War relics. (Daily; closed holidays) **$$**

Oaklawn Manor Plantation. *3296 E Oaklawn Dr, Franklin (70538). 5 miles NW off Hwy 90, Hwy 182. Phone 337/828-0434.* (1837) Restored in 1927, this massive Greek Revival house has walls 20 inches thick, is furnished with European antiques, and is surrounded by one of the largest groves of live oaks in the US. Home of Louisiana Governor Mike Foster. (Daily; closed holidays) **$$$**

Limited-Service Hotel

★ ★ **BEST WESTERN FOREST MOTOR INN.** *1909 Main St, Franklin (70538). Phone 337/828-1810; toll-free 800/828-1812; fax 337/828-1810. www.bestwestern.com.* 89 rooms, 2 story. Check-out noon. Restaurant. Outdoor pool. **$**

Henderson (D-3)

Restaurants

★ ★ **PAT'S FISHERMAN'S WHARF RESTAURANT.** *1008 Henderson Levee, Henderson (70517). Phone 337/228-7512; fax 337/228-7623.* Seafood, steak menu. Lunch, dinner. Bar. Children's menu. Casual attire. Outdoor seating. **$$**

★ ★ **ROBIN'S.** *1409 Henderson Hwy, Henderson (70517). Phone 337/228-7594; fax 337/228-7595.* Cajun, Creole menu. Lunch, dinner. Closed Thanksgiving, Dec 24-26. Children's menu. **$$**

Houma (E-4)

See also Morgan City, Thibodaux

Founded 1832
Population 32,393
Elevation 0-12 ft
Area Code 985
Information Houma-Terrebonne Tourist Commission, 114 Tourist Dr; phone 985/868-2732 or toll-free 800/688-2732
Web Site www.houmachamber.com

Situated on Bayou Terrebonne and the Intracoastal Waterway, Houma has for many years been a center for fishing, shrimping, and fur trapping. Known as the "Venice of America," Houma is famous for Cajun food and hospitality.

What to See and Do

Annie Miller's Swamp & Marsh Tours. *3718 Southdown Mandalay, Houma (70360). Phone 985/868-4758; toll-free 800/341-5441. www.annie-miller.com.* Boat trips (two to three hours) through winding waterways in swamps and wild marshlands. See birds, alligators, wild game, tropical plants, and flowers. (Mar-Oct, two departures daily) **$$$$**

Fishing. Excellent fresh and saltwater angling in nearby bays and bayous. Fishing is best May-Nov. Charter boats are available.

Southdown Plantation House/Terrebonne Museum. *1208 Museum Dr, Houma (70360). Hwy 311 and St. Charles St. Phone 985/851-0154. www.southdownmuseum.org.* (1893) The first floor, Greek Revival in style, was built in 1859; the second floor, late Victorian/Queen Anne in style, was added in 1893; 21-room house includes stained glass, Boehm and Doughty porcelain bird collection, Terreboone Parish history room, re-creation of Allen Ellender's senate office, antique furniture, Mardi Gras costumes. (Tues-Sat; closed holidays) **$$**

Special Events

Blessing of the Shrimp Fleet. *Hwy 56, Chauvin (70344). Phone 985/594-5859.* Apr.

Grand Bois Inter Tribal. *470 B Bourg Larose Hwy 24, Bourg (70343). Phone 985/594-7410.* Mar and Sept.

Jackson (C-4)

See also Baton Rouge, St. Francisville

Population 4,130
Elevation 180 ft
Area Code 225
Zip 70748
Information Feliciana Chamber of Commerce, 3406 College St, PO Box 667; phone 225/634-7155
Web Site www.felicianatourism.org

What to See and Do

Jackson Historic District. Includes 123 structures covering approximately 65 percent of town; structures range from storefronts and warehouses to cottages and mansions; architectural styles range from Renaissance and Greek Revival to Queen Anne and California stick-style bungalow.

Milbank Historic House. *3045 Bank St, Jackson (70748). Phone 225/634-5901. www.milbankbandb.com/milbank.htm.* (1836) Greek Revival town house, originally built as a banking house for the Clinton-Port Hudson Railroad, features first- and second-floor galleries supported by twelve 30-foot columns. Overnight stays available. Tours (daily; closed holidays). **$$**

Specialty Lodging

MILBANK HISTORIC HOUSE. *3045 Bank St, Jackson (70748). Phone 225/634-5901. www.milbankbandb.com/milbank.htm.* 4 rooms, 2 story. Complimentary full breakfast. Check-in 2 pm, check-out 11 am. Former bank and newspaper office (1836). **$**

Jean Lafitte National Historical Park and Preserve (E-5)

This park comprises six separate sites, one encompassing the French Quarter and one just a few miles outside New Orleans. The Barataria Preserves 20,000 acres gives you ample room to hike or stroll through three types of the Mississippi Deltas natural ecosystems: marsh, swamp, and uplands. Although much of the protected wildlife is nocturnal, the variety of vegetation (and insect lifelong pants and insect repellant are recommended) will hold your attention. More interested in sea than in shore? Rent a canoe and paddle the motorboat-free waterways. If your passion is for creatures of the air, don't miss this bird-observers paradise, where you may spot everything from egrets to herons. Carrying the proper permit lets you fish or hunt. Take advantage of guided tours tailored for birders, canoeists, or children. Closed Mardi Gras, Dec 25. Phone 504/589-3882 (recorded message), 504/589-2133 (visitor information).

What to See and Do

Acadian Unit. *501 Fisher Rd, Lafayette (70508). Phone 337/232-0789.* Consists of three Acadian cultural centers: the Acadian Cultural Center (Lafayette), the Wetlands Acadian Cultural Center (Thibodaux), and the Prairie Acadian Cultural Center (Eunice). **FREE**

Barataria Preserve Unit. *6588 Barataria Blvd, Marrero (70072). On W bank of the Mississippi, 15 miles S on Hwy 45 (Barataria Blvd). Phone 504/589-2330.* Visitor center has an information desk, exhibits, and movies. Trails run through bottomland hardwood forest, swamp, and marsh. Guided and self-guided walks. Canoeing and fishing. (Daily; closed Dec 25) **FREE**

Chalmette Unit. *Jean Lafitte National Historical Park and Preserve, 8606 W St. Bernard Hwy, Chalmette (70043). 6 miles E on St. Bernard Hwy (Hwy 46). From Canal St, take Rampart St, which merges into St. Claude Ave. Phone 504/589-4428.* On this national park site, daily talks discuss the importance of the Battle of New Orleans, where future president Andrew Jackson's troops soundly defeated the British in the last battle of the War of 1812. View living history demonstrations, audiovisual programs, and battleground memorabilia in the visitor center, or follow the marked road tour route. The adjacent cemetery holds the remains of soldiers who fought in the Civil War and every subsequent war. (Daily; closed Mardi Gras, Dec 25) **FREE**

Los Isleños Museum. *1357 Bayou Road, St. Bernard (70085). Approximately 14 miles SE on Hwy 46. Phone 504/682-0862.* Interprets the history and contemporary culture of the Canary Islanders who were settled here by the Spanish government in the late 1700s. Interpretive exhibits, information about self-guided auto tours to Isleo communities. (Wed-Sun; closed Mardi Gras, Dec 25)

New Orleans Unit. *Folklife/Visitor Center, 419 Decatur St, New Orleans (70130). Folklife/Visitor Center. Phone 504/589-2636.* Walking tours that leave from the Center include "History of New Orleans," an exploration of the French Quarter. The Folklife/Visitor Center also offers exhibits and audiovisual programs; performances and demonstrations by traditional artists and craftspeople; information about the ethnic population of the Delta. Unit and tours (daily; closed Mardi Gras, Dec 25). **FREE**

Jennings (D-3)

See also Lake Charles

Founded 1888
Population 10,986
Elevation 22 ft
Area Code 337
Zip 70546
Information Jeff Davis Business Alliance, 246 N Main St; phone 337/824-0933
Web Site www.jdbusinessalliance.com.com

The Southern Pacific Railroad urged Midwesterners to settle in Jennings soon after its line was built in 1880. The town was chartered in 1884. Louisiana's first oil well, 5 miles northeast, came in on September 21, 1901, bringing pioneer oil developers to the area. Today Jennings remains a center of beef, soybean, and rice production, while oil continues to contribute to the local economy.

What to See and Do

W. H. Tupper General Merchandise Museum. *311 N Main St, Jennings (70546). Phone 337/821-5532; toll-free 800/264-5521. www.oldmagnoliagiftshoppe. com/whtuppermuseum.* Over 10,000 items on display re-creating the atmosphere of early 20th-century life in rural Louisiana. Toy collection; period clothing; drugs and toiletries; Native American basketry. Gift shop. (Mon-Fri 9:30 am-5:30 pm; closed holidays) **$**

Zigler Museum. *411 Clara St, Jennings (70546). Phone 337/824-0114.* Museum contains galleries of wildlife and natural history, European, and American art; rotating exhibits. (Tues-Sat, Sun afternoons; closed holidays) **$**

Limited-Service Hotel

★ ★ **HOLIDAY INN.** *603 Holiday Dr, Jennings (70546). Phone 337/824-5280; toll-free 800/465-4329; fax 337/824-7941. www.holiday-inn.com.* 131 rooms, 2 story. Check-out noon. Restaurant, bar. Fitness room. Outdoor pool. **$**

Kenner (D-5)

See also Covington, Hammond, Metairie

Population 70,517
Elevation 5 ft
Area Code 504
Web Site www.kennercvb.com

What to See and Do

Treasure Chest Casino. *5050 Williams Blvd, Kenner (70065). Phone 504/443-8000; toll-free 800/298-0711. www.treasurechest.com.* A riverboat docked in Lake Ponchartrain, the 25,767 square feet of the *Treasure Chest* holds 1,000 slot machines and table games ranging from blackjack to Let It Ride to Caribbean Stud, which is in keeping with the casino's overall Caribbean theme. Food choices are an all-you-can-eat buffet or the upscale Bobby G's restaurant, while the Caribbean Showroom offers live entertainment. (Daily, 24 hours)

Full-Service Hotel

★ ★ ★ **HILTON NEW ORLEANS AIRPORT.** *901 Airline Dr, Kenner (70062). Phone 504/469-5000; toll-free 800/872-5914; fax 504/466-5473. www.hilton. com.* This first-class hotel caters to business travelers, but with a 21-station fitness center, outdoor pool and whirlpool, tennis courts, and putting green, it is great for leisure travelers as well. 317 rooms, 6 story. Pets accepted, some restrictions; fee. Check-out 1 pm. Restaurant, bar. Fitness room. Outdoor pool, whirlpool. Tennis. Airport transportation available. Business center. **$**

Lacombe

See also Covington, Hammond, Metairie

Restaurant

★ ★ ★ ★ **LA PROVENCE.** *Hwy 190 E, Lacombe (70445). Phone 985/626-7662; fax 985/626-9598. www. laprovencerestaurant.com.* For three decades, residents of New Orleans (and beyond) have been treated to the rustic, traditional cuisine of southern France lovingly prepared by Constantin Kerageorgiou, chef/owner of La Provence. Kerageorgiou opened La Provence, a country innstyle restaurant secreted in the pines of Lacombe, in 1972 and has been paying homage to his Mediterranean roots ever since. Steaming dishes brimming with garlic, tomatoes, olives, and fresh herbs are his signature. When the air fills with the heavy, intoxicating aromas coming from the kitchen, you are swept up and away from the real world to the charming French countryside. The restaurants blazing hearths, fresh flowers, and antique décor help prolong the fantasy. French menu. Lunch, dinner, brunch. Closed Mon-Tues; Jan 1, July 4, Dec 25. Casual attire. Reservations recommended. **$$**

Lafayette (D-3)

See also New Iberia, Opelousas, Saint Martinville

Founded 1823
Population 110,257
Elevation 41 ft
Area Code 337
Information Lafayette Convention & Visitors Commission, 1400 NW Evangeline Thrwy, PO Box 52066, 70505;
Web Site www.lafayettetravel.com

Acadians from Nova Scotia came to the Lafayette area to escape British persecution. A significant percentage of today's residents continue to speak French or a patois and maintain a strong feeling of kinship with Nova Scotia and France. These descendants of the French Acadians form the nucleus of the Louisiana Cajuns, who have contributed greatly to the state's rich culture.

Today, Lafayette is a commercial city built around retail trade, light industry, agriculture, and oil. Area farmers produce soybeans, rice, and sugarcane, as well as beef and dairy products. Many oil companies drilling for and pumping offshore oil have regional offices in the area, with headquarters in Lafayette's Heymann Oil Center.

Despite its industrial image, Lafayette has retained its "small-town" charm. Live oaks and azaleas abound around the town, as do clumps of native iris, the city's official flower. Tours of the navigable Bayou Vermilion are now available to visitors.

What to See and Do

Acadian Village: A Museum of Acadian Heritage and Culture. *200 Greenleaf Dr, Lafayette (70506). 5 miles S via Hwy 167, Johnston St S, Ridge Rd W.Phone 337/981-2364; toll-free 800/962-9133.* This restored 19th-century Acadian village features fine examples of unique Acadian architecture with houses, a general store, and a chapel. Crafts displays and sales. (Daily; closed Mardi Gras, holidays) **$$$**

Chretien Point Plantation. *665 Chretien Point Rd, Lafayette (70584). 5 miles W on I-10 to Hwy 93, 11 miles N to Hwy 356, W one block to Parish Rd 2-151, then 1 mile N. Phone 337/662-5876.* (1831) Restored Greek Revival mansion, site of a Civil War battle; stairway copied for Tara in the 1939 movie *Gone With the Wind.* (Daily; closed holidays) **$$$**

Lafayette Museum. *1122 Lafayette St, Lafayette (70501). Phone 337/234-2208.* (1800-1849) Once the residence of Alexandre Mouton, the first Democratic governor of the state, the house is now a museum with antique furnishings, Civil War relics, and carnival costumes. (Tues-Sun; closed Mardi Gras, holidays) **$$**

Lafayette Natural History Museum and Planetarium. *433 Jefferson St, Lafayette (70503). Phone 337/291-5544. www.lnhm.org.* Planetarium programs; changing exhibits. (Daily; closed Mardi Gras, holidays) **$$**

University Art Museum. *E Lewis and Girard Park Dr, Lafayette (70503). Phone 337/482-5326. www.louisiana.edu/UAM.* There are two locations: the permanent collection is at 101 Girard Park Dr (Mon-Fri; closed holidays); changing exhibits are staged at Fletcher Hall, East Lewis, and Girard Park Circle (Tues-Sat; closed holidays). **$**

University of Louisiana at Lafayette. *200 E University Ave, Lafayette (70503). Phone 337/482-1000. www.louisiana.edu.* (1900) (16,200 students.) The tree-shaded campus serves as an arboretum with many Southern plant species. Cypress Lake, a miniature Louisiana cypress swamp, has fish, alligators, and native irises.

Special Events

Azalea Trail. *Phone 337/232-3737.* Mid-Mar.

Festival International de Louisiane. *735 Jefferson St, Lafayette (70501). Downtown. Phone 337/232-8086. www.festivalinternational.com.* International and Louisiana performing and visual arts and cuisine. Last weekend in Apr.

Festivals Acadiens. *Phone 337/232-3737.* Cajun music and food festival. Third weekend in Sept.

Thoroughbred racing. *Evangeline Downs, 3620 NW Evangeline, Lafayette. 3 miles N on Hwy 167. Phone 866/472-2466. www.evangelinedowns.com.* Pari-mutuel betting. Proper attire required in clubhouse. Early Apr-Labor Day.

Limited-Service Hotels

★ ★ **BEST WESTERN HOTEL ACADIANA.** *1801 W Pinhook Rd, Lafayette (70508). Phone 337/233-8120; toll-free 800/826-8386; fax 337/234-9667. www.bestwestern.com.* 290 rooms, 6 story. Check-out noon. Restaurant, bar. Fitness room. Outdoor pool. Airport transportation available. Business center. **$**

★ ★ **COMFORT INN.** *1421 SE Evangeline Thrwy, Lafayette (70501). Phone 337/232-9000; toll-free 800/800-8752; fax 337/233-8629. www.choicehotels.com.* 200 rooms, 2 story. Pets accepted. Complimentary continental breakfast. Check-out noon. Restaurant, bar. Fitness room. Outdoor pool. Airport transportation available. **$**

★ **LA QUINTA INN.** *2100 NE Evangeline Thrwy, Lafayette (70507). Phone 337/233-5610; toll-free 800/531-5900; fax 337/235-2104. www.laquinta.com.* 140 rooms, 2 story. Pets accepted. Complimentary continental breakfast. Check-out noon. Outdoor pool. **$**

Full-Service Hotel

★ ★ ★ **HILTON LAFAYETTE AND TOWERS.** *1521 W Pinhook Rd, Lafayette (70503). Phone 337/235-6111; fax 337/237-6313. www.hilton.com.* 327 rooms, 15 story. Check-out noon. Restaurant, bar. Outdoor pool. Airport transportation available. **$**

Restaurants

★ **BLAIR HOUSE.** *1316 Surrey, Lafayette (70501). Phone 337/234-0357; fax 337/235-3377.* American, Cajun, French menu. Lunch, dinner. Closed holidays. Bar. Children's menu. Casual attire. Reservations recommended. **$$**

★ ★ **BLUE DOG CAFE.** *1211 W Pinhook, Lafayette (70501). Phone 337/237-0005; fax 337/237-0065.* Cajun/Creole, seafood, steak menu. Lunch, dinner, brunch. Closed holidays. Bar. Casual attire. Reservations recommended. Outdoor seating. **$$**

★ ★ **DON'S SEAFOOD & STEAK HOUSE.** *301 E Vermilion St, Lafayette (70501). Phone 337/235-3551; fax 337/235-6707. www.donsdowntown.com.* Cajun, seafood, steak menu. Lunch, dinner. Closed Mardi Gras, Dec 25. Bar. Children's menu. Casual attire. **$$**

★ ★ **I MONELLI.** *4017 Johnston St, Lafayette (70503). Phone 337/989-9291; fax 337/981-5618.* Italian menu. Lunch, dinner. Closed Sun-Mon; holidays; Mardi Gras. Bar. Business casual attire. Reservations recommended. **$$**

★ ★ **LA FONDA.** *3809 Johnston St, Lafayette (70503). Phone 337/984-5630; fax 337/984-5639.* Mexican menu. Lunch, dinner. Closed Sun-Mon; also Thanksgiving week. Bar. Casual attire. **$$**

★ ★ **POOR BOY'S RIVERSIDE INN.** *240 Tubing Rd, Lafayette (70508). Phone 337/235-8559; fax 337/837-4265. www.poorboysriversideinn.com.* Cajun, seafood menu. Lunch, dinner. Closed Sun; holidays. Bar. Children's menu. Casual attire. Reservations recommended. **$$**

★ **PREJEAN'S RESTAURANT.** *3480 I-49N, Lafayette (70507). Phone 337/896-3247; fax 337/896-3278. www.prejeans.com.* Cajun menu. Breakfast, lunch, dinner. Closed holidays. Bar. Children's menu. Casual attire. Mounted and stuffed wildlife on display, including a 14-foot alligator believed to have been 65 years old when captured. **$$**

★ **RANDOL'S.** *2320 Kaliste Saloom Rd, Lafayette (70508). Phone 337/981-7080; toll-free 800/962-2586; fax 337/981-7083. www.randols.com.* Seafood menu. Dinner. Closed holidays. Bar. Children's menu. Casual attire. **$$**

★ ★ ★ **RUTH'S CHRIS STEAK HOUSE.** *620 W Pinhook Rd, Lafayette (70503). Phone 337/237-6123; fax 337/237-8013. www.ruthschris.com.* Prime steaks broiled in a custom-built oven and served sizzling in a pool of butter on a very hot plate characterize this upscale chain. A la carte vegetables include creamed spinach; asparagus with hollandaise sauce; and baked, mashed, lyonnaise, or au gratin potatoes. Steak menu. Lunch, dinner. Closed holidays. Bar. Children's menu. Business casual attire. Reservations recommended. Valet parking. **$$$**

Lake Charles (D-2)

See also Jennings

Founded circa 1781
Population 71,757
Elevation 20 ft
Area Code 337
Information Southwest Louisiana Convention & Visitors Bureau, off I-10 on North Beach, 1205 N Lakeshore Dr, PO Box 1912, 70602; phone 337/436-9588 or toll-free 800/456-7952
Web Site www.visitlakecharles.org

Around 1781, a Frenchman named Charles Sallier settled on the shore of a pleasant lake, married, and built a house. His property became known to travelers as "Charlie's Lake," and his hospitality became famous. However, the town grew slowly until the Southern Pacific Railroad's link between Houston and New Orleans was finished. Stimulated by railroad transportation and under the more sedate name of "Lake Charles," the town began its real growth, mainly via timber and rice culture. Captain J. B. Watkins began a tremendous penny-postcard publicity campaign in 1887. It was effective, but not so effective as the discovery of oil and sulphur early in the 20th century. In 1926, when a deepwater port was opened, the city's future was assured.

A massive reforestation project, centered around Lake Charles, began in the 1950s, and revitalized the area's lumber industry. Now oil, rubber, and chemicals have joined cattle and rice to make this a vital industrial center. McNeese State University is located in Lake Charles.

What to See and Do

Brimstone Historical Society Museum. *800 Picard Rd, Sulphur (70663). In Frasch Park, 11 miles W via I-10, exit N onto Ruth St, then W on Logan St.* Commemorates turn-of-the-century birth of the local sulphur industry with exhibits explaining the development of the Frasch mining process; other exhibits deal with southwest Louisiana. (Mon-Fri; closed holidays) **FREE**

Creole Nature Trail National Scenic Byway. *1205 N Lakeshore Dr, Sulphur (70601). Begins 15 miles SW off I-10 via Hwy 27. Phone toll-free 800/456-7952. www.creolenaturetrail.org.* Follows Hwy 27 in a circular route ending back at Lake Charles. Unique composite of wildflowers, animals, shrimp, crab, and many varieties of fish, plus one of the largest alligator populations in the world; winter habitat of thousands of ducks and geese; views of several bayous, Intracoastal Waterway, oil platforms, beaches, four wildlife refuges, and a bird sanctuary. Automobile nature trail (180 miles); walking nature trail (1 1/2 miles). (Daily) For map contact the Convention & Visitors Bureau. **FREE**

Fishing, hunting. On and around Lake Calcasieu. Fishing in Calcasieu River; deep sea, jetty fishing at Cameron, Gulf of Mexico.

⭐ Historic "Charpentier". District includes 20 square blocks of downtown area; architectural styles range from Queen Anne, Eastlake, and "Carpenter's Gothic" (known locally as "Lake Charles style") to Western stick-style bungalows. Tours (fee) and brochures describing self-guided tours may be obtained at the Convention & Visitors Bureau.

Imperial Calcasieu Museum. *204 W Sallier St, Lake Charles (70601). Phone 337/439-3797.* Items of local historical interest. Complete rooms and shops; toy collection, rare Audubon prints. Gibson-Barham Gallery houses art exhibits. On premises is the 300-year-old Sallier Oak tree. (Tues-Sat; closed holidays) **$**

Port of Lake Charles. *150 Marine St, Lake Charles (70601). W end of Shell Beach Dr. www.portlc.com.* Docks and turning basin. Ships pass down the Calcasieu ship channel and through Lake Calcasieu.

Sam Houston Jones State Park. *107 Sutherland Rd, Lake Charles (70611). 12 miles N, off Hwy 171 on Hwy 378. Phone 337/855-2665; toll-free 888/677-7264. www.lastateparks.com/sanhoust/Shjones.htm.* The approximately 1,000 acres includes lagoons in a densely wooded area at the confluence of the west fork of the Caslcasieu and Houston Rivers and the Indian Bayou. Fishing, boating (rentals, launch); nature trails, hiking, picnicking, tent and trailer sites (hookups, dump station), cabins. Standard fees. (Daily) **$**

Special Events

CFMA Cajun Music and Food Festival. *Burton Coliseum., 7001 Gulf Hwy, Lake Charles (70607). Phone toll-free 800/456-7952.* Entertainment, contests, arts and crafts. Late July.

Contraband Days. *Lake Charles Civic Center, 900 Lake Shore Dr, Lake Charles (70601). Phone 337/436-5508; toll-free 800/456-7952. www.contrabanddays.com.*

Honors "gentleman pirate" Jean Lafitte. Boat races, midway, concerts, arts and crafts display. Two weeks in early May.

Horse racing. *2717 Hwy 3063, Vinton (70668). Phone 337/589-7441; toll-free 800/737-3358.* Delta Downs. 30 miles W via I-10. Minimum age 18. Jacket required in Clubhouse, Skyline. Thoroughbreds Sept-Mar, Thurs-Sat evenings; Sun matinee; no racing holidays. Also quarterhorse racing Apr-Labor Day.

Limited-Service Hotel

⭐ BEST WESTERN RICHMOND SUITES HOTEL. *2600 Moeling St, Lake Charles (70615). Phone 337/433-5213; toll-free 800/643-2582; fax 337/439-4243. www.bestwestern.com.* 140 rooms, 2 story. Complimentary full breakfast. Check-out noon. Fitness room. Outdoor pool, whirlpool. Airport transportation available. **$**
🏃 🏊

Specialty Lodgings

A RIVER'S EDGE BED & BREAKFAST. *2035 Gus St, Westlake (70669). Phone 337/497-1525. www.lakecharlesbedbreakfast.com.* Set between a winding bayou and its own private island. Guests are greeted with smoothies, homemade cookies, cold cuts, cheese and crackers. 3 rooms, 1 story. Outdoor pool. **$**
🏊

AUNT RUBY'S BED & BREAKFAST. *504 Pujo St, Lake Charles (70601). Phone 318/430-0603. www.auntrubys.com.* Constructed in 1911, it has six guest rooms with private baths and offers a gourmet breakfast in the morning. 6 rooms, 2 story. **$**

C.A.'S HOUSE BED & BREAKFAST. *624 Ford St, Lake Charles (70601). Phone 337/439-6672. www.waltersattic.com.* A three-story colonial house originally built in the early 1900s. It is located in the Charpentier Historic District and was once owned by the president of the Huber Motor Oil Company and Quality Oil Company and then later owned by C.A. King II. 5 rooms, 3 story. **$$**

WALTER'S ATTIC BED & BREAKFAST. *618 Ford St, Lake Charles (70601). Phone 337/439-6672; toll-free 866/439-6672. www.waltersattic.com.* This inn is located in the Charpentier Historic District and caters to honeymoon and anniversary couples. It features a heated pool and fireplaces. 5 rooms, 2 story. Outdoor pool. **$$**
🏊

Restaurants

★ ★ ★ **CAFE MARGAUX.** *765 Bayou Pines E, Lake Charles (70601). Phone 337/433-2902; fax 337/494-0606.* An interesting location in a business park leads you to this pleasing French restaurant. Indulge in some of the entrées including the house filet with sautéed crabmeat, duck with sautéed mushrooms, and red snapper. French menu. Lunch, dinner, brunch. Closed Sun; Dec 25. Bar. Business casual attire. Reservations recommended. **$$**

★ ★ **PAT'S OF HENDERSON.** *1500 Siebarth Dr, Lake Charles (70615). Phone 337/439-6618; fax 337/439-4399. www.patsofhenderson.com.* Cajun menu. Lunch, dinner. Closed Thanksgiving, Dec 25. Bar. Children's menu. Casual attire. **$$**

★ ★ **PEKING GARDEN.** *2433 E Broad St, Lake Charles (70601). Phone 337/436-3597; fax 337/439-5002.* Chinese menu. Lunch, dinner. Closed Thanksgiving, Dec 25. Bar. Casual attire. **$$**

★ ★ **PUJO STREET CAFE.** *901 Ryan St, Lake Charles (70601). Phone 337/439-2054. www.pujo-street.com.* Updated Creole cuisine in downtown Lake Charles. Cajun/Creole menu. Lunch, dinner. Closed Sun evening. **$**

★ **STEAMBOAT BILL'S.** *732 Martin Luther King Hwy, Lake Charles (70601). Phone 337/494-1700.* Famous for its catfish and po' boys. Creole menu. Lunch, dinner. **$**

★ **TONY'S PIZZA.** *335 E Prien Lake Rd, Lake Charles (70601). Phone 337/477-1611; fax 337/477-4469.* Italian menu. Lunch, dinner. Closed Thanksgiving, Dec 25. Casual attire. **$**

Laplace (D-5)

What to See and Do

Cajun Pride Swamp Tours. *Manchac Swamp, Laplace (70069). Phone toll-free 800/467-0758. www.cajun-prideswamptours.com.* This private wildlife refuge in the Manchac Swamp provides swamp and plantation tours as well as guided canoe trips. You're bound to see a number of bird species, along with lizards, raccoons, and, of course, alligators. On a boat tour, your guide may even get you a close-up with a jumping gator. (Daily; schedule varies by season) **$$$$**

Mandeville (D-5)

Restaurant

★ ★ ★ **TREY YUEN.** *600 N Causeway, Mandeville (70448). Phone 985/626-4476; fax 985/626-8293.* This ornate structure showcases magnificent Eastern accoutrements. Custom-built carvings enhance an outdoor setting of koi ponds and foot bridges. The rich abundance of fresh seafood available in the area defines their signature dishes. Alligator dishes are popular, as well as the local soft-shell crab and crawfish creations. All prepared with an Oriental twist. Chinese menu. Lunch, dinner. Closed holidays; Mardi Gras. Bar. **$$**

Many (B-2)

See also Natchitoches

Settled 1837
Population 2,889
Elevation 321 ft
Area Code 318
Zip 71449
Information Sabine Parish Tourist Commission, 1601 Texas Hwy; phone 318/256-5880; or contact the Louisiana Tourist Center, Hwy 6 W; phone 318/256-4114

What to See and Do

Fort Jesup State Historic Site. *32 Geohagan Rd, Many (71449). 6 miles E on Hwy 6 to Hwy 3118. Phone 318/256-4117; toll-free 888/677-5378. www.lastate-parks.com/fortjes/ftjesup.htm.* This fort on 21 acres, established in 1822 by Zachary Taylor, features a restored 1830s army kitchen, reconstructed officers' quarters, and a museum. Picnic facilities. (Daily; closed Jan 1, Thanksgiving, Dec 25) **$**

Hodges Gardens. *110 Hodges Loop, Many (71449). 12 miles S on Hwy 171. Phone 318/586-3523. www.hodges-gardens.com.* Has 4,700 acres of gardens, greenhouses; 225-acre lake. Wild and cultivated flowers and plants all year. Terrazzo map commemorating Louisiana Purchase. Wildlife, fishing boat rentals, picnic facilities. Special events include Easter service, July 4 festival, and Christmas lights festival. (Daily; closed Jan 1, Dec 24-25) **$$**

Toledo Bend Dam and Reservoir. *W on Hwy 6.*

Special Events

Battle of Pleasant Hill Re-Enactment. *18 miles N on Hwy 175, N of Pleasant Hill.* Phone 318/872-1310. Three-day event includes beauty pageant, Confederate ball, parade, and battle reenactment. Early Apr.

Sabine Free State Festival. *237 W Port Arthur Ave, Florien (71429).* Phone 318/586-7286. *www.sabineparish.com/fest/freestate.asp.* Ten miles S in Florien. Beauty pageant; syrup-making, basket-weaving, and quilting demonstrations; arts and crafts exhibits; flea market. First weekend in Nov.

Sawmill Days. *4 L Dr, Fisher (71426).* Phone 318/256-2001. *www.sabineparish.com/fest/sawmill.asp.* 8 miles S via Hwy 171. Third weekend in May.

Metairie (D-5)

See also Covington, Kenner, New Orleans

Population 146,136
Elevation 5 ft
Area Code 504
Web Site www.metairie.com

What to See and Do

New Orleans Zephyrs. *6000 Airline Hwy (Hwy 61), Metairie (70003).* Phone 504/734-5155. *www.zephyrsbaseball.com.* The Zephyrs first took the field in 1993 as the AAA farm team for the Houston Astros. They play ball at the 10,000-seat Zephyr Field, cheered on by team mascots Boudreaux D. Nutria and his wife, Clotile, as well as their numerous offspring. (Nutria are a species of water-dwelling rodent, which are beneficial in Louisiana and Texas but viewed as destructive in other areas.) (Early Apr-Aug)

Limited-Service Hotel

★ ★ **MARRIOTT HOTEL.** *3838 N Causeway Blvd, Metairie (70002).* Phone 504/836-5253; fax 504/846-4562. *www.marriott.com.* This hotel offers guests a stunning view of Lake Pontchartrain and the New Orleans skyline. 210 rooms, 16 story. Check-out noon. Restaurant, bar. Fitness room. Indoor pool, whirlpool. Tennis. Airport transportation available. **$$**

Restaurants

★ ★ ★ **ANDREA'S.** *3100 19th St, Metairie (70002).*

Phone 504/834-8583; fax 504/834-6698. *www.andreasrestaurant.com.* Italian menu. Lunch, dinner, Sun brunch. Closed July 4, Labor Day. Bar. Children's menu. **$$$**

★ ★ **IMPASTATO'S.** *3400 16th St, Metairie (70002).* Phone 504/455-1545; fax 504/833-1816. *www.impastatos.com.* Italian menu. Dinner. Closed Sun-Mon; also Mardi Gras, Thanksgiving, Dec 25. Bar. **$$$**

★ **MORNING CALL.** *3325 Severn Ave, Metairie (70002).* Phone 504/885-4068. Deli menu. Breakfast, lunch, dinner, late-night. Closed Jan 1, Mardi Gras, Dec 25. No credit cards accepted. **$**

Minden (A-2)

See also Bossier City, Shreveport

Founded 1836
Population 13,027
Information Chamber of Commerce, 110 Sibley Rd, PO Box 819, 71058; phone 318/377-4240 or toll-free 800/264-6336
Web Site www.minden.org

What to See and Do

Germantown Museum. *120 Museum Rd, Minden (71055).* 8 miles NE via I-20 and Parish Rd 114. Phone 318/377-6061. Museum includes three buildings completed in 1835 by Germans seeking freedom from persecution; replicas of commune smokehouse and blacksmith shop; records and artifacts used by settlers. (Wed-Sun) **$$**

Lake Bistineau State Park. *101 State Park Rd, Minden (71023).* 9 miles SW on Hwy 79, 80, then 13 miles S on Hwy 163. Phone 318/745-3503; toll-free 888/677-2478. *www.lastateparks.com/lakebist/bistino.htm.* This 750-acre park in the heart of a pine forest includes a large lake. Swimming, waterskiing, fishing, boating (rentals, launch); tent and trailer sites, cabins. Standard fees. (Daily) **$**

Monroe and West Monroe (A-3)

See also Bastrop

Settled 1785
Population 54,909

Elevation 74 ft
Area Code 318
Zip West Monroe: 71291
Information Monroe-West Monroe Convention &
Visitors Bureau, 601 Constitution Drive, West Monroe
71292; PO Box 1436; phone 318/387-5691 or toll-free
800/843-1872

In March, 1783, a swashbuckling young French adven-
turer named Jean Baptiste Filhiol, then in the service
of the King of Spain, married the beautiful daughter
of a wealthy Opelousas family. Shortly thereafter he
took her in a keelboat up the Mississippi, Red, Black,
and Ouachita rivers into the wilderness to establish
a great personal estate. Flooded out, Filhiol and his
bride moved downstream to the site of Monroe, where
he settled, calling his post Fort Miro in honor of the
Spanish governor.

Filhiol was an excellent administrator and the post
prospered. In 1819 the first steamboat, the *James Monroe*, traveled up the Ouachita. After some shipboard
conviviality, residents decided to rename their town
for the boat.

The Monroe natural gas field, one of the world's largest,
affords the city a great industrial advantage; nearby
forests provide raw materials for the paper products,
furniture, and chemicals produced in Monroe.

What to See and Do

⭐ **Emy-Lou Biedenharn Foundation.** *2006 Riverside
Dr, Monroe (71201). Phone 318/387-5281.* Includes
Bible Museum, Biedenharn Family House, and Elsong
Gardens and Conservatory. (Mon-Sat, Sun afternoons;
closed holidays) **FREE** Includes

> **Bible Museum.** *Phone toll-free 800/362-0983.*
> Museum-library contains early and rare Bibles,
> archaeological artifacts, coins, antique musical
> instruments, and furnishings.

> **Biedenharn Family House.** *Phone toll-free 800/362-
> 0983.* (1914) Built by Joseph Biedenharn, first
> bottler of Coca-Cola; contains antiques, fine
> furnishings, silver dating from the 18th century,
> and Coca-Cola memorabilia.

> **Elsong Gardens & Conservatory.** *Phone toll-free
> 800/362-0983.* These formal gardens enclosed
> within brick walls, were originally designed
> to accommodate musical events. Today back-
> ground music is triggered by lasers as visitors

stroll through separate gardens linked by winding paths. There are four fountains, including a
porcelain fountain from the garden of Russian
Empress Catherine the Great.

Fishing, water sports. *Ouachita River in city; Chenire
Lake (3,600 acres) 4 miles W; D'Arbonne Lake (15,000
acres) 35 miles N; Bayou DeSiard (1,200 acres) 3 miles
NE; Black Bayou (2,600 acres) 6 miles N.*

Louisiana Purchase Gardens and Zoo. *1405 Bernstien
Park Dr, Monroe (71202). Phone 318/329-2400. www.
monroezoo.org.* Formal gardens, moss-laden live oaks,
waterways, and winding paths surround naturalistic
habitats for more than 850 exotic animals in this 80-
acre zoo; boat rides. Picnicking, concessions. (Daily;
closed Thanksgiving, Dec 25; rides, concessions, Apr-
Oct only). Special trail for disabled. **$$**

Masur Museum of Art. *1400 S Grand St, Monroe and
West Monroe (71202). Phone 318/329-2237.* Permanent
and changing exhibits. (Tues-Sun; closed holidays)
FREE

University of Louisiana at Monroe. *700 University Ave,
Monroe (71203). Phone 318/342-1000. www.ulm.edu.*
(1931) (11,000 students.) On campus are

> **Bry Hall Art Gallery.** *Phone 318/342-1376.* Art
> exhibits, photographs by American and foreign
> artists, students, faculty. (Mon-Fri; closed Easter,
> July 4, Thanksgiving, mid-Dec-early Jan) **FREE**

> **Museum of Natural History.** *Third floor of Hanna
> Hall. Phone 318/342-1868.* Geological exhibits
> include Native American, Latin American, and
> African artifacts. (Mon-Fri; closed Easter, July 4,
> Thanksgiving, also mid-Dec-early Jan) **FREE**

> **Museum of Zoology.** *First floor of Garret Hall.
> Phone 318/342-1799.* Fish collection is one of the
> largest and most complete in the nation. (Mon-
> Fri; closed Easter, July 4, Thanksgiving, also mid-
> Aug-early-Sept, mid-Dec-early-Jan) **FREE**

Limited-Service Hotels

★ ★ **HOLIDAY INN.** *1051 Hwy 165 Bypass, Monroe
(71203). Phone 318/387-5100; toll-free 800/465-4329;
fax 318/329-9126. www.holiday-inn.com.* 260 rooms, 2
story. Check-out noon. Restaurant, bar. Fitness room.
Indoor pool, outdoor pool, children's pool, whirlpool.
Airport transportation available. **$**
🧍 🛁

★ **LA QUINTA INN.** *1035 Hwy 165 Bypass, Monroe (71203). Phone 318/322-3900; toll-free 800/531-5900; fax 318/323-5537. www.laquinta.com.* 130 rooms, 2 story. Pets accepted, some restrictions; fee. Complimentary continental breakfast. Outdoor pool. **$**
🐾🏊

Restaurants

★ ★ **CHATEAU.** *2007 Louisville Ave, Monroe (71201). Phone 318/325-0384; fax 318/325-7600.* American, Italian menu. Lunch, dinner. Closed Sun; holidays. Bar. **$$**

★ ★ **WAREHOUSE NO. 1.** *1 Olive St, Monroe (71201). Phone 318/322-1340; fax 318/322-1176. www.warehouseno1.com.* Seafood menu. Dinner. Closed Sun; holidays; Mon after Easter. Bar. Children's menu. Valet parking. Outdoor seating. **$$$**

Morgan City (E-4)

See also Franklin, Houma, Thibodaux

Founded circa 1850
Population 12,703
Elevation 5 ft
Area Code 985
Information St. Mary Parish Tourist Commission, 112 Main St, PO Box 2332, 70381; phone 985/395-4905 or toll-free 800/256-2931

Originally named Brashear City for the Brashear family, upon whose plantation the town was laid out, the name was later changed to Morgan City in honor of Charles Morgan, president of the New Orleans, Opelousas and Great Western Railroad, which established its western terminus in the town. Morgan, a shipping and railroad magnate, was responsible for dredging Morgan City's first port as well as operating the first steamboat on the Gulf of Mexico (1835).

Morgan City was a strategic point during the Civil War. Today it is an important inland port and commercial fishing center. In addition to its large shrimp industry, Morgan City has become a headquarters for offshore oil drilling.

What to See and Do

Brownell Memorial Park & Carillon Tower. *3359 Hwy 70, Morgan City (70380). N off Hwy 70 on Lake Palourde. Phone 985/384-2283.* Park preserves swamp in its natural state; on the property is a 106-foot carillon tower with 61 bronze bells. (Daily) **FREE**

Cajun Jack's. *118 Main St, Morgan City (70392). Hwy 90 to Patterson. Phone 985/395-7420. www.cajunjack. com.* Go back and see how Cajun people lived over 200 years ago. Explore the area where the first Tarzan movie was filmed. Two scheduled tours daily (three in summer). **$$$$**

Fishing and hunting. A vast interlocking network of bayous, rivers, and lakes with cypress, tupelo, gumwood forests, and sugarcane fields makes the whole area excellent for small game and duck hunting, and for fishing.

Kemper Williams Park. *Patterson. 8 miles W via Hwy 90, Cotton Rd exit in Patterson. Phone 985/395-2298.* This 290-acre park offers nature and jogging trails, tennis courts, golf driving range, baseball diamonds, picnicking, camping (hookups; additional fee). (Daily; closed holidays) **$**

Lake End Park. *On Lake Palourde along Hwy 70. Phone 504/380-4623.* Swimming beach, fishing in lake and bayous, boating (launch, marina); picnicking (shelter), tent and trailer sites (hookups; fee). (Daily) **$**

Scully's. *3141 Hwy 70, Morgan City (70380). Phone 985/385-2388.* See local wildlife while enjoying authentic Cajun seafood on two-hour tours. (Tues-Sat; closed holidays) **$$$$**

Swamp Gardens and Wildlife Zoo. *725 Myrtle St, Morgan City (70380). In Heritage Park. Phone 985/384-3343.* Outdoor exhibits depict both the history of the human settlement of the great Atchafalaya Basin and the natural flora and fauna of the swamp. Guided walking tours only. (Daily; closed Jan 1, Dec 25) **$$**

Turn-of-the-Century House. *715 Second St, Morgan City (70380). Phone 504/380-4651.* Restored 1906 house with period furnishings and artifacts relating to local history; also elaborate Mardi Gras costumes. Guided tours. (Mon-Fri; closed holidays) **$$**

Special Event

Louisiana Shrimp and Petroleum Festival and Fair. *Phone 985/384-3830. www.shrimp-petrofest.org.* Saturday: Children's Day activities, amusement rides, parade, hands-on children's village, storytelling; coronation of adult court, coronation ball. Sunday: blessing of shrimp and petroleum fleets on Berwick Bay, parade, fireworks. Also arts and crafts fair; entertainment, gospel tent, music in the park; food fest. Labor Day weekend.

Limited-Service Hotel

★ ★ **HOLIDAY INN.** *520 Roderick St, Morgan City (70381). Phone 985/385-2200; fax 985/384-3810. www. holiday-inn.com.* 219 rooms, 2 story. Pets accepted; fee. Check-out noon. Restaurant, bar. Outdoor pool. **$**

Natchitoches (B-2)

See also Many

Founded 1714
Population 17,865
Elevation 125 ft
Area Code 318
Zip 71457
Information Natchitoches Parish Tourist Commission, 781 Front St, 71458; phone 318/352-8072 or toll-free 800/259-1714
Web Site www.natchitoches.net

Natchitoches (NACK-a-tish) is the oldest permanent settlement in the Louisiana Purchase Territory. In 1714, a French expedition led by Louis Juchereau de St. Denis established a post on the site of the present city to open trade with the Native Americans and Spaniards in Texas. The following year Fort St. Jean Baptiste was constructed to provide protection against the Native Americans and to prevent the Spaniards from extending the frontier of Texas any farther eastward. The name Natchitoches is derived from the name of a Native American tribe. The town is on the Cane River a few miles from the Red River. A Ranger District office of the Kisatchie National Forests (see ALEXANDRIA) is in Natchitoches.

What to See and Do

Bayou Folk Museum. *243 Hwy 495, Cloutierville (71416). 20 miles S, off Hwy 1. Phone 318/379-2233.* Displays depict the history of Cane River country in the restored house of writer Kate Chopin; period furniture. Also reconditioned blacksmith shop, doctor's office. (Daily; closed holidays) **$$**

Beau Fort Plantation. *4078 Hwy 494, Bermuda (71458). 10 miles S via Hwy 1, 119. Phone 318/352-9580.* (1790) Restored Creole cottage (1 1/2-story) at the head of an *allee* of live oaks boasts an 84-foot front

gallery, enclosed courtyard, and landscaped gardens. (Daily; closed holidays) **$$**

Fort St. Jean Baptiste State Historic Site. *130 Moreau St, Natchitoches (71457). Downtown on the Cane River. Phone 318/357-3101. www.lastateparks.com/fortstj/ft-stjean.htm.* On this 5-acre site is a replica of the fort as it was when first built to halt Spanish movement into Louisiana; the restoration includes barracks, a warehouse, a chapel, and a mess hall. (Daily; closed Jan 1, Thanksgiving, Dec 25) Standard fees. **$**

Melrose Plantation. *3533 Hwy 119, Natchitoches (71452). 16 miles S on Hwy 119. Phone 318/379-0055. www.natchitoches.net/melrose.* Complex of eight plantation buildings including Yucca House (circa 1795), the original cabin, the Big House, and the African House. Originally the residence of Marie Therese Coincoin, a former slave whose son developed the Spanish land grant into a thriving antebellum plantation. Melrose was restored at the turn of the 20th century by "Miss Cammie" Garrett Henry, who turned it into a repository of local arts and crafts. (Daily; closed holidays) **$$$**

National Fish Hatchery & Aquarium. *615 Hwy 1 S, Natchitoches (71457). Phone 318/352-5324. natchitoches.fws.gov.* Sixteen tanks of indigenous fish, turtles, and alligators. (Daily; closed holidays) **FREE**

Northwestern State University. *College Ave at the end of 2nd St, Natchitoches (71457). Phone 318/357-6361. www.nsula.edu.* (1884) (9,400 students.) The 916-acre campus is on Chaplin's Lake. On campus are the Louisiana Sports Writers Hall of Fame in Prather Coliseum, the Archives Room of Watson Memorial Library, the Folklife Center, the Williamson Archaeological Museum in Kyser Hall, and the Normal Hill Historic District.

Special Events

Christmas Festival of Lights. *781 Front St, Natchitoches (71457). Landmark Historic District and along Cane River Lake. Phone 318/352-8072. www.christmasfestival.com.* More than 140,000 lights are turned on after a full day of celebration to welcome the Christmas season. First Sat in Dec.

Melrose Plantation Arts & Crafts Festival. *3533 Hwy 119, Natchitoches (71457). Phone 318/379-0055.* Juried works of more than 100 artists and craftspeople. Second weekend in June.

Natchitoches Pilgrimage. *781 Front St, Natchitoches (71457). Phone 318/352-8072.* City and Cane River tours of houses and plantations; also candlelight tour Sat. Second full weekend in Oct.

Natchitoches-Northwestern Folk Festival. *NSU Prather Coliseum., 938 S Jefferson, Natchitoches (71497). Phone 318/357-4332. www.nsula.edu/folklife.* Festival spotlights a different industry or occupation each year and works to preserve Louisiana folk art forms; music, dance, crafts, storytelling, foods. Third weekend in July.

Limited-Service Hotel

★ **COMFORT INN.** *5362 Hwy 6, Natchitoches (71457). Phone 318/352-7500; toll-free 800/228-5150; fax 318/352-7500. www.choicehotels.com.* 59 rooms, 2 story. Complimentary continental breakfast. Check-out noon. Outdoor pool. **$**

Specialty Lodging

FLEUR DE LIS B & B. *336 Second St, Natchitoches (71457). Phone 318/352-6621; toll-free 800/489-6621. www.fleurdelisbandb.com.* 5 rooms, 2 story. Complimentary full breakfast. Check-in 3 pm, check-out 11 am. This turn-of-the-century house is located in the historic district of the oldest settlement in the Louisiana Purchase. **$**

Restaurants

★ ★ **LANDING.** *530 Front St, Natchitoches (71457). Phone 318/352-1579; fax 318/357-8616. www.thelandingrestaurantandbar.com.* Cajun menu. Lunch, dinner, Sun brunch. Closed Mon; Thanksgiving, Dec 25. Bar. Children's menu. **$$**

★ **LASYONE MEAT PIE KITCHEN.** *622 2nd St, Natchitoches (71457). Phone 318/352-3353.* American, Cajun menu. Breakfast, lunch, dinner. Closed Sun; holidays. Built in 1859. **$**

★ ★ **MARINERS SEAFOOD & STEAK HOUSE.** *5948 Hwy 1 Bypass, Natchitoches (71457). Phone 318/357-1220; fax 318/352-5529. www.marinersrestaurant.com.* Seafood, steak menu. Dinner, Sun brunch. Closed holidays. Bar. Children's menu. Outdoor seating. **$$**

New Iberia (D-3)

See also Franklin, Lafayette, Saint Martinville

Founded 1779
Population 32,623
Elevation 20 ft
Area Code 337
Zip 70560
Information Iberia Parish Tourist Commission, 2513 Hwy 14; phone 337/365-1540
Web Site www.cityofnewiberia.com

New Iberia was settled by French and Acadians but named by the first Spanish settlers. Many families of original settlers still reside in and around New Iberia.

This area is known for its swamps, bayous, alligators, antebellum homes, factories, and cuisine. Sugarcane grows in the surrounding country and raw sugar is processed in and around New Iberia. The parish is composed of not only New Iberia, the parish seat, but Jeanerette, Delcambre, and the Village of Loreauville as well. Each city contributes to the unique culture of Iberia Parish, located in the heart of Cajun Country.

What to See and Do

Avery Island. *New Iberia. 7 miles SW via Hwy 14, 329.* An enormous mass of rock salt underlies the area. The salt was first mined in 1862, when a Union blockade left the Confederate army and entire South in dire need of salt. Toll road onto island (fee); no bicycles or motorcycles permitted. On the island are

> **Jungle Gardens.** *PO Box 126, Hwy 329, Avery Island. On Avery Island. Phone 337/369-6243.* Avery Island's most spectacular feature was developed by the late Edward Avery McIlhenny. Camellias, azaleas, irises, and tropical plants, in season, form a beautiful display. Enormous flocks of egrets, cranes, and herons, among other species, are protected here and may be seen in early spring and summer; ducks and other wild fowl in winter. Chinese Garden contains a fine Buddha dating from AD 1000. (Daily) **$$$**

> **McIlhenny Company.** *1 Main Rd, Avery Island (70513). Phone 337/365-8173.* Tabasco brand pepper sauce is made on the island. Guided tours of the factory and Tabasco Country Store. (Mon-Sat; closed holidays). **FREE**

Bouligny Plaza. *On Main St in center of town.* In the park are depictions of the history of the area; gazebo, historic landmarks, beautiful view along the bayou.

Konriko Rice Mill and Company Store. *309 Ann St, New Iberia (70560). Phone 337/367-6163; toll-free 800/551-3245.* Tours of the oldest rice mill in the US; next door is a replica of the original company store, with antique fixtures and merchandise typical of Acadiana and Louisiana. Tours; film (Mon-Sat; closed holidays). **$$**

Rip van Winkle Gardens. *5505 Rip Van Winkle Rd, New Iberia (70560). On Jefferson Island, 8 miles W off Hwy 14. Phone 337/359-8525; fax 337/359-8526. www. ripvanwinklegardens.com.* Twenty acres of landscaped gardens and nature preserve. Also on the premises is the Victorian residence of 19th-century actor Joseph Jefferson (tours). Restaurant. Gift shop. (Daily; closed Jan 1, Thanksgiving, Dec 24-25) **$$$**

⭐ **Shadows-on-the-Teche.** *317 E Main St, New Iberia (70560). Phone 337/369-6446. www.shadowsontheteche.org.* (1834) Red brick and white-pillared Greek Revival house was built on the banks of the Bayou Teche by sugar planter David Weeks. Home to four generations of his family, it served as the center of an antebellum plantation system. The house was restored and its celebrated gardens created in the 1920s by the builder's great-grandson, Weeks Hall, who used the estate to entertain such celebrities as D. W. Griffith, Anais Nin, and Walt Disney. The house is surrounded by 3 acres of azaleas, camellias, and massive oaks draped in Spanish moss. A National Trust for Historic Preservation property. (Daily 9 am-4:30 pm; closed holidays) **$$**

Special Events

Andalusia Mardi Gras Parade. *Main St, New Iberia (70650). Phone 337/365-1540; toll-free 888/942-3742.* Fri before Mardi Gras.

Sugar Cane Festival and Fair. *various locations in New Iberia. Phone 337/365-1540; toll-free 888/942-3742. www.hisugar.org.* Last full weekend in Sept.

Limited-Service Hotel

★ ★ **HOLIDAY INN.** *2915 Hwy 14, New Iberia (70560). Phone 337/367-1201; toll-free 800/465-4329; fax 337/367-7877. www.holiday-inn.com.* 177 rooms, 2 story. Pets accepted, some restrictions; fee. Check-out 11 am. Restaurant, bar. Fitness room. Outdoor pool. **$**
🖼 🏃 🌊

Specialty Lodging

LE ROSIER. *314 E Main St, New Iberia (70560). Phone 337/367-5306; toll-free 888/804-7673; fax 337/367-1009. www.lerosier.com.* This 1870 country inn is complete with guest rooms furnished with lovely appointments. The inn is tucked behind a mainhouse and is framed by a rear deck and patio, as well as a front veranda. The gardens of antique roses, day lilies, and other perennials provide an ideal setting for cocktails and wine tastings. 6 rooms, 2 story. Children over 12 years only. Complimentary full breakfast. Check-in 3 pm, check-out 11 am. **$**

Restaurant

★ **LITTLE RIVER INN.** *833 E Main, New Iberia (70560). Phone 337/367-7466; fax 337/365-3991. www.poorboysriversideinn.com.* Cajun, seafood menu. Lunch, dinner. Closed Sun; holidays. Bar. Children's menu. Casual attire. Reservations recommended. **$$**

New Orleans (D-5)

See also Covington, Kenner, Metairie, Slidell

Founded 1718
Population 484,674
Elevation 5 ft
Area Code 504
Information New Orleans Metropolitan Convention & Visitors Bureau, 220 St. Charles Ave, 70130; phone 504/566-5011 or toll-free 800/672-6124
Web Site www.neworleanscvb.com
Suburbs Covington, Kenner, Metairie, Slidell.

New Orleans is a beguiling combination of old and new. Named for the Duc d'Orlans, Regent of France, it was founded by Jean Baptiste Le Moyne, Sieur de Bienville. From 1763-1801, the territory of Louisiana was under Spanish rule. In 1801, Napoleon regained it for France, though no one in Louisiana knew of this until 1803, only 20 days before the Louisiana Purchase made it US territory. The first institution of higher learning in Louisiana, the College of Orleans, opened in New Orleans in 1811. The following year, the first steamboat went into service between New Orleans and Natchez. Louisiana was admitted to the Union on April 30, 1812, with New Orleans as the capital. The War of 1812 was over on January 8, 1815, when General Sir Edward Pakenham attacked New Orleans with a British force and was decisively defeated by General Andrew Jackson at Chalmette Plantation (now a

National Historical Park). During the Civil War, New Orleans was captured by Union forces and held under tight military rule for the duration.

The population is extremely cosmopolitan, with its Creoles (descendants of the original French and Spanish colonists), Cajuns (descendants of the Acadians who were driven from Nova Scotia by the British in 1755), and other groups whose ancestors came from Italy, Africa, and the islands of the Caribbean.

Among tourists, New Orleans is famous for the old-world charm of its French Quarter. Visitors come from all over the country to dine in superb restaurants, listen to incomparable jazz, and browse in Royal Street's fine antique shops. In the world of trade, New Orleans is known as one of the busiest and most efficient international ports in the country. More than 100 steamship lines dock here. As many as 52 vessels can be berthed at one time.

What to See and Do

Adelina Patti's House and Courtyard. *631 Royal St, New Orleans (70130).* Former residence of the famous 19th-century opera diva.

Ampersand. *1100 Tulane Ave, New Orleans (70112). Phone 504/587-3737. www.ampersandnola.com.* Sophisticatedly naughty, this converted bank building features two levels, two bars, a huge dance floor, an outdoor courtyard, and several sitting roomsone in the former bank vault. Appealing to serious clubbers of all stripes, Ampersand offers DJs from around the world spinning music of the techno and industrial persuasion. (Fri and Sat at 11 pm) **$$$$**

Audubon Park. *6500 Magazine St, New Orleans (70118). Phone 504/861-2537. www.auduboninstitute. org.* This 400-acre park designed by the Olmstead brothers is nestled between St. Charles Avenue and the Mississippi River and is surrounded by century-old live oak trees. The park features a par-62 18-hole golf course ($$$$), bicycle and jogging paths, and tennis courts. (Daily)

Audubon Zoo. *6500 Magazine St, New Orleans (70118). Phone 504/861-2537; toll-free 866/487-2966. www. auduboninstitute.org/zoo.* More than 1,800 animals from every continent call this top-ranked zoo, part of the Audubon Nature Institute, home. Check out kangaroos from Australia, llamas from South America, white tigers from Asia, and zebras from Africa, all in naturalistic habitats. Indigenous furry, feathered, and

scaly creatures are featured at the Louisiana Swamp Exhibit. You can get up close during the sea lion show and personal in the Embraceable Zoo. Discovery walks, the EarthLab, and other interactive programs make the zoo an "edutaining" experience. Combination Zoo/Aquarium and Zoo/Aquarium/IMAX tickets are available. (Tues-Sun from 9:30 am; closed Thanksgiving, Christmas, Mardi Gras, and the first Fri in May) **$$$**

Auto or streetcar tour of universities and Audubon Park. *St. Charles Ave and Canal St, New Orleans (70130).* The St. Charles Avenue streetcar can be boarded here. **$** Points of interest includes

Audubon Aquarium of the Americas. *#1 Canal St, Riverfront Area, New Orleans (70130). Phone 504/861-2537; toll-free 800/774-7394.* True to its name, this aquarium houses more than 10,000 aquatic creatures from all areas of the Americas. For total immersionwithout getting wetwalk through the aquatic tunnel in the Caribbean Reef section or catch a glimpse of a rare white alligator through the RiverView window in the Mississippi section. Boasting the largest collection of jellyfish in the world, the aquarium also houses penguins, sea otters, and sharksand lets you actually touch one! Combination Aquarium/Zoo, Aquarium/ IMAX, and Aquarium/IMAX/Zoo tickets are available. (Sun-Thurs 9:30 am-6 pm, Fri-Sat until 7 pm; closed Mardi Gras Day, Dec 25) **$$$**

Lafayette Square. *6000 St. Charles Ave, New Orleans (70118).* With statues of Franklin, Clay, and McDonough.

Lee Circle. *Howard Ave.* With a statue of Robert E. Lee by Alexander Doyle.

Loyola University. *6363 St. Charles Ave, New Orleans (70118). Phone 504/865-3240; toll-free 800/465-9652.* (1912) (3,500 students.) Buildings on the 21-acre campus are Tudor Gothic in style. Tours are arranged through the Office of Admissions (Mon-Fri, twice daily).

The Garden District. *Magazine St and Washington Ave, New Orleans (70130).* It was once the social center of New Orleans American (as opposed to Creole) aristocracy. There are still beautiful Greek Revival and Victorian houses with palms, magnolias, and enormous live oaks on the spacious grounds in this area. A walking tour of the Garden District, conducted by a national park ranger,

Books and Movies To Set The Mood

Movies

The Flame of New Orleans (1941), starring Marlene Dietrich and Bruce Cabot. Set in 1891 New Orleans, Clare Ledoux (Dietrich) convinces her wealthy banker fiancé that she is two different women, a complicated but necessary exploit in order to simultaneously dally with a poor, but handsome, sea captain. Who will end up with the beautiful adventuress?

A Streetcar Named Desire (1951), starring Vivien Leigh, Marlon Brando, Kim Hunter, and Karl Malden. Tennessee Williams' masterpiece about the descent into madness of Blanche DuBois, a faded Southern belle, while visiting her earthy sister and brother-in-law in post-World War II New Orleans. It was a star-making vehicle for Brando and won Oscars for Hunter, Leigh, and Malden.

Abbott and Costello Go to Mars (1953). Winner of the "So Bad You *Must* See It" award is this long-forgotten (but available on DVD) gem, considered the duo's worst film. In it, the pair manage to climb aboard a rocket ship and launch it into space. On their way, they land in New Orleans, convinced that theyve reached Mars when they see aliens walking the street. The aliens are, of course, Mardi Gras revelers.

Live and Let Die (1973), starring Roger Moore. Who could forget the jazz funeral?

The Big Easy (1987), starring Dennis Quaid and Ellen Barkin. A New Orleans mystery/romance with a Cajun soundtrack. Quaid plays a detective investigating a series of mob-related murders, and Barkin plays an assistant district attorney looking into allegations of cop corruption.

Interview with the Vampire (1994), starring Tom Cruise, Brad Pitt, and Kirsten Dunst. Many scenes of Anne Rice's now-classic novel-turned-movie were filmed on location in New Orleans. Lafayette Cemetery #1 figures prominently in many scenes.

Books

The Awakening by Kate Chopin (1899). Edna Pontellier, a fiery 28-year-old wife and mother living in conventional Creole society, has difficulty channeling her passion into traditional roles. She enters into an affair with a younger man and begins a journey of self-discovery. The novel shocked society, and the reaction haunted Chopin for the remainder of her life.

All the Kings Men by Robert Penn Warren (1946). A story of politics, morality, and the price of success, based loosely on Louisiana Governor Huey Long. The story is narrated by aide Jack Burden, who witnesses the governor become a powerful leader at a very high price. The book won the 1947 Pulitzer Prize for fiction.

The Moviegoer by Walker Percy (1961). As he approaches 30, Binx Bolling, rake, hedonist, and cinephile, senses that something is missing in his life. Along with Kate, a friend and cousin with whom he has a complex relationship, he begins an existential quest to rise above his ennui. Percy's book takes place during Mardi Gras in the late 1950s. It won the 1962 National Book Award.

A Confederacy of Dunces by John Kennedy Toole (1980). The twists and turns, subplots and secondary characters met by Ignatius J. Reilly, a 30-year-old self-proclaimed genius, as he wends his way through the working world of New Orleans earned this book the 1981 Pulitzer Prize for fiction. The author committed suicide and never lived to see his novels success.

New Orleans Mourning by Julie Smith (1991). During Mardi Gras week, Chauncy St. Amant is in high spirits, having finally achieved his dream of being crowned Rex, King of Carnival, when he is shot and killed by someone dressed in a Dolly Parton costume. This is the first of Smith's Skip Langdon mystery series. It won the 1991 Edgar for best mystery.

Remembering Dixie by Ignatus DAquila (1997). A highly readable, frequently funny story of the life and friends of a New Orleans newspaper editor.

departs from the corner of 1st and St. Charles (by appointment; closed Mardi Gras, Dec 25).

Tulane Green Wave. *Tulane University, New Orleans.* Tulane University fields 13 sports teams, all using the Green Wave nickname. The logo for Tulane evolved from a pelican riding a surfboard to the fierce Riptide pelican mascot. The Superdome is home to the football team; other Tulane teams play at a variety of venues including Fogelman Arena and Turchin Stadium.

Tulane University. *6823 St. Charles Ave, New Orleans (70118). Phone 504/865-5000.* (1834) (12,381 students.) The 110-acre main campus, located uptown, offers art galleries and other exhibits. The Tulane University Medical Center, located downtown, includes the School of Medicine, the School of Public Health and Tropical Medicine, and a 300-bed private hospital.

Auto tour to City Park and Lake Pontchartrain. *Drive NW on Esplanade or NE on N Carrollton Ave to the Esplanade entrance.* Allow two to four hours. Proceed along Lelong Drive to the

Dueling Oaks. *1 Palm Dr, New Orleans (70124).* Where many an affair of honor was settled in the early 18th century. Located in City Park.

Lake Pontchartrain. *Lakeshore Dr, New Orleans (70122).* A favorite spot of locals for picnicking, fishing, running, cycling, skating, or simply watching sailboats pass by.

Lake Pontchartrain Causeway. This, the longest bridge in the world, is 24-miles-long (toll).

New Orleans Botanical Garden. *1 Palm Dr, New Orleans (70124). Phone 504/483-9386.* This beautiful public garden features a collection of antique roses, as well as azaleas, camellias, and gardenias. In the center of the garden is the Pavilion of the Two Sisters, named for Eminia Wadsworth and Marion Wadsworth Harve, who helped fund the Education Pavilion. (Tues-Sat 10 am-4:30 pm; Sun noon-5 pm; closed Mon) **$**

New Orleans Museum of Art. *City Park,1 Collins Diboll Cir, New Orleans (70124). Phone 504/488-2631.* Established in 1911, NOMA boasts more than 40,000 objects in its permanent collection. The strengths of the permanent collection lie in its photography and glassware exhibits, as well as notable collections of American, African, Japanese, and French art, including works by Edgar Degas, who visited New Orleans in the early 1870s. World-class traveling exhibits, extensive children's programs, and a sculpture garden, which opened in 2002 in the adjacent City Park, round out the attractions. (Wed-Sun 10 am-4:30 pm; closed holidays) **$$$**

Southern Regional Research Center. *1100 Robert E. Lee Blvd, New Orleans (70124). Phone 504/286-4200.* Part of the US Department of Agriculture, which finds and develops new and improved uses for Southern farm crops. Guided tours by appointment. (Mon-Fri; closed holidays) **FREE**

University of New Orleans. *2000 Lake Shore Dr, New Orleans (70122). Phone 504/280-6000.* (1958) 17,000 students.) On the shores of Lake Pontchartrain, the 345-acre campus is the center of a residential area. Fine Arts Gallery (Mon-Fri; closed holidays).

Bally's Casino. *1 Stars and Stripes Blvd, New Orleans (70126). Phone toll-free 800/572-2559. www.parkplace.com/ballys/neworleans.* Floating in Lake Pontchartrain, Ballys boasts high-limit gambling with games including blackjack, mini baccarat, craps, and roulette. You can choose from traditional or video slot machines and participate in weekly tournaments. The Showroom brings in musical acts from the 1960s, '70s, and '80s. You can also find live entertainment at the Wild Card Sports Bar, along with 16 sports-filled TV screens. Food choices include an all-you-can-eat buffet, a bakery specializing in desserts, and a deli. (Daily, 24 hours)

Bayou Barriere Golf Course. *7427 Hwy 23, Belle Chasse (70037). Phone 504/394-9500.* This course is fairly flat but strives to offer variety from hole to hole. The fairways differ in width and water comes into play, but at different points in each hole. The prices are reasonable, and the course is open year-round. With 27 holes on site, the facility accommodates high levels of traffic well, and you can explore various combinations of holes to find your favorite 18. The most challenging nine is the third, as the tee boxes are mostly on the courses levee. **$$$$**

Bayou Oaks. *1040 Fillmore Ave, New Orleans (70124). Phone 504/483-9396. www.neworleanscitypark.com/golf.html.* The four courses at Bayou Oaks vary greatly in length in order to appeal to every type of golfer at every skill level. The two best courses are the championship West and the Wisner. The West course is more than 7,000 yards long and features water on many holes, like a lot of New Orleans courses do. White cranes, alligators, and great blue herons can often been seen on the course, which uses the natural borders of the bayou for many of its boundaries. Wide fairways, large greens, and easy access from downtown make this one of the best places for any golfer to spend time while in the Big Easy. **$$$$**

Composing History

He usually played sitting in a chair, leaning against a wall, with a derby tilted over one eyehis bad eye, which was blinded when he was a kid. It is said that when we talk about "hot jazz," we are talking about the style he perfected: the art of playing collective improvisations instead of solos. He used mutes, bottles, cups, and derbies to coax different sounds out of his horn, and he mesmerized a young boy named Louis Armstrong who used to sit in the smoky New Orleans clubs to hear him play. The guy's name was Joe Oliver. He gave Armstrong his first cornet and became his mentor. Until the day Oliver died broke, in pain from a bad back, and working as a janitor in a pool room in Georgia Louis referred to him as Papa Joe.

Papa Joe Oliver is one of the legends of turn-of-the-century New Orleans, a time when jazz was becoming jazz; Buddy Bolden, whose band began playing in 1895, was another. "The blowingest man ever lived since Gabriel," Jelly Roll Morton called him, himself a French Quarter luminary. While Jelly Roll is credited with being the first true jazz composer the first to put notes to paper Bolden established the organization of the jazz ensembleone or two cornets, a clarinet, trombone, double bass, guitar, and drums. Like Joe Oliver, he died tragically. After suffering a breakdown while playing his cornet in a street parade, he was committed to a mental institution and never emerged. He died 25 years later.

New Orleans is filled with the echoes of musicians like Buddy Bolden and Papa Joe, people who carved out Americas musical heritage. Take a walk through the French Quarter and youll hear them all. Over there is Jelly Roll Morton, smiling at the audience with a diamond in his teeth, tickling the ivories and creating the transition between ragtime and jazz. There are the strains of Mahalia Jackson singing gospel in a Baptist church. There's Louis Prima, singing and playing his trumpet before heading to New York,

where he all but created swing and composed Benny Goodman's greatest hit, "Sing Sing Sing."

The legendary musician known as Professor Longhair started here. "The first instrument I played was the bottom of my feet, working out rhythms," he once said. He danced for tips in the French Quarter before becoming one of the fathers of rhythm and blues. His style greatly influenced Fats Domino, who brought popular appeal to the "classic New Orleans R&B sound." However, Domino's first recording, 1949's "The Fat Man," is considered a contender (along with many, many others) for the first rock and roll record. That always confused Fats. Rock and roll? He was only doing what hed been doing in New Orleans for many years.

Farther down the block, you hear the horns of Al Hirt and Pete Fountain, the bluesy voice of Marva Wright, and the R&B trumpet of Charlie Miller. And then, finally, you hear the sounds of The Man himself: Satchmo. Louis Armstrong's musical ability, knowledge, technique, and irrepressible inventiveness all honed here made him one of the greatest of all jazz musicians. And in this town, even more than in most, he is legendary. His rags-to-riches story includes picking up his first cornet at reform school. He made a name for himself in the French Quarter, left, came back, and left, but never forgot his roots, they say. And because he popularized the "New Orleans sound," he paved the way for musicians to head north to play in cities like Chicago and New York and create even newer sounds.

Still, the New Orleans notes keep coming. From the Marsalis boys, Wynton and Branford. From the Neville Brothers. From Harry Connick, Jr. They sing with different voices, perhaps, and with different rhythms and beats. But that is New OrleansNew Orleans as it has always been.

Beauregard-Keyes House and Garden. *1113 Chartres St, New Orleans (70116). Phone 504/523-7257.* (Circa 1826) Greek Revival, Louisiana-raised cottage restored by its former owner, the novelist Frances Parkinson Keyes. Confederate Army General Pierre G. T. Beauregard lived here for more than a year following the Civil War. Exhibits include the main house and

servant quarters, which together form a handsome shaded courtyard. (Keyes actually lived informally in the servant quarters, which are filled with her books, antiques, and family heirlooms.) To the side of the main house is a formal garden (visible from both Chartres and Ursulines streets) that is part of the guided tour conducted by costumed docents. (Mon-Sat 10 am-3 pm; closed holidays) **$**

Bourbon Street. No place in the world can match Bourbon Street for 24-hours-a-day, gaudy, bawdy fun. With elegant hotels next door to garish strip clubs, Bourbon Street encapsulates the ever-beating heart of the French Quarter. Visit its shops and restaurants in the daytime if you're not up for the always-rowdy nighttime crowds. But if you're visiting the Big Easy to let the good times roll, there's no better place to start a night of rambunctious partying.

Brechtel Park Golf Course. *4401 Lennox Blvd, New Orleans (70131). Phone 504/364-4014.* Built in 1965, Brechtel Park has been a favorite recreational course in New Orleans for some time. Not as challenging as some of the more exclusive clubs in the area, the course still requires a moderate level of skill to hit shots accurate enough to keep scores down. Brechtel Park is a good bargain if you're looking for a quick, fun, and inexpensive round of golf. **$$$$**

Brulatour Courtyard. *520 Royal St, New Orleans (70130).* The Courtyard is lined with interesting shops.

The Cabildo. *701 Chartres St, New Orleans (70118). Phone 504/568-6968. lsm.crt.state.la.us.* Part of the Louisiana State Museum, the Cabildo offers exhibits on life in early New Orleans, including plantation and slave life. Construction was completed in 1799, and the building housed the city council and the Louisiana Supreme Court at various times. In 1803, the transfer of the Louisiana Purchase took place here. Though a 1988 fire did significant damage, many artifacts were saved, the structure was authentically restored, and the building re-opened in 1994. (Tues-Sun 9 am-5 pm) **$$**

Cathedral Garden. *615 Pére Antoine Alley, New Orleans (70116).* The monument in the center of the garden was erected in honor of French marines who died while nursing New Orleans' citizens during a yellow fever outbreak. Picturesque, narrow Pirate's Alley, bordering the garden, is a favorite spot for painters. On the Alley is the house in which William Faulkner lived when he wrote his first novel. The garden is also called St. Anthony's Square in memory of a beloved priest known as Pére Antoine.

Cemetery & Voodoo History Tour. *Café Beignet, 334-B Royal St, New Orleans (70130). In the courtyard of Café Beignet. Phone 504/947-2120.* Tour (approximately two hours) features St. Louis Cemetery #1, the oldest and most significant burial ground in New Orleans;

visits to a practicing Voodoo priestess at her temple; Congo Square, the site of early slave gatherings; and a visit to the home of legendary Voodoo Queen Marie Laveau. (Mon-Sat 10 am and 1pm; Sun 10 am) **$$$**

Center of Banking. *403 Royal, New Orleans (70130). At the corner of Royal and Bienville, turn right, away from the river, four blocks to N Rampart, turn right and walk five blocks.* The old Louisiana State Bank was designed in 1821 by Benjamin Latrobe, one of the architects of the Capitol in Washington. The 343 Royal building was completed in the early 1800s for the old Bank of the United States. The old Bank of Louisiana, 334 Royal, was built in 1826; it is now the French Quarter Police Station.

City Park. *1 Palm Dr, New Orleans (70124). Phone 504/482-4888. www.neworleanscitypark.com.* The 1,500 acres of City Park provide room for all sorts of family fun. Step into Storyland to slide down the dragon-flame slide, board Captain Hook's ship, or engage with actors portraying storybook characters. Board one of two minitrains and mount a steed on one of the oldest wooden carousels in the US. Catch some spray from Popp Fountain, get a license and catch some fish in one of the many lagoons, or bask in Marconi Meadow and catch some rays. Admire a range of architectural styles in various buildings and bridges. Appreciate the natural beauty in the Botanical Garden and see more mature oak trees than anyplace in the world. Get active and rent a boat or play tennis, golf, or softball in the park's facilities. Check for events at Tad Gormley Stadium. Also in City Park are

> **Bandstand and Peristyle.** The latter is an attractive classical structure.

> **Recreation areas.** Four 18-hole golf courses, a driving range, lighted tennis courts, and lagoons for boating (fee).

Contemporary Arts Center. *900 Camp St, New Orleans (70130). Phone 504/528-3800. www.cacno.org.* Established in 1976, the Contemporary Arts Center (CAC) is housed in an award-winning building renovated in 1990. Each year, CAC hosts as many as two dozen exhibitions in its 10,000 square feet of gallery space. Taking a multidisciplinary approach, the center promotes art forms as traditional as painting, photography, and sculpture, and as diverse as performance art, dance, music, and video. Artists Studio Days offer children and their elders a glimpse into the creative process. The Dog & Pony Theater company-in-residence presents workshops, rehearsals, and dance and theater

Demystifying New Orleans-Speak

Cajun: Nickname for a Louisianan descended from the French-speaking people who began migrating to Louisiana from Nova Scotia (then Acadia) in 1755.

Creole: A white person descended from early French or Spanish settlers of the US Gulf states, who preserve their speech and culture.

creole: Highly seasoned food typically prepared with rice, okra, tomatoes, and peppers.

Fais-do-do (FAY-doe-doe): When Cajuns partied in days gone by, they would bring their children along, bundle them in their blankets at bedtime, put them to sleep, and party into the wee hours. Fais-do-do means put the kids to sleep.

Faubourg (FOE-burg): Faubourgs are neighborhoods near the French Quarter. Literally, Faubourg means suburb.

French Quarter: The 90 square blocks that used to be the entire city of New Orleans and today encompasses 2,700 European- and Creole-style buildings.

Gris-gris (GREE-gree): Means X marks the spot. An X on a tomb indicates a voodoo spell, like that on the tomb of the mysterious Marie Laveau, New Orleans hairdresser-turned-legendary Voodoo Queen.

Gumbo ya-ya: Everybody talking at once.

Jazz: Louis Armstrong said, If you gotta ask, you'll never know. With apologies to Armstrong, jazz mixes African and Creole rhythms with European styles; Irish, Germans, and Italians added the brass.

Krewe: Wealthy 19th-century New Orleans citizens who bankrolled Mardi Gras balls and parades were members of carnival organizations with names like Rex (King of the Carnival). Members were called Krewe of Rex, a variation of the word crew.

Pass a Good Time: Live it up.

Vieux Carre (VYEUH kah-RAY): Old Square or Old Quarter, referring to the French Quarter.

Voodoo: A combination of the West African Yoruba religion and the Catholicism of French colonists in Haiti. It means god, spirit, or insight in the Fon language of Dahomey, a former country in West Africa on the Gulf of Guinea.

Yat: A citizen. This term comes from the Ninth Ward greeting, Where yat?

---

productions. CAC also hosts the annual Black Theater Festival during the first two weekends in October. (Tues-Sun 11 am-5 pm; closed Mon) **$$**

Crescent City Farmers' Market. *700 Magazine St, New Orleans (70116). Phone 504/861-5898. www.crescentcityfarmersmarket.org.* Choose the day and location to suit your needs. At this market, regional vendors offer fresh produce, seafood, baked goods, and other edibles, as well as cut flowers and bedding plants. Each location offers frequent cooking demonstrations with area chefs and a variety of food-related events. Market founders promote sound ecological and economic development in the greater New Orleans area. The Tuesday Market is situated between Levee and Broadway in the parking lot of Uptown Square, at 200 Broadway from 10 am to 1 pm. The Wednesday Market is located between French Market Place and Governor Nicholls Street from 10 am to 2 pm. The Thursday Market sits on the recently renovated American Can

Company residential development at 3700 Orleans Avenue from 3-7 pm. The Saturday Market is in the downtown neighborhood known as the Warehouse District (originally known as the American Sector), on the corner of Magazine and Girod streets, at 700 Magazine Street from 8 am-noon.

Destrehan Plantation. *13034 River Rd, Destrehan (70047). Approximately 30 miles W via Hwy 48. Phone 985/764-9315. www.destrehanplantation.org.* Built in 1787, this is the oldest plantation house left intact in the lower Mississippi Valley, with ancient live oaks adorning the grounds. Guided tours are available. (Daily; closed holidays) **$$$**

Dragon's Den. *435 Esplanade Ave, New Orleans (70116). Phone 504/945-7744.* Located above a Thai restaurant, the Den echoes the Eastern atmosphere with a dark, red-lit ambience and tasseled pillows strewn on the floor. Live music styles range from jazz to bluegrass to hip-hop to the latest local sounds. The club also hosts spoken-word performances, which feature local poets. (After 2 am)

Entergy IMAX Theatre. *#1 Canal St, New Orleans (70130). Phone 504/581-IMAX; toll-free 800/774-7394. www.auduboninstitute.org/imax.* Adjacent to the Audubon Aquarium of the Americas (see) and part of the Audubon Nature Institute, this theater showcases several films at a time in larger-than-life format and hosts a summer film festival. Combination IMAX/ Aquarium and IMAX/Aquarium/Zoo tickets are available. (Daily from 10 am; closed Mardi Gras Day, Dec 25) **$$**

F & F Botanica. *801 N Broad St, New Orleans (70119).* The oldest and largest spiritual supply store in the French Quarter, F & F Botanica offers herbs, oils, potions, candles, incensewhatever you need to enhance your spiritual practice, whether it be Santeria, Voodoo, or what have you. The store offers free spiritual consultations to help you figure out how to find what your spirit is searching for. At least one staffer is sure to speak Spanish to help customers who share owner Felix Figueroa's heritage. (Mon-Sat 8 am-6 pm)

French Market. *813 Decatur St, New Orleans (70116).* Which has been a farmers' market for nearly two centuries. The market's "Café du Monde" (see RES-TAURANTS) is a popular and famous coffee stand specializing in café au lait (half coffee with chicory, half hot milk) and beignets (square-shaped doughnuts sprinkled with powdered sugar). The café never closes (except Dec 25), and café au lait and beignets are inexpensive. The downriver end of the French Market houses booths in which produce is sold.

French Quarter. *Bourbon St, New Orleans (70130). From Canal St to Esplanade Ave, and from Decatur St on the Mississippi River to Rampart St. www.french-quarter.com.* Whether you're in New Orleans to party hearty, shop 'til you drop, soak up Creole (or voodoo) charms, sample Southern hospitality, delve into history, or admire architecture, you can find what you want in the Vieux Carr. The oldest—and only remaining—French and Spanish settlement in the country, the Quarter offers sights, sounds, tastes, and treasures to suit every interest.

★ **French Quarter Walking Tours.** *Phone 504/523-3939.* Both the Friends of Cabildo (1850 House Museum Store, 523 St. Ann St on Jackson Square; phone 504/523-3939) and the French Quarter Visitor Center (419 Decatur St; phone 504/589-2636) offer walking tours that cover the Quarters history and architecture.

The pace isn't strenuous, but factor in the heat and humidity, and dress accordingly. Licensed guides conduct the two-hour Friends of Cibaldo tours, while interpreters from the National Park Service lead a 90-minute free tour, which is restricted to the first 25 people who show up each day. A Cibaldo tour ticket entitles you to a discount on items at the 1850 House Museum Store. (Daily; no tours holidays, Mardi Gras) **$$$**

Gallier House. *1126 Royal St, New Orleans (70116). Phone 504/525-5661. www.gnofn.org/~hggh.* For a slice of pre-Civil War life in New Orleans, check out the home of architect James Gallier, Jr., which he designed for himself in 1857. Thoroughly modern for its time, the house boasts hot-and-cold running water and an indoor bathroom. Painstakingly restored, the house is one of New Orlean's more beautiful historic landmarks. (Mon-Fri 10 am-4 pm; closed holidays) **$$$**

Gray Line bus tours. *#1 Toulouse St, New Orleans (70130). Phone 504/569-1401; toll-free 800/535-7786. www.graylineneworleans.com.* See all of New Orlean's must-see sites from the comfort of an air-conditioned coach. Besides its comprehensive city tour, Gray Line offers numerous other sightseeing options, including tours of plantations, swamps and bayous, the Garden District, and cemeteries. An off-the-beaten path trek takes you to such places as the childhood neighborhood of jazz great Louis Armstrong and Faubourg Marigny, one of the earliest Creole suburbs, where the striking architecture will surely grab your attention. If you want to ply the Mississippi, the company also offers a riverboat cruise. (Closed Mardi Gras) **$$$$**

Griffin Fishing Charters. *2629 Privateer Blvd, Lafitte (70036). Phone toll-free 800/741-1340. www.griffin-fishing.com.* Specializing in shallow-sea fishing for speckled trout and redfish in saltwater marshes from Lafitte down to the Gulf of Mexico, owners Raymond and Belinda Griffin can also set you up for a day of deep-sea fishing. Or combine two pursuitsplay golf in the morning and then head out to the water for some fishing. Prices include an out-of-state fishing license, rods, reels, bait, tackle, ice, Po-boy sandwiches, soda, water, and cleaning and packaging of caught fish. Package plans that include lodging, meals, and transportation are also available. **$$$$**

Harrah's New Orleans. *8 Canal St, New Orleans (70130). Phone 504/533-6000; toll-free 800/847-5299. www.harrahs.com.* The oldest of New Orleans's land-based casinos, Harrah's is 115,000 square feet of non-stop gambling fun. More than 100 tables offer 10 different games, including poker, craps, Baccarat, and

Kings, Krewes, Beads, and Balls

Behold the Tuesday before Lent: Mardi Gras. It is a day given to great feasting and even greater revelry as befits the day before a time of fasting and repentance. And in New Orleans, behold the feasting and revelry. Mardi Gras here is celebrated on a bigger scale, is more elaborate, and is celebrated with more abandon than anywhere else in the world.

There are plenty of other places in the world where the celebration is big and bold. Venice, Rio de Janeiro, and areas in Germany, Italy, and Switzerland are just some of the places where elaborate festivals and masked balls ring in the Carnival. In Nice, the French wear giant masks in the Mardi Gras parade, making it look as though everyone is a walking head with a tiny body. In Belgium, people dress as clowns, wear bright costumes, and decorate their heads with ostrich feathers, carrying baskets and tossing oranges to the crowd. In Trinidad, Mardi Gras is celebrated with a two-day festival of the arts featuring calypso music, steel drums, and masquerade balls.

Veracruz has a week-long celebration said to be the most exciting in Mexico. Each year, the city bulges with thousands of visitors. The celebration begins with an opening ceremony of *Quema del Mal Humor* or the *Burning of Bad Humor* and concludes on Ash Wednesday with the last courtship and Funeral of Juan Carnaval, the most lavish of the city's several parades.

And in New Orleans? The Mardi Gras season, as its called, begins on Twelfth Night January 6, 12 days after Christmas when the festive holiday season traditionally ends. In New Orleans, however, Twelfth Night kicks off a season of merriment. Festivities reach a fevered pitch 12 days before Mardi Gras and peak the Saturday prior to Fat Tuesday, exploding with four days of nonstop jazz, food, drink, masked

balls, and general reckless abandon. Perhaps most closely associated with the celebrations aside from mayhem in the French Quarter are the elaborate, colorful parades in which walkers dress in magical costumes and plastic beads in Mardi Gras colors of purple, green, and gold are tossed to onlookers. Other tosses include roses, stuffed animals, and plastic alligators, rubber snakes, or other swamp creatures.

You'll see something fascinating everywhere you turn in this feast for the senses. Here are some tips to make your experience even better:

On Fat Tuesday, the French Quarter is alive with visitors in mysterious, beautiful masks. Accent Annex at 1420 Sams Avenue, Suite F, is a good place to check out costumes, beads, doubloons, and other Mardi Gras items.

Taste a King Cake a large cake round, plain or filled with fruit or cream cheese, coated with purple, green, and gold sugar. A tiny plastic baby is hidden inside. Traditionally, whoever gets the slice with the baby provides the King Cake for the next party.

At 6 pm on Fat Monday, the King of Rex lands at the Riverfront near the French Quarter. The mayor turns over the city to him for the duration of Mardi Gras. Earlier that day, the Zulu King arrives at the Riverfront and the Zulus celebrate in Woldenberg Park. The meeting of the two Kings is widely celebrated.

The meaning of the parades is that Kings and Queens ride floats to the balls and loyal krewes follow on foot. Balls have always been by invitation only, but some krewes now allow the public to attend. One of the newer krewes, the Krewe of Orpheus, provides information on their Web site: www.kreweoforpheus.net.

---

roulette. You can play the slots for a penny, a dollar, or up to $500 at any of 2,500 slot machines. Live jazz, Creole cuisine, Mardi Gras décor, and an attached hotel means that you can immerse yourself in a total Harrah's New Orleans experience. (Daily, 24 hours)

Hermann-Grima House. *820 St. Louis St, New Orleans (70112). Phone 504/525-5661. www.gnofn.org/~hggh.* (1831) The Georgian design reflects the post-Loui-

siana Purchase American influence on traditional French and Spanish styles in the Quarter; the furnishings typify a well-to-do lifestyle during the period of 1831-1860. The restored house has elegant interiors, two landscaped courtyards, slave quarters, a stable, and a working period kitchen; Creole cooking demonstrations on open hearth (Oct-May, Thurs). Tours. (Mon-Fri; closed holidays) **$$$**

Historic New Orleans Collection. *533 Royal St, New Orleans (70130). Phone 504/523-4662. www.hnoc.org.* Established in 1966 by local collectors, General and Mrs. Kemper Williams, the Collection is composed of several historic buildings housing a museum and comprehensive research center for state and local history. The main exhibition gallery presents changing displays on Louisiana's history and culture. The 1792 Merieult House features a pictorial history of New Orleans and Louisiana; the Williams Residence shows the elegant lifestyle of the collection's founders. Changing exhibits grace several galleries. There is also a touch tour for the visually impaired. (Tues-Sat 9:30 am-4:30 pm)

House of Blues. *225 Decatur St, New Orleans (70130). Phone 504/529-2624.www.hob.com.*Even in the eye-catching French Quarter, its hard to miss the gaudy, neon-lit entrance to the House of Blues. Past the wildly decorated porch and inside, you're liable to hear musical styles ranging from Cajun to country and reggae to rock and roll, not to mention pure, soulful blues. And the music is live, of course. The Sunday Gospel Brunch is justly famous and surprisingly inexpensive.

The Howlin' Wolf. *907 S Peters, New Orleans (70130). Phone 504/522-9653. www.howlin-wolf.com.* The live music here tends more toward local and national rock and roll and alternative sounds than traditional New Orleans jazz and blues. After opening in 1988 in nearby Metairie, the Wolf successfully transplanted its relaxed ambience to the Warehouse District in 1991, where it remains popular with college students and those looking for original music and up-and-coming acts. Check out the acoustic open-mike nights on Mondays. **$$$$**

Jackson Brewery. *600 Decatur St, New Orleans (70130). Phone 504/566-7245. www.jacksonbrewery. com.* This historic brewery was converted into a large retail, food, and entertainment complex with 75 shops and restaurants, outdoor seating, and a riverfront promenade. (Mon-Sat 10 am-8 pm; Sun 10 am-7 pm; closed Dec 25)

Jackson Square. *615 Pére Antoine Alley, New Orleans (70116). www.jackson-square.com.* Bordered by Chartres, St. Peter, Decatur, and St. Ann streets, this area was established as a drill field in 1721 and was called the *Place d'Armes* until 1848, when it was renamed for Andrew Jackson, hero of the Battle of New Orleans. The statue of Jackson, the focal point of the square, was the world's first equestrian statue with more than one hoof unsupported; the American sculptor, Clark Mills, had never seen an equestrian statue and therefore did not know that the pose was thought impossible. Today, the square and surrounding plaza is one of the best places in the Quarter to catch your breath, watch people, and listen to jazz. It attracts local artists, food vendors, and street performers such as mimes, magicians, and musicians.

Jean Bragg Antiques & Gallery. *600 Julia St, New Orleans (70115). Phone 504/895-7375. www.jeanbraggantiques.com.* The focus of this shop and gallery is on Louisianian and Southern art, especially paintings, watercolors, and etchings of Louisiana and the French Quarter. Specializing in George Ohr pottery and Newcomb College pottery and craft work, the shop also offers museum-quality pieces from the late 19th and early 20th centuries. Discover vintage linens, jewelry, and glassware along with Victorian furniture. (Mon-Sat 10 am-5 pm)

Lafitte's Blacksmith Shop. *941 Bourbon St, New Orleans (70116). www.atneworleans.com/body/blacksmith.htm.* This popular bar is arguably the oldest French-style building left in the French Quarter after the Spanish style dominated rebuilding efforts following two fires in the 1700s that destroyed much of the city. Local lore has it that the original smithy, built sometime before 1772, served as a front for pirate Jean Lafittes more notorious activities. The bar retains a dark, historical feel, although the local and exotic patrons lighten the atmosphere. (Daily from 11 am)

Le Chat Noir. *715 St. Charles Ave, New Orleans (70130). Phone 504/581-6333. www.cabaretlechatnoir.com.* Get decked out (no jeans or shorts) to check out the Cat (*chat noir* means black cat) for an ever-changing schedule of cabaret, live theater, and musical performances. The Bar Noir is a cozier room, perfect for a pre-show cocktail (try the house specialty Black Cat) or for quiet conversation with friends.

Levee and docks. *Canal St and Mississippi River, New Orleans.* From the foot of Canal Street, turn right and walk along the busy docks to the coffee and general cargo wharves, which are most interesting. Smoking is forbidden in the dock area. Rides on the Canal Street Ferry are free. Along the docks are paddlewheel and other excursion boats.

Longue Vue House & Gardens. *7 Bamboo Rd, New Orleans (70124). I-10, Metairie Rd exit. Phone 504/488-5488. www.longuevue.com/.* A grand city estate furnished with original English and American antiques is

The Big Easy

The number of nicknames for New Orleans is almost as long as a krewe parade at Mardi Gras. Most are easily understood. Because of the way the Mississippi River curves around one side of town, New Orleans is called The Crescent City. Its lively, colorful French Quarter gave way to The City That Care Forgot. Parade City USA is a tribute to Mardi Gras; Birthplace of Jazz is self-explanatory; Queen City of the South is an understandable chauvinistic dazzler. And anyone who has ever set foot inside a New Orleans restaurant understands the moniker City of the Chefs.

But what of the nickname most closely associated with the City of Saints and Sinners (football and revelers): The Big Easy?

Some say that the nickname is a relatively recent one. In the early 1970s, a columnist for *The Times-Picayune* compared New Orleans's relaxed style with the hurry-up pace of New York; if New York is the Big Apple, she wrote, then New Orleans is the Big Easy. In 1970, police reporter James Conaway wrote a novel of corruption and romance in New Orleans and called it *The Big Easy*. The term became firmly planted in American lexicon when the novel became a 1987 movie starring Dennis Quaid and Ellen Barkin.

But the nickname's origins are actually thought to have taken root nearly a century earlier, at the dawn of the Jazz Age. In the early 1900s, Buddy Bolden became the first of the great New Orleans jazz legends, playing his cornet in all the hot areas of town Uptown, Gretna, and the new Storyville district at Rampart and Perdido streets. He took smoky center stage at clubs like the Come Clean and the Funky Butt (which became his theme song, and where a very young Louis Armstrong listened nightly). Bolden was said to have played in a dance club called Big Easy Hall. Another early 1900s jazz legend, bass man George Pops Foster, made reference to the Big Easy club in his book *Pops Foster: The Autobiography of a New Orleans Jazz Man*. Because jazz musicians are known to give nicknames to everything and everybody, the name might refer to a dance hall, or it might have been a dance itself.

But in the end, the names relevance to the city is best summed up in the reaction a visitor is likely to get when asking about its origin. Query any two people, and the answer is likely to be the same: Just like anything else in New Orleans, they will say, it just *is*.

located on 8 acres of formal and picturesque gardens; changing exhibits in galleries and seasonal horticultural displays in gardens. Tours on the hour. (Mon-Sat 10 am-5 pm; Sun 1-5 pm; closed holidays) **$$**

Louis Armstrong Park. *N Rampart St, New Orleans (70130).* To the left of the entrance—built to resemble a Mardi Gras float—is a stand of very old live oak trees. This area was originally known as Congo Square, where slaves were permitted to congregate on Sunday afternoons; it was also the scene of voodoo rites. After the Civil War, the square was named for General P. G. T. Beauregard. Louis Armstrong Park, which includes an extensive water garden that focuses upon a larger-than-life-size statue of Armstrong, was expanded from the original square and contains the municipal auditorium and the Theatre of the Performing Arts. Located in the 800 block of North Rampart Street.

Louisiana Nature Center. *5601 Read Blvd, New Orleans (70127). Phone 504/246-5672; toll-free 800/774-7394.*

www.auduboninstitute.org/lnc. You can lead yourself on an audio tour of local plant and animal life through the nature centers trails and boardwalks, or set off to explore some of the 86 acres on your own. On Turtle Pond offers, yes, turtles and tortoises, along with other amphibian life. The public is invited to a schedule of shows in the planetarium on Saturdays and Sundays. (Tues-Fri 9 am-5 pm, Sat 10 am-5 pm, Sun noon-5 pm) **$**

Louisiana State Museum. *751 Chartres, New Orleans (70116). Phone 504/568-6968; toll-free 800/568-6968. lsm.crt.state.la.us.* The Museum comprises five properties in the French Quarter city (see the separate listing for The Cabildo) and three sites outside of the city. Though only the residence is open to the public (a kitchen and servants' quarters complete the complex), Madame John's Legacy is a fine example of Creole architecture. Built in 1789 after the great fire of 1788, it's notable for also surviving the 1795 fire. The 1850 House, named for the year it was built, holds an authentic collection of period furnishings. Built in 1791 on the site of a monastery, one of the Presbytere's functions was as a courthouse. It currently holds not-to-be-missed Mardi Gras exhibits. The Old US Mint was the only mint in the country that printed currency for both the Confederacy and the US government. The Mint now holds state and local research materials and exhibits. (Tues-Sun 9 am-5 pm; closed holidays) **$**

Louisiana Superdome. *Sugar Bowl Dr, New Orleans (70112). Phone 504/587-3663. www.superdome.com.* The Dome is home field for the New Orleans Saints (NFL football), Tulane University Green Wave (NCAA Division I football), and host to a variety of other sports events, including college baseball and the 2003 NCAA men's basketball Final Four. The annual Endymion Extravaganza Mardi Gras Parade and Party happens here, as well as the New Orleans Home & Garden Show, the Boat & Sport Fishing Show, the Kid's Fair & Expo, and numerous concerts and other special events.

Louisiana's Children's Museum. *420 Julia St, New Orleans (70130). Phone 504/523-1357. www.lcm.org.* Catering to toddlers and the young at heart of any age, this museum encourages hands-on exploration. Take a ride in a simulated police cruiser in the Safety First area, anchor a newscast in the Kidswatch Studio, or experience bayou life in the Cajun Cottage. Other areas include Waterworks, Big City Port, Art Trek, and the Challenge area, where you can try your hand at reading Braille, a print language for the blind. Children under 16 must be accompanied by an adult. (Tues-Sun; open Mon during the summer; closed holidays) **$$**

M. S. Rau Antiques. *630 Royal St, New Orleans (70130). Phone 504/523-5660; toll-free 800/544-9440. www.rauantiques.com.* Founded in 1912, this family-owned and family-run business is so confident of its merchandise that it offers a 125 percent guarantee on all in-store purchases (online purchases include a slightly modified guarantee). Internationally known names such as Paul Revere, Meissen, Faberg, Wedgwood, Tiffany, and Chippendale are represented in the 25,000-square-foot showroom and extensive catalogue. You can also pick up fabulous diamonds, jewelry, silver, and objets d'art among the vast array of American and European antiques. (Mon-Sat 9 am-5:15 pm; closed Sun)

Madame John's Legacy. *632 Dumaine St, New Orleans (70116). Phone 504/568-6968. lsm.crt.state.la.us/madam.htm.* This home is one of the oldest domestic buildings in the Mississippi Valley, built about 1727, rebuilt in 1788, and restored in 1981. It is part of the Louisiana State Museum. (Tues-Sun 9 am-5 pm) **$**

Magazine Street. *Magazine St, New Orleans (70115). Phone toll-free 866/679-4764. www.magazinestreet.com.* Fun and funky, Magazine Street offers 6 miles of clothing retailers, antique establishments, gift shops, eateries, and more. Most of the businesses are housed in 19th-century buildings or brick-faced cottages, which helps the area maintain its other-worldly charm. You can stroll from the French Quarter through Magazine Street to the Audubon Zoo, picking up a piece of jewelry, a piece of furniture, a book, or some food along the way. Make a point to stop off at the Magazine Arcade, a mini-mall that houses eclectic shops offering antique music boxes and musical instruments, period medical equipment, dolls and their furnishings, as well as antique household items for real people. Most shops open daily 10 am-5 pm.

Maison Le Monnier. *640 Royal St (private), New Orleans (70130).* Built in 1811 and sometimes called the "skyscraper," this was the first building in the Vieux Carr more than two stories high. This house was used as the setting of George W. Cable's novel *Sieur George*. Notice the YLR, for Yves LeMonnier, worked into the grillwork.

⭐ **Mardi Gras World.** *233 Newton St, New Orleans (70114). Phone 504/361-7821; toll-free 800/362-8213. www.mardigrasworld.com.* For a fascinating look at where about 75 percent of Mardi Gras props and floats are made, visit this unique establishmentthe world's largest. You can try on costumes; watch painters, sculptors, and carpenters at work; and tour rooms filled with props and Mardi Gras paraphernalia. The Kern family's business also provides floats and props for parades across the country. (Daily 9:30 am-4:30 pm) **$$$**

Memorial Hall—Confederate Museum. *929 Camp St, New Orleans (70130). Phone 504/523-4522. www.confederatemuseum.com.* Louisiana veterans of the War Between the States founded the Hall as a repository for artifacts and memorabilia of the Confederate side of the Civil War. Opened in 1891, it is the nation's longest continuously operating museum. The museum houses flags, swords, and uniforms from both officers and foot solders as well as an extensive collection of photographs. The widow of Confederate president Jefferson Davis donated many family items. (Mon-Sat 10 am-4 pm; closed holidays, Mardi Gras) **$**

The French Quarter

Since the founding of New Orleans, Royal Street has been the most prestigious address in the city. Today it remains the most refined street in the Quarter, lined with historic buildings, famous restaurants, galleries, and of course, banks. A good starting point for exploring this part of New Orleans is behind St. Louis Cathedral, a block up from Jackson Square, where a lush collection of tropical plants fills the compact St. Anthonys Garden. Follow the alleyway upriver to 324 Pirates Alley, where author William Faulkner lived in 1925. His fans still flock to that corner, now the home of a popular bookstore featuring the works of this bard of Southern letters. Continue down Pirate's Alley and away from the river along St. Peter to return to Royal Street.

Near the corner of St. Peter and Royal streets, the brick Labranche buildings, with their dramatic cast-iron galleries, were built starting in 1835. Proceed upriver along Royal Street. Beyond Toulouse Street, the 1798 Court of Two Lions at 541 Royal Street features marble lions atop the entry posts. The same architect built the neighboring house (527-533 Royal Street) in 1792. Now home to the Historic New Orleans Collection (phone 504/523-4662), the house museum displays exhibits on New Orleans history. At 613 Royal, the Court of Two Sisters is among the city's most venerable restaurants for French-Creole cuisine.

Between St. Louis and Conti streets, the huge, white marble State Supreme Court Building dominates the block; between Conti and Bienville streets, its the block-long Monteleone Hotel. You might turn around before you hit the harsher realities of contemporary life outside the Quarter at Canal Street. Loop around Bourbon Street for a change of scene, pass restaurants, nightclubs, and saloons, and drop down St. Ann Street back to Royal Street, where the Café des Exiles marks the historical gathering spot of French refugees from the Revolution. Further downriver, a detour down Dumaine toward the river lands you in front of Madame Johns Legacy (632 Dumaine; phone 504/568-6968). This French cottage was one of the few structures to survive the fire that destroyed most of the city in 1794. Returning to Royal and proceeding downriver, the cornstalk fence at 915 Royal draws onlookers and carriage tours, who stop to admire the intricate tasseled design of the ironwork.

The Gallier House museum at 1118-32 Royal Street (phone 504/525-5661) was built in the 1860s by acclaimed local architect James Gallier, Jr. Drop down Ursulines Avenue here to the old Ursulines Convent at the corner of Chartres Street. The 1745 convent is among the oldest structures in the city. Continue down Ursulines towards the River to visit the French Market, or return upriver along Chartres Street to return to Jackson Square.

Metairie Cemetery. *5100 Pontchartrain Blvd, New Orleans (70112). Phone 504/486-6331.* On the former grounds of the Metairie Race Course, the largest (150 acres) and loveliest of New Orleans' cemeteries is home to a variety of eye-catching memorials and mausoleums. Styles range from Egyptian pyramids to Celtic crosses to European castles. At least one of the numerous bronze statues is said to wander the grounds, a lovely setting for a quiet stroll. You can rent a taped audio tour or choose to drive around the grounds. (Daily 8:30 am-5 pm)

Mid-19th-century townhouse. *826 St. Ann St, New Orleans (70116). Phone 504/581-1367.* Headquarters of the New Orleans Spring Fiesta Association (see SPECIAL EVENTS). Early 19th-century antiques, Victorian pieces; *objets d'art.* Guided tours (Mon-Fri afternoons). **$$**

Moonwalk. *615 Pére Antoine Alley, New Orleans (70116). www.neworleansonline.com.* Running the length of the French Quarter along the river levee, the Moonwalk is a pedestrian thoroughfare that connects many attractions along the river, including the Aquarium of the Americas and paddleboat cruises, as well as shops and restaurants. Or, you can park yourself on a bench and watch the crowds and the river flow by. Locals and tourists make this a popular venue for an evening stroll, especially on a clear, moonlit night.

Musee Conti Historical Wax Museum. *917 rue Conti, New Orleans (70112). Phone 504/581-1993; toll-free 800/233-5405. www.get-waxed.com.* In addition to the obligatory dungeon of horrors featuring Dracula and the Wolfman, more than 150 wax figures illustrate the history of the city. Catch Napolean Bonaparte in his bath, Voodoo Queen Marie Laveau and her dancers, and Duke Ellington playing some jazz. The figures are painstakingly constructed (even clean-shaven men have stubble) using a process that makes them seem nearly life-like, and are set in historically accurate tableaux. (Mon-Sat 10 am-5:30 pm; closed Mardi Gras, Thanksgiving, Dec 20-26) **$$**

National D-Day Museum. *945 Magazine St, New Orleans (70130). Phone 504/527-6012. www.ddaymuseum.org.* Opened on June 6, 2000, the 16,000 square feet of gallery space houses exhibits, many interactive, that trace the political and economic events leading up to the D-Day invasion in 1944. Founded by the late historian and author Stephen Ambrose, the museum offers oral histories of the men and women who participated and rare film footage that help bring World War II to life. Free lunchbox lectures on Wednesdays give insight into specific topics or personalities. (Tues-Sun 9 am-5 pm; Thurs 9 am-7 pm; closed Thanksgiving, Dec 24-25, Mardi Gras) **$$$**

New Orleans Centre. *1400 Poydras, New Orleans (70112). Phone 504/568-0000.* This three-story mall is located in the heart of the business district adjacent to the Louisiana Superdome, the New Orleans Sports Arena, and the Hyatt Regency New Orleans. Anchored by Macy's and Lord & Taylor, the mall houses more than 60 shops including national chains and local specialty shops. Food offerings run the gamut from fast-food outlets to well-reviewed restaurants. (Mon-Sat 10 am-8 pm, Sun noon-6 pm)

New Orleans Custom House. *423 Canal St, New Orleans (70130). Decatur and Canal sts.* Begun in 1848, interrupted by the Civil War, and completed in 1881, the Greek Revival building with neo-Egyptian details was used in part as an office by Major General Benjamin "Spoons" Butler during Union occupation, and in part as a prison for Confederate soldiers. A great dome was planned but the great weight of the existing building caused the foundation to settle and the dome was never completed. (In 1940, the building had sunk 30 inches, while the street level had been raised three feet.) Of particular interest is the famed Marble Hall, an architectural wonder. Self-guided tour. (Mon-Fri) **FREE**

New Orleans Fair Grounds. *1751 Gentilly Blvd, New Orleans (70119). Phone 504/944-5515. www.fgno.com.* The horses have been darting out of the starting gates at this Mid-City racetrack since 1852, making it the oldest one still operating in the United States. When you're not placing bets and watching the fast-paced action on the track, wander through the Racing Hall

of Fame, which honors 110 of the sports most revered, such as legendary jockey Bill Shoemaker and Duncan Kenner, the founding father of racing in this country. The 145-acre facility also hosts the city's annual Jazz and Heritage Festival. (Thanksgiving Day-Mar: races start at 12:30 pm) **$**

New Orleans Ghost Tour. *625 St. Phillip, New Orleans (70129). Phone 504/628-1722. www.neworleansghosttour.com.* This walking tour carries on rain or shine (though not gloom of night) and covers creepy happenings in the French Quarter ranging from the mad butcher, who may have butchered more than beef, to the sultan reportedly buried alive. Tour host Thomas Duran has extensive ghost-hunting credentials from England and is a licensed New Orleans tour guide. **$$$$**

⭐ **New Orleans Historic Voodoo Museum.** *724 rue Dumaine, New Orleans (70116). www.voodoomuseum.com.* Marie Laveau reigned as Voodoo Queen of New Orleans throughout much of the 19th century. The Voodoo Museum displays her portrait and memorabilia. Although it sells the stereotypical voodoo supplies, the museum also offers serious exhibits on voodoo history and its artifacts. You can also purchase your own *gris-gris* bag filled with herbs, bones, and charms to bring luck or love into your life (a local addition to the trappings of the practice). (Daily 10 am-dusk) **$$$$**

New Orleans Hornets (NBA). *New Orleans Arena, 1501 Girod St, New Orleans (70113). Phone 504/301-4000. www.nba.com/hornets.* The Hornets moved from Charlotte for the 20022003 NBA season to give New Orleans a National Basketball Association team for the first time since the Jazz moved to Utah in 1979. They play home games at the New Orleans Arena, where the Honeybees cheer them on and mascot Hugo the Hornet is a three-time NBA Mascot Slam Dunk Champion. **$$$$**

New Orleans Opera. *Tulane University, MacAlester Auditorium, New Orleans (70116). Phone 504/529-2278; toll-free 800/881-4459. www.neworleansopera.org.* Operating from the Mahalia Jackson Theatre of the Performing Arts, the New Orleans Opera Association presents four operas each season, which runs from October through March. The association was founded in 1943 and stages high-quality performances of renowned operas as well as world premieres. (The 2003-2004 season opened with the world premiere of the *Louisiana Purchase Opera*). English translations appear in subtitles above the stage. **$$$$**

You Can't Keep A Good Man Down

On the way into New Orleans from Louis Armstrong International Airport stands a curious sight: clusters of miniscule buildings set on 150 acres of land, looking for all intents and purposes like tiny cities glistening in the hot New Orleans sun.

But exit at Metairie Road and take a closer look. These are not buildings, they are monuments; and this is not a city, it's a cemetery. What you're seeing is an example of what New Orleans residents call their Cities of the Dead.

The cemeteries of New Orleans tell a fascinating story of the city's history, geology, and culture. It begins with New Orleans's elevation, which is below sea level. It was a literal horror story for the city's settlers. A hole dug for a 6-foot grave would fill with 6 feet of water, causing caskets to float. Rocks placed in and on top of the coffins to weigh them down worked until a rainstorm occurred, causing the water level to rise and popping the airtight coffin right out of the ground.

Eventually, large holes were drilled into the underside of the coffin so it would quickly fill with water and sink. This method, too, was abandoned, due in part to the painful sound of loved ones gurgling their way down to their final resting place.

Meanwhile, Estaban Miro, an early governor of the city, had introduced the wall vault burial system that was popular in Spain for those who wanted to be buried above ground. Economical vaults were stacked on top of one another, while wealthier families built large, ornate tombs with crypts, many of which looked like tiny mansions. Rows of tombs looked like streets, clusters of monuments looked like communities, and cemeteries have thus become known as Cities of the Dead.

Most of New Orleans's 42 cemeteries offer tours. Each has its own story to tell. St. Louis Cemetery #1, for instance, commissioned in 1789, was the first to offer above-ground burials. Notables buried there include Homer Plessy (of legal case *Plessy vs. Ferguson* fame) and Marie Laveau, New Orleans mysterious Voodoo Queen.

Lafayette Cemetery #1, laid out in 1833, figures prominently in Anne Rice's vampire books and was the film location for *Interview with the Vampire*. In 1980, it was also the site of a real-life wedding when a bride and groom and a plane full of guests flew in from Houston. The reason for the unusual location, the couple said, was that in addition to getting married, they wanted to bury their past.

Metairie Cemetery has a broad range of architecture and is considered one of the most beautiful cemeteries in the world. It is the final resting place of nine Louisiana governors and notorious Storyville madam Josie Arlington.

Holt is the New Orleans oddity, a below-ground cemetery and perhaps the most touching of any cemetery in the city. It is a graveyard for indigents. As such, graves are either unmarked or marked by a collection of poignant, hand-made headstones. Buddy Bolden, the great early 20th-century jazz musician who spent the second half of his life in a mental institution, is buried here.

New Orleans Pharmacy Museum (La Pharmacie Francaise). *514 Chartres St, New Orleans (70130). www.pharmacymuseum.org.* Louis Dufilho, the first licensed pharmacist in the US, operated an apothecary shop here from 1823 to 1855. The ground floor contains pharmaceutical memorabilia of the 1800s, such as apothecary jars filled with medicinal herbs and voodoo powders, surgical instruments, pharmacy fixtures, and a black-and-rose Italian marble soda fountain (circa 1855). (Tues-Sun 10 am-5 pm; closed Mon, holidays) **$**

New Orleans Saints (NFL). *Louisiana Superdome, Sugar Bowl Dr, New Orleans (70112). Phone 504/731-1700. www.neworleanssaints.com.* One of the few NFL teams that remains in its original city, the Saints joined the National Football League in 1967. They play their home games in the Superdome, which also regularly hosts the Super Bowl, a game the team itself has never been to. **$$$$**

New Orleans School of Cooking & Louisiana General Store. *524 St. Louis St, New Orleans (70130). Phone 504/525-2665; toll-free 800/237-4841. www.nosoc.com.* After a session at the School of Cooking, you'll be a convert to Louisiana cuisine—"ga-ron-teed." Make a reservation for a three-hour or a two-hour lunch class to learn the basics of Louisiana cooking, and, even better, to sample the four dishes cooked up. An early 1800s-era converted molasses warehouse is home to the school and to the Louisiana General Store, where you can pick up ingredients, a cookbook, and cooking utensils. **$$$$**

New Orleans Steamboat Company. *#2 Canal St, Suite 2500, New Orleans (70130). Phone 504/586-8777; toll-free 800/233-2628. www.neworleanssteamboat.com.* Cruise from the heart of the French Quarter on the steamboat *Natchez.* She's the ninth steamer to have the name. Her predecessor, *Natchez VI,* won the race against the *Robert E. Lee* in the most famous steamboat race of all time. The *Natchez* has never lost a race. She was launched in 1975, and is one of only six true steam-powered sternwheelers sailing on the Mississippi today. Cruises last two hours, and there is an optional creole lunch available for an additional fee. Each cruise features live narration of historical facts and highlights, jazz music in the main dining room, and a calliope concert during boarding times. The Harbor/Jazz Cruises at 11:30 am and 2:30 pm offer jazz by Duke Heitger and the Steamboat Stompers. The 7 pm Dinner/Jazz Cruise features the world-renowned Dukes of Dixieland performing nightly. The Dinner/Jazz Cruise offers buffet-style dining and indoor/outdoor seating. Cruises depart from the Toulouse Street Wharf. **$$$$**

New Orleans Walking and Driving Tour. *2020 Saint Charles Ave, New Orleans (70115). Phone 504/566-5011. www.neworleanscvb.com.* For a more thorough tour of the many interesting points in the Vieux Carr and surrounding area, see the visitor information center.

No Problem Raceway Park. *6470 Hwy 996, Bella Rose (70341). Phone 985/369-3692. www.noproblemraceway.com.* This drag racing park hosts, you guessed itdrag raceson its 4,000-foot dragstrip. Part of the Grand Bayou Circuit, the park also has a 1.8-mile, 15-turn asphalt road course and sponsors kart races as well. (Wed, Fri, Sat, some Sun; race times vary with event) Also here is

> **Grand Bayou Circuit.** *Bella Rose (70341).* You can race your own car on the 1.8-mile asphalt track.

Oak Alley Plantation. *3645 Hwy 18 (Great River Rd), Vacherie (70090). W on I-10, Gramercy exit 194, S on Hwy 641, W on Hwy 18. Phone 225/265-2151; toll-free 800/442-5539. www.oakalleyplantation.com.* (1839) This quintessential antebellum, Greek Revival plantation house has been featured in many films: an *allee* of 300-year-old live oaks leads to the mansion surrounded by first- and second-floor galleries supported by massive columns. The interior was remodeled in the 1930s with antiques and modern furnishings of the day. Extensive grounds with many old trees. Picnicking, restaurant. Cottages. (Daily tours 9 am-5 pm; closed Thanksgiving, Dec 25) **$$**

The Old US Mint. *400 Esplanade Ave, New Orleans (70116). Esplanade and Decatur sts. Phone 504/568-6968. lsm.crt.state.la.us.* Designed by William Strickland in 1835, the mint produced coins for both the US and for the Confederate States. Today, the Mint houses permanent exhibitions of jazz and the Louisiana State Museum's Historical Center, a research facility. (Tues-Sun 9 am-5 pm; historical center also Mon, by appointment; closed holidays) **$**

Pitot House. *1440 Moss St, New Orleans (70119). Phone 504/482-0312. www.pitothouse.org/.* (1799) One of the last remaining French colonial/West Indies-style plantation houses along Bayou St. John. It was the residence of James Pitot, the first elected mayor of incorporated New Orleans. Restored; furnished with antiques. (Wed-Sat 10 am-3 pm; closed Sun-Tues, holidays)**$**

Pontalba Building. *523 St. Anne St, New Orleans (70116). Phone 504/524-9118.* Completed in 1850 and 1851 by the Baroness Pontalba to beautify the square. Still occupied and used as intended (with duplex apartments above ground-floor offices and shops), the buildings are now owned by the city and the Louisiana State Museum. The 1850 House is furnished in the manner of the period (Tues-Sun 10 am-4 pm; closed holidays). **$**

⭐ **Preservation Hall.** *726 St. Peter St, New Orleans (70116). Phone 504/522-2841. www.preservationhall.com.* Since 1961, people have been warming the benches at this rustic music hall in the French Quarter for one reasonto hear traditional New Orleans Jazz, which dates back to the early 1900s. If you know your music, you know this type of jazz is slower than other forms and features simple arrangements usually led by the sweet sounds of the trumpet. But even if you're no jazzman, you'll still want to jive to the beat at this swingin joint. Bring the kids, too; the hall welcomes all ages. (Daily 8 pm-midnight) **$**

The Presbytere. *751 Chartres St, New Orleans (70116). Phone 504/568-6968. lsm.crt.state.la.us.* Architecturally similar to the Cabildo, this 1791 building was intended to house clergy serving the parish church. A series of fires kept the Presbytére incomplete until 1813, when it was finished by the US government. It is now a museum with a permanent exhibit on the history of Mardi Gras. The Presbytére, like the Cabildo, is part of the Louisiana State Museum complex. (Tues-Sun; closed holidays) **$$**

River cruises. *2 Canal St, New Orleans (70130).* Daily excursions depart from the riverfront.

Delta Queen and **Mississippi Queen** Sternwheelers. *Phone 504/586-0631; toll-free 800/543-1949.* The sternwheelers *Delta Queen* and *Mississippi Queen* offer 3- to 12-night cruises on the Mississippi, Ohio, Cumberland, and Tennessee rivers year-round. Contact the Delta Queen Steamboat Co, 30 Robin St Wharf, 70130-1890.

John James Audubon Riverboat. *1 Canal St, New Orleans (70130). Phone 504/586-8777; toll-free 800/233-2628.* The riverboat *John James Audubon* provides river transportation between the Aquarium of the Americas and the Audubon Zoo 7 miles upriver, round-trip or one-way; return may be made via the St. Charles Avenue Streetcar (additional fee). Round-trip ticket price includes admission to both the Audubon Zoo and the Aquarium of the Americas.

Paddlewheeler *Creole Queen* and **Riverboat** *Cajun Queen.* *610 S Peters, New Orleans (70130). Phone 504/524-0814.* The paddlewheeler *Creole Queen* offers 2 1/2-hour sightseeing cruises to Chalmette National Historical Park, the site of the Battle of New Orleans, as well as three-hour dinner jazz cruises. The riverboat *Cajun Queen* offers harbor cruises from the Aquarium of the Americas (one-hour tour with narration).

Steamboat *Natchez.* *2 Canal St, New Orleans (70130). Toulouse St Wharf in the French Quater behind Jackson Brewery. Phone 504/586-8777; toll-free 800/233-2628.* This sternwheeler steamboat, the only one in New Orleans, takes passengers on two- and three-hour harbor cruises and evening dinner cruises. Live jazz is featured on all cruises. Tours depart from the Toulouse Street Wharf. **$$$$**

Riverfront Streetcar Line. *www.norta.com.* Vintage streetcars follow a 1 1/2-mile route along the Mississippi riverfront from Esplanade past the French Quarter to the World Trade Center, Riverwalk, Convention Center, and back. **$**

Riverwalk. *1 Poydras St, New Orleans (70130). Phone 504/522-1555. www.riverwalkmarketplace.com.* This 1/2-mile-long festival marketplace has more than 140 national and local shops, restaurants, and cafés. The Riverwalk structure was converted from World's Fair pavilions. (Mon-Sat 10 am-9 pm; Sun 11 am-7 pm; closed Thanksgiving, Dec 25)

Saenger Theatre. *143 N Rampart St, New Orleans (70112). Phone 504/525-1052. www.saengertheatre. com.* Opened in 1927 as a movie house, the Saenger now hosts national theatrical tours, musical acts, and other performing arts organizations. Entered in the National Register of Historic Places in 1977, the buildings Italian Baroque interior includes Greek and Roman statuary and a ceiling embedded with lights to evoke a starry night sky. The 778-pipe organ is the largest the Robert Morton Wonder Organ Company ever built.

San Francisco Plantation. *2646 Hwy 44 (River Rd), Garyville (70051). Approximately 35 miles W via Hwy 61 or I-10 and Hwy 44. Phone 985/535-2341; toll-free 888/322-1756. www.sanfranciscoplantation.org.* (1853-1856) While a remarkable example of the "Steamboat Gothic" style in detail, the structure is typical of a Creole building: galleried with the main living quarters on the second floor, dining room and various service rooms on the ground floor. Authentically restored, the interior features five decorated ceilings (two are original). The house was used as the setting of Frances Parkinson Keyes's novel *Steamboat Gothic.* (Daily tours 9:30 am-4:40 pm, 4 pm in winter; closed holidays, Mardi Gras) **$$**

Shim-Sham Club and Juke Joint. *615 Toulouse St, New Orleans (70130). www.shimshamclub.com.* Nothing if not distinctive, the Shim-Sham Club offers everything from punk/heavy metal karaoke nights to alternative live theater. Boogie to the tunes at the weekly '80s dance party, or spin your own discs at the Juke Joint's jukebox. The Shim-Sham Revue offers burlesque complete with striptease and comedy acts. (Daily 2 pm-6 am)

The Shops at Canal Place. *333 Canal St, New Orleans (70130). Phone 504/522-9200. www.theshopsatcanal-place.com.* Three levels of name and designer shops give this shopping center at the edge of the French Quarter lots of cachet. Saks Fifth Avenue anchors the mall, which also offers Gucci, Kenneth Cole, and Betsey Johnson stores, along with Williams-Sonoma, Pottery Barn, and other clothing, jewelry, and shoe shopsabout 30 in all. Additional amenities include a fitness club, a post office, and, of course, an ATM. The Southern Repertory Theater stage is located here also. (Mon-Sat 10 am-7 pm, Sun noon-6 pm)

Southern Repertory Theater. *365 Canal St, New Orleans (70118). Phone 504/522-6545. www.southern-rep.com.* Permanently housed in The Shops at Canal Place mall since 1991, the Southern Repertory Theater (SRT) was founded in 1986 to promote Southern plays and playwrights. Plays by Southern luminaries such as Tennessee Williams, Pearl Cleage, Beth Henley, and SRT founding member Rosary H. O'Neill form the basis of the theater's September-to-May season. (Thurs-Sat 8 pm, Sun 3 pm) **$$$$**

St. Bernard State Park. *501 St. Bernard Pkwy, Braithwaite (70040). 18 miles SE on Hwy 39. Phone 504/682-2101; toll-free 888/677-7823. www.lastateparks.com/st-bernar.* Approximately 358 acres near the Mississippi River, with many viewing points of the river and a network of artificial lagoons. Swimming; picnicking, playground, trails, camping. (Daily) **FREE**

★ **St. Charles Avenue Streetcar.** *6700 Plaza Dr, New Orleans (70127). Phone 504/827-7802. www.regionaltransit.org.* The streetcars (never call them trolleys!) entered the National Registry of Historic Places in 1973. A ride is a quaint and relaxing way to view the varied architecture and exotic greenery of the aptly named Garden District. The 13.2-mile route can take you to tour Tulane University, drop you off at Audubon Park (where the zoo is located), and provide you with safe transport after imbibing in the French Quarter. **$**

St. Louis Cathedral. *615 Pre Antoine Alley, New Orleans (70116). Phone 504/525-9585. www.saintlouiscathedral.org.* Consecrated in 1794 and named for French king and Saint Louis IX, this is the oldest cathedral in the United States and is the third church to stand on the site. (The two earlier churches were destroyed by hurricane and fire, respectively.) A mural inside depicts Louis announcing the seventh crusade. The triple steeple makes this French Quarter landmark easy to spot. (Daily; closed during Mardi Gras)

St. Louis Cemetery #1. *425 Basin St, New Orleans (70112). Phone 504/525-9585.* It's not a place to be after dark if you care about your physical health (it's in a high-crime area), but the oldest cemetery in the city is still worth a visit with a tour guide. Because New Orleans itself is below sea level, all the tombs are above ground and range in size and opulence from small, simple crypts to towering, ornate mausoleums. Don't be surprised to see flowers at Voodoo Queen Marie Laveau's tomb. (Mon-Sat 9 am-3 pm, Sun 9 am-noon)

Tipitina's. *501 Napoleon Ave, New Orleans (70125). Phone 504/895-8477. www.tipitinas.com.* Live music is what you find at Tip's, as it's known to the locals. The emphasis is on rock, but funk, Cajun, and jazz all make the calendar. Tuesdays feature various local artists at the no-cover 8th Floor "Homegrown Nights," and Sundays often offer a $5 cover for the Cajun Fais Do Do. Shows featuring nationally and locally known talent start at 10 pm. (Thurs-Sun)

Toulouse Street Wharf. *At the foot of Toulouse St and the river.* Sales office and departure point for riverboat cruises and bus tours of the city and countryside.

Washington Artillery Park. *Frenchman and Royal sts, New Orleans (70152).* Between the muddy Mississippi and elegant Jackson Square lies this park named for the 141st Field Artillery, which has fought in every major conflict since the 1845 Mexican War. Broad steps serve as an amphitheater from which you can catch the escapades of the kids in the playground, the antics of the street performers, the lazy flow of the river, or a great view of the French Quarter.

Whiskey Blue. *333 Poydras St, New Orleans (70130). Phone 504/525-9444. www.whotels.com.* Located in the nouveau-chic W Hotel, Whiskey Blue upholds the hotel's chic, edgy tone with low-slung chairs, clear blue lighting, and pricey, (and expertly made) martinis. Smallish (it holds just 91 patrons) and intimate (there's a queen-sized bed in the middle of the place), the Blue caters to a stylish crowd taking a break from the French Quarter's free-for-all atmosphere. (Mon-Sat 4 pm-4 am, Sun to 2 am)

Woldenberg Riverfront Park. *1 Canal St, New Orleans (70130). Between Toulouse and Canal sts. Phone 504/565-3033.* Covering 17 acres on the riverfront, Woldenberg Park offers the city its first direct access to the river in 150 years; ships and paddlewheelers dock along the park. Visitors can choose from a variety of riverboat tours. (Sun-Thurs 6 am-10 pm, Fri-Sat 6 am-12 am)

World Trade Center of New Orleans. *2 Canal St, New Orleans (70130). Phone 504/529-1601. wtc-no.org.* This center houses the offices of many maritime companies and foreign consulates involved in international trade. Top of the Mart, a revolving restaurant and cocktail lounge on the 33rd floor, offers fine views of the city and the Mississippi River. (Daily; closed holidays) **$**

Special Events

Allstate Sugar Bowl College Football Classic. *Louisiana Superdome, Sugar Bowl Dr, New Orleans (70112). Phone 504/828-2400. www.allstatesugarbowl.com.* Each year, two top-ranked college football teams compete in this prestigious bowl game, part of the Bowl Championship Series. From 4 pm to kickoff, all football lovers can party at Fan Jam, on the Gate C Bridge located on the Superdomes east side. The spirited event features live music, contests, hot food, and ice-cold beverages. Sugar Bowl week also includes a basketball classic and a regatta on Lake Pontchartrain. Jan.

Bridge City Gumbo Festival. *Gumbo Festival Park on Angel Square, 1701 Bridge City Ave, New Orleans (70130). Gumbo Festival Park on Angel Square. On the other side of Huey P. Long Bridge from New Orleans. Phone 504/436-4712. www.hgaparish.org/gumbo-festival.htm.* In the Gumbo Capital of the World, festival organizers cook up more than 2,000 gallons of chicken, sausage, and seafood gumbos. Jambalaya, another local specialty, is also available, along with a variety of accompaniments. You can enter a cooking contest, listen to live music, enjoy carnival rides, and participate in many other activities. Early Nov.

French Quarter Festival. *French Quarter, 100 Conti St, New Orleans (70130). Phone 504/522-5730; toll-free 800/673-5725. www.frenchquarterfestival.com.* Fabulous and free, the French Quarter Festival showcases local musicians on 15 stages throughout the Vieux Carr. Marching bands, brass bands, and jazz and Dixieland bands play early to late three days running, usually the second weekend in April. You can also hear Cajun, country, zydeco, and everything in between. Music stages are located at Jackson Square, Woldenberg Riverfront Park, Bourbon Street, Royal Street, the French Market, Le Petit Theatre at St. Peter and Chartres, and Louisiana State Musuem's Old US Mint at Esplanade and Decatur. Don't miss the "World's Largest Jazz Brunch" booths can be found in Jackson Square, Woldenberg Riverfront Park, and Louisiana State Museums Old US Mint. Art exhibits, dance troupes, and workshops for young and young at heart guarantee something for everyone.

Horse racing. Fair Grounds Racetrack. *1751 Gentilly Blvd, New Orleans (70119). Phone 504/944-5515. www.fgno.com.* (1872) America's third-oldest racetrack. Pari-mutuel betting. Jacket required in clubhouse. Wed-Sun, late Nov-Mar.

Louisiana Crawfish Festival. *8200 W Judge Perez Dr, Chalmette (70043) Phone 504/329-6411.* Rides, games, live entertainment, and an array of dishes featuring crawfish. Early Apr.

Louisiana Swampfest. *6500 Magazine St, New Orleans (70118). Phone 504/581-4629; toll-free 866/487-2966.*

www.auduboninstitute.org/swampfest/. Ever wondered how alligator tastes? Head to the Swampfest to try fried gator tidbits while listening to local bands play Cajun and Zydeco tunes. You may want to participate in the 5K run before indulging in the food and music treats, checking out the craft village, or getting some hands-on experience with live creatures in the swamp exhibit. Early-mid-Nov.

Mardi Gras Festival. *New Orleans. The main parade route travels down St. Charles Ave and the heart of Bourbon St. Phone 504/566-5011. www.mardigras. com or www.mardigrasday.com.* The biggest party of the year offers something for everyone—especially if you're into raucous, bawdy partying. The party starts weeks before the actual date of Mardi Gras, which, because it's 46 days before Easter, varies each year. Parades and parties are scheduled throughout the weeks leading up to Ash Wednesday and Lent (the French term *mardi gras* means "fat Tuesday"). Though most of the balls are invitation-only, you pay nothing to watch the numerous parades sponsored by the secret societies (krewes) that organize the festivities. The parades range in theme and name from Barkus (animals of all kinds), to the Phunny Phorty Phellows, to Comus, New Orleans' oldest krewe. If you're looking to enjoy the festivities without offending too many sensibilities, head to the family-friendly Garden District and avoid the French Quarter, where it's nearly impossible to avoid seeing lots of flesh and usually concealed body parts. Early Jan-Late Feb.

New Orleans Jazz & Heritage Festival. *Fair Grounds Racetrack, 1751 Gentilly Blvd, New Orleans (70119). Phone 504/522-4786. www.nojazzfest.com.* Each year, Jazz Fest draws 500,000 visitors from around the world for an experience that embraces music, food, art exhibits, and craft workshops. You know that the music is eclectic when the acts for one day range from Lil Romeo to Crosby, Stills & Nash to Buckwheat Zydeco. The main action is at the Fair Grounds, but the fun spreads to venues throughout the city. New Orleanss own Neville Brothers are always a big draw. Late Apr-early May. **$$$$**

Spring Fiesta. *826 St. Ann St, New Orleans (70116). Phone 504/581-1367.* For two weekends every year, New Orleans celebrates its unique heritage with this springtime festival. The fun-packed festivities include a parade of horse-drawn carriages through the French Quarter, the coronation of the festivals queen at Jackson Square, and tours of private homes and courtyards and the historic Metairie Cemetery. Mid-late Apr.

Tennessee Williams New Orleans Literary Festival.
French Quarter, Le Petit Theatre du Vieux Carr, 616 St. Peter St, New Orleans (70116). Phone 504/581-1144; toll-free 800/965-4827. www.tennesseewilliams.net. Born in Mississippi, playwright Tennessee Williams adopted New Orleans as his spiritual home. The city honors him with an annual festival held around his March 26 birthday. The five days of the festival are filled with workshops on writing and publishing, a one-act play competition, and a book fair, as well as performances of some of Williams' plays. You can join a literary walking tour or compete in a Stanley and Stella contest. Le Petit Theatre du Vieux Carr is the festival headquarters, but other venues also house activities. Late Mar.

White Linen Night. *900 Camp St, New Orleans (70130). Phone 504/528-3805. www.cacno.org.* Catch some culture during this annual art walk and street party. August in the bayou is always hot and humid, so patrons and partiers don their coolest clotheswhite linen is a popular choiceand stroll through the Arts District, popping into galleries that stay open late, catching live dance and theater performances, and ending up at the Contemporary Arts Center for a party that goes on until the wee hours. First Sat in Aug. **FREE**

Limited-Service Hotels

★ ★ **BEST WESTERN FRENCH QUARTER LANDMARK.** *920 N Rampart St, New Orleans (70116). Phone 504/524-3333; toll-free 800/780-7234; fax 504/523-5431. www.bestwestern.com.* 100 rooms, 3 story. Check-in 4 pm. Check-out noon. Restaurant, bar. Outdoor pool. **$**

★ ★ **BIENVILLE HOUSE HOTEL.** *320 Decatur St, New Orleans (70130). Phone 800/535-7836; toll-free 800/535-9603; fax 504/525-6079. www.bienvillehouse. com.* One of the first things to strike you about the Bienville House Hotel is how much the lobby feels like your living roomassuming that your living room has a chandelier and looks somewhat like a French Quarter manor home from the late-18th-century. Elegantly cushy chairs and coffee tables aside, a recent multi-million-dollar renovation that included the creation of hand-painted wall murals has steeped this French Quarter treat with a stately, old-world charm. The allure continues outside in a lush courtyard surrounding a pool with four sundecks and wonderful city views. 83 rooms, 4 story. Complimentary continental breakfast. Check-out noon. Restaurant. Outdoor pool. **$**

★ ★ **DOUBLETREE HOTEL.** *300 Canal St, New Orleans (70130). Phone 504/581-1300; fax 504/522-4100. www.doubletree.com.* Location is what distinguishes this fairly standard hotel. It's conveniently located in the business district, just three blocks from the convention center and overlooking the river. Harrah's Casino is next door, and the French Quarter is just across the street. 363 rooms, 17 story. Check-in 3 pm, check-out noon. Restaurant, bar. Fitness room. Outdoor pool. Business center. **$$**

★ ★ **EMBASSY SUITES.** *315 Julia St, New Orleans (70130). Phone 504/525-1993; toll-free 800/362-2779; fax 504/525-3437. www.embassyneworleans.com.* This hotel is located in the convention center and is convenient to the French Quarter, the St. Charles Streetcar, and the waterfront. 282 rooms, 16 story, all suites. Complimentary full breakfast. Check-in 3 pm, check-out noon. Restaurant, bar. Fitness room. Outdoor pool, whirlpool. **$$**

★ ★ **HOTEL PROVINCIAL.** *1024 rue Chartres, New Orleans (70116). Phone 504/581-4995; toll-free 800/535-7922; fax 504/581-1018. www.hotelprovincial. com.* Haunted? Rumor has that it soldiers who were treated here when it was a Civil War hospital still come around every once in a while. If you see one, ask him to bring you a beignet; if he's anything like any other employee at the hotel, you'll have it before the request leaves your lips. The service at Hotel Provincial is nearly as wonderful as its award-winning architecture, which is nearly as wonderful as the warm, relaxing atmosphere that can be soaked up within its restored old buildings. 105 rooms, 4 story. Check-out noon. Restaurant, bar. Fitness room. Outdoor pool. **$**

★ ★ **IBERVILLE SUITES.** *910 Iberville St, New Orleans (70112). Phone 504/523-2400; fax 504/524-1320. www.ibervillesuites.com.* It's location in the historic Maison Blanche building in the French Quarter gives you a clue as to what you'll find inside this hotel: warm Southern hospitality from check-in to check-out. The antique-filled lobby, with classic wood touches, comfortable chairs and sofas, and plenty of sitting room for relaxing and people-watching, is the sort of place you want to sit for a while, or perhaps take tea. If you'd prefer to have tea in your room or suite, take comfort in the fact that your tea (or coffee) will be served in a silver pot and poured into china cups. Guests also enjoy signing privileges at the Ritz-Carlton's food and beverage outlets and spa and fitness facilities. Elegantly decorated guest rooms boast warm, rich colors and more antiques. 230 rooms, 7 story, all suites. Pets accepted, some restrictions; fee. Complimentary continental breakfast. Check-in 3 pm, check-out noon. Restaurant, bar. Fitness room, spa. Indoor pool, whirlpool. Airport transportation available. Business center. **$$**

★ ★ MAISON DE VILLE AND AUDUBON COTTAGES. *727 rue Toulouse, New Orleans (70130). Phone 504/561-5858; fax 504/528-9939.* In the heart of the French Quarter, this charming hotel offers antique-filled main-house rooms and historic Audubon Cottages (believed to be former slave quarters). All accommodations include continental breakfast and evening port and sherry served in the courtyard or salon. 23 rooms, 3 story. Children over 12 years only. Complimentary continental breakfast. Check-in 3 pm, check-out noon. Restaurant. **$$**

★ ★ MAISON DUPUY. *1001 rue Toulouse, New Orleans (70112). Phone 504/586-8000; toll-free 800/535-9177; fax 504/566-7450. www.maisondupuy. com.* A low-key, semitropical courtyard complete with gas lamps and potted palms may be just the thing after a long day of hustle-bustling your way through the nearby French Quarter. The courtyard emerged as part of the renovation and preservation project that took seven French Quarter townhouses and created Maison Dupuy. It is the heart of this quiet hotel, the place where guests can be found starting their day, relaxing before dinner, and enjoying a dip in the whirlpool before retiring for the night. 200 rooms, 5 story. Check-out 11 am. Restaurant, bar. Fitness room. Outdoor pool. **$$**

★ ★ PRYTANIA PARK HOTEL. *1525 Prytania St, New Orleans (70130). Phone 504/524-0427; toll-free 888/498-7591; fax 504/522-2977. www.prytaniapark-hotel.com.* Huey Long's girlfriend slept here. No doubt she wanted to be a tad removed from the center of things; but the Pyrtania Park has a shuttle to take you to the French Quarter, the Convention Center, and the Central Business District. A group of 1980 buildings wrapped around an 1834 townhouse, the Prytania Park is a tourist-class hotel with peaceful courtyards

and outside stairwells, provoking a sense of old New Orleans. Several wooden picnic tables and chairs line shady, narrow walkways, providing a lovely place for breakfast. 62 rooms, 2 story. Complimentary continental breakfast. Check-out noon. **$**

★ ★ RIVERFRONT HOTEL. *701 Convention Center Blvd, New Orleans (70130). Phone 504/524-8200; fax 504/524-0600.* The Riverfront is a pleasant hotel in the heart of New Orlean's business district, across the street from the Ernest N. Memorial Convention Center. This is a business travelers delightgreat amenities and a staff that understands the importance (and occasional urgency) of getting a job done. Its location adjacent to downtown New Orleans and the French Quarter, near Cafe du Monde, Pat O'Briens, Jackson Square, Canal Place, and the Audubon Aquarium of the Americas means that the staff is also well versed in the art of having fun and can give you guidance on things to do. 202 rooms, 6 story. Check-out noon. Restaurant, bar. Fitness room. **$$**

★ ★ W NEW ORLEANS-FRENCH QUARTER. *316 Chartres St, New Orleans (70130). Phone 504/581-1200; fax 504/523-2910. www.whotels.com.* 98 rooms, 5 story. Pets accepted, some restrictions. Check-out noon. Restaurant, bar. Outdoor pool. **$$**

★ ★ WYNDHAM BOURBON ORLEANS HOTEL. *717 Orleans St, New Orleans (70116). Phone 504/523-2222; fax 504/525-8166. www.bourbonorleans.com.* After a wild beginning as the famous Orleans Ballroom, the site of the city's earliest masquerade balls, things took a 180 turn and this property was purchased by an order of African-American nuns devoted to teaching, who turned it into a school. Today, the hotel has recaptured its lavish roots: a huge spiral staircase, columns, chandeliers, marble floors, and Queen Anne and Chippendale furnishings in the lobby and foyer create an air of restrained opulence. And Mardi Gras balls again take place here, now in the sumptuous banquet room. 216 rooms, 6 story. Check-out noon. Restaurant, bar. Fitness room. Outdoor pool. **$**

Full-Service Hotels

★ ★ ★ CHATEAU SONESTA HOTEL. *800 Iberville St, New Orleans (70112). Phone 504/586-0800; fax 504/586-1987. www.chateausonesta.com.* Not only are the guest rooms extra large (with 12-foot ceilings), but most come with good views of well-landscaped court-

yards or Bourbon Street, which sits just steps away. As an added bonus for business travelers, all the rooms come with T-1 high-speed Internet access. If you wake up hungry, La Chatelaine serves breakfast. For lunch or dinner, savor scrumptious seafood dishes at Ralph Brennans Red Fish Grill. The unique-looking hotel dates all the way back to 1849, when Daniel Henry Holmes opened his D. H. Holmes Department Store, which did a booming business on this very site until 1989. 251 rooms, 4 story. Pets accepted, some restrictions; fee. Check-in 3 pm, check-out noon. High-speed Internet access. Two restaurants, bar. Fitness room. Outdoor pool. Business center. Credit cards accepted. **$$**

★ ★ **DAUPHINE ORLEANS HOTEL.** *415 Dauphine St, New Orleans (70112). Phone 504/586-1800; toll-free 800/521-7111; fax 504/586-1409. www. dauphineorleans.com.* Head to the French Quarter and step back into the New Orleans of yesteryear when you check into this jewel with quite a past. May Baily's Place, the hotel's bar, was one of the more popular bordellos in the city's red-light district in 1857. In the Audubon Cottage, now the main meeting room, John James Audubon painted his well-known "Birds of America" series from 1821 to 1822. And a townhome built for a wealthy merchant in 1834 now houses 14 patio rooms. Besides all this history, the charming boutique hotel also serves guests a welcome cocktail, continental breakfast, and afternoon tea (with cookies) all complimentary. 111 rooms, 4 story. Complimentary continental breakfast. Check-in 3 pm, check-out noon. Bar. Fitness room. Outdoor pool, whirlpool. Credit cards accepted. **$$**

★ ★ ★ **THE FAIRMONT NEW ORLEANS.** *123 Baronne St, New Orleans (70112). Phone 504/529-7111; toll-free 800/441-1414; fax 504/522-2303. www. fairmont.com.* The genteel Fairmont offers the perfect introduction to the sultry city of New Orleans. Situated at the edge of the French Quarter in the center of the business district, this posh hotel has been the preferred choice of gentlemen and ladies since 1893. Eight presidents have slept here. When it was called The Roosevelt (in honor of Teddy), rumor has it that Governor Huey Long built a 90-mile road from the state capital in Baton Rouge to the hotel so that he could get there more easily; a right turn upon leaving The Fairmont does indeed put you on Highway 61 to Baton Rouge. Its location makes it ideal for exploring the city's renowned streets by foot, although it is the Victorian-era elegance and sparkling interiors that really make this hotel a standout. Its atmosphere is distinctly historic, yet the hotel remains relevant with the latest technology and amenities. The elegance of the glorious lobby, with huge bouquets of fresh flowers and a snap-to-it bellstaff, parallels that of the guest rooms, most with huge bathrooms, and many with claw-foot bathtubs and marble showers. Foodies flock to New Orleans for its top-notch restaurants, and The Fairmonts Sazerac Bar & Grill rarely disappoints with its fantastic Creole cuisine. 700 rooms, 14 story. Pets accepted, some restrictions; fee. Check-in 4 pm, check-out 1 pm. Restaurant, bar. Fitness room. Outdoor pool. Tennis. Business center. **$$**

★ ★ ★ **HILTON NEW ORLEANS RIVERSIDE.** *2 Poydras St, New Orleans (70140). Phone 504/561-0500; fax 504/568-1721. www.neworleans.hilton.com.* With its multiple levels, intimate sitting areas, soaring ceilings, a long crosswalk, and entrances in several different lobbies, the Hilton New Orleans Riverside lives up to its own moniker: a city within a city. This is not a quaint, cozy hotel. A feeling of excitement and high energy prevails from check-in, past the main street of shops and dining venues and up to the guest rooms. Although this sophisticated hotel can't be summed up by any one particular style, the rooms can be termed either traditional or French Provinial, the latter perhaps fitting with the hotels location on the banks of the Mississippi. Privileges to a nearby racquet and health club are available to guests for a small fee. 1,616 rooms, 29 story. Check-in 3 pm, check-out noon. Restaurant. Fitness room. Two outdoor pools, whirlpool. Tennis. Business center. **$**

★ ★ ★ **HOTEL LE CIRQUE.** *2 Lee Cir, New Orleans (70130). Phone 504/962-0900. www.hotellecirque. com.* A stylish and hip crowd checks into this chic hotel, thanks to its location in the oh-so-funky Arts and Warehouse District, home to many cutting-edge galleries, restaurants, and shops. You'll feel positively cosmopolitan in one of its smart-looking guest rooms, and you'll feel like a local when you dine in its Lee Circle Restaurant, which dishes up tasty French Creole cuisine. The hotel has one of the best locations for enjoying Mardi Gras festivities because more than 23 krewes parade right by its front doors. 137 rooms, 10 story. Check-out noon. Restaurant, bar. Fitness room. Airport transportation available. Business center. **$**

★ ★ ★ **HOTEL MONTELEONE.** *214 rue Royal, New Orleans (70130). Phone 504/523-3341; fax 504/528-1019. www.hotelmonteleone.com.* Since 1886, the French Quarter's oldest and largest hotel has been rolling out the red carpet for its guests, many of them celebrated authors, movie stars, royalty, and other notables. The guest rooms in this family-owned and - operated property are spacious and well appointed, as one would expect after seeing the elegant and ornate lobby, with its fluted columns, crystal chandeliers, and mural-painted ceilings. For decades, locals have favored the Monteleones Carousel Bar, where some seats revolve around the room (hence the watering holes name). After cocktails, take a seat inside the Hunt Room Grill for fine dining. For recreation, head up to the rooftop for a dip in the pool or a workout in the well-equipped fitness center, which offers splendid views of the French Quarter and the Mississippi River. The Spa Aria offers guests a variety of services to relax and rejuvenate. 570 rooms, 17 story. Check-in 3 pm, check-out noon. High-speed Internet access. Three restaurants, two bars. Fitness room, spa. Outdoor pool. Business center. **$$**
🏋 🛏 🚶

★ ★ ★ **INTERCONTINENTAL HOTEL NEW ORLEANS.** *444 St. Charles Ave, New Orleans (70130). Phone 504/525-5566; toll-free 800/445-6563; fax 504/523-7310. www.new-orleans.interconti.com.* With translation services available, a foreign currency exchange on the premises, a global newspaper service, and a staff that speaks 14 languages, the InterContinental Hotel New Orleans can't help but have a European flair. This large, modern hotel is a mecca for business travelers. Yet while the furnishings are modern and the business accoutrements are top-notch, so are the elements that bring pleasure to even have to travela terrific health club and a restaurant that serves lavish breakfast and lunch buffets, fine traditional New Orleans cuisine, and a traditional jazz Sunday brunch. 482 rooms, 15 story. Check-in 3 pm, check-out noon. Restaurant, bar. Fitness room. Outdoor pool. Airport transportation available. Business center. **$$$**
🏋 🛏 🚶

★ ★ ★ **INTERNATIONAL HOUSE.** *221 Camp St, New Orleans (70130). Phone 504/553-9550; toll-free 800/633-5770; fax 504/553-9560. www.ihhotel.com.* At this top-rated boutique hotel, the décor is a winning mix of New Orleans style and contemporary chic. The charming folk art and handmade furniture created by Louisiana artisans serve as a pleasant reminder you're in Cajun country, but the stainless steel and marble accents give the ritzy, intimate hotel a cosmopolitan feel. Get in touch with the spirits at Loa (the Voodoo word for deities), a dark bar lighted only by candles. And dine at Lemon Grass (see) for Vietnamese cuisine with some French touches. After drinks and dinner, could romance come next? At the International House, definitely. 119 rooms, 12 story. Check-in 4 pm, check-out noon. Fitnesss room. Restaurant, bar. Golf. **$$**
🏋 🛏

★ ★ ★ **LAFAYETTE HOTEL.** *600 St. Charles Ave, New Orleans (70130). Phone 504/524-4441; toll-free 888/524-4441; fax 504/523-7327. www.thelafayette-hotel.com.* In 1916, this small and luxurious hotel originally opened in the same Beaux Arts building in which it still pampers guests. Located on Lafayette Square in the Central Business District, it often hosts executives in town on business. Its old-world-style rooms and suites are individually decorated and come well appointed—many have French doors and wrought-iron balconies, and all have English botanical prints, overstuffed easy chairs, and marble bathrooms with French-milled soaps and thick terry bathrobes. Off its small but elegant lobby, guests can dine at Mike Ditka's, a gourmet steakhouse that also serves Creole and Cajun favorites. 44 rooms, 5 story. Check-in 4 pm, check-out 11 am. Restaurant, bar. **$**

★ ★ ★ **LE PAVILLON HOTEL.** *833 Poydras St, New Orleans (70112). Phone 504/581-3111; fax 504/620-4130.* This historic hotel has seen it all: wars, prohibition, and the birth of the horseless carriage. Through it all, it has kept its reputation as a Great Lady of New Orleans. In 1970, the Hotel Denechaud, as it was called, passed into new hands and was renamed Le Pavillon, receiving a facelift and some spectacular accoutrements: crystal chandeliers from Czechoslovakia, railings from the lobby of Paris's Grand Hotel, and fine art and antiques from around the world. The Crystal Suite contains a hand-carved marble bathtub, a gift from Napoleon to a wealthy Louisiana plantation ownerjust like the one in the Louvre. 226 rooms, 10 story. Check-in 3 pm, check-out noon. Restaurant, bar. Fitness room. Outdoor pool, whirlpool. Airport transportation available. This 90-year-old hotel is listed on the National Register of Historic Places. **$**
🏋 🛏

★ ★ ★ **LE RICHELIEU IN THE FRENCH QUARTER.** *1234 Chartres St, New Orleans (70116).*

Phone 504/529-2492; toll-free 800/535-9653; fax 504/524-8179. www.lerichelieuhotel.com. This family-owned hotel offers an amenity you won't find at any other hotel in the French Quarter: free self-parking. As good as that sounds, many guests keep coming back to this people-pleaser for other reasons as well including affordable rates; comfortable, homey rooms decorated in Creole style with mirrored walls and ceiling fans; a cozy bar and caf; and an attractive courtyard with a pool. All these pluses got the attention of ex-Beatle Paul McCartney, who checked in here for two months in the late 1970s while in town doing some recording work. A suite is now named after him. 86 rooms, 4 story. Check-in 3 pm, check-out 1 pm. Restaurant, bar. Outdoor pool. **$**

★ ★ ★ **OMNI ROYAL CRESCENT HOTEL.**
535 Gravier St, New Orleans (70130). Phone 504/527-0006; toll-free 800/578-3200; fax 504/571-7575. www.omniroyalcrescent.com. A first impression of the Omni Royal Crescent makes you want to straighten your posture: this is a place where the staff will allow no slouching, and you just don't want to. The lobby is an impeccable blend of modern and traditional, with shiny brass elevators, a concierge stand, and colorful fresh flowers, plus refined artwork and potted palms. Unusual in New Orleans, the Omni has a restaurant serving Thai food (with American food for breakfast). The comfortable guest rooms feature touches of wood and brass. 98 rooms, 8 story. Pets accepted; fee. Check-in 3 pm, check-out noon. Restaurant. Fitness room. Outdoor pool, whirlpool. **$**

★ ★ ★ **OMNI ROYAL ORLEANS.** *621 St. Louis St, New Orleans (70140). Phone 504/529-5333; fax 504/529-7089. www.omniroyalorleans.com.* For royal treatment in the French Quarter, settle into one of the many plush rooms at this luxury hotel, which has been pampering visitors to the city since 1960. In the comfort of your room, this chain property will spoil you with Irish linen sheets, marble baths, and windows overlooking all the action in the Quarter. Dine on steak and seafood in the award-winning Rib Room, a local favorite for decades; or refresh yourself with a mint julep or two at the Touche Bar or the Esplanade Lounge (in the lobby). Up on the rooftop, go for a relaxing swim in the pool, work up a sweat in the fitness center, or take in the sensational views. 346 rooms, 7 story. Pets accepted, some restrictions; fee. Check-in 4 pm, check-out noon. Restaurant, bar. Fitness room. Outdoor pool. Business center. **$$$**

★ ★ ★ **THE PONTCHARTRAIN HOTEL.** *2031 St. Charles Ave, New Orleans (70140). Phone 504/524-0581; fax 504/529-1165.* For more than 75 years, this *grande dame* has been mixing European elegance with Southern hospitality in the city's charming Garden District. In years gone by, dignitaries and celebrities frequently registered here, explaining why some of the suites bear the names of famous folks—Richard Burton, Joan Fontaine, and Mary Martin, among them. But these days, business travelers like to settle into its comfortable rooms, all of which are individually decorated with antiques and original art. At breakfast, lunch, or dinner, savor classic Creole and Cajun specialties at Lafittes Restaurant. If you start your morning there, you'll likely spot local politicos and civic leaders drinking café au lait and biting into beignets. After the workday, local professionals often wind down in the Bayou Bar. 104 rooms, 12 story. Pets accepted; fee. Check-in 3 pm, check-out noon. Restaurant, bar. Airport transportation available. **$**

★ ★ ★ **RENAISSANCE PERE MARQUETTE HOTEL.** *817 Common St, New Orleans (70112). Phone 504/525-1111; fax 504/525-0688. www.renaissancehotels.com.* Although its housed in a historic building, this hotel has a contemporary look that appeals to those who like modern, chic décor. Given its location in the Central Business District, the Renaissance attracts plenty of business travelers, especially since every room comes with high-speed Internet access, two-line phones with data ports, and work desks with lamps. But leisure travelers book its rooms, as well, because of its close proximity to some of the city's best shopping, restaurants, and attractions, including the French Quarter. Rene Bistrot serves award-winning French cuisine at affordable prices, so you'll be vying for a table with the locals who work downtown and know where to find the best deals. 275 rooms, 7 story. Check-in 3 pm, check-out noon. High-speed Internet access. Restaurant, bar. Fitness room. Outdoor pool, whirlpool. Business center. **$$**

★ ★ ★ **ROYAL SONESTA HOTEL NEW ORLEANS.** *300 Bourbon St, New Orleans (70130). Phone 504/586-0300; fax 504/586-0335. www.royalsonestano.com.* This cozy but elegant property occupies a full block right on Bourbon Street, and it looks like it belongs in this historic district. Gabled windows, French doors, wrought-iron lace balconies, and gilded mirrors add to the décor of this newer building designed to evoke the past. The furniture is reminiscent of 18th-century France, and the courtyards are tranquil and beautifully landscaped. If you crave a gourmet meal, sample the contemporary French and Creole cuisine served at Begues Restaurant (see). For something more casual, opt for the Desire Oyster Bar (see), where the chefs cook up both Creole and seafood dishes. Party at the Mystick Den cocktail lounge or the Can-Can Café and Jazz Club. If you just want to rest and relax, lounge out by the pool on an appealing third-floor terrace. 483 rooms, 7 story. Pets accepted, some restrictions; fee. Check-in 3 pm, check-out noon. High-speed Internet access. Two restaurants, two bars. Fitness room. Outdoor pool. Business center. Credit cards accepted. **$$**

★ ★ ★ **THE RITZ-CARLTON, NEW ORLEANS.** *921 Canal St, New Orleans (70112). Phone 504/524-1331; toll-free 800/241-3333; fax 504/524-7675. www. ritzcarlton.com.* The Ritz-Carlton transports visitors to 19th-century New Orleans with its French *savoir-faire* and gracious styling. On the edge of the French Quarter, this refined hotel is a delightful refuge in the vibrant Crescent City. The guest rooms have a timeless elegance. Feather beds and deep-soaking tubs add to the luxurious atmosphere. The bistro-style FQB is a casually elegant spot, while Victor's dazzles with its formal setting and refined cuisine. The exquisite lounge offers an unrivaled afternoon tea set to the gentle strains of a harp. Reviving many treatments favored by royals like Marie Antoinette and Princess Eugenie and incorporating the citrus scent created for Napoleon, the sensational spa is a celebration of all things French. 527 rooms, 14 story. Pets accepted, some restrictions; fee. Check-in 3 pm, check-out noon. Restaurant, bar. Fitness room, spa. Indoor pool, whirlpool. Airport transportation available. Business center. **$$**

★ ★ ★ **ST. JAMES HOTEL.** *330 Magazine St, New Orleans (70130). Phone 504/304-4000; toll-free 888/856-4485; fax 504/569-0640. www.saintjameshotel. com.* The St. James has the look of a distinguished older property because it occupies a renovated building that dates back to the 1850s. Business travelers like its downtown location in the Central Business District and the two-line phones in every room. The theme at this intimate boutique hotel is tropical, with a tropical fish tank in the lobby, rattan furniture, and palms. Rooftop terraces overlook a small pool in a charming courtyard. Cuvee restaurant (see) offers contempo-

rary Creole cuisine and more than 500 wine choices. 83 rooms, 3 story. Pets accepted; fee. Check-in 3 pm, check-out 11 am. Wireless Internet access. Restaurant, bar. Outdoor pool. Credit cards accepted. **$$**

★ ★ ★ **ST. LOUIS HOTEL.** *730 rue Bienville, New Orleans (70130). Phone 504/581-7300; toll-free 888/535-9111; fax 504/524-8925. www.stlouishotel.com.* Located in the French Quarter, this quaint hotel, with its pastel stucco exterior, is within walking distance to all area attractions. Guest rooms, traditionally furnished and good-sized, are centered around a large courtyard, lush with tropical greenery, banana trees, flowering plants, and a Baroque fountain. Fabulous French cuisine is featured in the Louis XVI Restaurant, a New Orleans tradition. At breakfast, however, the hotel serves Eggs Sardou and other local favorites in its courtyard. This tranquil oasis gives guests an opportunity to find serenity in the midst of the bustling French Quarter. 85 rooms, 5 story. Check-in 3 pm, check-out noon. Restaurant, bar. Credit cards accepted. **$**

★ ★ ★ **W NEW ORLEANS.** *333 Poydras St, New Orleans (70130). Phone 504/525-9444; toll-free 800/522-6963; fax 504/581-7179. www.whotels.com.* This style-soaked chain is designed for savvy business travelers, but even leisure guests won't mind the down comforters, Aveda products, and great fitness center. Near the convention center and many area restaurants, it is located in the Central Business District and adjacent to the French Quarter. The ultracontemporary space is decorated with chrome, mirrors, and a lipstick red accent wall—the overall effect is minimalist. Guest rooms are contemporary as well, with upscale bedding and large desks. Zoe Bistro offers creative French food, and the lobby's Whiskey Blue (see) bar delivers a dose of Randy Gerber-style nightlife. 423 rooms, 23 story. Pets accepted, some restrictions; fee. Check-in 3 pm, check-out noon. High-speed Internet access. Two restaurants, two bars. Fitness room. Outdoor pool. Business center. Credit cards accepted. **$$**

★ ★ ★ **WINDSOR COURT HOTEL.** *300 Gravier St, New Orleans (70130). Phone 504/523-6000; fax 504/596-4513. www.windsorcourthotel.com.* Not far from the French Quarter, in the city's Business District, the Windsor Court Hotel welcomes guests with open arms. Set around a courtyard, this elegant hotel brings a bit of the English countryside to New Orleans. Traditional English furnishings and unique artwork define the rooms, while bay windows focus attention on lovely views of the city or the Mississippi River. This full-service hotel also includes a pool, sundeck, and comprehensive business and fitness centers under its roof. In a city hailed for its works of culinary genius, the Windsor Court is no exception. The Grill Room (see) is one of the hottest tables in town; the Polo Club Lounge is ideal for enjoying brandy and cigars; and Le Salon is the in spot for afternoon tea. 324 rooms, 23 story. Pets accepted, some restrictions; fee. Check-in 3 pm, check-out noon. High-speed Internet access. Restaurant, bar. Fitness room. Outdoor pool. Business center. Credit cards accepted. **$$$**

★ ★ ★ **WYNDHAM NEW ORLEANS AT CANAL PLACE.** *100 rue Iberville, New Orleans (70130). Phone 504/566-7006; fax 504/553-5133. www.wyndham.com.* Its downtown location isn't the only reason business travelers give this upscale hotel a thumbs up. They also like the oversized guest rooms and the worker-friendly amenities in them, including direct high-speed Internet access, ergonomic work chairs, and cordless telephones. But the Wyndham also appeals to leisure travelers since its convenient to most of the city's main attractions. In fact, it's in the Canal Place Tower, home to the Shops at Canal Place, where visitors (and locals) like to go on buying sprees in the many top-name stores, such as Saks Fifth Avenue. Everyone who beds down here appreciates the stellar views of the city from both the marble-adorned lobby (on the towers 11th floor) and the rooms that rise above it. For the hungry, the Wyndham dishes up American cuisine with a Louisiana twist in the Riverbend Grill. 438 rooms, 18 story. Check-in 3 pm, check-out noon. Restaurant, bar. Fitness room. Outdoor pool. Business center. **$$$**

★ ★ ★ **WYNDHAM WHITNEY HOTEL.** *610 Poydras St, New Orleans (70130). Phone 504/581-4222; fax 504/207-0101. www.wyndham.com.* The fact that this building used to be a branch of the Whitney National Bank is what puts the fun in functional. Take some time to check out the private dining room, once the banks vault; the grand public dining room, once the actual bank space; the impossibly thick doors, which once kept out bank robbers; and the intricate old plasterwork in the public spaces. The atmosphere makes it easy to understand what it all must have been like, although your imagination is helped by the hotels location—right next to the US federal buildings. 293 rooms, 7 story. Check-in 3 pm, check-out noon. Restaurant, bar. Fitness room. Business center. **$**

Full-Service Inns

★ ★ ★ **HOUSE ON BAYOU ROAD.** *2275 Bayou Rd, New Orleans (70119). Phone 504/945-0992; toll-free 800/882-2968; fax 504/945-0993. www.houseonbayouroad.com.* Experience old New Orleans at this converted plantation home, offering 2 acres of gardens, ponds, and patios, as well as a plantation-style breakfast. 9 rooms, 2 story. Children over 12 years only. Complimentary full breakfast. Check-in 3 pm, check-out noon. Restaurant. Outdoor pool, whirlpool. Indigo plantation house built in 1798; antiques. **$**

★ ★ ★ **LAFITTE GUEST HOUSE.** *1003 Bourbon St, New Orleans (70116). Phone 504/581-2678; toll-free 800/331-7971; fax 504/581-2677. www.lafitteguesthouse.com.* If you want to feel like you're staying with friends in the mid-19th century, this three-story bed-and-breakfast will do the trick. At this guest house-cum-small inn—there is a concierge to attend to your needs—you'll receive the type of warm welcome that only a guest house can truly provide. One can just imagine a proper cup of tea while sitting in the 1849 Victorian ground-floor sitting room, a fire crackling, couches and chairs adorning an Oriental rug. Most of the guest rooms have private balconies with views of what makes New Orleans New Orleans—Bourbon Street or the French Quarter. 14 rooms, 4 story. Complimentary continental breakfast. Check-in 2 pm, check-out noon. **$**

★ ★ ★ **MELROSE MANSION.** *937 Esplanade Ave, New Orleans (70116). Phone 504/944-2255; toll-free 800/650-3323; fax 504/945-1794. www.melrose-group.com.* The Melrose Mansion, overlooking the French Quarter, was built in 1884 and purchased a few years later by a New Orleans nightclub owner as a home for the girls in his conga line. Conga girls don't live there anymore, but those who love the atmosphere in which they did can, at least for a night or two. Approaching the front door of a brick welcome path, you'll walk past a wrought-iron gate and ascend the grand staircase to your suite (the suites have names like Prince Edward and Miss Kitty). You'll descend the next morning for fresh-baked pastries and hazelnut coffeetaken in the parlor, of course. 8 rooms, 2 story. Complimentary continental breakfast. Check-in 3 pm, check-out noon. Outdoor pool. **$$**

★ ★ ★ **SONIAT HOUSE HOTEL.** *1133 Chartres St, New Orleans (70116). Phone 504/522-0570; toll-free 800/544-8808; fax 504/522-7208. www.soniathouse.*

com. Don't let its location in the bustling French Quarter fool you. The quiet and intimate Soniat House offers an elegant respite from all the revelry out on the streets of this boisterous entertainment district. Its cozy rooms are housed in three Creole-style town houses dating back to the early 1800s, and they're tastefully decorated with English, French, and Louisiana antiques. What the property lacks in amenities—no pool, restaurant, or fitness center—it more than makes up for with all its charm and the superior service of its friendly, attentive staff. 33 rooms, 3 story. Children over 12 years only. Check-in 3 pm, check-out noon. **$$**

Specialty Lodgings

CHIMES BED & BREAKFAST. *1146 Constantinople St, New Orleans (70115). Phone 504/342-4861; toll-free 800/729-4640; fax 504/488-4639. www. historiclodging.com/chimes.* Jill and Charles Abbyad were pioneers in 1987 when they opened a B&B in the servants' quarters behind their charming Victorian home near the French Quarter. The bed-and-breakfast craze had not yet caught on in this city of historic hotels. They are warm, inviting hosts, offering both comfort and good cheer to their guests. Breakfast is served in the main house along with knowledgeable advice on where to go and what to do in the city the owners know so well. 5 rooms. Pets accepted, some restrictions; fee. Complimentary full breakfast. **$**

HISTORIC FRENCH MARKET INN. *501 rue Decatur, New Orleans (70130). Phone 504/561-5621; toll-free 888/256-9970; fax 504/566-0160. www.neworleansfinehotels.com.* Built in the 1800s for the fabulously wealthy Baron Joseph Xavier de Pontalba, the Historic French Market Inn was the official government house when Louisiana was still a French colony. The atmosphere has changed since the baron shot his daughter-in-law and then turned the gun on himself: today, the original 19th-century brick walls, elegant brass beds, and lush courtyard speak of romance. The wrought-iron gates guarding the entrance whisper of a different pace; a grand staircase sweeps from the ground floor rotunda to the second-floor lobby, and antique period pieces convey two centuries of New Orleans history. 108 rooms, 4 story. Complimentary continental breakfast. Check-out 11 am. Bar. Outdoor pool. **$**

Spa

★ ★ ★ THE SPA AT THE RITZ-CARLTON, NEW ORLEANS. *921 Canal St, New Orleans (70112). Phone 504/670-2929; toll-free 800/241-3333. www.ritzcarlton.com.* Soft lighting, gleaming marble, brass chandeliers, and gentle colors set a regal tone for The Spa at The Ritz-Carlton, New Orleans. This tranquil spa lets you relax and indulge like the royals once did with a treatment menu inspired in part by favorite practices of French aristocrats. From the four-hands massage that Marie Antoinette adored to the citrus scent that Napoleon once wore, this spa takes you on a fascinating journey, enabling you to unwind in splendor. Your body is primped and pampered in style here, whether you opt for a massage, a hydrotherapy soak, or a body treatment. The Napoleon royal massage is a spa signature that includes a heavenly citrus-scented bath prior to a lemon verbena-scented Swedish massage. Hydrotherapy soaks include therapeutic, couples, and even color therapy-themed baths. The body treatments are superb, and the spa's signature magnolia sugar scrub gently exfoliates and polishes your skin while the heady scent of Louisiana's luscious magnolias blended with botanical extracts envelops you. The magie violete therapy uses marine clay with lemon, lavender, pine, cinnamon, cypress, sweet marjoram, and ylang ylang essential oils and offers an innovative approach to the body wrap without the actual wrapping. In the magie noire treatment, moor mud draws out the skin's impurities and is followed by an exfoliating massage and a refreshing Vichy shower. Whether you want to add a glow to your skin with a body bronzing treatment or to banish unwanted cellulite with a body contour treatment, this spa satisfies all requests, while manicures, pedicures, and hair care services ensure that you leave looking your best. A delightful café invites you to linger before or after a treatment and is a lovely spot to enjoy salads, sandwiches, and light dishes that please your palate without adding to your waistline. The spa's well-stocked gift shop warrants some retail therapy; the magnolia-scented signature products are wonderful reminders of this sweet Southern getaway.

Restaurants

★ ★ **ALLEGRO BISTRO.** *1100 Poydras, New Orleans (70163). Phone 504/582-2350; fax 504/582-2351.* American menu. Lunch. Closed Sat-Sun; one week in July; also Mardi Gras, holidays. Bar. Business casual attire. Reservations recommended. Outdoor seating. **$$**

★ ★ ANDREW JAEGER'S HOUSE OF SEAFOOD. *300 Decatur St, New Orleans (70130). Phone 504/581-2534; fax 504/581-9314. www.andrewjaegers. com.* Creole, seafood menu. Dinner. Closed Thanksgiving, Dec 25. Bar. Casual attire. Reservations recommended. Three distinct levels of dining in an 1832 Creole cottage. **$$**

★ ★ ★ ANTOINE'S. *713 rue St. Louis, New Orleans (70130). Phone 504/581-4422; fax 504/581-3003. www. antoines.com.* A fixture since 1840, this Creole/classic French dining spot still exudes quality fare. It is in the French Quarter, just a short distance from Bourbon Street. The locals know which entrées are the best— the filet and any oyster dish—Rockefeller, Bienville, and Foch included. Creole menu. Lunch, dinner, Sun brunch; holidays. Bar. Jacket required. Reservations recommended. **$$$**

★ ★ ★ ARNAUD'S. *813 rue Bienville, New Orleans (70112). Phone 504/523-5433; toll-free 866/230-8891; fax 504/581-7908. www.arnauds.com.* In the French Quarter near Bourbon Street, this exquisite restaurant heaps refined service on diners. Partake of the trout meuiere and shrimp remoulade. A wonderful romantic atmosphere prevails. French, Creole menu. Dinner, Sun brunch. Closed Dec 25. Bar. Jacket required. Built in 1790 and opened in 1918, it has been restored to its original design. **$$$**

★ ★ ★ BACCO. *310 Chartres St, New Orleans (70130). Phone 504/522-2426; fax 504/521-8323. www. bacco.com.* A member of the Brennan family, located at the W Hotel in the French Quarter (see), this romantic Creole/Italian restaurant fuses local products with traditional Italian recipes. Guests can even pick up some Italian; they play tapes in the rest rooms. Italian menu. Lunch, dinner. Closed Mardi Gras, Dec 24-25. Bar. Children's menu. Business casual attire. Reservations recommended. Valet parking. **$$$**

★ ★ ★ BAYONA. *430 Dauphine St, New Orleans (70112). Phone 504/525-4455; fax 504/522-0589. www. bayona.com.* A little slice of the romantic Mediterranean awaits you at Bayona, a jewel of a restaurant tucked into a 200-year-old Creole cottage, in the heart of the French Quarter. The warm, cozy room is often set with fresh flowers and is warmed by sunny lighting and bright colors. Settle in and get ready for chef Susan Spicers terrific interpretation of New Orleans cuisine, blending the ingredients of the Mediterranean with the flavors of Alsace, Asia, India, and the Southwest. Spicer is indeed a talented chef, capable of surprising her loyal fans by successfully combin-

ing textures and spices that have never before met on a plate. To match the exquisite fare, you'll find an outstanding waitstaff eager to guide you and answer questions about the menu. A great selection of beers, including several local brews, plus an extensive wine list, make it difficult to choose a beverage to accompany dinner, so you may just have to come back a few times. International menu. Lunch, dinner. Closed Sun-Mon; Jan 1, Mardi Gras, Dec 25. Business casual attire. Reservations recommended. Outdoor seating. Credit cards accepted. **$$$**

★ ★ ★ BEGUE'S. *300 Bourbon St, New Orleans (70140). Phone 504/586-0300. www.sonesta.com/begues.* This elegant French Quarter restaurant is located in the Royal Sonesta Hotel (see). Meals are served in a serene, airy atmosphere overlooking a tropical courtyard filled with orange trees and a fountain. The specialty here is Creole cuisine, prepared beautifully, and an all-you-can-eat Sunday brunch (with live piano music) that makes you wonder if there are any crawfish or snapper left in any other part of the world. Creole, French menu. Breakfast, lunch, dinner, Sun brunch. Casual attire. Reservations recommended. Valet parking. Credit cards accepted. **$$$**

★ ★ ★ BELLA LUNA. *914 N Peters St, New Orleans (70116). Phone 504/529-1583; fax 504/522-4858. www.bellalunarestaurant.com.* Guests get a choice of two views, the French Quarter on one side and a great romantic view of the Mississippi River on the other side. The cuisine is mostly American, with a spicy Creole flavor. Local favorites are the pecan-crusted pork chops, battered soft shell crabs, and the giant stuffed gulf shrimp. Cajun/Creole, Mediterranean menu. Dinner. Closed Dec 25, Mardi Gras. Bar. Valet parking. **$$$**

★ ★ BISTRO AT MAISON DE VILLE. *733 Toulouse St, New Orleans (70130). Phone 504/528-9206; toll-free 800/634-1600; fax 504/528-9939. www. maisondeville.com.* This intimate restaurant in an 18th-century house is steps from Bourbon Street. The lustrous mahogany and soft lighting relax guests prior to a fine dining experience. There are stylish, flavorful Creole and American creations like grilled salmon with pecan-flavored wild rice, and saffron-sage broth with quail ravioli. Patio dining is also available, weather permitting. Creole menu. Lunch, dinner. Closed first week in Aug. Bar. Business casual attire. Reservations recommended. Outdoor seating. **$$$**

★ ★ **BON TON CAFE.** *401 Magazine St, New Orleans (70130). Phone 504/524-3386; toll-free 888/524-5611.* Cajun menu. Lunch, dinner. Closed Sat-Sun; holidays. Bar. Children's menu. Business casual attire. Reservations recommended. Wrought-iron chandelier, shuttered windows, wildlife prints on exposed brick walls. **$$**

★ ★ ★ **BRENNAN'S.** *417 Royal St, New Orleans (70130). Phone 504/525-9711; fax 504/525-2302. www. brennansneworleans.com.* Breakfast is king at this sister restaurant to Commander's Palace (see) in the heart of the French Quarter, but guests will enjoy the classic upscale Creole cuisine at any meal of the day. Dine in the courtyard on the decadent egg dishes. French, Creole menu. Breakfast, lunch, dinner, brunch. Closed Tues-Wed; Dec 24-25. Bar. Children's menu. Business casual attire. Reservations recommended. **$$$**

★ ★ ★ **BRIGTSEN'S.** *723 Dante St, New Orleans (70118). Phone 504/861-7610; fax 504/866-7397. www. brigtsens.com.* Frank Brigsten is the chef/owner of this delightful Uptown spot with excellent food and even better service. It is a local favorite and offers Cajun/Creole dishes, with specialties of the house including blackened tuna and roast duck. Creole menu. Dinner. Closed Sun-Mon; holidays. In a restored 1900s house built from river barge timbers. Reservations recommended. **$$**

★ ★ ★ **BROUSSARD'S.** *819 Conti St, New Orleans (70112). Phone 504/581-3866; fax 504/581-3873. www.broussards.com.* This award-winning restaurant has been family-owned for 75 years, albeit by different families. The current owners run things with as much loving care and attention to detail as the Broussards did in the early 1800s, with wife Evelyn tending to personal touches—impeccable table settings, romantic candles, courtyard greenery, and blooming flowers. Her husband, classically French-trained chef Gunter, prepares unmatched Creole fantasies; try the lump crab in ravigote sauce with shrimp rémoulade and house-cured salmon; or grilled pompano on puff pastry accompanied by shrimp, scallops, and mustard-caper sauce. Wine aficionados: prepare for the 20-page wine list. French menu. Dinner. Closed Dec 25. Bar. Reservations recommended. Outdoor seating. **$$$**

★ **CAFE DE MELLO.** *81 French Market Pl, New Orleans. Phone 504/522-3121.* French menu. Breakfast, lunch, dinner. Closed holidays. Casual attire. Outdoor seating. **$**

★ **CAFE DU MONDE.** *800 Decatur St, New Orleans (70116). Phone 504/525-4544; toll-free 800/772-2927; fax 504/587-0847. www.cafedumonde.com.* The appeal of fried dough blanketed in powdered sugar cannot be understood or underestimated. The Café du Monde is world famous for its beignets, as well as for its roasted chicory-and-coffee combinations. The original café is located on the edge of the French Quarter and provides a perfect place to stop in for a sweet treat between bouts of shopping at the adjacent French Market or before or after whooping it up in the Quarter. French menu. Breakfast, late-night. Closed Dec 25. Casual attire. Outdoor seating. No credit cards accepted. **$**

★ ★ **CAFE GIOVANNI.** *117 rue Decatur, New Orleans (70130). Phone 504/529-2154; fax 504/529-3352. www.cafegiovanni.com.* Creole, Italian menu. Dinner. Closed Sun-Mon; holidays; Mardi Gras. Bar. Business casual attire. Reservations recommended. **$$** ▣

★ **CAFE PONTALBA.** *546 St. Peter St, New Orleans (70116). Phone 504/522-1180; fax 504/522-1186.* Cajun, Creole menu. Lunch, dinner. Closed Dec 25. Bar. **$$** ▣

★ ★ **CAFE VOLAGE.** *720 Dublin St, New Orleans (70118). Phone 504/861-4227; fax 504/861-4207.* French, Mediterranean menu. Lunch, dinner, Sun brunch. Closed holidays; Mardi Gras. Children's menu. This restaurant comprised of two intimate dining areas in an 1800s Victorian cottage. Outdoor seating. **$$** ▣

★ **CENTRAL GROCERY.** *923 Decatur St, New Orleans (70116). Phone 504/523-1620; toll-free 866/620-0174; fax 504/523-1670.* Italian menu. Lunch. Closed holidays. Casual attire. **$** ▣

★ ★ ★ **COMMANDER'S PALACE.** *1403 Washington Ave, New Orleans (70130). Phone 504/899-8221; fax 504/891-3242. www.commanderspalace. com.* In the center of the Garden District stands this turquoise and white Victorian monument to Creole cuisine. The famed Brennan family has presided over the dining room since 1974, but Emile Commander originally founded it in 1880 as a fine restaurant for distinguished neighborhood families. The lush garden setting hosts live Dixieland music for the lively Saturday and Sunday jazz brunches. Creole menu. Lunch, dinner, brunch. Closed Mardi Gras, Dec 25. Bar. Business casual attire. Reservations recommended. Valet parking. Outdoor seating. **$$$**

★ ★ **COURT OF TWO SISTERS.** *613 Royal St, New Orleans (70130). Phone 504/522-7261; fax*

504/581-5804. *www.courtoftwosisters.com.* Creole menu. Breakfast, lunch, dinner, brunch. Closed Dec 25. Bar. Children's menu. Casual attire. Reservations recommended. Outdoor seating. Built in 1832 with a spacious patio and courtyard. **$$**

★ ★ **CRESCENT CITY BREWHOUSE.** *527 Decatur St, New Orleans (70130). Phone 504/522-0571; toll-free 888/819-9330; fax 504/522-0577. www.crescentcitybrewhouse.com.* American, Cajun/Creole menu. Lunch, dinner. Closed Thanksgiving, Dec 25. Bar. Children's menu. Casual attire. Outdoor seating. **$$**

★ ★ ★ **CUVEE.** *322 Magazine St, New Orleans (70130). Phone 504/587-9001; fax 504/587-9006. www.restaurantcuvee.com.* Excellent advice on wine and food pairings is just one of the highlights of this New Orleans bright star. Opened in 1999 and considered an upstart in this city of decades-old dining establishments, Cuvee nevertheless has gained a reputation as one of New Orleans's finest gourmet restaurants. Housed in a landmark 1833 building in the heart of the Central Business District, the restaurant is intimate, with just 85 seats, and features a stylish, understated décor. The nouveau New Orleans cuisine includes dishes such as sugar cane-smoked duck breast and crispy confit leg served with Hudson Valley foie gras and Roquefort-pecan risotto. Cajun/Creole menu. Dinner. Closed Sun. Bar. Business casual attire. Reservations recommended. Credit cards accepted. **$$$**
🅳

★ ★ **DESIRE OYSTER BAR.** *300 Bourbon St, New Orleans (70140). Phone 504/586-0300; fax 504/586-0335.* American, Creole, seafood menu. Lunch, dinner. Bar. Children's menu. Casual attire. **$$**

★ ★ ★ **DOMINQUE'S.** *1001 rue Toulouse St, New Orleans (70112). Phone 504/586-8000; fax 504/525-5334. www.dominiquesrestaurant.com.* This French Quarter location in the beautiful Maison Dupuy Hotel (see) features the innovative cuisine of chef Dominique Macquet. Ingredients are always the freshest available, and the breads and pastries are baked on the premises. French menu. Dinner. Bar. Children's menu. Business casual attire. Reservations recommended. Valet parking. Outdoor seating. **$$$**

★ ★ **DOOKY CHASE.** *2301 Orleans Ave, New Orleans (70119). Phone 504/821-0600; fax 504/821-0600.* Creole menu. Lunch, dinner. Closed Dec 25. Bar. **$$**

★ ★ ★ ★ **EMERIL'S RESTAURANT.** *800 Tchoupitoulas St, New Orleans (70130). Phone 504/528-9393; toll-free 800/980-8474; fax 504/558-3925. www.emerils.com.* Emeril's is a chic and stylish hot spot located in the Central Business District. With lofty ceilings, an open kitchen, custom-made cast metal door handles, and a towering wooden wine wall, the restaurant is a dynamic space that suits its urban Warehouse District neighborhood. The slick food bar is a fun spot to take in the buzzing see-and-be-seen crowd. If you are looking for intimacy and romance, this is not the place. The room can get loud, but like a ride on a roller coaster, its a great rush. The French Creole-meets-the-Southwest-meets-Emeril menu liberally employs a world of herbs, spices, and chiles that awaken the palate with a wonderful jolt. Emeril's trademarks include barbecued shrimp served over flaky, rosemary-scented buttermilk biscuits and a tamarind-glazed double-cut Niman ranch pork chop with green chili mole and roasted sweet potatoes. Cajun/Creole menu. Dinner. Closed Sun. Bar. Business casual attire. Reservations recommended. Valet parking. Credit cards accepted. **$$$**

★ ★ **FEELINGS CAFE.** *2600 Chartres St, New Orleans (70117). Phone 504/945-2222; fax 504/945-7019. www.feelingscafe.com.* Creole menu. Lunch, dinner, Sun brunch. Closed Thanksgiving, Dec 25; Mardi Gras. Located in an outbuilding of an 18th-century plantation, this restaurant features antiques and original artwork. Outdoor seating. **$$**

★ ★ **FIVE HAPPINESS.** *3605 S Carrollton Ave, New Orleans (70118). Phone 504/482-3935; fax 504/486-0743. www.fivehappiness.com.* Chinese menu. Lunch, dinner. Closed Thanksgiving. Bar. Casual attire. **$**

★ **FRENCH MARKET.** *1001 Decatur St, New Orleans (70116). Phone 504/525-7879; fax 504/568-1522.* Cajun/Creole, French menu. Lunch, dinner. Closed Good Friday, Thanksgiving, Dec 25. Bar. Children's menu. Casual attire. Outdoor seating. **$$**

★ ★ ★ **GABRIELLE.** *438 Henry Clay Ave, New Orleans (70119). Phone 504/948-6233; fax 504/949-7459. www.gabriellerestaurant.com.* This is a place where locals go or used to, when they could get in. Tourists have discovered it, and Gabrielle's popularity has overtaken its 62 seats (which, divided between two dining rooms, make this a wonderfully cozy dining experience). The menu is contemporary Creole, lighter than what many think of as traditional New Orleans cooking. Entrées include Creole cream cheese-crusted lamb chops and a very un-Creole dish of chicken served with tomatoes, provolone, and mixed greens with balsamic vinaigrette. Creole menu. Lunch, dinner. Closed Sun-Mon; holidays; Mardi Gras. Bar. Outdoor seating. **$$$**

★ ★ ★ **GALATOIRE'S.** *209 Bourbon St, New Orleans (70130). Phone 504/525-2021; fax 504/525-5900.* Jean Galatoire, a Frenchman from the foothills of the Pyrenees, founded this landmark French Quarter restaurant in 1905. To this day, it continues on in the hands of his descendants. Cajun/Creole menu. Lunch, dinner. Closed Mon; holidays; also Mardi Gras, week of July 4. Bar. Jacket required. Reservations recommended. **$$$**

★ ★ ★ **GAUTREAU'S.** *1728 Soniat St, New Orleans (70115). Phone 504/899-7397; fax 504/899-0154. www.gautreaus.net.* This quintessential neighborhood bistro in Uptown is in an old pharmacy, with an antique apothecary serving as a liquor cabinet and embossed tin ceilings. Chef John Harris lends his classical French-trained style to a Creole-influenced menu. American, seafood menu. Dinner. Closed Sun; holidays. From the early 1900s. Valet parking. **$$$**

★ ★ **GUMBO SHOP.** *630 St. Peter St, New Orleans (70116). Phone 504/525-1486; fax 504/524-0747. www.gumboshop.com.* Creole, seafood menu. Lunch, dinner. **$$**
🅳

★ ★ **K-PAUL'S LOUISIANA KITCHEN.** *416 Chartres St, New Orleans (70130). Phone 504/524-7394; fax 504/596-2540. www.chefpaul.com.* Cajun/Creole menu. Lunch, dinner. Closed Sun; Jan 1, Mardi Gras, Dec 24-25. Bar. Business casual attire. Reservations recommended. Outdoor seating. **$$$**

★ ★ **LA MADELEINE.** *601 S Carollton, New Orleans (70116). Phone 504/861-8662; fax 504/525-1680. www.lamadeleine.com.* French menu. Breakfast, lunch, dinner. Closed Dec 25. Children's menu. Casual attire. Outdoor seating. **$**

★ **LUCY'S RETIRED SURFERS BAR & RESTAURANT.** *701 Tchoupitoulas St, New Orleans (70130). Phone 504/523-8995; fax 504/523-9198. www.lucysretiredsurfers.com.* Mexican, California menu. Lunch, dinner, late-night, brunch. Closed holidays. Bar. Children's menu. Casual attire. Outdoor seating. **$**

★ ★ ★ **MARTINIQUE.** *5908 Magazine St, New Orleans (70115). Phone 504/891-8495; fax 504/862-8549.* French menu. Lunch, dinner, Sun brunch. Closed Jan 1, Dec 25. Outdoor seating. **$$**

★ **MICHAUL'S.** *840 St. Charles Ave, New Orleans (70130). Phone 504/522-5517; toll-free 800/563-4055; fax 504/529-2541. www.michauls.com.* Cajun menu. Dinner. Closed Sun; Easter, Thanksgiving, Dec 25; also Aug. Bar. Children's menu. Casual attire. Reservations recommended. **$$**

★ **MOTHER'S RESTAURANT.** *401 Poydras St, New Orleans (70130). Phone 504/523-9656; fax 504/525-7671. www.mothersrestaurant.net.* Creole menu. Breakfast, lunch, dinner. Bar. Casual attire, casual attire. Cafeteria-style service. Former residence (1830); extensive collection of US Marine memorabilia. **$**

★ ★ ★ **MR B'S BISTRO.** *201 Royal St, New Orleans (70130). Phone 504/523-2078; fax 504/521-8304. www.mrbsbistro.com.* This famous Brennan family institution in the French Quarter offers Creole cuisine specializing in local and organically grown products. It is the power lunch spot in the French Quarter and is very popular among locals and tourists alike for dinner. Creole menu. Lunch, dinner. Closed Mardi Gras, Dec 24-25. Bar. Business casual attire. Reservations recommended. Valet parking. **$$$**

★ ★ ★ ★ **THE NEW ORLEANS GRILL.** *300 Gravier St, New Orleans (70130). Phone 504/522-1994; toll-free 888/596-0955; fax 504/596-4649. www.windsorcourthotel.com.* Dining at The New Orleans Grill (located inside the Windsor Court Hotel) may be one of the most luxurious ways to spend an evening in New Orleans. With a menu that changes monthly and features locally grown and organic foods whenever possible, The New Orleans Grill is known for its fabulous contemporary American cuisine. The kitchen's robust and inventive brand of cuisine—jazzed up with a bold mixture of Creole and Southern style is complemented by one of the finest wine cellars in the city. And the restaurant's lounge, the Polo Room, offers live music on Friday nights. The room is lavishly appointed with cushy, nap-worthy armchairs and banquettes, brocade drapes, and suntan-glow lighting. Add to the serene surroundings the extreme pampering the warm and attentive staff will treat you to, and you'll come to realize that The New Orleans Grill experience is nothing short of marvelous. French-influenced menu. Breakfast, lunch, dinner. Bar. Children's menu. Jacket required. Reservations recommended. Valet parking. Credit cards accepted. **$$$**

★ ★ ★ **NOLA.** *534 St. Louis Street, New Orleans (70130). Phone 504/522-6652; fax 504/524-6178. www. emerils.com.* As the most accessible of Emeril's restaurants, the innovative cuisine at this French Quarter location complements the unique Art Deco ambience. Efficient service and elegant presentations bring life to the "Bam!" Creole menu. Lunch, dinner. Closed Mardi Gras, Thanksgiving, Dec 24-25. Bar. Casual attire. Reservations recommended. **$$$**

★ ★ ★ **PALACE CAFE.** *605 Canal St, New Orleans (70130). Phone 504/523-1661. www.palacecafe.com.* Crabmeat cheesecake, anyone? Both contemporary and classic Creole seafood dishes are available at this upscale, lively café on historic Canal Street. Owned by Dickie Brennan of the famous restaurant family, Palace Cafés signature dishes include a creamy oyster pan roast and white chocolate bread pudding. If you can't bear to leave said bread pudding, fear not: that, plus 169 other Palace Café recipes, are available in *The Flavor of New Orleans Palace Café* cookbook, available for purchase. What must be experienced in person, however, is the popular Sunday brunch with live blues music. Cajun/Creole menu. Lunch, dinner, Sun brunch. Closed Mardi Gras, Dec 24-25. Bar. Children's menu. Casual attire. **$$**

★ ★ ★ **PELICAN CLUB.** *312 Exchange Alley, New Orleans (70130). Phone 504/523-1504; fax 504/522-2331. www.pelicanclub.com.* For fine dining in the French Quarter, look no further than this restaurant tucked away in a converted townhouse in charming Exchange Alley. Excellent cuisine and professional service make for an enjoyable dining experience. International menu. Dinner. Closed holidays; Mardi Gras. Bar. **$$$**

★ ★ ★ **PERISTYLE.** *1041 Dumaine St, New Orleans (70116). Phone 504/593-9535; fax 504/529-6942.* A fire in 1999 was the catalyst for the present look of this two-story 19th-century French Quarter building, once a family-owned oyster house near the red light district. A basement office was converted into a wine cellar with something to complement every dish on the decidedly French menu, with items like lassiette du charcutier and rosemary lamb loin chop with red onion marmalade and pine nut-sultana red wine reduction. Also on the menu: a touch of romance, with antique-framed mirrors on the walls, a polished copper-topped bar, fresh flowers, and a row of hopper-transom windows above the bars banquette. French menu. Dinner. Closed Sun-Mon; holidays. Bar. Reservations recommended. Free valet parking. **$$$**

★ **PRALINE CONNECTION.** *542 Frenchmen St, New Orleans (70116). Phone 504/943-3934; fax 504/943-7903. www.pralineconnection.com.* Creole menu. Lunch, dinner. Closed Dec 25. Bar. Children's menu. **$$**

★ ★ **RED FISH GRILL.** *115 Bourbon St, New Orleans (70130). Phone 504/598-1200; fax 504/598-1211. www.redfishgrill.com.* Seafood menu. Lunch, dinner. Closed Mardi Gras, Dec 24-25. Bar. Children's menu. Casual attire. In a converted department store. **$$$**

★ ★ ★ **RESTAURANT AUGUST.** *301 Tchoupitoulas St, New Orleans (70130). Phone 504/299-9777; fax 504/299-1199. www.rest-august.com.* The instant you walk into Restaurant Augusta—a beautiful place set in an 18th-century townhouse in New Orleans historic Warehouse District—you feel at ease. The host, who greets you at the door, smiles and welcomes you heartily, then escorts you to your table set in a warm, exposed-brick room with vaulted ceilings, old-world antiques, and floral arrangements. Chef Jon Besh does a wonderful job creating an innovative and delicious menu of dishes that marry robust ingredients from Spain and France with regional flavors. His menu changes seasonally, but two flawless signatures are the Moroccan-spiced duck with polenta and tempura dates and the BLT, made from fat, meaty fried Buster crabs (the owners uncle farms them), lettuce, and heirloom tomatoes on a slab of brioche. You'll leave warm, full, and very happy indeed. American, French menu. Lunch, dinner. Closed Sun-Mon. Bar. Business casual attire. Reservations recommended. Credit cards accepted. **$$$**

★ **SNUG HARBOR JAZZ BISTRO.** *626 Frenchmen St, New Orleans (70116). Phone 504/949-0696. www.snugjazz.com.* Seafood, steak menu. Dinner. Closed Dec 25. Bar. **$$**

★ ★ **TONY MORAN'S.** *240 Bourbon St, New Orleans (70130). Phone 504/523-4640; fax 504/524-0146. www.tonymorans.com.* Italian menu. Dinner. Closed Mardi Gras. Bar. Children's menu. Casual attire. Reservations recommended. Outdoor seating. **$$$**
🄳

★ ★ **TUJAGUE'S.** *823 Decatur St, New Orleans (70116). Phone 504/525-8676; fax 504/525-8785. www. tujagues.com.* This restaurant opened its doors before New Orleans had a name. Back then, it was a Spanish armory. Today, it's the second-oldest restaurant in New Orleans, boasts the city's first stand-up bar, and has a mirror over the bar that's been there for more than 150 years. The restaurant has a decidedly 19th-century atmosphere. Located in the middle of the French Quarter, facing the historic French Market, Tujagues (pronounced two Jacks) plays to repeat customers—no menu, six courses (five plus coffee), and you take whatever entrée they give you. Creole menu. Lunch, dinner. Bar. Children's menu. Casual attire. Reservations recommended. **$$**

★ ★ ★ **UPPERLINE.** *1413 Upperline St, New Orleans (70115). Phone 504/891-9822. www.upperline. com.* The gracious service and excellent Creole food make this neighborhood restaurant in Uptown a local favorite. Cajun/Creole menu. Dinner. Closed Mon-Tues; Mardi Gras, July 4, Thanksgiving, Dec 25. Bar. Children's menu. **$$**

★ ★ ★ **VERANDA.** *444 St. Charles Ave, New Orleans (70130). Phone 504/525-5566; fax 504/585-4377.* Situated on the second floor of the InterContinental Hotel New Orleans (see), opening onto the hotel's enormous faux-streetlamp-lined atrium, Veranda is an open, airy, delightful arena for a calming meal. Regional fare is the ticket here; Cajun, gumbo, crawfish, and other New Orleans cuisine is done up in imaginative ways, but Veranda is known primarily for its lavish breakfast and lunch buffets. And the Sunday champagne jazz brunch draws both locals and visitors from throughout the city. American, Creole menu. Breakfast, lunch, dinner, Sun brunch. Bar. Children's menu. Reservations recommended. Valet parking. Outdoor seating. **$$**

Opelousas (D-3)

See also Covington, Slidell

Founded circa 1720
Population 22,860
Elevation 70 ft
Area Code 337
Information Tourist Information Center, 828 E Landry, phone 337/948-6263 or toll-free 800/424-5442; or contact the Tourism & Activities Committee, 441 E Grolee, PO Box 712; phone 337/948-4731
Web Site www.cityofopelousas.com

French is spoken as often as English in this charming old town, the third oldest in the state. Opelousas was a trading post from the early 1700s until 1774, when St. Landry's church was established. Farm specialties are yams, cotton, corn, rice, and soybeans. These crops, along with beef, pork, and dairy products, bring millions into the parish annually.

What to See and Do

Chicot State Park. *3469 Chicot Park Rd, Opelousas (70586). 36 miles NW via Hwy 167, Hwy 3042 near Ville Platte.Phone 337/363-2503; toll-free 888/677-2442. www.lastateparks.com/chicot/chicot.htm.* Nearly 6,000 acres of rolling woodland surround a 2,000-acre artificial lake stocked with bream, bass, and crappie. Swimming, fishing, boating (launch, rentals); hiking, picnicking, tent and trailer sites (hookups, dump station). Cabins. (Daily) **$** Also here is

> **Louisiana State Arboretum.** *Opelousas (70586). Phone 337/363-6289; toll-free 888/677-6100.* The 300-acre arboretum on Lake Chicot includes more than 150 species of plant life indigenous to Louisiana; nature trails. (Daily) **$**

Jim Bowie Museum. *Hwy 90 and Academy St, Opelousas . Phone 337/948-6263; toll-free 800/424-5442.* Bowie memorabilia. Local historical items; 18th-century colonial house built by a woman named Venus. (Daily; closed holidays) **DONATION**

Washington. *404 N Main St, Washington (70570). 6 miles N via I-49 at Hwy 103. Phone 337/826-3627.* Built between 1780-1835, the antebellum buildings in this historic river port include Hinckley House (1803), House of History (1820), Camellia Cove (1825), and De la Morandiere (1830). Check locally for hours and fees. Many houses are open for tours (fee).

Special Events

Louisiana Yambilee. *Fairgrounds, Hwy 190 W, Opelousas (70570). Phone 985/447-4658.* Held in honor of the yam; although often confused, the yam and the sweet potato are, technically, two distinct species. Last full weekend in Oct.

Original Southwest Louisiana Zydeco Music Festival. *457 Zydeco Rd, off Hwy 167, Opelousas (70570). Phone 337/942-2392.* Celebrates the spicy culture of the Creoles. Concerts, interpretive stage, 5K run. Labor Day weekend.

Limited-Service Hotel

★ ★ **AMERICAN BEST VALUE INN.** *4165 I-49 Service Rd, Opelousas (70570). Phone 337/948-9500; fax 337/942-5035.* 67 rooms, 2 story. Check-out noon. Restaurant, bar. Outdoor pool, whirlpool. **$**

Ruston (A-3)

Founded 1884
Population 20,546
Elevation 319 ft
Area Code 318
Zip 71270
Information Ruston/Lincoln Convention and Visitors Bureau, 104 E Mississippi; phone 318/255-2031 or toll-free 800/392-9032
Web Site www.rustonlincoln.com

What to See and Do

Lincoln Parish Museum. *609 N Vienna St, Ruston (71270). Phone 318/251-0018.* Restored house (1886) with items of local history. (Tues-Fri; closed holidays) **FREE**

Louisiana Tech University. *152 Kenny Cir, Ruston (71270). Phone 318/257-3036; toll-free 800/528-3241. www.latech.edu.* (1894) (10,150 students.) The campus, which is wooded and hilly, is on the west side of Ruston; the Horticulture Center, with more than 500 species of native and exotic plants, is south of town, off Hwy 80 W (Mon-Fri; free); also the Louisiana Tech Equine Center (daily; free).

Special Events

Louisiana Passion Play. *Phone 318/255-2031.* First weekend in Sept-second weekend in Oct.

Louisiana Peach Festival. *N Trenton St, Ruston (71270). Phone 318/255-2031; toll-free 800/392-9032.* Second weekend in June.

Limited-Service Hotels

★ ★ **HOWARD JOHNSON.** *401 N Service Rd, Ruston (71270). Phone 318/255-5901; fax 318/255-3729. www.howardjohnson.com.* 228 rooms, 2 story. Pets accepted; fee. Check-out noon. Restaurant. Two outdoor pools, children's pool. **$**

★ **KINGS INN.** *I-20; Hwy 167 S, Ruston (71270). Phone 318/251-0000; fax 318/251-1453.* 52 rooms, 2 story. Complimentary continental breakfast. Check-out noon. Outdoor pool. **$**

Saint Martinville (D-3)

See also Lafayette, New Iberia

Settled circa 1760
Population 6,989
Elevation 19 ft
Area Code 337
Zip 70582
Information Chamber of Commerce, Box 436; phone 337/394-7578

Few towns in Louisiana have a more colorful history than St. Martinville. On the winding, peaceful Bayou Teche, St. Martinville was first settled about 1760. In the years thereafter, Acadians driven out of Nova Scotia by the British drifted into St. Martinville with the hope of finding religious tolerance. The town is the setting for part of Henry Wadsworth Longfellow's "Evangeline." Although based on an actual romance between Emmeline Labiche and Louis Arceneaux, Longfellow took considerable liberty with the facts.

During the French Revolution many Royalist refugees came to St. Martinville, and for a time barons, marquises, and counts, with their elegantly gowned ladies, attended luxurious balls and operas, which led to the town being called *Le Petit Paris.* Members of the colony steadfastly believed they would one day return to France and rule again.

In quick succession, yellow fever, a terrible fire, a hurricane, and the end of steamboat travel on the bayou triggered the decline of the town at about the time of the Civil War. Today St. Martinville is a quiet, old-fashioned hamlet.

What to See and Do

Evangeline Oak. *On the bayou at end of Port St.* This ancient, moss-draped live oak is said to be the meeting place of the real Evangeline and her Gabriel.

Longfellow-Evangeline State Commemorative Area. *1200 N Main St, Saint Martinville (70582). Just N of town on Hwy 31. Phone 337/394-3754.* This 157-acre park on the banks of the Bayou Teche is a reconstruction of a typical 19th-century plantation. The Olivier plantation (now restored) was begun in approximately 1810 by Pierre Olivier du Clozel, a French Creole. The structure employs wooden pegs; walls are made of Spanish moss-mixed bousillage and cypress; period furnishings; replica of 1840s kitchen and kitchen garden. Picnicking. (Daily; closed Jan 1, Thanksgiving, Dec 25) Standard fees. **$**

St. Martin of Tours Catholic Church. *103 S Main St, Saint Martinville. Phone 337/394-7334.* (1837) Established in 1765 as mother church of the exiled Acadians, the present, restored building contains stained glass windows, an exquisite carved baptismal font, which was a gift of Louis XVI of France, a gold and silver sanctuary light, a painting of St. Martin de Tours by Jean Francois Mouchet, and other religious artifacts. Guided tours (by appointment only). **$$** Behind the church's left wing is

> **Evangeline Monument.** Monument marks the spot where Emmeline Labiche, "Evangeline," is believed to be buried. Monument was erected by Dolores del Rio, who portrayed Evangeline in a 1929 silent movie filmed in St. Martinsville.

> **Petit Paris Museum.** Museum contains a collection of elaborate carnival costumes, local memorabilia, and gift shop. (Daily) **$$**

> **Presbytere.** On St. Martin of Tours Church Square. The priest's residence, Greek Revival in style, was constructed in 1856. By legend, it was built in such a grand manner in the hope that St. Martinville would be designated as the seat of the diocese.

Specialty Lodging

LA PLACE D'EVANGELINE. *220 Evangeline Blvd, Saint Martinville (70582). Phone 337/394-4010; toll-free 800/621-3017; fax 337/394-7983. www.oldcastillo. com.* This historic hotel, built in the early 1800s, is located on the banks of Bayou Teche, beneath the Evangeline Oak, and near Evangeline Oak Park. 5 rooms, 2 story. Complimentary full breakfast. Check-in 1 pm, check-out 11 am. **$**
🅳

Shreveport (A-2)

See also Bossier City, Minden

Founded 1839
Population 200,145
Elevation 204 ft
Area Code 318
Information Shreveport-Bossier Convention & Tourist Bureau, 629 Spring St, PO Box 1761, 71166; phone 318/222-9391 or toll-free 800/551-8682

Web Site www.shreveport-bossier.org

Until 1835, the Red River was jammed for nearly 165 miles of its course with driftwood, snags, and tree trunks; then Henry Miller Shreve, river captain and steamboat inventor, bulled his way through this "Great Raft" to cut a channel. He founded Shreveport, which thrived as a river town until the river silted up and steamboats could no longer navigate it. The river is in the process of being rehabilitated to allow barge traffic to travel from the Gulf to Shreveport. Oil and gas were discovered in the area in 1905. Now Shreveport is a heavily industrialized city and lumber-producing center.

What to See and Do

American Rose Center. *8877 Jefferson-Paige Rd, Shreveport (71119). 14 miles W via I-20 to exit 5, then N. Phone 318/938-5402. www.ars.org.* Center consists of 60 individually-designed rose gardens donated by rose societies from across the US; 20,000 rosebushes. (Apr-Oct: Mon-Fri 9 am-5 pm, Sat to 6 pm, Sun 1-6 pm) **$**

C. Bickham Dickson Park. *2283 E Bert Kouns Loop, Shreveport (71105). Jct 70th St and Bert Kouns.* Shreveport's largest park (585 acres) contains a 200-acre oxbow lake with pier. Fishing; hayrides, picnicking, playground. Some fees. (Tues-Sun; closed holidays)

Louisiana State Exhibit Museum. *3015 Greenwood Rd, Shreveport (71109). I-20, Fairgrounds exit. Phone 318/632-2020.* Remarkable dioramas and murals of the prehistory and resources of the Louisiana area; exhibits of antique and modern items; historical gallery. (Daily; closed holidays) **$**

R. S. Barnwell Memorial Garden and Art Center. *601 Clyde Fant Pkwy, Shreveport (71101). Phone 318/673-7703. www.nwlagardener.org.* Combination art and horticulture facility has permanent and changing exhibits. Flower displays include seasonal and native plantings of the area; sculpture garden with a walk-through bronze sculpture; fragrance garden for the visually impaired. (Mon-Fri, also Sat-Sun afternoons; closed holidays) **FREE**

R. W. Norton Art Gallery. *4747 Creswell Ave, Shreveport (71106). Phone 318/865-4201. www.rwnaf.org.* American and European paintings, sculpture, decorative arts, and manuscripts from the 15th-20th centuries, including a large collection of Western art by Frederic Remington and Charles M. Russell. (Tues-Fri 10 am-5 pm, Sat-Sun 1-5 pm; closed Mon, holidays) **FREE**

The Strand Theatre. *619 Louisiana Ave, Shreveport (71101). Phone 318/226-8555. www.thestrandtheatre. com.* This restored ornate theater was built in 1925.

Water Town USA. *7670 W 70th St, Shreveport (71149). I-20 W, Industrial Loop exit.Phone 318/938-5475. www. watertownusa.com.* This 20-acre water activity theme park features speed slides, adventure slides, and a wave pool, plus two other pools; restaurant and concessions. (June-late Aug: daily; May: Sat-Sun; also Labor Day weekend) **$$$$**

Special Events

Louisiana State Fair. *Fairgrounds, 3701 Hudson Ave, Shreveport (71109). Phone 318/635-1361. www. statefairoflouisiana.com.* One of the largest fairs in the country, it annually draws more than 300,000 people. Entertainment; agriculture and livestock competition. Late Oct-early Nov.

Red River Revel Arts Festival. *Riverfront area, Shreveport (71101). Phone 318/424-4000. www.redriver-revel.com.* National festival featuring fine arts, crafts, pottery, jewelery; music and performing arts; creative writing, poetry; ethnic foods. Late Sept-early Oct.

Limited-Service Hotels

★ ★ **BEST WESTERN CHATEAU SUITE HOTEL.** *201 Lake St, Shreveport (71101). Phone 318/222-7620; toll-free 800/845-9334; fax 318/424-2014. www.bestwestern.com.* 103 rooms, 5 story. Check-out 1 pm. Restaurant, bar. Fitness room. Outdoor pool. Airport transportation available. **$**

★ **DAYS INN.** *4935 W Monkhouse Dr, Shreveport (71109). Phone 318/636-0080; toll-free 800/329-7466; fax 318/635-4517. www.daysinn.com.* 148 rooms, 3 story. Complimentary continental breakfast. Check-out 11 am. Outdoor pool. **$**

★ **FAIRFIELD INN.** *6245 Westport Ave, Shreveport (71129). Phone 318/686-0102; toll-free 800/228-2800; fax 318/688-8791. www.fairfieldinn.com.* 105 rooms, 3 story. Complimentary continental breakfast. Check-out noon. Fitness room. Outdoor pool. **$**

★ ★ **HOLIDAY INN.** *5555 Financial Plz, Shreveport (71129). Phone 318/688-3000; toll-free 800/465-4329; fax 318/687-4462. www.holiday-inn.com.* 230 rooms, 6 story. Check-out noon. Restaurant, bar. Indoor pool,

outdoor pool, children's pool, whirlpool. Airport transportation available. Business center. **$**

Full-Service Hotel

★ ★ ★ **CLARION HOTEL.** *1419 E 70th St, Shreveport (71105). Phone 318/797-9900; fax 318/798-2923. www.choicehotels.com.* 267 rooms, 6 story. Check-out noon. Restaurant, bar. Fitness room. Outdoor pool. Business center. **$**

Specialty Lodgings

FAIRFIELD PLACE BED & BREAKFAST. *2221 Fairfield Ave, Shreveport (71104). Phone 318/222-0048; fax 318/226-0631. www.fairfieldbandb.com.* 6 rooms, 2 story. Complimentary full breakfast. Check-in 2 pm, check-out 11 am. Built in 1880 for a Louisiana Supreme Court justice. **$$**

TWENTY-FOUR THIRTY-NINE FAIRFIELD. *2439 Fairfield Ave, Shreveport (71104). Phone 318/424-2424; fax 318/459-1839. www.shreveportbedandbreakfast.com.* The bright turquoise, white-pillared façade of this 1905 bed-and-breakfast beckons guests to explore an interior of Victorian-style charm, lace, and antiques. Downtown Shreveport, Louisiana Downs, and riverboat casinos are located nearby. 4 rooms, 3 story. Complimentary full breakfast. Check-in 1 pm, check-out 11 am. Landscaped gardens, carved oak staircase, crystal chandeliers. **$$**

Restaurants

★ ★ **DON'S SEAFOOD.** *3100 Highland, Shreveport (71104). Phone 318/865-4291; fax 318/869-1925.* Cajun, Creole menu. Lunch, dinner. Closed Jan 1, Thanksgiving, Dec 25. Bar. Children's menu. **$$**

★ **SUPERIOR GRILL.** *6123 Line Ave, Shreveport (71106). Phone 318/869-3243; fax 318/869-4879. www. superiorgrill.com.* Mexican menu. Lunch, dinner. Closed Thanksgiving, Dec 25. Bar. **$$**

Slidell (D-5)

See also Covington, New Orleans

Population 25,695
Elevation 9 ft
Area Code 985
Information St. Tammany Parish Tourist & Convention Commission, 68099 Hwy 59, Mandeville 70471; phone 985/892-0520 or toll-free 800/634-9443
Web Site www.neworleansnorthshore.com

Slidell offers natural attractions and scenery in southeast Louisiana. The Honey Island Swamp encompasses the parish's eastern border. Slidell's historic district, called Olde Town, is filled with antique shops and restaurants.

What to See and Do

Fort Pike State Commemorative Area. *8 miles E via Hwy 190, then 6 miles SW on Hwy 90. Phone 504/662-5703; toll-free 888/662-5703. www.lastateparks. com/fortpike/fortpike.htm.* The fort was constructed in the 1820s to defend navigational channels leading to New Orleans. Visitors can stroll through authentic brick archways and stand overlooking the Rigolets as sentries once did. Picnicking. (Daily; closed Jan 1, Thanksgiving, Dec 25)

Oak Harbor Golf Course. *201 Oak Harbor Blvd, Slidell (70458). Phone 985/646-0110. www.oakharborgolf. com.* Oak Harbor forces smart, often conservative play in order to score well, with water on 12 holes and challenging approaches to many greens. Designed in the style of Pete Dye, with railroad ties and bulkheads along the course, Oak Harbor is still only a touch over 6,200 yards in length from the mens tees. A GPS system in each cart helps players estimate distances and speed play along one of New Orleans's newer courses, opened in 1992. **$$$$**

Slidell Cultural Center. *444 Erlanger St, Slidell (70458). Phone 985/646-4375. www.slidell.la.us/arts_center.htm.* Art gallery. (Mon-Fri 9 am-4 pm, Sat 10 am-2 pm) **FREE**

Limited-Service Hotel

★ **LA QUINTA INN.** *794 E I-10 Service Rd, Slidell (70461). Phone 985/643-9770; fax 985/641-4476.* 177 rooms, 2 story. Pets accepted, some restrictions. Complimentary continental breakfast. Check-out noon.

Bar. Fitness room. Outdoor pool. **$**

St. Francisville (C-4)

See also Baton Rouge, Jackson

Population 1,712
Elevation 115 ft
Area Code 225
Zip 70775
Information West Feliciana Historical Society, 11757 Ferdinand St, PO Box 338; phone 225/635-6330
Web Site www.stfrancisville.net

This picturesque old town, chartered under Spanish dominion, has been called "2 miles long and 2 yards wide" because it was built on a narrow ridge. St. Francisville is listed on the National Register of Historic Places and is the second-oldest incorporated town in the state.

What to See and Do

Louisiana State Penitentiary Museum. *Hwy 66, Angola (70712). 20 miles from Hwy 61. Phone 225/655-2592. www.angolamuseum.org.* Museum operated within an active prison. Exhibits include an original electric chair, original inmate record books dating from 1889, and weapons used by guards. Historic artifacts. (Mon-Fri 8 am-4:30 pm, Sat 9 am-5 pm, Sun 1-5 pm; closed holidays) **FREE**

⭐ **Plantations and historic buildings.** *St. Francisville.* (For details, see BATON ROUGE; the following directions are from St. Francisville.) **Catalpa**, 4 miles N on Hwy 61; **Oakley**, 1 mile S via Hwy 61, then 3 miles E on Hwy 965; **Cottage**, 5 miles N on Hwy 61; **Butler Greenwood**, 3 miles N on Hwy 61; **Greenwood**, 3 miles N on Hwy 61, then 4 1/2 miles W on Hwy 66 to Highland Rd; **Rosedown**, E of town on Hwy 10. Also of interest are **Grace Episcopal Church** (1858), in town on Hwy 10; **Afton Villa Gardens**, 4 miles N on Hwy 61; and the **Myrtles Plantation**, 1 mile N on Hwy 61.

Special Events

Angola Prison Rodeo. *L. S. P. Rodeo Arena, Louisiana State Prison, Hwy 66, Angola (70712). Phone 225/655-2592. angolarodeo.com.* Every Sun in Oct.

Audubon Pilgrimage. *11757 Ferdinand St, St. Francisville (70775). Phone 225/635-6330. www.audubonpil-*

grimage.info. Tour of historic plantation houses, two gardens, and a rural homestead. Third weekend in Mar.

Southern Garden Symposium. *Hwy 61 S and Hwy 965, St. Francisville (70775). Phone 225/635-3738.* Tribute to Southern gardening. Workshops, field trips. Mid-Oct.

Specialty Lodging

BARROW HOUSE INN. *9779 Royal St, St. Francisville (70775). Phone 225/635-4791; fax 225/635-1863. www.topteninn.com.* 5 rooms. Closed Dec 22-25. Check-in 3-7 pm, check-out 11 am. Built in 1809; antiques. **$**
🅑

Sulphur

Restaurant

★ **CAJUN CHARLIE'S SEAFOOD RESTAU-RANT.** *202 Henning Dr, Sulphur (70663). Phone 337/527-9044. www.cajuncharlies.com.* Known for authentic Creole seafood recipes and being a very local attraction. Creole menu. Lunch, dinner. **$**

Thibodaux (E-4)

See also Houma, Morgan City

Population 14,431
Elevation 15 ft
Area Code 504
Zip 70301
Information Chamber of Commerce, 318 E Bayou Rd, PO Box 467, 70302; phone 504/446-1187

What to See and Do

Laurel Valley Village. *595 Hwy 308, Thibodaux (70301). 2 miles S on Hwy 308. Phone 504/446-7456.* Village consists of the remains of a turn-of-the-century sugarcane plantation, including the sugar mill (1845), schoolhouse, two-story boarding house, country store, blacksmith shop, and more than 50 other support buildings; also museum. (Mon-Fri 10 am-3 pm, Sat-Sun from 11 am; closed holidays). **FREE**

Madewood Plantation House. *4250 Hwy 308, Napoleonville (70390). NW on Hwy 308. Phone 504/369-7151. www.madewood.com.* (1846) Refined example of domestic Greek Revival is furnished with period

antiques and houses an extensive art collection. This house served as the setting for the movie *A Woman Called Moses.* On the grounds are the family cemetery and other historic buildings. (Daily; closed Jan 1, Thanksgiving, Dec 25) **$$**

Limited-Service Hotel

★ ★ **HOWARD JOHNSON.** *203 N Canal Blvd, Thibodaux (70301). Phone 985/447-9071; toll-free 800/952-2968; fax 985/447-5752. www.hojo.com.* 118 rooms, 2 story. Pets accepted, some restrictions; fee. Complimentary full breakfast. Check-out noon. Restaurant, bar. Fitness room. Outdoor pool. Tennis. **$**
🐾 🏋 🏊 🎿

Washington

Restaurant

★ ★ **STEAMBOAT WAREHOUSE.** *525 N Main St, Washington (70589). Phone 337/826-7227; fax 337/826-7684. www.steamboatwarehouse.com.* Cajun, seafood menu. Dinner. Closed Mon; Dec 25. Bar. Children's menu. Casual attire. Restored 1830s steamboat warehouse. **$$**

White Castle

Restaurant

★ ★ **RANDOLPH HALL.** *30970 Hwy 405, White Castle (70788). Phone 225/545-2730; fax 225/545-8632. www.nottoway.com.* Cajun, Creole menu. Lunch, dinner. Closed Dec 25. Bar. Children's menu. **$$**

Mississippi

Bearded Spaniards in rusted armor followed De Soto across Mississippi in search of gold 80 years before the *Mayflower* landed in Massachusetts. De Soto died in the fruitless search. Pierre Le Moyne, Sieur d'Iberville, established Mississippi's first permanent settlement near Biloxi in 1699. There was no gold to be found, but the mighty Mississippi River had created something of infinitely greater valuean immense valley of rich, productive land on which cotton could be grown. Cotton established the great plantations, but while cotton still ranks first in agricultural production, the state also produces forestry, poultry, soybeans, and catfish. However, manufacturing is the number-one industry in the state.

Andrew Jackson became a hero in Mississippi after he defeated the Creek Indian nation and was again honored during a triumphal return through the state after winning the Battle of New Orleans in 1815. Mississippians enthusiastically named their capital after "Old Hickory," and they entertained him royally when he returned as an elder statesman in 1840.

For two years, northern Mississippi was the scene of some of the fiercest fighting in the Civil War. Following the Union defeat of Confederate forces at the Battle of Shiloh (Tennessee) in April 1862, General Ulysses S. Grant moved southwest into Mississippi. The following year, Grant besieged Vicksburg for 47 days. When the city finally fell, the fate of the Confederacy, according to some historians, was sealed. Yet battles still seesawed across and up and down the beleaguered state as railroads and telegraph lines were sliced by northern raiders. Mississippi was left in shambles. It was after General William Tecumseh Sherman burned Jackson

Population: 2,573,216

Area: 47,234 square miles

Elevation: 0-806 feett

Peak: Woodall Mountain (Tishomingo County)

Entered Union: December 10, 1817 (20th state)

Capital: Jackson

Motto: By Valor and Arms

Nickname: Magnolia State

Flower: Magnolia

Bird: Mockingbird

Tree: Magnolia

Time Zone: Central

Web Site: www.visitmississippi.org

Fun Fact:

• In 1963, the University of Mississippi Medical Center accomplished the world's first human lung transplant, and on January 23, 1964, Dr. James D. Hardy performed the world's first heart transplant surgery.

that he said, "War is Hell!" For Mississippi, the war was indeed hell, and the Reconstruction period was nearly as chaotic.

Today, Mississippi's subtropical Gulf Coast provides vast quantities of shrimp and oysters; it is also a tremendously popular resort and vacation area. Fishing is good in many streams; hunting for waterfowl along the Mississippi River and for deer in other areas is also excellent. The state has beautiful forests, the antebellum traditions and pageantry of Natchez, the beautiful Natchez Trace Parkway, and many other attractions.

Calendar Highlights

MARCH

National Cutting Horse Association Show
(Jackson). Phone 601/960-1891. Entries from across the US participate in amateur to professional rider competitions.

Spring Pilgrimage *(Vicksburg). Contact Convention and Visitors Bureau, phone 601/636-9421 or 800/221-3536.* Twelve antebellum houses are open to the public. Three tours daily.

MAY

Blessing of the Fleet *(Biloxi).* Hundreds of vessels manned by descendants of settlers participate in this ritual of European origin.

JUNE

Delta Jubilee *(Clarksdale). Contact Convention and Visitors Bureau, phone 662/627-7337 or 800/626-3764.* Statewide arts and crafts festival, Mississippi championship pork barbecue contest, 5K run, and antique car show.

JULY

Mississippi Deep-Sea Fishing Rodeo *(Gulfport). Phone 228/863-2713 or 228/832-0079.* Anglers from the US, Canada, and Latin America compete in various types of sport fishing.

SEPTEMBER

Mississippi Delta Blues and Heritage Festival *(Greenville). Phone 662/335-3523 or toll-free 888/812-5837.* Showcase of Blues greats.

OCTOBER

Great Mississippi River Balloon Race Weekend *(Natchez). Contact Convention and Visitors Bureau, phone 601/446-6345 or toll-free 800/647-6724.* Food, music, and entertainment.

Mississippi State Fair *(Jackson). Phone 601/961-4000.* Agricultural and industrial exhibits and contests; entertainment.

When to Go/Climate

Mild winters and hot summers are the norm in Mississippi. Rain is common, but snow is unusual. Hurricane season runs from June through October along the Gulf Coast.

AVERAGE HIGH/LOW TEMPERATURES (°F)

Jackson

Jan 56/33	**May** 84/60	**Sept** 88/64
Feb 60/36	**June** 91/67	**Oct** 79/50
Mar 69/44	**July** 92/71	**Nov** 69/42
Apr 77/52	**Aug** 92/70	**Dec** 60/36

Tupelo

Jan 49/31	**May** 81/60	**Sept** 85/63
Feb 55/34	**June** 88/67	**Oct** 75/50
Mar 64/43	**July** 91/71	**Nov** 64/42
Apr 74/51	**Aug** 90/69	**Dec** 53/34

Parks and Recreation

Water-related activities, hiking, various other sports, picnicking, and visitor centers, as well as camping, are available in many of Mississippi's state parks. Parks provide fishing ($3); boating, rentals ($5/day), launching ($5); swimming ($2; children $1); picnicking; tent and trailer facilities ($9-$14/night; 14-day maximum); primitive tent camping ($9) and cabins ($30-$70/night; 14-day maximum). Pets on leash only; not allowed in cabins or on property. Scattered throughout the state are 89 roadside parks with picnic facilities. For further information, contact Information Services and Marketing, Department of Wildlife, Fisheries and Parks, 1505 Eastover Dr, Jackson 39211-6374; phone 601/432-2400 or toll-free 800/467-2757.

FISHING AND HUNTING

Anglers find limitless possibilities in Mississippi. There are no closed seasons, and size limits are imposed on game fish in only some areas (excluding sea-run striped bass and black bass on a few state waters). The Chickasawhay, Pearl, Homochitto, and Pascagoula rivers are endless sources for large-

THE BLUES HIGHWAY

"If I ever die before you think my time has come, I want you to bury my body out on Highway 61."

—Mississippi Fred McDowell

From Vicksburg north to the Tennessee line, Highway 61 travels the length of the Mississippi Delta. Blues music originated here around the turn of the 20th century, and the sound spread north to Memphis and clear up to Chicago along the Highway 61 corridor. Today Highway 61 is known as "the Blues Highway."

The Mississippi Delta is roughly a diamond-shaped basin, approximately 160 miles long and 50 miles wide. The land is practically treeless, and what's not a cotton field is a catfish pond. The region's main tourist attractionsbeyond raw blues history and musical landmarksare the casinos along the Mississippi riverbank in Vicksburg, Greenville, and Tunica County near Memphis.

From Vicksburg, take I-20 east to Highway 61 north. In Onward, Highway 1 (the Great River Road) splits off from Hwy 61 to follow a more rural route along the Mississippi River. Here at the crossroads outside the 1913 Onward Store, a historical marker tells the story of the "Teddy" bear that originated here. The legend goes that President Theodore Roosevelt was hunting nearby and refused to shoot at a captured bear cub. Thus the nickname "Teddy" was adopted for baby bears. Up the road a piece, Rolling Fork is the birthplace of blues musician Muddy Waters (19151983). There's also a ranger station here, off the side of the road, where they can direct you to trails and campsites in the surrounding Delta National Forest.

A short detour east off Highway 61 in Cleveland leads to Dockery Farms, a few miles east on Highway 8 between Cleveland and Ruleville. The legendary birthplace of the Delta Blues, Dockery Farms has a rich blues lineage: it's where fieldworker Henry Sloan showed Charley Patton how to play. Back up

Highway 61 north of Cleveland, Mound Bayou is the oldest African-American town in the state. Isaiah Montgomery, once enslaved on the plantation of the brother of Confederate President Jefferson Davis, founded the community here in 1888.

Clarksdale is the holy grail for pilgrims on a blues tour of the Mississippi Delta. The home of Junior Parker, Sam Cooke, and John Lee Hooker, Clarksdale is also the site of the Delta Blues Museum (phone 662/624-4461 or 662/627-6820) at 1 Blues Alley. Set in a newly restored 1916 freight depot, the museum chronicles the history and heritage of blues music from its African roots to its rock-and-roll offshoots. The most notorious piece in its collection is the famous "Muddywood" guitar, constructed of wood cannibalized from Muddy Waters's cabin by ZZ Top guitarist Billy Gibbons. This is a great place to ask about what music might be in town.

Clarksdale's other musical landmarks include the legendary crossroads (at the junction of Highways 61 and 49) where the original bluesman Robert Johnson is alleged to have sold his soul to the devil. The shack where Muddy Waters livedthe original House of Blueswas located at Stovall Farms, 7 miles west of town via Oakhurst Avenue. Bessie Smith died downtown in what is now the Riverside Hotel boardinghouse at 615 Sunflower Avenue. Even the local barber is renowned as a blues artistyou can hear him wailing at Walton's Barber Shop at 317 Issaquena Street, near the museum.

Between Clarksdale and Memphis, dozens of Las Vegas-style casinos shoot up incongruously along the banks of the Mississippi River. To speed the flow of money into its till, the county has widened this stretch of Highway 61 into a four-lane expressway. The fastest route back south is I-55.

(Approximately 160 miles)

mouth bass, crappie, bluegill, bream, and catfish, as are six large reservoirs and more than 170,000 acres of lakes. There are fishing camps at many lakes and reservoirs and on the Gulf Coast, where boats, bait, and tackle are available. Complete charter services for deep-sea fishing and fishing piers are featured along Hwy 90 as well as at Gulf Coast resorts. Non-

resident fishing license, 16 years and over: annual, $30; three-day, $15.

Hunting on some 1 million acres of the more than 30 state-managed public hunting areas is seasonal: quail, late Nov-late Feb; wild turkey (gobblers only), late Feb-late Apr; squirrel, mid-Oct-mid-Jan;

deer, usually Oct-Jan; duck, reservoir areas and major river lowlands, usually Dec-Jan; doves, Sep-Oct and winter. Public waterfowl management areas are located on some reservoirs and river lowlands. Licenses for nonresidents: all game (annual $300, seven-day $125); small game (annual $75, seven-day $30); archery and primitive firearms (must also purchase annual all-game permit) $75; waterfowl, state waterfowl stamp required $10. Agent fee for all licenses is $3. For detailed information, contact the Department of Wildlife, Fisheries, and Parks, 1505 Eastover Dr, Jackson 39211-6374; phone 601/432-2400 or toll-free 800/467-2757.

Driving Information

Safety belts are mandatory for front-seat passengers. Children under 4 years must be in approved safety seats anywhere in a vehicle. In addition, safety belts are mandatory for all persons anywhere in a vehicle when traveling on the Natchez Trace Parkway.

INTERSTATE HIGHWAY SYSTEM

The following alphabetical listing of Mississippi towns in this book shows that these cities are within 10 miles of the indicated interstate highways. Check a highway map for the nearest exit.

Highway Number	Cities/Towns Within 10 Miles
Interstate 10	Biloxi, Gulfport, Ocean Springs, Pascagoula, Pass Christian.
Interstate 20	Jackson, Meridian, Vicksburg.
Interstate 55	Grenada, Jackson, McComb, Sardis.
Interstate 59	Hattiesburg, Laurel, Meridian.

Additional Visitor Information

Information booklets are available from the Division of Tourism, PO Box 1705, Ocean Springs 39566; phone toll-free 800/927-6378.

There are many welcome centers in Mississippi; visitors who stop by will receive information, brochures, and personal assistance in planning stops at points of interest. Their locations are at the northern end of the state, on I-55 S of Hernando; along the southern border, on I-55 south of Chatawa, on I-59 N of Nicholson, on I-10 at Waveland, and on I-10 at Pas-

cagoula; by the eastern border, on I-20 E of Toomsuba; in the western section, on Hwy 82 and Reed Rd in Greenville, on I-20 near Vicksburg, on Hwy 61 Bypass and Seargent S. Prentiss Dr N of Natchez, and on I-78 W of border. Centers are open daily 8 am-5 pm. For information about road conditions, phone the Mississippi Highway Patrol, 601/987-1211.

Biloxi (E-3)

See also Gulfport, Ocean Springs, Pascagoula, Pass Christian, Gulf Islands National Seashore

Settled 1699
Population 50,644
Elevation 25 ft
Area Code 228
Information Visitor Center, 710 Beach Blvd, 39530; phone 228/374-3105 or toll-free 800/245-6943
Web Site www.biloxi.ms.us

The oldest town in the Mississippi Valley, Biloxi has been a popular resort since the 1840s. It has, since the 1870s, been a leading oyster and shrimp fishing headquarters; shrimp were first canned here in 1883.

The Sieur d'Iberville's first French fort was established at Ocean Springs, just east of Biloxi. In 1721, the third shipment of "Cassette Girls" (so called after the boxes or "cassettes" in which they carried their possessions) landed at Ship Island, 12 miles south in the Gulf of Mexico. These 89 girls, carefully selected by a French bishop, were sent to become wives to the settlers. The area continues to reflect a strong ethnic heritage representing the eight flags that have flown over Biloxi during the past 300 years.

Magnolia trees, camellias, azaleas, roses, and crepe myrtle bloom along Biloxi's streets among the oaks draped with Spanish moss. There is freshwater, saltwater, and deep-sea fishing all year; crabbing, floundering, and mullet net casting. Biloxi is the home of Keesler AFB, the electronics and computer training center of the US Air Force. In recent years, casinos have become a popular attraction in Biloxi, and many have been built along the Gulf of Mexico beach.

What to See and Do

Gulf Coast Research Lab/J. L. Scott Marine Education Center & Aquarium. *703 E Beach Dr (lab), and 115 Beach Blvd (aquarium), Biloxi (39530). Phone 228/818-*

8890. www.usm.edu/aquarium. This facility features more than 40 aquariums showcasing native fish and other creatures. Also here is a 42,000-gallon Gulf of Mexico tank, featuring sharks, sea turtles, and eels; seashell collection and hands-on exhibits for children. (Mon-Sat; closed Jan 1, Thanksgiving, Dec 25) **$$**

Harrison County Sand Beach. *842 Commerce St, Biloxi (39507). Phone 228/896-0055. www.co.harrison.ms.us.* This 300-foot-wide white sand beach stretches the entire 26-mile length of the county; a seawall separates the beach from the highway.

Old Biloxi Cemetery. *1166 Irish Hill Dr, Biloxi (39530).* Burial ground of French pioneer families of Biloxi and the Gulf Coast. John Cuevas, hero of Cat Island (War of 1812), is buried here.

Small Craft Harbor. *Main St and Hwy 90, Biloxi (39530).* View fishing boats unloading the day's catch of Gulf game fish. Deep-sea fishing charter boats.

Special Events

Blessing of the Fleet. *177 1st St, Biloxi (39530). Gulf of Mexico.* Hundreds of vessels manned by descendants of settlers participate in this ritual of European origin. First weekend in May.

Garden Club Pilgrimage. *261 Lovers Ln, Biloxi (39530).* Guided tour of historic houses, sites, and gardens. Mar or Apr.

Mardi Gras. *2501 Beachview Dr, Biloxi (39531).* Carnival and parade. Feb.

Seafood Festival. *Point Cadet Plaza, 120 Cadet St, Biloxi (39530). E on Hwy 90.* Arts and crafts show, entertainment, seafood booths, contests. Last weekend in Sept.

Full-Service Hotel

★ ★ ★ **GRAND CASINO HOTEL BILOXI.** *265 Beach Blvd, Biloxi (39530). Phone 228/432-2500; toll-free 800/946-2946; fax 228/435-8966.* 491 rooms, 12 story. Check-out 11 am. Restaurant, bar. Children's activity center. Fitness room. Outdoor pool, whirlpool. Airport transportation available. **$**

Full-Service Resort

★ ★ ★ **BEAU RIVAGE BY MIRAGE RESORTS.** *875 Beach Blvd, Biloxi (39530). Phone 228/386-7111; toll-free 888/567-6667; fax 228/386-7446.*

www.beaurivage.com. The Beau Rivage revs things up on Mississippis Gulf Coast. The placid waters are a scenic backdrop for the excitement of this first-class destination that brings a bit of Las Vegas and the French Riviera to the South. This resort is truly a world of its own, with a 31-slip marina, casino, and endless recreational and entertainment choices. The guest rooms and suites lift spirits with cheery prints and pastel tones recalling the English countryside, while bay and ocean views calm and relax. Sophisticated dining is enjoyed here, where the eight dining establishments span the world for inspiration. Sports enthusiasts charter boats for relaxing rides or thrilling sport-fishing adventures, while the spa and salon invite landlubbers with a penchant for pampering. 1,780 rooms, 32 story. Check-in 11 am, check-out 3 pm. Restaurant, bar. Fitness room, spa. Outdoor pool. Casino. **$**

Restaurant

★ ★ ★ **MARY MAHONEY'S OLD FRENCH HOUSE.** *Magnolia and Water sts, Biloxi (39530). Phone 228/374-0163; fax 228/432-1387. www.marymahoneys.com.* Mary Mahoney, daughter of Yugoslavian immigrants, founded this Gulf Coast landmark establishment in 1964. The restaurant, built in 1737, is on the National Register of Historic Places. American menu. Lunch, dinner. Closed Sun; Dec 24-25. Bar. Children's menu. Colonial house and slave quarters; antiques, fireplaces. Outdoor seating. **$$$**

Clarksdale (B-2)

See also Cleveland

Founded 1869
Population 20,645
Elevation 175 ft
Area Code 662
Zip 38614
Information Coahoma County Tourism Commission, 1540 Desoto, PO Box 160; phone 662/627-7337 or toll-free 800/626-3764
Web Site www.clarksdaletourism.com

Named for John Clark, an Englishman who laid out the town in 1869, Clarksdale shared dual status with Friars Point as Coahoma County seat from 1892 until 1930. Sunflower Landing, near Clarksdale, is said to be the site where De Soto discovered the Mississippi River.

Clarksdale is located in the heart of the rich delta farmland, one of the state's top-ranking areas in cotton, soybean, and grain production. Three lakes in the area make this a water sports center.

What to See and Do

Carnegie Public Library. *114 Delta Ave, Clarksdale (38614). Phone 662/624-4461. www.cplclarksdale.lib. ms.us.* (Mon-Sat; closed holidays) Located within the library is

> **Archaeology Museum.** Native American pottery and other artifacts on exhibit. Collection of books and reports on Lower Mississippi Valley archaeology. **FREE**

Delta Blues Museum. *1 Blues Alley, Clarksdale (38614). Phone 662/627-6820.* Videotapes, recordings, and memorabilia about blues music. Permanent and changing exhibits; performances. (Mar-Oct 15: Mon-Sat 9 am-5 pm; rest of year: from 10 am) **$$**

Special Events

Delta Jubilee. *114 Delta Ave, Clarksdale (38614).* Statewide arts and crafts festival; Mississippi championship pork barbecue cooking contest; 5K run; antique car show. First weekend in June.

Sunflower River Blues and Gospel Festival. *www. sunflowerfest.org.* Weekend of outdoor concerts—blues on Fri and Sat, gospel on Sat—with local barbecue and other Southern specialties. Early Aug.

Limited-Service Hotel

★ **BEST WESTERN EXECUTIVE INN.** *710 S State St, Clarksdale (38614). Phone 662/627-9292; fax 662/624-4763. www.bestwestern.com.* 93 rooms, 2 story. Complimentary breakfast. Check-out noon. Restaurant. Fitness room. Indoor pool, outdoor pool, whirlpool. **$**

Cleveland (B-2)

See also Clarksdale

Population 13,841
Elevation 142 ft
Area Code 662
Zip 38732
Information Cleveland-Bolivar County Chamber

of Commerce, 600 Third St, PO Box 490; phone 662/843-2712 or toll-free 800/295-7473
Web Site www.clevelandmschamber.com

What to See and Do

Delta State University. *Hwy 8 W, Cleveland. Phone 662/846-3000. www.deltastate.edu.* (1924) (4,200 students.) On campus are

> **Bologna Performing Arts Center.** *Phone 662/846-4626.* Performances in music, theater, and dance. **$$$$**

> **Wright Art Gallery.** Exhibits works by southern artists.

Great River Road State Park. *Hwy 1 S, Rosedale. 18 miles W on Hwy 8.Phone 662/759-6762. www.mdwfp. com.* This 800-acre park is situated on the bluffs of the Mississippi River and has the state's largest campground inside the levee. Fishing in Perry Martin Lake; boating (ramp, rentals). Nature, bicycle trails. Picnicking (shelters), playground, playing field, snack bar, lodge, coin laundry. Improved and primitive camping. Four-level observation tower. Standard fees.

Limited-Service Hotel

★ ★ **HOLIDAY INN EXPRESS HOTEL & SUITES.** *808 N Davis Ave, Cleveland (38732). Phone 662/843-9300; fax 662/843-9342.* 119 rooms, 2 story. Complimentary full breakfast. Check-out noon. Restaurant, bar. Fitness room. Outdoor pool. **$**

Columbus (B-4)

See also Starkville

Settled 1817
Population 25,944
Area Code 662
Information Columbus Convention & Visitors Bureau, PO Box 789, 39703; phone 662/329-1191 or toll-free 800/327-2686 (exc MS)
Web Site www.columbus-ms.org

On the Tennessee-Tombigbee Waterway (also on the Buttahatchie and Luxapalila), Columbus progressed from a trading post to an educational center and repository for traditions and architecture of the Old South.

Mentioned in the state's oldest records, Columbus became a stopover on the Military Road ordered built by Andrew Jackson between New Orleans and Nashville (1817-1820). It was first called "Possum Town" because Native Americans thought that the tavernkeeper who served them looked like a wizened old possum. Columbus welcomed its first steamboat, the *Cotton Plant*, in 1822, a year after Mississippi's first public school, Franklin Academy, was established in the town.

Commerce and education went forward together. The Columbus Female Institute, founded in 1847, later became the first state-supported school in the United States to offer education exclusively to women—Mississippi University for Women (1884). Columbus was a favored place for planters to build imposing houses, and in antebellum days it became the cultural center of the rich Black Prairie. During the Civil War, a large Confederate arsenal was located in the town, and the state capital was moved here after Jackson fell. Columbus Air Force Base, an ATC training facility, is 9 miles north.

What to See and Do

Blewett-Harrison-Lee Museum. *316 7th St N, Columbus (39701). Phone 662/327-8888.* Contains articles of local history as well as Civil War exhibits. (Fri; closed holidays) **$$**

Friendship Cemetery. *4th St S and 13th Ave, Columbus.* Where the first Memorial Day, Apr 25, 1866 was said to have been observed, as women of Columbus gathered to decorate graves of Union and Confederate soldiers alike.

Historic houses. Columbus boasts more than 100 antebellum houses. Some are open for tours (daily; fee). For information, free 30-minute auto tour map, and narrative of houses contact the Convention & Visitors Bureau. Tour fee per home. **$$**

Lake Lowndes State Park. *3319 Lake Lowndes, Columbus (39702). 6 miles SE off Hwy 69. Phone 662/328-2110. mdwfp.com.* One of the finest recreation complexes among all the state parks. Approximately 600 acres with a 150-acre lake. Swimming beach, waterskiing, fishing, boating (ramps, rentals). Nature trail, tennis, game fields. Picnicking, playground, concession, indoor recreation complex, coin laundry. Improved and primitive camping, cabins. Standard fees.

Waverly Plantation. *Waverly Rd, West Point. 10 miles NW via Hwy 45, Hwy 50 near West Point. Phone 662/494-1399. (1852).* Mansion with twin, circular, self-supporting stairways leading to a 65-foot-high, octagonal observation cupola; original gold-leaf mirrors and Italian marble mantels. (Daily) **$$$**

Special Event

Pilgrimage. *Phone 601/329-3533. historic-columbus. org.* Costumed guides conduct tours through 15 historic houses. Special events. First two weeks of Apr.

Limited-Service Hotels

★ **COMFORT INN.** *1210 Hwy 45 N, Columbus (39705). Phone 662/329-2422; toll-free 800/228-5150; fax 662/327-0311. www.choicehotels.com.* 64 rooms, 2 story. Complimentary continental breakfast. Check-out 11 am. Wireless Internet access. **$**

★ ★ **MATER HOST INN & SUITES.** *506 Hwy 45 N, Columbus (39701). Phone 662/328-5202; toll-free 800/465-4329; fax 662/241-4979.* 153 rooms, 2 story. Check-out noon. Wireless Internet access. Bar. Outdoor pool. **$**

Restaurant

★ ★ **HARVEY'S.** *200 Main St, Columbus (39703). Phone 662/327-1639; fax 662/327-1675. www.eatwithus.com.* American menu. Lunch, dinner. Closed Sun; holidays. Bar. Children's menu. Restored tannery; antiques. **$$**

Corinth (A-4)

Founded 1854
Population 14,054
Elevation 455 ft
Area Code 662
Information Corinth Area Tourism Promotion Council, 602 E Waldron St, 38834; phone 662/287-8300 or toll-free 800/748-9048
Web Site www.corinth.net

The Memphis and Charleston and the Mobile and Ohio railroads selected this spot as a junction point, calling the town Cross City. Later the name was changed to honor the Greek city.

After being defeated at the Battle of Shiloh (April 6-7, 1862), Confederate General P.G.T. Beauregard retreated to Corinth. On October 3-4, 1862, Union forces, aiming at Vicksburg, took the town and held it until January 25, 1864. The only effort made to regain Corinth by the Confederates ended in defeat.

What to See and Do

Battery Robinett. *W on Linden St.* Union fort constructed on inner defense lines during the Battle of Corinth (1862). Monuments mark spots where Confederate heroes died; headstones commemorate color-bearers who fell while trying to plant a flag during battle. **FREE**

Curlee House. *705 Jackson St, Corinth (38834). Phone 662/287-9501. www.curleehouse.org.* (1857). Restored antebellum house; served as headquarters for Generals Bragg, Halleck, and Hood during the Civil War. (Daily; closed Dec 25) **$$**

Jacinto Courthouse. *15 miles SE. Phone toll-free 800/748-9048.* (1854). Fine example of early federal architecture was first the courthouse for old Tishomingo County; later used as both a school and a church. (Tues-Sat) **FREE**

Flowood

Restaurant

★ ★ **PRIMOS CAFE.** *2323 Lakeland Dr, Flowood (39232). Phone 601/936-3701; fax 601/981-8109. www.primoscafe.com.* Seafood, steak menu. Breakfast, lunch, dinner. Closed Sun; Dec 24-25. Bar. Children's menu. **$$**

Gautier (F-4)

Restaurant

★ ★ **TIKI RESTAURANT, LOUNGE AND MARINA.** *3212 Mary Walker Dr, Gautier (39553). Phone 228/497-1591; fax 228/497-1575.* Seafood, steak menu. Lunch, dinner. Closed Jan 1, Dec 24-25. Bar. Children's menu. On the bayou. **$$**

Greenville (C-1)

Settled 1828
Population 41,633
Area Code 662

Information Greenville Area Chamber of Commerce, 915 Washington Ave, PO Box 933, 38702-0933; phone 662/378-3141 or the Washington County Convention & Visitors Bureau, 410 Washington Ave, 38702; phone 662/334-2711.
Web Site www.visitgreenville.org

Greenville, which is not even on the Mississippi, is the state's largest river port. The Mississippi River was, in 1935, finally broken of its habit of stealing whole areas of the town, block by block. Levees forced the channel 6 miles westward and left a lake for a harbor. Before this, in 1927, the whole town was under water for 70 days. The first Greenville settlement was on the Blantonia Plantation (1828), which was purchased for the site of the third county seat. The first was flooded out; the second burned during shelling by Union gunboats in 1863.

What to See and Do

Birthplace of the Frog Exhibit. *S Deer Creek Dr E, Leland. 8 miles E via Hwy 82. Phone 662/686-7383. www.lelandms.org/kermit.html.* Muppet memorabilia from collectors and the family of the late Jim Henson, creator of the Muppets. (Mon-Sat 10 am-5 pm, Sun from 2 pm; daily to 5 pm from June-Aug)

Leroy Percy State Park. *Hwy 61 W, Hollandale (38703). 18 miles S on Hwy 1, then 6 miles E on Hwy 61. Phone 662/827-5436. www.mdwfp.com/.* The oldest of Mississippi's state parks is composed of approximately 2,400 acres. One of the four hot artesian wells provides water for an alligator pond (view from boardwalk). Nature trails lead through Delta lowlands. Nearby is live alligator exhibit. Swimming pool (Memorial Day-Labor Day, daily); fishing, hunting; boating (rentals). Picnicking (shelters), playground, game field, snack bar, restaurant, lodge, coin laundry. Improved and primitive camping, cabins. Standard fees.

River Road Queen. *7 miles E of bridge via Hwy 82. Phone 662/332-2378.* Replica of 19th-century paddlewheel steamboat. Built for 1984 World's Fair; now serves as the town's welcome center. (Daily)

Winterville Mounds State Park. *2415 Hwy 1 N, Greenville (38703). 7 miles N off of Hwy 1. Phone 662/334-4684.* One of the largest groups of Native American mounds in the Mississippi Valley, the area was a religious site and an economic and military center for thousands of Native Americans of the Mississippian era, who disappeared sometime after De Soto's exploration. Great Temple mound, 55 feet high, is surrounded by ten smaller mounds used for a variety of purposes. Picnicking (shelters), concession, playground. The museum houses artifacts from the mound site and adjoining territory (Wed-Sat and Sun afternoons; closed Dec 25). **$**

Special Event

Mississippi Delta Blues and Heritage Festival. *Hwy 1 S and Hwy 454, Greenville (38701). Phone 601/335-3523. www.deltablues.org.* Showcase of blues greats. Sept.

Limited-Service Hotels

★ **DAYS INN.** *2701 Hwy 82 E, Greenville (38703). Phone 662/334-1818; fax 662/332-1761. www.daysinn. com.* 120 rooms, 2 story. Complimentary continental breakfast. Check-out noon. Fitness room. Outdoor pool. Business center. **$**

★ ★ **OVINA.** *2700 Hwy 82 E, Greenville (38701). Phone 662/332-4411; toll-free 800/272-6232; fax 662/332-4411.* 121 rooms, 2 story. Complimentary continental breakfast. Wireless Internet access. Check-out noon. Outdoor pool. **$**

Restaurant

★ **SHERMAN'S.** *1400 S Main St, Greenville (38701). Phone 662/332-6924; fax 662/332-6928.* American, Italian menu. Lunch, dinner. Closed Sun; holidays. Bar. Children's menu. **$$**

Greenwood (B-2)

See also Grenada

Settled 1834
Population 18,425
Elevation 140 ft
Area Code 662
Zip 38930
Information Convention & Visitors Bureau, PO Drawer 739; phone 662/453-9198 or toll-free 800/748-9064
Web Site www.greenwoodms.org

Lying on both banks of the Yazoo River and surrounded by rich, black delta lands, Greenwood was a river port shipping cotton before the US Civil War and a rail center after Reconstruction.

The town grew from a river landing, established on 162 acres of land bought for $1.25 an acre by John Williams. Planters who used his landing to ship their cotton included Choctaw Chief Greenwood Leflore. After a quarrel about Williams' storage methods, the chief built his own landing with a warehouse 3 miles up the river, calling it Point Leflore. However, the original landing flourished and absorbed the trade of its rival. Today Greenwood is one of the nation's largest cotton markets.

What to See and Do

Cottonlandia Museum. *1608 Hwy 82 W, Greenwood (38903). 2 miles W on Hwy 49 E, Hwy 82 Bypass W. Phone 662/453-0925. www.cottonlandia.org.* Exhibits highlight the history of the Mississippi Delta, its people, and its land from 10,000 BC to the present. Also Mississippi art exhibit; garden; gift shop. (Mon-Fri 9 am-5 pm, Sat-Sun from 2 pm; closed holidays) **$**

Florewood River Plantation. *Greenwood. 2 miles W on Hwy 82. Phone 601/432-2400. www.mdwfp.com.* A re-creation of an 1850s plantation and outbuildings; crops worked and harvested; cotton museum; steam engine displays; crafts demonstrations. Tours (Mar-Nov, Tues-Sun; limited tours rest of year). **$$**

Limited-Service Hotels

★ **BEST WESTERN GREENWOOD.** *635 Hwy 82, Greenwood (38930). Phone 662/455-5777; toll-free 888/455-5770; fax 662/455-4239. www.bestwestern. com.* Sitting at the edge of an industrial park 1 mile south of city center, cotton-capital property offers complimentary continental breakfast, and an indoor-outdoor pool. 100 rooms, 2 story. Check-out noon. Fitness room. Indoor, outdoor pool; children's pool. Tennis. **$**

★ **ECONO LODGE.** *401 W Hwy 82, Greenwood (38930). Phone 662/453-5974; toll-free 800/228-5150; fax 662/455-6401. www.choicehotels.com.* 60 rooms, 2 story. Complimentary continental breakfast. Check-out noon. Outdoor pool. **$**

Restaurant

★ ★ **CRYSTAL GRILL.** *423 Carrollton Ave, Greenwood (38930). Phone 662/453-6530; fax 662/453-4744.* Seafood, steak menu. Lunch, dinner. Closed Mon; holidays. Bar. Children's menu. **$$**

Grenada (B-3)

See also Greenwood

Population 14,879
Elevation 195 ft
Area Code 662
Zip 38901
Information Grenada Tourism Commission, 95 SW Frontage Rd, PO Box 1824; phone 662/226-2571 or toll-free 800/373-2571
Web Site www.grenadamississippi.com

The economy of Grenada had from early days been based on cotton. Today, it is diversified; industry and tourism, as well as agriculture, support this town located on the eastern edge of the Mississippi Delta. Founded as two towns by political rivals, the two communities united in 1836. The union was literally symbolized by a wedding in which the bride came from one town and the groom from the other. Confederate General John C. Pemberton headquartered in Grenada while opposing Grant's second Vicksburg campaign.

What to See and Do

Grenada Lake. *2088 Scenic Loop 333, Grenada (38901). 5 miles NE off Hwy 8.* Phone 662/226-5911. Covers approximately 35,000 acres, with 200 miles of shoreline. Swimming, water sports; fishing, hunting; boat launch. Fitness trails; archery, tennis, ball fields. Picnicking. Primitive and improved camping (fee at some sites). Visitor center at Grenada Dam on Scenic Loop 333. (Daily) **FREE** On the lake is

> **Hugh White State Park.** *3170 Hugh White State Park Rd, Grenada (38901). 5 miles E on Hwy 8.* Phone 662/226-4934. A 1,581-acre park with swimming beach, pool, waterskiing; fishing; boating (ramp, rentals). Nature, bicycle trails; tennis nearby. Picnicking (shelter), playground, lodge. Primitive and improved camping, cabins, camp store. Standard fees.

Historic Old Grenada. Motor and walking tour of houses and churches. Contact Chamber of Commerce.

Special Event

Thunder on Water Festival. *Grenada Lake.* Parade, children's fishing rodeo, antique car show, boat light parade, and several speed boat races. Second weekend in June.

Limited-Service Hotels

★ ★ **AMERICAS BEST VALUE INN.** *1750 Sunset Dr, Grenada (38901).* Phone 662/226-7816; toll-free 800/880-8866; fax 662/226-5623. 61 rooms, 2 story. Pets accepted, some restrictions; fee. Complimentary full breakfast. Check-out noon. High-speed Internet access. Restaurant. Outdoor pool. **$**

★ **COMFORT INN.** *1552 Sunset Dr, Grenada (38901).* Phone 662/226-1683; toll-free 800/228-5150; fax 662/226-9484. www.choicehotels.com. 66 rooms, 2 story. Complimentary continental breakfast. Check-out noon. High-speed Internet access. Fitness room. Outdoor pool, whirlpool. **$**

Gulf Islands National Seashore (F-4)

See also Biloxi, Gulfport, Ocean Springs

Web Site www.nps.gov/guis/.
Information Park Office, 3500 Park Rd, Ocean Springs; phone 228/875-0821

Headquarters and campground for the Mississippi district of this beautiful area are in Ocean Springs. Sparkling beaches, coastal marshes, and wildlife sanctuaries may be found on the four offshore islands (Petit Bois, Horn, East and West Ship) and the mainland area (Davis Bayou). The mainland areas are open year-round and are accessible from Highway 90.

In 1969, Hurricane Camille split Ship Island in two, leaving East Ship and West Ship Islands. Ship Island was once a base for French exploration and settlement (1699-1753) of the Gulf Coast from Mobile, Alabama, to the mouth of the Mississippi River. What is now East Ship Island once served as the staging area for a 50-ship British armada and an unsuccessful attempt to capture New Orleans in 1815 at the end of the War of 1812.

On West Ship Island is Fort Massachusetts. Construction of this brick coastal defense began in 1859, prior to the outbreak of the Civil War. Two years later, the Mississippi militia took control of the fort from the US Army Corps of Engineers after the state seceded from the Union. The Confederates later fortified it, naming it Fort Twiggs in honor of the New Orleans Confederate general. Repeated threats by Northern forces caused the Confederates to withdraw in September 1861. The fort was then reoccupied by Union soldiers, who called it Fort Massachusetts. For a time, the area east of the fort served as a prisoner-of-war camp, confining some 4,300 Confederate prisoners at one point. Completed in 1866, the fort was never fully armed. Free tours of the fort are offered daily (March-November). Concession boats run to Fort Massachusetts and West Ship Island from Gulfport (March-October), depending on weather conditions.

All four offshore islands are accessible year-round by boat only and are open to wilderness camping (except on West Ship Island), surf fishing, surf swimming (Memorial Day-Labor Day), boating, picnicking, and hiking. No motor vehicles or glass are allowed on the islands. Horn and Petit Bois are designated as wilderness areas, and special restrictions apply.

The mainland campground has water and electric hookups (fee) at 51 sites, a public boat dock, and picnic areas. The visitor center offers audiovisual programs, exhibits, boardwalks, and nature trails. Pets are allowed on leash only. **FREE**

Gulfport (F-4)

See also Biloxi, Gulf Islands National Seashore, Ocean Springs, Pass Christian

Founded 1880
Population 71,127
Elevation 20 ft
Area Code 228
Information Chamber of Commerce, 1401 20th Ave, PO Drawer FF, 39502; phone 228/863-2933
Web Site www.biloxi.org

Although chosen as an ideal site for a port and a railroad terminus in 1887, it was 1902 before the Gulf & Ship Island Railroad's New York owner fulfilled the plan. As a planned city, Gulfport has broad streets laid out in a regular rectangular pattern paralleling the seawall. This was in marked contrast to the narrow-streeted antebellum towns along the rest of the coast. When completed, the railroad, which ran through sparsely settled sections rich in timber, transformed southern Mississippi.

Gulfport turned to the resort business in the 1920s and had a real estate boom in 1925 when the Illinois Central Railroad bought the Gulf & Ship Island line. The boom collapsed a year later after having produced Gulfport's tower apartments and many hotels. After World War II, luxury motels took over. With the Mississippi Sound and a great number of lakes, rivers, bays, and bayous within a few minutes drive from downtown, and with excellent facilities for deep-sea fishing, Gulfport is an angler's paradise.

Mississippi City, which has been incorporated into Gulfport, was the scene of the bare-knuckles fight for the heavyweight championship of the world on February 7, 1882, when John L. Sullivan beat Paddy Ryan under the live oaks now at the corner of Highway 90 and Texas Street.

What to See and Do

⭐ **John C. Stennis Space Center.** *NASA Space Center, 38 miles W via I-10. Phone 228/688-2370. www.ssc.nasa.gov.* Second-largest NASA field installation. Testing site of *Saturn V*, first and second stages for the Apollo manned lunar program, including those for *Apollo 11*, which landed the first men on the moon in 1969. Original test stands were later modified to develop and test space shuttle main engines. The Stennis Space Center hosts NASA and 18 federal and state agencies involved in oceanographic, environmental, and national defense programs. Visitor center with 90-foot Space Tower; films, demonstrations; indoor, outdoor exhibits; guided tours. (Daily; closed Easter, Thanksgiving, Dec 25) **FREE**

Port of Gulfport. *Mississippi Technical Center, 1 Research Blvd, Gulfport (39759). Phone 228/863-2942.* Extends seaward from the junction of Hwy 49 and 90, located equidistant to New Orleans and Mobile, Alabama. One of the largest banana import facilities in the US; the projected depth of the channel is 32 feet; the depth of the harbor is 30 feet at mean low water with a tidal variation of approximately 2 feet. The 1,320-foot-wide harbor separates the port's two parallel piers; 11 berths are available.

Ship Island Excursions. *Gulfport Yacht Harbor,Hwy 90, Gulfport (39501). Phone 228/864-1014. www.msship-island.com.* Passenger ferry leaves from the Gulfport Yacht Harbor for a one-hour trip to Ship Island, 12 miles off the coast. You can spend as much time on the island as you like, as long as you catch the last ferry of the day, at either 2:30 or 5 pm depending on the day and time of year. No reservations are accepted. (Mar-Oct, schedule varies, one to three cruises daily) **$$$$**

Small Craft Harbor. *Hwy 49 and Hwy 90, Gulfport (39501).* Launching ramps, charter boats, and pleasure craft docking.

Limited-Service Hotels

★ **BEST WESTERN BEACH VIEW INN.** *2922 W Beach Blvd, Gulfport (39501). Phone 228/864-4650; toll-free 800/748-8969; fax 228/863-6867. www.best-western.com.* 150 rooms, 5 story. Check-out noon. Bar. Outdoor pool. Overlooks the harbor. **$**

★ ★ **COURTYARD BY MARRIOTT.** *1600 E Beach Blvd, Gulfport (39501). Phone 228/864-4310; toll-free 800/441-0887; fax 228/865-0525. www.gulfportbeach-fronthotel.com.* 229 rooms, 5 story. Check-out noon. Restaurant, bar. Outdoor pool, children's pool. Opposite the beach. **$**

Restaurant

★ ★ **VRAZEL'S.** *3206 W Beach Blvd (Hwy 90), Gulfport (39501). Phone 228/863-2229; fax 228/633-2240. www.vrazelsfinefood.com.* A view of the gardens or the beach can be enjoyed from this restaurant. American menu. Lunch, dinner. Closed Sun; holidays. **$$$**

Hattiesburg (E-3)

See also Laurel

Founded 1882
Population 44,479
Elevation 161 ft
Area Code 601
Information Convention and Visitors Bureau, 1 Convention Center Plaza, PO Box 16122, 39401; phone 601/268-3220 or 601/638-6877
Web Site www.hattiesburg.org

Once known as Twin Forks and Gordonville, the settlement was renamed by an early settler in honor of his wife, Hattie. When railroads were routed through Hattiesburg during the late 19th century, the town began to thrive. Unlike other towns that came and went with the lumber boom of the 1920s, Hattiesburg

was able to diversify its economic base with a number of industries. The University of Southern Mississippi makes the town the educational center of the southern sector of the state.

What to See and Do

De Soto National Forest. *654 W Frontage Rd, Chickasaw Ranger District, Wiggins (39577).* 10 miles SE on Hwy 49.Phone 601/965-4391. Approximately 500,000 acres. Black Creek Float Trip offers 50 miles of scenic streams. Black Creek Trail has 41 miles of trails, ten of which go through 5,000 acres of Black Creek Wilderness. Fees may be charged at designated recreation sites. Swimming, fishing. Hiking, bridle trails. Picnicking. Primitive camping. Ranger District offices are located in Laurel, Wiggins and McHenry. Contact Forest Supervisor, 100 W Capitol St, Suite 1141, Jackson 39269.

Paul B. Johnson State Park. *319 Geiger Lake Rd, Hattiesburg (39401).* 15 miles S off Hwy 49. Phone 601/582-7721. *mdwfp.com.* More than 805 acres of pine forest. A spring-fed lake provides excellent facilities for water sports. Swimming beach, waterskiing, fishing, boating (ramp, rentals). Nature trail. Picnicking (shelters), playground, playing fields, snack bar, lodge with game room, coin laundry. Improved and primitive camping, cabins. Visitor center. Standard fees.

University of Southern Mississippi. *2700 Hardy St, Hattiesburg (39401). Phone 601/266-4491. www.usm.edu.* (1910) (12,000 students.) Library houses large collection of original illustrations and manuscripts for children's books by authors and artists from here and abroad. American Rose Society garden on campus, blooms spring-mid-Dec. Also Science and Technology Building, Performing Arts Center, Danforth Chapel, Polymer Research Center, art gallery, natatorium, and golf course.

Limited-Service Hotels

★ ★ **INN ON THE HILL.** *6595 Hwy 49 N, Hattiesburg (39401). Phone 601/599-2001; toll-free 800/228-5150; fax 601/599-2002. www.hattiesburginn.com.* 119 rooms, 2 story. Pets accepted; fee. Complimentary full breakfast. Check-out noon. Wireless Internet access. Restaurant, bar. Outdoor pool. **$**

★ ★ **LA QUINTA INN.** *6563 Hwy 49 N, Hattiesburg (39401). Phone 601/268-2850; toll-free 800/465-4329; fax 601/268-2823.* 128 rooms, 2 story. Check-out noon. Restaurant, bar. Wireless Internet access. Fitness room. Outdoor pool. **$**

Restaurants

★ ★ **CHESTERFIELD'S.** *2507 Hardy St, Hattiesburg (39401). Phone 601/582-2778; fax 601/544-0006.* Seafood, steak menu. Lunch, dinner. Closed Thanksgiving, Dec 25. Bar. Children's menu. **$$**

★ ★ **CRESCENT CITY GRILL.** *3810 Hardy St, Hattiesburg (39402). Phone 601/264-0657; fax 601/264-0681. www.nsrg.com.* Creole, French menu. Lunch, dinner. Closed Thanksgiving, Dec 25. Bar. Children's menu. **$$**

Holly Springs (A-3)

Also see Memphis, TN

Founded 1835
Population 7,957
Elevation 609 ft
Area Code 662
Zip 38635
Information Chamber of Commerce, 154 S Memphis St; phone 662/252-2943

Holly Springs crowns the ridge along which a Native American trail once led from the Mississippi to the tribal home of the Chickasaw Nation. William Randolph, descendant of Virginia's famed John Randolph, is credited with founding the town.

Wealth from cotton went into buying more and more land, driving up real estate prices. Soon lawyers, who were needed to cope with squabbles over land and deeds, outnumbered all other professionals. The town skipped the frontier stage as Georgian and Greek Revival mansions rose instead of log cabins.

Holly Springs suffered 61 raids during the Civil War; the most devastating was by a Southern force led by Confederate General Van Dorn in 1862; the Confederates destroyed General Grant's supply base, delaying the fall of Vicksburg by a year.

What to See and Do

Holly Springs National Forest. *1000 Front St, Oxford (38655).* Intensive erosion control measures are carried out within this 152,200-acre area. Fishing, large and small game hunting; boating at Puskus, Chewalla, and Tillatoba lakes. Picnicking. Primitive camping. Fees are charged at designated recreation sites. Contact Forest Supervisor, 100 W Capitol St, Suite 1141, Jackson 39269.

Kate Freeman Clark Art Gallery. *300 E College Ave, Holly Springs (38635). College Ave. Phone 662/252-1563.* Endowed by the artist to permanently house her works, the gallery contains more than 1,000 paintings done while Clark studied under William Merritt Chase in New York in the early 1900s. Clark returned to her native Holly Springs in 1923 and simply stored her work until her death 40 years later. Also here are three canvasses by Chase and one by Rockwell Kent. Contact Bank of Holly Springs. **$**

Marshall County Historical Museum. *220 E College Ave, Holly Springs (38635). At Randolph St. Phone 662/252-3669.* Local historical artifacts; Civil War Room; quilts; dolls, toys; antique clothing; wildlife exhibits. Library. (Mon-Sat; closed the week before Christmas) **$**

Rust College. *150 Rust Ave, Holly Springs (38635). Memphis and Rust aves. Phone 662/252-8000. www. rustcollege.edu.* (1866) (1,075 students.) Site of campground for General Grant's troops. On campus is Leontyne Price Library, which houses the Roy Wilkins Collection on civil rights. Tours.

Wall Doxey State Park. *3946 Hwy 7 S, Holly Springs (38635). 7 miles S off Hwy 7. Phone 662/252-4231. mdwfp.com.* Park covering 850 acres located on a spring-fed lake. Swimming beach (three-level diving pier); fishing, boating (ramp, rentals). Nature trail. Picnicking (shelters), playground, playing field, snack bar, lodge. Improved and primitive camping, cabins. Standard fees. **$**

Special Event

Pilgrimage. *154 S Memphis St, Holly Springs. Phone 662/252-2943.* Historic houses and gardens open to visitors. Mid-Apr.

Jackson (D-2)

See also Mendenhall, Yazoo City

Founded 1821
Population 184,256
Elevation 294 ft
Area Code 601
Information Convention & Visitors Bureau, 921 N President St, PO Box 1450, 39215; 601/960-1891 or 800/354-7695
Web Site www.visitjackson.com

The beautiful site of Jackson, along the bluffs above the Pearl River, was selected as a perfect location for commerce by a young French Canadian trader. Although Louis LeFleur succeeded in his aim and set up a trading post after his exploratory voyage up the Pearl from the Gulf of Mexico, the city has, throughout its existence, been a center of government rather than business.

It is impossible to separate the town's history from its role as state capital; it was designated such as soon as the state's boundaries had expanded sufficiently, by the ceding of Native American lands, to make Jackson the state's geographical center. The first session of the legislature held in the town convened in January of 1822. By then the city had already been named for Andrew Jackson, idol of Mississippi, and laid out in a checkerboard pattern in accordance with Thomas Jefferson's recommendation to Governor Claiborne 17 years earlier. Evidence still remains of the original plan, which reserved every other square as a park or green.

There were attempts in 1829 to move the capital to Clinton and in the following year to Port Gibson, but these were averted by a legislative act of 1832 that named Jackson as the capital until 1850—by which time it had a permanent stature. Andrew Jackson addressed the legislature in what is now the Old Capitol in 1840, the year after its completion, and a Mississippi Convention assembled to consider Henry Clay's last compromise in 1850. The building was the scene of the Secession Convention in January 1861.

Jackson was the junction of two great railroads by the time of the Civil War; it played an important role as Confederate capital of Mississippi until it was besieged in 1863, when the capital was removed and the city destroyed. All that was recorded in Jackson of the state's turbulent politics and government went up in smoke when General Sherman's army reduced the city to ashes, bringing it the ironic nickname, "Chimneyville."

The so-called "Black and Tan" convention that met at Jackson in January 1868, was the first political organization in Mississippi with black representation. It framed a constitution under which Mississippi lived for 22 years, giving blacks the franchise and enabling a few to attain high political office. In the same year, the governor was ejected from his office, and the carpetbaggers reigned until 1876. Jefferson Davis made his last public appearance in Jackson in 1884.

With the coming of the 20th century and half a dozen railroads connecting Jackson with the whole South, the population doubled within five years. Further growth came with the discovery of natural gas fields in 1930. The Ross Barnett Reservoir, covering 31,000 acres in central Mississippi, created tourist and recreational attractions as well as residential and industrial sites in the greater Jackson area.

What to See and Do

Battlefield Park. *Porter St and Langley Ave, Jackson.* Site of Civil War battle; original cannon and trenches.

Davis Planetarium/McNair Space Theater. *201 E Pascagoula St, Jackson (39201). Phone 601/960-1550. www. thedavisplanetarium.com.* Programs change quarterly; 230-seat auditorium. (Daily; closed holidays) **$$**

Governor's Mansion. *300 E Capitol St, Jackson (39201). Between N Congress and N West sts. Phone 601/359-3175.* (1842). Restored to original plan and Greek Revival style; antiques and period furnishings. Grounds occupy entire block and feature gardens, gazebos; tours. (Tues-Fri, mornings only; closed during official state functions) **FREE**

Jackson Zoological Park. *2918 W Capitol St, Jackson (39209). Phone 601/352-2580. www.jacksonzoo. org.* More than 400 mammals, birds, and reptiles in naturalized habitats. (Daily 9 am-5 pm; closed Jan 1, Dec 25) **$$**

Manship House. *420 E Fortification St, Jackson (39202). Phone 601/961-4724. www.mdah.state.ms.us/museum/ manship.html.* Restored Gothic Revival cottage (circa 1855), was the residence of Charles Henry Manship, mayor of Jackson during the Civil War. Period furnishings; fine examples of wood graining and marbling. (Tues-Fri 9 am-4 pm, Sat from 10 am; closed holidays) **FREE**

Mississippi Agriculture & Forestry Museum and National Agricultural Aviation Museum. *1150 Lakeland Dr, Jackson (39216). 1 mile NE on I-55, exit 98 at Lakeland Dr.Phone 601/713-3365; toll-free 800/844-8687. www.msagmuseum.org.* Complex, covering 39 acres, includes museum exhibit center, forest trail, 1920s living history town and farm. Picnicking. (Mon-Sat 9 am-5 pm; closed Jan 1, Dec 24-25) **$$**

Mississippi Museum of Art. *201 E Pascagoula, Jackson (39201). Phone 601/960-1515. www.msmuseumart. org.* Exhibitions of 19th- and 20th-century works by local, regional, national, and international artists. The museum's collection includes African-American folk art; photographs. Special exhibitions; sculpture garden; hands-on children's gallery; restaurant, gallery programs, films; instruction, sales gallery. (Mon-Sat 10 am-5 pm, Sun from noon; closed holidays) **$**

Jackson Fun Fact

• The rarest of North America cranes lives in Mississippi in the grassy savannas of Jackson County. The Mississippi Sandhill Crane stands about 44 inches tall and has an 8-foot wingspan.

Mississippi Petrified Forest. *124 Forest Park Rd, Flora. 11 miles N on Hwy 49, 1 1/2 miles W via access road. Phone 601/879-8189.* Surface erosion exposed giant (up to 6 feet in diameter) petrified logs that were deposited in the Mississippi area as driftwood by a prehistoric river. Self-guided nature trail. Museum at visitor center has dioramas; wood, gem, mineral, fossil displays; ultraviolet (black light) room. Picknicking. Camping. Gift shop. (Daily; closed Dec 25) **$$**

Mississippi Sports Hall of Fame and Museum. *1152 Lakeland Dr, Jackson (39216). Phone 601/982-8264; toll-free 800/280-3263. www.msfame.com.* A variety of interactive exhibits can be found here, such as touch-screen television kiosks that access archival sports footage. Through interactive technology, visitors can play championship golf courses, soccer, or pitch horseshoes. (Mon-Sat 10 am-4 pm) **$**

Municipal Art Gallery. *839 N State St, Jackson (39202). Phone 601/960-1582.* Changing exhibits in a variety of media displayed in an antebellum house. (Tues-Sat, also Sun afternoons; closed holidays, Fri of Thanksgiving week; also Aug) **FREE**

Museum of Natural Science. *2148 Riverside Dr, Jackson (39202). Phone 601/354-7303. www.mdwfp. com/museum.* Collections, designed for research and education, cover Mississippi's vertebrates, invertebrates, plants, and fossils. Exhibits and aquariums depict the ecological story of the region; educational programs and workshops offered for all ages. Professional library. Division of Mississippi Department of Wildlife Conservation. (Mon-Fri 8 am-5 pm, Sat from 9 am, Sun from 1 pm; closed holidays) **$**

Mynelle Gardens. *4736 Clinton Blvd, Jackson (39209). Two blocks off Hwy 220. Phone 601/960-1894.* A 5-acre display garden with thousands of azaleas, camellias, daylilies, flowering trees, and other perennials; reflecting pools and statuary; Oriental garden, miniature flower gardens, and an all-white garden. Turn-of-the-century Westbrook House is open for viewing. Changing art and photography exhibits. Gift shop. Picnicking. (Daily; closed holidays) **$**

The Oaks House Museum. *823 N Jefferson St, Jackson (39202). Phone 601/353-9339.* (1846). Greek Revival cottage, built of hand-hewn timber by James H. Boyd, former mayor of Jackson, was occupied by General Sherman during the siege of 1863. Period furniture; garden. (Tues-Sat; closed Jan 1, Thanksgiving, Dec 25)**$**

Ross R. Barnett Reservoir. *115 Madison Landing Cir, Ridgeland (39157). 7 miles N on I-55, 3 miles E on Natchez Trace Pkwy. Phone 601/354-3448.* Reservoir (43 miles in length) created by damming Pearl River. Swimming, waterskiing, fishing, boating. Picnicking. Camping. Standard fees. (Daily) **$**

Smith Robertson Museum. *528 Bloom St, Jackson (39202). Phone 601/960-1457. www.city.jackson. ms.us/CityHall/robertson.htm.* History and culture of African-American Mississippians from Africa to present; large collection of photos, books, documents, arts and crafts. (Mon-Fri 9 am-5 pm, Sat 10 am-1 pm, Sun 2-5 pm; closed holidays) **$**

State Capitol. *400 High St, Jackson (39201). Phone 601/359-3114.* (1903). Impeccably restored in 1979, the lavish, beaux-arts capitol building was patterned after the national capitol in Washington. Houses legislature and governor's office. Tours (by appointment). **FREE**

Special Events

Dixie National Livestock Show and Rodeo. *Mississippi Coliseum., 1207 Mississippi St, Jackson (39202). Phone 601/961-4000.* Late Jan-mid Feb. Rodeo second week in Feb.

Jackson County Fair. *Fairgrounds, 200 W Ganson St, Jackson (49201).* Mid-Oct.

Mississippi State Fair. *State Fairgrounds, Jefferson St, Jackson. Phone 601/961-4000.* Agricultural and industrial exhibits and contests; midway, entertainment. Early-mid Oct.

National Cutting Horse Association Show. *Mississippi Coliseum., 1207 Mississippi St, Jackson (39202). Phone 601/961-4000.* Entries from across the US participate in amateur to professional rider competitions. Late Mar.

Limited-Service Hotels

★ ★ **EDISON WALTHALL HOTEL.** *225 E Capitol St, Jackson (39201). Phone 601/948-6161; toll-free 800/932-6161; fax 601/948-0080. www.edisonwalthall-hotel.com.* Guests are sure to enjoy their stay at this hotel. A dining room, lounge and bar are available along with a fitness center and outdoor pool. A complimentary van is available for airport pick up and drop off, as well as for the local area. 208 rooms, 8 story. Pets accepted; fee. Check-out noon. Restaurant, bar. Fitness room. Outdoor pool, whirlpool. Airport transportation available. **$**

★ **HOLIDAY INN EXPRESS.** *310 Greymont Ave, Jackson (39202). Phone 601/948-4466; toll-free 800/465-4329; fax 601/355-8919. www.hiexpress. com.* 110 rooms, 5 story. Complimentary continental breakfast. Check-out noon. **$**

★ **LA QUINTA INN.** *616 Briarwood Dr, Jackson (39211). Phone 601/957-1741; toll-free 800/687-6667; fax 601/956-5764. www.lq.com.* 101 rooms, 3 story. Pets accepted. Check-out noon. Outdoor pool. Airport transportation available. **$**

Full-Service Hotel

★ ★ **HILTON JACKSON.** *1001 E County Line Rd, Jackson (39211). Phone 601/957-2800; toll-free 888/263-0524; fax 601/957-3191. www.hilton.com.* This is a finely decorated hotel; no detail was overlooked. It offers a full-service restaurant, a courtyard pool, a poolside fitness center, a complimentary airport shuttle and more. The property is near many of the local area attractions. 300 rooms, 14 story. Check-out 1 pm. Restaurant, bar. Fitness room. Outdoor pool, whirlpool. Airport transportation available. Business center. **$**

Restaurants

★ ★ **DENNERY'S.** *330 Greymont Ave, Jackson (39202). Phone 601/354-2527; fax 601/354-2554.* Steak, seafood menu. Lunch, dinner. Closed Sun; holidays. Children's menu. **$$**

★ ★ **NICK'S.** *1501 Lakeland Dr, Jackson (39216). Phone 601/981-8017; fax 601/982-9640. www.nicksres-taurant.com.* For over 15 years Nick's has delighted the palate of Jackson residents with fine dining. The char-grilled blackfish served over grilled zucchini, yellow squash, red onions, yellow peppers, and finished with fresh basil and lemon oil is very popular. The pan-roasted duck and pork tenderloin will also please. Explore the very extensive wine list for a delightful wine to accompany dinner. Seafood menu. Lunch, dinner. Closed Sun; holidays. Bar. Children's menu. **$$**

Kosciusko (C-3)

See also Mendenhall, Yazoo City

Population 7,372
Area Code 662
Zip 39090
Information Kosciusko-Attala Chamber of Commerce, 301 E Jefferson, PO Box 696; phone 662/289-2981
Web Site www.kosciuskotourism.com

What to See and Do

Holmes County State Park. *5369 State Park Rd, Kosciusko (39063). 25 miles W on Hwy 12, then S on Hwy 51, between Hwy 51 and I-55. Phone 662/653-3351. mdwfp.com.* Approximately 450-acre park has two lakes. Fishing; boating (rentals). Nature trails; archery range. Picnicking (shelters), playground, skating rink (call for schedule), coin laundry. Camping (water, electric hookups), cabins. Standard fees.

Kosciusko Museum-Information Center. *1 1/2 miles S via S Huntington St, Natchez Trace Pkwy exit. Contact Chamber of Commerce.* Museum features information on the area, Natchez Trace Pkwy, and Polish general Tadeusz Kosciuszko; revolving displays. (Daily; closed Dec 25) **FREE**

Special Event

Central Mississippi Fair. *124 N Jackson St, Kosciusko. www.centralmsfair.com.* Central Mississippi Fairgrounds. Aug.

Laurel (E-4)

See also Hattiesburg

Settled 1882
Population 18,393
Elevation 246 ft

Area Code 601
Information Jones County Chamber of Commerce, PO Box 527, 39441; phone 601/428-0574
Web Site www.edajones.com

Laurel was built by two sawmill men in the piney woods of southeastern Mississippi after Reconstruction. Pushing through northeast Mississippi's pinelands, they picked a spot on the Southern Railroad that they thought was the forest's center. They called it Laurel for the abundant flowering shrubs, but it remained a rough lumber camp for a decade. Laurel bloomed after a midwestern company took over the lumber mill, laying out streets, and encouraging workers to buy houses. The ladies of Laurel organized the state's first garden club in the 1890s.

Laurel has been fortunate in the development of a reforestation program and diversified industry.

What to See and Do

Landrum's Homestead. *1356 Hwy 15 S, Laurel (39443). Phone 601/649-2546. www.landrums.com.* Re-creation of a late 1800s settlement. Blacksmith shop, watermill grist mill, gem mining, general store. (Mon-Sat 9 am-5 pm; closed holidays) **$$**

Lauren Rogers Museum of Art. *565 N 5th Ave, Laurel (39441). 5th Ave and 7th St. Phone 601/649-6374. www.lrma.org.* Collections of 19th- and 20th-century American and European paintings, 18th-century Japanese woodblock prints, English Georgian silver, Native American baskets. (Tues-Sat 10 am-4:45 pm, Sun 1-4 pm; closed holidays) **FREE**

Limited-Service Hotel

★ ★ **RAMADA.** *1105 Sawmill Rd, Laurel (39441). Phone 601/649-9100; toll-free 800/272-6232; fax 601/649-6045. www.ramada.com.* 207 rooms, 4 story. Check-out 1 pm. Restaurant, bar. Outdoor pool. **$**
🛏

Louisville (C-4)

See also Kosciusko, Philadelphia

Population 7,006
Elevation 525 ft
Information Louisville-Winston County Chamber of Commerce, 311 W Park, PO Box 551; phone 662/773-3921

Web Site www.winstoncounty.com

What to See and Do

Legion State Park. *635 Legion State Park Rd, Louisville (39339). On Old Hwy 25. Phone 662/773-8323. mdwfp. com.* One of the first parks developed by the Civilian Conservation Corps; original stone lodge still in use. Swimming beach; two fishing lakes; boating (ramp, rentals). Nature trail. Picnicking (shelters). Tent camping, cabins. (Daily) Standard fees.

Nanih Waiya State Park. *4496 Hwy 393, Louisville (39339). 18 miles SE via Hwy 397. Phone 662/773-7988. mdwfp.com/parks.asp.* The legendary birthplace of the Choctaw and the site of their Sacred Mound; the area was occupied from approximately the time of Christ until the arrival of Europeans. A swinging bridge leads to a cave under the mound. Picnicking (shelters). Near the Pearl River. For further information, contact the Site Manager, Hwy 3, Box 251-A. (Daily; closed Dec 25) **$**

Tombigbee National Forest. *Hwy 15, Louisville (39735). N on Hwy 15, which borders W side of forest. Phone 662/965-4391. www.fs.fed.us/r8/tombigbee.* This southern section of the forest contains Choctaw Lake. Swimming (fee), fishing, boating. Picnicking. Camping (Mar-mid-Nov; hookups, fee; dump station). Fees are charged at recreation sites. There is a Ranger District station near Ackerman and another section of the forest S of Tupelo (see). Contact Forest Supervisor, 100 W Capitol St, Suite 1141, Jackson 39269. **$$**

McComb (E-2)

Founded 1872
Population 13,337
Elevation 460 ft
Area Code 601
Zip 39649
Information Chamber of Commerce, 120 N Railroad Blvd, PO Box 83; phone 601/684-2291 or toll-free 800/399-4404
Web Site www.pikeinfo.com

What to See and Do

Bogue Chitto Water Park. *1068 Dogwood Trail, Mc-Comb (39648). 12 miles E on Hwy 98. Phone 601/684-9568. www.boguechittowaterpark.com.* Swimming, tubing, canoeing. Nature trail. Picnicking, playground, pavilion. Primitive/improved camping, cabins (**$$-**

$$$$**). Visitor center. (Daily) **$

Percy Quin State Park. *6 miles S on I-55, exit 13.Phone 601/684-3931. mdwfp.com.* Park covering 1,700 acres on 700-acre Tangipahoa Lake in oak and pine forests. Lodge area includes arboretum and Liberty White Railroad Museum, housed in a caboose. Pool, bathhouse, waterskiing, fishing, boating (ramp, rentals). Nature; miniature golf, 27-hole golf course. Picnicking (shelters), snack bar, playing field, lodge. Improved and primitive camping, cabins. Standard fees. **$**

Special Event

Lighted Azalea Trail. In keeping with the Japanese tradition of lighting cherry blossoms, McComb citizens illuminate their azaleas; arts festival, music programs. Two weeks in mid-Mar.

Restaurant

★ **DINNER BELL.** *229 5th Ave, McComb (39648). Phone 601/684-4883.* American menu. Lunch, dinner. Closed Mon; July 4, Dec 23-mid-Jan. Children's menu. **$**

Mendenhall (D-3)

See also Jackson

Population 2,555
Elevation 323 ft
Area Code 601
Zip 39114
Information Chamber of Commerce, PO Box 635; phone 601/847-1725

What to See and Do

Bienville National Forest. *Hwy 35 through Raleigh, Mendenhall (39074). NW on Hwy 49 to Hwy 13, then N, in forest. Phone 601/469-3811. www.southernregion. fs.fed.us/mississippi/bienville.* This central Mississippi tract of 178,374 acres has numerous forest management demonstration areas of second-growth pine and hardwood. Swimming, boating. Hiking, bridle trails. Picknicking. Camping. Ranger District office is located in Forest. Contact District Ranger, Bienville Ranger District, 3473 Hwy 35 S, Forest 39074. Two major recreation areas are

> **Marathon.** *47 miles NE via hwys 540, 18, 501, forest service roads.* A 58-acre lake. Swimming (fee), fishing, boating. Picnicking. Camping (fee).

> **Shongelo.** *22 miles E and N via hwys 540, 35.*A 5-acre lake. Swimming (fee), bathhouse; fishing. Picnicking. Camping (fee).

D'Lo Water Park. *3 miles NW via Hwy 49. Phone 601/847-4310.* Park includes 85 acres. Swimming, bathhouse, fishing, canoeing (rentals). Nature trails, lighted playing fields. Picnicking. Camping (hookups; fee). (Daily; closed Jan 1, Thanksgiving, Dec 25) **FREE**

Meridian (D-4)

See also Philadelphia

Settled 1831
Population 39,968
Elevation 333 ft
Area Code 601
Information East Mississippi Development Corporation, 1915 Front St, Union Station, 39302; phone 601/693-1306 or toll-free 800/748-9970
Web Site www.meridianms.org

Founded at the junction of two railroads, Meridian is now an industrial, agricultural, and retailing center in the heart of the South's finest timber-growing country.

What to See and Do

Bienville National Forest. *3473 Hwy 35 S, Forest (39074). 45 miles W off I-20. Phone 601/469-3811. www.fs.fed.us/r8/miss.* (see MENDENHALL)

Clarkco State Park. *Hwy 45 N, Quitman. 18 miles S off Hwy 45. Phone 601/776-6651. mdwfp.com.* Park covering 815 acres situated on a 65-acre lake. Swimming beach, waterskiing, fishing, boating (ramp, rentals). Nature trail; lighted tennis. Picnicking (shelters), playground, playing field, lodge, coin laundry. Primitive and improved camping, cabins (each with lake pier). **$**

Jimmie Rodgers Museum. *1725 Jimmie Rodgers Dr, Meridian (39307). Highland Park, 19th St and 41st Ave. Phone 601/485-1808. www.jimmierodgers.com.* Fashioned after an old train depot, the museum houses souvenirs and memorabilia of the "Father of Country Music," including a rare Martin 00045 guitar. (Daily; closed Jan 1, Thanksgiving, Dec 25) **$**

Meridian Museum of Art. *628 25th Ave, Meridian (39301). 25th Ave at 7th St. Phone 601/693-1501.* Permanent and changing exhibits of paintings, graphics, photographs, sculpture, and crafts by regional artists. (Tues-Sun, afternoons; closed holidays) **FREE**

Merrehope. *905 Martin Luther King, Jr. Memorial Dr, Meridian (39301). Phone 601/483-8439.* Stately 20-room mansion, begun in 1859, features unusual woodwork, handsome columns, mantels, and stairway. (Mon-Sat; closed holidays) Special Christmas tours. **$$** Nearby is

> **Frank W. Williams House.** *Phone 601/483-8439.* Victorian home (circa 1886) features stained glass, oak paneling, parquet floors, and detailed gingerbread. (Days same as Merrehope) Admission to both houses. **$$**

Okatibbee Dam and Reservoir. *7 miles NW off Hwy 19. Phone 601/626-8431.* A 3,800-acre lake with swimming (seasonal), waterskiing, water slides; fishing; boating (ramps, marina). Picnicking, lodging. Camping at Twiltley Branch Park (fee; phone 601/626-8068) and at Okatibbee Water Park (seasonal, fee; phone 601/737-2370).

Special Events

Arts in the Park. *Phone 601/693-2787. www.meridianms.org/artcalendar.htm.* Concerts, plays, art shows, children's programs. First weekend in Apr. **FREE**

Jimmie Rodgers Memorial Festival. *Phone 601/693-2686. www.jimmierodgers.com/festival.html.* Country and western music. May.

Queen City State Fair. *Phone 601/693-5465.* Agricultural exhibits, carnival. Oct.

Limited-Service Hotels

★ **BEST WESTERN OF MERIDIAN.** *2219 S Frontage Rd, Meridian (39301). Phone 601/693-3210; toll-free 800/528-1234; fax 601/693-3210. www.bestwestern.com.* 120 rooms, 2 story. Check-in 2 pm, check-out noon. Restaurant. Outdoor pool. **$**

★ **HOWARD JOHNSON.** *110 Hwy 80 E, Meridian (39302). Phone 601/483-8281; fax 601/485-2015. www.hojo.com.* 142 rooms, 2 story. Check-in 1 pm, check-out noon. Indoor pool, whirlpool. **$**

Natchez (E-1)

See also Woodville

Settled 1716
Population 18,464
Elevation 215 ft
Area Code 601
Information Convention and Visitors Bureau; 640 S Canal, Box C, PO Box 1485, 39120; phone 601/446-6345 or toll-free 800/647-6724
Web Site www.natchez.ms.us

Natchez lives in the enchantment of the Old South, a plantation atmosphere where everything seems beautiful and romantic. Greek Revival mansions, manicured gardens and lawns, tree-shaded streets, and southern hospitality abound in this museum of the antebellum South.

Natchez, named for a Native American tribe, is also a manufacturing town with a history of trapping, trading, hunting, and farming. French, Spanish, English, Confederate, and US flags have flown over this town, one of the oldest in the Mississippi Valley. Vestiges of the Spanish influence can still be seen along South Wall Street, near Washington Street, a charming neighborhood once restricted to the Spanish dons. The city's modern stores and buildings serve to emphasize how lovingly the citizens of Natchez have preserved their past.

What to See and Do

Isle Capri Casino. *21 Silver St, Natchez (39120). On the riverfront. Phone 601/445-0605; toll-free 800/722-5825. www.islecapricasino.com.*

⭐ **Canal Street Depot.** *Canal and State sts, Natchez.* Houses the official Natchez Pilgrimage Tour and Tourist Headquarters. (Daily) Information on historic Natchez and the surrounding area. Offers tours (fee) of 15 antebellum mansions and tickets for spring, fall, and Christmas pilgrimages (see SPECIAL EVENTS).

Dunleith. *84 Homochitto St, Natchez (39120). Phone 601/446-8500; toll-free 800/433-2445. www.natchezdunleith.com.* (Circa 1856). National Historic Landmark. Restored antebellum, Greek Revival mansion completely surrounded by colonnaded galleries. Estate includes 40 acres of green pastures and wooded bayous within Natchez. French and English antiques.

Sightseeing in the Historic District

Natchez is a delightful town to visit. It's beautifully set on a high bluff overlooking the Mississippi River. The compact downtown area, designated a National Historic District for its many antebellum buildings and distinguished architecture, has many attractive house museums with guided tours that illuminate the interesting town history. There are plenty of restaurants, cafés, and shops to break up a day of sightseeing.

You might want to start upriver and work your way back down. The oldest house in town, built in 1799, is the small two-story House on Ellicott Hill (North Canal at Jefferson; phone 601/442-2011). Andrew Elliott raised the American flag here in defiance of Spain, which claimed the broad plain along the gulf to the Mississippi River as Spanish West Florida.

Walk away from the river down Jefferson, then up Pearl Street a block to Stanton Hall off High Street (phone 601/442-6282). A stately mansion built in 1857, Stanton Hall perhaps better fits the classic image of opulent antebellum architecture. Find fine dining and inner theater in the cottage house. Return down Pearl Street toward the commercial district.

Two blocks down, carriage tours depart from the entranceway of the Natchez Eola Hotel. Around the corner on Main Street, in the old Post Office building, the Museum of Afro-American History and Culture (phone 601/445-0728) shows a different side of the towns revered antebellum history.

Two blocks farther south along Pearl, Magnolia Hall (215 South Pearl Street; phone 601/442-6672), a Greek Revival mansion built in 1858, is now a house museum. A block west (toward the river), the Governor Holmes House (207 South Wall Street; phone 601/442-2366), opens the home of the last governor of the Mississippi Territory, who then became the first state governor when Mississippi joined the Union in 1817. Like many of the historic houses in town, it also operates as an inn for overnight lodging.

A collection of shops right here at Wall Street and Washington includes cafés and a great bookshop. Cross Canal Street and skip down a block to visit Rosalie, on the bluff at South Broadway (phone 601/445-4555), a lovely brick mansion that served as Union Army headquarters during the Civil War.

Walk upriver a couple of blocks until you see the steep road leading down the bluff. This leads to Natchez Under-the-Hill, once the disreputable bawdytown that catered to the seamier side of the steamboat trade. Today it is thoroughly sanitized, though it retains an Old West frontier look and spirit. There are several family restaurants and a tavern called the Saloon, all with great river views. Down at the water, the *Lady Luck* riverboat casino operates around the clock. If you've parked at the visitor center; you car is right up the hill from here.

(Daily 9 am-4:30 pm; closed Jan 1, Thanksgiving, Dec 25) Guest rooms. **$$**

Emerald Mound. *2680 Natchez Trace Pkwy, Natchez (39120). 10 miles NE of Natchez on Natchez Trace Pkwy.Phone 601/442-2658. www.cr.nps.gov/nr/travel/ mounds/eme.htm.* (see) **FREE**

Grand Village of the Natchez. *400 Jefferson Davis Blvd, Natchez (39120). Phone 601/446-6502. www.mdah. state.ms.us/hprop/gvnivisit.html.* Museum, archaeological site, nature trails, picnic area, gift shop. (Daily; closed Jan 1, Thanksgiving, Dec 25) **FREE**

Historic Jefferson College. *16 Old North St, Washington. 6 miles E on Hwy 61. Phone 601/442-2901. www.mdah. state.ms.us/hprop/hjc.html.* The Jefferson College campus was the site, in 1817, of the first state Constitutional Convention. Jefferson Davis was among the famous Mississippians who attended the school. No longer in use as a school, it is now listed on the National Register of Historic places. A museum interprets the early history of the territory, state, and campus; nature trails; picnicking. (Mon-Sat 9 am-5 pm, Sun 1-5 pm; closed Jan 1, Thanksgiving, Dec 25) **FREE**

Historic Springfield Plantation. *20 miles NE via Hwy 61, Natchez Trace Pkwy, then 12 miles N on Hwy 553. Phone 601/786-3802.* (1786-1790). Believed to be the first mansion erected in Mississippi; remains nearly intact with little remodeling over the years; original hand-carved woodwork. Built for Thomas Marston Green, Jr., wealthy planter from Virginia; site of Andrew Jackson's wedding. Displays include Civil

War equipment, railroad memorabilia, narrow-gauge locomotive. (Daily; closed Dec 25) **$$$**

Homochitto National Forest. *NE and SE via Hwy 84, 98, Hwy 33. Phone 601/965-4391. www.southernregion. fs.fed.us/mississippi/homochitto.* This 189,000-acre forest is located near the picturesquely eroded loess country. Visitors view the regular timber management activities. Swimming (Clear Springs Recreation Area); fishing and hunting. Picnicking, camping (Clear Springs Recreation Area). Fees may be charged at recreation sites. Ranger District offices are located in Meadville and Gloster. Contact Forest Supervisor, 100 W Capitol St, Suite 1141, Jackson 39269.

The House on Ellicott Hill. *211 N. Canal St, Natchez (39120). Jefferson and Canal sts. Phone 601/442-2011.* Site where, in 1797, Andrew Ellicott raised the first American flag in the lower Mississippi Valley. Built in 1798, the house overlooks both the Mississippi and the terminus of the Natchez Trace. Restored and authentically furnished. (Daily) **$$$**

Longwood. *140 Lower Woodville Rd, Natchez (39120). Phone 601/442-5193.* Enormous, Italianate detailed "octagon house" crowned with an onion dome. Under construction at the start of the Civil War, interiors were never completed above first floor; circa 1840 furnishings. Owned and operated by the Pilgrimage Garden Club. (Daily; days vary during Pilgrimages) (See SPECIAL EVENTS)**$$$**

Magnolia Hall. *S Pearl and Washington, Natchez. Phone 601/442-6672.* (1858). Last great mansion to be erected in the city before the outbreak of the Civil War, an outstanding example of Greek Revival architecture; period antiques; costume museum. (Daily)**$$**

Melrose Estate Home. *1 Melrose Ave, off Hwy 61., Natchez (39120). Phone 601/446-5790.* The National Park Service oversees this historic mansion and grounds, and tells the plantation story from a more national perspective. House open for guided tours only; self-guided tours of slave quarters. (Daily)

Monmouth. *36 Melrose Ave, Natchez (39120). Phone 601/442-5852. www.monmouthplantation.com.* (Circa 1818). Registered as a National Historic Landmark, the monumental Greek Revival house and auxiliary buildings, once owned by Mexican War hero General John Anthony Quitman, have been completely restored; antique furnishings; extensive gardens. Guest rooms. Tours (daily; closed Dec 25). **$$$**

Mount Locust. *2680 Natchez Trace Pkwy, Natchez. 15 miles NE on Natchez Trace Pkwy. Phone 601/445-4211.* (see) **FREE**

Natchez State Park. *230B Wickliff Rd, Natchez. 10 miles N off Hwy 61. Phone 601/442-2658. mdwfp.com.* Park has horse trails believed to be abandoned plantation roads that lead to Brandon Hall, house of the first native Mississippi governor, Gerard Brandon (1826-1831). Fishing lake; boating (ramp, rentals). Nature trail. Picnicking. Primitive and improved camping, cabins. Standard fees.

Natchez Visitor Center. *640 S Canal, Natchez (39120). On Hwy 84. Phone toll-free 800/647-6742. www.cityof-natchez.com.* Spacious modern visitor center on the bluff above the Mississippi River offers comprehensive tourist services, including a film on the city's history and heritage. (Daily)

Rosalie. *100 Orleans St, Natchez (39120). Phone 601/445-4555. www.rosaliemansion.com.* (1820-23) Red brick Georgian mansion with Greek Revival portico served as the headquarters for the Union Army during occupation of Natchez. Original furnishings date from 1857; gardens on bluff above Mississippi. (Daily, 9:30 am-4:30 pm; closed Easter, Thanksgiving, Dec 25) Fees vary during scheduled times at the Pilgrimages (see SPECIAL EVENTS). **$$**

Stanton Hall. *401 High St, Natchez (39120). Phone 601/446-6631. www.natchezmansions.com/html/stanton_hall.html.* (1851-57) Highly elaborate antebellum mansion surrounded by giant oaks; original chandeliers, marble mantels, Sheffield hardware, French mirrors. Owned and operated by the Pilgrimage Garden Club. Tours every 1/2 hour (daily 9 am-4:30 pm; closed Dec 25 and during pilgrimages) (See SPECIAL EVENTS) **$$**

Special Events

Great Mississippi River Balloon Race Weekend. *640 S Canal St # C, Natchez (39120). www.natchezms. com/balloonrace.* Third weekend in Oct. **$**

Natchez Opera Festival. *64 Homochitto St, Natchez (39120). www.alcorn.edu/opera.* Apr-May. **$$$$**

Natchez Pilgrimage Tours. *640 S Canal, Natchez (39120). Phone toll-free 800/647-6742. www.natchezpilgrimage.com. Headquarters, Canal Street Depot.* Tours of antebellum houses sponsored by the Natchez Pilgrimage Association (daily). Also Confederate Pageant at City Auditorium (Mon, Wed, Fri, Sat). Contact

PO Box 347 for details. Mar-early Apr; Fall Pilgrimage mid-Oct; Christmas Dec.

Limited-Service Hotels

★★ **ISLE OF CAPRI CASINO & HOTEL.** *645 S Canal St, Natchez (39120). Phone 601/445-0605; toll-free 800/722-5825; fax 601/442-9823. www.isleof-capricasino.com.* 147 rooms, 6 story. Check-in 4 pm, check-out 1 pm. Restaurant. Outdoor pool, whirlpool. Casino. **$**

★★ **NATCHEZ EOLA HOTEL.** *110 N Pearl, Natchez (39121). Phone 601/445-6000; fax 601/446-5310.* 125 rooms, 7 story. Check-out 11 am. Restaurant, bar. **$**

Full-Service Inns

★★★ **DUNLEITH PLANTATION.** *84 Homochitto St, Natchez (39120). Phone 601/446-8500; toll-free 800/433-2445; fax 601/442-8554. www.dunleithplantation.com.* This luxurious home has recently been restored to its pre-Civil War excellence. With exceptional cuisine and lavish grounds, this location is ideal for weddings and large parties. 9 rooms, 2 story. Closed Easter, Thanksgiving, Dec 24-25. Children over 14 years only. Complimentary full breakfast. Check-in 2 pm, check-out 11 am. Antebellum mansion (circa 1856) on 40 acres; courtyard. **$$**

★★★ **MONMOUTH PLANTATION.** *36 Melrose Ave, Natchez (39120). Phone 601/442-5852; toll-free 800/828-4531; fax 601/446-7762. www.monmouthplantation.com.* This plantation offers an atmosphere of beautifully restored luxury. The dining experience is as exceptional as its décor. Enjoy the vast courtyards or a five-course dinner in the evening or take advantage of the historic plantation tours and carriage rides during the day. 30 rooms, 2 story. Children over 14 years only. Complimentary full breakfast. Check-in 3 pm, check-out 11 am. Tennis. **$$**

Specialty Lodgings

BRIARS BED & BREAKFAST. *31 Irving Ln, Natchez (39120). Phone 601/446-9654; toll-free 800/634-1818; fax 601/445-6037. www.thebriarsinn.com.* Listed on the National Register of Historic Places, this 19-acre property is covered with manicured gardens, brick walkways, and pecan and magnolia trees. The owners, both interior designers, have meticulously restored and renovated all guest rooms. Jefferson Davis was married here in 1845. 14 rooms, 2 story. Children over 12 years only. Complimentary full breakfast. Check-in 2 pm, check-out 11 am. Outdoor pool. **$$**

THE BURN ANTEBELLUM BED & BREAKFAST INN. *712 N Union St, Natchez (39120). Phone 601/442-1344; toll-free 800/654-8859; fax 601/445-0606. www.theburnbnb.com.* 7 rooms, 2 story. Closed Dec 25. Children over 12 years only. Complimentary full breakfast. Check-in 2-6 pm, check-out 11 am. Outdoor pool. Early Greek Revival house (1834) with semi-spiral staircase in central hall; used as headquarters and hospital by Union troops during Civil War. Free tour of house. **$**

Restaurants

★★ **CARRIAGE HOUSE.** *401 High St, Natchez (39120). Phone 601/445-5151; fax 601/445-6108.* American menu. Lunch. Closed Tues-Wed; Jan 1, July 4. Bar. **$$**

★ **COCK OF THE WALK.** *200 N Broadway, Natchez (39120). Phone 601/446-8920; fax 601/446-7733.* American menu. Dinner. Closed holidays. Children's menu. **$$**

Natchez Trace Parkway (E-1)

Web Site www.nps.gov/natr/

One of the earliest "interstates," the Natchez Trace stretched from Natchez, Mississippi, to Nashville, Tennessee, and was the most heavily traveled road in the Old Southwest from approximately 1785 to 1820. Boatmen floated their products downriver to Natchez or New Orleans, sold them, and walked or rode home over the Natchez Trace. A "trace" is a trail or road. This one was shown on French maps as far back as 1733. It was still in use, to some extent, as late as the 1830s, though its importance diminished after the invention of the steam engine.

The 444-mile-long parkway crosses and recrosses the original trace, passing many points of historic interest, including Emerald Mound (see NATCHEZ).

The parkway headquarters and visitor center are 5 miles north of Tupelo, at junction Hwy 45 Business (sign reads Hwy 145) and the parkway. Interpretive facilities include a visitor center with exhibits depicting the history of the trace and an audiovisual program that tells the story of the trace (daily; closed Dec 25; free). Park Service personnel can furnish information on self-guided trails, wayside exhibits, interpretive programs, camping, and picnicking facilities along the parkway. For further information contact Superintendent, 2680 Natchez Trace Pkwy, Tupelo 38804; phone 662/680-4025 or toll-free 800/305-7417.

Ocean Springs (F-4)

See also Biloxi, Gulf Islands National Seashore, Gulfport, Pascagoula

Population 17,225
Elevation 20 ft
Area Code 228
Zip 39566
Information Chamber of Commerce, 1000 Washington Ave, PO Box 187; phone 228/875-4424
Web Site www.oceanspringschamber.com

This is the site of Old Biloxi, settled by d'Iberville in 1699. The site of the original Fort Maurepas was verified by the discovery here of cannons dredged from the bay and cannonballs unearthed from the land.

Although some soldiers and settlers remained after the French colonial capital was moved to Mobile in 1702, the area languished until the first large influx of summer visitors arrived in the 1850s. It has since become a popular resort.

Headquarters and campground for the Mississippi District of the Gulf Islands National Seashore (see) are in Ocean Springs.

Special Event

Garden and Home Pilgrimage. Late Mar or early Apr.

Restaurant

★ ★ **JOCELYN'S.** *Hwy 90 E, Ocean Springs (39564). Phone 228/875-1925.* French, Creole menu. Dinner. Closed Sun-Mon. Bar. Children's menu. **$$**
🅳

Oxford (A-3)

Settled 1836
Population 11,756
Elevation 416 ft
Area Code 662
Zip 38655
Information Oxford Tourism Council, PO Box 965; phone 662/234-4680 or toll-free 800/758-9177
Web Site www.touroxfordms.com

Oxford was named for the English university city in an effort to lure the University of Mississippi to the site; in 1848 the university was opened. Today, "Ole Miss," with its forested, hilly 1,194-acre campus, dominates the area, and the town that boasted an opera house before the Civil War still reveres its role as a university town.

William Faulkner, Nobel Prize winning author, lived near the university at "Rowan Oak." Many landmarks of his fictional Yoknapatawpha County can be found in surrounding Lafayette County.

What to See and Do

University of Mississippi. *1 mile W on University Ave. Phone 662/915-5993. www.olemiss.edu.* (1848). (12,000 students.) Greek Revival-style buildings grouped around the Lyceum Building. Newer buildings follow the Classical Revival style.

Blues Archive. *340 Farley Hall, Oxford (38677). Farley Hall, Grove Loop. Phone 662/232-7753.* Extensive collection of blues recordings and related material. Three major collections form the nucleus of the archive: The B.B. King Collections, The Kenneth S. Goldstein Folklore Collection, and The Living Blues Archival Collection. (Mon-Fri; closed school holidays) **FREE**

University Archives. *University Library. Phone 662/232-7408.* Historical and literary works of and by Mississippians; works by William Faulkner in 35 languages, exhibit of his awards, including Nobel Prize, manuscripts, and first editions. (Mon-Fri 8 am-5 pm; closed university holidays) **FREE**

University Museums. *University Ave and Fifth St, Oxford (38677). Phone 662/232-7073.* Housed in two adjoining buildings, the collections include Greek and Roman antiquities, antique scientific instruments, other historic objects; also African-American, Caribbean, and Southern folk art. (Tues-Sat 9:30 am-4:30 pm, Sun 1-4 pm; closed Mon; university holidays) **FREE**

Limited-Service Hotels

★ **DAYS INN.** *1101 Frontage Rd, Oxford (38655). Phone 662/234-9500; fax 662/236-2772. www.daysinn. com.* 100 rooms, 2 story. Check-out 11 am. Wireless Internet access. Outdoor pool. **$**
⌷

★ **DOWNTOWN OXFORD INN & SUITES.** *400 N Lamar Blvd, Oxford (38655). Phone 662/234-3031; toll-free 800/780-7234; fax 662/234-2834. www.downtownox-fordinnandsuites.com.* 123 rooms, 2 story. Pets accepted; fee. Check-in 2 pm, check-out 1 pm. Fitness room. Outdoor pool. Airport transportation available. **$**
⌷ ⌷ ⌷

★ **SUPER 8.** *2201 Jackson Ave W, Oxford (38655). Phone 662/234-7013; fax 662/236-4378. www.super8. com.* 116 rooms, 2 story. Check-out noon. Wireless Internet access. Fitness room. Outdoor pool. **$**
⌷ ⌷

Specialty Lodging

OLIVER-BRITT HOUSE INN & TEAROOM. *512 Van Buren Ave, Oxford (38655). Phone 662/234-8043; fax 662/281-8065.* Restored manor house built in 1905; some period furnishings. 5 rooms, 2 story. Complimentary full breakfast. Check-in 2 pm, check-out 11 am. **$**
⌷

Restaurant

★ ★ **DOWNTOWN GRILL.** *110 Courthouse Sq, Oxford (38655). Phone 662/234-2659; fax 662/234-3933.* American menu. Breakfast, lunch, dinner. Closed Sun; holidays. Bar. **$$**

Pascagoula (F-4)

See also Biloxi, Ocean Springs, also see Mobile, AL

Population 26,200
Elevation 15 ft
Area Code 228
Information Jackson County Chamber of Commerce, 720 Krebs Ave, PO Box 480, 39568-0480; phone 228/762-3391
Web Site www.jcchamber.com

This resort, shipbuilding center, and port offers fresh and saltwater fishing, swimming, and many other recreational opportunities. The city has a long and fascinating history. Pine ridges and mysterious bayous surround it, and its "singing river" is famous.

The Pascagoula River gives forth a peculiar singing music, which resembles a swarm of bees in flight. According to legend, the Pascagoula Indians (for whom the city is named) had a young chieftain who wooed and won a princess of the neighboring Biloxi tribe, even though she was betrothed. The Biloxi chief, enraged, attacked the Pascagoula tribe with an overwhelming force. The Pascagoula, realizing they could not win, joined hands and walked, singing, into the river to their death.

What to See and Do

Mississippi Sandhill Crane National Wildlife Refuge. *7200 Gautier Vancleave Rd, Pascagoula (39553). Off Gautier-Vancleave Rd, 1/2 miles N of I-10 exit 61, follow signs. Phone 228/497-6322. mississippisandhillcrane. fws.gov.* Established to protect endangered cranes, the refuge's three units total 18,000 acres. Visitor center has slide programs (by request), wildlife exhibit, paintings, and maps (Mon-Fri; closed legal holidays). Tours (Jan-Feb, by appointment). Also here is wildlife trail (3/4 mile) with interpretive panels; outdoor exhibit; bird-watching. Visitor center (Mon-Fri 8 am-4 pm). **FREE**

Old Spanish Fort and Museum. *4602 Fort St, Pascagoula (39567). Five blocks N of Hwy 90. Phone 228/769-1505.* (1718). Built by the French, later captured by the Spanish, the fort's walls of massive cypress timbers cemented with oyster shells, mud, and moss are 18 inches thick. Said to be the oldest structure in the Mississippi Valley. Museum has Native American relics, historic items. (Daily; closed holidays) **$**

Scranton Nature Center. *IG Levy Park at Pascagoula River, Pascagoula. Phone 228/762-6017.* Nautical, marine, and wetlands exhibits housed in restored shrimp boat. (Tues-Sat, also Sun afternoons) **$**

★ **Singing River.** *Pascagoula River, two blocks W of the courthouse.* The singing sound is best heard on late summer and autumn nights. The music seems to increase in volume, coming nearer until it seems to be underfoot. Scientists have said it could be made by fish, sand scraping the hard slate bottom, natural gas escaping from sand bed, or current sucked past a hidden cave. None of the explanations offered has been proven.

Special Events

Garden Club Pilgrimage. Tours of historic houses and gardens in town. Late Mar-early Apr.

Jackson County Fair. *Fairgrounds., 200 W Ganson St, Jackson (49201).* Mid-Oct.

Mardi Gras. Month leading to Ash Wednesday.

River Jamboree. *Moss Point. N on Hwy 63.* Arts and crafts, games. First Sat in May.

Limited-Service Hotel

★ ★ **LA FONT INN.** *2703 Denny Ave, Pascagoula (39567). Phone 228/762-7111; toll-free 800/647-6077; fax 228/934-4324. www.lafontinn.com.* A festive atmosphere, located conveniently near all of the Mississippi Gulf golf courses. Dining is available for breakfast, lunch, and dinner and the menus feature seasonal local delicacies. The inn is ideal for business travelers as well as private parties. 192 rooms, 2 story. Pets accepted, some restrictions; fee. Check-out 1 pm. Restaurant, bar. Outdoor pool, children's pool, whirlpool. Tennis. **$**

Pass Christian (F-3)

See also Biloxi, Gulfport

Settled 1704
Population 6,579
Elevation 10 ft
Area Code 228
Zip 39571
Information Chamber of Commerce, PO Box 307; phone 228/452-2252

The town was a resort before the Civil War and the site of the South's first yacht club, which was founded in 1849. It is Mrs. Jane Murphy Manders who is generally credited with the "bed sheet surrender" of Pass Christian on April 4, 1862; attempting to save the city from further shelling by the Union fleet after the Confederate forces evacuated, she waved a sheet from her doorway. Pass Christian has hosted six vacationing US presidents—Jackson, Taylor, Grant, Theodore Roosevelt, Wilson, and Truman. The world's largest oyster reef is offshore.

What to See and Do

Buccaneer State Park. *1150 S Beach Blvd, Waveland (39576). 20 miles W on Hwy 90. Phone 800/467-2757. mdwfp.com.* Located on the Gulf of Mexico, the park features two waterslides. Swimming beach, pool, wading pool; gulf fishing for speckled trout, flounder, redfish, crab, shrimp. Nature, bicycle trails; lighted tennis. Picnicking (shelters), playground, basketball courts, snack bar, lodge with game room, coin laundry. Primitive and improved camping. **$**

The Friendship Oak. *6 miles E on Hwy 90, located on the University of Southern Mississippi's Gulf Park campus, beside Hardy Hall in Long Beach. Phone 228/865-4500.* The oak's 16-foot trunk and 5-foot-plus-diameter limbs dwarf Hardy Hall. A plaque dates the tree back to 1487, five years before Columbus's arrival to the new world. Legend proclaims that those who enter the tree's shadow shall remain lifetime friends. Wooden platform provides a peaceful haven. American poet Vachel Lindsay regularly held classes in the shade of the majestic oak.

Special Events

Blessing of the Fleet. Festival; boat decorations competition; band; entertainment. Last Sun in May.

Garden Club Pilgrimage. Information at Chamber of Commerce Building, Small Craft Harbor. Visits to several historic houses and gardens in town. Late Mar.

Mardi Gras. Carnival Ball and Parade. Sat, Sun before Shrove Tuesday.

Limited-Service Hotel

★ ★ **CASINO MAGIC BAY TOWER HOTEL.** *711 Casino Magic Dr, Bay St. Louis (39521). Phone 228/467-9257; toll-free 800/562-4425; fax 228/469-2689. www.casinomagic.com.* 201 rooms, 4 story. Check-out 11 am. Four restaurants, bars. Outdoor pool, whirlpool. **$**

Philadelphia (C-4)

See also Louisville, Meridian

Population 7,303
Elevation 424 ft
Area Code 601
Zip 39350
Information Philadelphia-Neshoba County Chamber of Commerce, 410 Poplar Ave, Suite 101, PO Box 51; phone 601/656-1742

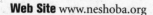
Web Site www.neshoba.org

This town was settled on Choctaw land. Several thousand Choctaws continue to live in the area. The Choctaw tribe, which once numbered more than 25,000, ceded its lands to the United States by the Treaty of Dancing Rabbit Creek in 1830. The Choctaw Indian Agency, which was founded shortly after the treaty was signed, is located in Philadelphia.

Special Events

Choctaw Indian Fair. *Choctaw Indian Reservation, 8 miles W via Hwy 16. Phone 601/650-1685. www.choctawindianfair.com.* Entertainment, arts and crafts, cultural programs, princess pageant, music. Mid-July. **$$$**

Neshoba County Fair. *8 1/2 miles SW via Hwy 21 S. www.neshobacountyfair.org.* Late July.

Restaurants

★★ **AMADA.** *217 Chestnut St, Philadelphia (19106). Phone 215/625-2450; fax 215/625-2470. www.amadarestaurant.com.* This authentic Spanish tapas restaurant is located in Philadelphia's historic district, just steps from many historical sites—so it's a great choice for tourists. The majority of the menu is tapas, but paella and steak for two are also available. The restaurant also offers a whole pig carved tableside (48 hours advance notice required). Chef's counter seating is available for those guests wishing to watch the kitchen while they eat. And flamenco dancing is performed twice a week—Wednesdays and Fridays. Spanish, tapas menu. Lunch, dinner, late-night. Bar. Casual attire. Reservations recommended. Valet parking. Credit cards accepted. **$$$**

★ **CAPOGIRO.** *119 S 13th St, Philadelphia (19107). Phone 215/351-0900. www.capogirogelato.com.* If you have a craving for gelato, this is the place you want to go. The gelato is made fresh daily. The menu also offers coffees, paninis, salads, assorted sweets, and juices. There are two locations in Philly—the other is at 117 South 20th Street. American menu. Breakfast, lunch, dinner. Children's menu. Casual attire. Outdoor seating. Credit cards accepted. **$**

★ **CAPOGIRO.** *117 S 20th St, Philadelphia (19103). Phone 215/636-9250. www.capogirogelato.com.* If you have a craving for gelato, this is the place you want to go. The gelato is made fresh daily. The menu also offers coffees, paninis, salads, assorted sweets, and juices. There are two locations in Philly—the other is at 119

South 13th Street. American menu. Breakfast, lunch, dinner. Children's menu. Casual attire. Outdoor seating. Credit cards accepted. **$**

★★ **DARK HORSE PUB.** *421 S 2nd St, Philadelphia (19147). Phone 215/928-9307; fax 215/928-0232. www.darkhorsepub.com.* Foodies may not want to overlook this English-style pub in the middle of Head House Square, where even a basic hamburger features goat cheese and is served on a brioche roll. Don't let the atmosphere of dart boards and televised soccer and rugby games fool you—the menu is more than just bangers and mash (which, by the way, is served with a caramelized onion demi-glaze). Braised free-range chicken steak with wild mushrooms and brie and Vietnamese mussels in a lemongrass broth are just a few of the tasty surprises found on the jazzed-up menu of English and American fare. American, Continental menu. Lunch, dinner, brunch. Closed Jan 1, Dec 25. Bar. Casual attire. **$$**

Port Gibson (D-1)

See also Louisville, Meridian

Settled 1788
Population 1,840
Elevation 120 ft
Area Code 601
Zip 39150
Information Port Gibson-Claiborne County Chamber of Commerce, PO Box 491; phone 601/437-4351
Web Site www.portgibson.org

Many antebellum houses and buildings remain in Port Gibson, lending support to the story that General Grant spared the town on his march to Vicksburg with the words: "It's too beautiful to burn."

The Samuel Gibson House (circa 1805), the oldest existing structure in town, has been restored and now houses the Port Gibson-Claiborne County Chamber of Commerce and Visitor Information Center.

What to See and Do

✪ **Antebellum houses.** *1601 Church St, Port Gibson (39150). Phone 601/437-4351.* Open year-round by appointment; special schedule during the Spring Pilgrimage. **$$**

Energy Central. *Port Gibson. 2 miles N on Hwy 61 to Grand Gulf Rd. On the grounds of Grand Gulf Nuclear*

Station. *Phone 601/437-6393.* Exhibits and hands-on displays about nuclear energy and electricity. (Mon-Fri) **FREE**

First Presbyterian Church. *Church and Walnut sts, Port Gibson. www.fpcportgibson.org.* (1859). Gold-leaf hand with a finger pointing skyward tops the steeple; interior features old slave gallery and chandeliers taken from the steamboat *Robert E. Lee.* **FREE**

Grand Gulf Military Park. *Grand Gulf Rd, Port Gibson. 8 miles NW off Hwy 61. Phone 601/437-5911. www. grandgulfpark.state.ms.us.* This site marks the former town of Grand Gulf, which lost 55 of 75 city blocks to Mississippi floods between 1855 and 1860. The Confederacy chose to fortify the banks when the population was only 160 and the town was dying. In the spring of 1862, Admiral David G. Farragut sent his powerful naval squadron upriver; Baton Rouge and Natchez fell, but Vicksburg refused to surrender. Confederate artillery and supporting troops were sent to Grand Gulf, where intermittent fighting between Union warships and Confederate shore batteries continued until a Union column landed at Bayou Pierre, marched on Grand Gulf and burned what remained of the town. War returned to Grand Gulf when Admiral D. D. Porter's ironclads opened fire on forts Cobun and Wade on the morning of Apr 29, 1863. After more than five hours, two ironclads were disabled and the guns of Fort Wade silenced. The park today includes fortifications, an observation tower, a cemetery, sawmill, dog-trot house, memorial chapel, water wheel and grist mill, a carriage house with vehicles used by the Confederates, a four-room cottage reconstructed from the early days of Grand Gulf, and several other pre-Civil War buildings. A museum in the visitor center displays Civil War, Native American, and prehistoric artifacts (daily 8 am-5 pm; closed Jan 1, Thanksgiving, Dec 25; fee). Park (daily). Picnic facilities, 42 camper pads (hookups). **$**

Oak Square. *1207 Church St, Port Gibson (39150). 1 mile off Natchez Trace Pkwy. Phone 601/437-4350.* (Circa 1850). Restored 30-room mansion with six fluted, Corinthian columns, each standing 22 feet tall. Antique furnishings from the 18th and 19th centuries. Extensive grounds, courtyard, gazebo. Guest rooms available (see SPECIALTY LODGINGS). Tours by appointment. **$$$**

Rosswood Plantation. *Lorman. 9 miles S on Hwy 61 to Lorman, then 2 1/2 miles E on Hwy 552. Phone toll-free 800/533-5889. www.rosswood.net.* (1857). Classic Greek Revival mansion designed by David Shroder, architect

of Windsor, features columned galleries, ten fireplaces, 15-foot ceilings, a winding stairway, and slave quarters in the basement. The first owner's diary has survived and offers details of antebellum life on a cotton plantation. The 14 rooms are furnished with antiques. Guest rooms available (see SPECIALTY LODGINGS). (Tours Mar-Dec; closed some holidays) **$$$**

The Ruins of Windsor. *Port Gibson. Old Rodney Rd. Phone 601/437-4351.* These 23 stately columns are all that is left of a four-story mansion built in 1860 at a cost of $175,000 and destroyed by fire in 1890. Its proximity to the river and size made it a natural marker for Mississippi River pilots, including Samuel Clemens.

Specialty Lodgings

OAK SQUARE COUNTRY INN. *1207 Church St, Port Gibson (39150). Phone 601/437-4350; toll-free 800/729-0240; fax 601/437-5768.* 12 rooms, 2 story. Complimentary full breakfast. Check-out 11 am. Restored antebellum mansion (circa 1850) and guest house. Free tour of mansion, grounds. **$** 🄳

ROSSWOOD PLANTATION. *Hwy 552 E, Lorman (39096). Phone 601/437-4215; toll-free 800/533-5889; fax 601/437-6888. www.rosswood.net.* 4 rooms, 2 story. Complimentary full breakfast. Check-in 2-5 pm, check-out 11 am. Outdoor pool, whirlpool. This landmark 1857 Greek Revival mansion is located on a working Christmas tree plantation. **$$** 🄳 🛌

Ridgeland (D-2)

Restaurant

★ ★ **TICO'S STEAK HOUSE.** *1536 E County Line Rd, Ridgeland (39157). Phone 601/956-1030; fax 601/956-2375.* Steak menu. Dinner. Closed Sun; holidays. Bar. **$$** 🄳

Sardis (A-3)

See also Louisville, Meridian

Population 2,038
Elevation 379 ft
Area Code 662
Zip 38666

Information Chamber of Commerce, 114 W Lee St, PO Box 377; phone 662/487-3451

What to See and Do

Enid Lake and Dam. *21 miles S on I-55, then 1 mile E. Phone 662/563-4571.* Shoreline with swimming, boating. Picnicking. Camping (hookups; fee). Amphitheater. Golden Age and Golden Access passports accepted (see MAKING THE MOST OF YOUR TRIP). The dam is part of the Yazoo Basin Flood Control Plan. On the S shore of the lake is

> **George Payne Cossar State Park.** *25 miles S on I-55, then 4 miles E on Hwy 32. Phone 662/623-7356.* The park, covering 900 acres, is situated on a peninsula jutting into Enid Lake. Swimming pool, water-skiing, fishing, boating (ramp). Nature, bicycle trails (rentals); miniature golf. Picnicking (shelters), playground, concession, restaurant (year-round, Wed-Sun), lodge, coin laundry. Improved camping, cabins. **$**

Heflin House Museum. *304 S Main, Sardis (38666).* (1858). One of the few remaining antebellum structures in Sardis and Panola County; houses exhibits on history of Panola County from Native American times through 1900. (Mon-Fri by appointment; closed holidays). Contact Chamber of Commerce.

Sardis Lake and Dam. *9 miles E off I-55. Phone 662/563-4531.* This lake, with a 260-mile shoreline formed by damming the Little Tallahatchie River, is part of the Yazoo Basin flood control project. Noted for its natural white sand beaches. Swimming, water-skiing, fishing, boating (launching ramps). Picnicking. Camping (some fees). Interpretive programs. **FREE** Overlooking the lake is

> **John W. Kyle State Park.** *4235 State Park Rd, Sardis (38666). Phone 662/487-1345.* Pool (summer, Tues-Sun), water-skiing, fishing, boating (ramps). Nature trails; lighted tennis courts. Picnicking (shelters), playground, playing field, snack bar, lodge, coin laundry. Improved camping, cabins. **$**

Starkville (C-4)

See also Columbus

Founded 1831
Population 21,869
Elevation 374 ft
Area Code 662

Zip 39759
Information Convention and Visitors Bureau, 322 University Dr; phone 662/323-3322 or toll-free 800/649-8687
Web Site www.starkville.org

Starkville is the seat of Oktibbeha County and the home of Mississippi State University.

What to See and Do

Mississippi State University. *1 mile E, on University Dr. Phone 662/325-2323. www.msstate.edu.* (1878). (16,000 students.) Originally Mississippi Agricultural and Mechanical College, the college became a state university in 1958. On a 4,200-acre tract, approximately 750 acres make up the campus; the Mississippi Agricultural and Forestry Experiment Station utilizes much of the remaining land for cultivation, pasture, and buildings. On campus are the Dunn-Seiler Geology Museum, Cobb Institute of Archaeology, University Art Gallery, and the Chapel of Memories.

National Wildlife Refuge. *SE off Hwy 25; follow signs from stadium at Mississippi State University. Phone 662/323-5548.* This 48,000-acre refuge, which includes a 1,200-acre Bluff Lake, offers space for more than 200 species of birds, including waterfowl, wild turkey, the endangered bald eagle and red-cockaded woodpecker, as well as alligators and deer. Fishing (Mar-Oct), hunting (fall; some fees). Hiking. Refuge (daily). **FREE**

Oktibbeha County Heritage Museum. *206 Fellowship St, Starkville (39759). Fellowship and Russell sts. Phone 662/323-0211.* Artifacts from the county's past housed in the former GM&O railroad station. (Tues-Thurs; or by appointment; closed holidays) **FREE**

Limited-Service Hotel

★ **RAMADA.** *403 Hwy 12, Starkville (39759). Phone 662/323-6161; fax 662/323-8073. www.ramada. com.* 173 rooms, 2 story. Pets accepted. Check-in 2 pm, check-out noon. High-speed Internet access. Bar. Outdoor pool. **$**

Restaurant

★ ★ **HARVEY'S.** *406 Hwy 12 E, Starkville (39759). Phone 662/323-1639; fax 662/323-2897.* Seafood, steak menu. Lunch, dinner. Closed Sun; holidays. Bar. Children's menu. **$$**

Tupelo (B-4)

See also Louisville, Meridian

Settled 1833
Population 34,211
Elevation 290 ft
Area Code 662
Information Convention & Visitors Bureau, 399 E Main St, PO Drawer 47, 38802; phone 662/841-6521 or toll-free 800/533-0611
Web Site www.tupelo.net

Tupelo is built on what was formerly Chickasaw land. On May 26, 1736, two forces of French colonists and their Choctaw allies unsuccessfully attacked the Chickasaw in an attempt to rescue prisoners and avenge an attack by the Natchez on the French settlement of Natchez. Failure to conquer the Chickasaw prevented the extension of French authority into northern Alabama, Mississippi, and western Tennessee.

When the town was ceded by the Treaty of Pontotoc in 1832, settlers moved in and began farming. After the Battle of Shiloh, April 6-7, 1862, Confederate General P.G.T. Beauregard and his defeated troops retreated to Tupelo.

This was the first city to sign for TVA power—on October 11, 1933. Less than four months later, service was begun at a tremendous savings. Tupelo is also the birthplace of Elvis Presley.

What to See and Do

Brices Cross Roads National Battlefield Site. *2680 Natchez Trace Pkwy, Tupelo (38804). Phone 601/680-4025. www.nps.gov/brcr.* **FREE**

Elvis Presley Park and Museum. *306 Elvis Presley Dr, Tupelo (38804). Phone 662/841-1245. www.elvispresleybirthplace.com.* In the park is a small white frame house where Presley lived for the first three years of his life. Museum houses a collection of Elvis memorabilia. Chapel (free). (May-Sept: Mon-Sat 9 am-5:30 pm; rest of year to 5 pm; also Sun 1-5 pm year-round; closed Thanksgiving, Dec 25) **$$**

Natchez Trace Parkway Visitor Center. *300 W Main St, Tupelo (38804). 5 miles N at junction Pkwy, Hwy 45 Business. www.nps.gov/natr.* (see NATCHEZ TRACE PARKWAY)

Oren Dunn Museum of Tupelo. *689 Rutherford Dr, Tupelo (38801). 2 miles W via Hwy 6 at Ballard Park. Phone 662/841-6438.* Displays include NASA space equipment used in Apollo missions; Elvis Presley room; reproductions of Western Union office, general store, train station, log cabin; Civil War and Chickasaw items. (Daily; closed holidays) **$**

Private John Allen National Fish Hatchery. *111 Elizabeth St, Tupelo (38804). Phone 662/842-1341.* This federal hatchery, one of the oldest (1902), operates 15 ponds totaling 17 acres. A warmwater hatchery, it produces striped and largemouth bass, bluegill, and walleye; it distributes one million fish annually for use in management of reservoirs and coastal waters. (Mon-Fri)

Tombigbee National Forest. *20 miles S, off Natchez Trace Pkwy. Phone 601/965-4391. www.fs.fed.us/r8/tombigbee.* This section of the forest, along with a tract to the south on Highway 15 near Louisville (see), totals 66,341 acres. Davis Lake provides swimming (fee); fishing. Picnicking. Camping (electric hookups; fee; dump station). Recreation area (Mar-mid-Nov). Standard fees are charged at recreation sites. A Ranger District office is located in Ackerman. Contact Forest Supervisor, 100 W Capitol St, Suite 1141, Jackson 39269. **$$**

Tombigbee State Park. *264 Cabin Dr, Tupelo (38804). 6 miles SE off Hwy 6. Phone 662/842-7669. mdwfp.com/parks.* A 702-acre park with a 102-acre spring-fed lake. Fishing; (ramp). Nature trail; tennis; archery range. Picnicking (shelters), playground, lodge. Primitive and improved camping, cabins. **$**

Trace State Park. *2139 Faulkner Rd, Belden (38826). 10 miles W via Hwy 6. Phone 662/489-2958.* On 2,500 acres with a 600-acre lake. Water-skiing; fishing for bass, catfish, bluegill, and crappie; boating (ramp, rentals). Hiking, horseriding trail; golf. Picnicking. Tent and trailer camping (electric and water hookups, dump station), cabins. **$**

Tupelo National Battlefield. *2680 Natchez Trace Pkwy, Tupelo (38804). 1 mile W on Hwy 6. Phone 601/680-4025. www.nps.gov/tupe.* One-acre tract near the area where the Confederate line was formed to attack the Union position. Marker with texts and maps explains battle. (Daily) **FREE**

Limited-Service Hotels

★ **HOLIDAY INN EXPRESS.** *923 N Gloster St, Tupelo (38801). Phone 601/842-8811; toll-free 800/465-4329; fax 601/844-6884. www.hiexpress.com.* 124 rooms, 2 story. Pets accepted, some restrictions; fee. Complimentary continental breakfast. Outdoor pool. **$**

★ **RAMADA.** *854 N Gloster St, Tupelo (38801). Phone 662/844-4111; toll-free 800/272-6232; fax 662/840-7960. www.ramadatupelo.com.* 230 rooms, 3 story. Check-out 1 pm. Restaurant, bar. Fitness room. Outdoor pool, children's pool. Airport transportation available. Business center. **$**

Specialty Lodging

MOCKINGBIRD INN BED & BREAKFAST. *305 N Gloster St, Tupelo (38804). Phone 662/841-0286; fax 662/840-4158. www.bbonline.com/ms/mockingbird.* 7 rooms, 2 story. Children over 10 years only. Complimentary full breakfast. Check-in 3-8 pm. Check-out noon. **$**

Restaurants

★ **JEFFERSON PLACE.** *823 Jefferson St, Tupelo (38801). Phone 662/844-8696; fax 662/842-6026.* American menu. Lunch, dinner. Closed Sun; Thanksgiving, Dec 25. Bar. **$$**

★ **MALONE'S FISH & STEAK HOUSE.** *1349 Hwy 41, Tupelo (38801). Phone 662/842-2747.* Steak menu. Dinner. Closed Sun-Mon; Thanksgiving; 2 weeks in late Dec. Children's menu. **$**

★ ★ **PAPA VANELLI'S.** *1302 N Gloster, Tupelo (38801). Phone 662/844-4410; fax 662/680-4746. www.vanellis.com.* Greek, Italian menu. Lunch, dinner. Closed Dec 25. Bar. Children's menu. **$$**

Vicksburg (D-2)

See also Port Gibson

Settled 1790
Population 26,407
Elevation 200 ft
Area Code 601
Information Convention & Visitors Bureau, 1221 Washington St, PO Box 110, 39181; phone 601/636-9421 or toll-free 800/221-3536
Web Site www.vicksburgcvb.org

In June 1862, the Union controlled the Mississippi River with the exception of Vicksburg, which was in Confederate hands. The location of the town, partly on high bluffs above the river, made it impossible to move traffic up or down the river without subjecting the boats to withering fire from strong Confederate batteries. This position made it possible to maintain communication lines with Louisiana, which were vital to the Confederacy.

Grant's purpose was to gain complete control of the Mississippi as a waterway and, in doing so, to split the South. In June, Admiral David Farragut sent his fleet of Union gunboats upriver from New Orleans and shelled the town; he was, however, forced to withdraw before taking the city or silencing its guns. General William Tecumseh Sherman, also attempting to take Vicksburg, moved along the west banks of the river, south from Memphis with 30,000 troops. He was repelled. Meanwhile, Grant's supply lines were being broken and harassed by Confederate cavalry.

Grant was now desperate. He had to take Vicksburg. He ordered Admiral David Porter to move his gunboats south from Memphis and to pass Vicksburg at night. The boats were sighted; two transports were lost. The others got through, and Grant, with an army west of the river, now had transportation across the river. Once in Mississippi, the Union army, living off the land, moved around Vicksburg in a series of brilliant diversionary maneuvers that kept the Confederate cavalry busy accomplishing nothing. Grant now took Jackson and moved toward Vicksburg from the east. He attacked the city with three corps, setting the time of attack and synchronizing watches to make sure all attacked together. But his forces were driven back.

Grant was a more modern and committed general than most of the other Union commanders in the war. He would settle for nothing less than total victory, including unconditional surrender of the city of Vicksburg. He realized that to take Vicksburg, the town must be starved; so he surrounded it and laid siege. For 47 days and nights Grant pounded Vicksburg with mortar and cannon fire; and the populace, hiding in caves, nearly starved.

The caves dug by the residents of Vicksburg and the Union army's trenches and tunneling were made easier because the city was built on loess, a wind-blown silt that forms a compacted, but soft, soil. Grant dug tunnels and planted mines under Confederate positions, but only one charge was set off. On July 4, the Confederates agreed to surrender the city. On that day, the South's cause was dealt a mighty blow from which it never recovered.

Modern Vicksburg is nearly surrounded by the Vicksburg National Military Park, which is as much a part of the town as the streets and antebellum houses. Originally an important river port, Vicksburg has a fascinating riverfront along the Mississippi River and the Yazoo Canal. Plan to spend several days; the town offers much to see and do.

What to See and Do

Anchuca Historic Mansion and Inn. *1010 First East St, Vicksburg (39183). Phone 601/661-0111.* (1830). Restored Greek Revival mansion furnished with period antiques and gas-burning lanterns. Landscaped gardens, brick courtyard. (Daily; closed Dec 25) Guest rooms. **$$$**

Biedenharn Museum of Coca-Cola Memorabilia. *1107 Washington St, Vicksburg (39183). Phone 601/638-6514.* The building in which Coca-Cola was first bottled in 1894. Restored candy store; old-fashioned soda fountain; collection of Coca-Cola advertising and memorabilia. (Daily; closed holidays) **$$**

Cedar Grove. *2200 Oak St, Vicksburg. Phone 601/636-1000; toll-free 800/862-1300. cedargroveinn.com.* (1840). Elegant mansion shelled by Union gunboats in siege; restored, but a cannonball is still lodged in the parlor wall; roof garden with view of the Mississippi and Yazoo rivers; tea room; many original furnishings. More than 4 acres of formal gardens; courtyards, fountains, gazebos. (Daily) Guest rooms available. **$$**

Duff Green. *1114 First East St, Vicksburg (39183). Phone 601/636-6968; toll-free 800/992-0037. www.duffgreenmansion.com.* (1856). Mansion of Paladian architecture shelled by Union forces during siege, then used as a hospital for Confederate and Union troops. Restored; antique furnishings. Guided tours. High tea and tour (by reservation). Guest rooms available. (Daily) **$$**

Martha Vick House. *1300 Grove St, Vicksburg (39183). Phone 601/638-7036.* (1830). Built by the daughter of the founder of Vicksburg, Newit Vick. Greek Revival façade; restored original interior furnished with 18th- and 19th-century antiques; outstanding art collection. (Daily; closed holidays) **$$**

McRaven Home. *1445 Harrison St, Vicksburg (39183). Phone 601/636-1663.* Heaviest-shelled house during the Siege of Vicksburg; provides an architectural

record of Vicksburg history, from frontier cottage (1797) to Empire (1836) and finally to elegant Greek Revival townhouse (1849); many original furnishings. Original brick walks surround the house; garden of live oaks, boxwood, magnolia and many plants. Guided tours. (Mar-Nov, daily) **$$**

Old Court House Museum. *1008 Cherry St, Vicksburg (39183). Court Square. Phone 601/636-0741. www.oldcourthouse.org.* (1858). Built with slave labor, this building offers a view of the Yazoo Canal from its hilltop position. Here, Grant raised the US flag on July 4, 1863, signifying the end of fighting after 47 days. Courthouse now houses an extensive display of Americana: Confederate Room contains weapons, documents on the siege of Vicksburg; also Pioneer Room; Furniture Room; Native American displays and objets d'art. (Mon-Sat 8:30 am-4:30 pm, Sun 1:30-4:30 pm; closed Jan 1, Thanksgiving, Dec 24-25) **$**

Tourist Information Center. *3300 Clay St, Vicksburg (39183). At I-20. Phone 601/636-9421; toll-free 800/221-3536.* Furnishes free information, maps, and brochures on points of interest and historic houses. Guide service (fee). House (daily; closed Jan 1, Thanksgiving, Dec 25).

"The Vanishing Glory". *717 Clay St, Vicksburg (39183). Phone 601/634-1863.* A 30-minute dramatization of the Civil War siege of Vicksburg; story based upon diaries and writings of people who lived through the campaign; wide-screen production, quadraphonic sound. (Shown every hour, daily)

⭐ **Vicksburg National Military Park & Cemetery.** *3201 Clay St, Vicksburg (39183). Phone 601/636-0583. www.nps.gov/vick.* This historic park, the site of Union siege lines and a brave Confederate defense, borders the eastern and northern sections of the city. A visitor center is at the park entrance, on Clay Street at I-20. Museum; exhibits and audiovisual aids. Self-guided, 16-minute tour. (Daily 8 am-5 pm; closed Dec 25) **$**

Special Event

Spring Pilgrimage. Fifteen antebellum houses are open to the public at this time. Two tours daily. Mid-Mar-early Apr.

Limited-Service Hotels

★ ★ **BATTLEFIELD INN.** *4137 I-20 N Frontage Rd, Vicksburg (39183). Phone 601/638-5811; toll-free 800/359-9363; fax 601/638-9249. www.battlefieldinn.*

org. 117 rooms, 2 story. Pets accepted, some restrictions; fee. Complimentary continental breakfast. Check-in 3 pm, check-out 12:30 pm. Restaurant, bar. Outdoor pool. **$**

★ **BEST INN.** *2390 S Frontage Rd, Vicksburg (39180). Phone 601/634-8607; toll-free 800/237-8466; fax 601/634-6053. www.bestinn.com.* 70 rooms, 2 story. Complimentary continental breakfast. Check-out 11 am. Outdoor pool. **$**

★ **MOTEL 6.** *4127 N Frontage Rd, Vicksburg (39180). Phone 601/638-5077; toll-free 800/466-8356; fax 601/638-6004. www.motel6.com.* 62 rooms, 2 story. Pets accepted. Check-out 11 am. Outdoor pool. **$**

Full-Service Inns

★ ★ ★ **ANCHUCA.** *1010 1st E St, Vicksburg (39183). Phone 601/661-0111; toll-free 800/469-2597. www.anchucamansion.com.* Climb the narrow, greenery-lined steps to this pre-Civil-War mansion offering guest rooms with private baths, a full breakfast, and afternoon tea. Built around 1830 in Greek Revival style, the common rooms are furnished with period antiques and romantic, gas-burning chandeliers. 7 rooms, 2 story. Complimentary full breakfast. Check-in 4-7 pm, check-out 11 am. Outdoor pool, whirlpool. Tour of house. **$**

★ ★ ★ **CEDAR GROVE MANSION INN.** *2300 Washington St, Vicksburg (39180). Phone 601/636-1000; toll-free 800/862-1300; fax 601/634-6126. www.cedargroveinn.com.* Choose from the many spacious guest rooms, suites, or cottages at this 5-acre, garden-like property. All accommodations include a full breakfast, afternoon tea, and evening sherry and chocolates. The inn's chef, Andre Flowers, turns out splendid New Orleans cuisine at Andre's Restaurant. 34 rooms, 4 story. Check-in 2 pm, check-out noon. Restaurant. Fitness room. Outdoor pool. Tennis. **$**

★ ★ ★ **DUFF GREEN MANSION.** *1114 First East St, Vicksburg (39181). Phone 601/638-6662; toll-free 800/992-0037; fax 601/661-0079. www.duffgreen-mansion.com.* This 12,000-square-foot, 1856 Palladian mansion was pressed into service as a hospital for both Confederate and Union soldiers during the Siege of Vicksburg. Each of the bedrooms has fireplaces and

porches; luxuriously furnished in period antiques and reproductions. A complimentary bar is offered during happy hour. 7 rooms, 3 story. Pets accepted. Complimentary full breakfast. Check-in 3 pm, check-out 11 am. Outdoor pool, whirlpool. Business center. Shelled during siege, it was completely restored. **$**

Specialty Lodgings

ANNABELLE BED AND BREAKFAST. *501 Speed St, Vicksburg (39180). Phone 601/638-2000; toll-free 800/791-2000; fax 601/636-5054. www.annabellebnb.com.* Perched along the Mississippi River Valley, shaded by magnolia trees, sits this Victorian-Italianate home and its neighboring guest house, built in 1868 and 1881 respectively. 8 rooms, 2 story. Complimentary full breakfast. Check-in 3 pm, check-out 11 am. Outdoor pool. **$**

CORNERS BED & BREAKFAST INN. *601 Klein St, Vicksburg (39180). Phone 601/636-7421; toll-free 800/444-7421; fax 601/636-7232. www.thecorners.com.* 15 rooms, 2 story. Complimentary full breakfast. Check-in 2 pm, check-out 11 am. **$**

Restaurants

★ ★ **CEDAR GROVE.** *2200 Oak St, Vicksburg (39180). Phone 601/636-1000; fax 601/634-6126. www.cedargroveinn.com.* American menu. Dinner. Closed Mon. Bar. Reservations recommended. **$$**

★ ★ **EDDIE MONSOUR'S.** *127 Country Club Dr, Vicksburg (39180). Phone 601/638-1571.* American menu. Lunch, dinner. Closed Sun; holidays. Bar. Children's menu. **$$**

★ **WALNUT HILLS ROUND TABLES.** *1214 Adams St, Vicksburg (39183). Phone 601/638-4910. www.walnuthillsms.com.* American menu. Lunch, dinner. Closed Sat; holidays. Bar. Children's menu. Built in 1880. **$$**

Woodville (E-1)

See also Natchez

Founded 1811
Population 1,192
Elevation 410 ft
Area Code 601
Zip 39669

Information Woodville Civic Club, PO Box 1055; phone 601/888-3998

First settled in the 18th century, Woodville grew steadily and became the seat of Wilkinson County. It is the home of *The Woodville Republican,* the oldest newspaper and the oldest business institution in Mississippi. The town still has many beautiful 19th-century houses and some of the state's first churches. These include the Woodville Baptist (1809), the Woodville Methodist (1824), and St. Paul's Episcopal (1823), which has an Erben organ, installed in 1837.

What to See and Do

★ **Rosemont Plantation.** *Woodville. 1 mile E on Hwy 24 (Main St). Phone 601/888-6809.* (Circa 1810) The home of Jefferson Davis and his family. His parents, Samuel and Jane Davis, moved to Woodville and built the house when the boy was two years old. The Confederate president grew up here and returned to visit his family throughout his life. Many family furnishings remain, including a spinning wheel that belonged to Jane Davis. Original working atmosphere of the 300-acre plantation. Five generations of the Davis family are buried here. (Tues-Sat 10 am-5 pm) **$$$**

Wilkinson County Museum. *Bank St, Woodville. Court House Square. Phone 601/888-3998.* Housed in a Greek Revival-style building; changing exhibits, period room settings. (Mon-Fri, also Sat mornings) **FREE**

Yazoo City (C-2)

See also Jackson

Founded 1823
Population 14,550
Elevation 120 ft
Area Code 662
Zip 39194
Information Convention and Visitors Bureau, 323 N Main St, PO Box 186; phone 662/746-1815 or toll-free 800/381-0662
Web Site www.yazoo.org

What to See and Do

Yazoo Historical Museum. *Triangle Cultural Center., 332 N Main St, Yazoo City (39194). Phone 662/746-2273.* Exhibits cover history of Yazoo County from prehistoric time to present; Civil War artifacts; fossils. Tours. (Mon-Fri; closed Jan 1, Thanksgiving, Dec 24-26) **FREE**

Tennessee

Handsomely rugged and rough-hewn, Tennessee reveals itself most characteristically in a 480-mile stretch from Mountain City at its northeastern boundary, southwest to Memphis and the Mississippi River, with its twisting western shore. In a place of individualistic, strong-minded people, history and legend blend into folklore based on the feats of Davy Crockett, Daniel Boone, Andrew Jackson, and Sam Houston. It is a state of mountain ballads and big-city ballet, of water-powered mills and atomic energy plants.

Population: 4,877,185
Area: 42,244 square miles
Elevation: 182-6,643 feet
Peak: Clingmans Dome (Sevier County)
Entered Union: June 1, 1796 (16th state)
Capital: Nashville
Nickname: Volunteer State
Flower: Iris
Bird: Mockingbird
Tree: Tulip Poplar
Time Zone: Eastern and Central
Web Site: www.state.tn.us/tourdev/
Fun Facts:
- Tennessee has more than 3,800 documented caves.
- Graceland, Elvis Presley's home, is the second most visited home in the country.

The state's economy and its basic patterns of life and leisure were electrified in the 1930s by the Tennessee Valley Authority (TVA), the Depression-born, often denounced, and often praised grand-scale public power, flood control, and navigation project. TVA harnessed rampaging rivers, saved cities from the annual plague of floods, created a broad system for navigation, and produced inexpensive power and a treasury of recreational facilities. TVA altered the mainstream of the state's economy, achieving a dramatic switch from agriculture to industry. Cheap power, of course, sparked that revolution. Today, Tennessee has manufacturing payrolls in excess of farm income. Chemicals, textiles, foods, apparel, tourism, healthcare, printing and publishing, metalworking, and lumber products are its chief industries.

Farms and forests still produce more than 50 different crops, but the emphasis is changing from cotton and tobacco to livestock. With more than 200 species of trees, Tennessee is the nation's hardwood producing center. Mining is also a leading industry in Tennessee, with limestone the major product. The state also ranks high in the production of zinc, pyrite, ball clay, phosphate rock, and marble.

In 1541, it is believed, the explorer de Soto planted the flag of Spain on the banks of the Mississippi near what is now Memphis. Although French traders explored the Tennessee Valley, it was their English counterparts who came over the mountain ranges, settling among the Cherokee and establishing a claim to the area. By the end of the 17th century, the Tennessee region was a territory of North Carolina. With the construction of Fort Loudoun (1756), the first Anglo-American fort garrisoned west of the Alleghenies, settlement began. The first permanent colonies were established near the Watauga River in 1769 and 1771 and are known as the Watauga settlements.

The free-spirited settlers in the outlying regions found themselves far from the seat of their formal government in eastern North Carolina. Dissatisfied and insecure, they formed the independent state of Franklin in 1784. But formal recognition of the independent state was never to come. After four chaotic years, the federal government took over and in 1790 established "The Territory of the United

Calendar Highlights

APRIL

Dogwood Arts Festival *(Knoxville)*. Phone 865/637-4561. Arts and crafts exhibits and shows; more than 80 public and private gardens on display; music; parades; sporting events; more than 60 miles of marked dogwood trails or auto or free bus tours; special children's and senior citizen activities.

MAY

Memphis in May International Festival *(Memphis)*. Phone 901/525-4611. Month-long celebration of the cultural and artistic heritage of Memphis. Major events occur on weekends, but activities are held daily. Includes the Beale St Music Festival, World Championship Barbecue Cooking Contest, and Sunset Symphony.

JUNE

International Country Music Fan Fair *(Nashville)*. Phone 866/326-3247. Country music fans have an opportunity to mix and mingle with their favorite stars. Autograph sessions and special concerts.

Riverbend Festival *(Chattanooga)*. Phone 423/265-4112. Music and sporting events, children's activities, and a fireworks display.

AUGUST

Tennessee Walking Horse National Celebration *(Shelbyville)*. Phone 931/684-5915. More than 2,100 horses participate. Events conclude with crowning ceremonies for world grand champion walking horse.

SEPTEMBER

Labor Day Fest *(Memphis)*. Beale St. Phone 901/529-0999. Memphis musicians perform rhythm and blues, jazz, country, and rock at clubs and restaurants throughout the historic district.

Mid-South Fair and Exposition *(Memphis)*. Mid-South Fairgrounds. Phone 901/274-8800. Agricultural, commercial, industrial exhibits; rides and concerts. Largest rodeo east of the Mississippi.

Tennessee State Fair *(Nashville)*. Phone 615/862-8980.

Tennessee Valley Fair *(Knoxville)*. Chilhowee Park. Phone 865/637-5840. Entertainment; livestock and agricultural shows; contests, exhibits, fireworks, and carnival rides.

OCTOBER

Fall Color Cruise & Folk Festival *(Chattanooga)*. Phone 706/275-8778. Riverboat trips, arts and crafts, and entertainment.

National Storytelling Festival *(Johnson City)*. Phone 423/753-2171. Three-day gathering from across the nation features some of the country's best storytellers.

NOVEMBER

A Country Christmas *(Nashville)*. Opryland Hotel. Phone 615/871-7637. Offers events ranging from a musical stage show to an art, antique, and craft show.

States South of the River Ohio." Tennessee was admitted to the Union six years later. Among the first representatives it sent to Washington was a raw backwoodsman named Andrew Jackson.

During the War of 1812, Tennessee riflemen volunteered in such great numbers that Tennessee was henceforth called the "Volunteer State," and Andrew Jackson emerged from the war a national hero.

Although there was strong abolitionist sentiment in parts of the state, Tennessee finally seceded in 1861 and became a battleground; some of the bloodiest battles of the war, including Shiloh, Stones River, Missionary Ridge, Fort Donelson, and the Battle of Franklin, were fought within the state's boundaries. In 1866, shortly after former Tennessee governor Andrew Johnson became president, the state was accepted back into the Union.

When to Go/Climate

Tennessee usually experiences cool winters and warm summers. There is little variation in temperatures from north to south; however, temperatures do drop from west to east due to the rise in elevation. The eastern mountains occasionally see significant snowfall. The following temperature chart offers a representative sampling of high/low temperatures in the state.

AVERAGE HIGH/LOW TEMPERATURES (°F)

Knoxville

Jan 46/26	**May** 78/53	**Sept** 81/59
Feb 51/29	**June** 85/62	**Oct** 71/46
Mar 61/37	**July** 87/66	**Nov** 60/38
Apr 70/45	**Aug** 87/65	**Dec** 50/30

Memphis

Jan 49/31	**May** 81/61	**Sept** 84/65
Feb 54/35	**June** 89/69	**Oct** 74/52
Mar 63/43	**July** 92/73	**Nov** 62/43
Apr 73/52	**Aug** 91/71	**Dec** 53/35

Parks and Recreation

Water-related activities, hiking, riding, various other sports, picnicking and visitor centers, as well as camping, are available in many of Tennessee's state parks. Most parks have supervised swimming (June-Labor Day, $2.50-$3), golf in resort parks (18 holes, $14-$24; 9 holes, $7.50-$13), boating ($3-$3.50/hour), fishing and tent camping (one-two people, at least one over 17 years: $7-$19/day, each additional over 7 years, $.50; two-week maximum). Cabins, rustic to very modern, are available in several parks (daily, $50-$220; reservations should be made at park of choice; one-night deposit required; two-night minimum). Reservations are required for camping at some parks. There is also camping in Cherokee National Forest and Great Smoky Mountains National Park (see both). For further information, contact the Tennessee Department of Environment & Conservation, Bureau of State Parks, 401 Church St, 7th floor, Nashville 37243-0446; phone 615/532-0001, 800/421-6683, or 888/867-2757.

FISHING AND HUNTING

There are more than 30 different kinds of fish in the state's mountain streams and lakes, including striped, largemouth, smallmouth, and white bass; rainbow trout; walleye; muskie; crappie; and catfish. Nonresident licenses: three-day all species, $20.50; ten-day all species, $30.50; three-day, no trout $10.50; ten-day, no trout $15.50; annual, no trout $26; annual, all species $51.

Within the constraints of season and limits, everything from squirrel and deer to wild boar can be hunted. Nonresident licenses: seven-day small game and water fowl, $30.50; annual small game and water fowl, $56; seven-day all game, $105.50; annual all game, $156. For detailed information, contact the Tennessee Wildlife Resources Agency, Ellington Agricultural Center, PO Box 40747, Nashville 37204; phone 615/781-6500.

Driving Information

Safety belts are mandatory for all persons in the front seat of a vehicle. Children under 4 years must be in child/passenger restraint systems that meet federal motor vehicle safety standards. For more information, phone 615/741-3073.

INTERSTATE HIGHWAY SYSTEM

The following alphabetical listing of Tennessee towns and parks in this book shows that these cities are within 10 miles of the indicated interstate highways. Check a highway map for the nearest exit.

Highway Number	Cities/Towns within 10 Miles
Interstate 24	Chattanooga, Clarksville, Manchester, Monteagle, Murfreesboro, Nashville.
Interstate 40	Cherokee National Forest, Cookeville, Crossville, Dickson, Hurricane Mills, Jackson, Knoxville, Lebanon, Lenoir City, Memphis, Nashville, Natchez Trace State Resort Park, Oak Ridge, Sevierville.
Interstate 65	Columbia, Franklin, Lewisburg, Nashville.
Interstate 75	Caryville, Chattanooga, Cleveland, Jellico, Knoxville, Lenoir City, Sweetwater.
Interstate 81	Kingsport, Morristown.

THE COPPER BASIN

A driving tour along Highway 64 east of Chattanooga takes visitors through the scenic Cherokee National Forest, alongside the notorious Ocoee River, and through the badlands of the Copper Basin at the Georgia border for a 75-mile driving trip through Tennessee's remote southeast corner. From Chattanooga, take I-75 north to Cleveland, and then Highway 64 east to the Georgia border (take the bypass around Cleveland). From outside the town of Ocoee, Highway 64 runs east through 24 miles of the Cherokee National Forest alongside the Ocoee River.

The Ocoee River, which hosted the 1996 Olympic Whitewater Competition, draws daring paddlers to one of the premiere whitewater runs in the country. A continuous series of Class III and IV rapids with nicknames like "Broken Nose," "Diamond Splitter," "Tablesaw," and "Hell Hole" hints at the river's reputation as one of the Southeast's greatest whitewater runs (overall rating: Class IV). The acclaimed whitewater lies between two dams built and managed by the Tennessee Valley Authority (TVA) for hydroelectric powerthe TVA can dry up or "turn on" the whitewater as easily as turning a spigot. Two dozen outfitters around Ocoee lead guided rafting expeditions downriver for half-day or full-day excursions; try Nantahala Outdoor Center (phone 800/232-7238), Ocoee Outdoors (phone 800/533-7767), or Southeastern Expeditions (phone 800/868-7238).

Eleven miles from Ocoee off Highway 64, the Parksville Lake Recreation Area, operated by the National Forest Service, offers a nice spot for picnics, boating, or camping in stands of pine and dogwood trees. Enjoy a few leisurely hours here before continuing on to the Copper Basin.

Centered between Ducktown and Copperhill at the Georgia border off Highway 64, the Copper Basin draws its name from the copper mines that flourished here in the 1800s. Unfortunately, the industry clear-cut the forest and generated copper sulfide fumes that devastated what was then left of the local environment, creating a stark desert out of the once-lush forested terrain. In the 1930s, the Civilian Conservation Corps was sent in to restore the area, and after five forgiving decades and active land reclamation, the Copper Basin is beginning to recover. Today the devastation is locally considered a distinguishing historic legacy.

The Ducktown Basin Museum, on Highway 68 1/4-mile north of Highway 64 (phone 423/496-5778), tells the story of the copper industry as well as the history of the Cherokee Indians in the region, who were forced to emigrate along the "Trail of Tears" to Oklahoma in 1838. You can see what remains of Ducktown's first copper mine outside near the museum. Two miles south of Ducktown are the neighboring border towns of Copperhill, Tennessee and McCaysville, Georgia, across the Ocoee River from one another. Both Copperhill and McCaysville offer beautiful historic districts.

From downtown Copperhill, the Blue Ridge Scenic Railway (phone toll-free 800/934-1898) runs passengers 13 1/2 miles to Blue Ridge, Georgia. An antique locomotive with a red caboose powers the railway. There are several restaurants and cafés right across the street from the depot. Self-guided walking- and driving-tour maps are available at the visitor center in downtown Copperhill (phone 615/496-1012). **(Approximately 75 miles)**

Additional Visitor Information

The Department of Tourist Development, 320 6th Ave N, 5th floor, Rachel Jackson Building, Nashville 37243, publishes a state map and a Tennessee vacation guide magazine highlighting attractions, historic sites, and major events and will provide information about vacationing in Tennessee. Phone 615/741-2158.

The TVA and the US Army Corps of Engineers have transformed muddy rivers into lovely lakes, making Tennessee home to the "Great Lakes of the South" with more than 29 big lakes in the public province. Also, TVA has developed Land Between the Lakes (see KENTUCKY), a giant national recreation area spanning the Kentucky-Tennessee border.

There are 13 welcome centers in Tennessee; visitors may find the information and brochures helpful in their state travels. These centers operate year-round; they are located on interstate highway entrances to the state.

Andrew Johnson National Historic Site (E-9)

See also Greeneville

Web site www.nps.gov/anjo/

(*Monument Ave, College and Depot sts, Greeneville.*)

The tailor shop, two houses, and the burial place of the 17th president of the United States are preserved. Apprenticed to a tailor during his youth, Andrew Johnson came to Greeneville from his native Raleigh, NC, in 1826. After years of service in local, state, and federal governments, Senator Johnson chose to remain loyal to the Union when Tennessee seceded. After serving as military governor of Tennessee, Johnson was elected vice president in 1864. On April 15, 1865, he became president following the assassination of Abraham Lincoln. Continued opposition to the radical program of Reconstruction led to his impeachment in 1868. Acquitted by the Senate, he continued to serve as president until 1869. In 1875, Andrew Johnson became the only former president to be elected to the US Senate.

What to See and Do

Grave and monument. *Monument Ave, Andrew Jackson National Historic Site. Phone 423/639-5912.* An eagle-capped marker sits over the president's grave. Members of his immediate family are also buried in what is now a national cemetery. (Daily)

Johnson Homestead. *Andrew Jackson National Historic Site.* Occupied by Johnson family from 1851 to 1875, except during Civil War and presidential years, the house is restored and furnished with family heirlooms. (Daily; closed Jan 1, Thanksgiving, Dec 25) Tickets at visitor center. **$**

Park area. *101 N College St, Greeneville (37743). Phone 423/638-3551.* Camping (mid-Mar-Oct) at Kinser Park, phone 423/639-5912, or call US Forest Service, 423/638-4109. Contact Historic Site Superintendent, PO Box 1088, Greeneville 37744.

Visitor center. *Depot and College sts, Greenville.* The visitor center houses the Johnson tailor shop, pre-

served with some original furnishings and tools of the craft, as well as a museum with exhibits and memorabilia relating to Johnson's career. (Daily; closed Jan 1, Thanksgiving, Dec 25) Opposite is the Johnson house (1830s-1851), occupied during his career as a tailor and as a congressman. **FREE**

Caryville (E-7)

Population 2,243
Elevation 1,095 ft
Area Code 423
Zip 37714

What to See and Do

Cove Lake State Park. *110 Cove Lake Ln, Caryville (37714). N, off Hwy 25 W. Phone 423/566-9701. www. state.tn.us/environment/parks/CoveLake.* Approximately 1,500 acres include 300-acre Cove Lake, where hundreds of Canadian geese winter. Pool, wading pool, lifeguard; fishing, boat rentals. Nature trails, programs. Picnicking, concession, restaurant, playground, game courts. Camping, tent and trailer sites. **$**

Limited-Service Hotels

★ **DAYS INN.** *221 Colonial Ln, Lake City (37769). Phone 865/426-2816; toll-free 800/329-7466; fax 865/426-4626. www.daysinn.com.* 60 rooms, 2 story. Complimentary continental breakfast. Check-out 11 am. Outdoor pool. **$**

★ **HAMPTON INN.** *4459 Veterans Memorial Hwy, Caryville (37714). Phone 423/562-9888; toll-free 800/426-7866; fax 423/562-7474. www.hamptoninn. com.* 64 rooms, 2 story. Complimentary full breakfast. Check-out 11 am. Fitness room. Outdoor pool, whirlpool. **$**

Celina (D-6)

Population 1,379
Elevation 562 ft
Area Code 931
Zip 38551
Information Dale Hollow-Clay County Chamber of Commerce; phone 931/243-3338
Web site www.dalehollowlake.org

Located in the scenic Upper Cumberland section of Tennessee, Celina is the location of the first law office of revered statesman Cordell Hull. Involved in both agriculture (especially cattle raising and truck farming) and industry (notably work clothes and denim sportswear), Celina is also noted for its nearby recreational facilities.

What to See and Do

Dale Hollow Lake. *Phone 931/243-3136. www.dalehollow-lake.net.* Controlling and harnessing the Obey River is a concrete dam 200 feet high and 1,717 feet long; it creates a 61-mile-long lake with 620 miles of shoreline. Swimming, bathhouse, fishing, boating (14 commercial docks); hunting, primitive and improved camping (May-Oct; fee; dump station). (Daily) Headquarters are 3 miles E on Hwy 53.

Dale Hollow National Fish Hatchery. *145 Fish Hatchery Rd, Celina (38551). 2 miles N off Hwy 53. Phone 931/243-2443. www.fws.gov/dalehollow.* More than 300,000 pounds of rainbow, brown, and lake trout are raised annually for stocking streams and reservoirs; aquarium, visitor center. (Daily 7:30 am-3:30 pm) **FREE**

Standing Stone State Park. *10 miles S on Hwy 52. Phone 931/823-6347. www.state.tn.us/environment/parks/parks/StandingStone.* Approximately 11,000 acres of virgin forest. Swimming pool, bathhouse, fishing, boating (rentals). Hiking; tennis. Picnicking, playground, concessions. Tent and trailer sites, cabins. **$**

Full-Service Resort

★ ★ **CEDAR HILL RESORT.** *705 Cedar Hill Rd, Celina (38551). Phone 931/243-3201; toll-free 800/872-8393; fax 931/243-4892. www.cedarhillresort.com.* 47 rooms. Pets accepted; fee. Check-in 1 pm, check-out 10 am. Restaurant. Outdoor pool. **$**

Chattanooga (F-6)

See also Chatsworth, Cleveland, Chickamauga and Chattanooga National Military Park, Dalton

Settled 1835
Population 155,554
Elevation 685 ft
Area Code 423
Information Chattanooga Area Convention and Visitors Bureau, 2 Broad St, 37402; phone 423/756-8687

or toll-free 800/964-8600
Web site www.chattanoogafun.com

Walled in on three sides by the Appalachian Mountains and the Cumberland Plateau, Chattanooga is a diversified city. It is the birthplace of miniature golf, the site of the first Coca-Cola bottling plant, and has the steepest passenger incline railway in the country.

It's a city celebrated in song and heralded in history. The Cherokees called it *Tsatanugi* (rock coming to a point), describing Lookout Mountain, which stands like a sentinel over the city. They called the creek here "Chickamauga" (river of blood).

Cherokee Chief John Ross founded the city. One of the starting points of the tragic "Trail of Tears" was from Chattanooga; Native Americans from three states were herded by Federal troops and forced to march in bitter winter to distant Oklahoma. The Battle of Chickamauga in the fall of 1863 was one of the turning points of the Civil War. It ended when Union forces overpowered entrenched Confederate forces on Missionary Ridge; there were more than 34,500 casualties. Sherman's march to the sea began immediately thereafter.

Chattanooga emerged as an important industrial city at the end of the Civil War, when soldiers from both sides returned to stake their futures in this commercially strategic city. Only 1,500 persons lived in Chattanooga at the war's end, but by 1880 the city had 77 industries.

In 1878, Adolph S. Ochs moved to Chattanooga from Knoxville, purchased the *Chattanooga Times* and made it one of the state's most influential newspapers. Although he later went on to publish the *New York Times,* Ochs retained control of the Chattanooga journal until his death in 1935.

Sparked by the Tennessee Valley Authority, the city's greatest period of growth began in the 1930s. In the past few years, millions of dollars have been spent along Chattanooga's riverfront, making it a popular visitor destination.

What to See and Do

Booker T. Washington State Park. *5801 Champion Rd, Chattanooga (37416). 13 miles NE on Hwy 58. Phone 423/894-4955. www.state.tn.us/environment/parks/*

parks/BookerTWashington. More than 350 acres on Chickamauga Lake. Swimming pools; fishing, boating (rentals, launch). Nature trail. Picnicking, playground, lodge. Some facilities seasonal. **$**

Chattanooga African-American Museum. *200 E Martin Luther King Blvd, Chattanooga (37403). Phone 423/266-8658. www.caamhistory.com.* Educational institution that portrays African-American contributions to the growth of Chattanooga and the nation. (Mon-Fri 10 am-5 pm, Sat noon-4 pm; closed Sun) **$**

Chattanooga Choo-Choo. *Terminal Station, 1400 Market St, Chattanooga (37402). Phone 423/266-5000; toll-free 800/872-2529. www.choochoo.com.* Converted 1909 train station with hotel and restaurants. Formal gardens, fountains, pools, turn-of-the-century shops, gaslights, trolley ride $), model railroad museum $).

Chester Frost Park. *2318 Gold Point Cir N, Hixson (37343). 17 miles NE off I-75 exit 4, then Hwy 153 to Hixson Pike, N to Gold Point Circle, on W shore of Chickamauga Lake. Phone 423/842-0177.* Swimming, sand beach, bathhouse, fishing, boating (ramps). Hiking, picnicking, concessions, camping (fee; electricity, water). Islands in the park are accessible by causeways. **FREE**

Creative Discovery Museum. *321 Chestnut St, Chattanooga (37402). Phone 423/756-2738. www.cdmfun.org.* Encourages children to learn about their world hands-on through creativity and individual achievement. Exhibit areas include Artist's Studio, Inventor's Workshop, Musician's Studio, and Scientist's Field Laboratory. (Mon-Fri 8:30 am-5 pm, Sun noon-5 pm; Memorial Day-Labor Day: daily 10 am-6 pm; closed Wed from Sept-May; also Thanksgiving, Dec 24-25) **$$**

Harrison Bay State Park. *8411 Harrison Bay Rd, Harrison (37341). 11 miles NE off Hwy 58. Phone 423/344-6214. www.state.tn.us/environment/parks/parks/HarrisonBay.* More than 1,200 acres on Chickamauga Lake. Swimming pool, fishing, boating (ramp, marina). Picnicking, playground, snack bar, restaurant, camp store (all seasonal). Camping. Recreation building (seasonal). (Daily 8 am-10 pm) **$$**

Houston Museum of Decorative Arts. *201 High St, Chattanooga (37403). In Bluff View Art District. Phone 423/267-7176. www.thehoustonmuseum.com.* Glass, porcelain, pottery, music boxes, dolls, collection of pitchers; country-style furniture. (Mon-Fri 9:30 am-4 pm, Sat from noon; closed Sun, holidays) **$$**

Hunter Museum of American Art. *10 Bluff View, Chattanooga (37403). In Bluff View Art District. Phone 423/267-0968. www.huntermuseum.org.* Paintings, sculpture, glass, drawings; permanent collection of major American artists; changing exhibits. Gift shop. (Mon-Tues, Fri-Sat 10 am-5 pm; Wed, Sun noon-5 pm; Thurs 10 am-9 pm; closed holidays) **$**

International Towing & Recovery Hall of Fame & Museum. *3315 Broad St, Chattanooga (37402). Phone 423/267-3132. www.internationaltowingmuseum.net.* An entire museum dedicated to the people and vehicles that are reliable as soon as your car decides that it isn't. Dedicated in the autumn of 1995, this museum is just a block away from where the Ernest Holmes Company made the very first automobile wrecker. The museum has a large collection of antique toy trucks and towing and wrecking equipment, as well as a hall of fame. (Mon-Fri 10 am-4:30 pm, Sat-Sun 11 am-5 pm; closed holidays) **$$**

⭐ **Lookout Mountain.** *S of town via Ochs Hwy and Scenic Hwy. www.lookoutmountainattractions.com.* Mountain towers more than 2,120 feet above the city, offering clear-day views of Tennessee, Georgia, North Carolina, South Carolina, and Alabama. During the Civil War the "Battle Above the Clouds" was fought on the slope. On or near the mountain are

Battles for Chattanooga Museum. *1110 E Brow Rd, Lookout Mountain (37350). Adjacent to Point Park. Phone 423/821-2812.* Automated, 3-D display re-creates Civil War Battles of Chattanooga using 5,000 miniature soldiers, flashing lights, smoking cannons, and crackling rifles. Also here are dioramas of area history prior to Civil War. (Summer: 9 am-6:30 pm; rest of year: 10 am-5 pm; closed Dec 25) **$$**

Chattanooga Nature Center at Reflection Riding. *400 Garden Rd, Chattanooga (37419). 6 miles SW, near junction Hwy 11/64, Hwy 41 and Hwy 72, on Lookout Mountain. Phone 423/821-1160. www.chattanooganaturecenter.org.* Park meant for leisurely driving offers winding 3-mile drive with vistas: historic sites, trees, wildflowers, shrubs, reflecting pools. Also wetland walkway; nature center; hiking trails; programs. (Mon-Sat) **$$$**

Cravens House. *Phone 423/821-7786.* (1866) Oldest surviving structure on the mountain, restored with period furnishings. Original house (1856), center of the "Battle Above the Clouds," was largely destroyed; present structure was erected on the original foundations in 1866. (Mid-June-mid-Aug, Wed-Mon). **FREE**

Lookout Mountain Incline Railway. *3917 St. Elmo Ave, Chattanooga (37409). Lower Station. Phone 423/821-4224.* World's steepest passenger incline railway climbs Lookout Mountain to 2,100-feet altitude; near top, grade is at a 72.7 angle; passengers ride glass-roofed cars; Smoky Mountains (200 miles away) can be seen from Upper Station observation deck. Round trip approximately 30 minutes. (Daily; closed Thanksgiving, Dec 25) **$$$**

Point Park. *110 Point Park Rd, Lookout Mountain (37350). Phone 423/821-7786.* View of Chattanooga and Moccasin Bend from observatory. Monuments, plaques, museum tell the story of battle. Visitor center. Part of Chickamauga and Chattanooga National Military Park. (Daily; closed Dec 25) **$**

Rock City Gardens. *1400 Patten Rd, Lookout Mountain (37350). 2 1/2 miles S on Hwy 58, on Lookout Mountain. Phone 706/820-2531.* Fourteen acres of mountaintop trails and vistas. Fairyland Caverns and Mother Goose Village, rock formations, swinging bridge, observation point. Restaurant; shops. (Daily from 8:30 am; closing times vary, call or visit the Web site for schedule) **$$$**

Ruby Falls-Lookout Mountain Caverns. *1720 S Scenic Hwy, Chattanooga (37409). Scenic Hwy 148, on Lookout Mountain. Phone 423/821-2544.* Under the battlefield are twin caves with onyx formations, giant stalactites and stalagmites of various hues; at 1,120 feet below the surface, Ruby Falls is a 145-foot waterfall inside Lookout Mountain Caverns. View of the city from the tower above entrance building. Guided tours. (Daily; closed Dec 25) **$$$$**

Nickajack Dam and Lake. *3490 TVA Rd, Jasper (37347). 25 miles W on Hwy 41, 64, 72 or I-24. Phone 423/942-1633.* TVA dam impounds lake with 192 miles of shoreline and 10,370 acres of water surface. Fishing; boat launch. **FREE**

Raccoon Mountain Caverns and Campground. *319 W Hills Dr, Chattanooga (37419). Approximately 5 miles W; exit 174 off I-24, 1 mile N on Hwy 41. Phone toll-free 800/823-2267.* Guided tours offer views of beautiful formations, stalagmites, and stalactites; also "wild" cave tours through undeveloped sections. Full-facility campground (fee). (Daily) **$$$**

Raccoon Mountain Pumped Storage Plant. *6 miles W. Phone 423/825-3100. www.tva.gov/sites/raccoonmt.htm.* Raccoon Mountain is the largest of the TVA's rock-filled dams, measuring 230 feet high and 8,500 feet long. Water pumped from the Tennessee River flows from the reservoir atop the mountain to the powerhouse below. Cut 1,350 feet inside the mountain, the powerhouse chamber has four of the largest reversible pump turbines in the world. Visitor center and picnic area atop mountain (daylight hours); fishing at base of the mountain; overlooks with spectacular views of Tennessee River gorge and Chattanooga. **FREE**

Signal Point. *9 miles N on Ridgeway Ave (Hwy 127).* Mountain was used for signaling by Cherokees and later by Confederates. View of "Grand Canyon of the Tennessee" can be seen by looking almost straight down to the Tennessee River from Signal Point Military Park, off St. James Blvd.

Southern Belle riverboat. *201 Riverfront Pkwy, Chattanooga (37402). Phone 423/266-4488; toll-free 800/766-2784. www.chattanoogariverboat.com.* Sightseeing, breakfast, lunch, and dinner cruises on a 500-passenger riverboat. (Apr-Dec, daily) **$$$$**

⭐ **Tennessee Aquarium.** *1 Broad St, Chattanooga (37402). On the banks of the Tennessee River. Phone 423/265-0695; toll-free 800/262-0695. www.tennesseeaquarium.com.* First major freshwater life center in the country, focusing primarily on the natural habitats and wildlife of the Tennessee River and related ecosystems. Within this 130,000-square-foot complex are more than 9,000 animals in their natural habitats. The Aquarium re-creates riverine habitats in seven major freshwater tanks and two terrestial environments and is organized into five major galleries: **Appalachian Cove Forest** re-creates the mountain source of the Tennessee River; **Tennessee River Gallery** examines the river at midstream and compares the "original" river with the river as it now exists; **Discovery Falls** is a series of interactive displays and small tanks; **Mississipi Delta** explores the river as it slows to meet the sea; and **Rivers of the World** explores six of the world's great river systems. Highlight of the Aquarium is the 60-foot-high central canyon, designed to give visitors a sense of immersion into the river. (Daily 10 am-7:30 pm; last ticket sold at 6 pm; closed Thanksgiving, Dec 25). **$$$** Adjacent is

IMAX 3D Theater. *201 Chestnut St, Chattanooga (37402). Phone toll-free 800/262-0695.* Six-story movie screen. Discounted combination tickets with the Tennessee Aquarium are available. (Daily) **$$**

Tennessee Valley Railroad. *4119 Cromwell Rd, Chattanooga (37421). Phone 423/894-8028. www.tvrail.com.*

The South's largest operating historic railroad, with steam locomotives, diesels, and passenger coaches of various types. Trains take passengers on a 6-mile ride, including tunnel. Audiovisual show, displays; gift shop. (June-Labor Day: daily; Apr-May and Sept-mid-Nov: Mon-Fri) **$$$**

University of Tennessee at Chattanooga. *615 McCallie Ave, Chattanooga (37403). Phone 423/425-4416; toll-free 800/882-6627. www.utc.edu.* (1886) (7,800 students) Fine Arts Center has McKenzie Arena for entertainment and special events. Tours of campus by appointment.

Special Events

Fall Color Cruise & Folk Festival. *1902 Dug Gap Rd # B, Chattanooga (37402). Phone 706/275-8778.* Riverboat trips, arts and crafts, entertainment. Last two weekends in Oct.

Riverbend Festival. *1001 Market St, Chattanooga (37402). Phone 423/756-2211. www.riverbendfestival. com.* Music and sporting events, children's activities, fireworks display. Mid-June. **$$$$**

Theatrical, musical productions. *709 Broad St, Chattanooga (37402).* **Tivoli Theater.** Variety of events, includes plays, concerts, opera; box office, phone 423/757-5042. **Chattanooga Theatre Centre,** 400 River St, box office, phone 423/267-8534. **Memorial Auditorium,** 399 McCallie Ave; box office, phone 423/757-5042. **Chattanooga Symphony and Opera Association,** 25 concerts and two opera productions yearly, phone 423/267-8583. **Backstage Playhouse,** 3264 Brainerd Rd, dinner theater, phone 423/629-1565.

Limited-Service Hotels

★ ★ **CLARION HOTEL.** *407 Chestnut St, Chattanooga (37402). Phone 423/756-5150; fax 423/265-8708. www.chattanoogaclarion.com.* 201 rooms, 12 story. Check-in 3 pm, check-out 11 am. Restaurant, bar. Fitness room. Outdoor pool. Business center. **$**
🧍 ⛱ 🏃

★ **DAYS INN.** *901 Carter St, Chattanooga (37402). Phone 423/266-7331; toll-free 800/329-7466; fax 423/266-9357. www.daysinn.com.* 138 rooms, 3 story. Check-in 2 pm, check-out 11 am. Fitness room. Outdoor pool. **$**
🧍 ⛱

★ **HAMPTON INN.** *7013 Shallowford Rd, Chattanooga (37421). Phone 423/855-0095; toll-free 800/426-7866; fax 423/894-7600. www.hamptoninn.com.* 167 rooms, 2 story. Complimentary continental breakfast. Check-in 3 pm, check-out 11 am. Fitness room. Outdoor pool. **$**
🧍 ⛱

★ ★ **HOLIDAY INN.** *1400 Market St, Chattanooga (37402). Phone 423/266-5000; toll-free 800/872-2529; fax 423/265-4635. www.choochoo.com.* A railway terminal from 1909 to 1970, this 23-acre complex offers some rooms and suites in restored Victorian-traincars. Trolley rides, historic displays and three pools make it attractive for families. 1880 Chattanooga Choo-Choo engine. 363 rooms. Pets accepted, some restrictions; fee. Check-in 3 pm, check-out 11 am. Five restaurants, two bars. Children's activity center. Fitness room. Indoor pool, two outdoor pools, whirlpool. **$**
🐾 🧍 ⛱

★ **LA QUINTA INN.** *7015 Shallowford Rd, Chattanooga (37421). Phone 423/855-0011; toll-free 800/531-5900; fax 423/499-5409. www.laquinta.com.* 132 rooms, 2 story. Pets accepted. Complimentary continental breakfast. Check-in 3 pm, check-out noon. Outdoor pool. **$**
✈ 🐾 ⛱

★ **QUALITY SUITES.** *7324 Shallowford Rd, Chattanooga (37421). Phone 423/892-1500; fax 423/892-0111. www.choicehotels.com.* 62 rooms, 2 story. Complimentary continental breakfast. Check-in 2 pm, check-out 11 am. High-speed Internet access. Fitness room. Indoor pool, whirlpool. Business center. **$**
🧍 ⛱ 🏃

Full-Service Hotel

★ ★ ★ **MARRIOTT CHATTANOOGA CONVENTION CENTER.** *2 Carter Plz, Chattanooga (37402). Phone 423/756-0002; toll-free 800/228-9290; fax 423/308-1010. www.marriott.com.* This high-rise hotel is located in the downtown area near shopping, restaurants, and great nightlife. 342 rooms, 16 story. Pets accepted, some restrictions; fee. Check-in 4 pm, check-out noon. High-speed Internet access. Restaurant, bar. Fitness room. Indoor pool, outdoor pool, whirlpool. Business center. **$**
🐾 🧍 ⛱ 🏃

Specialty Lodging

BLUFF VIEW INN BED & BREAKFAST. *411 E 2nd St, Chattanooga (37403). Phone 423/265-5033; fax 423/757-0120. www.bluffviewartdistrict.com.* Located in the historic Bluff View art district, this property includes three turn-of-the-century homes; an English Tudor, a Colonial, and a Victorian. Some rooms feature bluff views overlooking the Tennessee River. 16 rooms, 2 story. Complimentary full breakfast. Check-in 3 pm, check-out noon. **$$**

Restaurants

★ ★ **212 MARKET.** *212 Market St, Chattanooga (37402). Phone 423/265-1212; fax 423/267-2428. www.212market.com.* American menu. Lunch, dinner. Closed Jan 1, Dec 25. Bar. Children's menu. Outdoor seating. **$$**

★ **COUNTRY PLACE.** *7320 Shallowford Rd, Chattanooga (37421). Phone 423/855-1392; fax 423/855-5738.* American menu. Breakfast, lunch, dinner. Closed Dec 25. Children's menu. Casual attire. **$**

★ ★ **MOUNT VERNON.** *3535 Broad St, Chattanooga (37409). Phone 423/266-6591; fax 423/266-4216.* American, seafood menu. Lunch, dinner. Closed Sat-Sun; also late Dec-early Jan. Bar. Children's menu. Casual attire. **$**

Cherokee National Forest (E-9)

See also Cleveland, Greeneville, Johnson City

Web site www.southernregion.fs.fed.us/cherokee/

NE, SE, and SW of Johnson City via Hwy 23, 321, Hwy 91; E of Cleveland on Hwy 64. Phone 423/476-9700.

This 630,000-acre forest, slashed by river gorges and creased by rugged mountains, lies in two separate strips along the Tennessee-North Carolina boundary, northeast and southwest of Great Smoky Mountains National Park (see). A region of thick forests, streams, and waterfalls, the forest takes its name from the Native American tribe. There are more than 500 miles of hiking trails, including the Appalachian Trail. There are 29 campgrounds, 28 picnic areas, 8 swimming sites, and 13 boating sites. Hunting for game, including wild boar, deer, and turkey, is permitted under Tennessee game regulations. Fees may be charged at recreation sites.

Clarksville (D-4)

Also see Hopkinsville, KY

Founded 1784
Population 103,455
Elevation 543 ft
Area Code 931
Information Clarksville/Montgomery County Tourist Commission, 312 Madison St, PO Box 883, 37040; phone 931/647-2331 or toll-free 800/530-2487
Web site www.clarksville.tn.us

Clarksville, named for General George Rogers Clark, has achieved a balanced economy with many industries and heavy traffic in tobacco, grain, and livestock. Clarksville has long been considered one of the top dark-fired tobacco markets in the world. Natural gas and low-cost TVA power have contributed to the town's industrial development. Clarksville is the home of Austin Peay State University.

What to See and Do

Beachhaven Vineyard & Winery. *1100 Dunlap Ln, Clarksville (37040). I-24, exit 4. Phone 931/645-8867.* Tours of vineyard and winery; tasting room; picnic area. (Daily; closed Jan 1, Thanksgiving, Dec 25) **FREE**

Customs House Museum. *200 S 2nd St, Clarksville (37040). Phone 931/648-5780. www.customshousemuseum.org.* Built in 1898 as a US Post Office and Customs House, the museum houses changing history, science, and art exhibits. (Tues-Sat 10 am-5 pm, Sun from 1 pm; closed Mon, holidays) **$**

Dunbar Cave State Natural Area. *5 miles SE via Hwy 79, Dunbar Cave Rd exit. Phone 931/648-5526.* This 110-acre park with small scenic lake was once a fashionable resort; the cave itself housed big band dances. The old bathhouse has been refurbished to serve as a museum and visitor center. Park (daily); cave (June-Aug, weekends, by reservation only). **$**

Fort Campbell Military Reservation. *Hwy 41A, in both TN and KY. Phone 270/439-9466; toll-free 866/439-9465. www.fortcampbell.com.* Home of the army's famed 101st Airborn Division (Air Assault). The post visitors center is just inside Gate 4; Don F. Pratt Museum is located in Wickham Hall. (Daily; closed Jan 1, Dec 25) **FREE**

Port Royal State Historic Area. *5 miles E via Hwy 76, near Adams; follow signs. Phone 931/358-9696. www.state.tn.us/environment/parks/PortRoyal.* At the confluence of Sulphur Fork Creek and the Red River, Port Royal was one of the state's earliest communities and trading centers. A 300-foot covered bridge spans the river. (Daily 8 am-sundown)

Special Event

Old-Time Fiddlers Championship. Late Mar.

Limited-Service Hotels

★ **COUNTRY INN & SUITES BY CARLSON CLARKSVILLE.** *3075 Wilma Rudolph Blvd, Clarksville (37040). Phone 931/645-1400; toll-free 800/531-1900; fax 931/472-1002. www.countryinns.com.* 125 rooms, 4 story. Complimentary full breakfast. Check-out noon. Indoor pool, outdoor pool, whirlpool. **$**
⌫

★ **HAMPTON INN.** *190 Holiday Rd, Clarksville (37040). Phone 931/552-2255; fax 931/552-4871. www.hamptoninn.com.* 77 rooms, 2 story. Complimentary continental breakfast. Check-out noon. Fitness room. Outdoor pool, whirlpool. **$**
🏃 ⌫

★ **QUALITY INN.** *803 N 2nd St, Clarksville (37040). Phone 931/645-9084; fax 931/645-9084. www.quality-inn.com.* 130 rooms, 2 story. Pets accepted; fee. Complimentary continental breakfast. Check-out noon. Bar. Indoor pool, whirlpool. **$**
🐾 ⌫

★ ★ **RIVERVIEW INN.** *50 College St, Clarksville (37041). Phone 931/552-3331; toll-free 877/487-4837; fax 931/647-5005. www.theriverviewinn.com.* 154 rooms, 7 story. Check-out noon. Restaurant, bar. Indoor pool. **$**
⌫

Cleveland (F-7)

See also Chattanooga, Cherokee National Forest

Population 37,192
Elevation 920 ft
Area Code 423
Information Cleveland/Bradley Chamber of Commerce, 2145 Keith St, PO Box 2275, 37320; phone 423/472-6587
Web Site www.clevelandchamber.com

Cleveland is the location of the Superintendent's office of the Cherokee National Forest (see).

Limited-Service Hotels

★ **BAYMONT INN.** *107 Interstate Dr NW, Cleveland (37312). Phone 423/339-1000; fax 423/339-2760. www.baymontinns.com.* 100 rooms, 3 story. Complimentary continental breakfast. Check-in 3 pm, check-out noon. Fitness room. Outdoor pool. **$**
🏃 ⌫

★ **QUALITY INN.** *2595 Georgetown Rd NW, Cleveland (37311). Phone 423/476-8511; toll-free 800/228-5151; fax 423/476-8511. www.qualityinn.com.* 97 rooms, 3 story. Pets accepted; fee. Complimentary continental breakfast. Check-in 2 pm, check-out 11 am. Restaurant, bar. Outdoor pool, whirlpool. **$**
🐾 ⌫

Columbia (E-4)

See also Franklin

Settled 1807
Population 33,055
Elevation 637 ft
Area Code 931
Information Maury County Convention & Visitors Bureau, #8 Public Square, 38401; phone 931/381-7176 or toll-free 888/852-1860
Web site www.columbiatn.com

James K. Polk, 11th president of the United States, spent his boyhood in Columbia and returned here to open his first law office. The town is known for its many antebellum houses.

What to See and Do

Ancestral home of James K. Polk. *301 W 7th St, Columbia (38401). Phone 931/388-2354. www.jamesk-polk.com.* (1816). Built by Samuel Polk, father of the president, the Federal-style house is furnished with family possessions, including furniture and portraits used at the White House. Gardens link the house to an adjacent 1818 building owned by the president's sisters. Visitor center. (Apr-Oct: Mon-Sat 9 am-5 pm, Sun 1-5 pm; rest of year: Mon-Sat 9 am-4 pm, Sun 1-5 pm; closed Jan 1, Thanksgiving, Dec 24-25) **$**

The Athenaeum. *808 Athenaeum St, Columbia (38401). Phone 931/381-4822. www.athenaeumrectory.com.* (1835-1837) Buildings of Moorish design were used as a girls' school after 1852; during the Civil War, the rectory became headquarters of Union Generals Negeley and Schofield. (Feb-Dec, Tues-Sun; fall tour Sept) **$$**

Special Events

Majestic Middle Tennessee Fall Tour. *808 Athenaeum St, Columbia (38401). Phone 931/381-4822.* Last weekend in Sept.

Maury County Fair. *Maury County Park Fairgrounds, 1018 Maury County Park Dr, Columbia (38401). Phone 931/375-6101. www.maurycountyfair.com.* Late Aug-early Sept. **$**

Mule Day. *Mule Day Office, 1018 Maury County Park Dr, Columbia (38401). Phone 931/381-9557. www.muleday.com.* Liar's contest, auction, parade, mule pull, square dance, bluegrass night, pioneer craft festival, knife and coin show. First weekend in Apr. **$**

National Tennessee Walking Horse Jubilee. *Maury County Park, 1018 Maury County Park Dr, Columbia (38401). Phone 931/375-6101.* Contact the park, Experiment Station Lane. Late May-early June.

Plantation Christmas Tour of Homes. First weekend in Dec.

Limited-Service Hotel

★ **DAYS INN.** *1504 Nashville Hwy, Columbia (38401). Phone 931/381-3297; fax 931/381-8692. www.daysinn.com.* 54 rooms, 2 story. Complimentary continental breakfast. Check-out 11 am. Outdoor pool. **$**
🖼

Restaurants

★ ★ **THE OLE LAMPLIGHTER.** *1000 Riverside Dr, Columbia (38401). Phone 931/381-3837; fax 931/381-5382.* Seafood, steak menu. Dinner. Closed holidays; also first week in July. Bar. Children's menu. **$$$**
🖼

★ **RANCH HOUSE.** *900 Riverside Dr, Columbia (38401). Phone 931/381-2268; fax 931/381-5382.* Dinner. Closed Sun. Children's menu. **$$**

Cookeville (E-6)

See also Jamestown

Settled 1854
Population 23,923
Elevation 1,118 ft

Area Code 931
Zip 38501
Information Cookeville Area-Putnam County Chamber of Commerce, 1 W 1st St; phone 931/526-2211 or toll-free 800/264-5541
Web site www.cookevillechamber.com

Cookeville, a cultural and industrial center for the upper Cumberland area, is the home of Tennessee Technological University.

What to See and Do

Burgess Falls State Natural Area. *4000 Burgess Falls Dr, Sparta (38583). 8 miles S of I-40 exit 286 on Hwy 135. Phone 931/432-5312. www.state.tn.us/environment/parks/parks/BurgessFalls.* Scenic riverside trail (3/4 mile) leads to an overlook of a 130-foot waterfall, considered one of the most beautiful in the state, located in a gorge on the Falling Water River. Fishing (Burgess Falls Lake and River below dam). Hiking trails. Picnicking (below dam). (Daily 8 am until 30 minutes before sundown)

Center Hill Dam and Lake. *Resource Manager's Office, 158 Resource Ln, Lancaster (38569). 25 miles W via I-40, Hwy 141. Phone 931/858-3125. www.smithvilletn.com/lake/index.htm.* This 250-foot-high, 2,160-foot-long concrete and earth-fill dam controls the flood waters of the Caney Fork River and provides electric power. The lake has a 415-mile shoreline. Swimming, waterskiing, fishing; boating; hunting. Picnicking at six recreation areas around the reservoir. Camping (fee; hookups). Eight commercial docks. Some facilities are closed Oct-mid-Apr. Also here are

Appalachian Center for Crafts. *1560 Craft Center Dr, Smithville (37166). W on I-40, 6 miles S on Hwy 56. Phone 615/597-6801.* On 600 acres overlooking Center Hill Lake. Operated by Tennessee Technological University. Teaching programs in fiber, metal, wood, glass, and clay. Exhibition galleries. (Daily 9 am-5 pm; closed Easter, Thanksgiving; also end of Dec, last 2-3 business days of June) **FREE**

Edgar Evins State Park. *1630 Edgar Evins State Park Rd, Silver Point (38582). Phone 931/858-2446; toll-free 800/250-8619.* This approximately 6,000-acre park has boat launch facilities. It also offers camping (dump station) and cabins. (Daily 6 am-10:30 pm) **$**

Limited-Service Hotels

★ **BEST VALUE INN.** *897 S Jefferson Ave, Cookeville (38501). Phone 931/526-9521; toll-free 800/826-2791; fax 931/528-2285. www.bestvalueinn.com.* 78 rooms. Complimentary continental breakfast. Check-in 1 pm, check-out 11 am. High-speed Internet access. Outdoor pool. **$**
🌊

★ **BEST WESTERN THUNDERBIRD MOTEL.** *900 S Jefferson Ave, Cookeville (38501). Phone 931/526-7115; toll-free 800/528-1234; fax 931/526-7115. www.bestwestern.com.* 76 rooms, 3 story. Pets accepted, some restrictions; fee. Complimentary continental breakfast. Check-in 3 pm, check-out noon. Fitness room. Outdoor pool. Business center. **$**
🐾 🏋 🌊 🚶

★ ★ **HOLIDAY INN.** *970 S Jefferson Ave, Cookeville (38501). Phone 931/526-7125; toll-free 800/465-4329; fax 931/520-7944. www.holiday-inn.com.* This property is located 1 mile from downtown, near the Cookeville Mall, and is within easy traveling distance of recreational areas. 200 rooms, 3 story. Pets accepted. Complimentary continental breakfast. Check-in 3 pm, check-out noon. High-speed Internet access. Two restaurants. Children's activity center. Fitness room. Indoor pool, outdoor pool, children's pool, whirlpool. Business center. **$**
🐾 🏋 🌊 🚶

Restaurant

★ ★ **NICK'S.** *895 S Jefferson Ave, Cookeville (38501). Phone 931/528-1434.* American menu. Lunch, dinner. Bar. Casual attire. **$$**

Covington (E-1)

See also Memphis

Population 8,463
Elevation 339 ft
Area Code 901
Zip 38019

What to See and Do

Fort Pillow State Historic Area. *3122 Park Rd, Henning (38041). 33 miles NW via Hwy 51 N and Hwy 87 W. Phone 731/738-5581. www.state.tn.us/environment/parks/parks/FortPillow.* This archaeologically significant area consists of 1,646 acres on the Chickasaw Bluffs, overlooking the Mississippi River. It contains substantial remains of a large fort named for a Confederate general, and 5 miles of earthworks. Fishing. Wooded trails (15 miles). Picnicking. Tent and primitive camping. Visitors center (Mon-Fri), nature exhibits. (Daily; closed Dec 25) **$**

Crossville (E-9)

Population 8,981
Elevation 1,863 ft
Area Code 931
Zip 38555
Information Greater Cumberland County Chamber of Commerce, 34 S Main St, 38555; phone 931/484-8444
Web site www.crossville-chamber.com

More than 36,000 tons of multicolored quartzite are quarried in the Crossville area each year and sold for construction projects throughout the country. This Cumberland Plateau town also markets cattle, dairy products, strawberries, beans, and potatoes. Hickory handles, charcoal, liquid smoke, rubber mats, office supplies, ceramic tile, exercise equipment, bus and truck mirrors, yarn, and apparel are also produced locally.

What to See and Do

Cumberland County Playhouse. *221 Tennessee Ave, Crossville (38555). 2 1/2 miles W on Hwy 70S, overlooking Lake Holiday. Phone 931/484-5000. www.ccplayhouse.com.* Indoor stage presentations by both professional and community actors. Picnic facilities, concession. For schedule, reservations, and ticket prices call or visit the Web site.

Cumberland Mountain State Park. *24 Office Dr, Crossville (38555). I-40 E from Nashville, W from Knoxville exit on #317. S on Hwy 127 for 9 miles. Phone 931/484-6138. www.state.tn.us/environment/parks/parks/CumberlandMtn.* This 1,548-acre park, located along the Cumberland Plateau, is 1,820 feet above sea level. It stands on the largest remaining timberland plateau in America and has a 35-acre lake. Swimming pool, bathhouse, lifeguards; fishing, boating (rentals). Nature trails and programs, tennis. Picnicking, playground, concession, snack bar, dining room. Camping, tent and trailer sites, cabins. (Daily 7 am-10 pm) **$**

Homesteads Tower Museum. *96 Hwy 68, Crossville (38555). 4 miles S on Hwy 127. Phone 931/456-9663.* The tower was built in 1937-1938 to house administrative offices of the Cumberland Homesteads, a New Deal-era project. A winding stairway leads to a lookout platform at the top of the octagonal stone tower. At the base of the tower is a museum with photos, documents, and artifacts from the 1930s and 1940s. (Mar-Dec, daily; closed Easter, Labor Day, Thanksgiving). **$**

Special Event

Cumberland County Fair. *4000 Burgess Falls Rd, Sparta (38583). Phone 931/484-9454.* Exhibits, horse, cattle, and other animal shows, mule pulls, fiddlers' contest. Late Aug. **$$**

Limited-Service Hotel

★ **LA QUINTA INN.** *4038 Hwy 127 N, Crossville (38571). Phone 931/456-9338; toll-free 800/531-5900; fax 931/456-8758. www.laquinta.com.* 60 rooms, 3 story. Pets accepted. Complimentary continental breakfast. Check-in 2 pm, check-out 11 am. High-speed Internet access. Fitness room. Indoor pool, whirlpool. Business center. **$**

Dickson (E-4)

See also Hurricane Mills, Nashville

Founded 1873
Population 12,244
Elevation 794 ft
Area Code 615
Zip 37055
Information Chamber of Commerce, 119 Hwy 70 E; phone 615/446-2349
Web site www.dicksoncountychamber.com

What to See and Do

Montgomery Bell State Park. *1020 Jackson Hill Rd, Burns (37029). 7 miles E on Hwy 70. Phone 615/797-9052. www.state.tn.us/environment/parks/parks/Mont-gomeryBell.* A 5,000-acre, wooded park with streams, brooks, and three lakes in the Highland Rim. Replica of a church on the site where Cumberland Presbyterian Church was founded in 1810. Swimming, bathhouse; fishing, boating (rentals). Nature trails, backpacking; golf, tennis. Picnicking, playground, restaurant. Tent and trailer sites, lodging, cabins. (Daily 6 am-10 pm) **$**

Special Event

Old-Timers' Day Festival. Parades, entertainment, and special events. First weekend in May.

Specialty Lodging

EAST HILLS BED & BREAKFAST INN. *100 E Hill Terrace, Dickson (37055). Phone 615/441-9428. www.easthillsbb.com.* This inn was originally built by the owner's father in the early 1940s and features complete seclusion with five rooms having private bathrooms. 7 rooms, 1 story. **$**

Dyersburg (E-2)

Population 17,452
Elevation 295 ft
Area Code 731
Information Dyersburg/Dyer County Chamber of Commerce, 2000 Commerce Ave, 38025; phone 731/285-3433
Web Site www.dyerchamber.com

Limited-Service Hotel

★ **COMFORT INN.** *815 Reelfoot Dr, Dyersburg (38024). Phone 731/285-6951; toll-free 800/228-5150; fax 731/285-6956. www.comfortinn.com.* 80 rooms, 2 story. Pets accepted, some restrictions; fee. Complimentary continental breakfast. Check-in 1 pm, check-out 11 am. Fitness room. Outdoor pool. **$**

Elizabethton (D-10)

See also Johnson City

Population 13,372
Elevation 1,530 ft
Area Code 423
Zip 37643
Information Elizabethton/Carter County Chamber of Commerce, 500 Veterans Memorial Pkwy, PO Box 190, 37644; phone 423/547-3850
Web site www.tourelizabethton.com

A monument on the lawn of Carter County Courthouse marks the spot where the Watauga Association was formed in 1772 by settlers in these hills. Isolated from the seaboard colonies, the pioneers were determined to organize for law and self-protection. Their constitution was the first to be adopted by independent Americans. Little is now known about this constitution except that it helped unite the people of eastern Tennessee to fight in the American Revolution.

What to See and Do

Roan Mountain State Park. *1015 Hwy 143, Roan Mountain (37687). 17 miles SE via Hwy 19 E, S on Hwy 143. Phone 423/772-3303; toll-free 800/250-8620. www.state.tn.us/environment/parks/parks/RoanMtn.* The 2,104-acre park includes 6,285-foot Roan Mountain, one of the highest peaks in the eastern US. Atop the mountain is a 600-acre garden of rhododendron, in bloom late June (see SPECIAL EVENTS). Swimming pool; fishing. Nature trail. Cross-country skiing. Picnicking, playground, snack bar. Camping, cabins. (Daily 8 am-4:30 pm) **$**

Sycamore Shoals State Historic Area. *1651 W Elk Ave, Elizabethton (37643). 1 1/2 miles W on Hwy 321. Phone 423/543-5808. www.state.tn.us/environment/parks/parks/SycamoreShoals.* The first colonial settlement west of the Blue Ridge Mountains has a reconstructed fort consisting of five buildings and palisade walls; visitor center with museum and theater (daily). Tours of nearby Carter Mansion available by appointment. Picnic sites. Visitor center (Mon-Sat 8 am-4:30 pm, Sun 1-4:30 pm). **FREE**

Special Events

Covered Bridge Celebration. *Elk Ave Bridge, downtown.* Arts and crafts festival, antique show. Area country music stars and local talent perform. Four nights in early June.

Outdoor Drama. *Sycamore Shoals State Historic Area, 1651 W Elk Ave, Elizabethton (37643). Phone 423/543-5808.* Depicts muster of Overmountain Men, who marched to King's Mountain, SC, and defeated the British. Mid-July.

Overmountain Victory Trail Celebration. *Phone 815/543-5808.* Reenactment in period costume of original 200-mile march. Late Sept.

Rhododendron Festival. *Roan Mountain State Park, 1015 Hwy 143, Elizabethton (37687).* Mid-late June.

Roan Mountain Wild Flower Tours and Bird Walks. *Roan Mountain State Park, 1015 Hwy 143, Elizabethton (37687).* May.

Fort Donelson National Battlefield and Cemetery (D-3)

Web site www.nps.gov/fodo/

(1 mile W of Dover on Hwy 79) Phone 931/232-5348.

"Unconditional and immediate surrender!" demanded General Ulysses S. Grant when Confederate General Simon B. Buckner proposed a truce at Fort Donelson. Thus did Grant contribute to the long list of appropriate and pithy remarks for which American military men have become justly famous.

Nothing helped Grant so much during this four-day battle as weak generalship on the part of Confederate commanders John B. Floyd and Gideon J. Pillow. Although the Confederates repulsed an attack by Federal ironclad gunboats, the responsibility of surrendering the Confederate garrison of 15,000 was thrust upon Buckner on February 16, 1862. Grant's victory at Fort Donelson, coupled with the fall of Fort Henry ten days earlier, opened the Tennessee and Cumberland rivers into the heart of the Confederacy. In Grant, the people had a new hero. His laconic surrender message stirred the imagination, and he was quickly dubbed "Unconditional Surrender" Grant.

The fort walls, outer defenses, and river batteries still remain and are well-marked to give the story of the battle. A visitor center features a ten-minute slide program, museum, and touch exhibits (daily; closed Dec 25). A 6-mile, self-guided auto tour includes a visit to the fort, the cemetery, and the Dover Hotel, where General Buckner surrendered. The park is open year-round, dawn to dusk. Contact the Superintendent, PO Box 434, Dover 37058. **FREE**

Franklin (E-5)

See also Columbia, Nashville

Founded 1799
Population 41,842
Elevation 648 ft
Area Code 615
Information Williamson County Convention and

Visitors Bureau, City Hall, PO Box 156, 37065-0156; phone 615/794-1225 or toll-free 800/356-3445 **Web site** www.williamsoncvb.org

Franklin is a favorite of Civil War buffs, who come to retrace the Battle of Franklin, a decisive clash that took place November 30, 1864. General John B. Hood, attempting to prevent two Union armies from uniting, outflanked the troops of General John Schofield. The Union troops, dug-in around the Carter House, were discovered by Hood late in the afternoon. For five hours the battle raged. In the morning Hood found that the Schofield troops had escaped across the river to join forces with the Union army at Nashville. The Confederates suffered 6,252 casualties, including the loss of five generals at Carnton Plantation and a sixth general ten days after the battle. The North suffered 2,326 casualties.

What to See and Do

Carter House. *1140 Columbia Ave, Franklin (37064). On Hwy 31. Phone 615/791-1861. www.carter-house. org.* (1830) Served as the command post for the Union forces during the Battle of Franklin. Confederate museum has documents, uniforms, flags, guns, maps, Civil War prints. Guided tour of house and grounds, video presentation. (Mon-Sat 9 am-5 pm, Sun from 1 pm; closed Sun in Jan; also major holidays) **$$**

⭐ **Heritage Trail.** *N and S on Hwy 31.* Scenic drive along the highway from Brentwood through Franklin to Spring Hill, an area that was, in the mid-1800s, plantation country. Southern culture is reflected in the drive's many antebellum and Victorian houses; Williamson County was one of the richest areas in Tennessee by the time of the Civil War.

Historic Carnton and McGavock Confederate Cemetery. *1345 Carnton Ln, Franklin (37064). 1 mile SE off Hwy 431 (Lewisburg Pike). Phone 615/794-0903.* Federal house (1826) modified in the 1840s to reflect Greek Revival style. Built by an early mayor of Nashville, the house was a social and political center. At the end of the Battle of Franklin, which was fought nearby, four Confederate generals lay dead on the back porch. The nation's largest private Confederate cemetery is adjacent. (Daily; closed holidays) **$$$**

Historic District. *1st Ave and N Margin St, Franklin. Downtown area within 1st Ave S to 5th Ave S and N Margin St to S Margin St, centered around the Town Square and the Confederate Monument.* Earliest buildings of Franklin, dating back to 1800; those along Main St are exceptional in their architectural designs and are part of a historic preservation project.

Special Events

Carter House Christmas Candlelight Tour. *1140 Columbia Ave, Franklin (37064). Phone 615-791-1861. www.carter-house.org/events.* Early Dec. **$$$$**

Heritage Foundation Town & Country Tour. *Phone 615/591-8500. www.historicfranklin.com/events_tourof-homes.html.* Tour of the interiors of nine Franklin and Williamson County historic homes. First weekend in May. **$$$$**

Limited-Service Hotel

⭐ **BEST WESTERN FRANKLIN INN.** *1308 Murfreesboro Rd, Franklin (37064). Phone 615/790-0570; fax 615/790-0512.* 142 rooms, 2 story. Pets accepted, some restrictions. Complimentary continental breakfast. Check-out noon. Outdoor pool. **$**

Specialty Lodgings

A HOMEPLACE BED & BREAKFAST. *7826 Nolensville Rd, Nolensville (37135). Phone 615/776-5181.* A pre-Civil War era home hidden in dense forests. Each room has a canopy bed and fireplace. 3 rooms, 1 story. **$**

THE INN AT WALKING HORSE FARM. *1490 Lewisburg Pike, Franklin (37064). Phone 615/790-2076.* Set on forty acres of rolling pastureland with eight walking horses. Guests are welcome to bring their own horses as well with boarding, meals, and grooming available. 4 rooms, 1 story. **$$**

Gallatin (D-5)

See also Nashville

Founded 1802
Population 23,230
Elevation 526 ft
Area Code 615
Zip 37066
Information Chamber of Commerce, 118 W Main, PO Box 26; phone 615/452-4000
Web site www.gallatintn.org

The county seat and market for tobacco and livestock, Gallatin is named for Albert Gallatin, Secretary of the Treasury under John Adams and Thomas Jefferson.

What to See and Do

Bledsoe Creek State Park. *400 Zieglers Fort Rd, Gallatin (37066). 6 miles E on Hwy 25 to Ziegler Fort Rd, then 1 1/2 miles S to Main Park Rd and the park entrance. Phone 615/452-3706.* Waterskiing, fishing; boating (launch). Nature trails. Playground. Camping (hookups, dump station). (Daily 7 am-sunset) **$**

Cragfont. *200 Cragfont Rd, Castalian Springs (37031). 5 miles E on Hwy 25. Phone 615/452-7070. www.srlab. net/cragfont.* (1798) This late Georgian-style house was built for General James Winchester, Revolutionary War hero, by masons and carpenters brought from Maryland. It is named for the rocky bluff (with spring below) on which it stands. Galleried ballroom, weaving room, wine cellar; Federal period furnishings. Restored gardens. (Mid-Apr-Nov: Tues-Sat 10 am-5 pm, Sun from 1 pm; rest of year: by appointment) **$**

Trousdale Place. *183 W Main St, Gallatin (37066). Phone 615/452-5648. www.trousdaleplace.com.* Two-story brick house built in the early 1800s was the residence of Governor William Trousdale; period furniture, military history library. **$$**

Wynnewood. *210 Old Hwy 25, Castalian Springs (37031). 7 miles E on Hwy 25. Phone 615/452-5463.* (1828) Log inn, considered the oldest and largest log structure ever built in Tennessee, was originally constructed as a stagecoach stop and mineral springs resort; Andrew Jackson visited here many times. (Apr-Oct: daily; rest of year: Mon-Sat; closed holidays) **$$**

Special Event

Sumner County Pilgrimage. *200 Cragfont Rd, Castalian Springs (37031). Phone 615/452-7070.* Tour of historic houses. Last Sat in Apr.

Limited-Service Hotels

★ **GUESTHOUSE INN GALLATIN.** *221 W Main St, Gallatin (37066). Phone 615/452-5433; fax 615/452-1665.* 86 rooms, 2 story. Check-out noon. Outdoor pool. **$**

★ **HOLIDAY INN EXPRESS.** *615 E Main St, Hendersonville (37075). Phone 615/824-0022; fax 615/824-7977. www.holiday-inn.com.* This property is located 25 minutes from the Nashville International Airport.

93 rooms, 4 story. Check-out noon. Fitness room. Outdoor pool. **$**

Gatlinburg (E-8)

See also Pigeon Forge, Sevierville, Townsend

Population 3,382
Elevation 1,289 ft
Area Code 865
Zip 37738
Information Chamber of Commerce, 811 E Parkway, PO Box 527; phone 865/430-4148 or toll-free 800/900-4148
Web site www.gatlinburg.com

Gatlinburg has retained most of its mountain quaintness while turning its attention to tapping into the stream of tourists that flows through the town en route to Great Smoky Mountains National Park, the country's most visited national park. The city has accommodations for 40,000 guests and a $22-million convention center. At the foot of Mount LeConte and at the head of the Pigeon River, Gatlinburg is noted for its many shops that make and sell mountain handicrafts—brooms, candles, candies, pottery, and furniture.

What to See and Do

Aerial Tramway-Ober Gatlinburg Ski Resort. *1001 Parkway, Gatlinburg (37738). Phone 865/436-5423. www.obergatlinburg.com.* Ten-minute, 2-mile tram ride to the top of Mount Harrison. (Daily; closed two weeks in Mar) **$$**

Christus Gardens. *510 River Rd, Gatlinburg (37738). Phone 865/436-5155. www.christusgardens.com.* Events from the life of Jesus portrayed in life-size dioramas; music and narration. Floral gardens in season. (Apr-Oct: daily 8 am-9 pm; rest of year: daily 9 am-5 pm; closed Dec 25) **$$**

Craft shops. *Along Main Street and E along Hwy 321 on Glades Rd.*

Gatlinburg Space Needle. *115 Historic Nature Trail, Gatlinburg (37738). Phone 865/436-4629. www. gatlinburgspaceneedle.com.* Glass-enclosed elevator to a 342-foot-high observation deck for a view of the Smokies. (Daily) **$$**

Ober Gatlinburg Ski Resort. *1001 Parkway, Gatlinburg (37738). Ski Mountain Rd, on Harrison. Phone*

865/436-5423; toll-free 800/251-9202. www.obergatlin-burg.com. Double, two quad chairlifts; patrol, school, rentals; snowmaking; concession area, restaurant, bar. Longest run 5,000 feet; vertical drop 600 feet. Night skiing. (Dec-mid-Mar, daily) Also alpine slide, indoor ice skating arena (daily; closed two weeks in Mar; fees); aerial tramway and sightseeing chairlift. **$$$$**

Sightseeing Chairlift-Ober Gatlinburg Ski Resort. *Ski Mountain Rd.* Double chairlift operates to top of Mount Harrison. (Mar-Memorial Day, daily) **$$**

Sky Lift. *765 Parkway (Hwy 441), Gatlinburg (37738).* *Phone 865/436-4307.* Double chairlift ride up Crockett Mountain to 2,300 feet. View of Smokies en route and from observation deck at summit; snack bar; gift shop. (Daily, weather permitting) **$$$**

Special Events

Craftsmen's Fairs. *121 Silverbell Ln, Gatlinburg (37738). www.craftsmenfair.com.* Craft demonstrations, folk music. Late July-early Aug; also mid-Oct. **$**

Dulcimer Harp Festival. *20 miles NE on Hwy 321 to Hwy 32 S. 267 S Hwy 32, Gatlinburg. Phone 865/487-5543.* Dulcimer convention; folk music; crafts demonstrations, storytelling, workshops. Participants from throughout the Appalachian region. Cosby 37722. Second weekend in June.

Scottish Festival and Games. *www.gsfg.org.* Bagpipe marching bands, highland dancing, sheep dog demonstrations. Third weekend in May. **$$$**

Smoky Mountain Lights & Winterfest. *107 Park Head-quarters Rd, Gatlinburg (37738). Phone 865/453-6411. www.smokymountainwinterfest.com.* Citywide winter celebration including Yule log burnings, more than 2 million lights, and other special events. Late Nov-Feb.

Spring Wildflower Pilgrimage. *Contact the Gatlin-burg Chamber of Commerce, 811 E Pkwy, Gatlinburg (37738). Phone 865/947-2256. www.springwildflower-pilgrimage.org.* This event offers numerous wildflower, fauna, and natural history walks, seminars, art classes, and a variety of other programs. It is held outdoors at the Great Smoky Mountains National Park, as well as in a variety of indoor venues around Gatlinburg. Seven days in late Apr.

Sweet Fanny Adams Theater. *461 Parkway, Gatlinburg (37738). Phone 865/436-4039. www.sweetfannyadams. com.* Professional theater presenting musical com-

edies, Gay '90s revue, old-time sing-along. Nightly except Sun. Reservations advisable. Late Apr-Nov.

Limited-Service Hotels

★ ★ **BENT CREEK GOLF VILLAGE.** *3919 East Parkway, Gatlinburg (37738). Phone 865/436-2875; toll-free 800/251-9336; fax 865/436-3257. www.bent-creekgolfvillage.com.* 108 rooms, 3 story. Check-out 11 am. Restaurant. Outdoor pool, children's pool. Golf. **$**

★ **BEST WESTERN CROSSROADS INN.** *440 Parkway, Gatlinburg (37738). Phone 865/436-5661; toll-free 800/925-8889; fax 865/430-9713. www.best-western.com.* 78 rooms, 4 story. Check-in 2 pm, check-out 11 am. Outdoor pool, children's pool. **$**

★ ★ **EDGEWATER HOTEL - GATLINBURG.** *402 River Rd, Gatlinburg (37738). Phone 865/436-4151; toll-free 800/423-9582; fax 865/436-6947. www. edgewater-hotel.com.* 205 rooms, 8 story. Check-out 11 am. Restaurant, bar. Indoor pool, outdoor pool, whirlpool. **$**

★ **GREYSTONE LODGE.** *559 Parkway, Gatlinburg (37738). Phone 865/436-5621; toll-free 800/451-9202; fax 865/430-4471. www.greystonelodgetn.com.* 257 rooms, 5 story. Complimentary continental breakfast. Check-in 4 pm, check-out 11 am. Outdoor pool, children's pool. **$**

★ **HAMPTON INN.** *967 Parkway, Gatlinburg (37738). Phone 865/436-4878; toll-free 888/476-6597; fax 865/436-4088. www.hamptoninn.com.* 92 rooms, 4 story. Complimentary full breakfast. Check-in 3 pm, check-out 11 am. High-speed Internet access, wireless Internet access. Outdoor pool, whirlpool. **$**

★ ★ **HOLIDAY INN.** *520 Historic Nature Trail, Gatlinburg (37738). Phone 865/436-9201; toll-free 800/435-9201; fax 865/436-7974. www.holiday-inn. com.* Just two blocks from downtown, this resort is adjacent to the Great Smoky Mountain National Park. Hop the convenient trolley for a short ride to Dollywood, music shows, theaters, and shops. LeConte Creek winds through this mountain retreat. 402 rooms, 8 story. Pets accepted; fee. Check-out 11 am. Restaurant, bar. Children's activity center. Fitness room. Indoor pool, outdoor pool, children's pool. **$**

★ **JOHNSON'S INN.** *242 Bishop Ln, Gatlinburg (37738). Phone 865/436-4881; fax 865/436-2582. www. johnsonsinn.com.* 80 rooms, 4 story. Check-out 11 am. Outdoor pool, children's pool. **$**

★ **MIDTOWN LODGE.** *805 Parkway, Gatlinburg (37738). Phone 865/436-5691; toll-free 800/633-2446; fax 865/430-3602. www.midtownlodge.com.* 135 rooms, 6 story. Pets accepted, some restrictions; fee. Complimentary continental breakfast. Check-in 2 pm, check-out 11 am. Outdoor pool, children's pool. **$**

★ ★ **RIVER TERRACE RESORT.** *125 Leconte Creek Dr, Gatlinburg (37738). Phone 865/436-5161; toll-free 800/473-8319; fax 865/436-3392. www.riverterrace.com.* 69 rooms, 3 story. Complimentary continental breakfast. Check-out 11 am. Two outdoor pools, children's pool. **$**

★ **ROCKY WATERS MOTOR INN.** *333 Parkway, Gatlinburg (37738). Phone 865/436-7861; toll-free 800/824-1111; fax 865/436-0241. www.rockywaters.com.* 102 rooms, 3 story. Check-in 2 pm, check-out 11 am. Outdoor pool, children's pool, whirlpool. **$**

★ **RODEWAY INN SKYLAND.** *223 E Parkway, Gatlinburg (37738). Phone 865/436-5821; toll-free 800/255-8738; fax 865/436-6876. www.choicehotels.com.* 56 rooms, 2 story. Complimentary continental breakfast. Check-out 11 am. Outdoor pool. **$**

Full-Service Resort

★ ★ **PARK VISTA HOTEL & CONVENTION CENTER.** *705 Cherokee Orchard Rd, Gatlinburg (37738). Phone 865/436-9211; toll-free 800/421-7275; fax 865/430-7533. www.parkvista.com.* Each room at this full-service resort hotel offers a spectacular view of the Great Smoky Mountains. The hotel is great for a family vacation or a weekend getaway. 312 rooms, 15 story. Check-out 11 am. Restaurant, bar. Fitness room. Indoor pool, children's pool, whirlpool. **$**

Full-Service Inns

★ ★ **CHRISTOPHER PLACE, AN INTIMATE RESORT.** *1500 Pinnacles Way, Newport (37821). Phone 423/623-6555; toll-free 800/595-9441; fax 423/613-4771. www.christopherplace.com.* Tucked away in the scenic Smoky Mountains of Tennessee, this antebellum inn is restored to its original splendor. Enjoy the romantic ambience of the Mountain View dining room while savoring four courses selected daily by the chef. 8 rooms, 3 story. Children over 13 years only. Complimentary full breakfast. Check-in 3 pm, check-out 11 am. Fitness room. Outdoor pool. Tennis. **$$**

★ ★ ★ **EIGHT GABLES INN.** *219 N Mountain Trail, Gatlinburg (37738). Phone 865/430-3344; toll-free 800/279-5716. www.eightgables.com.* Its wooded setting inviting tranquility, this welcoming country inn is perfect for a romantic getaway. If you don't get out and enjoy the nearby attractions, including fly fishing, golf, and whitewater rafting, you can while away the hours on the porch and admire the grounds. Guest rooms are quaintly furnished, with feather-top beds; suites have fireplaces and two-person whirlpool tubs. In addition to a five-course breakfast, the room rate includes nightly dessert and access to the inn's pantry. The Magnolia Tea Room serves lunch (open to the public), and candlelight dinners of regional Southern cuisine tempt guests three days a week. 20 rooms. Children over 10 years only. Complimentary full breakfast. Check-in 3 pm, check-out noon. Restaurant. **$$**

Specialty Lodging

BUCKHORN INN. *2140 Tudor Mountain Rd, Gatlinburg (37738). Phone 865/436-4668; fax 865/436-5009. www.buckhorninn.com.* 9 rooms, 2 story. Complimentary full breakfast. Check-in 3 pm. Check-out 11 am. Restaurant. Porch overlooks Mount LeConte. **$**

Restaurants

★ **BRASS LANTERN.** *710 Parkway, Gatlinburg (37738). Phone 865/436-4168; fax 865/436-4376. www.thebrasslanternrestaurant.com.* American menu. Lunch, dinner. Closed Dec 25. Bar. Children's menu. Casual attire. Outdoor seating. **$$**

★ ★ **MAXWELL'S STEAK AND SEAFOOD.** *1103 Parkway, Gatlinburg (37738). Phone 865/436-3738; fax 865/436-3739. www.maxwells-inc.com.* This elegant restaurant specializes in regional dishes. The management is so committed to fine beef that a disclaimer on the menu refuses to guarantee steaks cooked past medium. American menu. Dinner. Bar. Children's menu. Casual attire. Reservations recommended. **$$**

★ ★ **PARK GRILL.** *110 Parkway, Gatlinburg (37738). Phone 865/436-2300; fax 865/436-2836. www. peddlerparkgrill.com.* American menu. Dinner. Closed Dec 24-25. Bar. Children's menu. Casual attire. Reservations recommended. **$$**

★ ★ **THE PEDDLER RESTAURANT.** *820 River Rd, Gatlinburg (37738). Phone 865/436-5794; fax 865/436-2836. www.peddlerparkgrill.com.* American menu. Dinner. Closed Dec 24-25. Bar. Children's menu. Converted log cabin. Casual attire. Reservations recommended. **$$**

Great Smoky Mountains National Park (E-8)

See also Gatlinburg

Web site www.nps.gov/grsm

44 miles SE of Knoxville via Hwy 441.

The lofty peaks of the Appalachian Mountains stand tall and regal in this 800-square-mile area. They are products of a slow and powerful uplifting of ancient sediments that took place more than 200 million years ago. Red spruce, basswood, eastern hemlock, yellow birch, white ash, cucumber trees, silverbells, Fraser fir, tulip poplar, red maple, and Fraser magnolias tower above hundreds of other species of flowering plants. Perhaps the most spectacular of these are the purple rhododendron, mountain laurel, and flame azalea in bloom from early June to mid-July.

The moist, moderate climate has helped make this area a rich wilderness. From early spring to late fall the "coves" (open valleys surrounded by peaks) and forest floors are covered with a succession of flowers unmatched in the United States for colorful variety. Spring and summer bring heavy showers to the mountains, days that are warm, though 15°-20° F cooler than in the valleys below, and cool nights. Autumn is breathtaking as the deciduous trees change to almost every color in the spectrum. Winter brings snow, which is occasionally heavy, and fog over the mountains; while winter discourages many tourists, it can be a very good time to visit the park. (Some park roads, however, may be temporarily closed.)

A wonderful place to hike, half of the park is in North Carolina, while the other half is in Tennessee. The Appalachian Trail follows the state line for 70 miles along the high ridge of the park. The park preserves cabins, barns, and mills of the mountain people, whose ancestors came from England and Scotland. It is also a place to see the descendants of the Cherokee Indian Nation, whose ancestors hid in the mountains from the soldiers during the winter of 1838-1839 to avoid being driven over the "Trail of Tears" to Oklahoma. This is the tribe of Sequoya, a brilliant chief who invented a written alphabet for the Cherokee people.

Stop first at one of the three visitor centers: **Oconaluftee** (daily; closed December 25) in North Carolina, 2 miles north of Cherokee on Newfound Gap Road, designated Hwy 441 outside of the park; **Sugarlands** (daily; closed December 25) in Tennessee, 2 miles south of Gatlinburg; and **Cades Cove** (daily; closed December 25) in Tennessee, 10 miles southwest of Townsend. All have exhibits and information about the park. There are hundreds of miles of foot trails and bridle paths. Camping is popular; ask at any visitor center for locations and regulations. Developed campgrounds (inquire for fee) are available. Reservations may be made up to three months in advance by phoning 800/365-2267 from mid-May-Oct for Elkmont, Cades Cove, and Smokemont; reservations are not taken for other sites.

The views from Newfound Gap and the observation platform at Clingmans Dome (closed winter), about 7 miles southwest, are spectacular. Cades Cove, about 25 miles west of Sugarlands, is an outdoor museum reflecting the life of the original mountain people. It has log cabins and barns. Park naturalists conduct campfire programs and hikes during summer. There are also self-guided nature trails. LeConte Lodge, reached only on foot or horseback, is a concession within the park (late Mar-mid-Nov).

Fishing is permitted with a Tennessee or North Carolina state fishing license. Obtain regulations at visitor centers and campgrounds. The park is a wildlife sanctuary; any disturbance of plant or animal life is forbidden. Dogs and cats are not permitted on trails, but may be brought in if kept on leash or under other physical restrictive controls. Never feed, tease, or frighten bears; always give them a wide berth, as they may inflict serious injury. Watch bears from a car with the windows closed. Park (daily). **FREE**

CCInc Auto Tape Tours, a 90-minute cassette, offers a mile-by-mile self-guided tour of the park. It provides information on history, points of interest, and flora and fauna of the park. Available in Gatlinburg at motels and gift shops; in Cherokee, NC, at Raven Craft Shop on Main Street, and at Log Cabin Trading Post, across from the cinema. Tapes also may be purchased directly from CCInc, PO Box 227, 2 Elbrook Dr, Allendale, NJ 07401; phone 201/236-1666.

For further information, contact the Superintendent, Great Smoky Mountains National Park, 107 Park Headquarters Rd, Gatlinburg 37738; phone 865/436-1200. Lodging is available in the park at LeConte Lodge, phone 423/429-5704. **$$$$**

Greeneville (E-9)

Settled 1783
Population 15,198
Elevation 1,531 ft
Area Code 423
Information Greene County Partnership, 115 Academy St, 37743; phone 423/638-4111
Web site www.greeneville.com

Greeneville was the capital of the independent sovereign state of Franklin (1785-1788), formed by the rugged, independent-minded Scotch-Irish settlers who seceded from North Carolina. A Greeneville tailor, Andrew Johnson, was elected to the Board of Aldermen in 1829 and went on to become president of the United States. Davy Crockett was born a few miles outside of town in 1786. Manufacturing, lumber, dairying, and tobacco are most important today. A Ranger District office of the Cherokee National Forest is located in Greeneville.

What to See and Do

Davy Crockett Birthplace State Park. *1245 Davy Crockett Park Rd, Limestone (37681). 3 miles E off Hwy 11 E. Phone 423/257-2167. www.state.tn.us/environment/ parks/parks/DavyCrockettSHP.* A 100-acre site overlooking Nolichuckey River serves as a memorial to Crockett—humorist, bear hunter, congressman, and hero of the Alamo. Small monument marks birthplace; nearby is a replica of the log cabin in which Crockett was born in 1786. Swimming pool (fee). Picnicking. Camping (hook-ups). Museum and visitors center (Mon-Fri, or by appointment). Park (daily). **$**

Kinser Park. *650 Kinser Park Ln, Greeneville (37743). 6 miles S via Hwy 70S. Phone 423/639-5912.* A 285-acre park surrounded by woodland, overlooking Nolichuckey River. Swimming pool (bathhouses, waterslide); boating (ramp). Nature trails; tennis courts, golf course, miniature golf, playing fields, go-cart track. Picnic facilities, playgrounds. Camping (fee; hookups). Fee for some activities. (Mid-Mar-Oct, daily) **FREE**

Limited-Service Hotels

★ ★ **CHARRAY INN.** *121 Serral Dr, Greeneville (37743). Phone 423/638-1331; toll-free 800/852-4682; fax 423/639-5289. www.charrayinn.com.* 36 rooms, 2 story. Complimentary full breakfast. Check-in 1 pm, check-out 11 am. Restaurant. Airport transportation available. **$**
🅳

★ **COMFORT INN.** *1790 E Andrew Johnson Hwy, Greeneville (37745). Phone 423/639-4185; toll-free 888/557-5007; fax 423/639-7280. www.choicehotels. com.* 90 rooms, 2 story. Check-out noon. Restaurant, bar. Outdoor pool. **$**
🌊

Restaurant

★ ★ **AUGUSTINO'S.** *3465 E Andrew Johnson Hwy, Greeneville (37745). Phone 423/639-5612.* Italian menu. Lunch, dinner. Closed Sun, holidays. Bar. Children's menu. Casual attire. **$$**

Harrogate (D-8)

Population 2,865
Elevation 1,300 ft
Area Code 423
Zip 37752
Web site www.harrogate-tn.com

What to See and Do

Abraham Lincoln Library and Museum. *Hwy 25 E, Greeneville (37752). S on Cumberland Gap Pkwy, Hwy 25 E, on the Lincoln Memorial University campus. Phone 423/869-6235. www.lmunet.edu/Museum/index.htm.* The collection, one of the largest of its type in the world, contains more than 25,000 pieces of Lincolniana and items related to the Civil War. Research center. (Mon-Fri 9 am-4 pm, Sat from 11 am, Sun from 1 pm; Library by appointment only Mon-Fri; closed Easter, Thanksgiving, Dec 25) **$**

Hurricane Mills (E-4)

See also Dickson

Population 40
Area Code 931
Zip 37078
Information Humphreys County Chamber of Commerce, 124 E Main St, PO Box 733, Waverly 37185; phone 931/296-4865
Web site www.waverly.net/hcchamber

What to See and Do

Loretta Lynn's Ranch. *44 Hurricane Mills Rd, Hurricane Mills (37078).* On Hwy 13. Phone 931/296-7700. *www.lorettalynn.com.* Tours of country music star's house, museum, Mooney's Ranch Office, Butcher Holler Home and simulated coal mine; Western and general stores, and Loretta Lynn's Record Shop. Swimming, fishing. Hiking; tennis. Camping. Special events including concerts, trail rides, campfires. (Apr-Oct daily) Fee for most activities.

Nolan House. *375 Hwy 13 N, Waverly (37185). 8 miles N via Hwy 13.* Phone 931/296-2511. Restored, 12-room Victorian house (circa 1870); period furnishings; redoubt trail; dog-trot; family graveyard. Overnight stays available. Tours (Mon-Sat). **$**

Limited-Service Hotels

★★ **BEST WESTERN OF HURRICANE MILLS.** *15542 Hwy 135, Hurricane Mills (37078).* Phone 931/296-4251; fax 931/296-9104. *www.bestwestern.com.* 89 rooms, 2 story. Pets accepted; fee. Check-out 11 am. Restaurant. Outdoor pool, whirlpool. **$**
🐾 ⊠

★ **DAYS INN.** *15415 Hwy 13 S, Hurricane Mills (37078).* Phone 931/296-7647; fax 931/296-5488. 78 rooms, 2 story. Pets accepted, some restrictions; fee. Check-out noon. Restaurant. Outdoor pool. **$**
🐾 ⊠

Jackson (E-2)

Founded 1822
Population 59,643
Elevation 401 ft
Area Code 731
Information Jackson County Convention and Visitors Bureau, 314 E Main St, 38301; phone 731/425-8333 or toll-free 800/498-4748
Web site www.jacksontncvb.com

Railroading is both the tradition and past livelihood of Jackson, home and burial place of John Luther "Casey" Jones, hero of ballad and legend. Because many of General Andrew Jackson's soldiers and many of his wife's relatives settled here, the town was named in his honor. Today Jackson is an industrial center of western Tennessee.

What to See and Do

Casey Jones Village. *30 Casey Jones Ln, Jackson (38305). 5 miles NW at Hwy 45 Bypass and I-40.* Phone 731/668-1222. *www.caseyjones.com.* Complex of turn-of-the-century shops and buildings centered around the life of one of America's most famous railroad heroes. (Daily 9 am-8 pm; closed Easter, Thanksgiving, Dec 25) **FREE** In the village are

> **Brooks Shaw & Son Old Country Store.** *56 Casey Jones Ln, Jackson (38305).* Phone 731/668-1223. Turn-of-the-century general store with more than 15,000 antiques on display; restaurant (see), ice-cream parlor, confectionery shop. (Daily; closed Easter, Thanksgiving, Dec 25)

> **Casey Jones Home and Railroad Museum.** *30 Casey Jones Ln, Jackson (38305).* Phone 731/668-1222. The original house of the high-rolling engineer who, on Apr 30, 1900, climbed into the cab of "Old 382" on the Illinois Central Railroad and took his "farewell trip to that promised land"—and a place in American folklore. On display are personal effects of Jones and railroad memorabilia, including railroad passes, timetables, bells, and steam whistles; also steam locomotive of the type driven by Casey Jones and restored 1890s coach cars. (Daily; closed Easter, Thanksgiving, Dec 25) **$**

Chickasaw State Rustic Park. *20 Cabin Lake, Henderson (38340). 16 miles SE on Hwy 45, then 8 miles SW on Hwy 100.* Phone 731/989-5141; toll-free 800/458-1752. *www.state.tn.us/environment/parks/parks/ Chickasaw.* Park covering 11,215 acres features two lakes. Swimming, fishing, boating (rentals). Horseback riding. Picnicking, playground, recreation lodge. Tent and trailer sites, cabins. **$**

Cypress Grove Nature Park. *866 Hwy 70 W, Jackson (38301).* Phone 731/425-8364. *www.cityofjackson. net/departments/recpark/facilities/cypressgrove.html.*

Boardwalk more than 1 mile long winds through a 165-acre cypress forest; observation tower, nature center, picnic shelter. (Daily) **FREE**

Pinson Mounds State Archaeological Area. *460 Ozier Rd, Pinson (38366). 9 miles S on Hwy 45, then 2 1/2 miles E of Pinson on Ozier Rd. Phone 731/988-5614. www.state. tn.us/environment/parks/parks/PinsonMounds.* Remains of ancient mounds of the Middle Woodland Mound period and more than ten ceremonial and burial mounds of various sizes, including Sauls (72 feet high). Nature trail. Picnicking. Museum (Mar-Nov: daily; rest of year: Mon-Fri); video programs. **FREE**

Limited-Service Hotels

★ **BEST WESTERN CROSSROADS INN.** *21045 Hwy 22 N, Wildersville (38388). Phone 731/968-2532; toll-free 800/780-7234; fax 731/968-2082. www.bestwestern.com.* 40 rooms. Pets accepted; fee. Complimentary continental breakfast. Check-in 1 pm, check-out 11 am. High-speed Internet access. Outdoor pool. **$**

★ **COMFORT INN JACKSON.** *1963 Hwy 45 Bypass, Jackson (38305). Phone 731/668-4100; toll-free 800/850-1131; fax 731/664-6940. www.comfortin-njackson.com.* 203 rooms, 4 story. Pets accepted. Complimentary continental breakfast. Check-in 3 pm, check-out 11 am. Fitness room. Outdoor pool. **$**

★ ★ **HOLIDAY INN.** *541 Carriage House Dr, Jackson (38305). Phone 731/668-6000; toll-free 800/222-3297; fax 731/668-9516. www.holiday-inn.com.* This hotel is directly across the street from Casey Jones Village, a development celebrating the famous railroad engineer. 136 rooms, 5 story. Check-in 3 pm, check-out noon. Restaurant, bar. Fitness room. Indoor pool. **$**

★ ★ **THE OLD ENGLISH INN.** *2267 N Highland Ave, Jackson (38305). Phone 731/668-1571; fax 731/664-8070. www.oldenglishinn.com.* The English manor-style façade and gardenlike landscaping of this property create an inviting exterior. Beveled-glass doors open to public rooms filled with authentic antiques. Historic parks and several antique shops are located nearby. 80 rooms, 2 story. Complimentary continental breakfast. Check-in 3 pm, check-out noon. High-speed Internet access. Outdoor pool. English Tudor décor. **$**

Restaurant

★ **OLD COUNTRY STORE.** *56 Casey Jones Ln, Jackson (38305). Phone 731/668-1223; fax 731/668-6889. www.caseyjonesvillage.com.* American menu. Breakfast, lunch, dinner. Closed Easter, Thanksgiving, Dec 25. Children's menu. Turn-of-the-century décor. Casual attire. **$**

Jamestown (D-7)

See also Cookville

Population 1,839
Elevation 1,716 ft
Area Code 931
Zip 38556
Information Fentress County Chamber of Commerce, 114 Central Ave W, PO Box 1294; phone 931/879-9948 or toll-free 800/327-3945
Web site www.jamestowntn.org

Once a hunting ground for Davy Crockett and later Sergeant Alvin C. York, Jamestown was also the home of Cordell Hull, FDR's secretary of state.

What to See and Do

Big South Fork National River/Recreation Area. *4564 Leatherwood Rd, Oneida (37841). 20 miles NE on Hwy 154, then Hwy 297. Phone 423/569-9778. www.nps.gov/ biso.* Approximately 105,000 acres on the Cumberland Plateau. Swimming pool, fishing, whitewater canoeing, rafting, kayaking. Nature trails, hiking, backpacking, bridle trails; hunting. Primitive and improved camping (year-round; **$$$$**). Brandy Creek Visitor Center (Daily 8 am-4:30 pm). Stearns Visitor Center (Apr-Late Oct: daily 9:30 am-5 pm).

Historic Rugby. *Hwy 52, Rugby (37733). 17 miles SE via Hwy 52. Phone 423/628-2441; toll-free 888/214-3400. www.historicrugby.org.* English colony founded in 1880s by author-statesman-social reformer Thomas Hughes. Highest priority was placed on beauty, culture, parks, and recreational facilities. When it became difficult to make a living, the colony floundered. However, much has been preserved, and of the 17 original Victorian buildings remaining, four are open to the public. Hughes Public Library, unchanged since opening in 1882, contains a unique 7,000-volume collection from the Victorian era. Visitor center in Rugby Schoolhouse; guided walking tours (daily). Also picnicking, hiking in surrounding river gorges on trails built by original colonists. Bookshop, traditional craft commissary, lodging in historic houses and café. **$$**

Pickett State Rustic Park. *4465 Pickett Park Hwy, Jamestown (38556). 2 miles N on Hwy 127, then 11 miles NE on Hwy 154 N. Phone 931/879-5821.* Park covering 14,000 acres in Cumberland Mountains; unusual rock formations, caves, natural bridges. Sand beach. Swimming, fishing, boating (rentals). Nature trails, backpacking. Picnicking, concession, recreation lodge. Camping, cabins. Standard fees. **$**

Jellico (D-8)

See also Carryville

Population 2,447
Elevation 982 ft
Area Code 423
Zip 37762
Information Jellico Tourism Office, 906 5th St; phone 423/784-3275
Web site www.jellico.com/jellico/jellico.htm

What to See and Do

Indian Mountain State Park. *3 miles off I-75, exit 160. Phone 423/784-7958.* More than 200 acres. Swimming pool; fishing. Hiking trail. Picnicking, shelters; playgrounds. Camping. Standard fees. **$**

Limited-Service Hotel

★ **DAYS INN.** *I-75 Hwy 25 W, Jellico (37762). Phone 423/784-7281; toll-free 800/329-7466; fax 423/784-4529. www.daysinn.com.* 126 rooms, 3 story. Checkout 11 am. Restaurant. Outdoor pool. **$**
◩

Johnson City (D-10)

See also Cherokee National Forest, Elizabethton, Kingsport

Settled 1782
Population 55,469
Elevation 1,692 ft
Area Code 423
Information Convention and Visitors Bureau, 603 E Market St, PO Box 180, 37605; phone 423/461-8000 or toll-free 800/852-3392
Web site www.johnsoncitytn.com

Johnson City is a leading burley tobacco sales center, as well as a market and shipping point for Washington County's cattle, eggs, and alfalfa. Chemicals, textiles, building materials, electronics, and furniture are also produced in the town.

What to See and Do

Appalachian Caverns. *420 Cave Hill Rd, Blountville (37617). Phone 423/323-2337. www.appalachiancaverns.net.* When it's hot, caving will cool you right off. These giant underground chambers, made colorful by deposits of manganese, copper, calcium, and other elements, served Native Americans in need of shelter, hid soldiers during the Civil War, and protected moonshiners during Prohibition. Guided tours (daily; fee). **$$**

East Tennessee State University. *807 University Pkwy, Johnson City (37614). Phone 423/439-1000. www.etsu.edu.* (1911) (12,028 students) Campus has 63 buildings on 366 acres; Slocumb Galleries; Memorial Center (sports); James H. Quillen College of Medicine (1974). Tours of campus. Also on campus is

> **Carroll Reece Museum.** *Phone 423/439-4392.* Contemporary art and regional history exhibits; gallery tours; concert, film, and lecture series. (Daily; closed holidays) **FREE**

Hands On! Regional Museum. *315 E Main St, Johnson City (37601). Phone 423/434-4263. www.handsonmuseum.org.* More than 20 hands-on exhibits designed for children of all ages. Traveling shows. (June-Aug: Mon-Fri 9 am-5 pm, Sat from 10 am, Sun from 1 pm; closed Mon from Sept-May; also holidays) **$$**

⭐ **Jonesborough.** *6 miles W off Hwy 11 E.* Oldest town in Tennessee and the first capital of the state of Franklin.

> **Historic District.** *Visitors Center, 117 Boone St, Jonesborough (37659). Phone 423/753-5961.* Four-by-six-block area through the heart of town reflecting 200 years of history. Private residences, commercial and public buildings of Federal, Greek Revival, and Victorian styles; brick sidewalks, old-style lampposts, shops. Obtain walking tour brochures at visitors center.

> **Jonesborough History Museum.** *117 Boone St, Johnson City (37659). In visitors center. Phone 423/753-1015.* Exhibits highlight history of Jonesborough from pioneer days to early 20th century. (Daily; closed holidays) **$**

Rocky Mount Historic Site & Overmountain Museum.
*200 Hyder Hill Rd, Piney Flats (37686). 4 miles NE on
Hwy 11 E.* Phone 423/538-7396. Log house (circa 1770),
territorial capitol under Governor William Blount
from 1790 to 1792, is restored to original simplicity
with much 18th-century furniture; log kitchen, slave
cabin, barn, blacksmith shop, smokehouse. Costumed
interpreters reenact a day in the life of a typical pioneer
family; tour (1 1/2 hours) includes Cobb-Massengill
house, kitchen, and slave cabin, as well as self-guided
tour through the adjacent Museum of Overmountain
History. (Mon-Sat; closed Dec 20-Jan)

Rocky Top Campground. *496 Pearl Ln, Blountville
(37617). I-81, exit 63, about 15 miles S of Bristol Motor
Speedway.* Phone 423/323-2535. *www.rockytopcamp-
ground.com.* 35 wooded, level, pull-thru sites with wa-
ter/electric hook-ups. Modem and cable TV hookups are
also available. Air-conditioned restrooms with hot showers, tent platforms, and cabins. Reservations required.

Tipton-Haynes Historic Site. *2620 S Roan St, Johnson
City (37601). 1 mile off I-181 exit 31, at S edge of town.*
Phone 423/926-3631. Site of the 1788 "Battle of the
Lost State of Franklin." Six original buildings and four
reconstructions span American history from pre-co-
lonial days through the Civil War. Visitor center with
museum display; gift shop. (Apr-Oct: daily; rest of
year: Mon-Fri) Special programs, events. **$$**

Watauga Dam and Lake. *About 20 minutes E of Johnson
City off Hwy 321. www.tennesseelakeinfo.com/watauga.*
Surrounded by the Cherokee National Forest and
flanked by the Appalachian Mountains, Watauga
Reservoir is arguably one of the most beautiful in the
world and boasts excellent fishing. Below Watauga Dam
is a wildlife observation area, where visitors can view
waterfowl. The Appalachian Trail passes nearby. Phone
423/587-7037 to purchase fishing licenses. **FREE**

Whitewater rafting. *Cherokee Adventures, 2000 Jones-
borough Rd, Erwin (37650). 17 miles S on Hwy 19/23,
exit 18, then 1 mile N on Hwy 81.* Phone 423/743-7733;
toll-free 800/445-7238. *www.cherokeeadventures.com.*
Variety of guided whitewater rafting trips through the
Nolichucky Canyon and some of the deepest gorges
east of the Mississippi River and along the Watauga and
Russell Fork rivers. Mountain biking programs. Other
tours operated by USA Raft (Jones Branch Rd, Erwin,
phone toll-free 800/872-7238). (Mar-Nov) **$$$$**

Special Events

Appalachian Fair. *100 Lakeview St, Gray (37615).*
Phone 423/477-3211. *www.appalachianfair.com.* N, just
off I-181 in Gray at fairgrounds. Regional fair featur-
ing livestock, agriculture and youth exhibits, antique
display; entertainment. Nine days in late Aug. **$$**

Christmas in Jonesborough. *6 miles W. www.his-
toricjonesborough.com/events.html.* Tours of historic
houses, tree decoration, workshops, old-time holiday
events. Dec.

Jonesborough Days. *6 miles W.* Includes parade, art
show, crafts, old-time games, traditional music, square
dancing and clogging, food. July 4th weekend.

National Storytelling Festival. *8 miles W in Jonesborough. 116 W Main St, Johnson City (37659).* Phone
423/753-2171. *www.storytellingcenter.com/festival/fes-
tival/htm.* Three-day gathering from across the nation
features some of the country's best storytellers. First
weekend in Oct. **$$$$**

Limited-Service Hotels

★ ★ BEST WESTERN JOHNSON CITY
HOTEL & CONFERENCE CENTER. *2406 N
Roan St, Johnson City (37601).* Phone 423/282-2161;
toll-free 877/504-1007; fax 423/282-2488. *www.bw-
johnsoncity.com.* Visitors to the Johnson City area, as
well as business travelers, will appreciate everything
this extensive hotel has to offer. Enjoy a great meal
at Galloway's Restaurant, laze around in the huge
outdoor pool (the largest one in town), and check out
the jukebox in the hotel lounge area. 180 rooms, 4
story. Pets accepted; fee. Complimentary full breakfast.
Check-in 3 pm, check-out 11 am. High-speed Internet
access. Restaurant, bar. Fitness room. Outdoor pool.
Airport transportation available. **$**

★ ★ DOUBLETREE HOTEL JOHNSON CITY.
211 Mockingbird Ln, Johnson City (37604). Phone
423/929-2000; toll-free 800/222-8733; fax 423/929-
1783. *www.doubletreejohnsoncity.com.* This hotel is
near Interstate 81 and other major highways and
within walking distance of shopping at the Roan Centre and multiscreen movie theater. 184 rooms. Pets
accepted. Check-in 3 pm, check-out noon. High-speed
Internet access, wireless Internet access. Restaurant,
bar. Fitness room. Indoor pool, outdoor pool. Airport
transportation available. Business center. **$**

★ HAMPTON INN. *508 N State of Franklin Rd,
Johnson City (37604).* Phone 423/929-8000; toll-free
800/426-7866; fax 423/929-3336. *www.hamptoninn.*

com. 77 rooms, 3 story. Complimentary full breakfast. Check-in 3 pm, check-out noon. High-speed Internet access, wireless Internet access. Fitness room. Outdoor pool. Business center. **$**

★ ★ **HOLIDAY INN.** *101 W Springbrook Dr, Johnson City (37604). Phone 423/282-4611; toll-free 866/400-0541; fax 423/283-4869. www.holiday-inn. com.* 204 rooms, 6 story. Pets accepted. Check-in 3 pm, check-out 11 am. High-speed Internet access, wireless Internet access. Restaurant, bar. Fitness room. Outdoor pool. **$**

Restaurants

★ **FIREHOUSE.** *627 W Walnut St, Johnson City (37604). Phone 423/929-7377; fax 423/929-2080. www.thefirehouse.com.* Set in an old firehouse right in downtown Johnson City, this family restaurant prides itself on friendly service and hickory-smoked specialties. Kids will be fascinated by the old fire engine in the entrance area and all the old fireman memorabilia throughout the dining room. American menu. Lunch, dinner. Closed Sun; Thanksgiving, Dec 25. Children's menu. Casual attire. **$**

★ ★ **PEERLESS.** *2531 N Roan St, Johnson City (37601). Phone 423/282-2351; fax 423/282-4224. www. thepeerlessinc.com.* This award-winning restaurant is often recognized as Johnson City's best. It specializes in banquets and large groups. American menu. Dinner. Closed Sun; holidays. Bar. Children's menu. Casual attire. Reservations recommended. **$$**

Kingsport (D-9)

See also Johnson City

Settled 1761
Population 44,905
Elevation 1,208 ft
Area Code 423
Information Convention and Visitors Bureau, 151 E Main St, PO Box 1403, 37662; phone 423/392-8820 or toll-free 800/743-5282
Web site ci.kingsport.tn.us

Located at a natural gateway to the Southwest, this area saw the passage of the Great Indian Warrior & Trader Path and Island Road (1761), the first road built in Tennessee. The trail later became the Great Stage Road and was used for 150 years, marking the beginning of Daniel Boone's Wilderness Road. Kingsport was a little town on the Holston River, but it was converted to a planned industrial city during World War I. The first council-manager form of government in the state was installed in the town. The Eastman Chemical Company, the largest private employer in the state, is located in Kingsport.

What to See and Do

Bays Mountain Planetarium. *853 Bays Mountain Park Rd, Kingsport (37660). 6 miles SE off Hwy 93. Phone 423/229-9447. www.baysmountain.com.* Plant and animal sanctuary covers 3,000 acres, 25 miles of trails; nature interpretive center, aviary, deer pen; otter, bobcat, and wolf habitats; nature programs (summer, daily; rest of year, weekends); ocean pool; planetarium (shows daily in summer; rest of year, weekends). Exhibition gallery and library. Observation tower. 19th-century farmstead museum. Barge rides on 44-acre lake. Picnic tables. Park (daily). Fee for activities. **$$**

Boat Yard Park. *Netherland Inn Rd, Kingsport (37660). Phone 423/229-9457.* On the banks of the north and south forks of the Holston River. Historical complex includes Netherland Inn museum, picnic areas, playgrounds, boating, fishing; footpaths along the river (2 miles). Fees for some activities. **FREE** Here is

   Netherland Inn. *2144 Netherland Inn Rd, Kingsport (37660). Phone 423/246-6262.* (1818) Large frame and stone structure on site of King's Boat Yard (1802) was a celebrated stop on the Great Stage Road and was operated for over 150 years as an inn and the town's entertainment center; it was especially popular from 1818 to 1841 and was visited by many prominent individuals, including Andrew Jackson, Andrew Johnson, and James K. Polk. Now a museum with 18th- and 19th-century furnishings. The complex also includes a wellhouse, flatboat, garden, log cabin (1773), children's museum, museum shop. Interpreters. (May-Sept: Sat-Mon; Apr and Oct: Sat-Sun) **$$**

Boone Dam and Lake. *12 miles SE via Hwy 36, Hwy 75. Phone 423/279-3500.* TVA dam, 160 feet high and 1,640 feet long, impounds a 33-mile-long lake with 130 miles of shoreline. Swimming, fishing, boating (marina). Picnicking. Overlook (daily). **FREE**

Exchange Place. *4812 Orebank Rd, Kingsport (37664). Phone 423/288-6071. www.exchangeplace.info.* Restored 19th-century farm once served as a facility for exchanging horses and Virginia currency for Tennessee currency; crafts center; special events (fee). (May-Oct, weekends or by appointment) **FREE**

Fort Patrick Henry Dam and Lake. *490 Hemlock Park, Kingsport (37664). 4 miles S on Hwy 36. Phone 423/247-7891.* Companion to Boone Dam, this TVA dam, 95 feet high, 737 feet long, impounds a 10-mile-long lake. Swimming, fishing, boating. Overlook. (Daily) **FREE** Along the lakeshore is

Warriors' Path State Park. *490 Hemlock Rd, Kingsport (37663). I-81, exit 59, about 25 miles S of Bristol Motor Speedway. Phone 423/239-8531. www.state.tn.us/environment/parks.* This campground is on the shores of Patrick Henry Reservoir on the Holston River. The first-come, first-served wooded sites have picnic tables and grills. The sites are usually full by Tuesday of race week. 135 sites, 94 full hook-ups. Water stations, restrooms, showers. Pool, boat rentals, horseback riding.

Special Event

Kingsport Fun Fest. *Director's office, 151 E Main St, Kingsport (37662). Phone 423/392-8800. www.funfest.net.* Citywide, with more than 100 events including hot-air balloon races, sports events, entertainment. Nine days in late July.

Limited-Service Hotels

★ ★ **DAYS INN.** *805 Lynn Garden Dr, Kingsport (37660). Phone 423/246-7126; toll-free 800/329-7466; fax 423/247-8785. www.daysinn.com.* The downtown location and comfortable furnishings of this hotel make it a great choice for visitors to the area. Pet lovers will also appreciate the hotel's pet acceptance policy, which charges no extra fee to bring Fluffy along. 65 rooms, 2 story. Pets accepted, some restrictions. Complimentary continental breakfast. Check-in 11 am, check-out 11 am. High-speed Internet access. Outdoor pool, children's pool. Business center. **$**

★ ★ **RAMADA.** *2005 La Masa Dr, Kingsport (37660). Phone 423/245-0271; toll-free 800/272-6232; fax 423/245-7992. www.kingsportramada.com.* In addition to every convenience a seasoned traveler could want, the real draws of this hotel are its close proximity to the Bristol Raceway and its deluxe buffet continental breakfast, including favorites like scrambled eggs and waffles. 195 rooms, 2 story. Complimentary continental breakfast. Check-in 3 pm, check-out

noon. Restaurant, bar. Outdoor pool. Tennis. Airport transportation available. **$**

Full-Service Resort

★ ★ ★ **MARRIOTT MEADOWVIEW RESORT.** *1901 Meadowview Pkwy, Kingsport (37660). Phone 423/578-6600; toll-free 800/228-9290; fax 423/578-6630. www.meadowviewresort.com.* Whether you decide to stick around the beautiful grounds of this vast resort or catch the excitement of a race at Bristol, the amenities and atmosphere here will not disappoint. For sporty types, the resort offers tennis, basketball, golf, mountain biking, freshwater fishing, and volleyball; for those looking to relax, a dip in the outdoor pool or a nap in one of the resorts 195 rooms is a surefire way to recharge. 195 rooms, 7 story. Check-in 4 pm, check-out noon. High-speed Internet access. Restaurant, bar. Fitness room. Outdoor pool, whirlpool. Golf, 18 holes. Tennis. Airport transportation available. Business center. **$**

Knoxville (E-8)

Settled 1791
Population 173,890
Elevation 936 ft
Area Code 865
Information Convention and Visitors Bureau, 601 W Summitt Hill Dr, Suite 200B, 37902-2011; phone 865/523-7263 or toll-free 800/727-8045
Web site www.knoxville.org

First capital of Tennessee, Knoxville today is the manufacturing center for the east Tennessee Valley. In its early days, Knoxville was a frontier outpost on the edge of the Cherokee nation, last stop on the way west. Headquarters of the Tennessee Valley Authority, marketplace for tobacco and livestock, Knoxville is also a diversified industrial city, a product of power plant rather than plantation and of the atomic age rather than the Old South (Oak Ridge is only 22 miles away). It is a gracious city with the University of Tennessee as a cultural center and dogwood-lined streets in its residential sections.

Founded by an American Revolution veteran from North Carolina and named after Secretary of War Henry Knox, Knoxville quickly became a provisioning place for westward-bound wagons. It was known for its whiskey and wild times. East Tennessee had many Union sympathizers; during the Civil War Knoxville was seized by Confederates and became headquarters for an army of occupation. In 1863, Southern troops withdrew to Chattanooga and a Union army moved in, only to be besieged by Confederates. While the battle for Knoxville saw large sections of the city destroyed, the Confederate attack was rebuffed, and Knoxville remained in Union hands for the rest of the war.

The postwar years brought many former Union soldiers, skilled Northern workmen, and investment capital to Knoxville. Within two decades, its population more than tripled. During and since World War II, it has enjoyed a similar period of industrial growth and commercial well-being. The University of Tennessee, Knoxville (1794) is located here.

What to See and Do

Beck Cultural Exchange Center-Museum of Black History and Culture. *1927 Dandridge Ave, Knoxville (37915). Phone 865/524-8461.* Research, preservation, and display of the achievements of Knoxville's black citizens from the early 1800s. Gallery features changing exhibits of local and regional artists. (Tues-Sat; closed holidays) **FREE**

Confederate Memorial Hall. *3148 Kingston Pike SW, Knoxville (37919). Phone 865/522-2371.* Antebellum mansion with Mediterranean-style gardens served as headquarters of Confederate General James Longstreet during the siege of Knoxville. Maintained as a Confederate memorial, the 15-room house is furnished with museum pieces, a collection of Southern and Civil War relics; library of Southern literature. (Tues, Thurs-Fri afternoons) **$$**

Crescent Bend (Armstrong-Lockett House) and W. Perry Toms Memorial Gardens. *2728 Kingston Pike, Knoxville (37919). Phone 865/637-3163.* (1834) Collections of American and English furniture; English silver (16401820); extensive terraced gardens. (Mar-Dec, Tues-Sun) **$$**

East Tennessee Discovery Center & AKIMA Planetarium. *516 N Beaman St, Knoxville (37914). Chilhowee Park. Phone 865/594-1494. www.etdiscovery. org.* Science center with exhibits on life, energy, transportation, minerals, fossils; includes aquarium and planetarium. (Mon-Sat; closed holidays) **$**

Governor William Blount Mansion. *200 W Hill Ave, Knoxville (37902). Phone 865/525-2375. www.*

blountmansion.org. (1792) House of William Blount, Governor of the Southwest Territory and signer of the US Constitution, was the center of political and social activity in the territory. Restored to condition of late 1700s with period furnishings, Blount memorabilia; 18th-century garden. Tennessee's first state constitution was drafted in the governor's office behind the mansion. (Apr-mid-Dec: Mon-Sat 9:30 am-5 pm; early Jan-late Mar: Mon-Fri 9:30 am-5 pm; closed holidays) **$**

James White's Fort. *205 E Hill Ave, Knoxville (37915). Phone 865/525-6514.* Original pioneer house (1786) built by founder and first settler of Knoxville; restored buildings include smokehouse, blacksmith shop, museum. (Mar-mid-Dec: Mon-Sat; Jan, Feb: Mon-Fri; closed holidays) **$$**

Knoxville Museum of Art. *1050 World's Fair Park, Knoxville (37916). Phone 865/525-6101. www.knoxart. org.* Four galleries, gardens, great hall, ARTcade, exploratory gallery; collection of graphics. Changing exhibits. Gift shop. Free admission Tues 5-8 pm. (Tues-Wed noon-8 pm, Thurs-Fri to 9 pm, Sat-Sun 11 am-5 pm; closed holidays) **$**

Knoxville Zoo. *3500 Knoxville Zoo Dr, Knoxville (37914). E via I-40, Rutledge Pikes exit. Phone 865/637-5331. www.knoxville-zoo.org.* More than 1,000 animals, including big cats, gorillas, reptiles, elephants; petting zoo. (Daily; closed Dec 25) **$$$**

Marble Springs. *Approximately 6 miles S via Hwy 441, Hwy 33, then W on Hwy 168. Phone 865/573-5508.* Restored house of John Sevier, state's first governor (1796-1801, 1803-1809); original cabin and other restored buildings on 36 acres. (Tues-Sun) **$**

McClung Historical Collection. *East Tennessee Historical Center, 314 W Clinch Ave, Knoxville (37902). Phone 865/544-5744.* More than 38,000 volumes of history and genealogy covering Tennessee and Southeastern US. (Daily; closed holidays) **FREE**

Ramsey House (Swan Pond). *2614 Thorngrove Pike, Knoxville (37914). 6 miles NE. Phone 865/546-0745.* (1797) First stone house in Knox County, built for Colonel Francis A. Ramsey, was social, religious, and political center of early Tennessee. Restored gabled house with attached kitchen features ornamental cornices, keystone arches, and period furnishings. Picknicking available. (Apr-Oct: Tues-Sat and Sun afternoons; rest of year: by appointment) **$$**

Sunsphere. *810 Clinch Ave, Knoxville (37902). Phone toll-free 800/523-4227.* Built for the 1982 World's Fair, this 266-foot tower has an observation deck that provides views of downtown and Smoky Mountains. The Convention and Visitors Bureau Information Center is located here. **FREE**

University of Tennessee, Knoxville. *W Cumberland Ave, Hwy 11, 70. www.utk.edu.* (1794) (27,018 students.) On campus are Frank H. McClung Museum (daily; closed holidays; phone 865/974-2144); Clarence Brown Theater on Andy Holt Dr; special collections, 1401 Cumberland Ave (Mon-Fri; phone 865/974-4480).

Special Events

Dogwood Arts Festival. *111 N Central St, Knoxville (37902). Phone 865/637-4561. www.dogwoodarts.com.* More than 150 events and activities throughout the community including arts and crafts exhibits and shows; more than 80 public and private gardens on display; musical entertainment; parades; sporting events; more than 60 miles of marked dogwood trails for auto or free bus tours; special children's and senior citizen activities. Mid-late Apr.

Tennessee Valley Fair. *Chilhowee Park, 3301 E Magnolia Ave, Knoxville (37914). Phone 865/637-5840. www. tnvalleyfair.org.* Entertainment; livestock and agricultural shows; contests, exhibits, fireworks, carnival rides. Ten days in early-mid-Sept. **$$**

Limited-Service Hotels

★ ★ **COURTYARD BY MARRIOTT.** *216 Langley Pl, Knoxville (37922). Phone 865/539-0600; fax 865/539-4488. www.cyknoxville.com.* This neat-as-a-pin Courtyard assures guests a comfortable stay with well-appointed rooms that include television with cable, in-room coffee and tea, and luxurious bedding with fluffy down comforters and pillows. 72 rooms, 3 story. Check-in 3 pm, check-out noon. High-speed Internet access, wireless Internet access. Fitness room. Indoor pool, whirlpool. Business center. **$**

★ **HAMPTON INN.** *117 Cedar Ln, Knoxville (37912). Phone 865/689-1011; fax 865/689-7917. www. hamptoninnknoxvillenorth.com.* Clean and well-maintained accommodations make this Hampton Inn a comfortable and pleasant place to stay in Knoxville. With free in-room movies, a complimentary breakfast bar, and an on-site exercise room among the amenities here, this hotel makes guests feel right at home. 129 rooms, 3 story. Complimentary full breakfast. Check-

in 3 pm, check-out 11 am. High-speed Internet access, wireless Internet access. Fitness room. Outdoor pool. Business center. **$**

★ ★ **HOLIDAY INN.** *525 Henley St, Knoxville (37902). Phone 865/522-2800; fax 865/523-0738. www. holiday-inn.com.* 293 rooms, 11 story. Check-out 11 am. Restaurant, bar. Fitness room. Indoor pool, whirlpool. Business center. **$**

★ ★ **HOLIDAY INN.** *1315 Kirby Rd, Knoxville (37909). Phone 865/584-3911; toll-free 800/854-8315; fax 865/588-0920. www.holiday-inn.com.* Guests visiting Knoxville will find easy access to everything at the Holiday Inn, including the University of Tennessee, the Knoxville Convention Center, and shopping, museums, and historical sites. Pets are welcomed here, kids eat free, and business travelers will find fax and copy services as well as wireless high-speed Internet access and seven meeting rooms. 240 rooms, 4 story. Pets accepted, some restrictions; fee. Check-in 3 pm, check-out 11 am. High-speed Internet access, wireless Internet access. Restaurant, bar. Outdoor pool, whirlpool. **$**

★ ★ **RADISSON SUMMIT HILL KNOXVILLE.** *401 Summit Hill Dr, Knoxville (37902). Phone 865/522-2600; fax 865/523-7200. www.radisson.com.* This hotel has a convenient location near many attractions, including the historic shopping district and the Old City. 197 rooms, 12 story. Pets accepted, some restrictions; fee. Check-out noon. Restaurant, bar. Fitness room. Indoor pool. **$**

Full-Service Hotel

★ ★ ★ **HILTON KNOXVILLE.** *501 W Church Ave, Knoxville (37902). Phone 865/523-2300; fax 865/525-6532.* With a great view of the Tennessee River, this hotel is located in Knoxville's business and financial district near many attractions and restaurants. 317 rooms, 18 story. Check-out noon. Restaurant, bar. Fitness room. Outdoor pool. Airport transportation available. Business center. **$$**

Restaurants

★ **APPLE CAKE TEA ROOM.** *11312 Station W Dr, Knoxville (37922). Phone 865/966-7848.* Pop into this unbelievably quaint café located among boutique shops and the Tennessee countryside for a quick lunch or snack. The interior beckons diners to settle in and get comfortable, with a fireplace, log cabin furnishings, and lace curtains. Also, be sure to check out their homemade jams, jellies, and craft items for sale. American menu. Lunch. Closed Sun; holidays. Children's menu. Casual attire. Reservations recommended. **$**

★ **BUTCHER SHOP.** *806 World Fair Park Dr, Knoxville (37902). Phone 865/637-0204. www.thebutchershop.com.* This popular steakhouse is located in an old freight depot at the World's Fair Park near downtown Knoxville, making it a great choice for groups, business dinners, and families. Diners keep coming back for the grain-fed Midwestern beef which is grilled over an open pit with hickory charcoal for a truly delicious meal. Steak menu. Dinner. Closed Thanksgiving, Dec 24-25. Bar. Children's menu. Casual attire. Reservations recommended. Valet parking. **$$**

★ ★ **CALHOUN'S.** *10020 Kingston Pike, Knoxville (37922). Phone 865/673-3444; fax 865/673-3445. www.calhouns.com.* Featuring its own microbrew, this popular American restaurant also serves a huge array of Southern pub and barbecue favorites, including prime rib, fried catfish, and, yes, fried green tomatoes. Antique farming implements and Western décor go well with the homey menu and cordial staff. American menu. Lunch, dinner. Closed Dec 25. Bar. Children's menu. Casual attire. **$$**

★ ★ **CHESAPEAKE'S.** *500 N Henley St, Knoxville (37902). Phone 865/673-3433; fax 865/673-3435. www.chesapeakes.com.* The seafood in this nautically themed, downtown Knoxville spot is just about as fresh as you can get in a landlocked statehence, why the restaurant is named after a known seafood mecca. Choose from menu items like Maryland crab cakes, a soft-shell crab sandwich, Maine lobster, and oysters Rockefeller, as well as plenty of other enticing aquatic and nonaquatic options. Seafood menu. Lunch, dinner. Closed Thanksgiving, Dec 25. Bar. Children's menu. Business casual attire. Reservations recommended. Outdoor seating. **$$**

★ ★ **COPPER CELLAR.** *1807 Cumberland Ave, Knoxville (37916). Phone 865/673-3411; fax 865/521-7390. www.coppercellar.com.* Owned by the same company that runs both Chesapeakes and Calhouns (see), this local favorite restaurant (which is located downstairs of the more casual Cumberland Grill restaurant) boasts a menu that seems to have the best of both worlds—great steaks teamed with amazingly fresh seafood dishes like baked stuffed shrimp. Also serving Calhouns specialty microbrew, this richly decorated restaurant caters to all tastes. And be sure not to miss the crab bisque—it's a favorite. Steak menu. Dinner. Closed Sun; Thanksgiving, Dec 25. Bar. Children's menu. Casual attire. Reservations recommended. **$$**

★ ★ **LITTON'S.** *2803 Essary Rd, Knoxville (37918). Phone 865/688-0429.* American menu. Lunch, dinner. Closed Sun; holidays, children's menu. Casual attire. Reservations recommended. **$**

★ ★ **NAPLES.** *5500 Kingston Pike, Knoxville (37919). Phone 865/584-5033; fax 865/584-9415.* Italian menu. Lunch, dinner. Closed holidays. Bar. Children's menu. **$$**

★ ★ ★ **THE ORANGERY.** *5412 Kingston Pike, Knoxville (37919). Phone 865/588-2964; fax 865/588-5499. www.theorangeryrestaurant.com.* A beautiful winding staircase is the first thing that diners notice when they enter this elegant Knoxville restaurant. Its interior is decorated with French Provincial furnishings, mirrors, chandeliers, and antiques. A grand piano sits in the lounge area and is played nightly for diners while they enjoy a pre- or post-dinner drink. Large windows provide natural lighting but also give diners a wonderful view of the beautiful gardens in the courtyard. The Continental menu features specialties such as veal porterhouse, prime New York strip steak, buffalo with caramelized shallots, and elk chop with vegetable puree, and the extensive wine list provides many choices for a perfect pairing. This established restaurant is the perfect place for special-occasion meals. Continental menu. Lunch, dinner. Closed Sun; holidays; also first week of Jan and week of July 4. Bar. Business casual attire. Reservations recommended. **$$$**

★ ★ ★ **REGAS.** *318 N Gay St, Knoxville (37917). Phone 865/637-3427; fax 865/637-7799. www.connorconcepts.com.* First opened as a stool-and-counter restaurant in 1919, Regas has since become one of Knoxville's most popular restaurants. The décor has a rich, old-world elegance with a cozy fireplace, beamed ceilings, and brick-and-wood walls. The hearty lunch and dinner menus features classic American cuisine: steaks, chops, seafood, and chicken. However, no meal here would be complete without inhaling Regas' famous red velvet cake. American, seafood, steak menu. Lunch, dinner. Closed Sun; holidays. Bar. Children's menu. Business casual attire. Reservations recommended. Valet parking. **$$**

Lawrenceburg (F-4)

Founded 1815
Population 10,796
Elevation 890 ft
Area Code 931
Zip 38464
Web site www.cityoflawrenceburgtn.com

What to See and Do

David Crockett State Park. *1400 W Gaines St, Lawrenceburg (38464). W on Hwy 64.* Phone 931/762-9408. *www.state.tn.us/environment/parks/parks/DavidCrockettSP.* This 1,000-acre area is located on the banks of Shoal Creek, where Crockett once operated a gristmill. Swimming pool, wading pool, bathhouse; fishing, boating (rentals). Nature, bicycle trails; lighted tennis. Picnicking, playground, concessions; park restaurant doubles as a dinner theater in summer (reservations required). Tent, trailer sites. Visitors center housed in water-powered gristmill (Memorial Day-Labor Day); amphitheater. (Daily 7 am-dark) **$**

Lebanon (E-5)

See also Murfreesboro, Nashville

Population 20,235
Elevation 531 ft
Area Code 615
Zip 37087
Information Convention and Visitors Bureau, 149 Public Sq; phone 615/453-9655 or toll-free 800/789-1327
Web site www.wilsoncounty.com

Tall red cedars thrive in this area as they did in the biblical lands of Lebanon. Thus the founding fathers named the city Lebanon. The dense cedar forest has been used for many industrial purposes including wood, paper, and pencils. Since 1842, Lebanon has been the home of Cumberland University.

What to See and Do

Cedars of Lebanon State Park. *328 Cedar Forest Rd, Lebanon (37090). 7 miles S on Hwy 231, Hwy 10.* Phone 615/443-2769; toll-free 800/713-5180. *www.state.*

tn.us/environment/parks/parks/Cedars. Approximately 831 acres within this 9,000-acre state forest. Limestone cavern and sinks were reforested, in 1930s, with juniper. Swimming and wading pools. Hiking; game courts. Picnicking, playground, concession, recreation lodge. Tent and trailer sites, cabins. Nature center. **$**

Countryside RV Resort. *2100 Safari Camp Rd, Lebanon (37090).* Phone 615/449-5527. *www.countrysideresort.com.* 100 sites, 61 full hook-ups, 39 water and electrical hook-ups. Laundry services, convenience store, ice. Outdoor pool; playground; horseshoe pits; volleyball, basketball, and tennis courts. Pavilion.

Old Hickory Lake. *6 miles NW. www.tennesseelakeinfo.com.* Waterskiing, fishing, boating.

Limited-Service Hotel

★ **HAMPTON INN.** *704 S Cumberland St, Lebanon (37087).* Phone 615/444-7400; toll-free 800/426-7866; fax 615/449-7969. *www.hamptoninn.com.* 87 rooms, 2 story. Pets accepted, some restrictions; fee. Complimentary continental breakfast. Check-in 1 pm, check-out 11 am. High-speed Internet access. Fitness room. Outdoor pool, whirlpool. **$**

Lenoir City (E-7)

See also Knoxville, Sweetwater

Founded 1890
Population 6,819
Elevation 798 ft
Area Code 865
Information Loudon County Chamber of Commerce, 318 Angel Row, PO Box 129, Loudon 37774; phone 865/458-2067
Web site www.loudoncountychamber.org

What to See and Do

Fort Loudoun Dam and Lake. *983 City Park Dr, Lenoir City (37771). On Hwy 11 at S end of city.* Phone 865/986-3737. This TVA dam, 4,190 feet long and 122 feet high, with a lock chamber to permit navigation of the river, transforms a 61-mile stretch of once unruly river into a placid lake extending to Knoxville. Fishing, boating on 14,600-acre lake. **FREE**

Tellico Dam and Lake. *983 City Park Dr, Lenoir City (37771). Approximately 3 miles S off Hwy 321.* Phone 865/986-3737. TVA dam on Little Tennessee River impounds 15,680-acre lake. Upper end of reservoir adjoins the Cherokee National Forest (see). Excellent fishing and boating with the Great Smoky Mountains as a backdrop. Summer pool; boat access sites. Picnicking. Camping.

Limited-Service Hotel

★ **DAYS INN.** *1110 Hwy 321 N, Lenoir City (37771). Phone 865/986-2011; toll-free 800/289-0822; fax 865/986-6454. www.daysinn.com.* 80 rooms, 2 story. Pets accepted. Complimentary continental breakfast. Check-in 2 pm, check-out 11 am. Outdoor pool, children's pool. **$**

Full-Service Inn

★ ★ ★ **WHITESTONE COUNTRY INN.** *1200 Paint Rock Rd, Kingston (37763). Phone 865/376-0113; fax 865/376-4454. www.whitestoneinn.com.* Countryside leisure abounds at this peaceful, 360-acre property bordering Watts Bar Lake, just 40 minutes west of Knoxville. The farmhouse and barn hold seven bedrooms and five suites, each with a private bath, whirlpool tub and fireplace. 21 rooms, 2 story. Complimentary full breakfast. Check-in 3 pm, check-out 11 am. Restaurant. Children's activity center. Whirlpool. Tennis. Airport transportation available. Business center. **$$**

Lewisburg (F-5)

See also Shelbyville

Settled 1837
Population 10,413
Elevation 734 ft
Area Code 931
Zip 37091
Information Marshall County Chamber of Commerce, 227 2nd Ave N; phone 931/359-3863
Web site www.lewisburgtn.com

Named for Meriwether Lewis, of the Lewis and Clark expeditions, Lewisburg is largely linked to the dairy industry and is a trading and shipping center for the surrounding farms. Milk processing plants are supplemented by factories producing air conditioners, furniture, and pencils.

What to See and Do

Dairy Experiment Station. *1070 New Lake Rd, Lewisburg (37901). 3 miles S on Hwy 31A. Phone 931/270-2240. dairy.tennessee.edu.* Operated cooperatively by the US Department of Agriculture and the University of Tennessee on 615 acres. (Mon-Fri; weekends, by appointment) **FREE**

Henry Horton State Resort Park. *4358 Nashville Hwy, Chapel Hill (37034). 11 miles NE of I-65, on Hwy 31A. Phone 931/364-2319; toll-free 800/250-8612. www.state. tn.us/environment/parks/parks/HenryHorton.* Park covering 1,135 acres located on the estate of a former Tennessee governor is bordered by the scenic Duck River, a popular canoeing and fishing river. Facilities include swimming and wading pools. Clubhouse, golf course, lighted tennis; skeet and trap range. Picnicking, restaurant. Tent and trailer sites, cabins, resort inn. **$**

Tennessee Walking Horse Breeders' & Exhibitors' Association. *250 N Ellington Pkwy, Lewisburg (37091). Phone 931/359-1574. www.twhbea.com.* All registrations, transfers and decisions concerning the walking horse breed are made at this world headquarters. Open to visitors, the building contains a gallery of world champions. (Mon-Fri) **FREE**

Manchester (F-5)

See also Monteagle

Population 8,294
Elevation 1,063 ft
Area Code 931
Zip 37355
Information Chamber of Commerce, 110 E Main St; phone 931/728-7635
Web site www.manchestertn.org

What to See and Do

Jack Daniel's Distillery. *280 Lynchburg Hwy, Lynchburg (37352). 25 miles SW on Hwy 55. Phone 931/759-4221. www.jackdaniels.com/distillerytour.asp.* Nation's oldest registered distillery. One-hour and 20-minute guided tours include rustic grounds, limestone spring cave, old office. (Daily 9 am-4:30 pm; closed Jan 1, Thanksgiving, Dec 25) **FREE**

Normandy Lake. *8 miles W, 2 miles upstream from Normandy.* Completed in 1976, the dam is 2,734 feet high and impounds a 3,160-acre lake. Controlled releases provide a scenic floatway (28 miles) below the dam with public access points along the way. Summer pool; excellent spring and fall fishing. Picnicking. Camping.

Old Stone Fort State Archaeological Park. *732 Stone Fort Dr, Manchester (37855). 1 1/2 miles W off I-24, exit 110. Phone 931/723-5073. www.state.tn.us.environment/parks/parks/OldStoneFort.* Park covering 600 acres surrounds earthen remains of a more than 2,000-year-old walled structure built along the bluffs of the Duck River. Fishing. Picnicking, playground. Camping. Museum (daily 8 am-4:30 pm). (Daily 8 am-sunset) **$**

Special Event

Old Timer's Day. *City Square, Manchester.* Parade, pet contest, entertainment, games, food. Late Sept-early Oct.

Limited-Service Hotel

★ **AMBASSADOR INN AND LUXURY SUITES.** *925 Interstate Dr, Manchester (37355). Phone 931/728-2200; toll-free 800/237-9228; fax 931/728-8376. www.ambassadorinn.com.* 105 rooms, 2 story. Complimentary continental breakfast. Check-out 11 am. Fitness room. Outdoor pool. **$**
🖼 🏊

Restaurant

★ **OAK.** *947 Interstate Dr, Manchester (37355). Phone 931/728-5777.* American menu. Lunch, dinner, brunch. Closed Mon; holidays. Children's menu. Casual attire. Reservations recommended. **$**

Maryville (E-8)

See also Knoxville, Townsend

Founded 1795
Population 23,120
Elevation 989 ft
Area Code 865
Information Blount County Chamber of Commerce, 201 S Washington St, 37804; phone 865/983-2241
Web site www.blountchamber.com

Maryville and its twin city, Alcoa, provide a scenic gateway to the Great Smoky Mountains National Park (see). The seat of Blount County, Maryville was once the home of Sam Houston, the only man in US history to serve as governor of two states; in 1807 he moved to this area from Virginia with his widowed mother and eight brothers.

What to See and Do

Maryville College. *Office of Admissions, 502 E Lamar Alexander Pkwy, Maryville (37804). Phone 865/981-8000. www.maryvillecollege.edu.* (1819) (850 students) Liberal arts college. Twenty buildings represent architectural trends from 1869-1922. Fine Arts Center has plays, concerts, and exhibits. Tours of the campus leave Fayerweather Hall from the admissions office twice daily Monday through Friday.

Sam Houston Schoolhouse. *3650 Old Sam Houston School Rd, Maryville (37804). 5 miles NE, off Hwy 411 (follow signs). Phone 865/983-1550. www.geocities.com/samhoustonschoolhouse.* (1794) Restored log building in which Sam Houston taught in 1812 at a tuition rate of $8/term. Museum of Houston memorabilia in nearby visitor center. Picnicking. (Tues-Sat 10 am-5 pm, Sun from 1 pm; closed holidays; also Jan) **$**

Full-Service Inn

★ ★ ★ **BLACKBERRY FARM.** *1471 W Millers Cove Rd, Walland (37886). Phone 865/984-8166; fax 865/681-7753. www.blackberryfarm.com.* Blackberry Farm welcomes well-traveled guests with open arms to its gracious country home. Set on 2,500 picturesque acres in the foothills of Tennessees Smoky Mountains, it is a quintessential mountain retreat. Warm Southern hospitality is the hallmark of Blackberry Farm, and guests instantly feel like family here. A decidedly country style is injected with sophistication in the lovely accommodations, where fine art and antiques reside alongside canopy beds and floral prints. Wood-burning fireplaces and covered porches with rocking chairs further enhance the romantic appeal. The property's two ponds and stream beckon anglers who travel here solely for the Orvis fly fishing; horseback riding, swimming, hiking, tennis, and other country pursuits attract others; and epicureans savor the renowned haute cuisine. Housed in a charming 1870s farmhouse, the Aveda Concept Spa offers signature treatments using local blackberries to soothe and rejuvenate the body. 44 rooms, 2 story. Children over 10 years only, excluding holidays. Check-in 4 pm, check-out noon. Restaurant. Fitness room. Outdoor pool. Tennis. Airport transportation available. **$$$**
🖼 🏊 ⛷

McMinnville (E-6)

Population 12,749
Elevation 976 ft
Area Code 931
Information McMinnville-Warren County Chamber of Commerce, 110 S Court Sq, PO Box 574, 37111; phone 931/473-6611
Web site www.warrentn.com

What to See and Do

Cumberland Caverns Park. *1437 Cumberland Caverns Rd, McMinnville (37110). 7 miles SE, just off Hwy 8. Phone 931/668-4396. www.cumberlandcaverns.com.* Mined for saltpeter as long ago as the Civil War but not yet fully explored, the Cumberland Caverns offer a variety of underground formations and sights: old saltpeter mines; "Hall of the Mountain King" (600 feet across, 140 feet high); underground dining room; "God of the Mountain," a dramatization of the Creation with spectacular lighting (shown on every tour). Constant 56° F. Picnic area above ground. Tours (May-Oct: daily; spring-fall: 10 am, noon, 2 pm, 4 pm; summer: every hour 9 am-5 pm). **$$$**

Fall Creek Falls State Resort Park. *Hwy 3, Box 300, Pikeville (37367). 11 miles E of Spencer and 18 miles W of Pikeville via Hwy 30 to Hwy 284 E. Phone 423/881-3241; toll-free 800/250-8611. www.state.tn.us/environment/parks/parks/FallCreekFalls.* More than 16,000-acre park offers mountain scenery, the 256-foot Fall Creek Falls and great fishing. Swimming pool; boating (rentals). Nature trails; backpacking, riding; 18-hole golf, sports facilities. Picnicking, concessions, restaurant, inn. Tent and trailer sites, cabins. (Daily 24 hours) **$**

Rock Island State Rustic Park. *82 Beach Rd, Rock Island (38581). 14 miles NE via Hwy 70S. Phone 931/686-2471. www.state.tn.us/environment/parks/parks/RockIsland.* Approximately 850 acres, located on Center Hill Reservoir. (Daily 7:30 am-10 pm) **$**

Specialty Lodging

FALCON MANOR. *2645 Faulkner Springs Rd, McMinnville (37110). Phone 931/668-4444; fax 931/815-4444. www.falconmanor.com.* 4 rooms, 2 story. Children over 11 years only. Complimentary full breakfast. Check-in 3-7 pm, check-out 11 am. The Falcon Manor is an authentically restored Victorian mansion that was built in 1896. **$**

Memphis (F-1)

Also see Covington, KY and Holly Springs, MS

Settled 1819
Population 650,100
Elevation 264 ft
Area Code 901
Information Convention and Visitors Bureau, 47 Union Ave, 38103; phone 901/543-5300
Web site www.memphistravel.com

Memphis, on the Mississippi, is an old town with a new face. It is both "Old South" and modern metropolis. The city has towering office buildings, flashy expressways, a $60 million civic center—and historic Beale Street, where W. C. Handy helped give birth to the blues.

General James Winchester is credited with naming the city for the Egyptian city Memphis, which means "place of good abode." The Nile-like Mississippi, of course, was the inspiration. Winchester, Andrew Jackson, and John Overton laid out the town on a land grant from North Carolina, selecting this site because of the high bluffs above the river and the natural harbor at the mouth of the Wolf River. The land deal was somewhat questionable, and General Jackson left under a barrage of criticism. River traffic quickly developed; stores, shops, and sawmills appeared, and Memphis became one of the busiest and most boisterous ports in America.

For a short time, Memphis was the Confederate capital of the state, also serving as a military supply depot and stronghold for the Southern forces. In 1862, however, Northern troops seized the city after a river battle dominated by an armada of 30 Union ships and held it throughout the war. Plagued by yellow fever epidemics, an impoverished Memphis made a slow postwar recovery. But by 1892 the city was back on its feet, becoming the busiest inland cotton market and hardwood lumber center in the world.

Memphis dominates the flat, crop-rich, alluvial Mississippi Delta. It serves as hub of six railroads, port for millions of tons of river cargo annually, and home of over 1,100 manufacturing plants in the Memphis area. In national competition it has been acclaimed as the Cleanest City, the Safest City, and the Quietest City.

As much as one-third of the country's cotton crop is bought or sold in Memphis, known as the cotton

Beale Street

Ever since W. C. Handy set up shop in the early 1900s, Beale Street has been known around the world as the home of the blues and the inspiration for rock-and-roll. This is graphically described by no lesser authority than the Smithsonian Institution, which has set up one of its few remote sites beyond Washington D.C. in Beale Streets backlot.

Beale Street was a thriving commercial center for Memphiss African-American community for much of the 20th century, though it declined to a state of decay in the latter half of that century. It was resurrected in the last decade or so and is once again a thriving commercial district, the citys prime entertainment district for people of all stripes. Some say the strip lost its character in the transition from a gritty no-mans-land, but the folks dancing on the sidewalks as street musicians play for free on warm weekend nights don't seem to mind a bit.

From the top of the hill at 2nd Street you can look down on all the action. Here you'll find B. B. King's club and Elvis Presley's, both upscale supper clubs with name entertainmentsometimes even the King of the Blues himself. Stay on the lookout for the ghost of Elvis.

At the corner of 3rd street and Beale, a statue of W. C. Handy stands in front of an amphitheater that is the venue for many local music festivals, concerts, and other events. At 3rd Street you can cut behind Beale to the Gibson Guitar plant, where the Smithsonian has set up shop for its Rockn Soul exhibit, which does an excellent job of tracing the lineage of the most popular musical movements of the 20th century. A two-block walk up 3rd Street leads to the historic Peabody Hotel, the city's premier hotel, famous for its resident ducks, who descend from their penthouse suite across a red carpet to the lobby fountain each morning and ascend back each evening. In an alleyway across Union Street from the Peabody Hotel is the famous basement joint, the Rendezvous, which almost single-handedly has built and preserved Memphiss reputation as a barbecue capital.

---

center of the world, but the agricultural segment of the city's economy is highly diversified—corn, alfalfa, vegetables, soybeans, rice, livestock, and even fish farming. Memphis has the largest medical center in the South and more than a dozen institutions of higher learning, including the University of Memphis and Rhodes College. A city with a civic ballet, a symphony orchestra, an opera company, a repertory theater, art galleries, and College of Art, Memphis is also a major convention city and distribution center.

Throughout the world Memphis has become associated with the legendary Elvis Presley. Graceland, Presley's home, and Meditation Gardens, site of his grave, have become a destination for thousands of visitors annually. Each August, memorial celebrations are held citywide in honor of the "King of Rock 'n' Roll."

What to See and Do

⭐ **Beale Street.** *Beale Street Corporate Offices, 203 Beale St, Suite 300, Memphis (38103). Downtown, off Riverside Dr. Phone 901/526-0110. www.bealestreet.* com. Part of a seven-block entertainment district stretching east from the Mississippi River bluffs with restaurants, shops, parks, and theaters. Statue of W. C. Handy in Handy Park (3rd and Beale sts). Also on Beale Street is

W. C. Handy's Home. *352 Beale St, Memphis (38103). Phone 901/522-1556.* House where W. C. Handy wrote "Memphis Blues," "St. Louis Blues," and other classic tunes. Collection of Handy memorabilia. (Mon-Sat 10 am-4 pm, Sun 1-5 pm) **$**

The Children's Museum of Memphis. *2525 Central Ave, Memphis (38104). Phone 901/458-2678. www. cmom.com.* This hands-on discovery museum has created an interactive "kid-sized city" including a bank, grocery store, and skyscraper, among others. Other exhibits include *Art Smart*, where kids sculpt, paint, and draw; *Going Places*, where children "fly" a real airplane and watch a hot-air balloon ride. Save time to explore other special workshops and exhibits. (Tues-Sat 9 am-5 pm, Sun from noon; closed holidays) **$$**

Circuit Playhouse. *1705 Poplar Ave, Memphis (38104).* *Phone 901/726-5523. www.playhouseonthesquare.org.* Comedies, musicals, and dramas. **$$$$**

Coach USA. *5275 Raleigh La Grange, Memphis (38134).* *Phone 901/384-3474; toll-free 800/222-0089. www. coachusa.com.* Offers 3- or 4-day Branson, Missouri escorted tours and casino tours to Tunica. **$$$$**

Crystal Shrine Grotto. *5668 Poplar Ave, Memphis (38119). In Memorial Park Cemetery. Phone 901/767-8930.* Crystal cave made of natural rock, quartz, crystal, and semiprecious stones carved out of a hillside by naturalistic artist Dionicio Rodriguez in the late 1930s. Also scenes by the artist depicting the life of Jesus and Biblical characters. (Daily) **FREE**

Delta Queen, Mississippi Queen, American Queen. *Phone toll-free 800/543-1949. www.deltaqueen.com.* Paddlewheelers offer 3- to 12-night cruises on the Mississippi, Ohio, Cumberland, and Tennessee rivers. Contact Delta Queen Steamboat Co, Robin St Wharf, 1380 Port of New Orleans Pl, New Orleans, LA 70130-1890.

Dixon Gallery and Gardens. *4339 Park Ave, Memphis (38117). Phone 901/761-5250. www.dixon.org.* Hugo Norton Dixon and Margaret Oates Dixon, philanthropists and community leaders, left their home, grounds, and a large portion of their estate to fund this museum and garden complex for the enjoyment and education of future generations in Memphis. The museum is surrounded by 17 acres of formal gardens with a camellia house and garden statuary. The exhibition galleries display American and French Impressionist and post-Impressionist art, British portraits and landscapes, English antique furnishings, and 18th-century German porcelain. (Tues-Fri 10 am-4 pm, Sat to 5 pm; closed holidays) **$**

Downtown Mall Trolley. *Phone 901/274-6282.* Antique electric trolley loop runs up Main St and back in the Pinch Historic District providing transportation to hotels, Beale St, and attractions such as Pyramid Arena and the National Civil Rights Museum. (Daily)

★ **Graceland.** *3734 Elvis Presley Blvd, Memphis (38186). Phone 901/332-3322; toll-free 800/238-2000. www.elvis. com.* No visit to Memphis is complete without a stop at Graceland to pay homage to the King of Rock n Roll. The 60- to 90-minute tour of the Elvis Presley mansion includes the living room, dining room, kitchen, music room, TV room, pool room, Elvis's parents bedroom, the jungle room, and the recent addition of Elvis's personal office and costumes. It also features the racquetball room, trophy room (where Elvis's gold records and

awards are kept), and Meditation Garden, where Elvis's own eternal flame blazes and visitors leave flowers and other mementos at his gravesite. You can take separate tours of the Automobile Museum, which features Elvis's collection of Cadillacs and other cars and motorcycles; Elvis's custom jets, the *Lisa Marie* and the *Hound Dog II*; and Sincerely Elvis, a small museum of fan-related items. Don't miss the nearby gift shops for an amazing assortment of Elvis-related kitsch. (Mar-Oct: Mon-Sat 9 am-5 pm, Sun 10 am-4 pm; Nov-Feb: Mon, Wed-Sun 10 am-4 pm; closed Jan 1, Thanksgiving, Dec 25) **$$$$**

Lichterman Nature Center. *1680 Lynnfield, Memphis (38119). Phone 901/767-7322.* Wildlife sanctuary (65 acres) includes 12-acre lake, greenhouse, and hospital for wild animals. Hiking trails (3 miles). Picnicking. (Tues-Sun; closed Jan 1, Thanksgiving, Dec 24-25) **$**

Meeman-Shelby Forest State Park. *910 Riddick Rd, Millington (38053). 13 miles N via Hwy 51. Phone 901/876-5215; toll-free 800/471-5293. www.state. tn.us/environment/parks/parks/MeemanShelby.* This 13,467-acre pristine state park features two lakes, a campground, fishing, boating, and a swimming pool, and is a beautiful setting for a leisurely hike or walk. Meeman-Shelby Foreset State Park has more than 20 miles of hiking trails. However, since some of the trails are located in the Mississippi River bottom, they are off limits during managed hunts. (Daily 7 am-10 pm) **$**

Memphis Botanic Garden. *750 Cherry Rd, Memphis (38111). In Audubon Park. Phone 901/685-1566. www. memphisbotanicgarden.com.* Garden encompasses 96 acres; 20 formal gardens here include the Japanese Garden of Tranquility, the Rose Garden, and the Wildflower Garden. (Mar 1-Oct 31: Mon-Sat 9 am-6 pm, Sun from 11 am; rest of year: Mon-Sat 9 am-4:30 pm, Sun from 11 am; closed Jan 1, Thanksgiving, Dec 25) **$**

Memphis Brooks Museum of Art. *1934 Poplar Ave, Memphis (38104). In Overton Park. Phone 901/544-6200. www.brooksmuseum.org.* The largest art museum in Tennessee features drawings, paintings, sculpture, prints, photographs, and decorative arts such as glass and textiles. Its collections contain three centuries worth of works from Africa, Asia, Europe, and North and South America, including paintings by Andrew Wyeth, Winslow Homer, and Georgia O'Keeffe; sculptures by Auguste Rodin; and prints by Thomas Hart Benton. The museums Brushmark Restaurant, with terrific views of Overton Park through the floor-to-ceiling windows or on the outdoor terrace, serves lunch. (Tues-Fri 10 am-4 pm, Sat to 5 pm, Sun 11:30 am-5 pm; closed holidays) **$$**

Memphis Motorsports Park. *5500 Taylor Forge Dr, Millington (38053). N on I-240. Phone 901/358-7223. www.memphismotorsports.com.* Multiuse park features four tracks hosting a variety of racing events: drag, circle track, tractor pulls, motorcycle, go-cart, and four-wheeler. (Mar-Nov) **$$$$**

Memphis Pink Palace Museum and Planetarium. *3050 Central Ave, Memphis (38111). Phone 901/320-6320. www.memphismuseums.org.* Exhibits at this recently expanded and remodeled museum focus on the natural and cultural history of the mid-South. Many facets of the region, including insects, birds, mammals, geology, pioneer life, medical history, commerce, and the Civil War, can be explored through dioramas, exhibits, and audio-visuals. The museum also has a planetarium and an IMAX Theater. (Mon-Thurs 9 am-4 pm, Fri-Sat to 9 pm, Sun noon-6 pm; closed holidays) Planetarium has shows weekends and in summer ($). **$$$**

Memphis Queen Line Riverboats. *45 Riverside Dr, Memphis (38103). Phone 901/527-5694. www.memphisqueen.com.* Troll the river on one of the sightseeing or Evening Music Cruises aboard a Mississippi riverboat. (Sightseeing, Mar-Nov: daily; evening cruises, Apr-Oct: Fri-Sat) **$$$$**

Memphis Rock 'n' Soul Museum. *FedExForum, 191 Beale St, Memphis (38103). Phone 901/205-2533. www.memphisrocknsoul.org.* Showcasing Memphis as the crossroads of blues, rock 'n' roll, and country music, this museum features exhibits such as B. B. King's first "Lucille" guitar and Dick Clark's podium from American Bandstand. (Daily 10 am-7 pm) **$$**

⭐ **Memphis Zoo.** *2000 Prentiss Pl, Memphis (38112). Bounded by N Parkway, E Parkway and Poplar Ave. Phone 901/333-6500; toll-free 800/290-6041. www.memphiszoo.org.* The Memphis Zoo houses more than 3,500 animals in naturalistic habitats such as Cat Country, Primate Canyon, Animals of the Night, China, and Once Upon a Farm. And two of the most popular animals at the zoo are Ya Ya and Le Le, the giant pandas from China—don't miss them. The zoo is large, but it's easy to get around, just board the tram and it will take you on a leisurely ride around the park. Take a break from viewing the animals to go for a ride on the carousel or get a bite to eat at the café. (Mar-Oct: daily 9 am-6 pm; Nov-Feb: daily 9 am-5 pm; closed Thanksgiving, Dec 24-25) **$$$**

Memphis-Graceland RV Park. *3691 Elvis Presley Blvd, Memphis (38116). Phone 901/396-7125; toll-free 866/571-9236.* 91 sites, 72 full hook-ups, 16 with water and electricity. Laundry services, convenience store, ice. Pool, playground, volleyball and basketball courts.

⭐ **Mud Island River Park.** *125 N Front St, Memphis (38103). Monorail to island at Front St exit off I-40. Phone 901/576-7241; toll-free 800/507-6507. www.mudisland.com.* This 52-acre island, accessible by monorail or pedestrian walkway, is a unique park designed to showcase the character of the river. The River Walk is a five-block-long scale model of the lower Mississippi River from Cairo, IL, to the Gulf of Mexico (guided tours $$). The River Museum ($$) features 18 galleries that chronicle the development of river music, art, lore, and history. Also here are films; a playground; riverboat excursions; shops; restaurants; and a 5,400-seat amphitheater. (Late May-Sept: daily 10 am-8 pm; early Sept-late Oct, mid-Apr-late May: Tues-Sun 10 am-5 pm) **FREE** Also on the island is

Memphis Belle. *Jim Webb Restoration Center, 8101 Hornet Ave, Millington (38053). Phone 901/412-8071; toll-free 800/507-6507.* Named for the pilot's wartime sweetheart, this B-17 bomber and her crew were the first to complete 25 missions over Nazi targets and return to the US during WWII without losing any crew members or incurring any major injuries. The *Memphis Belle* shot down eight enemy fighters, most likely destroyed five others, and damaged at least a dozen more. The famous plane is currently undergoing restoration at Millington Municipal Airport, after which she will be moved to a new museum. The public may visit the "Belle" at hangar N7 while she is under restoration. (Tues-Fri 10 am-3 pm, Mon, Sat by appointment) **$**

⭐ **National Civil Rights Museum.** *450 Mulberry St, Memphis (38103). Phone 901/521-9699. www.civilrightsmuseum.org.* Opened in 1991, this is the nation's first civil rights museum. It honors the American civil rights movement and the people behind it, from colonial to present times. The museum is located at the former Lorraine Motel, site of the 1968 assassination of Dr. Martin Luther King, Jr. Exhibits include sound and light displays, audiovisual presentations, and visitor participation programs; special exhibits. There is also an auditorium, gift shop, and courtyard. (June-Aug: Mon, Wed-Sat 9 am-6 pm, Sun 1-6 pm; rest of year: Mon, Wed-Sat 9 am-5 pm, Sun 1-5 pm; closed Jan 1, Thanksgiving, Dec 25) **$$$**

National Ornamental Metal Museum. *374 Metal Museum Dr, Memphis (38106). On the river bluff. Phone 901/774-6380. www.metalmuseum.org.* Architectural and decorative metalwork. (Tues-Sat 10 am-5 pm, Sun from noon; closed Dec 24-Jan 1) **$**

Playhouse on the Square. *51 S Cooper, Memphis (38104). In Overton Sq. Phone 901/725-0776. www. playhouseonthesquare.com.* Professional theater. **$$$$**

Pyramid Arena. *1 Auction Ave, Memphis (38105). Downtown Pinch Historic District, on the Wolf River at Auction St Bridge. Phone 901/521-9675. www.pyramidarena.com.* This 32-story, 22,500-seat stainless steel and concrete pyramid, overlooking the Mississippi River, is fashioned after the ancient Egyptian Great Pyramid of Cheops and is used as a multisports and entertainment arena. Group tours (Mon-Fri). **$$**

Race-On Driving Experience. *525 N Main St, Memphis (38105). Phone 901/527-6174; toll-free 866/472-2366. www.4raceon.com.* If you're jealous of watching the pros have all the fun, test your skills behind the wheel of a NASCAR vehicle around the 3/4-mile paved tri-oval track at Memphis Motorsports Park (on nonrace days, of course). The season runs from March to November, but times and dates vary, so call for a schedule.

Rhodes College. *2000 N Parkway, Memphis (38112). Phone 901/843-3000; toll-free 800/844-5969. www. rhodes.edu.* (1848) (1,500 students) On campus is the 140-foot-high Richard Halliburton Memorial Tower, with first editions of Halliburton's books; memorabilia. Clough-Hanson Gallery has changing art exhibits (Tues-Sat 10 am-7 pm; closed holidays). Tours of campus (daily during school year; Mon-Fri in summer).

Stax Museum of American Soul Music. *926 E McLemore Ave, Memphis (38106). Phone 901/942-7685. www.soulsvilleusa.com.* This museum is built on the original headquarter's site of Stax Records, the Memphis-based record label that launched the careers of Otis Redding, Isaac Hayes, Sam and Dave, and other stars of the 1960s and 1970s. Featured here are more than 2,000 exhibits including Hayes's gold-trimmed, peacock-blue "Superfly" Cadillac. (Mar-Oct: Mon-Sat 9 am-4 pm, Sun 1-4 pm; Nov-Feb: Mon-Sat 10 am-4 pm, Sun 1-4 pm; closed holidays) **$$**

★ **Sun Studio.** *706 Union Ave, Memphis (38103). At Marshall Ave. Phone 901/521-0664; toll-free 800/441-6249. www.sunstudio.com.* Music legends like Elvis Presley, Jerry Lee Lewis, Johnny Cash, B. B. King, Roy Orbison, and Carl Perkins made their first recordings in this small studio. The 45-minute tour (last tour begins 30 minutes before closing) is worth the stop, and you can make your own custom recording. (Daily 10 am-6 pm; closed Thanksgiving, Dec 25) **$$**

T. O. Fuller State Park. *1500 Mitchell Rd, Memphis (38109). S on Hwy 61, then 4 miles W on Mitchell Rd. Phone 901/543-7581. www.state.tn.us/environment/parks/parks/TOFuller.* A 384-acre park where De Soto is believed to have crossed the Mississippi. Swimming pool, bathhouse. Golf. Picnicking, concessions. Campsites (hookups). (Daily 8 am-sunset) **$** In the park is

Chucalissa Archaeological Museum. *1987 Indian Village Dr, Memphis (38109). Phone 901/785-3160.* Archaeological project of the University of Memphis at the site of a Native American village founded about AD 900 and abandoned circa 1500. Native houses and temple have been reconstructed; archaeological exhibits. Museum displays artifacts and dioramas; 15-minute slide program. (Tues-Sun; closed holidays; no admittance to village area after 4:30 pm) **$$**

Victorian Village. *600 Adams Ave, Memphis (38105). Within 1 mile of downtown area.* Eighteen landmark buildings, either preserved or restored, range in style from Gothic Revival to neo-Classical. The three houses open to the public are

Magevney House. *198 Adams Ave, Memphis (38150). Phone 901/526-4464.* (1836) Restored house of pioneer schoolmaster Eugene Magevney. Oldest middle-class dwelling in the city, furnished with artifacts of the period. (Fri-Sat noon-4 pm; closed Jan 1, Thanksgiving, Dec 24-25) **FREE**

Mallory-Neely House. *652 Adams Ave, Memphis (38150). Phone 901/523-1484.* (1852) Preserved Italianate mansion (25 rooms) with original furnishings. (Tues-Sat 10 am-4 pm, Sun from 1 pm; closed Jan-Feb, Thanksgiving, Dec 24-25) **$$**

Woodruff-Fontaine House. *680 Adams Ave, Memphis (38150). Phone 901/526-1469.* (1870) Restored and furnished Second Empire/Victorian mansion with antique textile/costume collection. Gift shop. (Mon, Wed-Sun 10 am-4 pm; closed July 4, Thanksgiving, Dec 24-25) **$**

Special Events

Beale Street Music Festival. *www.thebealestreetmusicfestival.com.* International roster of musicians returns to Memphis for a musical family reunion. Part of the Memphis in May festivities. Early May.

Carnival Memphis. *1060 Early Maxwell Blvd, Memphis (38104). Phone 901/278-0243. www.carnivalmemphis.*

org. Features parade, exhibits, salute to industry, and the Cottonmaker's Jubilee. Ten days in early June.

Elvis Presley International Tribute Week. *3734 Elvis Presley Blvd, Memphis (38186). Phone 901/332-3322; toll-free 800/238-2000. www.elvis.com/graceland/calendar/elvis_week.asp.* Thousands of people come to Memphis from all around the world for this event-packed week to celebrate and remember the King of Rock 'n' Roll. More than 30 events including concerts, tours, street parties, fan forums, and even an Elvis fashion show, take place mid-Aug. **$$$$**

Labor Day Fest. *203 Beale St #300, Memphis (38103). Phone 901/526-0110.* Memphis musicians perform blues, jazz, rhythm and blues, country, and rock; at clubs and restaurants throughout the historic district. Early Sept.

Memphis in May International Festival. *88 Union Ave, Suite 301, Memphis (38103). Phone 901/525-4611. www.memphisinmay.org.* Month-long community-wide celebration focuses on cultural and artistic heritage of Memphis while featuring a different nation each year. Major events occur weekends, but activities are held daily. Includes the Beale Street Music Festival, World Championship Barbecue Cooking Contest, and Sunset Symphony. May.

Mid-South Fair and Exposition. *Mid-South Fairgrounds, 940 Early Maxwell Blvd, Memphis (38104). Phone 901/274-8800.* Agricultural, commercial, industrial exhibits; midway rides and concerts. Largest rodeo east of the Mississippi. Late Sept-early Oct.

Outdoor concerts. *1928 Poplar Ave, Memphis (38104). Phone 901/274-6046. www.overtonparkshell.org.* Raoul Wallenberg Overton Park Shell, said to be the true birthplace of rock 'n' roll; Elvis Presley gave one of his first live performances here. Concerts feature local blues, rock, and jazz musicians; also theater, movies, and dance presentations. Apr-Oct.

Theatre Memphis. *630 Perkins Extended, Memphis (38117). Phone 901/682-8601.* Internationally acclaimed community theater. Mainstage offers six-play season Sept-June; Little Theatre features four-play season July-May.

Zydeco Festival. *Beale St, Memphis.* Beale St. Cajun-Creole and zydeco blues bands entertain in Beale Street clubs. Early Feb.

Limited-Service Hotels

★ ★ **COURTYARD BY MARRIOTT.** *6015 Park Ave, Memphis (38119). Phone 901/761-0330; toll-free 800/321-2211; fax 901/682-8422. www.memphisparkavecourtyard.com.* 146 rooms, 3 story. Check-in 3 pm, check-out noon. High-speed Internet access. Restaurant. Fitness room. Outdoor pool, whirlpool. Business center. **$**
🏃 ⌁ 🏃

★ ★ **EMBASSY SUITES.** *1022 S Shady Grove Rd, Memphis (38120). Phone 901/684-1777; toll-free 800/362-2779; fax 901/685-8185. www.embassysuites.com.* Located in East Memphis, each suite offers a view of the hotel's tropical atrium. This property is within walking distance of fine shops and restaurants at the Regalia Shopping Center. The Memphis International Airport is also nearby. 125 rooms, 5 story, all suites. Complimentary full breakfast. Check-in 2 pm, check-out noon. High-speed Internet access, wireless Internet access. Restaurant, bar. Children's activity center. Fitness room. Indoor pool, whirlpool. Airport transportation available. Business center. **$**
✈ 🏃 ⌁ 🏃

★ ★ **HOLIDAY INN.** *160 Union Ave, Memphis (38103). Phone 901/525-5491; toll-free 888/300-5491; fax 901/529-8950. www.hisdowntownmemphis.com.* This hotel is near many downtown restaurants and attractions, including the IMAX, the zoo, and Mud Island River Park. 192 rooms, 15 story. Check-in 3 pm, check-out 11 am. High-speed Internet access, wireless Internet access. Two restaurants, bar. Fitness room. Outdoor pool. Business center. **$$**
🏃 ⌁ 🏃

Full-Service Hotels

★ ★ **DOUBLETREE HOTEL.** *5069 Sanderlin Ave, Memphis (38117). Phone 901/767-6666; fax 901/683-8563. www.doubletree.com.* 265 rooms, 8 story. Check-in 3 pm, check-out noon. High-speed Internet access, wireless Internet access. Restaurant, bar. Fitness room. Indoor pool, outdoor pool. Airport transportation available. Business center. **$**
🅿 🏃 ⌁ 🏃

★ ★ **DOUBLETREE HOTEL MEMPHIS DOWNTOWN.** *185 Union Ave, Memphis (38103). Phone 901/528-1800; toll-free 800/222-8733; fax 901/526-3226.* This hotel is two blocks from the famous Beale Street, near many restaurants and the downtown entertainment district. 280 rooms, 10 story. Check-in 3 pm, check-out 11 am. High-speed

Internet access, wireless Internet access. Restaurant, bar. Fitness room. Outdoor pool. Business center. **$**

★ ★ ★ **HILTON MEMPHIS.** *939 Ridge Lake Blvd, Memphis (38120). Phone 901/684-6664; toll-free 800/445-8667; fax 901/762-7496. www.hilton.com.* Towering 27 stories above the Memphis area, this hotel looks ultramodern on the outside but proves to be very bright and roomy on the inside. The hotel is set in the entertainment and business district, just minutes from downtown Memphis, guaranteeing a host of opportunities for sightseeing and experiencing the city. 405 rooms, 27 story. Check-in 3 pm, check-out noon. High-speed Internet access, wireless Internet access. Restaurant, bar. Fitness room. Outdoor pool, children's pool, whirlpool. Airport transportation available. Business center. **$$**

★ ★ ★ **MADISON HOTEL.** *79 Madison Ave, Memphis (38103). Phone 901/333-1200; fax 901/333-1299. www.madisonhotelmemphis.com.* The jazzy spirit of Memphis is brought to life at the Madison Hotel. This boutique hotel dazzles the senses with its striking interiors. Its contemporary style is best defined by its bold use of colors, geometric patterns, and modern furnishings. Sexy yet comfortable, this stylish place is the top address for cosmopolitan travelers. The guest accommodations are fitted with state-of-the-art technology for those here on business, while luxurious Italian bed linens and whirlpool baths appeal to all visitors. The intimate restaurant and lounge echo the hotel's commitment to style, and the rooftop garden affords views of both downtown and the Mississippi River. A converted bank vault serves as the hotel's fitness center, and a beautiful indoor lap pool invites swimmers to take a dip. 110 rooms, 15 story. Complimentary continental breakfast. Check-in 3 pm, check-out noon. High-speed Internet access. Restaurant, bar. Fitness room. Indoor pool. Business center. **$$$**

★ ★ ★ **MARRIOTT MEMPHIS.** *2625 Thousand Oaks Blvd, Memphis (38118). Phone 901/362-6200; toll-free 800/627-3587; fax 901/360-8836. www.marriott.com.* Near this property are attractions such as Graceland and the Mall of Memphis. 320 rooms, 14 story. Check-in 3 pm, check-out 11 am. High-speed Internet access, wireless Internet access. Restaurant, bar. Fitness room. Indoor pool, outdoor pool, whirlpool. Airport transportation available. Business center. **$**

★ ★ ★ **MARRIOTT MEMPHIS DOWNTOWN.** *250 N Main St, Memphis (38103). Phone 901/527-7300; toll-free 888/557-8740; fax 901/526-1561. www.memphismarriottdowntown.com.* This hotel, offering spacious guest rooms, is located 20 minutes from the Memphis International Airport and near shopping, museums, the world-famous Beale Street, and Mud Island. 600 rooms, 19 story. Check-in 4 pm, check-out noon. High-speed Internet access, wireless Internet access. Restaurant, bar. Children's activity center. Fitness room. Indoor pool, whirlpool. Airport transportation available. **$$**

★ ★ ★ **THE PEABODY MEMPHIS.** *149 Union Ave, Memphis (38103). Phone 901/529-4000; toll-free 800/732-2639; fax 901/529-3600. www.peabodymemphis.com.* The Peabody is a Memphis landmark. Perhaps best known for its signature ducks who march twice daily to splash in the hotel's fountain, this grand hotel is equally well known as a shopping destination and the home of Lansky's, Elvis's favorite clothing store. This full-service downtown hotel caters to discriminating travelers with its array of services and sophisticated accommodations. A comprehensive health club, indoor pool, and Gould's Day Spa and Salon cater to fitness-minded visitors. Attention to detail is a hallmark of this hotel, and club-level rooms come with special benefits, including nightly cocktails, hors d'oeuvres, and personalized services. Delicious Italian cooking is prepared at the popular Capriccio Restaurant, Bar & Café, while classic French dishes are updated at Chez Philippe. 464 rooms, 13 story. Check-in 4 pm, check-out 11 am. High-speed Internet access, wireless Internet access. Two restaurants, two bars. Fitness room, spa. Indoor pool, whirlpool. Airport transportation available. Business center. **$$**

★ ★ ★ **SHERATON CASINO AND HOTEL.** *1107 Casino Center Dr, Robinsonville (38664). Phone 662/363-4900; fax 662/363-1677. www.sheraton.com.* What's your poison—blackjack, roulette, craps, caribbean stud poker, pai gow, or slots? Well, you can find these games and more at this 92,000-square-foot casino. The tudor-style mansion houses 31,000 square feet of gaming space including 40 table games and 1,300 slot and video poker machines, an adjoining hotel, a restaurant, a spa, and live entertainment seven days a week. 134 rooms, 6 story. Check-out noon. Restaurant, bar. Fitness room, spa. Airport transportation available. Business center. **$$**

Restaurants

★ **ALFRED'S.** *197 Beale St, Memphis (38103). Phone 901-525-3711; toll-free 888/433-7711; fax 901-527-7949. www.alfreds-on-beale.com.* If you want great live music, tasty Southern cuisine, and a place to let your hair down, you have to check out Alfred's. This restaurant and bar is located on world-famous Beale Street. It has nightly live music, a huge dance floor, DJs, karaoke, and outdoor patios. American menu. Lunch, dinner, late-night. Bar. Casual attire. Outdoor seating. **$$**

★ ★ **AUTOMATIC SLIM'S TONGA CLUB.** *83 S 2nd St, Memphis (38103). Phone 901-525-7948; fax 901-526-6642.* The fare is spicy Caribbean, and the décor straight from the islands at this hip restaurant, which offers a view of The Peabody hotel and seating on the mezzanine. Caribbean menu. Lunch, dinner, late-night. Closed Sun; holidays. Bar. Casual attire. Reservations recommended. Outdoor seating. **$$**

★ **BUCKLEY'S FINE FILET GRILL.** *5355 Poplar Ave, Memphis (38119). Phone 901/683-4538; fax 901/682-2825. www.buckleysgrill.com.* If you love steak, don't miss the specialty of this locally owned house: the Buckley's Filet, 8 ounces of tenderloin grilled in garlic butter, served with garlic mashed potatoes. Italian, steak menu. Dinner. Closed holidays. Bar. Children's menu. Casual attire. **$$**

★ ★ **CAFÉ 61.** *85 S Second St, Memphis (38103). Phone 901/523-9351; fax 901/523-9640.* Cajun, Southern, Asian menu. Lunch, dinner, late-night, brunch. Closed holidays. Bar. Casual attire. Reservations recommended. **$$**

★ **CHARLIE VERGOS RENDEZVOUS.** *52 S 2nd St, Memphis (38103). Phone 901/523-2746; toll-free 888/464-7359; fax 901/525-7688. www.hogsfly. com.* This restaurant is a Memphis favorite for wet barbecued ribsserved with beans and slaw, of course. Located in an 1890s building and decorated with fun Memphis memorabilia and collectibles, this family-run business has been going strong since 1948. Barbecue menu. Lunch, dinner. Closed Sun-Mon; holidays. Bar. Casual attire. **$**

★ ★ ★ ★ **CHEZ PHILIPPE.** *149 Union Ave, Memphis (38103). Phone 901/529-4188; toll-free 800/732-2639; fax 901/529-3600. www.peabodymemphis.com.* For more than a decade, this sexy, sophisticated restaurant located in the historic Peabody Hotel (see) has been a perennial favorite of foodies, movie stars, celebrity chefs, and well-heeled locals. Like clockwork, the crowds show up every evening, filling Chez Philippe's stunning dining room for the opportunity to feast on the culinary artwork on display. The formula for success here is straightforward and winning. The service is efficient and unobtrusive. The atmosphere is hushed, elegant, and refined. And the food is practiced and classic—the aria of a well-trained culinary composer. The kitchen applies simple, seasonal ingredients to the delicate dishes of French origin, occasionally accented with regional flair. Desserts are a wonderful display of sweet interpretation; imagine that you are in Gascony and enjoying the signature Grand Marnier souffl. Because of its longstanding reputation, the dining room has legions of fans, but it will always find seats so that more diners may enjoy the symphony of Chez Philippe. French menu. Dinner. Closed Sun-Mon. Business casual attire. Reservations recommended. Valet parking. **$$$**

★ **THE CUPBOARD.** *1400 Union Ave, Memphis (38104). Phone 901/276-8015; fax 901/728-5518. www. thecupboardrestaurant.com.* This restaurant has been around since 1943 and has been at its current location since 2000. Be prepared to wait in line at lunchtime— The Cupboard is always crowded. Once seated, try the popular "meat and three," macaroni and cheese, or eggplant casserole. And don't leave without tasting the corn pudding. American menu. Lunch, dinner. Closed holidays. Casual attire. Reservations recommended. **$**

★ ★ ★ **ERLING JENSEN.** *1044 S Yates Rd, Memphis (38119). Phone 901/763-3700; fax 901/763-3800. www. ejensen.com.* This cutting-edge restaurant is one of the most popular in Memphis. Savor the shrimp and lobster terrine trimmed with mesclun greens and champagne vinaigrette, the quail and red cabbage, or the rich creamy bisques and fois gras preparations. International menu. Dinner. Closed holidays. Business casual attire. Reservations recommended. Valet parking. **$$$**

★ ★ ★ **GRILL 83.** *83 Madison Ave, Memphis (38103). Phone 901/333-1224; fax 901/333-1299. www. grill83.com.* Steak menu. Breakfast, lunch, dinner. Bar. Business casual attire. Reservations recommended. Valet parking. **$$$**

★ **INDIA PALACE.** *1720 Poplar Ave, Memphis (38104). Phone 901/278-1199; fax 901/278-1177.* The Indian menu at this restaurant features a lunch buffet with curries and tandooris. Decorated with Indian art, including an elephant mural. Indian menu. Lunch, dinner. Casual attire. Reservations recommended. **$$**

★ ★ ★ **LA TOURELLE RESTAURANT.** *2146 Monroe Ave, Memphis (38104). Phone 901/726-5771;*

fax 901/272-0492. www.latourellememphis.com. French menu. Dinner, brunch. Closed Mon; holidays. Business casual attire. Reservations recommended. **$$$**

★ ★ **PAULETTE'S.** *2110 Madison Ave, Memphis (38104). Phone 901/726-5128; fax 901/726-5670. www. paulettes.net.* French menu. Lunch, dinner, brunch. Closed holidays. Bar. Casual attire. Reservations recommended. Outdoor seating. **$$**

★ ★ ★ **RONALDO GRISANTI AND SONS.** *2855 Poplar Ave, Memphis (38111). Phone 901/323-0007; fax 901/323-0070.* Everything is freshly prepared at this restaurant, which is located in a small strip mall east of downtown. Specialties of the northern Italian menu include Gorgonzola-stuffed filets; fresh sea bass; and pasta la elfo, with shrimp, garlic, and mushroom. Italian menu. Dinner. Closed Sun; holidays. Bar. Casual attire. Reservations recommended. **$$$**

Monteagle (F-6)

See also Manchester

Population 1,238
Elevation 1,927 ft
Area Code 931
Zip 37356
Information Monteagle Mountain Chamber of Commerce, PO Box 535; phone 931/924-5353
Web site www.monteaglemtnchamber.com

A popular summer resort for more than a century, Monteagle is also famous for its Chautauqua Assembly, which has been held every summer since 1882.

What to See and Do

South Cumberland State Park. *Hwy 41, Monteagle. Phone 931/924-2980. www.state.tn.us/environment/parks/parks/SouthCumberland.* Extensive park system in southeastern Tennessee composed of nine separate areas. Visitor Center is located east of Monteagle on Hwy 41. (Daily 7 am-sunset) Within the system are

> **Carter State Natural Area.** *5 miles S of Sewanee on Hwy 56. Phone 615/532-0436.* A 140-acre area that includes the Lost Cove Caves. **FREE**

> **Foster Falls Small Wild Area.** *7 miles S of Tracy City on Hwy 41.* Foster Falls has the largest volume of water of any falls in the South Cumberland Recreation Area. Hiking. Picnicking. Camping (mid-Apr-mid-Oct). **FREE**

Great Stone Door. *Monteagle. Near Bersheba Springs.* A unique rock formation that is a 150-foot-high crevice at the crest of the Cumberland Plateau above Big Creek Gulf. Panoramic view of the area. Hiking. Picnicking. **FREE**

Grundy Forest State Natural Area. *Tracy City.* Sycamore Falls, a 12-foot-high waterfall lying in the bottom of the Fiery Gizzard Gorge, and Chimney Rocks, a unique geological formation, are highlights of this 212-acre recreational area. The Fiery Gizzard Hiking Trail winds around moss-laden cliffs and mountain laurel to connect the forest with the Foster Falls Small Wild Area. Picnicking. **FREE**

Grundy Lakes State Park. *Monteagle.* An 81-acre site features the Lone Rock Coke Ovens. These ovens, operated in the late 1800s with convict labor, were used in making coke for the smelting of iron ore. Swimming. Hiking. Picnicking. **FREE**

Savage Gulf State Natural Area. *27 miles NE, near Palmer on County 399E.* Covering 11,500 acres, the area offers 70 miles of wilderness hiking trails, backcountry camping, and rock climbing. The Savage Gulf cuts deep into the Cumberland Plateau and shelters virgin timber, rock cliffs, caves, and many waterfalls. **FREE**

Sewanee Natural Bridge. *2 miles S of Sewanee on Hwy 56.* A 2-acre area that features a 25-foot sandstone arch overlooking Lost Cove. **FREE**

University of the South. *Sewanee. 6 miles SW via Hwy 41. Phone 931/598-1286. www.sewanee.edu.* (1857) (1,300 students) Campus covering 10,000 acres at an elevation of 2,000 feet features scenic mountain overlooks, hiking trails, waterfalls, and caves; Gothic Revival architecture. On campus are DuPont Library Collection of rare books and manuscripts (Mon-Sat); All Saints' Chapel; Leonidas Polk Carillon (concerts Sun). Guided tours available.

Special Events

Monteagle Chautauqua Assembly. *Hwy 41 and Hwy 64, Monteagle. Phone 931/924-2268.* Concerts, lectures, academic courses, art classes. Early July-late Aug.

Sewanee Summer Music Center Concerts. *Guerry Hall, University of the South, 735 University Ave, Sewanee (37383). Phone 931/598-1225.* Four-day festival concludes season. Weekends, late June-early Aug.

Limited-Service Hotel

★ ★ **BEST WESTERN SMOKEHOUSE LODGE.** *850 Main St, Monteagle (37356). Phone 931/924-2268; fax 931/924-3175.* 85 rooms, 2 story. Pets accepted; fee. Check-out 11 am. Restaurant. Outdoor pool. Tennis. **$**

Specialty Lodging

ADAMS HISTORIC EDGEWORTH INN. *Monteagle Assembly Grounds, Monteagle (37356). Phone 931/924-4000; toll-free 877/352-9466; fax 931/924-3236. www.relaxinn.com.* 11 rooms, 3 story. Complimentary full breakfast. Check-in 4 pm, check-out 11 am. Art collection in 1896 building. On grounds of Monteagle Chatauqua Assembly. **$**

Morristown (E-9)

Settled 1783
Population 24,965
Elevation 1,350 ft
Area Code 423
Zip 37814
Information Chamber of Commerce, 825 W 1st North St, PO Box 9, 37815; phone 423/586-6382
Web site www.morristownchamber.com

Bounded by Clinch Mountain and the Great Smoky Mountains, Morristown is a major manufacturing center. Davy Crockett lived here from 1794 to 1809.

What to See and Do

Cherokee Dam and Lake. *Jefferson City. 14 miles SW on Hwy 11E to Jefferson City, then 5 miles N on Hwy 92. www.cherokeelakeinfo.com.* TVA dam (6,760 feet long, 175 feet high) on Holston River. Fishing, boating. Visitor building and powerhouse tours (daily). **FREE**

Panther Creek State Park. *210 Panther Creek Rd, Morristown (37814). 4 miles S on Hwy 11 E, then 2 miles W on Panther Creek Rd. Phone 423/587-7046. www.state.tn.us/environment/parks/parks/PantherCreek.* More than 1,400 acres on Cherokee Lake. Swimming pool; fishing. Hiking trails. Picnic sites, playground. Campground. Visitors center. (Daily 6 am-dark) **$**

Rose Center. *442 W 2nd North St, Morristown (37814). Phone 423/581-4330. www.rosecenter.org.* Historic building serves as a cultural center and includes a children's "touch" museum, historical classroom art gallery, and historical museum. (Mon-Fri; closed holidays) **FREE**

Limited-Service Hotel

★ **DAYS INN.** *2512 E Andrew Johnson Hwy, Morristown (37814). Phone 423/587-2200; toll-free 800/329-7466; fax 423/587-9752. www.morristowndaysinn.com.* 64 rooms, 2 story. Pets accepted, some restrictions. Complimentary continental breakfast. Check-in 11 am, check-out 11 am. Outdoor pool. Business center. **$**

Full-Service Hotel

★ ★ **HOLIDAY INN.** *5435 S Davy Crockett Pkwy, Morristown (37815). Phone 423/587-2400; toll-free 800/465-4329; fax 423/581-7344. www.holiday-inn.com.* 111 rooms, 3 story. Pets accepted, some restrictions; fee. Check-in 3 pm, check-out noon. High-speed Internet access. Restaurant. Fitness room. Two outdoor pools, children's pool. Business center. **$**

Murfreesboro (E-3)

See also Lebanon, Nashville

Founded 1811
Population 68,816
Elevation 619 ft
Area Code 615
Information Rutherford County Chamber of Commerce, 501 Memorial Blvd, PO Box 864, 37133-0864; phone 615/893-6565 or toll-free 800/716-7560
Web site www.rutherfordchamber.org

Murfreesboro lies in the geographic center of Tennessee. Because of this strategic location, the town was almost named the state capital. The legislature did meet in Murfreesboro from 1819 to 1826, but it never returned after convening in Nashville. The area is rich in Civil War history and is known as the "antique center of the South." Rutherford County is also noted for its production of cattle and prize-winning Tennessee walking horses.

What to See and Do

Oaklands. *900 N Maney Ave, Murfreesboro (37130). 2 miles N of I-24. Phone 615/893-0022.* This 19th-century mansion, an architectural blend of four different periods, was a social center before the Civil War and was the command headquarters for Union Colonel W. W. Duffield, who surrendered Murfreesboro to Confederate General Nathan Bedford Forrest at the house. Rooms restored and furnished with items appropriate to the Civil War period. Grounds landscaped in period style. (Tues-Sat 10 am-4 pm, Sun from 1 pm; closed holidays) **$**

Special Events

International Grand Championship Walking Horse Show. *Tennessee Miller Coliseum, 304 W Thompson Ln, Murfreesboro (37129). Phone 615/494-8822. walking horseowners.com.* Late Sept. **$$**

Longhorn Championship Finals Rodeo. *Tennessee Miller Coliseum, 304B W Thompson Ln, Murfreesboro (37129). Phone toll-free 800/357-6336.* Professional cowboys compete for final championship. Second weekend in Nov.

Street Festival. Arts and crafts. Early May.

Uncle Dave Macon Days. *Cannonsburgh Village, 105 S Church St, Murfreesboro (37130). Phone 615/893-2369. www.uncledavemacondays.com.* Old-time music, dance, arts and crafts. Second weekend in July. **FREE**

Limited-Service Hotels

★ ★ **DOUBLETREE HOTEL MURFREES-BORO.** *1850 Old Fort Pkwy, Murfreesboro (37129). Phone 615/895-5555; toll-free 800/222-8733; fax 615/895-3557. www.doubletree.com.* This hotel is conveniently located within minutes of business centers, hundreds of Tennessee attractions, and the interstate system. 168 rooms, 5 story. Pets accepted; fee. Complimentary continental breakfast. Check-in 3 pm, check-out noon. Wireless Internet access. Restaurant, bar. Fitness room. Indoor pool, outdoor pool, whirlpool. Business center. **$**

★ **GUESTHOUSE MURFREESBORO.** *1954 S Church St, Murfreesboro (37130). Phone 615/896-6030; fax 615/896-6046.* 125 rooms. Check-in 2 pm, check-out noon. High-speed Internet access. Outdoor pool. **$**

★ **HAMPTON INN.** *2230 Armory Dr, Murfreesboro (37129). Phone 615/896-1172; toll-free 800/426-7866; fax 615/895-4277. www.hamptoninn.com.* 114 rooms, 2 story. Pets accepted, some restrictions. Complimentary full breakfast. Check-in 3 pm, check-out noon. Wireless

Internet access. Fitness room. Outdoor pool. **$**

★ **SUPER 8 MOTEL.** *1414 Princeton Pl, Hermitage (37076). Phone 615/871-4545; fax 615/871-4545. www.thesuper8.com.* 65 rooms, 2 story. Complimentary continental breakfast. Check-in 2 pm, check-out 11 am. Wireless Internet access. Fitness room. Indoor pool, outdoor pool, whirlpool. Business center. **$**

Full-Service Hotel

★ ★ **HOLIDAY INN.** *2227 Old Fort Pkwy, Murfreesboro (37129). Phone 615/896-2420; toll-free 800/465-4329; fax 615/896-8738. www.holiday-inn.com.* 179 rooms, 4 story. Pets accepted, some restrictions. Check-in 4 pm, check-out 11 am. Two restaurants, bar. Fitness room. Indoor pool, outdoor pool, whirlpool. Airport transportation available. **$**

Restaurants

★ ★ **PARTHENON MEDITERRANEAN.** *1935 S Church St, Murfreesboro (37130). Phone 615/895-2665; fax 615/895-8177.* Mediterranean menu. Lunch, dinner, late-night. Closed holidays. Bar. Children's menu. Casual attire. Reservations recommended. Valet parking. **$$**

★ **SANTA FE STEAK CO.** *1824 Old Fort Pkwy, Murfreesboro (37129). Phone 615/890-3030.* American menu. Lunch, dinner, late-night. Bar. Children's menu. Casual attire. **$$**

Nashville (E-5)

See also Dickson, Franklin, Gallatin, Lebanon, Murfreesboro

Settled 1779
Population 569,891
Elevation 440 ft
Area Code 615
Information Convention and Visitors Bureau, 150 4th Ave N, 37201; phone toll-free 877/259-4704
Web site www.nashvillecvb.com

Commercial center and capital city, Nashville's heritage is part Andrew Jackson's Hermitage and part Grand Ole Opry. It is often referred to as the "Athens of the South" because of its 16 colleges and universities, religious publishing firms, and some 750 churches. To prove this point, it has the Parthenon, the only full-size replica of the Athenian architectural masterpiece.

The Nashville region's economy is diverse, and the area has benefitted from low unemployment, consistent job growth, and a broadening of the labor force. The city is a leader in publishing, finance and insurance, healthcare, music and entertainment, transportation technology, higher education, and tourism.

In recent years, millions of dollars in investment capital have been used for new buildings and vast expansion programs. This redevelopment has given the lovely old capital a new, airy setting. Throughout this bustle of commerce and construction, Nashville retains an Old South quality, proud of its gracious homes and its traditions.

These traditions stem back to the days when a band of pioneers built a log stockade on the west bank of the Cumberland River in 1779, naming it Fort Nashborough. The Cumberland Compact established a governing body of 12 judges at this wilderness village. By an act of the North Carolina legislature, the name was changed to Nashville. Nearly 50 years after Tennessee became a state, Nashville was made the permanent capital.

During the Civil War, the city was taken by Union troops in March 1862. In December 1864, a Confederate force under General John Bell Hood moved to the hills south of the city in an attempt to recapture it. However, two Union counterattacks virtually wiped out the Confederate army.

Just as the Cumberland Compact of May 1780 was an innovation in government, so was a new charter that became effective in 1963, setting up Nashville and Davidson County under a single administration with a legislative body of 40 members.

Additional Visitor Information

The Nashville Convention and Visitors Bureau, 211 Commerce St, Suite 100, 37201, has maps, brochures, lists of tour companies, and calendar of events; phone 800/657-6910. Advance reservations are strongly advised for the summer season (mid-May-mid-Sept) and all weekends. The Visitor Information Center is located in the glass tower of the Nashville Arena at 501 Broadway; phone 615/259-4747.

What to See and Do

Adventure Science Museum. *800 Fort Negley Blvd, Nashville (37203). Phone 615/862-5160. www.adventuresci.com.* Kids will love this hands-on science museum. There are six main concept areas to explore here: Earth Science, Creativity and Invention, Sound and Light, Air and Space, Health, and Energy. You can find all of these concepts represented on the Adventure Tower, a 75-foot-tall structure with seven levels of activities. Other exhibits include Construction Junction, Mission Impossible, and Dino Rumble. (Tues-Sun; closed Mon, holidays) **$$**

Belle Meade Plantation. *5025 Harding Rd, Nashville (37205). Phone 615/356-0501; toll-free 800/270-3991. www.bellemeadeplantation.com.* The antebellum mansion (1853) and outbuildings were once part of a 5,300-acre working plantation. At the turn of the 20th century, John Harding's Belle Meade was considered the greatest thoroughbred breeding farm in the country. The 14-room Greek Revival mansion contains Empire and Victorian furnishings and an heirloom showcase with racing trophies and mementos. Also on the grounds are the Dunham Station log cabin (1793) and the Carriage House (1890s), containing one of the South's largest carriage collections. (Mon-Sat 9 am-5 pm, Sun 11 am-5 pm; closed Jan 1, Thanksgiving, Dec 25) **$$$**

Belmont Mansion. *1900 Belmont Blvd, Nashville (37212). At Acklen Ave, on Belmont University campus. Phone 615/460-5459. www.belmontmansion.com.* Built in the 1850s in the style of an Italian villa, this mansion, once considered one of the finest private residences in the US, has original marble statues, Venetian glass, gasoliers, mirrors, and paintings in the 15 rooms open to the public; gardens feature large collection of 19th-century ornaments and cast-iron gazebos. (Mon-Sat 10 am-4 pm, Sun from 1 pm) **$$**

Centennial Sportsplex. *222 25th Ave N, Nashville (37203). Phone 615/862-8480. www.nashville.org/sportsplex.* This 17-acre fitness and recreation facility is mainly for middle Tennessee residents, but visitors can purchase passes in blocks of ten visits. The complex includes an aquatic center, a fitness center, a tennis center, and two ice rinks (fee) that are open to the general public. It's also home to the Nashville Predators, the areas NHL team. **$$$$**

Cheatham Lake, Lock, and Dam. *Nashville. 30 miles NW on Hwy 12, near Ashland City. Phone 615/792-5697.* Some recreation areas have swimming, fishing, boating (commercial docks). Camping (fee; electricity additional). Camping closed Nov-Mar. Fees for some areas.

Cheekwood Botanical Garden and Museum of Art.
1200 Forrest Park Dr, Nashville (37205). 8 miles SW on Forrest Park Dr, next to Percy Warner Park. Phone 615/356-8000. www.cheekwood.org. Cheekwood, once the private home and estate of the Cheek family, is now a cultural center complex set on 55 acres. The site, which was opened to the public in 1960, includes a museum with a permanent collection of 19th- and 20th-century American art; a Botanic Hall with an atrium of tropical flora and changing plant exhibits; public greenhouses featuring orchids, camellias, and plants from Central American cloud forests; and five major gardens specializing in dogwood, wildflowers, herbs, daffodils, roses, and tulips. (Tues-Sat 9:30 am-4:30 pm, Sun from 11 am; closed holidays) **$$**

Country Music Hall of Fame and Museum. *222 Fifth Ave S, Nashville (37203). Phone 615/416-2001; toll-free 800/852-6437. www.countrymusichalloffame.com.* This $37 million complex includes displays with costumes and instruments donated by country music legends from Minnie Pearl to George Jones. The rotundas bronze plaques commemorating hall of fame members can cause goosebumps. You can also check out the restored Historic RCA Studio B, where more than 1,000 top 10 hits from Elvis Presley, Willie Nelson, and other stars were recorded (fee). (Daily 9 am-5 pm; closed Jan 1, Thanksgiving, Dec 25) **$$$$**

Ellington Agricultural Center. *440 Hogan Rd, Nashville. 6 miles S. Phone 615/837-5197. www.tnagmuseum. org.* Former horse barn on a historic estate. Oldest Agricultural Hall of Fame in the US. Farm tools, equipment, and household items of the 19th century. (Mon-Fri; closed state holidays) **FREE**

Ernest Tubb Record Shop. *417 Broadway, Nashville (37203). Phone 615/255-7503. www.ernesttubb.com.* When Ernest Tubb and the Texas Troubadours weren't out touring in a big silver bus, the country music star was tending to his other love, the Ernest Tubb Record Shop. The original E.T. died in 1984, but the store continues to sell nothing but country music releases. Offerings range from hard-to-find rarities to the newest smash hits. The store on Music Valley Drive (2416 Music Valley Dr, 37214, phone 615/889-2474) also features the Texas Troubadour Theatre, home of the Midnight Jamboree every Saturday.

Fisk University. *1000 17th Ave N, Nashville (37208). Phone 615/329-8500. www.fisk.edu.* (1866) (900 students.) A National Historic District with Jubilee Hall, a historic landmark. The Carl Van Vechten Art Gallery houses the Stieglitz Collection of modern art. The Aaron Douglas Gallery houses a collection of African art.

Fort Nashborough. *100 1st Ave N, Nashville (37201). At Church St, at N end of Riverfront Park. Phone 615/862-8400.* Patterned after the pioneer fort established several blocks from this site in 1779; the replica is smaller and has fewer cabins. Stockaded walls, exhibits of pioneer implements. (Tues-Sun, weather permitting; closed holidays) **FREE**

General Jackson Showboat. *Opry Mills, Opry Mills Dr, Nashville (37214). Phone 615/458-3900. www.general-jackson.com.* Named after the first steamboat working the Cumberland River as far back as 1817, this 300-foot paddlewheel riverboat—the world's largest showboat these days—offers lunch cruises (buffet plus country music show) and elegant dinner cruises (includes a Broadway-style show). Call for times. **$$$$**

Grand Ole Opry. *2802 Opryland Dr, Nashville (37214). Phone 615/871-6779. www.opry.com.* You haven't made it in Music City USA as a country star until you've graced the stage of the world's longest-running radio show. Every weekend, the Opry showcases the best of bluegrass, country, gospel, swing, and Cajun. Part of the thrill for the audience is never knowing which stars who happen to be in Nashville will make a surprise appearance. (From November to February, shows originate from the Ryman Auditorium; from March to October, they're at the Grand Ole Opry House.) (Fri 7:30 pm, Sat 6:30 pm and 9:30 pm; also Tues in summer, 7 pm) **$$$$**

Grand Ole Opry Tours. *2800 Opryland Dr, Nashville (37214). Phone 615/883-2211.* One-hour, three-hour, and all-day bus tours include houses of country music stars, Music Row, recording studios, backstage visit to Grand Ole Opry House. Contact 2810 Opryland Dr, 37214. **$$$$**

Opryland Museums. *2802 Opryland Dr, Nashville. Located just outside the Grand Ole Opry House. Phone 615/889-3060.* **Minnie Pearl Museum** features 50 years of memorabilia; **Roy Acuff Museum** includes musical instruments; **Grand Ole Opry Museum** pays tribute to country stars with audiovisual and interactive devices. (Daily) **FREE**

Gray Line bus tours. *2416 Music Valley Ln, Nashville (37214). Phone 615/883-5555; toll-free 800/251-1864. www.graylinenashville.com.* Offers daily one- to six-hour sightseeing tours that highlight Nashville's most popular attractions, such as the Country Music Hall of Fame, Opry Mills, and the homes of country music stars. **$$$$**

⭐ **The Hermitage.** *4580 Rachel's Ln, Nashville (37076). 12 miles E off I-40 exit 221A. Phone 615/889-2941. www.thehermitage.com.* Rebuilt after a fire in 1834, this Greek Revival residence of President Andrew Jackson is furnished almost entirely with original family pieces, many of which were associated with Jackson's military career and years in the White House. The mansion has been completely restored to its appearance from 1837-1845, Jackson's retirement years. Tours of the 660-acre estate are narrated by historically costumed interpreters. The tour includes a museum; the Tulip Grove Mansion; the Hermitage Church; a garden with graves of Jackson and his wife, Rachel; two log cabins; a visitor center; and a biographical film on Jackson. (Daily 9 am-5 pm; closed Thanksgiving, Dec 25; also third week in Jan) **$$$** Included in the fee is

Tulip Grove. (1836) Greek Revival house of Andrew Jackson Donelson, Mrs. Jackson's nephew and President Jackson's private secretary. Interior has examples of 19th-century faux marbling.

Holiday-Nashville Travel Park. *2572 Music Valley Dr, Nashville (37214). Phone 615/889-4225; toll-free 800/547-4480.* 256 sites, 168 full hook-ups, 67 water and electrical hook-ups. Laundry services, convenience store, ice. Outdoor pool, playground, volleyball and basketball courts, shuffleboard, recreation room.

J. Percy Priest Lake. *3737 Bell Rd, Nashville (37214). 11 miles E off I-40. Phone 615/889-1975.* Waterskiing, fishing, boating (ramps, commercial boat docks). Picnicking. Tent and trailer sites (fee). Visitor center near dam (Mon-Fri). Some areas closed Nov-Mar.

Nashville KOA Kampground. *2626 Music Valley Dr, Nashville (37214). Phone 615/889-0282; toll-free 800/562-7789. www.koa.com.* 426 sites, 291 full hook-ups, 77 water and electrical hook-ups. Laundry services, convenience store, ice. Outdoor pool, children's pool, playground, horseshoe pits, basketball courts, recreation room.

Nashville Zoo. *3777 Nolensville Rd, Nashville (37211). Phone 615/833-1534. www.nashvillezoo.org.* At the Nashville Zoo, designers have gone to great lengths to make it seem as if you're simply walking through the woods and stumbling upon otters, cheetahs, apes, macaws, and other animals. (Apr-Oct: daily 9 am-6

pm; Nov-Mar: daily 9 am-4 pm; closed Jan 1, Thanksgiving, Dec 25) **$$$**

Old Hickory Lake. *6 miles NE of Nashville on the Cumberland River. Phone 615/822-4846.* This 22,000-acre lake has 440 miles of shoreline, eight marinas, and an abundance of water fowl and wading birds—a perfect place to spend a lazy day on the water. The lake is shared by pleasure boats, sailboats, personal watercraft, fishing boats, and commercial barges. (Daily; some areas closed Oct-Apr)

Opry Mills. *433 Opry Mills Dr, Nashville (37214). Phone 615/514-1000; toll-free 800/746-7386. www.oprymills. com.* There's something for just about everyone at this 1.2 million-square-foot shopping, dining, and entertainment complex. With the malls unique combination of manufacturers outlets and specialty stores, shoppers can find everything from clothing bargains to high-end sporting and outdoor goods. Noteworthy stores include Banana Republic Factory Store; Off 5th, the Saks Fifth Avenue Outlet; and Barnes & Noble. Keep in mind the whopping 9.25 percent sales tax when making your purchasing decisions. When you're ready for a break from shopping, have a bite at Rainforest Café, enjoy a sundae at Ghirardelli Chocolate Shop, or take in a movie on one of 20 screens or at the IMAX theater. (Mon-Sat 10 am-9:30 pm, Sun 11 am-7 pm; closed Easter, Thanksgiving, Dec 25)

The Parthenon. *2600 West End Ave, Nashville (37203). In Centennial Park, West End Ave and 25th Ave N. Phone 615/862-8431. www.nashville.gov/parthenon.* Replica of the Parthenon of Pericles' time was built in plaster for the Tennessee Centennial of 1897 and later reconstructed in concrete aggregate. As in the original, there is not a straight horizontal or vertical line, and no two columns are placed the same distance apart. Houses 19th- and 20th-century artworks; changing art exhibits; replicas of Elgin Marbles; 42-foot statue of the goddess Athena. (Tues-Sat 9 am-4:30 pm; also Sun 12:30-4:30 pm from Apr-Sept; closed Jan 1, Dec 25) **$**

Radnor Lake State Natural Area. *1160 Otter Creek Rd, Nashville (37220). 7 miles S on Hwy 31, then 1 1/2 miles W on Otter Creek Rd. Phone 615/373-3467. www. state.tn.us/environment/parks/radnor.* Located just south of Nashville, this 1,100-acre environmental preserve features an 85-acre lake and some of the highest hills in the Nashville Basin. The area provides scenic, biological, and geological areas for hiking, observation, photography, and nature study. (Daily) **$**

Ryman Auditorium & Museum. *116 5th Ave N, Nashville (37219). Phone 615/458-8700. www.ryman.com.* The Mother Church of Country Music underwent an $8.5 million facelift in the 1990s. Now, this National Historic Landmark hosts concerts and a museum that tells its story. (Don'trepeat, don'tleave without buying a box of GooGoos in the museum gift shop.) Tour of auditorium available. (Daily 9 am-4 pm; evening show times vary; closed Jan 1, Thanksgiving, Dec 25). **$$**

Sam Davis Home. *1399 Sam Davis Rd, Nashville (37167). 20 miles S off I-24 in Smyrna. Phone 615/459-2341.* Described as "the most beautiful shrine to a private soldier in the US," this stately house and 168-acre working farm have been preserved as a memorial to Sam Davis, a Confederate scout caught behind Union lines and tried as a spy. Offered his life if he revealed the name of his informer, Davis chose to die on the gallows. His boyhood home is restored and furnished with many original pieces; the grounds include a kitchen, smokehouse, slave cabins, and family cemetery where Davis is buried. (Mon-Sat 10 am-4 pm, Sun 1-4 pm; closed Jan 1, Thanksgiving, Dec 25) **$$**

⭐ **State Capitol.** *600 Charlotte Ave, Nashville (37243). Between Sixth and Seventh aves. Phone 615/741-1886; fax 615/741-2665. www.state.tn.us.* Construction of the Capitol began in 1845 and lasted until 1859. The architect, William Strickland, died before the building was completed, and his body was entombed within the building's northeast wall. The Greek Revival structure has an 80-foot tower that rises above the city, and columns grace the ends and sides. The building houses the governor's offices, the chambers of the state Senate, and the House of Representatives and Constitutional offices. During Union occupation of Nashville from 1862-1865, the Capitol was used as Fortress Andrew Johnson. (Mon-Fri; closed holidays)

Tennessee State Museum. *Polk Cultural Center, 505 Deaderick St, Nashville (37243). Phone 615/741-2692; toll-free 800/407-4324. www.tnmuseum.org.* This museum is one of the largest in the nation, with 60,000 square feet of exhibition space. It also houses an awesome Civil War collection. The permanent exhibits illustrating life in Tennessee focus on the prehistoric, Frontier, Age of Jackson, Antebellum, Civil War, and Reconstruction periods. Artifacts on display include Andrew Jackson's 1829 inaugural hat, an 1850s-style parlor, a steatite shaman's medicine tube, and a hand-drawn map of the Shiloh battlefield prepared for Confederate General Beauregard. After visiting the main museum, walk across the street to check out

the Military Museum in the War Memorial Building. (Tues-Sat 10 am-5 pm, Sun from 1 pm; closed holidays) **FREE**

Tennessee Titans (NFL). *The Coliseum.,One Titans Way, Nashville (37213). Phone 615/565-4200. www.titansonline.com.* Tennesseans have enthusiastically embraced their NFL team, the Titans (formerly the Houston Oilers). The 68,000-seat Coliseum, an outdoor stadium set on the Cumberland River with a great view of downtown Nashville, regularly fills with rabid fans. If you stay downtown, the stadium is just a short walk across the river. Tickets can be tough to come by, so make sure to call well in advance. **$$$$**

Travellers Rest Plantation and Museum. *636 Farrell Pkwy, Nashville (37220). I-65 exit 78, S on Hwy 31 (Franklin Rd). Phone 615/832-8197. www.travellersrestplantation.org.* (1799) Restored Federal-style house of Judge John Overton. Maintained as a historical museum with period furniture, records, and letters, the building reflects the history and development of early Tennessee. Eleven-acre grounds with formal gardens, weaving house, smokehouse. Gift shop. Allow at least 45 minutes for your visit. (Mon-Sat 10 am-4 pm, Sun from 1 pm; closed Jan 1, Thanksgiving, Dec 25) **$$$**

Two Rivers Campground. *2616 Music Valley Dr, Nashville (37214). Phone 615/883-8559. www.tworiverscampground.com.* 105 sites, 78 full hook-ups, 27 water and electrical hook-ups. Laundry services, convenience store, ice. Outdoor pool, playground, recreation room.

The Upper Room Chapel and Museum. *1908 Grand Ave, Nashville (37203). Phone 615/340-7207. www.upperroom.org.* Chapel with polychrome wood carving of Leonardo da Vinci's *The Last Supper*, said to be the largest of its kind in the world; also World Christian Fellowship Window. Museum contains various religious artifacts including seasonal displays of 100 nativity scenes and Ukranian Easter eggs. (Mon-Fri; closed holidays)

Vanderbilt University. *West End and 21st Ave S, Nashville (37240). Phone 615/322-5000. www.vanderbilt.edu.* (1873) (10,000 students.) The 330-acre campus features 19th- and 20th-century architectural styles. Fine Arts Gallery has a permanent collection supplemented by traveling exhibits. Blair School of Music offers regular concerts. Campus tours (all year).

Wildhorse Saloon. *120 2nd Ave N, Nashville (37201). Phone 615/902-8200. www.wildhorsesaloon.com.* If you're into line dancing, the Wildhorse Saloon is the place to go. Owned by the same folks who own the Grand Ole Opry and set in a three-level historic warehouse on Nashvilles Music Row, the club features live country acts Tuesday-Saturday nights as well as DJ music and offers free dance lessons to keep your scootin boots in step with the music. If all that dancing makes you hungry, the restaurant serves award-winning Southern barbecue for lunch and dinner daily. Children younger than 18 allowed with parents. (Restaurant: daily 11 am-midnight; club: daily 11-2 am) **$$**

Special Events

A Country Christmas. *Gaylord Opryland Resort and Convention Center, 2800 Opryland Dr, Nashville (37214).* Phone 615/871-7637. Rockettes, Fantasy on Ice, Treasures for the Holidays, Enchanted Forest dinner, tour of the Country Music Hall of Fame.

Music festivals. Nashville is host to many festivals: the International Country Music Fan Fair with its Grand Master Old-Time Fiddling Championship (early June), Gospel Music Week (Apr), and the Franklin Jazz Festival (Aug).

Running of the Iroquois Memorial Steeplechase. *50 Vaughn Rd, Nashville (37221). www.iroquoissteeplechase.org.* At the entrance to Percy Warner Park. Natural amphitheater seats 100,000. Second Sat in May. **$$$$**

Tennessee State Fair. *Tennessee State Fairgrounds, 626 Smith Ave, Nashville (37203). Phone 615/862-8980. www.tennesseestatefair.org.* Music, art, baking contests, agricultural exhibits, and livestock competitions. Ten days starting on the first Fri after Labor Day. **$$**

Limited-Service Hotels

★ **AMERISUITES.** *202 Summit View Dr, Brentwood (37027). Phone 615/661-9477; fax 615/661-9936. http://www.amerisuites.com.* 126 rooms, 6 story, all suites. Pets accepted. Complimentary continental breakfast. Check-out noon. Fitness room. Outdoor pool. Business center. **$**

★★ **COURTYARD BY MARRIOTT.** *1901 West End Ave, Nashville (37203). Phone 615/327-9900; toll-free 800/245-1959; fax 615/327-8127. www.marriott.com.* 223 rooms, 8 story. Check-in 3 pm, check-out noon. Restaurant. Fitness room. Outdoor pool, whirlpool. **$**

★★ **DOUBLETREE HOTEL.** *315 4th Ave N, Nashville (37219). Phone 615/244-8200; toll-free 800/222-8733; fax 615/747-4815. www.doubletree.com.* Experience Southern charm and modern luxuries at the Doubletree Hotel Nashville, located just steps from Music City's most popular attractions. Guests of this hotel will find the Country Music Hall of Fame, state capitol, historic buildings, art galleries, and a busy nightlife nearby as well as comfortable rooms that include cozy "Sweet Dreams" bedding, televisions with cable and video games, work desks with ergonomic chairs, and high-speed Internet access. 337 rooms, 9 story. Pets accepted, some restrictions; fee. Check-in 3 pm, check-out noon. High-speed Internet access. Restaurant, bar. Fitness room. Spa. Indoor pool. Airport transportation available. Business center. **$**

★★ **EMBASSY SUITES.** *10 Century Blvd, Nashville (37214). Phone 615/871-0033; toll-free 800/362-2779; fax 615/883-9245. www.embassysuitesnashville.com.* The suites in this hotel encircle a large atrium with waterfalls and exotic birds. Just two minutes from the airport and ten minutes from the Grand Ole Opry, the hotel is convenient for all travelers. 296 rooms, 9 story, all suites. Pets accepted, some restrictions; fee. Complimentary full breakfast. Check-in 4 pm, check-out noon. Restaurant, bar. Children's activity center. Fitness room. Indoor pool, whirlpool. Airport transportation available. **$$**

★ **FAIRFIELD INN BY MARRIOTT NASHVILLE OPRYLAND.** *211 Music City Cir, Nashville (37214). Phone 615/872-8939; toll-free 800/228-2800; fax 615/872-7230. www.marriott.com/bnaop.* 109 rooms, 3 story. Complimentary continental breakfast. Check-in 3 pm, check-out noon. Fitness room. Indoor pool. Airport transportation available. **$**

★★ **HOLIDAY INN.** *2613 West End Ave, Nashville (37203). Phone 615/327-4707; fax 615/327-8034. www.holiday-inn.com.* Situated in the Vanderbilt University area, just west of downtown Nashville, the Holiday Inn is also near many of the city's best attractions, including the Ryman Auditorium, Country Music Hall of Fame, and Tennessee State Capitol. Guests will find accommodations to be clean and comfortable, with amenities that include high-speed Internet access, premium cable TV, in-room video games, and spacious work desks. 300 rooms, 13 story. Pets accepted; fee. Check-in 3 pm, check-out noon. Restaurant, bar.

Fitness room. Outdoor pool. Airport transportation available. Business center. **$**

Full-Service Hotels

★ ★ ★ GAYLORD OPRYLAND RESORT AND CONVENTION CENTER. *2800 Opryland Dr, Nashville (37214). Phone 615/889-1000; toll-free 888/777-6779; fax 615/871-5728. www.gaylordhotels. com.* The Gaylord Opryland Resort & Convention Center promises a toe-tapping good time. Adjacent to the Grand Ole Opry, this resort is a natural choice for music fans, but with championship golf, outlet mall shopping, riverboat cruises, and plenty of other activities nearby, this resort has something for everyone. Nine acres of tropical gardens and flowing rivers are tucked inside climate-controlled glass atriums, allowing guests to enjoy the "outdoors" year-round. Guests can even take a ride aboard the hotel's Delta Flatboats without ever going outside. For those who do want to venture beyond, two outdoor pools beckon sunbathers and swimmers. Variety is the spice of life here, with an endless supply of dining and recreational choices. 2,881 rooms, 6 story. Check-in 3 pm, check-out 11 am. Seven restaurants, five bars. Children's activity center. Fitness room. Outdoor pool, children's pool. Airport transportation available. Business center. **$**

★ ★ ★ ★ ★ THE HERMITAGE HOTEL. *231 Sixth Ave N, Nashville (37219). Phone 615/244-3121; toll-free 888/888-9414; fax 615/254-6909. www. thehermitagehotel.com.* The Hermitage Hotel is the pride of Nashville. Opened in 1910, this glorious hotel recalls the grace and charm of a former time. Its lobby virtually defines magnificence, with vaulted ceilings of stained glass, dazzling arches decorated with frescoes, and intricate stonework. When this hotel first opened, it represented the finest America could offer, and that tradition of excellence continues today. Travelers in the know book rooms at this posh urban palace for its white-glove service and historic elegance. Often considered one of Nashville's best restaurants, the Capitol Grille (see) delights the most demanding palates with its regionally focused cuisine. The adjacent Oak Bar, with its emerald green club chairs and dark wood paneling, is a top spot for relaxing before or after dinner. 123 rooms, 10 story. Pets accepted; fee. Check-in 4 pm, check-out 11 am. High-speed Internet access, wireless Internet access. Restaurant, bar. Fitness room. Spa. Business center. **$$$**

★ ★ ★ LOEWS VANDERBILT HOTEL NASH-VILLE. *2100 West End Ave, Nashville (37203). Phone 615/320-1700; toll-free 800/336-3335; fax 615/320-5019. www.loewshotels.com.* This well-kept, upscale property is conveniently located between Vanderbilt University and downtown. 340 rooms, 12 story. Pets accepted. Check-in 3 pm, check-out noon. Restaurant, bar. Children's activity center. Fitness room, spa. Business center. **$$**

★ ★ ★ MARRIOTT NASHVILLE AIRPORT. *600 Marriott Dr, Nashville (37214). Phone 615/889-9300; toll-free 800/228-9290; fax 615/889-9315. www.marriott.com/bnatn.* The fun and entertainment of Music City is just steps from the Nashville Airport Marriott, a beautiful resort-like property set on 17 meticulously landscaped acres. Richly decorated rooms in tones of warm golds and greens pamper guests with luxurious bedding with fluffy down comforters and pillows, fine bath amenities, and in-room coffee and tea, amenities for the business traveler, including spacious desks, ergonomic chairs, and high-speed Internet access. Recreational activities abound, with biking, hiking, golf, sailing, and water-skiing nearby, as well as swimming and tennis available on the property itself. 398 rooms, 18 story. Check-in 4 pm, check-out noon. High-speed Internet access. Restaurant, bar. Fitness room. Spa. Indoor pool, outdoor pool. Tennis. Airport transportation available. Business center. **$$**

★ ★ ★ MILLENNIUM MAXWELL HOUSE NASHVILLE. *2025 Metro Center Blvd, Nashville (37228). Phone 615/259-4343; toll-free 866/866-8086; fax 615/313-1327. www.millenniumhotels.com.* With a historic pedigree, this fully modern hotel offers personalized service and excellent accommodations. Just five minutes from downtown and 15 minutes from the Grand Ole Opry, the hotel is a perfect base for all travelers. 289 rooms, 10 story. Check-in 3 pm, check-out noon. Restaurant, bar. Fitness room. Outdoor pool, whirlpool. Tennis. **$**

★ ★ ★ RENAISSANCE NASHVILLE HOTEL. *611 Commerce St, Nashville (37203). Phone 615/255-8400; toll-free 800/327-6618; fax 615/255-8202. www. renaissancehotels.com/bnash.* Located between the business district and the city's tourist area, this hotel is near fine dining, great shopping, and plenty of attractions. 673 rooms, 25 story. Check-in 3 pm, check-out noon. Restaurant, bar. Fitness room. Indoor pool,

whirlpool. Business center. **$$**

★ ★ ★ SHERATON MUSIC CITY. *777 McGavock Pike, Nashville (37214). Phone 615/885-2200; toll-free 800/325-3535; fax 615/231-1134. www.sheratonmusic-city.com.* Boasting the largest guest rooms in Nashville, the Sheraton Music City is a bastion of comfort and luxury. Tennis courts, an indoor pool, a Jacuzzi, health club, spa, and jogging course provide plenty of on-site recreation options, while sleigh beds with pillow-top mattresses, work desks with ergonomic chairs, TVs with cable and video games, and spacious baths make guests willingly retreat to their rooms at the end of the day. The Grand Ole Opry and Opry Mills Shopping Mall are just minutes away, as are some of Tennessee's most beautiful state parks. 410 rooms, 4 story. Check-in 3 pm, check-out 11 am. High-speed Internet access. Restaurant, bar. Fitness room. Spa. Indoor pool, outdoor pool, children's pool, whirlpool. Tennis. Airport transportation available. Business center. **$**

★ ★ ★ SHERATON NASHVILLE DOWN-TOWN HOTEL. *623 Union St, Nashville (37219). Phone 615/259-2000; toll-free 800/447-9825; fax 615/742-6056. www.starwoodhotels.com.* This contemporary hotel in downtown Nashville offers guests a host of amenities and services that make a stay here not only pleasant, but pampering. Room service, turndown service, television with cable, coffee makers, plush bathrobes, and Sheraton's signature "Sweet Sleeper Bed" offer true relaxation in guest rooms, while the concierge offers carefree planning for both business and leisure needs. 476 rooms, 28 story. Pets accepted, some restrictions. Check-in 4 pm, check-out 11 am. High-speed Internet access, wireless Internet access. Restaurant, bar. Fitness room. Spa. Indoor pool. Business center. **$**

★ ★ ★ WYNDHAM UNION STATION HOTEL. *1001 Broadway, Nashville (37203). Phone 615/726-1001; fax 615/248-3554. www.wyndham.com.* A truly unique place to stay, the Wyndham Union Station is housed in a historic 1897 train station. Its spectacular décor features marble floors; a domed, stained-glass ceiling; and a limestone fireplace. Business services and concierge service help make each guest's stay pleasant and care-free, and nicely appointed rooms set around the spacious lobby offer many modern comforts like high-speed Internet and premium cable TV. With its location only a few blocks from 2nd

Avenue and Music Row, the Wyndham puts guests close to all of the entertainment, dining, and nightlife that Nashville has to offer, with complimentary shuttle service to nearby attractions. 124 rooms, 7 story. Pets accepted, some restrictions; fee. Check-in 3 pm, check-out noon. Restaurant, bar. Business center. **$$**

Restaurants

★ BOSCOS PIZZA KITCHEN AND BREWERY. *1805 21st Ave S, Nashville (37212). Phone 615/385-0050; fax 615/385-0170. www.boscos-beer.com.* Handcrafted beer and wood-fired pizzas are the stars at this large but friendly brewpub near Vanderbilt University. Choose from a half-dozen "always on tap" brews and a selection of special and seasonal beers to wash down pizzas like the Margherita, California, and Jamaican, as well as a number of salads, sandwiches, and fish dishes. American, pizza menu. Lunch, dinner, brunch. Closed Dec 25. Bar. Children's menu. Casual attire. Reservations recommended. **$$**

★ ★ BOUND'RY. *911 20th Ave S, Nashville (37212). Phone 615/321-3043; fax 615/321-0984. www.pan-south.com.* Eclectic décor with colorful murals and sculptures is the perfect accompaniment to the colorful plates of internationally influenced cuisine. Small plate offerings include barbecue egg rolls, lobster ravioli, and a variety of pizzas, while large plates include sesame seared duck breast, a double pork chop, and iron-baked ravioli with spinach ricotta mousse. The two-story dining room offers al fresco dining in pleasant weather, with a heated patio upstairs, and retractable doors and windows downstairs. International, tapas menu. Dinner. Closed Thanksgiving. Bar. Casual attire. Reservations recommended. Valet parking. Outdoor seating. **$$$**

★ ★ ★ CAPITOL GRILLE. *231 Sixth Ave N, Nashville (37219). Phone 615/345-7116; fax 615/254-6909. www.thehermitagehotel.com.* The elegant Hermitage Hotel (see) is the setting for an equally elegant dining experience at The Capitol Grille. Luxuriously appointed with European banquettes and ornate vaulted ceilings, the room welcomes diners with warm lighting and soft music. With its location adjacent to the state capitol, The Grille is the setting for many business power lunches, but is also popular for dinner before a show at the nearby Tennessee Performing Arts Center or for that special occasion. But you may enjoy the menu of Southern-influenced fare so much that you won't want to wait for another special occasion for a return visit. Executive Chef Tyler Brown oversees the creation of such dishes as Niman Ranch pork with sweet potato juice, and veal loin with root vegetables. Truffle mac and cheese and spicy fried green tomato with spicy pepper relish are just a few of the sides that you will find hard to resist, and desserts like flourless chocolate ganache torte end the evening on a perfect note. Downstairs in the historic Hermitage Hotel (see), this Southern-influenced restaurant offers a different menu each week. American menu. Breakfast, lunch, dinner, brunch. Bar. Children's menu. Business casual attire. Reservations recommended. Valet parking. **$$$**

★ ★ **DARFONS RESTAURANT & LOUNGE.** *2810 Elm Hill Pike, Nashville (37214). Phone 615/889-3032; fax 615/871-4119.* Known as the "Cheers" of Nashville, this pub is a fun, friendly place that attracts families for its American and Italian-influenced fare as well as after-work revelers who meet at the horseshoe-shaped bar for cocktails. American menu. Lunch, dinner. Closed Sun; holiays. Bar. Children's menu. Casual attire. Outdoor seating. **$$**

★ ★ ★ **F. SCOTT'S.** *2210 Crestmoor Rd, Nashville (37215). Phone 615/269-5861; fax 615/269-8948. www.fscotts.com.* This is a large, sophisticated restaurant, but the feeling is one of friendly elegance, with the dining area broken up into smaller rooms. The décor is contemporary Art Deco with black-and-white tile floors, etched glass, soft gold-colored walls, and lovely table settings. Popular jazz musicians play nightly, and the space is completely smoke-free. Chef Will Uhlhorn's menu features contemporary American dishes such as seared New York strip with spicy pecan sweet potato hash, squash casserole, and thyme chive Barnaise and spicy cornmeal-dusted pan-fried trout. And the frozen mixed berry souffl topped with mint crme fraiche is the perfect ending to a delicious meal. American menu. Dinner. Closed holidays. Bar. Business casual attire. Reservations recommended. Valet parking. Outdoor seating. **$$$**

★ ★ **GREEN HILLS GRILLE.** *2122 Hillsboro Dr, Nashville (37215). Phone 615/383-6444; fax 615/383-8661. www.greenhillsgrille.com.* Opened in 1990 and just south of downtown Nashville, this Southwestern restaurant makes each diner feel like part of the family. The fun menu, featuring such items as the adobo barbecue chicken salad, the tortilla club sandwich, and the cowboy ribeye, makes this restaurant a great choice for groups and families. Southwestern menu.

Lunch, dinner, brunch. Closed Thanksgiving, Dec 25. Bar. Children's menu. Casual attire. Valet parking. **$$**

★ **KOTO SUSHI BAR.** *137 7th Ave N, Nashville (37203). Phone 615/255-8122.* Authentic Japanese cuisine with an impressive display of live fish. Sushi menu. Lunch, dinner. Closed Sun. **$**

★ ★ **LOVELESS CAFÉ.** *8400 Hwy 100, Nashville (37221). Phone 615/646-9700; fax 615/646-1971. www.lovelesscafe.com.* This Nashville institution is a can't-miss. Set in a peaceful, rural area, the Loveless Café features a country dining room décor with checked tablecloths, old wood floors, and lovely old fireplaces. Breakfast is the most popular meal, but you can't go wrong if you order the brittle-crusted fried chicken for lunch. This restaurant is a local favorite, but you might spot some celebrities here also. The house specialties include award-winning country ham and red-eye gravy and scratch biscuits with homemade preserves. There is also a catalog of food items packed to go. American, Southern menu. Breakfast, lunch, dinner. Closed Dec 25. Children's menu. Casual attire. Outdoor seating. **$**

★ ★ **MAD PLATTER.** *1239 Sixth Ave N, Nashville (37208). Phone 615/242-2563; fax 615/254-0934. www.madplatter.citysearch.com.* Set in a historic German-town storefront, the Mad Platter is a casual restaurant with wood floors, local artwork, white linen-topped tables, and bookshelves lining exposed red brick walls. This charming, cozy atmosphere offers a great setting for dates as well as casual business lunches, and the seasonal American menu, with selection like roast duck, mushroom ravioli, and grilled filet of beef tenderloin, are definite palate-pleasers. American, International menu. Lunch, dinner. Closed holidays. Casual attire. Reservations recommended. Outdoor seating. **$$**

★ ★ ★ **MARIO'S RISTORANTE.** *2005 Broadway, Nashville (37203). Phone 615/327-3232; fax 615/321-2675. www.mariosfinedining.com.* This wonderful dining spot, with its creaky chairs, crystal chandeliers, and opulent art, has charmed Nashville since 1965. Choices on the award-winning wine list, which boasts more than 700 bottles, perfectly complement the menu of Northern Italian cuisine, which features dishes like fresh Dover sole with pine nuts, rack of lamb in rosemary sauce, and farfalle with prosciutto. Italian menu. Dinner. Closed Sun; holidays. Bar. Business casual attire. Reservations recommended. **$$$**

★ ★ **MERCHANTS.** *401 Broadway, Nashville (37201). Phone 615/254-1892; fax 615/254-3012. www.*

merchantsrestaurant.com. Housed in a lovely historic building—the former Merchants Hotel—Merchants offers pub-style dining on the main floor and white tablecloth dining upstairs. From a salmon BLT sandwich and burgers to ahi tuna and filet mignon, this popular restaurant pleases everyone from families to couples looking for a romantic night out. Steak, seafood menu. Lunch, dinner. Closed holidays. Bar. Casual attire. Reservations recommended. Valet parking. Outdoor seating. **$$$**

★ ★ **MIDTOWN CAFÉ.** *102 19th Ave S, Nashville (37203). Phone 615/320-7176; fax 615/320-0920. www.midtowncafe.com.* Sophisticated and cozy, Midtown Café is a small, upscale spot perfect for romantic dinners and celebrating special occasions. Lemon-artichoke soup is a favorite of loyal followers, but everything on the menu from fresh seafood to prime steaks and lamb dishes are sure to prompt return visits. Lunch, dinner. Closed holidays. Bar. Casual attire. Reservations recommended. Valet parking. **$$$**

★ **MONELL'S.** *1235 6th Ave N, Nashville (37208). Phone 615/248-4747. monellsdining.citysearch.com.* If you're craving an old-fashioned, like-Grandma-used-to-make meal, be sure to visit Monell's. Located in a mid-1880s Victorian brick home in Germantown, this down-home eatery features Southern regional cooking as well as Southern hospitality. Both service and seating are family-style, and you can eat as much as you want—all empty dishes are quickly refilled by the staff. American, Southern menu. Breakfast, lunch, dinner. Closed Jan 1, Dec 25. Bar. Casual attire. **$**

★ ★ ★ **THE OLD HICKORY STEAKHOUSE.** *2800 Opryland Dr, Nashville (37214). Phone 615/889-1000; fax 615/871-7872. www.gaylordopryland.com.* Located in the Opryland Hotel, this steakhouse offers refined dining in an atmosphere of dark wooden furniture and dimly-lit rooms. Steak menu. Dinner. Bar. Children's menu. Casual attire. Reservations recommended. Valet parking. Outdoor seating. **$$$**

★ ★ ★ **THE PALM.** *140 5th Ave S, Nashville (37203). Phone 615/742-7256. www.thepalm.com.* Serious-sized steaks, chops, and seafood dishes grace the menu at this legendary steakhouse, decorated with soft gold colored walls and caricatures of local luminaries. Also found among the meaty menu selections are Italian-tinged dishes like linguine and clams, spaghetti marinara, and tomato capri salad. Going strong since 1926, The Palm as expanded their empire to 25 cities across the country, including Philadelphia, Las Vegas, and Dallas. Steak menu. Lunch, dinner.

Closed Memorial Day, Labor Day, Dec 25. Bar. Business casual attire. Reservations recommended. Valet parking. **$$$**

★ ★ ★ **RUTH'S CHRIS STEAK HOUSE.** *2100 West End Ave, Nashville (37203). Phone 615/320-0163; fax 615/329-0062. www.ruthschris.com.* Born from a single New Orleans restaurant that Ruth Fertel bought in 1965 for $22,000, the Ruths Chris Steak House chain has made it to the top of every steak lovers list. Aged prime Midwestern beef is broiled to your liking and served on a heated plate, sizzling in butter, a staple ingredient used generously in most entrées; even healthier alternatives like chicken arrive at your table drenched in the savory substance. Sides like creamed spinach and fresh asparagus with hollandaise are not to be missed, and are the perfect companion to any entrée. And who can forget the potatoes? Choose from seven different preparations, from a 1-pound baked potato with everything to au gratin potatoes with cream sauce and topped with cheese. Steak menu. Dinner. Closed holidays. Bar. Business casual attire. Valet parking. **$$$**

★ **SITAR INDIAN RESTAURANT.** *116 21st Ave N, Nashville (37203). Phone 615/321-8889; fax 615/321-2688. www.sitar.com.* Try authentic Indian fare at this spot (known to offer some of the best in Nashville) located across from Vanderbilt University. Homemade Indian cheese, tandoori chicken, and karahai shrimp are a few of the flavorful items you'll find on the extensive menu, while a full lunch buffet offers several Indian curries and other favorites. Indian menu. Lunch, dinner. Casual attire. **$**

★ ★ **SPERRY'S.** *5109 Harding Rd, Nashville (37205). Phone 615/353-0809; fax 615/353-0814. www.sperrys.com.* Locals are big fans of this mainstay serving large portions of steaks and seafood and located just 4 miles southwest of downtown Nashville. The façade is unassuming and the interior simple and casual, but the dining room and small, serpentine bar have remained popular drinking and dining destinations for decades. Seafood, steak menu. Dinner. Closed holidays. Bar. Business casual attire. Reservations recommended. **$$$**

★ ★ ★ **STOCK-YARD.** *901 Second Ave N, Nashville (37201). Phone 615/255-6464; fax 615/255-9561. www.stock-yardrestaurant.com.* Richly furnished with dark woods, ornate window treatments, and lots of antiques, the impressive Stock-Yard restaurant has been a Nashville tradition since 1979. This historic building that was once the city's Union Stockyards is now a place where families, couples, and friends gather to celebrate special occasions over dinners that consist of prime rib, porterhouse, and New York strip sirloin—all certified angus beef—as well as selections from the sea such as stuffed salmon, lobster tails, and jumbo fried shrimp. Head to the restaurant's wine display to see the oldest bottle of wine in the country, a Madeira from the 1700's. Steak, seafood menu. Dinner. Closed holidays. Bar. Children's menu. Business casual attire. Reservations recommended. **$$$**

★ ★ **SUNSET GRILL.** *2001 Belcourt Ave, Nashville (37212). Phone 615/386-3663; fax 615/386-0495. www. sunsetgrill.com.* Located in the Historic Hillsboro Village, this contemporary yet elegant restaurant, with brightly colored walls adorned with Parisian art, specializes in seafood, pasta, steak, and eclectic specials. The extensive wine list, a winner of the *Wine Spectator* award for excellence, offers 100 wines by the glass and 300 bottles. American menu. Lunch, dinner. Closed Dec 25. Bar. Casual attire. Reservations recommended. Valet parking. Outdoor seating. **$$**

★ ★ **TIN ANGEL.** *3201 West End Ave, Nashville (37203). Phone 615/298-3444.* A popular low-key spot near Vanderbilt University, Tin Angel is an intimate American bistro where couples get cozy and health nuts get more options other than a steamed veg plate. Angel hair pasta with fresh parmesan and sun-dried tomatoes; chicken breast with pine nut mousse; and Tortilla Cats, a catfish fillet lightly fried in a tortilla crust with black beans, rice, and salsa, are just a few tasty choices on the menu, which also includes meatier options like steaks and chops. American menu. Lunch, dinner. Closed holidays. Bar. Casual attire. Valet parking. **$$**

★ **TOWNE HOUSE TEA ROOM AND RESTAURANT.** *165 8th Ave N, Nashville (37203). Phone 615/254-1277; fax 615/254-1261.* This restaurant is located in a historic 24-room mansion (1840s) with fireplaces, oak floors, antiques, and paintings. American menu. Breakfast, lunch. Closed Sat-Sun; holidays. Bar. Casual attire. Reservations recommended. **$**

★ ★ **THE TRACE.** *2000 Belcourt Ave, Nashville (37212). Phone 615/385-2200; fax 615/385-2005. www. tracerestaurant.com.* Chic and somewhat nightclubbish with black interior and a floor-to-ceiling glass facade that rolls up in nice weather, The Trace attracts an eclectic crowd, including professionals from nearby Music Row. Starters like ceviche and seared foie gras hint at the sophistication of entrées to come, like al-

mond-crusted pork tenderloin with goat cheese, chargrilled tuna with wasabi-infused creamer potatoes, and duck confit with Yukon gold whipped potatoes, while the late-night menu offers a good selection of appetizers, salads, sandwiches, and entrées, as well as sinful desserts like Tuaca Chocolate Cake. American, French menu. Dinner, Sun brunch. Closed holidays. Bar. Casual attire. Reservations recommended. Valet parking. Outdoor seating. **$$$**

★ ★ ★ **VALENTINO'S.** *1907 West End Ave, Nashville (37203). Phone 615/327-0148; fax 615/327-9482. www. valentinosnashville.com.* A popular spot for romantic dinners, Valentino's is set in a charming old house with several dining areas that feature beautiful old-world décor with brick and stucco walls and tables topped with black and white linens. A menu of rustic Italian fare such as vegetable ravioli, farfalle with salmon, and chicken Marsala are just a few of the freshly prepared dishes on the extensive menu. Italian menu. Lunch, dinner. Closed Sun; holidays. Bar. Business casual attire. Reservations recommended. Valet parking. **$$**

★ ★ **ZOLA.** *3001 West End Ave, Nashville (37203). Phone 615/320-7778; fax 615/320-6030. www.restaurantzola.com.* Mediterranean menu. Dinner. Closed holidays. Casual attire. Reservations recommended. **$$$**

Natchez Trace State Resort Park (E-3)

40 miles NE of Jackson, off I-40.

Named for the pioneer trail that connected Nashville and Natchez, this 48,000-acre park is the largest recreation area in western Tennessee and the location of a pecan tree that is said to be the world's third largest. Four lakes provide swimming, fishing, boating (launch, rentals); nature trails, backpacking, picnicking, playground, recreation lodge. Tent and trailer sites, cabins, inn. Standard fees. Phone 731/968-3742.

Limited-Service Hotels

★ **BEST WESTERN CROSSROADS INN.** *21045 Hwy 22 N, Wildersville (38388). Phone 731/968-2532; toll-free 800/780-7234; fax 731/968-2082. www.bestwestern.com.* 40 rooms. Pets accepted; fee. Complimentary continental breakfast. Check-in 1 pm, check-out 11 am. High-speed Internet access. Outdoor pool. **$**

★ **PIN OAK LODGE.** *567 Pin Oak Lodge Ln, Wildersville (38388). Phone 731/968-8176; toll-free 800/250-8616; fax 731/968-6515. www.tnstateparks. com.* 44 rooms, 2 story. Closed Dec-early Mar. Pets accepted; fee. Complimentary continental breakfast. Check-in 4 pm, check-out 11 am. Restaurant. Outdoor pool, children's pool. Tennis. **$**

🦅 🏊 ⛷

Oak Ridge (E-7)

See also Knoxville

Founded 1943
Population 27,387
Elevation 900 ft
Area Code 865
Zip 37830
Information Convention & Visitors Bureau, 302 S Tulane Ave; phone 865/482-7821 or toll-free 800/887-3429
Web site www.oakridgevisitor.com

Oak Ridge was built during World War II to house Manhattan Project workers involved in the production of uranium 235 (the first atomic bomb's explosive element). Once one of the most secret places in the United States, Oak Ridge is now host to thousands who come each year, drawn by the mysteries of nuclear energy. Built by the US government, Oak Ridge is known for scientific research and development. Although many of the installations are still classified, the city has not been restricted since March 1949.

What to See and Do

American Museum of Science and Energy. *300 S Tulane Ave, Oak Ridge (37830). Phone 865/576-3200. www. amse.org.* One of the world's largest energy exhibitions; fossil fuels, energy alternatives, resources and research. Hands-on exhibits, displays, models, films, games, and live demonstrations. (Tues-Sat 9 am-5 pm, Sun from 1 pm; closed Jan 1, Thanksgiving, Dec 25) **$**

Bull Run Steam Plant. *1265 Edgemoor Rd, Clinton (37716). 5 miles SE, on shore of Melton Hill Reservoir. Phone 865/945-7200.* TVA-built with an 800-foot-high chimney, the plant has a roadside overlook. Visitor lobby and tours to powerhouse overlook (Mon-Fri). **FREE**

Children's Museum of Oak Ridge. *461 W Outer Dr, Oak Ridge (37830). Phone 865/482-1074.childrens-museumofoakridge.org.* Hands-on exhibits and displays include the International Gallery, Discovery Lab, doll house, Playscape, Nature Walk, Pioneer Living, and Oak Ridge history. Performances, exhibits, seminars, workshops. (Sept-May: Mon-Fri 9 am-5 pm, Sat-Sun 1:30-4:30 pm; June-Aug: Mon-Fri 9 am-5 pm, Sat 11 am-4 pm; closed holidays) **$$**

The Department of Energy's Graphite Reactor. *300 S Inland Ave, Oak Ridge (37830). 10 miles SW on Bethel Valley Rd. Phone 865/574-7199.* The world's oldest nuclear reactor, the Graphite Reactor, was built during World War II as part of the Manhattan Project. Interpretive exhibits. ORNL visitor overlook with audiovisual presentation (daily). **FREE**

Frozen Head State Park. *964 Flat Fork Rd, Wartburg (37887). Approximately 18 miles NW on Hwy 62, then 4 miles N on Flat Fork Rd. Phone 423/346-3318. www. state.tn.us/environment/parks/parks/FrozenHead.* More than 12,000 acres in Cumberland Mountains. Trout fishing. Hiking trails (50 miles). Picnicking, playground. Primitive camping. Visitor center. (Daily 8 am-sunset) **$**

International Friendship Bell. *Bristol Park, adjacent to Municipal Building.* The bell was designed to celebrate the dedication of Manhattan Project workers as a symbol of everlasting peace. (Daily) **FREE**

Melton Hill Dam and Lake. *15 miles SW.* This TVA dam extends barge travel up the Clinch River to Clinton and provides electric power. Dam (103 feet high, 1,020 feet long) impounds 44-mile-long lake. Fishing, boating. Camping (fee). Visitor overlook. (Daily) **FREE**

Oak Ridge Art Center. *201 Badger Ave, Oak Ridge (37830). Phone 865/482-1441. www.korrnet.org/art.* Permanent collection of original paintings, drawings, and prints; temporary exhibits. (Tues-Fri 9 am-5 pm; Sat-Mon 1-4 pm; closed holidays) **FREE**

University of Tennessee Arboretum. *901 S Illinois Ave, Oak Ridge (37803). Phone 865/483-3571. forestry. tennessee.edu/arboretum.* Part of the University of Tennessee Forestry Experimental Station. More than 1,000 species of trees, shrubs, and flowering plants on 250 acres. Self-guided tours. Visitor center (Mon-Fri 8 am-noon, 1-5 pm). **FREE**

Special Event

Appalachian Fest. *Children's Museum of Oak Ridge, 461 Outer Dr, Oak Ridge (37830).* Traditional crafts and music. Late Nov.

Limited-Service Hotels

★ **DAYS INN.** *206 S Illinois Ave, Oak Ridge (37830).* Phone 865/483-5615; toll-free 800/329-7466; fax 865/483-5615. www.daysinn.com. 80 rooms, 2 story. Pets accepted; fee. Complimentary continental breakfast. Check-in 2 pm, check-out 11 am. Outdoor pool. **$**

★ ★ **DOUBLETREE HOTEL.** *215 S Illinois Ave, Oak Ridge (37830).* Phone 865/481-2468; fax 865/592-2474. www.doubletree.com. 168 rooms, 5 story. Check-in 3 pm, check-out noon. Restaurant, bar. Fitness room. Indoor pool, outdoor pool, whirlpool. Business center. **$**

★ **HAMPTON INN.** *208 S Illinois Ave, Oak Ridge (37830).* Phone 865/482-7889; toll-free 800/426-7866; fax 865/482-7493. www.hamptoninn.com. 60 rooms, 5 story. Complimentary continental breakfast. Check-in 2 pm, check-out 11 am. Fitness room. Indoor pool, whirlpool. **$**

Paris (D-3)

Also see Land Between the Lakes, KY

Founded 1821
Population 9,763
Elevation 519 ft
Area Code 731
Zip 38242
Information Paris-Henry County Chamber of Commerce, 2508 E Wood St, PO Box 8; phone 731/642-3431 or toll-free 800/345-1103
Web site www.paris.tn.org

Only 14 miles from Kentucky Lake, Paris is a growing recreational center. It was named in honor of the Marquis de Lafayette, who was visiting in Nashville when the city was founded. The downtown area is lined with many buildings dating back to 1900.

What to See and Do

Nathan Bedford Forrest State Park. *1825 Pilot Knob Rd, Eva (38333). 21 miles S on Hwy 641, E on Hwy 70, then 8 miles N on Hwy 191.* Phone 731/584-6356. www.state.tn.us/environment/parks/parks/NBForrest. On the west bank of Kentucky Lake, a monument marks the spot where, in 1864, Confederate General Forrest set up artillery. Undetected by Union forces, the hidden batteries destroyed both the Union base on the opposite shore and its protective warships on the Tennessee River. The area is now an 800-acre park offering fishing and canoe access to the lake. Nature trails and programs, backpacking. Picnicking, playground, concession. Camping, group lodge. View from Pilot Knob. Museum (Wed-Sun). Trace Creek Annex, located across Kentucky Lake, interprets a portion of the military history of the area. (Daily 7 am-10 pm) **$**

Paris Landing State Park. *16055 Hwy 79 North, Buchanan (38222). 16 miles NE on Hwy 79.* Phone 731/641-4465. www.state.tn.us/environment/parks/parks/ParisLanding. An 840-acre park on Kentucky Lake with swimming beach, pools, waterskiing, boating (launch, rentals, marina). Golf, tennis courts. Picnicking, playground, concessions, lodging, restaurant. Camping. (Daily, 24 hours) **$**

Special Events

Eiffel Tower Day & Hot-Air Balloon Festival. *Memorial Park, Paris.* Second weekend in Sept.

World's Biggest Fish Fry. *Henry County Fairgrounds, Paris.* www.paris.tn.org. Celebration includes rodeo, parade, contests, and tournaments. Last full week in Apr.

Limited-Service Hotel

★ **ECONO LODGE PARIS.** *1297 E Wood St, Paris (38242).* Phone 731/642-8881; fax 731/644-2881. 98 rooms, 2 story. Complimentary continental breakfast. Check-out noon. Outdoor pool. **$**

Pigeon Forge (E-8)

See also Gatlinburg, Sevierville

Population 5,083
Elevation 1,031 ft
Area Code 865
Information Deptartment of Tourism, 2450 Parkway, PO Box 1390, 37868-1390; phone 865/453-8574 or toll-free 800/251-9100
Web site www.mypigeonforge.com

Located in the shadow of the Smokies, this resort town was named for the river on which it sits and the iron forge built in the early 1800s.

What to See and Do

The Comedy Barn. *2775 Parkway, Pigeon Forge (37863). Phone 865/428-5222. www.comedybarn.com.* Family comedy variety show with magicians, jugglers, comedians, and live music. (Mar-Dec, daily) **$$$$**

Country Tonite Theatre. *129 Showplace Blvd, Pigeon Forge (37863). Phone 865/453-2003; toll-free 800/792-4308. www.countrytonitepf.com.* This two-hour show features singing, dancing, and comedy. (Mar-Dec, Tues-Sun) **$$$$**

Dollywood. *1020 Dollywood Ln, Pigeon Forge (37633). 1 mile E on Hwy 441. Phone 865/428-9488. www.dollywood.com.* Dolly Parton's entertainment park. More than 40 musical shows daily; more than 30 rides and attractions and more than 70 shops and restaurants. (Schedule varies by season; call or visit the Web site for more information; closed Jan-Mar) **$$$$**

Elwood Smooch's Ole Smoky Hoedown. *2135 Parkway, Pigeon Forge (37863). Phone 865/428-5600.* (Mid-Apr-Oct) **$$$$**

Flyaway Indoor Skydiving. *3106 Parkway, Pigeon Forge (37863). Phone 865/453-7777. www.flyawayindoorskydiving.com.* Vertical wind tunnel that simulates skydiving. Instructor assists participants in flight chamber and explains how to maneuver the body to soar, turn, and descend. Observation gallery (fee). (Mar-Nov, daily; winter schedule varies; closed Dec 25) **$$$$**

Memories Theatre. *2141 Parkway, Pigeon Forge (37863). Phone 865/428-7852; toll-free 800/325-3078. www.memoriestheatre.com.* Each show is a tribute to musical legends of the past and present, such as Tom Jones, Cher, Elvis Presley, Kenny Rodgers, and Buddy Holly. (Mon-Sat 8 pm; closed the week of Dec 25)

The Old Mill. *160 Old Mill Ave, Pigeon Forge (37868). Phone 865/453-4628. www.old-mill.com.* Water-powered mill in continuous operation since 1830; grinds cornmeal, grits, whole wheat, rye, and buckwheat flours; dam falls are illuminated at night. Guided tours available (Apr-Nov: Mon-Sat). **$$**

Smoky Mountain Car Museum. *2970 Parkway, Pigeon Forge (37863). Phone 865/453-3433.* More than 30 gas, electric, and steam autos, including Hank Williams, Jr.'s "Silver Dollar" car; James Bond's "007" Aston Martin; Al Capone's bulletproof Cadillac; the patrol car of Sheriff Buford Pusser from the movie *Walking Tall;* and Elvis Presley's Mercedes. Historic gas pump globe display; Burma Shave signs. (May-Oct, daily) **$$**

Smoky Mountain Jubilee. *2115 Parkway, Pigeon Forge (37863). Phone 865/428-1836.*

Limited-Service Hotels

★ **BEST WESTERN PLAZA INN.** *3755 Parkway, Pigeon Forge (37863). Phone 865/453-5538; toll-free 800/232-5656; fax 865/453-2619. www.bwplazainn.com.* 201 rooms, 5 story. Closed Dec 24-25. Complimentary continental breakfast. Check-in 2 pm, check-out 11 am. Indoor pool, outdoor pool, children's pool, whirlpool. **$**

★ **BRIARSTONE INN.** *3626 Parkway, Pigeon Forge (37868). Phone 865/453-4225; fax 865/453-2564. www.newbriarstoneinn.com.* 57 rooms, 3 story. Closed Jan-Mar weekends only. Check-in 3 pm, check-out 11 am. Outdoor pool, whirlpool. **$**

★ **COLONIAL HOUSE.** *3545 Parkway, Pigeon Forge (37863). Phone 865/453-0717; toll-free 800/662-5444; fax 865/453-8412. www.colonialhousemotel.com.* 63 rooms, 3 story. Complimentary continental breakfast. Check-in 3 pm, check-out 11 am. Indoor pool, outdoor pool, children's pool. **$**

★ **CREEKSTONE INN.** *4034 S River Rd, Pigeon Forge (37868). Phone 865/453-3557; fax 865/453-3557. www.creekstoneinnpigeonforge.com.* On Little Pigeon River. 112 rooms, 5 story. Complimentary continental breakfast. Check-in 3 pm, check-out 11 am. Outdoor pool. **$**

★ ★ **HOLIDAY INN.** *3230 Parkway, Pigeon Forge (37863). Phone 865/428-2700; toll-free 800/782-3119; fax 865/286-2732. www.4lodging.com.* This hotel is less than a mile from downtown Knoxville, about 1 mile from Dollywood, and 8 miles from the Great Smoky Mountains National Park. 210 rooms, 5 story. Pets accepted, some restrictions; fee. Check-in 4 pm, check-out 11 am. Restaurant. Children's activity center. Fitness room. Indoor pool, whirlpool. **$**

★ **LAUREL GROVE INN & SUITES.** *2179 Parkway, Pigeon Forge (37863). Phone 865/428-7305; toll-free 866/896-2950; fax 865/428-8977. www.laurelgroveinn.com.* 123 rooms, 4 story. Complimentary continental breakfast. Check-in 3 pm, check-out noon. Outdoor pool. **$**

★ **QUALITY INN.** *3756 Pkwy, Pigeon Forge (37863). Phone 865/453-3490; toll-free 800/925-4443; fax 865/429-5432. www.qualityinn/pigeonforge.com.* 126 rooms, 3 story. Complimentary continental breakfast. Check-in 3 pm, check-out 11 am. Outdoor pool, children's pool, whirlpool. **$**

Specialty Lodging

HILTON'S BLUFF B&B INN. *2654 Valley Heights Dr, Pigeon Forge (37863). Phone 865/428-9765; toll-free 800/441-4188; fax 865/428-8997. www.hiltonsbluff.com.* 10 rooms, 2 story. Children over 9 years only. Complimentary full breakfast. Check-in 3 pm, check-out 11 am. On hill with scenic mountain view; deck with rocking chairs. **$**

Restaurant

★ **OLD MILL.** *164 Old Mill Ave, Pigeon Forge (37863). Phone 865/429-3463; fax 865/429-2191.* American menu. Breakfast, lunch, dinner. Closed Dec 25. Children's menu. Casual attire. **$$**

Savannah (F-3)

See also Shiloh National Military Park

Population 6,917
Elevation 436 ft
Area Code 731
Zip 38372
Information Visitors Bureau, 495 Main St; phone 731/925-2364 or toll-free 800/552-3866
Web site www.tourhardincounty.org

What to See and Do

Pickwick Landing Dam, Lock, and Lake. *14 miles S on Hwy 128. Phone 731/689-3149.* This TVA dam (113 feet high, 7,715 feet long) impounds a 53-mile-long lake with 496 miles of shoreline. Also a 1,000-foot-long navigation lock. Powerhouse visitor lobby. Navigation Museum at lock. (Daily) Adjacent is

Pickwick Landing State Resort Park. *Hwys 57 and 128, Savannah (38365). 15 miles S on Hwy 128 to Hwy 57. Phone 731/689-3129.* Approximately 1,400 acres adjacent to Pickwick Dam. Swimming pool, beach, fishing, boating (marina, launch, rentals). Nature trails; golf, tennis. Picnicking,

playground, concession, café. Camping. Lodge (see). Standard fees. **$**

Limited-Service Hotel

★ ★ **PICKWICK INN.** *Hwy 57, Pickwick Dam (38365). Phone 731/689-3135; fax 731/689-3606. www.tnstateparks.com.* 78 rooms, 3 story. Check-out 11 am. Restaurant. Outdoor pool, children's pool. Golf. Tennis. **$**

Sevierville (E-8)

See also Gatlinburg, Pigeon Forge

Founded 1795
Population 11,757
Elevation 903 ft
Area Code 865
Information Chamber of Commerce, 110 Gary Wade Blvd, 37862; phone 865/453-6411 or toll-free 888/766-5948
Web site www.visitsevierville.com

Founded as part of the independent state of Franklin, this seat of Sevier County was named for John Sevier, who later became the first governor of Tennessee. Long a marketing center for a wide belt of farmland, Sevierville is only 16 miles from the Great Smoky Mountains National Park (see).

What to See and Do

Douglas Dam and Lake. *11 miles NE off Hwy 66. Phone 865/453-3889.* This TVA dam (202 feet high, 1,705 feet long) on the French Broad River was built on a 24-hour work schedule during World War II to furnish power for national defense. It impounds a lake that's 43 miles long with 555 miles of shoreline. Swimming, fishing, boating; camping. Overlook (daily). **FREE**

Forbidden Caverns. *455 Blowing Cave Rd, Sevierville (37876). 13 miles NE on Hwy 411. Phone 865/453-5972. www.forbiddencavern.com.* Natural chimneys, underground streams; stereophonic sound presentations. Temperature in cave is 58° F. (Apr-Nov: daily 10 am-6 pm; closed Thanksgiving) **$$$**

NASCAR SpeedPark. *1545 Parkway, Sevierville (37862). Phone 865/908-5500. www.nascarspeedpark.com.* Raring for some time on the racetrack? You can get into the action—and into the cars—at NASCAR Speed-

Park. Eight tracks offer levels ranging from the quarter-mile Smoky Mountain Speedway for drivers 16 and older, down to the Baby Bristol, a 200-foot starter track for kids. Or climb into a mock stock car and experience centrifugal forces, turns, and crash imapcts as you "drive" a full-motion NASCAR Silicon Motor Speedway simulator. Other attractions include a state-of-the-art arcade, kiddie rides, an indoor climbing wall, miniature golf, and bumper boats. **$$$$**

Smoky Mountain Deer Farm. *478 Happy Hollow Ln, Sevierville (37876). Phone 865/428-3337. www.deerfarmzoo.com.* Petting zoo includes deer, zebra, pygmy goats, and llamas. Pony rides and horseback riding (fee). (Daily 10 am-5:30 pm; closed Thanksgiving, Dec 25) **$$**

Limited-Service Hotels

★ **COMFORT INN MOUNTAIN RIVER SUITES.** *860 Winfield Dunn Pkwy, Sevierville (37876). Phone 865/428-5519; toll-free 800/441-0311; fax 865/428-6700. www.cisevierville.com.* 97 rooms, 3 story. Pets accepted; fee. Complimentary continental breakfast. Check-in 3 pm, check-out 11 am. Indoor pool, outdoor pool, whirlpool. **$**

★ **RAMADA.** *4010 Parkway, Sevierville (37863). Phone 865/453-1823; toll-free 800/269-1222; fax 865/429-8462. www.pigeonforgeramada.com.* 134 rooms, 3 story. Complimentary continental breakfast. Check-in 3 pm, check-out 11 am. Children's activity center. Fitness room. Indoor pool, whirlpool. **$**

Specialty Lodging

LITTLE GREENBRIER LODGE. *3685 Lyon Springs Rd, Sevierville (37862). Phone 865/429-2500; fax 865/429-4093. www.littlegreenbriarlodge.com.* Antiques and Victorian décor in lodge built in 1939. 9 rooms, 3 story. Closed Jan-Mar. Children over 12 years only. Complimentary full breakfast. Check-in 4 pm. Check-out 11 am. **$**

Restaurant

★ **APPLEWOOD FARM HOUSE.** *240 Apple Valley Rd, Sevierville (37862). Phone 865/428-1222; fax 865/428-5772.* American menu. Breakfast, lunch, dinner. Closed Dec 25. Children's menu. Casual attire. Grounds with gazebo, apple trees along river. **$**

Shelbyville (F-5)

See also Lewisburg

Founded 1809
Population 16,105
Elevation 765 ft
Area Code 931
Zip 37160
Information Shelbyville & Bedford County Chamber of Commerce, 100 N Cannon Blvd; phone 931/684-3482 or toll-free 888/662-2525
Web site www.shelbyvilletn.com

Enshrined in the hearts and thoughts of every true citizen of Shelbyville is the Tennessee walking horse, that most noble of animals whose high-stepping dignity and high-level intelligence is annually celebrated here. There are 50 walking horse farms and training stables within a 14-mile radius of town; obtain maps at the chamber of commerce.

Special Events

Spring Fun Show. *Celebration Grounds, 1110 Evans St, Shelbyville (37162). Phone 931/684-5915. www.twhnc.com/springfunshow.com.* Amateur and professional-class walking horses compete. Three days in late May.

Tennessee Walking Horse National Celebration. *Celebration Grounds,1110 Evans St, Shelbyville (37162). Phone 931/684-5915. www.twhnc.com/celebration.htm.* More than 2,100 horses participate. Events conclude with crowning ceremonies for world grand champion walking horse. Late Aug.

Limited-Service Hotel

★ ★ **BEST WESTERN CELEBRATION INN AND SUITES.** *724 Madison St, Shelbyville (37160). Phone 931/684-2378; toll-free 800/528-1234; fax 931/685-4936. www.bestwestern.com.* 58 rooms, 2 story. Complimentary continental breakfast. Check-in 2 pm, check-out noon. Fitness room. Indoor pool. **$**

Shiloh National Military Park (F-3)

See also Savannah

Web site www.nps.gov/shil/

(*10 miles SW of Savannah on Hwy 22.*) Phone 901/689-5696.

Bitter, bloody Shiloh was the first major Civil War battle in the West and one of the fiercest in history. In two days, April 6 and 7, 1862, nearly 24,000 men were killed, wounded, or missing. The South's failure to destroy Grant's army opened the way for the attack on and siege of Vicksburg, Mississippi (see). It was, however, a costly battle for the North as well.

General Grant's Army of the Tennessee, numbering almost 40,000, was camped near Pittsburg Landing and Shiloh Church, waiting for the Army of the Ohio under General Don Carlos Buell to attack the Confederates who, they thought, were near Corinth, Mississippi, 20 miles south. But the brilliant Southern General Albert Sidney Johnston surprised Grant with an attack at dawn on April 6.

Although General Johnston was mortally wounded on the first day, the Southerners successfully pushed the Union Army back and nearly captured their supply base at Pittsburg Landing. On the second day, however, the Northerners, reinforced by the 17,918-man Army of the Ohio, counterattacked and forced the Confederates to retreat toward Corinth.

At Shiloh, one of the first tent field hospitals ever established helped save the lives of many Union and Confederate soldiers. Among the men who fought this dreadful battle were John Wesley Powell, who lost an arm but later went down the Colorado River by boat and became head of the US Geological Survey; James A. Garfield, 20th president of the United States; Ambrose Bierce, famous satirist and short story writer; and Henry Morton Stanley, who later uttered the famous phrase, "Dr. Livingstone, I presume." The park is open all year; closed Dec 25.

What to See and Do

Auto tour. Self-guided, 10-mile tour begins at the visitor center, where brochures can be obtained. Numbered markers indicate 14 points of interest.

National Cemetery. *Ten acres on a bluff overlooking Pittsburg Landing and the Tennessee River.* Buried here are about 3,800 soldiers, two-thirds of whom are unidentified.

Visitor Center. *1 mile from park entrance, E off Hwy 22, near Pittsburg Landing.* Museum exhibits and 23-minute historical film; bookstore opposite. (Daily; closed Dec 25)

Sweetwater (E-7)

See also Lenoir City

Population 5,586
Elevation 917 ft
Area Code 423
Information Monroe County Chamber of Commerce Visitor Center, 520 Cook St, Suite A, Madisonville 37354; phone 423/442-9147 or toll-free 800/245-5428
Web site www.monroecounty.com

What to See and Do

Lost Sea. *140 Lost Sea Rd, Sweetwater (37874). 6 miles SE on Hwy 68.* Phone 423/337-6616. www.thelostsea.com. Glass-bottom boats explore the nation's largest underground lake (4 1/2 acres) in the Lost Sea Caverns. Guided tours (1 hour). Temperature is constant at 58° F. (Nov-Feb: daily 9 am-5 pm, Sept-Oct, Mar-Apr: daily 9 am-6 pm, May-June, Aug: daily 9 am-7 pm, July: daily 9 am-8 pm; closed Dec 25) **$$$**

McMinn County Living Heritage Museum. *522 W Madison Ave, Athens (37371). 13 miles S on Hwy 11.* Phone 423/745-0329. www.livingheritagemuseum.com. The museum contains 26 exhibit areas with more than 6,000 items that reflect life in this region during the time span from the Cherokees to the Great Depression. (Mon-Fri 10 am-5 pm, Sat to 4 pm; closed holidays) **$**

Limited-Service Hotel

★ **COMFORT INN.** *731 Main St, Sweetwater (37874).* Phone 423/337-6646; toll-free 800/638-7949; fax 423/337-5409. www.choicehotels.com. 54 rooms, 2 story. Pets accepted; fee. Complimentary full breakfast. Check-in 2 pm, check-out 11 am. High-speed Internet access. Indoor pool, whirlpool. **$**

Restaurant

★ **DINNER BELL.** *576 Oakland Rd, Sweetwater (37874)*. Phone *423/337-5825*. Breakfast, lunch, dinner. Closed Dec 24-25. Children's menu. Casual attire. **$**

Tennessee Valley Authority

Web site *www.tva.gov*

TVA projects are centered in and around the Tennessee River Valley, primarily in Tennessee, Kentucky, and Alabama.

The new prosperity and immense industrial expansion of a large portion of the South is directly linked to the Tennessee Valley Authority, an independent corporate agency of the federal government created by an Act of Congress on May 18, 1933. More than 80,000 square miles in Tennessee, North Carolina, Virginia, Georgia, Alabama, Mississippi, and Kentucky continue to benefit directly from its activities. In addition, the entire nation benefits indirectly from TVA research and development in a wide range of fields.

In 1933, most of the Tennessee Valley area was the scene of desperate poverty. It had never recovered from the Civil War; the depression that began in 1929 had struck another cruel blow. Senator George Norris of Nebraska, President Franklin D. Roosevelt, and other national leaders knew that in a river valley of rich potential this was unnecessary and illogical. They proposed that the nation provide the tools the valley's people needed to build a new prosperity through proper use of the Tennessee River, its tributaries, and its vast watershed.

Today TVA dams and reservoirs regulate floodwaters on the Tennessee River and help reduce floods downstream on the Ohio and Mississippi rivers. They provide a year-round river channel for modern barges from the Ohio to Knoxville, making the river a busy waterway for industry. The same dams produce power for residents and industries. In the watershed area, TVA helps advance erosion control and vital farming and forestry improvements. It has eliminated malaria from the region by destroying mosquito breeding habitats. It operates a national environmental research center where many modern products of the US fertilizer industry are made.

This resource development effort has helped the people of the region strengthen their economy and build an unprecedented prosperity. Per capita income in the TVA area was only 45 percent of the national average in 1933; today it stands at almost 80 percent.

Approximately eight million people live in the area served with TVA power. TVA power is distributed to local consumers through cooperatives owned by people of each area or by individual cities. Much of the original construction was financed by the federal government, and TVA has always earned appropriate income on this money. Today TVA power facilities are financed with the agency's own power revenues and through bond and note sales. Meanwhile, TVA is repaying the original appropriations invested in its power system, plus dividends on that investment.

TVA operates 39 dams on the Tennessee River and its tributaries; of these, TVA owns 35. Coal-burning power plants, built mostly in the 1950s and 1960s when power use exceeded the capacity of the dams, provide the primary souce of electricity today. Immense use by atomic and space installations was a main factor in requiring more power supply. Now the TVA system includes 11 coal-fired plants, one hydroelectric pumped-storage plant, and two nuclear plants.

For visitors interested in recreation, TVA lakes provide more than 600,000 surface acres of water and 11,000 miles of shoreline. Along these reservoirs, there are more than 100 public parks, 450 access areas, and 325 commercial recreation areas. The lakes provide excellent fishing for bass, walleye, crappie, and other fish, with no closed season, and many other recreational opportunities. In the 1960s, TVA developed a 40-mile-long recreation and environmental education area in western Kentucky and Tennessee called Land Between The Lakes.

Visitors are welcome at TVA dams and steam plants. Public Safety Officers who conduct tours are on duty from 9 am-5 pm at the Raccoon Mountain facility. Golden Age and Golden Access Passports (see MAKING THE MOST OF YOUR TRIP) are honored at all TVA fee recreation areas.

Recreation maps of TVA lakes with detailed routes to shoreline recreation areas, as well as navigation charts and maps for the major lakes, may be ordered by writing the TVA Map Sales Office, 1101 Market St, Chattanooga 37402. Specify the lake(s) of interest on each request. A free list of maps and their costs is available. Charts for mainstream lakes of the Tennessee River showing navigation channels, water depth, buoys, lights, other navigation aids, and recreation areas are also available.

Limited material on the TVA and its diverse programs is available from the Technical Library, TVA, 400 W Summit Hill Dr, Knoxville 37902; Phone 423/632-8000 or 423/632-2101.

Tiptonville (D-2)

See also Union City

Population 2,439
Elevation 301 ft
Area Code 901
Zip 38079
Information Reelfoot Area Chamber of Commerce, 130 S Court St; phone 731/253-8144
Web site www.reelfootareachamber.com

What to See and Do

Reelfoot Lake. *2 miles E on Hwy 21.* This 13,000-acre lake, 18 miles long and more than 2 miles wide, was created by the New Madrid earthquakes of 1811-1812. A bird and game refuge of unusual beauty, the lake has an untamed quality with vast expanses of lily pads and giant cypress trees growing from the water. More than 56 species of fish inhabit these waters, and 260 species of water and land fowl populate the area. Resorts around the lake provide boat rentals and guide services. On the south shore is

> **Reelfoot Lake State Park.** *Hwy 1, Box 2345, Tiptonville (38079). 5 miles E on Hwy 21.* Phone 731/253-7756; toll-free 866/836-6757. Approximately 300 acres with a visitor center/museum exhibiting Native American artifacts, natural and cultural displays, earthquake simulator, and specimens of local fauna (free). Fishing, duck hunting; boating (launch, rentals). Camping ($$$$). Tennis courts. Picnicking, concession, restaurant, lodge (see). Tent and trailer sites. Boat excursions at park (May-Sept). Bald eagle tours (Dec-mid-Mar).

Limited-Service Hotel

★ ★ **REELFOOT LAKE STATE PARK.** *Hwy 78 and Hwy 213, Tiptonville (38079).* Phone 731/253-7756; toll-free 800/250-8617; fax 731/253-8940. *www.reelfoottourism.com.* 3,500-foot landing strip. All facilities of Reelfoot Lake State Park available; overlooks Reelfoot Lake. 25 rooms, 2 story. Pets accepted; fee. Complimentary continental breakfast. Check-in 3 pm, check-out 11 am. Restaurant. Outdoor pool. Tennis. **$**
✈ 🐾 ♒ 🎾

Restaurant

★ **BOYETTE'S DINING ROOM.** *10 Boyette Rd, Tiptonville (38079).* Phone 901/253-7307; fax 901/253-7513. *www.boyettesbarbecue.com.* American menu. Lunch, dinner. Closed Thanksgiving, Dec 24-25. Children's menu. Casual attire. Reservations recommended. No credit cards accepted. **$**

Townsend (E-8)

See also Gatlinburg, Maryville

Population 244
Elevation 1,036 ft
Area Code 865
Zip 37882
Information Chamber of Commerce, 125 Townsend Park Rd, PO Box 247
Web site www.townsendchamber.org

What to See and Do

Cades Cove. *5 miles SE on Hwy 73, then 8 miles SW on unnumbered road in Great Smoky Mountains National Park (see).*

Tuckaleechee Caverns. *825 Caverns Rd, Townsend (37882). 3 miles S, off Hwy 321.* Phone 865/448-2274. *www.tuckaleecheecaverns.com.* Cathedral-like main chamber is the largest cavern room in the eastern US; drapery formations, walkway over subterranean streams, flowstone falls; waterfalls tour. Temperature is 58° F in the caverns. Guided tours every 15-20 minutes (mid-Mar-mid-Nov, daily 9 am-6 pm). **$$$**

Limited-Service Hotels

★ **BEST WESTERN VALLEY VIEW LODGE.** *7726 E Lamar Alexander Pkwy, Townsend (37882).* Phone 865/448-2237; toll-free 800/292-4844; fax 865/448-9957. *www.bestwestern.com.* 138 rooms, 2 story. Pets accepted, some restrictions; fee. Complimentary continental breakfast. Check-in 3 pm, check-out 11 am. Children's activity center. Indoor pool, two outdoor pools, two children's pools, whirlpool. **$**

★ **COMFORT INN.** *7824 E Lamar Alexander Pkwy, Townsend (37882). Phone 865/448-9000; toll-free 800/348-7090; fax 865/448-9254. www.choicehotels. com.* 53 rooms, 2 story. Pets accepted; fee. Complimentary continental breakfast. Check-in 2 pm, check-out 11 am. Outdoor pool. **$**

★ **TALLEY HO INN.** *8314 Hwy 73, Townsend (37882). Phone 865/448-2465; toll-free 800/448-2465; fax 865/448-3913. www.talleyhoinn.com.* 46 rooms, 2 story. Check-in 2 pm, check-out 11 am. Outdoor pool, children's pool. **$**

Full-Service Inn

★ ★ ★ **RICHMONT INN B&B.** *220 Winterberry Ln, Townsend (37882). Phone 865/448-6751; toll-free 866/267-7086; fax 865/448-6480. www.richmontinn. com.* Just ten minutes from the entrance to Great Smoky Mountains National Park, this charming inn affords an elegant respite. The comfort and coziness of the rustic accents, such as wide-planked and slate floors, high exposed-beam ceilings, and country furniture, are enhanced by the formal, attentive service. 14 rooms, 3 story. Children over 12 years only. Complimentary full breakfast. Check-in 3 pm, check-out 10:30 am. Restaurant. No credit cards accepted. **$**

Union City (D-2)

See also Tiptonville

Population 10,876
Elevation 337 ft
Area Code 901
Zip 38261

What to See and Do

Davy Crockett Cabin. *20 miles S on Hwy 45 W, in Rutherford. Phone 901/665-7166.* Frontiersman's cabin is now a museum with period artifacts; the grave of Crockett's mother is on the grounds. (Memorial Day-Labor Day) **$**

Special Event

Davy Crockett Days. *Rutherford. Phone 901/665-7253.* Parade, arts and crafts. Last week in Sept-first week in Oct.

Index

Johnson Homestead (Andrew Jackson National Historic Site, TN), *235*

Johnson's Inn (Gatlinburg, TN), *249*

Jonesborough (Jonesborough, TN), *254*

Jonesborough Days (Jonesborough, TN), *255*

Jonesborough History Museum (Johnson City, TN), *254*

Jonquil Festival (Washington, AR), *62*

Joseph T. Smitherman Historic Building (Selma, AL), *36*

Josephine Tussaud Wax Museum (Hot Springs, AR), *64*

Juban's (Baton Rouge, LA), *144*

Jubilee City Fest (Montgomery, AL), *33*

Jungle Gardens (Avery Island, LA), *158*

Junior League Horse Show (Lexington, KY), *111*

K

Ka-Do-Ha Indian Village (Murfreesboro, AR), *73*

Kate Freeman Clark Art Gallery (Holly Springs, MS), *209*

Kellogg Conference Center (Tuskegee Institute, AL), *42*

Kemper Williams Park (Patterson, LA), *156*

Kenlake State Resort Park (Hardin, KY), *108*

Kenlake State Resort Park (Kenlake State Resort Park,), *108*

Kent House (Alexandria, LA), *139*

Kentucky Action Park (Cave City, KY), *92*

Kentucky Apple Festival (Paintsville, KY), *129*

Kentucky Cardinal Inn (Elizabethtown, KY), *99*

Kentucky Center for the Arts (Louisville, KY), *116*

Kentucky Dam (Gilbertsville, KY), *102*

Kentucky Dam State Resort (Gilbertsville, KY), *102*

Kentucky Dam Village State Resort Park (Gilbertsville, KY), *102*

Kentucky Derby (Louisville, KY), *117*

Kentucky Derby Festival (Louisville, KY), *117*

Kentucky Derby Museum (Louisville, KY), *115*

Kentucky Diamond Caverns (Park City, KY), *128*

Kentucky Down Under/Kentucky Caverns (Horse Cave, KY), *107*

Kentucky Fair and Exposition Center (Louisville, KY), *116*

Kentucky Guild of Artists and Craftsmen's Fair (Berea, KY), *88*

Kentucky Heartland Festival (Elizabethtown, KY), *98*

Kentucky History Center (Frankfort, KY), *100*

Kentucky Horse Park (Lexington, KY), *110*

Kentucky Library (Bowling Green, KY), *89*

Kentucky Military History Museum (Frankfort, KY), *100*

Kentucky Museum (Bowling Green, KY), *89*

Kentucky Repertory Theatre (Horse Cave, KY), *107*

Kentucky Scottish Weekend (Carrollton, KY), *91*

Kentucky State Fair (Louisville, KY), *117*

Kentucky State University (Frankfort, KY), *100*

Kentucky Vietnam Veterans Memorial (Frankfort, KY), *100*

Kids Farm Education Center (Danville, KY), *97*

Kincaid Lake State Park (Williamstown, KY), *133*

King Biscuit Blues Festival (Helena, AR), *60*

Kings Inn (Ruston, LA), *192*

Kings, Krewes, Beads, and Balls (New Orleans,), *167*

Kingsport Fun Fest (Kingsport, TN), *257*

Kinser Park (Greeneville, TN), *251*

Kisatchie National Forest (Pineville, LA), *139*

Kiwanis West Kentucky-McCracken County Fair (Paducah, KY), *126*

Knoxville Museum of Art (Knoxville, TN), *258*

Knoxville Zoo (Knoxville, TN), *258*

Konriko Rice Mill and Company Store (New Iberia, LA), *159*

Kosciusko Museum-Information Center (Kosciusko, MS), *212*

Koto Sushi Bar (Nashville, TN), *282*

K-Paul's Louisiana Kitchen (New Orleans, LA), *189*

Kunz's Fourth and Market (Louisville, KY), *119*

Kurtz (Bardstown, KY), *87*

L

La Fonda (Lafayette, LA), *151*

La Font Inn (Pascagoula, MS), *221*

La Madeleine (New Orleans, LA), *189*

La Place D'Evangeline (Saint Martinville, LA), *193*

La Provence (Lacombe, LA), *149*

La Quinta (Little Rock, AR), *68*

La Quinta Inn (Birmingham, AL), *12*

La Quinta Inn (Huntsville, AL), *27*

La Quinta Inn (Mobile, AL), *31*

La Quinta Inn (Montgomery, AL), *34*

La Quinta Inn (Richmond, KY), *130*

La Quinta Inn (Slidell, LA), *195*

La Quinta Inn (Hattiesburg, MS), *208*

La Quinta Inn (Jackson, MS), *212*

La Quinta Inn (Chattanooga, TN), *239*

La Quinta Inn (Bossier City, LA), *145*

La Quinta Inn (Lafayette, LA), *150*

La Quinta Inn (Monroe, LA), *156*

La Quinta Inn (Crossville, TN), *244*

La Tourelle Restaurant (Memphis, TN), *271*

Labor Day Fest (Memphis, TN), *269*

Chain Restaurants

Alabama

Anniston

Ryan's Grill Buffet Bakery, 600 S Quintard Ave, Anniston, AL, 36201, (256) 236-0688, 10:45 am-9 pm

Athens

Cracker Barrel, 1212 Kelli Dr, Athens, AL, 35613, (256) 232-4141, 6 am-10 pm

Auburn

CiCi's Pizza, 1550 Opelika Rd, Auburn, AL, 36830, (334) 821-2600, 11 am-9 pm

Hooters, 1651 S College Dr, Auburn, AL, 36832, (334) 502-1332, 11 am-midnight

McAlister's Deli, 1651 E University Dr, Auburn, AL, (334) 502-0101, 10:30 am-10 pm

Auburn University

Godfather's Pizza, Auburn University Dining, Auburn University, AL, 36849, (334) 844-1275

Bessemer

Cracker Barrel, 5040 Academy Ln, Bessemer, AL, 35022, (205) 428-7080, 6 am-10 pm

Birmingham

Beef O'Brady's, 1477 USHwy 11, #138, Birmingham, AL, 35235, (205) 661-3660, 11 am-11 pm

Cheesecake Factory, 236 Summit Blvd, Birmingham, AL, 35243, (205) 262-1800, 11 am-11 pm

CiCi's Pizza, 5287 Hwy 280 S, Ste 209, Birmingham, AL, 35242, (205) 980-0099, 11 am-9 pm

CiCi's Pizza, 2477 1st St, NE, Birmingham, AL, 35215, (205) 854-2424, 11 am-9 pm

CiCi's Pizza, 428 Palisades Blvd, Ste 428, Birmingham, AL, 35209, (205) 870-0005, 11 am-9 pm

Cracker Barrel, 3415 Colonnade Pkwy, Birmingham, AL, 35243, (205) 969-1126, 6 am-10 pm

Golden Corral, 1185 Center Pt Pkwy E, Birmingham, AL, 35215, (205) 856-6170, 11 am-9 pm

Hooters, 5263 Hwy 280, #110, Birmingham, AL, 35242, (205) 437-1880, 11 am-midnight

Hooters, 1917 Edwards Lake Rd, Birmingham, AL, 35235, (205) 655-9475, 11 am-midnight

Hooters, 1278 Oak Grove Rd, Birmingham, AL, 35209, (205) 940-9145, 11 am-midnight

Hooters, 7401 Crestwood Dr, Birmingham, AL, 35210, (205) 591-4668, 11 am-midnight

Logan's Roadhouse, 100 Resource Center Pkwy, Birmingham, AL, 35242, (205) 981-9950, 11 am-10 pm

Logan's Roadhouse, 7724 Ludington Ln, Birmingham, AL, 35210, (205) 957-9775, 11 am-10 pm

McAlister's Deli, 2000 Riverchase Galleria E, Birmingham, AL, (205) 776-8769, 10:30 am-10 pm

McAlister's Deli, 5406 Hwy 280, Ste E-101, Birmingham, AL, (205) 408-7799, 10:30 am-10 pm

McAlister's Deli, 9340 Helena Rd, Ste I, Birmingham, AL, (205) 985-9797, 10:30 am-10 pm

McAlister's Deli, 1801 4th Ave S, Ste 111, Birmingham, AL, (205) 933-2828, 10:30 am-10 pm

O'Charley's, 9417 Pkwy E, Birmingham, AL, (205) 836-4400, 11 am-10 pm

On the Border, 245 Summit Blvd, Birmingham, AL, 35243, (205) 298-0877, 11 am-10 pm

P.F. Changs, 233 Summit Blvd, The Summit, Birmingham, AL, 35243, (205) 967-0040, 11 am-10 pm

Romano's Macaroni Grill, 241 Summit Blvd, Birmingham, AL, 35243, (205) 298-7998, 11 am-10 pm

Ryan's Grill Buffet Bakery, 7201 Crestwood Blvd, Birmingham, AL, 35210, (205) 592-9756, 10:45 am-9 pm

Boaz

Ryan's Grill Buffet Bakery, 568 US Hwy 431, Boaz, AL, 35957, (256) 593-1436, 10:45 am-9 pm

Calera

Cracker Barrel, 199 Supercenter Dr, Calera, AL, 35040, (205) 668-2027, 6 am-10 pm

Cullman

CiCi's Pizza, 1842 Patriot Way SW, Cullman, AL, 35055, (256) 736-2662, 11 am-9 pm

Cracker Barrel, 6020 State Hwy 157 NW, Cullman, AL, 35058, (256) 739-6950, 6 am-10 pm

Ryan's Grill Buffet Bakery, 1720 Cherokee Ave SW, Cullman, AL, 35055, (256) 775-1277, 10:45 am-9 pm

Daphne

Hooters, 28975 US Hwy 98, Daphne, AL, 36526, (251) 625-3910, 11 am-midnight

Longhorn Steakhouse, 6870 US Hwy 90, Daphne, AL, 36526, (251) 625-8960, 11 am-10 pm

McAlister's Deli, 6882 Hwy 90, Ste 1, Daphne, AL, (251) 621-7179, 10:30 am-10 pm

O'Charley's, 6840 US Hwy 90, Daphne, AL, (251) 447-0744, 11 am-10 pm

Decatur

CiCi's Pizza, 303 Beltline Pl SW, Bldg 1/ Unit B, Decatur, AL, 35603, (256) 301-5524, 11 am-9 pm

Cracker Barrel, 407 Beltline Rd SW, Decatur, AL, 35601, (256) 350-6263, 6 am-10 pm

Fire Mountain, 921 Wimberly Dr SW, Decatur, AL, 35603, (256) 306-9411, 10:45 am-9:30 pm

Logan's Roadhouse, 2315 Beltline Rd SW, Decatur, AL, 35603, (256) 432-2746, 11 am-10 pm

O'Charley's, 2148 Beltline Rd SW, Decatur, AL, (256) 355-0505, 11 am-10 pm

Dothan

Beef O'Brady's, 2743 Montgomery Hwy #1010, Dothan, AL, 36303, (334) 678-0010, 11 am-11 pm

Chili's, 3083 Montgomery Hwy, Dothan, AL, 36303, (334) 677-6767, 11 am-10 pm

CiCi's Pizza, 3702 Ross Clark Circle, Ste 7, Dothan, AL, 36303, (334) 673-3500, 11 am-9 pm

Cracker Barrel, 3431 Ross Clark Circle, Dothan, AL, 36303, (334) 673-8454, 6 am-10 pm

Golden Corral, 3340 Ross Clark Circle NW, Dothan, AL, 36301, (334) 677-9976, 11 am-9 pm

Hooters, 3385 Ross Clark Circle, Dothan, AL, 36303, (334) 673-4668, 11 am-midnight

Longhorn Steakhouse, 3411 Ross Clark Circle, Dothan, AL, 36303, (334) 794-4279, 11 am-10 pm

McAlister's Deli, 3106 Ross Clark Circle, Dothan, AL, (334) 794-3354, 10:30 am-10 pm

O'Charley's, 3320 Montgomery Hwy, Dothan, AL, (334) 673-1956, 11 am-10 pm

Ryan's Grill Buffet Bakery, 3240 S Oates St, Dothan, AL, 36301, (334) 678-6229, 10:45 am-9 pm

Enterprise

Ryan's Grill Buffet Bakery, 609 Boll Weevil Circle, Enterprise, AL, 36330, (334) 393-6225, 10:45 am-9 pm

Eufaula

Golden Corral, 1324 S Eufala Ave, Eufaula, AL, 36027, (334) 687-4978, 11 am-9 pm

Florence

CiCi's Pizza, 157 Cox Creek Pkwy S, Florence, AL, 35630, (256) 765-2424, 11 am-9 pm

Cracker Barrel, 150 Cox Creek Pkwy South, Florence, AL, 35630, (256) 766-2442, 6 am-10 pm

Godfather's Pizza, 2801 Mall Dr #15, Florence, AL, 35630, (256) 767-5504

Logan's Roadhouse, 2890 Florence Blvd, Florence, AL, 35630, (256) 764-5011, 11 am-10 pm

O'Charley's, 102 Cox Creek Pkwy S, Florence, AL, (256) 766-1997, 11 am-10 pm

Ryan's Grill Buffet Bakery, 362 Cox Creek Pkwy, Florence, AL, 35630, (256) 764-3862, 10:45 am-9 pm

Foley

CiCi's Pizza, 3061 S McKenzie St, Foley, AL, 36535, (251) 970-3242, 11 am-9 pm

Cracker Barrel, 3150 S McKenzie St, Foley, AL, 36535, (251) 943-7060, 6 am-10 pm

Fire Mountain, 2301 S Mckenzie St, Foley, AL, 36535, (251) 971-1121, 10:45 am-9:30 pm

O'Charley's, 3060 S McKenzie St, Foley, AL, (251) 943-3181, 11 am-10 pm

Fort Payne

Cracker Barrel, 201 Cracker Barrel Row SW, Fort Payne, AL, 35968, (256) 997-9204, 6 am-10 pm

Ryan's Grill Buffet Bakery, 1824 Glenn Blvd, SW, Fort Payne, AL, 35968, (256) 845-1783, 10:45 am-9 pm

Fultondale

O'Charley's, 1709 Fulton Rd, Fultondale, AL, (205) 849-6401, 11 am-10 pm

Gadsden

Cracker Barrel, 101 Taylor Dr, Gadsden, AL, 35904, (256) 538-5938, 6 am-10 pm

Logan's Roadhouse, 835 Rainbow Dr, Gadsden, AL, 35901, (256) 543-0470, 11 am-10 pm

Ryan's Grill Buffet Bakery, 127 River Rd, Gadsden, AL, 35901, (256) 547-3852, 10:45 am-9 pm

Gardendale

Cracker Barrel, 901 Fieldstown Rd, Gardendale, AL, 35071, (205) 631-8011, 6 am-10 pm

Fire Mountain, 838 Odum Rd, Gardendale, AL, 35071, (205) 608-0194, 10:45 am-9:30 pm

Greenville

Cracker Barrel, 180 Interstate Dr, Greenville, AL, 36037, (334) 382-2691, 6 am-10 pm

Gulf Shores

Godfather's Pizza, 1549 - G Gulf Shores Pkwy, Gulf Shores, AL, 36542, (251) 968-4616

Hooters, 300 E Beach Blvd, Gulf Shores, AL, 36542, (251) 948-4668, 11 am-midnight

Guntersville

O'Charley's, 11888 Hwy 431 S, Guntersville, AL, (256) 894-4469, 11 am-10 pm

Homewood

McAlister's Deli, 350 State Farm Pkwy, Ste 104, Homewood, AL, (205) 944-0060, 10:30 am-10 pm

O'Charley's, 109 Wildwood Pkwy, Homewood, AL, (205) 942-8001, 11 am-10 pm

Hoover

Golden Corral, 3117 Lorna Rd, Hoover, AL, 35216, (205) 822-8377, 11 am-9 pm

J. Alexander's, 3320 Galleria Circle, Hoover, AL, 35244, (205) 733-9995, 11 am-10 pm

Logan's Roadhouse, 2740 John Hawkins Pkwy, Hoover, AL, 35244, (205) 682-9530, 11 am-10 pm

Longhorn Steakhouse, 4775 Hwy 280, Hoover, AL, 35242, (205) 980-8361, 11 am-10 pm

McAlister's Deli, 1551 Montgomery Hwy, Hoover, AL, (205) 978-9334, 10:30 am-10 pm

O'Charley's, 2730 John Hawkins Pkwy, Hoover, AL, (205) 988-0780, 11 am-10 pm

Huntsville

CiCi's Pizza, 10004 Memorial Pkwy, Huntsville, AL, 35803, (256) 885-1595, 11 am-9 pm

CiCi's Pizza, 4925 University Dr, Ste 162, Huntsville, AL, 35816, (256) 864-2224, 11 am-9 pm

Donato's Pizza, 7500 Memorial Pkwy S, Huntsville, AL, 35802, (256) 881-9191, 11 am-midnight

Hooters, 4730 NW University, Huntsville, AL, 35806, (256) 722-0166, 11 am-midnight

Logan's Roadhouse, 6226 University Dr NW, Huntsville, AL, 35806, (256) 837-7885, 11 am-10 pm

Logan's Roadhouse, 4249 Balmoral Dr, Huntsville, AL, 35801, (256) 881-0584, 11 am-10 pm

Longhorn Steakhouse, 1450 Perimeter Pkwy, Huntsville, AL, 35806, (256) 895-6000, 11 am-10 pm

McAlister's Deli, 1480 Perimeter Pkwy NW, Huntsville, AL, (256) 425-0034, 10:30 am-10 pm

McAlister's Deli, 4800 Whitesburg Dr, Ste 32, Huntsville, AL, (256) 880-1557, 10:30 am-10 pm

O'Charley's, 6152 University Dr NW, Huntsville, AL, (256) 837-3431, 11 am-10 pm

O'Charley's, 4240 Balmoral Dr SW, Huntsville, AL, (256) 882-2626, 11 am-10 pm

Romano's Macaroni Grill, 5901 University Dr NW, Huntsville, AL, 35806, (256) 722-4770, 11 am-10 pm

Ryan's Grill Buffet Bakery, 10017 S Memorial Hwy, Huntsville, AL, 35803, (256) 882-0863, 10:45 am-9 pm

Ryan's Grill Buffet Bakery, 1808 University Dr, Huntsville, AL, 35801, (256) 536-0586, 10:45 am-9 pm

Jasper

Ryan's Grill Buffet Bakery, 2009 HWY78 East, Jasper, AL, 35501, (205) 302-0663, 10:45 am-9 pm

Leeds

Cracker Barrel, 2003 Village Dr, Leeds, AL, 35094, (205) 640-2478, 6 am-10 pm

Madison

Beef O'Brady's, 7429 Hwy 72 W, Madison, AL, 35758, (256) 489-3084, 11 am-11 pm

Cracker Barrel, 120 Cleghorn Blvd, Madison, AL, 35758, (256) 461-7670, 6 am-10 pm

Donato's Pizza, 8000 Madison Blvd, Ste D106, Madison, AL, 35758, (256) 772-6789, 11 am-midnight

Mobile

Beef O'Brady's, 4419 Rangeline Rd / PO Box 191734, Mobile, AL, 36619, (251) 661-3346, 11 am-11 pm

CiCi's Pizza, 6750 Airport Blvd, Ste 1, Mobile, AL, 36608, (251) 341-0880, 11 am-9 pm

CiCi's Pizza, 5441 Hwy 90 W, Mobile, AL, 36619, (251) 660-0414, 11 am-9 pm

Cracker Barrel, 845-A Schillinger Rd South, Mobile, AL, 36695, (251) 633-8200, 6 am-10 pm

Cracker Barrel, 43 E I-65 Service Rd South, Mobile, AL, 36606, (251) 473-6761, 6 am-10 pm

El Chico Café, 830 W I-65 Service Rd S, Mobile, AL, 36609, (251) 344-0134, 11 am-10 pm

Fire Mountain, 4439 Rangeline Rd, Mobile, AL, 36619, (251) 662-0880, 10:45 am-9:30 pm

Godfather's Pizza, 5015 Moffat Rd, Mobile, AL, 36618, (251) 342-1990

Godfather's Pizza, 3210 Dauphin St, Mobile, AL, 36606, (251) 476-0505

Godfather's Pizza, 6151 Airport Blvd, Mobile, AL, 36608, (251) 342-0055

Godfather's Pizza, 5442 Hwy 90 W, Mobile, AL, 36619, (251) 666-0106

Golden Corral, 5327 Halls Mill Rd, Mobile, AL, 36619, (251) 660-7122, 11 am-9 pm

Golden Corral, 675 S Schillenger Rd, Mobile, AL, 36695, (251) 639-9393, 11 am-9 pm

Hooters, 5470 Inn Rd, Mobile, AL, 36610, (251) 661-9117, 11 am-midnight

Hooters, 3869 Airport Blvd, Mobile, AL, 36608, (251) 473-9464, 11 am-midnight

Logan's Roadhouse, 3250 Airport Rd, Mobile, AL, 36606, (251) 473-2920, 11 am-10 pm

Longhorn Steakhouse, 6201 Airport Blvd, Mobile, AL, 36608, (251) 316-3880, 11 am-10 pm

McAlister's Deli, 6750 Airport Blvd, Mobile, AL, (251) 342-7707, 10:30 am-10 pm

McAlister's Deli, 1200 Satchel Paige Dr, Mobile, AL, (251) 478-1011, 10:30 am-10 pm

O'Charley's, 3649 Airport Blvd, Mobile, AL, (251) 344-0200, 11 am-10 pm

O'Charley's, 725 Schillinger Rd S, Mobile, AL, (251) 633-9710, 11 am-10 pm

Romano's Macaroni Grill, 3250 Airport Blvd, Ste B-6, Mobile, AL, 36606, (251) 450-4556, 11 am-10 pm

Smokey Bones, 4011 Airport Blvd, Mobile, AL, 36608, (251) 304-0444, 11 am-10 pm

Montgomery

CiCi's Pizza, 6268 Atlanta Hwy, Montgomery, AL, 36117, (334) 271-9989, 11 am-9 pm

Cracker Barrel, 9191 Boyd-Cooper Pkwy, Montgomery, AL, 36117, (334) 244-1085, 6 am-10 pm

Cracker Barrel, 1200 Eastern Blvd, Montgomery, AL, 36117, (334) 271-4308, 6 am-10 pm

Longhorn Steakhouse, 4095 Eastern Blvd, Montgomery, AL, 36116, (334) 613-7555, 11 am-10 pm

O'Charley's, 2690 Eastern Blvd, Montgomery, AL, (334) 279-7165, 11 am-10 pm

Red Star Tavern, 7078 E Chase Pkwy, Montgomery, AL, 36117, (334) 395-6665, 11:30- 1 am

Romano's Macaroni Grill, 3905 Troy Hwy, Montgomery, AL, 36116, (334) 281-0900, 11 am-10 pm

Ryan's Grill Buffet Bakery, 6561 Atlanta Hwy, Montgomery, AL, 36117, (334) 279-6007, 10:45 am-9 pm

Smokey Bones, 2465 Eastern Blvd, Montgomery, AL, 36117, (334) 270-1004, 11 am-10 pm

Northport

CiCi's Pizza, 929 McFarland Blvd E, Northport, AL, 35476, (205) 333-3920, 11 am-9 pm

McAlister's Deli, 3021 Tyler Rd, Northport, AL, (205) 330-7940, 10:30 am-10 pm

Opelika

Cracker Barrel, 1051 Fox Run Ave, Opelika, AL, 36801, (334) 749-2363, 6 am-10 pm

Golden Corral, 2301 Birmingham Hwy, Opelika, AL, 36801, (334) 741-0570, 11 am-9 pm

Logan's Roadhouse, 2400 Gateway Dr, Opelika, AL, 36801, (334) 742-8001, 11 am-10 pm

Longhorn Steakhouse, 2601 Gateway Dr, Opelika, AL, 36801, (334) 705-8800, 11 am-10 pm

O'Charley's, 2501 Gateway Dr, Opelika, AL, (334) 749-0719, 11 am-10 pm

Oxford

CiCi's Pizza, 657 Snow St, Oxford, AL, 36203, (256) 835-3595, 11 am-9 pm

Cracker Barrel, 220 Morgan Rd, Oxford, AL, 36203, (256) 835-6700, 6 am-10 pm

Logan's Roadhouse, 40 Ali Way, Oxford, AL, 36203, (256) 835-3116, 11 am-10 pm

McAlister's Deli, 815 Hamric Dr E, Oxford, AL, (256) 831-0079, 10:30 am-10 pm

O'Charley's, 4 Recreation Dr, Oxford, AL, (256) 831-8305, 11 am-10 pm

Pelham

Cracker Barrel, 655 Cahaba Valley Rd, Pelham, AL, 35124, (205) 987-1555, 6 am-10 pm

Golden Corral, 101 Cahaba Valley Pkwy E, Pelham, AL, 35124, (205) 682-0150, 11 am-9 pm

Hooters, 400 Cahalba Valley Rd, Pelham, AL, 35124, (205) 682-9464, 11 am-midnight

O'Charley's, 101 S Gate Dr, Pelham, AL, (205) 987-5044, 11 am-10 pm

Prattville

Cracker Barrel, 796 Business Park Dr, Prattville, AL, 36066, (334) 365-9600, 6 am-10 pm

Longhorn Steakhouse, 2295 Cobbs Ford Rd, Prattville, AL, 36066, (334) 285-7630, 11 am-10 pm

O'Charley's, 2301 Cobbs Ford Rd, Prattville, AL, (334) 285-2990, 11 am-10 pm

Ryan's Grill Buffet Bakery, 1915 Cobbs Ford Rd, Prattville, AL, 36066, (334) 358-1818, 10:45 am-9 pm

Rainbow City

CiCi's Pizza, 3225 Rainbow Dr, Ste 201C, Rainbow City, AL, 35906, (256) 413-0444, 11 am-9 pm

Saraland

Godfather's Pizza, 120 Saraland Loop Rd, Saraland, AL, 36571, (251) 679-0871

Spanish Fort

Cracker Barrel, 30227 Eastern Shore Court, Spanish Fort, AL, 36527, (251) 621-4826, 6 am-10 pm

Fire Mountain, 30179 Eastern Shore Court, Spanish Fort, AL, 36527, (251) 625-4632, 10:45 am-9:30 pm

Logan's Roadhouse, 30275 Eastern Shore Court, Spanish Fort, AL, 36527, (251) 625-0151, 11 am-10 pm

Sylacauga

Ryan's Grill Buffet Bakery, 41191 US Hwy 280, Sylacauga, AL, 35150, (256) 245-9500, 10:45 am-9 pm

Thomasville

Ryan's Grill Buffet Bakery, 33801 Hwy 43 North, Thomasville, AL, 36784, (334) 636-2800, 10:45 am-9 pm

Trussville

Cracker Barrel, 4710 Norrell Dr, Trussville, AL, 35173, (205) 655-8498, 6 am-10 pm

Tuscaloosa

Cracker Barrel, 4800 Doris Pate Dr, Tuscaloosa, AL, 35405, (205) 562-8282, 6 am-10 pm

Hooters, 5025 Oscar Baxter Dr, Tuscaloosa, AL, 35405, (205) 758-3035, 11 am-midnight

Logan's Roadhouse, 1511 Skyland Blvd E, Tuscaloosa, AL, 35403, (205) 349-3554, 11 am-10 pm

McAlister's Deli, 101 15th St, Tuscaloosa, AL, (205) 758-0039, 10:30 am-10 pm

O'Charley's, 3799 McFarland Blvd E, Tuscaloosa, AL, (205) 556-5143, 11 am-10 pm

Ryan's Grill Buffet Bakery, 4373 Courtney Dr, Tuscaloosa, AL, 35405, (205) 366-1114, 10:45 am-9 pm

Arkansas

Alma

Cracker Barrel, 431 US 71 North, Alma, AR, 72921, (479) 632-0767, 6 am-10 pm

Arkedelphia

Cracker Barrel, 173 Valley St, Arkedelphia, AR, 71923, (870) 230-8875, 6 am-10 pm

Benton

CiCi's Pizza, 17270 Interstate 30, Ste 501, Benton, AR, 72015, (501) 778-2424, 11 am-9 pm

Bentonville

McAlister's Deli, 900 S E Walton Blvd, Bentonville, AR, (479) 271-6263, 10:30 am-10 pm

Village Inn, 2300 SE Walton Blvd, Bentonville, AR, 72712, (479) 464-0777, 7 am-midnight

Bryant

Cracker Barrel, 318 Commerce St, Bryant, AR, 72022, (501) 847-7878, 6 am-10 pm

Conway

Chili's, 1111 E Oak, Conway, AR, 72032, (501) 730-0225, 11 am-10 pm

CiCi's Pizza, 1250 Old Morrilton Hwy, Conway, AR, 72032, (501) 329-6715, 11 am-9 pm

Cracker Barrel, 525 US 65 North, Conway, AR, 72032, (501) 327-6107, 6 am-10 pm

El Chico Café, 201 Hwy 65N, Conway, AR, 72032, (501) 327-6553, 11 am-10 pm

McAlister's Deli, 2465 Sanders Rd, Conway, AR, (501) 513-1311, 10:30 am-10 pm

Ryan's Grill Buffet Bakery, 1400 Hwy 64 West, Conway, AR, 72032, (501) 327-7926, 10:45 am-9 pm

Village Inn, 2490 Sanders Rd, Conway, AR, 72032, (479) 505-0840, 7 am-midnight

El Dorado

Ryan's Grill Buffet Bakery, 2740 N W Ave, El Dorado, AR, 71730, (870) 862-5151, 10:45 am-9 pm

Fayetteville

Chili's, 772 E Millsap St, Fayetteville, AR, 72703, (479) 521-9921, 11 am-10 pm

CiCi's Pizza, 637 E Joyce Blvd, Ste 101, Fayetteville, AR, 72703, (479) 582-9292, 11 am-9 pm

El Chico Café, 3854 Front St, Fayetteville, AR, 72701, (479) 521-5553, 11 am-10 pm

Fire Mountain, 3825 N Shiloh Dr, Fayetteville, AR, 72703, (479) 521-7926, 10:45 am-9:30 pm

Fuddruckers, 3675 N Mall Ave, Fayetteville, AR, 72703, 11 am-9 pm

Golden Corral, 4507 N College Ave, Fayetteville, AR, 72703, (479) 443-0433, 11 am-9 pm

Hooters, 4143 N Shiloh Dr, Fayetteville, AR, 72703, (479) 575-9464, 11 am-midnight

Logan's Roadhouse, 3611 N Shiloh Dr, Fayetteville, AR, 72703, (479) 251-7775, 11 am-10 pm

McAlister's Deli, 4055 N Steele Blvd, Fayetteville, AR, (479) 521-7900, 10:30 am-10 pm

O'Charley's, 3467 N Shiloh Dr, Fayetteville, AR, (479) 527-0903, 11 am-10 pm

Smokey Bones, 643 E Van Asche Dr, Fayetteville, AR, 72703, (479) 251-7517, 11 am-10 pm

Village Inn, 3364 No College Ave, Fayetteville, AR, 72703, (479) 521-1880, 7 am-midnight

Fort Smith

Chili's, 6720 Rogers Ave, Fort Smith, AR, 72903, (479) 452-6800, 11 am-10 pm

CiCi's Pizza, 8323 Rogers Ave, Fort Smith, AR, 72903, (479) 484-0909, 11 am-9 pm

El Chico Café, 12 Central Mall, Fort Smith, AR, 72903, (479) 452-1099, 11 am-10 pm

Fire Mountain, 3600 Massard Rd, Fort Smith, AR, 72903, (479) 452-3200, 10:45 am-9:30 pm

Golden Corral, 1801 S Waldron Ave, Fort Smith, AR, 72903, (479) 484-1040, 11 am-9 pm

Logan's Roadhouse, 6201 Rogers Ave, Fort Smith, AR, 72903, (479) 452-0303, 11 am-10 pm

Village Inn, 7620 Rogers Ave, Fort Smith, AR, 72903, (479) 452-7007, 7 am-midnight

Hot Springs

Chili's, 3815 Central Ave, Hot Springs, AR, 71913, (501) 520-0431, 11 am-10 pm

CiCi's Pizza, 3321 Central Ave, Hot Springs, AR, 71913, (501) 321-2400, 11 am-9 pm

Cracker Barrel, 170 Pakis St, Hot Springs, AR, 71913, (501) 525-4704, 6 am-10 pm

El Chico Café, 140 Hot Springs Mall, Hot Springs, AR, 71913, (501) 525-4055, 11 am-10 pm

McAlister's Deli, 3954 Central Ave, Ste A, Hot Springs, AR, (501) 525-5000, 10:30 am-10 pm

On the Border, 190 Pakis St, Hot Springs, AR, 71913, (501) 520-5045, 11 am-10 pm

Ryan's Grill Buffet Bakery, 4538 Central Ave, Hot Springs, AR, 71913, (501) 525-3007, 10:45 am-9 pm

Jacksonville

Chili's, 1800 W Main, Jacksonville, AR, 72076, (501) 241-1800, 11 am-10 pm

Jonesboro

Chili's, 1900 Stadium, Jonesboro, AR, 72401, (870) 268-6805, 11 am-10 pm

CiCi's Pizza, 2116 S Caraway, Jonesboro, AR, 72401, (870) 932-8300, 11 am-9 pm

Cracker Barrel, 2621 Phillips Dr, Jonesboro, AR, 72401, (870) 932-9732, 6 am-10 pm

El Chico Café, 2315 E Parker, Jonesboro, AR, 72404, (870) 910-0424, 11 am-10 pm

McAlister's Deli, 2400 S Caraway, Jonesboro, AR, (870) 802-2400, 10:30 am-10 pm

O'Charley's, 2312 E Parker Rd, Jonesboro, AR, (870) 933-7102, 11 am-10 pm

Ryan's Grill Buffet Bakery, 2809 E Highland Dr, Jonesboro, AR, 72401, (870) 932-3200, 10:45 am-9 pm

Little Rock

Chili's, 10700 Rodney Parham Ave, Little Rock, AR, 72212, (501) 224-0455, 11 am-10 pm

CiCi's Pizza, 11121 N Rodney Parham Rd, Ste 9A, Little Rock, AR, 72212, (501) 228-6560, 11 am-9 pm

Cozymel's Mexican Grill, 10 Shackleford, Little Rock, AR, 72211, (501) 954-7100, 11 am-10 pm

El Chico Café, 1315 Breckenridge Dr, Little Rock, AR, 72227, (501) 224-2550, 11 am-10 pm

El Chico Café, 8409 Interstate 30, Little Rock, AR, 72209, (501) 562-3762, 11 am-10 pm

McAlister's Deli, 5507 Ranch Dr, Ste 100, Little Rock, AR, (501) 367-5050, 10:30 am-10 pm

McAlister's Deli, 12019 Westh Aven Dr, Little Rock, AR, (501) 228-7727, 10:30 am-10 pm

McAlister's Deli, 9700 Rodney Parham, Little Rock, AR, (501) 537-4848, 10:30 am-10 pm

On the Border, 11721 Chenal Pkwy, Little Rock, AR, 72211, (501) 217-9275, 11 am-10 pm

P.F. Changs, 317 S Shackleford Rd, Little Rock, AR, 72211, (501) 225-4424, 11 am-10 pm

Romano's Macaroni Grill, 11100 W Markham, Little Rock, AR, 72211, (501) 221-3150, 11 am-10 pm

Ryan's Grill Buffet Bakery, 8815 Baseline Rd, Little Rock, AR, 72209, (501) 562-7400, 10:45 am-9 pm

Maumelle

Beef O'Brady's, 115 Audubon Dr, #10, Maumelle, AR, 72113, (501) 803-3500, 11 am-11 pm

Mountain Home

Chili's, 2785 Hwy 62 East, Mountain Home, AR, 72653, (870) 492-4294, 11 am-10 pm

El Chico Café, 45 Charles Blackburn Dr, Mountain Home, AR, 72653, (870) 492-4700, 11 am-10 pm

North Little Rock

Benihana, 2 Riverfront Pl, North Little Rock, AR, 72114, (501) 374-8081, 11:30 am-10 pm

Chili's, 4000 McCain Blvd, North Little Rock, AR, 72116, (501) 753-3333, 11 am-10 pm

CiCi's Pizza, 2815 Lakewood Village Dr, North Little Rock, AR, 72116, (501) 753-1182, 11 am-9 pm

Cracker Barrel, 3101 Springhill Dr, North Little Rock, AR, 72117, (501) 945-9373, 6 am-10 pm

Fire Mountain, 4000 Spring Hill Plz Ct, North Little Rock, AR, 72117, (501) 945-4737, 10:45 am-9:30 pm

Golden Corral, 5001 Warden Rd, North Little Rock, AR, 72116, (501) 771-4605, 11 am-9 pm

Hooters, 4110 Landers Rd, North Little Rock, AR, 72117, (501) 945-0444, 11 am-midnight

McAlister's Deli, 4842 N Hills Blvd, North Little Rock, AR, (501) 812-6920, 10:30 am-10 pm

Pine Bluff

Chili's, 5511 Olive St, Pine Bluff, AR, 71603, (870) 534-9763, 11 am-10 pm

Rogers

Chili's, 420 N 46th St, Rogers, AR, 72756, (479) 936-9990, 11 am-10 pm

CiCi's Pizza, 4408 W Walnut, Ste 5-6, Rogers, AR, 72756, (479) 636-1500, 11 am-9 pm

Copeland's, 463 N 46th St, Rogers, AR, 72756, (479) 246-9455, 11 am-10 pm

Fuddruckers, 3001 Market St, Rogers, AR, 72758, 11 am-9 pm

O'Charley's, 401 N 46th St, Rogers, AR, (479) 246-0708, 11 am-10 pm

On the Border, 577 N 46th St, Rogers, AR, 72756, (479) 636-7761, 11 am-10 pm

P.F. Changs, 2203 S 45th St, Ste 13100, Rogers, AR, 72758, 11 am-10 pm

Ryan's Grill Buffet Bakery, 102 S 21st St, Rogers, AR, 72758, (479) 636-5988, 10:45 am-9 pm

Russellville

CiCi's Pizza, 3063 E Main St, Ste C, Russellville, AR, 72173, (479) 967-4432, 11 am-9 pm

Cracker Barrel, 211 E Harrell Dr, Russellville, AR, 72802, (479) 968-5983, 6 am-10 pm

Ryan's Grill Buffet Bakery, 107 N Elmira Ave, Russellville, AR, 72802, (479) 967-6375, 10:45 am-9 pm

Searcy

Ryan's Grill Buffet Bakery, 3608 Race St, Searcy, AR, 72143, (501) 278-5400, 10:45 am-9 pm

Springdale

Cracker Barrel, 1022 S 48th St, Springdale, AR, 72762, (479) 872-2040, 6 am-10 pm

Sizzler, 4439 W Sunset Ave, Springdale, AR, 72762, (479) 750-7848, 11 am-10 pm

State University

Godfather's Pizza, 105 N Caraway, State University, AR, 72467, (870) 972-2059

Texarkana

El Chico Café, 300 Realtor Rd, Texarkana, AR, 75502, (870) 772-2626, 11 am-10 pm

West Memphis

Cracker Barrel, 1600 N 6th St, West Memphis, AR, 72301, (870) 733-0469, 6 am-10 pm

Kentucky

Ashland

Golden Corral, 21 Russell Plz Dr, Ashland, KY, 41101, (606) 324-6441, 11 am-9 pm

O'Charley's, 461 Riverhill Dr, Ashland, KY, (606) 326-0159, 11 am-10 pm

Auburn

Godfather's Pizza, 410 W Main St, Auburn, KY, 42206, (270) 542-7731

Bardstown

Golden Corral, 104 W John Rowan Blvd, Bardstown, KY, 40004, (502) 348-0153, 11 am-9 pm

Beaver Dam

Godfather's Pizza, 1989 US Hwy 231 S, Beaver Dam, KY, 42320, (270) 274-0344

Bellevue

Donato's Pizza, 15 Donnermeyer Dr, Bellevue, KY, 41073, (859) 261-5700, 11 am-midnight

Berea

Cracker Barrel, 101 McKinney Dr, Berea, KY, 40403, (859) 986-0512, 6 am-10 pm

Bowling Green

CiCi's Pizza, 2945 Scottsville Rd, Ste A-1, Bowling Green, KY, 42104, (270) 843-9299, 11 am-9 pm

Cracker Barrel, 1960 Mel Browning St, Bowling Green, KY, 42104, (270) 843-8087, 6 am-10 pm

Godfather's Pizza, 3810 Scottsville Rd, Bowling Green, KY, 42104, (270) 393-0308

Godfather's Pizza, 669 Three Springs Rd, Bowling Green, KY, 42104, (270) 842-9169

Godfather's Pizza, 4455 Russellville Rd, Bowling Green, KY, 42101, (270) 393-0370

Godfather's Pizza, 3411 Louisville Rd, Bowling Green, KY, 42101, (270) 842-0688

Godfather's Pizza, 810 Morgantown Rd, Bowling Green, KY, 42101, (270) 843-0449

Godfather's Pizza, 1051 Fairview Ave, Bowling Green, KY, 42103, (270) 842-4562

Godfather's Pizza, 3011 Nashville Rd, Bowling Green, KY, 42101, (270) 782-6701

Godfather's Pizza, 6607 Louisville Rd, Bowling Green, KY, 42101, (270) 796-3664

Godfather's Pizza, 1200 Campbell Ln, Bowling Green, KY, 42101, (270) 843-0590

Logan's Roadhouse, 2920 Scottsville Rd, Bowling Green, KY, 42103, (270) 846-2771, 11 am-10 pm

Longhorn Steakhouse, 2635 Scottsville Rd, Bowling Green, KY, 42104, (270) 746-0055, 11 am-10 pm

O'Charley's, 2717 Scottsville Rd, Bowling Green, KY, (270) 781-0806, 11 am-10 pm

Ryan's Grill Buffet Bakery, 1920 Mel Browning St, Bowling Green, KY, 42104, (270) 843-1439, 10:45 am-9 pm

Smokey Bones, 2450 Scottsville Rd, Bowling Green, KY, 42104, (270) 782-1888, 11 am-10 pm

Brownsville

Godfather's Pizza, Houchens Ferry Rd, Brownsville, KY, 42210, (270) 597-2180

Burlington

Donato's Pizza, 1800 Patrick Dr, Burlington, KY, 41005, (859) 689-7500, 11 am-midnight

Cadiz

Cracker Barrel, 74 Hospitality Ln, Cadiz, KY, 42211, (270) 522-0600, 6 am-10 pm

Godfather's Pizza, 267 Main St, Cadiz, KY, 42211, (270) 522-4658

Calvert City

Cracker Barrel, 314 Kennedy Ave, Calvert City, KY, 42029, (270) 395-0371, 6 am-10 pm

Godfather's Pizza, Hwy 95 & Fifth Ave, Calvert City, KY, 42029, (270) 395-1801

Campbellsville

Godfather's Pizza, 1581 E BRdway, Campbellsville, KY, 42719, (270) 465-4000

Cave City

Cracker Barrel, 800 Happy Valley St, Cave City, KY, 42127, (270) 773-4723, 6 am-10 pm

Godfather's Pizza, Hwy 31 & 70, Cave City, KY, 42127, (270) 773-4403

Cold Spring

Longhorn Steakhouse, 200 CrossRds Blvd, Cold Spring, KY, 41076, (859) 441-4820, 11 am-10 pm

O'Charley's, 100 CrossRds Blvd, Cold Spring, KY, (859) 442-9270, 11 am-10 pm

Corbin

Cracker Barrel, 857 E Cumberland Gap Pkwy, Corbin, KY, 40701, (606) 523-0522, 6 am-10 pm

Covington

Golden Corral, 488 Orphanage Rd, Covington, KY, 41017, (859) 578-3700, 11 am-9 pm

Crestview Hills

Max & Ermas, 2905 Dixie Hwy, Crestview Hills, KY, (859) 426-5501, 11 am-11 pm

Danville

Beef O'Brady's, 240 Skywatch Dr, Danville, KY, 40422, (859) 236-0197, 11 am-11 pm

CiCi's Pizza, 1560 Hustonville Rd, Ste 227, Danville, KY, 40422, (859) 936-1616, 11 am-9 pm

Cracker Barrel, 40 Cassady , Danville, KY, 40422, (859) 936-7792, 6 am-10 pm

Godfather's Pizza, 1096 Lexington Rd, Danville, KY, 40422, (859) 236-9815

O'Charley's, 1560 Hustonville Rd, Danville, KY, (859) 936-8040, 11 am-10 pm

Dry Ridge

Cracker Barrel, 1131 Fashion Ridge Rd, Dry Ridge, KY, 41035, (859) 823-0273, 6 am-10 pm

Elizabethtown

Cracker Barrel, 1047 Executive Dr, Elizabethtown, KY, 42701, (270) 765-5525, 6 am-10 pm

Godfather's Pizza, 2611 Leitchfield Rd, Elizabethtown, KY, 42701, (270) 769-2757

Golden Corral, 1835 N Dixie Hwy, Elizabethtown, KY, 42701, (270) 763-0822, 11 am-9 pm

O'Charley's, 1629 N Dixie Hwy, Elizabethtown, KY, (270) 763-9075, 11 am-10 pm

Ryan's Grill Buffet Bakery, 1034 Executive Dr, Elizabethtown, KY, 42701, (270) 766-1058, 10:45 am-9 pm

Erlanger

Donato's Pizza, 3044 Dixie Hwy, Erlanger, KY, 41018, (859) 331-0889, 11 am-midnight

Florence

CiCi's Pizza, 4989 Houston Rd, Florence, KY, 41042, (859) 525-6380, 11 am-9 pm

Cracker Barrel, 7399 Turfway Rd, Florence, KY, 41042, (859) 283-0101, 6 am-10 pm

Fuddruckers, 135 Hansel Ave, Florence, KY, 41042, 11 am-9 pm

Golden Corral, 4770 Houston Rd, Florence, KY, 41042, (859) 647-3900, 11 am-9 pm

Hooters, 7200 Houston Rd, Florence, KY, 41041, (859) 647-2848, 11 am-midnight

Logan's Roadhouse, 6835 Houston Rd, Florence, KY, 41042, (859) 525-2106, 11 am-10 pm

Longhorn Steakhouse, 7501 Foltz Dr, Florence, KY, 41042, (859) 282-9100, 11 am-10 pm

O'Charley's, 7414 Turfway Rd, Florence, KY, (859) 525-6622, 11 am-10 pm

Romano's Macaroni Grill, 7205 Houston Rd, Florence, KY, 41042, (859) 647-0500, 11 am-10 pm

Ryan's Grill Buffet Bakery, 40 Cavalier Blvd, Florence, KY, 41042, (859) 282-9199, 10:45 am-9 pm

Smokey Bones, 7848 Mall Rd, Florence, KY, 41042, (859) 371-5425, 11 am-10 pm

Fort Knox

Godfather's Pizza, Building #2013 Eisenhower, Fort Knox, KY, 40121, (502) 942-7485

Frankfort

Longhorn Steakhouse, 101 W Ridge Rd, Frankfort, KY, 40601, (502) 875-1500, 11 am-10 pm

O'Charley's, 325 Leonard Wood Rd, Frankfort, KY, (502) 223-3282, 11 am-10 pm

Franklin

Cracker Barrel, 155 Steele Rd, Franklin, KY, 42134, (270) 598-8812, 6 am-10 pm

Fulton

Godfather's Pizza, 101 Highland Ave, Fulton, KY, 42042, (270) 472-3034

Georgetown

CiCi's Pizza, 106 Osborn Way, Georgetown, KY, 40324, (502) 863-1605, 11 am-9 pm

Cracker Barrel, 1454 Cherry Blossom Way, Georgetown, KY, 40324, (502) 863-5670, 6 am-10 pm

Golden Corral, 100 Ikebana Path, Georgetown, KY, 40324, (502) 867-1600, 11 am-9 pm

O'Charley's, 100 Osborne, Georgetown, KY, (502) 868-9165, 11 am-10 pm

Glasgow

Godfather's Pizza, 557 SL Roger Wells Blvd, Glasgow, KY, 42141, (270) 659-0120

Greenville

Godfather's Pizza, 349 N Main St, Greenville, KY, 42345, (270) 338-2005

Hebron

Damon's Grill, 2939 Terminal Dr, Hebron, KY, 41048, (859) 767-1980

Henderson

Golden Corral, 1320 Green St, Henderson, KY, 42420, (270) 869-9310, 11 am-9 pm

Hopkinsville

Godfather's Pizza, 2701 Fort Campbell Blvd, Hopkinsville, KY, 42240, (270) 887-0909

O'Charley's, 4223 Fort Campbell Blvd, Hopkinsville, KY, (270) 885-3035, 11 am-10 pm

Ryan's Grill Buffet Bakery, 4131 Ft Campbell Blvd, Hopkinsville, KY, 42240, (270) 890-0406, 10:45 am-9 pm

Hurstbourne

Max & Ermas, 2901 S Hurstbourne Pkwy, Hurstbourne, KY, (502) 493-9662, 11 am-11 pm

P.F. Changs, 9120 Shelbyville Rd, Hurstbourne, KY, 40222, (502) 327-7707, 11 am-10 pm

Jeffersontown

Cracker Barrel, 1401 Kentucky Mills Dr, Jeffersontown, KY, 40299, (502) 266-8895, 6 am-10 pm

Lagrange

Beef O'Brady's, 1220 Market St, LaGrange, KY, 40031, (502) 225-5871, 11 am-11 pm

Cracker Barrel, 1414 E Crystal Dr, LaGrange, KY, 40031, (502) 222-1156, 6 am-10 pm

Leitchfield

Golden Corral, 624 S Main St, Leitchfield, KY, 42754, (270) 259-6041, 11 am-9 pm

Lexington

Beef O'Brady's, 3735 Palomar Centre Dr #12, Lexington, KY, 40515, (859) 223-0017, 11 am-11 pm

Beef O'Brady's, 125 Towne Centre Dr, #127, Lexington, KY, 40511, (859) 288-0078, 11 am-11 pm

CiCi's Pizza, 1315 Winchester Rd, Lexington, KY, 40505, (859) 246-1116, 11 am-9 pm

CiCi's Pizza, 2157 Harrodsburg Rd, Lexington, KY, 40504, (859) 275-1980, 11 am-9 pm

Cracker Barrel, 1927 Stanton Way, Lexington, KY, 40511, (859) 233-7684, 6 am-10 pm

Cracker Barrel, 2220 Elkhorn Rd, Lexington, KY, 40505, (859) 293-2555, 6 am-10 pm

Don Pablo's, 1924 Pavilion Way, Lexington, KY, 40509, (859) 543-1650, 11 am-10 pm

Donato's Pizza, 265 New Circle Rd NW, Lexington, KY, 40505, (859) 299-5000, 11 am-midnight

Donato's Pizza, 3120 Maple Leaf Dr, Lexington, KY, 40509, (859) 543-1818, 11 am-midnight

Donato's Pizza, 728 E Main St, Lexington, KY, 40502, (859) 269-5700, 11 am-midnight

Donato's Pizza, 3070 Lake Crest Circle, Lexington, KY, 40513, (859) 224-7772, 11 am-midnight

Donato's Pizza, 3851 Kennesaw Dr, Lexington, KY, 40515, (859) 271-6666, 11 am-midnight

El Chico Café, 3010 Lakecrest Circle, Lexington, KY, 40513, (859) 224-1002, 11 am-10 pm

Fire Mountain, 1973 Bryant Rd, Lexington, KY, 40509, (859) 263-0733, 10:45 am-9:30 pm

Golden Corral, 185 E New Circle Rd, Lexington, KY, 40505, (859) 299-1600, 11 am-9 pm

Hooters, 3101 Richmond Rd, Lexington, KY, 40509, (859) 269-8521, 11 am-midnight

Logan's Roadhouse, 1250 S BRdway, Lexington, KY, 40504, (859) 252-4307, 11 am-10 pm

Logan's Roadhouse, 1908 Pavillon Way, Lexington, KY, 40509, (859) 263-4716, 11 am-10 pm

Logan's Roadhouse, 140 Rojay Dr, Lexington, KY, 40503, (859) 273-0899, 11 am-10 pm

Longhorn Steakhouse, 2217 Harrodsburg Rd, Lexington, KY, 40504, (859) 313-5420, 11 am-10 pm

Max & Ermas, 3030 Lakecrest Circle, Lexington, KY, (859) 224-3440, 11 am-11 pm

Max & Ermas, 1848 Alysheba Way, Lexington, KY, (859) 543-8111, 11 am-11 pm

O'Charley's, 2895 Richmond Rd, Lexington, KY, (859) 266-8640, 11 am-10 pm

O'Charley's, 2270 Nicholasville Rd, Lexington, KY, (859) 278-4164, 11 am-10 pm

O'Charley's, 2099 Harrodsburg Rd, Lexington, KY, (859) 278-6984, 11 am-10 pm

P.F. Changs, Fayette Mall, Lexington, KY, 11 am-10 pm

Romano's Macaroni Grill, 116 MarketPl Dr, Lexington, KY, 40503, (859) 971-0292, 11 am-10 pm

Ryan's Grill Buffet Bakery, 701 Red Mile Rd, Lexington, KY, 40504, (859) 259-1736, 10:45 am-9 pm

Tony Roma's, 161 Lexington Green Circle, The Mall at Lexington Green, Lexington, KY, 40503, (859) 272-7526, 11 am-10 pm

London

Cracker Barrel, 80 Alamo Dr, London, KY, 40741, (606) 864-3102, 6 am-10 pm

Golden Corral, 204 Kings Way, London, KY, 40741, (606) 864-7062, 11 am-9 pm

Louisville

Beef O'Brady's, 3101 S 2nd St, Louisville, KY, 40208, (502) 637-3737, 11 am-11 pm

Beef O'Brady's, 5628 Bardstown Rd, Louisville, KY, 40291, (502) 239-2226, 11 am-11 pm

Beef O'Brady's, 241 Blankenbaker Pkwy, Louisville, KY, 40243, (502) 254-2322, 11 am-11 pm

Beef O'Brady's, 5501 Valley Station Rd, Louisville, KY, 40272, (502) 933-5919, 11 am-11 pm

Beef O'Brady's, 10000 US Hwy 22, Louisville, KY, 40241, (502) 327-8881, 11 am-11 pm

Cheesecake Factory, 5000 Shelbyville Rd, Ste 1585, Louisville, KY, 40207, (502) 897-3933, 11 am-11 pm

CiCi's Pizza, 5226 Dixie Hwy, Louisville, KY, 40216, (502) 448-8885, 11 am-9 pm

CiCi's Pizza, 3093 Breckenridge Ln, Louisville, KY, 40220, (502) 452-6700, 11 am-9 pm

Cracker Barrel, 10150 Brookridge Village Blvd, Louisville, KY, 40291, (502) 231-4663, 6 am-10 pm

Cracker Barrel, 2701 Crittenden Dr, Louisville, KY, 40209, (502) 636-2263, 6 am-10 pm

Golden Corral, 8013 Preston Hwy, Louisville, KY, 40219, (502) 966-4970, 11 am-9 pm

Golden Corral, 4032 Taylorsville Rd, Louisville, KY, 40220, (502) 485-0004, 11 am-9 pm

Golden Corral, 5362 Dixie Hwy, Louisville, KY, 40216, (502) 447-6660, 11 am-9 pm

Hometown Buffet, 3710 Chamberlain Ln, Louisville, KY, 40241, (502) 326-9777, 11 am-8:30 pm

Hometown Buffet, Bluegrass Commonwealth Park, 1700 Alliant Ave, Louisville, KY, 40299, (502) 267-7044, 11 am-8:30 pm

Hometown Buffet, 6641 Dixie Hwy, Louisville, KY, 40258, (502) 995-3320, 11 am-8:30 pm

Hooters, 7701 Preston Hwy, Louisville, KY, 40219, (502) 968-1606, 11 am-midnight

Hooters, 4120 Dutchman Ln, Louisville, KY, 40207, (502) 895-7100, 11 am-midnight

Hooters, 4948 Dixie Hwy, Louisville, KY, 40216, (502) 449-4194, 11 am-midnight

J. Alexander's, 102 Oxmoor Ct, Louisville, KY, 40222, (502) 339-2206, 11 am-10 pm

Logan's Roadhouse, 5229 Dixie Hwy, Louisville, KY, 40216, (502) 448-0577, 11 am-10 pm

Logan's Roadhouse, 5055 Shelbyville Rd, Louisville, KY, 40207, (502) 893-3884, 11 am-10 pm

Longhorn Steakhouse, 2535 Hurstbourne Gem Ln, Louisville, KY, 40220, (502) 671-5350, 11 am-10 pm

Melting Pot, 2045 S Hurstbourne Pkwy, Louisville, KY, 40220, (502) 491-3125, 5 pm-10:30 pm

O'Charley's, 4801 Outer Loop, Louisville, KY, (502) 968-8996, 11 am-10 pm

O'Charley's, 10641 Fischer Park Rd, Louisville, KY, (502) 339-2264, 11 am-10 pm

O'Charley's, 1901 S Hurstbourne Ln, Louisville, KY, (502) 491-8372, 11 am-10 pm

O'Charley's, 962 Breckenridge Ln, Louisville, KY, (502) 899-9430, 11 am-10 pm

On the Border, 10601 Fischer Park Dr, Louisville, KY, 40241, (502) 412-2461, 11 am-10 pm

Red Star Tavern, 450 S Fourth St, Lousiville, KY, 40202, (502) 568-5656, 11 am-2 am

Romano's Macaroni Grill, 401 S Hurstborne Pkwy, Louisville, KY, 40222, (502) 423-9220, 11 am-10 pm

Ryan's Grill Buffet Bakery, 5338 Bardstown Rd, Louisville, KY, 40291, (502) 491-1088, 10:45 am-9 pm

Smokey Bones, 2525 Hurstbourne Gem Ln, Louisville, KY, 40220, (502) 491-7570, 11 am-10 pm

Tony Roma's, 150 N Hurstbourne Pkwy, Louisville, KY, 40222, (502) 327-8500, 11 am-10 pm

Uno Chicago Grill, 6501 Bardstown Rd, Louisville, KY, 40291, (502) 239-0079, 11 am-12:30 am

Madisonville

Cracker Barrel, 1780 E Center St, Madisonville, KY, 42431, (270) 821-5444, 6 am-10 pm

Godfather's Pizza, Pkwy Plz Mall, Madisonville, KY, 42431, (270) 821-7575

Middlesboro

Ryan's Grill Buffet Bakery, 1238 N 12th St, Middlesboro, KY, 40965, (606) 242-2900, 10:45 am-9 pm

Morehead

CiCi's Pizza, 352 Kroger Center, Morehead, KY, 40351, (606) 783-1550, 11 am-9 pm

Morganfield

Godfather's Pizza, 600 E Fort St, Morganfield, KY, 42437, (270) 389-9588

Mt Vernon

Godfather's Pizza, 1475 Richmond Rd, Mt Vernon, KY, 40456, (606) 256-5079

Mt. Sterling

Cracker Barrel, 110 Stone Trace Dr, Mt. Sterling, KY, 40353, (859) 499-0200, 6 am-10 pm

Murray

Cracker Barrel, 650 N 12th St, Murray, KY, 42071, (270) 762-0081, 6 am-10 pm

Ryan's Grill Buffet Bakery, 801 Wal-Mart Dr, Murray, KY, 42071, (270) 759-3809, 10:45 am-9 pm

Newport

Don Pablo's, 401 Riverboat Row, Newport, KY, 41071, (859) 261-7100, 11 am-10 pm

Hooters, 301 Riverboat Row, Newport, KY, 41071, (859) 291-9191, 11 am-midnight

Nicholasville

CiCi's Pizza, 121 Bryant Dr, Nicholasville, KY, 40356, (859) 885-0666, 11 am-9 pm

Golden Corral, 110 Retail Rd, Nicholasville, KY, 40356, (859) 881-8122, 11 am-9 pm

Owensboro

Beef O'Brady's, 3189 Fairview Dr, Ste E, Owensboro, KY, 42303, (270) 685-4969, 11 am-11 pm

Cracker Barrel, 5311 Frederica St, Owensboro, KY, 42301, (270) 684-4118, 6 am-10 pm

O'Charley's, 5205 Frederica St, Owensboro, KY, (270) 686-8780, 11 am-10 pm

Ryan's Grill Buffet Bakery, 4500 Frederica St, Owensboro, KY, 42301, (270) 691-9787, 10:45 am-9 pm

Paducah

Cracker Barrel, 5035 Hinkleville Rd, Paducah, KY, 42001, (270) 443-9331, 6 am-10 pm

El Chico Café, 5015 Hinkleville Rd, Paducah, KY, 42001, (270) 443-0411, 11 am-10 pm

Logan's Roadhouse, 5137 Hinkleville, Paducah, KY, 42001, (270) 442-1939, 11 am-10 pm

O'Charley's, 3916 Hinkleville Rd, Paducah, KY, (270) 442-7770, 11 am-10 pm

Ryan's Grill Buffet Bakery, 5140 Hinkleville Rd, Paducah, KY, 42001, (270) 442-2868, 10:45 am-9 pm

Pembroke

Godfather's Pizza, 125 W Nashville, Pembroke, KY, 42266, (270) 475-9806

Providence

Godfather's Pizza, 200 E Main, Providence, KY, 42450, (270) 667-7177

Richmond

CiCi's Pizza, 256 Richmond Mall, Space F5, Richmond, KY, 40475, (859) 623-1555, 11 am-9 pm

Cracker Barrel, 1797 Lexington Rd, Richmond, KY, 40475, (859) 623-0037, 6 am-10 pm

Hooters, 241 Eastern Bypass, Richmond, KY, 40475, (859) 626-3900, 11 am-midnight

O'Charley's, 815 Eastern Bypass, Richmond, KY, (859) 624-8868, 11 am-10 pm

Ryan's Grill Buffet Bakery, 2019 Colby Taylor Rd, Richmond, KY, 40475, (859) 625-1996, 10:45 am-9 pm

Shelbyville

Cracker Barrel, 1565 Mt Eden Rd, Shelbyville, KY, 40065, (502) 633-9945, 6 am-10 pm

Shepherdsville

Cracker Barrel, 275 Brenton Way, Shepherdsville, KY, 40165, (502) 955-4008, 6 am-10 pm

Shively

O'Charley's, 4402 Dixie Hwy, Shively, KY, (502) 447-9203, 11 am-10 pm

Ryan's Grill Buffet Bakery, 4711 Dixie Hwy, Shively, KY, 40216, (502) 447-4781, 10:45 am-9 pm

Somerset

Cracker Barrel, 1899 S Hwy 27, Somerset, KY, 42503, (606) 451-9944, 6 am-10 pm

Donato's Pizza, 92 S Hwy 27, Somerset, KY, 42501, (606) 677-1700, 11 am-midnight

Golden Corral, 2020 S Hwy 27, Somerset, KY, 42501, (606) 677-0700, 11 am-9 pm

Sturgis

Godfather's Pizza, 620 N Main, Sturgis, KY, 42459, (270) 333-9245

Summit

Max & Ermas, 3921 Summit Plz Dr, Summit, KY, (502) 412-5229, 11 am-11 pm

Union

Beef O'Brady's, 1597 Cavalry Dr, Union, KY, 41091, (859) 384-9464, 11 am-11 pm

Winchester

Golden Corral, 1501 Bypass Rd, Winchester, KY, 40391, (859) 745-2972, 11 am-9 pm

Louisiana

Abbeville

Chili's, 3009 Veterans Memorial Dr, Abbeville, LA, 70510, (337) 893-3370, 11 am-10 pm

Golden Corral, 1910 Veterans Memorial Dr, Abbeville, LA, 70510, (337) 898-9427, 11 am-9 pm

Alexandria

Chili's, 2291 S Mac Arthur Dr, Alexandria, LA, 71301, (318) 442-3222, 11 am-10 pm

CiCi's Pizza, 1420 MacArthur Dr, Alexandria, LA, 71301, (318) 442-6969, 11 am-9 pm

Copeland's, 2421 S McArthur, Alexandria, LA, 71031, (318) 561-2040, 11 am-10 pm

Cracker Barrel, 6108 W Calhoun Dr, Alexandria, LA, 71303, (318) 767-0500, 6 am-10 pm

El Chico Café, 1730 Metro Dr, Alexandria, LA, 71301, (318) 442-4950, 11 am-10 pm

Fire Mountain, 3024 W Macarthur Dr, Alexandria, LA, 71303, (318) 445-8796, 10:45 am-9:30 pm

Logan's Roadhouse, 2820 McArthur Dr, Alexandria, LA, 71301, (318) 443-3550, 11 am-10 pm

Baton Rouge

Beef O'Brady's, 4710 OíNeal Ln, Baton Rouge, LA, 70817, (225) 752-1992, 11 am-11 pm

Chili's, 10305 N Mall Dr, Baton Rouge, LA, 70809, (225) 292-0702, 11 am-10 pm

Chili's, 4550 Constitution Ave E, Baton Rouge, LA, 70808, (225) 927-0035, 11 am-10 pm

CiCi's Pizza, 7060 Siegen Ln, Baton Rouge, LA, 70809, (225) 291-2424, 11 am-9 pm

CiCi's Pizza, 5260 Corporate Dr, Baton Rouge, LA, 70808, (225) 201-0611, 11 am-9 pm

Copeland's, 4957 Essen Ln, Baton Rouge, LA, 70809, (225) 769-1800, 11 am-10 pm

Cracker Barrel, 10250 Plz Americana Dr, Baton Rouge, LA, 70816, (225) 926-1328, 6 am-10 pm

Fire Mountain, 11650 Coursey Blvd, Baton Rouge, LA, 70816, (225) 296-5470, 10:45 am-9:30 pm

Godfather's Pizza, 14241 Coursey Blvd, Ste B1, Baton Rouge, LA, 70817, (225) 752-9292

Golden Corral, 5252 S Sherwood Forest Dr, Baton Rouge, LA, 70816, (225) 295-9595, 11 am-9 pm

Hooters, 5120 Corporate Blvd, Baton Rouge, LA, 70806, (225) 928-7221, 11 am-midnight

Hooters, 6454 Siegen Ln, Baton Rouge, LA, 70809, (225) 293-1900, 11 am-midnight

J. Alexander's, 6457 Bluebonnet Rd, Baton Rouge, LA, 70809, (225) 766-8630, 11 am-10 pm

Logan's Roadhouse, 6571 Blue Bonnet Blvd, Baton Rouge, LA, 70810, (225) 757-9449, 11 am-10 pm

McAlister's Deli, 7242 Perkins Rd, Baton Rouge, LA, (225) 303-0268, 10:30 am-10 pm

McAlister's Deli, 6808 Seigen Ln, Baton Rouge, LA, (225) 810-4000, 10:30 am-10 pm

Melting Pot, 5294 Corporate Blvd, Baton Rouge, LA, 70808, (225) 928-5677, 5 pm-10:30 pm

O'Charley's, 2562 CitiPl Blvd, Baton Rouge, LA, (225) 926-9969, 11 am-10 pm

On the Border, 2552 CitiPl Ct, Baton Rouge, LA, 70808, (225) 924-7400, 11 am-10 pm

P.F. Changs, 7341 Corporate Blvd, Baton Rouge, LA, 70809, (225) 216-9044, 11 am-10 pm

Romano's Macaroni Grill, 2572 CitiPl St, Baton Rouge, LA, 70808, (225) 927-6637, 11 am-10 pm

Ryan's Grill Buffet Bakery, 9607 Florida Blvd, Baton Rouge, LA, 70815, (225) 927-1432, 10:45 am-9 pm

Smokey Bones, 6330 Siegen Ln, Baton Rouge, LA, 70810, (225) 295-1888, 11 am-10 pm

Sullivan's Steakhouse, 5252 Corporate Blvd, Baton Rouge, LA, 70808, (225) 925-1161, 11 am-11 pm

Bossier City

Chili's, 3025 E Texas, Bossier City, LA, 71111, (318) 752-8700, 11 am-10 pm

CiCi's Pizza, 2142 Airline Dr, Ste 100, Bossier City, LA, 71111, (318) 741-2424, 11 am-9 pm

El Chico Café, 2050 Old Minden Rd, Bossier City, LA, 71111, (318) 742-4685, 11 am-10 pm

Fire Mountain, 2400 Airline Dr, Bossier City, LA, 71111, (318) 549-2133, 10:45 am-9:30 pm

Hooters, 545 Boardwalk Blvd, Bossier City, LA, 71111, (318) 752-4447, 11 am-midnight

McAlister's Deli, 2511 Beene Blvd, Bossier City, LA, 71111, (318) 550-0367, 10:30 am-10 pm

Covington

Copeland's, 680 N Hwy 190 , Covington, LA, 70433, (985) 809-9659, 11 am-10 pm

McAlister's Deli, 206 Lake Dr, Ste 15, Covington, LA, (985) 898-2800, 10:30 am-10 pm

Crowley

Chili's, 827 Odd Fellows Rd, Crowley, LA, 70526, (337) 783-1493, 11 am-10 pm

De Ridder

Ryan's Grill Buffet Bakery, 645 N Pine St, De Ridder, LA, 70634, (337) 462-1122, 10:45 am-9 pm

Denham Springs

Chili's, 135 Rushing Rd W, Denham Springs, LA, 70726, (225) 667-7151, 11 am-10 pm

Ryan's Grill Buffet Bakery, 910 S Range Ave, Denham Springs, LA, 70726, (225) 667-4882, 10:45 am-9 pm

Gonzales

Chili's, 2227 S Tanger Blvd, Gonzales, LA, 70737, (225) 647-8534, 11 am-10 pm

Cracker Barrel, 2313 S Tanger Blvd, Gonzales, LA, 70737, (225) 647-5277, 6 am-10 pm

Gretna

CiCi's Pizza, 605 Lapalco Blvd, Gretna, LA, 70056, (504) 393-7447, 11 am-9 pm

Hooters, 2781 Bell Chasse Hwy, Gretna, LA, 70053, (504) 393-7177, 11 am-midnight

Hammond

Chili's, 2907 US Hwy 190 West, Hammond, LA, 70401, (985) 230-2388, 11 am-10 pm

CiCi's Pizza, 1905 W Thomas St, Ste A, Hammond, LA, 70401, (985) 419-2200, 11 am-9 pm

Cracker Barrel, 201 Westin Oaks Dr, Hammond, LA, 70403, (985) 542-1828, 6 am-10 pm

Ryan's Grill Buffet Bakery, 1748 SW RailRd Ave, Hammond, LA, 70403, (985) 543-0144, 10:45 am-9 pm

Harvey

Chevy's, 1201 Manhattan Blvd, Harvey, LA, 70058, (504) 368-2100, 11 am-10 pm

Chili's, 1741 Manhattan Blvd, Harvey, LA, 70058, (504) 367-5594, 11 am-10 pm

Copeland's, 1700 Lapalco Blvd, Harvey, LA, 70058, (504) 364-1575, 11 am-10 pm

Houma

Chili's, 1539 Martin Luther King Jr Blvd, Houma, LA, 70360, (985) 580-0810, 11 am-10 pm

Copeland's, 1634 Martin Luther King Blvd, Houma, LA, 70364, (504) 873-9600, 11 am-10 pm

Golden Corral, 1724 Martin Luther King Blvd, Houma, LA, 70360, (985) 857-9500, 11 am-9 pm

Ryan's Grill Buffet Bakery, 1520 Martin Luther King, Houma, LA, 70360, (985) 868-1755, 10:45 am-9 pm

Jefferson

Copeland's, 1001 S Clearview Pkwy, Jefferson, LA, 70121, (504) 733-7843, 11 am-10 pm

Kenner

Chevy's, 1325 W Esplanade Ave, Kenner, LA, 70065, (504) 469-5657, 11 am-10 pm

CiCi's Pizza, 3501 Chateau Blvd, Ste 103, Kenner, LA, 70065, (504) 466-2442, 11 am-9 pm

Golden Corral, 3920 Williams Blvd, Kenner, LA, 70065, (504) 464-9696, 11 am-9 pm

McAlister's Deli, 1000 W Esplanade Ste A13, Kenner, LA, (504) 466-1500, 10:30 am-10 pm

La Place

Chili's, 1820 W Airline Hwy, La Place, LA, 70068, (985) 652-1227, 11 am-10 pm

Lafayette

Chili's, 3220 NE Evangeline Thruway, Lafayette, LA, 70507, (337) 266-8013, 11 am-10 pm

Chili's, 3905 Ambassador Caffery Pkwy, Lafayette, LA, 70503, (337) 984-6658, 11 am-10 pm

Chili's, 1734 W Pinhook, Lafayette, LA, 70508, (337) 235-6570, 11 am-10 pm

CiCi's Pizza, 2622 Johnston St, Lafayette, LA, 70503, (337) 237-6466, 11 am-9 pm

Copeland's, 3920 Ambassador Caffery Pkwy, Lafayette, LA, 70360, (337) 991-0320, 11 am-10 pm

Cracker Barrel, 116 Alcide Dominique Dr, Lafayette, LA, 70506, (337) 233-4220, 6 am-10 pm

Godfather's Pizza, 600 McKinley Room 189, Lafayette, LA, 70504, (337) 482-6179

Golden Corral, 3110 Ambassador Caffery Pkwy, Lafayette, LA, 70506, (337) 993-7858, 11 am-9 pm

Hooters, 3221 Ambassador Caffery Pkwy, Lafayette, LA, 70506, (337) 216-9464, 11 am-midnight

Logan's Roadhouse, 3323 Ambassador Caffery Pkwy, Lafayette, LA, 70506, (337) 991-9150, 11 am-10 pm

McAlister's Deli, 4409 Ambassador Caffery Pkwy, Ste 800, Lafayette, LA, (337) 988-3876, 10:30 am-10 pm

O'Charley's, 4301 Ambassador Caffrey Pkwy, Lafayette, LA, (337) 988-4563, 11 am-10 pm

Ryan's Grill Buffet Bakery, 3253 Ambassador Caffery, Lafayette, LA, 70506, (337) 989-8028, 10:45 am-9 pm

Lake Charles

Chili's, 3205 Gertsner Memorial Dr, Lake Charles, LA, 70601, (337) 477-8005, 11 am-10 pm

CiCi's Pizza, 3533 Ryan St, Lake Charles, LA, 70605, (337) 562-2223, 11 am-9 pm

Logan's Roadhouse, 3509 Gerstner Memorial Pkwy, Lake Charles, LA, 70605, (337) 562-2005, 11 am-10 pm

McAlister's Deli, 635 W Prien Lake Rd, Lake Charles, LA, (337) 990-0085, 10:30 am-10 pm

O'Charley's, 1780 W Prien Lake Rd, Lake Charles, LA, (337) 478-9927, 11 am-10 pm

Ryan's Grill Buffet Bakery, 4051 Ryan St, Lake Charles, LA, 70605, (337) 477-2107, 10:45 am-9 pm

Laplace

CiCi's Pizza, 1338 W Airline Hwy, Ste 7A, Laplace, LA, 70068, (985) 651-6272, 11 am-9 pm

Mandeville

Chili's, 3420 US Hwy 190, Mandeville, LA, 70471, (985) 727-2771, 11 am-10 pm

Romano's Macaroni Grill, 3410 US Hwy 190, Mandeville, LA, 70471, (985) 727-1998, 11 am-10 pm

Marrero

CiCi's Pizza, 1963 Barataria Blvd, Marrero, LA, 70072, (504) 340-2424, 11 am-9 pm

Ryan's Grill Buffet Bakery, 5101 Lapalco Blvd, Marrero, LA, 70072, (504) 347-4811, 10:45 am-9 pm

Meraux

CiCi's Pizza, 4308 E Judge Perez Dr, Meraux, LA, 70075, (504) 276-0404, 11 am-9 pm

Metairie

Chevy's, 3330 Veterans Blvd, Metairie, LA, 70002, (504) 887-7788, 11 am-10 pm

Chili's, 4201 Veterans Blvd, Metairie, LA, 70006, (504) 885-1381, 11 am-10 pm

CiCi's Pizza, 6311 Airline Park Shopping Center, Metairie, LA, 70003, (504) 818-2422, 11 am-9 pm

Hooters, 4748 Veterans Blvd, Metairie, LA, 70006, (504) 889-0160, 11 am-midnight

McAlister's Deli, 2701 Airline Hwy, Ste T, Metairie, LA, (504) 830-4030, 10:30 am-10 pm

P.F. Changs, 3301 Veterans Memorial Blvd, Lakeside Mall, Metairie, LA, 70002, (504) 828-5288, 11 am-10 pm

Monroe

Copeland's, 3851 Pecanland Mall Rd, Monroe, LA, 71203, (318) 324-1212, 11 am-10 pm

El Chico Café, 4700 Millh Aven Rd, Monroe, LA, 71203, (318) 388-8831, 11 am-10 pm

McAlister's Deli, 1202 Pecanland Rd, Monroe, LA, (318) 324-9219, 10:30 am-10 pm

O'Charley's, 4101 Pecanland Mall Dr, Monroe, LA, (318) 651-2034, 11 am-10 pm

R.J Gator's, 1119 Garrett Rd, Monroe, LA, 71203, (318) 342-8776, 11 am-10 pm

Ryan's Grill Buffet Bakery, 2400 Louisville Ave, Monroe, LA, 71201, (318) 324-8050, 10:45 am-9 pm

Morgan City

Ryan's Grill Buffet Bakery, 1101 Hwy 90 East, Morgan City, LA, 70380, (985) 395-6556, 10:45 am-9 pm

Natchitoches

Chili's, 932 Keyser Ave, Natchitoches, LA, 71457, (318) 357-0972, 11 am-10 pm

Ryan's Grill Buffet Bakery, 950 Keyser Ave, Natchitoches, LA, 71457, (318) 357-7926, 10:45 am-9 pm

New Iberia

Chili's, 2910 Hwy 14, New Iberia, LA, 70560, (337) 364-0904, 11 am-10 pm

Ryan's Grill Buffet Bakery, 1201 E Admiral Doyle Dr, New Iberia, LA, 70560, (337) 367-6387, 10:45 am-9 pm

New Orleans

Bubba Gump Shrimp, 429 Decatur St, New Orleans, LA, 70130, (504) 522-5800, 11 am-10 pm

Fuddruckers, Harrah's 4 Canal St, New Orleans, LA, 70130, 11 am-9 pm

Hooters, 301 N Peters St, New Orleans, LA, 70130, (504) 522-9222, 11 am-midnight

McAlister's Deli, 4 Canal St, New Orleans, LA, (504) 598-1930, 10:30 am-10 pm

Melting Pot, 1820 St Charles Ave, Ste 120, New Orleans, LA, 70130, (504) 525-3225, 5 pm-10:30 pm

Opelousas

Ryan's Grill Buffet Bakery, 5675 I-49 Service Rd South, Opelousas, LA, 70570, (337) 948-4300, 10:45 am-9 pm

Pineville

Fire Mountain, 3632 Monroe Hwy, Pineville, LA, 71360, (318) 641-9377, 10:45 am-9:30 pm

Prairieville

Godfather's Pizza, 36520 Oak Plz Ln, Ste E, Prairieville, LA, 70769, (225) 744-4622

Ruston

Chili's, 649 N Service Rd East, Ruston, LA, 71270, (318) 242-0155, 11 am-10 pm

Ryan's Grill Buffet Bakery, 1101 N Service Rd East, Ruston, LA, 71270, (318) 255-3020, 10:45 am-9 pm

Shreveport

Chili's, 6620 Youree Dr, Shreveport, LA, 71105, (318) 798-8800, 11 am-10 pm

Copeland's, 1665 E Industrial Loop , Shreveport, LA, 71106, (318) 797-0143, 11 am-10 pm

Cracker Barrel, 6251 Westport Ave, Shreveport, LA, 71129, (318) 688-6080, 6 am-10 pm

El Chico Café, 4015 Fern Ave, Shreveport, LA, 71105, (318) 865-4687, 11 am-10 pm

El Chico Café, 1513 E Bert Kouns, Shreveport, LA, 71105, (318) 798-5777, 11 am-10 pm

El Chico Café, 2127 Greenwood Rd, Shreveport, LA, 71103, (318) 425-7928, 11 am-10 pm

Golden Corral, 7250 Youree Dr, Shreveport, LA, 71105, (318) 798-5783, 11 am-9 pm

McAlister's Deli, 1671 E 70th St, Shreveport, LA, (318) 797-1232, 10:30 am-10 pm

On the Border, 6614 Youree Dr, Shreveport, LA, 71105, (318) 798-5666, 11 am-10 pm

Romano's Macaroni Grill, 7031 Youree Dr, Shreveport, LA, 71105, (318) 795-0491, 11 am-10 pm

Ryan's Grill Buffet Bakery, 2941 Ind Loop Expressway, Shreveport, LA, 71118, (318) 687-8240, 10:45 am-9 pm

Smokey Bones, 7231 Youree Dr, Shreveport, LA, 71105, (318) 797-4880, 11 am-10 pm

Slidell

Chili's, 116 Northshore Blvd, Slidell, LA, 70460, (985) 661-8550, 11 am-10 pm

CiCi's Pizza, 140 Gause Blvd W, Slidell, LA, 70460, (985) 639-8100, 11 am-9 pm

Copeland's, 1337 Gause Blvd, Slidell, LA, 70458, (985) 643-0001, 11 am-10 pm

Cracker Barrel, 790 I-10 E Service Rd, Slidell, LA, 70461, (985) 645-9631, 6 am-10 pm

Ryan's Grill Buffet Bakery, 1100 Robert Rd, Slidell, LA, 70458, (985) 847-0544, 10:45 am-9 pm

Sulphur

Chili's, 317 S Cities Service Hwy, Sulphur, LA, 70663, (337) 625-3837, 11 am-10 pm

Cracker Barrel, 2490 S Cities Service Hwy, Sulphur, LA, 70665, (337) 626-9500, 6 am-10 pm

Thibodaux

Chili's, 620 N Canal Blvd, Thibodaux, LA, 70301, (985) 447-8144, 11 am-10 pm

Godfather's Pizza, Nicholls State University, Thibodaux, LA, 70310, (985) 448-4513

West Monroe

Chili's, 301 Constitution, West Monroe, LA, 71292, (318) 323-7112, 11 am-10 pm

CiCi's Pizza, 3426 Cypress St, Ste 14-5, West Monroe, LA, 71291, (318) 396-3441, 11 am-9 pm

Cracker Barrel, 309 Constitution Dr, West Monroe, LA, 71292, (318) 325-5505, 6 am-10 pm

El Chico Café, 226 Blanchard St, West Monroe, LA, 71291, (318) 322-8500, 11 am-10 pm

Hooters, 505 Constitution Dr, West Monroe, LA, 71292, (318) 322-3224, 11 am-midnight

Logan's Roadhouse, 201 Constitution Dr, West Monroe, LA, 71292, (318) 361-9961, 11 am-10 pm

McAlister's Deli, 198 Thomas Rd, West Monroe, LA, (318) 387-2345, 10:30 am-10 pm

Zachary

Chili's, 5520 Main St, Zachary, LA, 70791, (225) 658-7748, 11 am-10 pm

Ryan's Grill Buffet Bakery, 5755 Main St, Zachary, LA, 70791, (225) 658-0045, 10:45 am-9 pm

Mississippi

Batesville

Cracker Barrel, 225 Lakewood Dr, Batesville, MS, 38606, (662) 563-6363, 6 am-10 pm

Biloxi

CiCi's Pizza, 2650 Beach Blvd, Ste 39, Biloxi, MS, 39531, (228) 388-4886, 11 am-9 pm

Hooters, 1845 Beach Blvd, Biloxi, MS, 39531, (228) 388-4496, 11 am-midnight

McAlister's Deli, 2422 Pass Rd, Unit A, Biloxi, MS, (228) 388-9393, 10:30 am-10 pm

Brandon

CiCi's Pizza, 1303 W Government, Brandon, MS, 39042, (601) 591-0977, 11 am-9 pm

McAlister's Deli, 1490 W Government St, Brandon, MS, (601) 824-7465, 10:30 am-10 pm

Brookhaven

Cracker Barrel, 1207 Hampton Dr, Brookhaven, MS, 39601, (601) 823-6800, 6 am-10 pm

Byram

McAlister's Deli, 7385 Siwell Rd, Byram, MS, (601) 346-0040, 10:30 am-10 pm

Clinton

McAlister's Deli, 620 Hwy 80 East, Clinton, MS, (601) 924-9222, 10:30 am-10 pm

Columbus

Fire Mountain, 1201 Hwy 45 North, Columbus, MS, 39705, (662) 329-9216, 10:45 am-9:30 pm

Corinth

McAlister's Deli, 1510 S Harper Rd, Corinth, MS, (662) 286-9007, 10:30 am-10 pm

Ryan's Grill Buffet Bakery, 2210 Harper Rd, Corinth, MS, 38834, (662) 287-4008, 10:45 am-9 pm

D'Iberville

Beef O'Brady's, 3680-L Sangani Blvd, D'Iberville, MS, 39540, (228) 392-4496, 11 am-11 pm

Chili's, 12017 Indian River Rd, D'Iberville, MS, 39540, (228) 396-1266, 11 am-10 pm

Flowood

CiCi's Pizza, 361 Ridge Way, Flowood, MS, 39232, (601) 992-4550, 11 am-9 pm

Fire Mountain, 205 Belle Meade Point, Flowood, MS, 39232, (601) 992-9221, 10:45 am-9:30 pm

Golden Corral, 988 Top St, Flowood, MS, 39232, (601) 420-9990, 11 am-9 pm

Logan's Roadhouse, 277 Dogwood Blvd, Flowood, MS, 39232, (601) 919-9845, 11 am-10 pm

McAlister's Deli, 1065 River Oaks Dr, Flowood, MS, (601) 939-6810, 10:30 am-10 pm

McAlister's Deli, 276 Dogwood Blvd, Flowood, MS, (601) 919-2520, 10:30 am-10 pm

Grenada

McAlister's Deli, 1650 Sunset Dr, Grenada, MS, (662) 229-9920, 10:30 am-10 pm

Gulfport

Chili's, 15291 CrossRds, Gulfport, MS, 39503, (228) 831-2251, 11 am-10 pm

CiCi's Pizza, 11240B Hwy 49 N, Gulfport, MS, 39505, (228) 539-5440, 11 am-9 pm

Cracker Barrel, 15255 CrossRds Pkwy, Gulfport, MS, 39503, (228) 831-1622, 6 am-10 pm

Hooters, 9495 Hwy 49, Gulfport, MS, 39503, (228) 864-1185, 11 am-midnight

Logan's Roadhouse, 15189 CrossRds Pkwy, Gulfport, MS, 39503, (228) 539-1135, 11 am-10 pm

McAlister's Deli, 15140 Creosote Rd, Gulfport, MS, (228) 822-0550, 10:30 am-10 pm

O'Charley's, 10510 Hwy 49, Gulfport, MS, (228) 328-1350, 11 am-10 pm

Hattiesburg

Chili's, 4500 Hardy St, Hattiesburg, MS, 39402, (601) 296-1131, 11 am-10 pm

CiCi's Pizza, 3720 Hardy St, Ste 6, Hattiesburg, MS, 39402, (601) 264-2393, 11 am-9 pm

Copeland's, 4591 Hardy St, Hattiesburg, MS, 39402, (601) 296-9300, 11 am-10 pm

Cracker Barrel, 6659 US 49, Hattiesburg, MS, 39401, (601) 296-7950, 6 am-10 pm

Fire Mountain, 6082 US Hwy 98 West, Hattiesburg, MS, 39402, (601) 268-0488, 10:45 am-9:30 pm

Logan's Roadhouse, 6147 US Hwy 98, Hattiesburg, MS, 39402, (601) 268-9588, 11 am-10 pm

Longhorn Steakhouse, 4503 Hardy St, Hattiesburg, MS, 39403, (601) 296-9279, 11 am-10 pm

McAlister's Deli, 1000 Turtle Creek Dr, Ste 255, Hattiesburg, MS, (601) 261-6101, 10:30 am-10 pm

McAlister's Deli, 122 Sheffield Loop, Hattiesburg, MS, (601) 271-2002, 10:30 am-10 pm

McAlister's Deli, 2300 Hardy St, Hattiesburg, MS, (601) 545-1876, 10:30 am-10 pm

O'Charley's, 4640 Hardy St, Hattiesburg, MS, (601) 268-1193, 11 am-10 pm

Horn Lake

Cracker Barrel, 706 Desoto Cove, Horn Lake, MS, 38637, (662) 349-4203, 6 am-10 pm

Fire Mountain, 988 Goodman Rd, Horn Lake, MS, 38637, (662) 349-5929, 10:45 am-9:30 pm

Hooters, 982 Goodman Rd, Horn Lake, MS, 38637, (662) 349-7300, 11 am-midnight

Jackson

Chili's, 475 Briarwood, Jackson, MS, 39206, (601) 957-7090, 11 am-10 pm

Cracker Barrel, 6020 I-55 North, Jackson, MS, 39211, (601) 977-1055, 6 am-10 pm

El Chico Café, 4240 Robinson Rd, Jackson, MS, 39209, (601) 969-5997, 11 am-10 pm

Hooters, 4565 Frontage Rd, Jackson, MS, 39206, (601) 981-0480, 11 am-midnight

McAlister's Deli, 220 E Amite St, Ste PG01, Jackson, MS, (601) 985-9108, 10:30 am-10 pm

McAlister's Deli, 1240 E Northside Dr, Jackson, MS, (601) 982-3883, 10:30 am-10 pm

On the Border, 6352 Ridgewood Ct, Jackson, MS, 39211, (601) 977-9447, 11 am-10 pm

Romano's Macaroni Grill, 6376 Ridgewood Court Dr, Jackson, MS, 39211, (601) 957-3999, 11 am-10 pm

Laurel

McAlister's Deli, 1106 Sawmill Rd, Laurel, MS, (601) 649-1178, 10:30 am-10 pm

Ryan's Grill Buffet Bakery, 2132 Hwy 15 North, Laurel, MS, 39440, (601) 649-0060, 10:45 am-9 pm

Madison

Chili's, 1893 Main St, Madison, MS, 39110, (601) 853-6102, 11 am-10 pm

McAlister's Deli, 2129 Main St, Madison, MS, (601) 898-2515, 10:30 am-10 pm

Mccomb

Golden Corral, 1601 Delaware Ave, Mccomb, MS, 39648, (601) 684-8601, 11 am-9 pm

Meridian

CiCi's Pizza, 547 Bonita Lakes Dr, Ste A, Meridian, MS, 39301, (601) 581-2110, 11 am-9 pm

Cracker Barrel, 609 Hwy 11 East, Meridian, MS, 39305, (601) 482-3003, 6 am-10 pm

McAlister's Deli, 4909 27th Pl, Meridian, MS, (601) 693-9100, 10:30 am-10 pm

O'Charley's, 539 Bonita Lakes Dr, Meridian, MS, (601) 482-6505, 11 am-10 pm

Ryan's Grill Buffet Bakery, 207 S Frontage Rd, Meridian, MS, 39301, (601) 482-6700, 10:45 am-9 pm

Moss Point

Cracker Barrel, 6805 SR 63 North, Moss Point, MS, 39563, (228) 475-8856, 6 am-10 pm

Natchez

Ryan's Grill Buffet Bakery, 355 D'Evereaux Dr, Natchez, MS, 39120, (601) 445-0730, 10:45 am-9 pm

New Albany

McAlister's Deli, 217 State Hwy 30 West, New Albany, MS, (662) 534-2700, 10:30 am-10 pm

Ocean Springs

McAlister's Deli, 1530 Bienville Blvd, Ocean Springs, MS, (228) 818-9998, 10:30 am-10 pm

Olive Branch

McAlister's Deli, 8120 Camp Creek Blvd, Ste 110, Olive Branch, MS, (662) 893-4120, 10:30 am-10 pm

O'Charley's, 7880 Craft Goodman Rd, Olive Branch, MS, (662) 893-2334, 11 am-10 pm

Oxford

Chili's, 2576 W Jackson Ave, Oxford, MS, 38655, (662) 281-3951, 11 am-10 pm

McAlister's Deli, 1515 University Ave, Oxford, MS, (662) 234-1363, 10:30 am-10 pm

Pearl

Cracker Barrel, 410 Riverwind Dr, Pearl, MS, 39208, (601) 936-9990, 6 am-10 pm

O'Charley's, 430 Riverwind Dr, Pearl, MS, (601) 932-6575, 11 am-10 pm

Ryan's Grill Buffet Bakery, 438 River wind Dr, Pearl, MS, 39208, (601) 932-4481, 10:45 am-9 pm

Picayune

Godfather's Pizza, 1702 Hwy 11 N, Ste D, Picayune, MS, 39466, (601) 799-3507

Ryan's Grill Buffet Bakery, 232 Frontage Rd, Picayune, MS, 39466, (601) 799-5995, 10:45 am-9 pm

Richland

McAlister's Deli, 1040 Hwy 49 South, Ste A, Richland, MS, (601) 936-4441, 10:30 am-10 pm

Ridgeland

Logan's Roadhouse, 600 E County Line Rd, Ridgeland, MS, 39157, (601) 957-2254, 11 am-10 pm

McAlister's Deli, 731 S Pear Orchard Rd, Ste 49, Ridgeland, MS, (601) 956-0030, 10:30 am-10 pm

McAlister's Deli, 1200 E County Line Rd, Ste 1530, Ridgeland, MS, (601) 896-0007, 10:30 am-10 pm

O'Charley's, 1270 E County Line Rd, Ridgeland, MS, (601) 956-6693, 11 am-10 pm

Saltillo

Cracker Barrel, 1270 Cross Creek Dr, Saltillo, MS, 38866, (662) 620-0820, 6 am-10 pm

Southaven

Chili's, 287 Goodman Rd W, Southaven, MS, 38671, (662) 349-7002, 11 am-10 pm

CiCi's Pizza, 1055 Goodman Rd, Ste A, Southaven, MS, 38671, (662) 349-9296, 11 am-9 pm

Logan's Roadhouse, 6685 Airways Blvd, Southaven, MS, 38671, (662) 772-5015, 11 am-10 pm

McAlister's Deli, 975 E Goodman Rd, Ste 21, Southaven, MS, (662) 349-3354, 10:30 am-10 pm

O'Charley's, 357 Goodman Rd W, Southaven, MS, (662) 349-6663, 11 am-10 pm

Smokey Bones, 6575 Airways Blvd, Southaven, MS, 38671, (662) 349-3520, 11 am-10 pm

Starkville

McAlister's Deli, 500 Russell St, Ste 7, Starkville, MS, (662) 324-2565, 10:30 am-10 pm

Tupelo

Chili's, 3196 N Gloster, Tupelo, MS, 38804, (662) 620-8883, 11 am-10 pm

CiCi's Pizza, 3834-3882 Market Center Dr, Tupelo, MS, 38804, (662) 842-2848, 11 am-9 pm

Logan's Roadhouse, 3954 N Gloster St, Tupelo, MS, 38804, (662) 840-7552, 11 am-10 pm

McAlister's Deli, 495 S Gloster, Tupelo, MS, (662) 680-3354, 10:30 am-10 pm

O'Charley's, 3876 N Gloster St, Tupelo, MS, (662) 840-4730, 11 am-10 pm

Ryan's Grill Buffet Bakery, 3990 Gloster, Tupelo, MS, 38801, (662) 842-9700, 10:45 am-9 pm

Vicksburg

Cracker Barrel, 4001 S Frontage Rd, Vicksburg, MS, 39180, (601) 636-2115, 6 am-10 pm

McAlister's Deli, 4200 E Clay St, Vicksburg, MS, (601) 619-8222, 10:30 am-10 pm

Ryan's Grill Buffet Bakery, 3419 Pemberton Square Blvd, Vicksburg, MS, 39180, (601) 629-9005, 10:45 am-9 pm

Tennessee

Alcoa

Chili's, 204 Hamilton Crossing Dr, Alcoa, TN, 37701, (865) 984-1121, 11 am-10 pm

CiCi's Pizza, 248 S Calderwood, Alcoa, TN, 37701, (865) 983-1118, 11 am-9 pm

Cracker Barrel, 771 Louisville Rd, Alcoa, TN, 37701, (865) 982-1277, 6 am-10 pm

Hooters, 1099 Hunter Crossing Dr, Alcoa, TN, 37701, (865) 983-1366, 11 am-midnight

O'Charley's, 364 Fountainview Circle, Alcoa, TN, (865) 379-9424, 11 am-10 pm

Ryan's Grill Buffet Bakery, 1053 Hunters Crossing Dr, Alcoa, TN, 37701, (865) 681-7776, 10:45 am-9 pm

Algood

Godfather's Pizza, 340 W Main, Algood, TN, 38506, (931) 537-6285

Antioch

Cracker Barrel, 504 Collins Park Dr, Antioch, TN, 37013, (615) 731-4014, 6 am-10 pm

Logan's Roadhouse, 5300 Hickory Hollow Ln, Antioch, TN, 37013, (615) 731-4022, 11 am-10 pm

O'Charley's, 923 Bell Rd, Antioch, TN, (615) 731-7606, 11 am-10 pm

Bartlett

CiCi's Pizza, 6600 Stage Rd, Ste 123, Bartlett, TN, 38134, (901) 387-0999, 11 am-9 pm

McAlister's Deli, 6600 Stage Rd, Ste 120, Bartlett, TN, (901) 213-3311, 10:30 am-10 pm

O'Charley's, 6045 Stage Rd No 74, Bartlett, TN, (901) 373-5602, 11 am-10 pm

Ryan's Grill Buffet Bakery, 6105 Stage Rd, Bartlett, TN, 38134, (901) 373-3870, 10:45 am-9 pm

Smokey Bones, 8324 Hwy 64, Bartlett, TN, 38133, (901) 213-4690, 11 am-10 pm

Brentwood

Beef O'Brady's, 1724 Carouthers Pkwy, #100, Brentwood, TN, 37027, (615) 371-7712, 11 am-11 pm

Chili's, 107 Creekside Crossing, Brentwood, TN, 37027, (615) 370-0114, 11 am-10 pm

Cozymel's Mexican Grill, 1654 Westgate Circle, Brentwood, TN, 37027, (615) 377-6363, 11 am-10 pm

Cracker Barrel, 1735 Mallory Ln, Brentwood, TN, 37027, (615) 376-8120, 6 am-10 pm

Longhorn Steakhouse, 774 Old Hickory Blvd, Brentwood, TN, 37027, (615) 376-5555, 11 am-10 pm

McAlister's Deli, 330 Franklin Rd, Brentwood, TN, (615) 221-4680, 10:30 am-10 pm

O'Charley's, 100 E Park Dr, Brentwood, TN, (615) 370-0274, 11 am-10 pm

Smokey Bones, 1634 Service Merchandise Rd, Brentwood, TN, 37024, (615) 309-1662, 11 am-10 pm

Chattanooga

Chili's, 509 Northgate Mall, Chattanooga, TN, 37415, (423) 877-4344, 11 am-10 pm

Chili's, 408 Market St, Chattanooga, TN, 37402, (423) 265-1511, 11 am-10 pm

Chili's, 5637 Brainerd Rd, Chattanooga, TN, 37411, (423) 855-0376, 11 am-10 pm

CiCi's Pizza, 2260 Gunbarrel Rd, Ste 302-A, Chattanooga, TN, 37421, (423) 485-0900, 11 am-9 pm

Cracker Barrel, 2346 Shallowford Village Rd, Chattanooga, TN, 37421, (423) 892-0977, 6 am-10 pm

Golden Corral, 1808 Gunbarrel Rd, Chattanooga, TN, 37421, (423) 894-3337, 11 am-9 pm

Hooters, 5912 Brainerd Rd, Chattanooga, TN, 37411, (423) 499-8668, 11 am-midnight

J. Alexander's, 2215 Hamilton Pl Blvd, Chattanooga, TN, 37421, (423) 855-5559, 11 am-10 pm

Logan's Roadhouse, 504A Northgate Mall, Chattanooga, TN, 37415, (423) 875-4443, 11 am-10 pm

Logan's Roadhouse, 2119 Gunbarrell Rd, Chattanooga, TN, 37421, (423) 499-4339, 11 am-10 pm

Longhorn Steakhouse, 5771 Brainerd Rd, Chattanooga, TN, 37411, (423) 490-0573, 11 am-10 pm

McAlister's Deli, 2288 Gunbarrel Rd, Chattanooga, TN, (423) 510-8299, 10:30 am-10 pm

O'Charley's, 5031 Hixson Pike, Chattanooga, TN, (423) 877-8966, 11 am-10 pm

O'Charley's, 2340 Shallowford Village Dr, Chattanooga, TN, (423) 892-3343, 11 am-10 pm

P.F. Changs, 2110 Hamilton Pl Blvd, Hamilton Pl Mall, Chattanooga, TN, 37421, 11 am-10 pm

Romano's Macaroni Grill, 2271 Gunbarrel Rd, Chattanooga, TN, 37421, (423) 894-2221, 11 am-10 pm

Ryan's Grill Buffet Bakery, 6734 Lee Hwy, Chattanooga, TN, 37421, (423) 855-5443, 10:45 am-9 pm

Ryan's Grill Buffet Bakery, 5326 Ringgold Rd, Chattanooga, TN, 37412, (423) 894-0592, 10:45 am-9 pm

Smokey Bones, 2225 Gunbarrel Rd, Chattanooga, TN, 37421, (423) 893-7850, 11 am-10 pm

Clarksville

Chili's, 2127 Lowes Dr, Clarksville, TN, 37040, (931) 552-5529, 11 am-10 pm

CiCi's Pizza, 76 Dover Crossing Rd, Clarksville, TN, 37042, (931) 905-2424, 11 am-9 pm

Cracker Barrel, 200 Cracker Barrel Dr, Clarksville, TN, 37040, (931) 645-1446, 6 am-10 pm

Fire Mountain, 2702 Wilma Rudolph Blvd, Clarksville, TN, 37040, (931) 647-9792, 10:45 am-9:30 pm

Godfather's Pizza, 523 Dover Rd, Clarksville, TN, 37042, (931) 906-6594

Godfather's Pizza, 1230 Peachers Mill Rd, Clarksville, TN, 37092, (931) 221-0235

Golden Corral, 2811 Wilma Rudolph Blvd, Clarksville, TN, 37040, (931) 906-9101, 11 am-9 pm

Hooters, 750 N Riverside Dr, Clarksville, TN, 37040, (931) 920-8400, 11 am-midnight

Logan's Roadhouse, 3072 Wilma Rudolph Blvd, Clarksville, TN, 37040, (931) 645-8333, 11 am-10 pm

Longhorn Steakhouse, 2788 Wilma Rudolph Blvd, Clarksville, TN, 37040, (931) 551-3800, 11 am-10 pm

O'Charley's, 674 N Riverside Dr, Clarksville, TN, (931) 552-7800, 11 am-10 pm

O'Charley's, 2792 Wilma Rudolph Blvd, Clarksville, TN, (931) 552-6335, 11 am-10 pm

Cleveland

Chili's, 385 Paul Huff Pkwy, NW, Cleveland, TN, 37312, (423) 473-7008, 11 am-10 pm

CiCi's Pizza, 355 Paul Huff Pkwy NW, Cleveland, TN, 37312, (423) 473-9550, 11 am-9 pm

Cracker Barrel, 1650 Clingan Ridge Dr NW, Cleveland, TN, 37312, (423) 728-4045, 6 am-10 pm

Golden Corral, 350 Stuart Rd, Cleveland, TN, 37312, (423) 473-1662, 11 am-9 pm

Logan's Roadhouse, 3940 Kieth St, Cleveland, TN, 37212, (423) 478-0094, 11 am-10 pm

O'Charley's, 148 Paul Huff Pkwy NW, Cleveland, TN, (423) 472-2192, 11 am-10 pm

Ryan's Grill Buffet Bakery, 138 Paul Huff Pkwy NW, Cleveland, TN, 37312, (423) 476-9255, 10:45 am-9 pm

Collierville

Chili's, 237 Market Blvd, Collierville, TN, 38017, (901) 853-7520, 11 am-10 pm

CiCi's Pizza, 930 W Poplar, Ste 1, Collierville, TN, 38017, (901) 854-4030, 11 am-9 pm

McAlister's Deli, 336 Market Blvd, Collierville, TN, (901) 853-1492, 10:30 am-10 pm

O'Charley's, 656 W Poplar Ave, Collierville, TN, (901) 861-5811, 11 am-10 pm

Columbia

CiCi's Pizza, 1202 S James Campbell Blvd, Ste 1-A, Columbia, TN, 38401, (931) 381-6485, 11 am-9 pm

Cracker Barrel, 1534 Bear Creek Pike, Columbia, TN, 38401, (931) 490-2250, 6 am-10 pm

Cookeville

Chili's, 1428 Interstate Dr, Cookeville, TN, 38501, (931) 372-0014, 11 am-10 pm

CiCi's Pizza, 541 S Willow Ave, Cookeville, TN, 38501, (931) 528-2424, 11 am-9 pm

Golden Corral, 1380 Interstate Dr, Cookeville, TN, 38501, (931) 526-2352, 11 am-9 pm

Logan's Roadhouse, 1395 Interstate Dr, Cookeville, TN, 38501, (931) 526-9595, 11 am-10 pm

O'Charley's, 1401 Interstate Dr, Cookeville, TN, (931) 520-1898, 11 am-10 pm

Ryan's Grill Buffet Bakery, 791 S Jefferson Ave, Cookeville, TN, 38501, (931) 526-1679, 10:45 am-9 pm

Cookville

Cracker Barrel, 1295 S Walnut Ave, Cookville, TN, 38501, (931) 372-2002, 6 am-10 pm

Cordova

Chili's, 1260 N Germantown Pkwy, Cordova, TN, 38016, (901) 756-7771, 11 am-10 pm

CiCi's Pizza, 1425 Germantown Pkwy, Ste 1, Cordova, TN, 38016, (901) 752-5554, 11 am-9 pm

McAlister's Deli, 7990 Trinity Rd, Ste 129, Cordova, TN, (901) 737-7282, 10:30 am-10 pm

O'Charley's, 1040 N Germantown Pkwy, Cordova, TN, (901) 754-6201, 11 am-10 pm

Crossville

Cracker Barrel, 23 Executive Dr, Crossville, TN, 38555, (931) 456-9622, 6 am-10 pm

Ryan's Grill Buffet Bakery, 2854 N Main, Crossville, TN, 38555, (931) 456-9228, 10:45 am-9 pm

Dickson

CiCi's Pizza, 454 Hwy 46 S, Dickson, TN, 37055, (615) 446-5665, 11 am-9 pm

Cracker Barrel, 115 Gumbranch Rd, Dickson, TN, 37055, (615) 441-3353, 6 am-10 pm

O'Charley's, 2409 Hwy 46 South, Dickson, TN, (615) 446-8085, 11 am-10 pm

Dyersburg

Ryan's Grill Buffet Bakery, 2730 Mall Loop Rd, Dyersburg, TN, 38024, (731) 287-7926, 10:45 am-9 pm

East Ridge

Cracker Barrel, 1460 N Mack Smith Rd, East Ridge, TN, 37412, (423) 899-5729, 6 am-10 pm

Fairfield Glade

Godfather's Pizza, 5461 Pea Vine Rd, Fairfield Glade, TN, 38558, (931) 484-7982

Farragut

Cracker Barrel, 716 Campbell Station Rd, Farragut, TN, 37922, (865) 675-1446, 6 am-10 pm

Franklin

Chili's, 3084 Columbia Ave, Franklin, TN, 37064, (615) 794-1499, 11 am-10 pm

Chili's, 7083 Bakers Bridge Rd, Franklin, TN, 37067, (615) 771-7497, 11 am-10 pm

CiCi's Pizza, 202 Williamson Square, Franklin, TN, 37064, (615) 791-4499, 11 am-9 pm

Cracker Barrel, 4210 Franklin Commons Court, Franklin, TN, 37067, (615) 794-8195, 6 am-10 pm

Golden Corral, 3020 Mallory Ln, Franklin, TN, 37067, (615) 771-8834, 11 am-9 pm

J. Alexander's, 1721 Galleria Blvd, Franklin, TN, 37064, (615) 771-7779, 11 am-10 pm

Logan's Roadhouse, 7087 Baker's Bridge Ave, Franklin, TN, 37064, (615) 771-7288, 11 am-10 pm

McAlister's Deli, 401-A Cool Springs Blvd, Ste 100, Franklin, TN, (615) 771-7380, 10:30 am-10 pm

O'Charley's, 1202 Murfreesboro Rd, Franklin, TN, (615) 794-9438, 11 am-10 pm

P.F. Changs, 439 Cool Springs Blvd, Franklin, TN, 37067, (615) 503-9640, 11 am-10 pm

Romano's Macaroni Grill, 1712 Galleria Blvd, Franklin, TN, 37064, (615) 771-7002, 11 am-10 pm

Gallatin

Chili's, 600 Village Green Dr, Gallatin, TN, 37066, (615) 230-8267, 11 am-10 pm

CiCi's Pizza, 565C Village Green Dr, Gallatin, TN, 37066, (615) 230-5777, 11 am-9 pm

Cracker Barrel, 1005 Village Green Crossing, Gallatin, TN, 37066, (615) 451-2420, 6 am-10 pm

Logan's Roadhouse, 1007 Village Green Crossing, Gallatin, TN, 37066, (615) 206-9393, 11 am-10 pm

McAlister's Deli, 142 N Belvedere Dr, Gallatin, TN, (615) 230-1800, 10:30 am-10 pm

O'Charley's, 1009 Village Green Crossing, Gallatin, TN, (615) 230-8103, 11 am-10 pm

Gatlinburg

Damon's Grill, 146 Pkwy, Gatlinburg, TN, 37738, (865) 430-7707, 11 am-9 pm

Germantown

Chili's, 7810 Poplar Ave, Germantown, TN, 38138, (901) 756-5203, 11 am-10 pm

McAlister's Deli, 7710 Poplar Ave, Germantown, TN, (901) 753-1507, 10:30 am-10 pm

Romano's Macaroni Grill, 6705 Poplar Ave, Germantown, TN, 38138, (901) 753-6588, 11 am-10 pm

Goodlettsville

Cracker Barrel, 235 Long Hollow Pike, Goodlettsville, TN, 37072, (615) 859-4383, 6 am-10 pm

El Chico Café, 928 Two Mile Pkwy, Goodlettsville, TN, 37072, (615) 859-1112, 11 am-10 pm

Godfather's Pizza, 219 S Main St, Goodlettsville, TN, 37072, (615) 859-6510

Godfather's Pizza, 1721 Hwy 41 S, Goodlettsville, TN, 37072, (615) 851-1974

Hooters, 654 Wade Circle, Goodlettsville, TN, 37072, (615) 851-6499, 11 am-midnight

O'Charley's, 912 Rivergate Pkwy, Goodlettsville, TN, (615) 859-4704, 11 am-10 pm

Greeneville

Ryan's Grill Buffet Bakery, 2645 E Andrew Johnson Hwy, Greeneville, TN, 37745, (423) 638-9727, 10:45 am-9 pm

Harriman

Cracker Barrel, 1839 S Roane St, Harriman, TN, 37748, (865) 882-1442, 6 am-10 pm

Harrogate

Godfather's Pizza, 915 Patterson Rd, Harrogate, TN, 37752, (423) 869-4771

Hendersonville

Chili's, 218 Indian Lake Blvd, Hendersonville, TN, 37075, (615) 826-1711, 11 am-10 pm

O'Charley's, 212 Indian Lake Blvd, Hendersonville, TN, (615) 826-9543, 11 am-10 pm

Hermitage

Chili's, 5005 Old Hickory Blvd, Hermitage, TN, 37076, (615) 872-7188, 11 am-10 pm

CiCi's Pizza, 4451 Lebanon Rd, Hermitage, TN, 37076, (615) 232-0950, 11 am-9 pm

Hooters, 4119 Lebanon Pike, Hermitage, TN, 37076, (615) 883-0257, 11 am-midnight

Longhorn Steakhouse, 4774 Lebanon Rd, Hermitage, TN, 37076, (615) 885-6290, 11 am-10 pm

O'Charley's, 5500 Old Hickory Blvd, Hermitage, TN, (615) 883-6993, 11 am-10 pm

Ryan's Grill Buffet Bakery, 3435 Lebanon Pike, Hermitage, TN, 37076, (615) 391-5141, 10:45 am-9 pm

Hixson

CiCi's Pizza, 5425 Hwy 153, #100, Hixson, TN, 37343, (423) 876-1000, 11 am-9 pm

Golden Corral, 4506 Hixson Pike, Hixson, TN, 37343, (423) 877-4343, 11 am-9 pm

Longhorn Steakhouse, 5583 Hwy 153, Hixson, TN, 37343, (423) 870-2722, 11 am-10 pm

Ryan's Grill Buffet Bakery, 5104 Hixson Pike Rd, Hixson, TN, 37343, (423) 875-8135, 10:45 am-9 pm

Jackson

Chili's, 2200 Emporium Dr, Jackson, TN, 38305, (731) 660-4440, 11 am-10 pm

CiCi's Pizza, 99 Old Hickory Blvd, Jackson, TN, 38305, (731) 668-3333, 11 am-9 pm

Cracker Barrel, 188 Vann Dr, Jackson, TN, 38305, (731) 664-1028, 6 am-10 pm

El Chico Café, 565 Carriage House Dr, Jackson, TN, 38305, (731) 668-2313, 11 am-10 pm

Logan's Roadhouse, 604 Carriage House Dr, Jackson, TN, 38305, (731) 664-9902, 11 am-10 pm

Longhorn Steakhouse, 631 Vann Dr, Jackson, TN, 38305, (731) 661-0980, 11 am-10 pm

O'Charley's, 644 Carriage House Rd, Jackson, TN, (731) 661-0840, 11 am-10 pm

Ryan's Grill Buffet Bakery, 71 Stonebrook Pl, Jackson, TN, 38305, (731) 668-7472, 10:45 am-9 pm

Johnson City

Chili's, 3040 Franklin Terrace Dr, Johnson City, TN, 37604, (423) 283-4229, 11 am-10 pm

Cracker Barrel, 2692 Boones Creek Rd, Johnson City, TN, 37615, (423) 282-8113, 6 am-10 pm

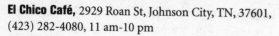

El Chico Café, 2929 Roan St, Johnson City, TN, 37601, (423) 282-4080, 11 am-10 pm

Fuddruckers, 2519 Knob Creek Rd, Johnson City, TN, 37604, 11 am-9 pm

Golden Corral, 3104 Browns Mill Rd, Johnson City, TN, 37604, (423) 854-9400, 11 am-9 pm

Hooters, 2288 N Roane St, Johnson City, TN, 37601, (423) 610-1484, 11 am-midnight

Logan's Roadhouse, 3112 Browns Mill Rd, Johnson City, TN, 37604, (423) 915-1122, 11 am-10 pm

O'Charley's, 112 Broyles Dr, Johnson City, TN, (423) 854-9110, 11 am-10 pm

Ryan's Grill Buffet Bakery, 205 E Mountcastle Dr, Johnson City, TN, 37601, (423) 282-2157, 10:45 am-9 pm

Smokey Bones, 1905 N Roan St, Johnson City, TN, 37601, (423) 979-1706, 11 am-10 pm

Kimball

Cracker Barrel, 550 Kimball Crossing Dr, Kimball, TN, 37347, (423) 837-5618, 6 am-10 pm

Kingsport

Chili's, 1921 N Eastman, Kingsport, TN, 37660, (423) 246-4173, 11 am-10 pm

Cracker Barrel, 10132 Airport Pkwy, Kingsport, TN, 37663, (423) 323-9212, 6 am-10 pm

Damon's Grill, 1221 Stewball Circle, Kingsport, TN, 37660, (423) 245-2221, 11 am-11 pm

Golden Corral, 1910 N Eastman Rd, Kingsport, TN, 37664, (423) 247-7810, 11 am-9 pm

McAlister's Deli, 2003 N Eastman Rd, Kingsport, TN, (423) 378-3354, 10:30 am-10 pm

O'Charley's, 1920 N Eastman Rd, Kingsport, TN, (423) 246-8868, 11 am-10 pm

Ryan's Grill Buffet Bakery, 2404 Memorial Dr, Kingsport, TN, 37664, (423) 245-5178, 10:45 am-9 pm

Knoxville

Beef O'Brady's, 11083 Parkside Dr, Knoxville, TN, 37922, (865) 671-2134, 11 am-11 pm

Chili's, 7304 Kingston Pike, Knoxville, TN, 37919, (865) 584-8195, 11 am-10 pm

Chili's, 120 W Mabry Hood Rd, Knoxville, TN, 37922, (865) 470-8664, 11 am-10 pm

Chili's, 6635 Clinton Hwy, Knoxville, TN, 37912, (865) 938-4372, 11 am-10 pm

Chili's, 1824 Cumberland Ave, Knoxville, TN, 37916, (865) 523-1911, 11 am-10 pm

CiCi's Pizza, 8414 Kingston Pike, Knoxville, TN, 37919, (865) 694-5060, 11 am-9 pm

CiCi's Pizza, 2885 Tazewell Pike, Knoxville, TN, 37918, (865) 281-2255, 11 am-9 pm

Cozymel's Mexican Grill, 7727 Kingston Pike, Knoxville, TN, 37919, (865) 694-9811, 11 am-10 pm

Cracker Barrel, 5001 Central Ave Pike, Knoxville, TN, 37912, (865) 688-7396, 6 am-10 pm

Cracker Barrel, 9214 Park W Blvd, Knoxville, TN, 37923, (865) 690-6060, 6 am-10 pm

Cracker Barrel, 2920 S Mall Rd, Knoxville, TN, 37924, (865) 971-4421, 6 am-10 pm

Cracker Barrel, 1510 Cracker Barrel Ln, Knoxville, TN, 37914, (865) 522-8232, 6 am-10 pm

Don Pablo's, 2904 E Towne Mall Circle, Knoxville, TN, 37924, (865) 633-4978, 11 am-10 pm

El Chico Café, 116 Cedar Ln, Knoxville, TN, 37912, (423) 687-4242, 11 am-10 pm

Fuddruckers, 8851 Towne & Country Circle, Knoxville, TN, 37923, 11 am-9 pm

Godfather's Pizza, 315 Merchant's Dr, Knoxville, TN, 37912, (865) 686-0354

Golden Corral, 6612 Clinton Hwy, Knoxville, TN, 37912, (865) 938-8901, 11 am-9 pm

Hooters, 5005 Central Ave Pike, Knoxville, TN, 37912, (865) 688-8066, 11 am-midnight

Hooters, 8050 Kingston Pike Hwy, Knoxville, TN, 37919, (865) 694-4668, 11 am-midnight

McAlister's Deli, 1801 Cumberland Ave, Knoxville, TN, (865) 633-8001, 10:30 am-10 pm

McAlister's Deli, 2758 Schaad Rd, Knoxville, TN, (865) 938-4300, 10:30 am-10 pm

McAlister's Deli, 11140 Parkside Dr, Knoxville, TN, (865) 966-1011, 10:30 am-10 pm

McAlister's Deli, 232 Morrell Rd, Knoxville, TN, (865) 769-5001, 10:30 am-10 pm

Melting Pot, 111 N Central Ave, Knoxville, TN, 37902, (865) 971-5400, 5 pm-10:30 pm

O'Charley's, 11820 Kingston Pike, Knoxville, TN, (865) 671-1232, 11 am-10 pm

O'Charley's, 3050 S Mall Rd, Knoxville, TN, (865) 524-9114, 11 am-10 pm

O'Charley's, 11036 Parkside Dr (Turkey Creek), Knoxville, TN, (865) 675-4244, 11 am-10 pm

O'Charley's, 117 Cedar Ln, Knoxville, TN, (865) 689-2870, 11 am-10 pm

O'Charley's, 8077 Kingston Pike, Knoxville, TN, (865) 691-5885, 11 am-10 pm

P.F. Changs, 6741 Kingston Pike, Knoxville, TN, 37919, (865) 212-5514, 11 am-10 pm

Romano's Macaroni Grill, 7723 Kingston Pike, Knoxville, TN, 37919, (865) 691-0809, 11 am-10 pm

Ryan's Grill Buffet Bakery, 213 Cedar Ln, Knoxville, TN, 37912, (865) 689-1398, 10:45 am-9 pm

Ryan's Grill Buffet Bakery, 9645 Kingston Pike, Knoxville, TN, 37922, (865) 690-1214, 10:45 am-9 pm

Kodak

Cracker Barrel, 154 Stadium Dr, Kodak, TN, 37764, (865) 932-1840, 6 am-10 pm

Lake City

Cracker Barrel, 111 Colonial Ln, Lake City, TN, 37769, (865) 426-6429, 6 am-10 pm

Lakeland

Cracker Barrel, 9649 E Davies Plantation Rd, Lakeland, TN, 38002, (901) 385-0976, 6 am-10 pm

Lebanon

Chili's, 909 S Hartmann Dr, Lebanon, TN, 37090, (615) 443-7121, 11 am-10 pm

Cracker Barrel, 635 S Cumberland, Lebanon, TN, 37087, (615) 444-4995, 6 am-10 pm

Godfather's Pizza, 1112 N Cumberland, Lebanon, TN, 37087, (615) 444-0674

O'Charley's, 902 Murfreesboro Rd, Lebanon, TN, (615) 453-1185, 11 am-10 pm

Ryan's Grill Buffet Bakery, 405 S Cumberland St, Lebanon, TN, 37087, (615) 453-6184, 10:45 am-9 pm

Lenoir City

Chili's, 320 Fort Loudon Medical Center, Lenoir City, TN, 37772, (865) 988-4061, 11 am-10 pm

Cracker Barrel, 325 Ft Loudoun Medical Center Dr, Lenoir City, TN, 37772, (865) 988-3201, 6 am-10 pm

Madison

Chili's, 1820 Gallatin Pike N, Madison, TN, 37115, (615) 851-9377, 11 am-10 pm

CiCi's Pizza, 1765 Gallatin Rd N, Madison, TN, 37115, (615) 860-4227, 11 am-9 pm

Hometown Buffet, MarketPl At Rivergate, 2151 Gallatin Pike North, Madison, TN, 37115, (615) 859-2185, 11 am-8:30 pm

Logan's Roadhouse, 1715 Gallatin Pk North, Madison, TN, 37115, (615) 860-9220, 11 am-10 pm

Longhorn Steakhouse, 2021 N Gallatin Rd, #296, Madison, TN, 37115, (615) 859-2202, 11 am-10 pm

Manchester

Cracker Barrel, 103 Paradise St, Manchester, TN, 37355, (931) 723-1358, 6 am-10 pm

O'Charley's, 2367 Hillsboro Blvd, Manchester, TN, (931) 728-6336, 11 am-10 pm

Martin

Godfather's Pizza, 609 Elm St, Martin, TN, 38237, (731) 587-5871

Maryville

Uno Chicago Grill, 743 Watkins Rd, Maryville, TN, 37801, (865) 982-1070, 11 am-12:30 am

McMinnville

Ryan's Grill Buffet Bakery, 918 N Chancery St, McMinnville, TN, 37110, (931) 473-0963, 10:45 am-9 pm

Memphis

Benihana, 912 Ridgelake Blvd, Memphis, TN, 38120, (901) 683-7390, 11:30 am-10 pm

Chili's, 8100 Giacosa Dr, Memphis, TN, 38133, (901) 372-3132, 11 am-10 pm

Chili's, 4609 Poplar, Memphis, TN, 38117, (901) 685-2257, 11 am-10 pm

CiCi's Pizza, 3637 Hickory Hill Rd, Memphis, TN, 38115, (901) 368-0006, 11 am-9 pm

CiCi's Pizza, 3474 Plz Ave, Memphis, TN, 38111, (901) 452-6225, 11 am-9 pm

Cozymel's Mexican Grill, 6450 Poplar Ave, Memphis, TN, 38119, (901) 763-1202, 11 am-10 pm

Cracker Barrel, 8000 Lowrance Rd, Memphis, TN, 38125, (901) 757-0269, 6 am-10 pm

Cracker Barrel, 6081 Shelby Oaks Dr, Memphis, TN, 38134, (901) 382-5465, 6 am-10 pm

El Chico Café, 3491 Poplar Ave, Memphis, TN, 38111, (901) 323-9609, 11 am-10 pm

Hooters, 2653 Mt Mariah, Memphis, TN, 38115, (901) 795-7123, 11 am-midnight

Hooters, 2838 New Brunswick Rd, Memphis, TN, 38133, (901) 266-4404, 11 am-midnight

Hooters, 250 Peabody Pl, Ste 101, Memphis, TN, 38103, (901) 523-9464, 11 am-midnight

J. Alexander's, 2670 N Germantown Pkwy, Memphis, TN, 38133, (901) 381-9670, 11 am-10 pm

Logan's Roadhouse, 2710 N Germantown Pkwy, Memphis, TN, 38133, (901) 381-5254, 11 am-10 pm

Logan's Roadhouse, 7755 Winchester Rd, Memphis, TN, 38125, (901) 759-1430, 11 am-10 pm

McAlister's Deli, 1 Commerce Square, Ste 150, Memphis, TN, (901) 522-9123, 10:30 am-10 pm

McAlister's Deli, 2857 Kirby Pkwy, Ste 119, Memphis, TN, (901) 756-2943, 10:30 am-10 pm

McAlister's Deli, 580 S Mendenhall, Memphis, TN, (901) 763-2711, 10:30 am-10 pm

McAlister's Deli, 3855 Hacks Cross Rd, Memphis, TN, (901) 881-6068, 10:30 am-10 pm

McAlister's Deli, 3482 Plz Ave, Memphis, TN, (901) 452-6009, 10:30 am-10 pm

Melting Pot, 2828 Wolfcreek Pkwy, Memphis, TN, 38133, (901) 380-9500, 5 pm-10:30 pm

On the Border, 8101 Giacosa Pl, Memphis, TN, 38133, (901) 372-8883, 11 am-10 pm

On the Border, 7935 Winchester Rd, Memphis, TN, 38125, (901) 755-6404, 11 am-10 pm

On the Border, 4552 Poplar Ave, Memphis, TN, 38117, (901) 763-0569, 11 am-10 pm

P.F. Changs, 1181 Ridgeway Rd, Park Pl Centre, Memphis, TN, 38119, (901) 818-3889, 11 am-10 pm

Romano's Macaroni Grill, 2859 N Germantown, Memphis, TN, 38133, (901) 266-4565, 11 am-10 pm

Ryan's Grill Buffet Bakery, 3813 Riverdale Rd, Memphis, TN, 38115, (901) 795-6287, 10:45 am-9 pm

Smokey Bones, 6980 Winchester Rd, Memphis, TN, 38115, (901) 365-2650, 11 am-10 pm

Millington

Chili's, 8526 Hwy 51, Millington, TN, 38053, (901) 872-0555, 11 am-10 pm

Ryan's Grill Buffet Bakery, 8165 US Hwy 51 N, Millington, TN, 38053, (901) 873-2900, 10:45 am-9 pm

Morristown

Cracker Barrel, 133 Cracker Rd, Morristown, TN, 37813, (423) 586-4555, 6 am-10 pm

Golden Corral, 2905 W Andrew Johnson Hwy, Morristown, TN, 37814, (423) 318-1024, 11 am-9 pm

O'Charley's, 3412 W Andrew Johnson Hwy, Morristown, TN, (423) 587-0175, 11 am-10 pm

Ryan's Grill Buffet Bakery, 203 S Davy Crockett Pkwy, Morristown, TN, 37814, (423) 317-9079, 10:45 am-9 pm

Mt. Juliet

Cracker Barrel, 350 S Mt Juliet Rd, Mt. Juliet, TN, 37122, (615) 754-8300, 6 am-10 pm

Logan's Roadhouse, 401 S Mt Juliet Rd, Mt. Juliet, TN, 37122, (615) 773-5505, 11 am-10 pm

Murfreesboro

Chili's, 755 NW BRd St, Murfreesboro, TN, 37129, (615) 867-2855, 11 am-10 pm

CiCi's Pizza, 710 Memorial Blvd, Ste 220, Murfreesboro, TN, 37129, (615) 867-4424, 11 am-9 pm

Cracker Barrel, 138 Chaffin Pl, Murfreesboro, TN, 37129, (615) 893-4980, 6 am-10 pm

Cracker Barrel, 2115 S Church St, Murfreesboro, TN, 37130, (615) 890-0789, 6 am-10 pm

Don Pablo's, 1835 Old Fort Pkwy, Murfreesboro, TN, 37129, (615) 896-8098, 11 am-10 pm

Hooters, 1310 NW BRd St, Murfreesboro, TN, 37129, (615) 867-2337, 11 am-midnight

Logan's Roadhouse, 740 NW BRd, Murfreesboro, TN, 37129, (615) 895-4419, 11 am-10 pm

McAlister's Deli, 1624 Memorial Blvd, Murfreesboro, TN, (615) 890-0330, 10:30 am-10 pm

O'Charley's, 2450 Old Fort Pkwy, Murfreesboro, TN, (615) 895-4441, 11 am-10 pm

O'Charley's, 1006 Memorial Blvd, Murfreesboro, TN, (615) 898-0390, 11 am-10 pm

Ryan's Grill Buffet Bakery, 1829 Old Fort Pkwy, Murfreesboro, TN, 37129, (615) 895-4272, 10:45 am-9 pm

Nashville

Cheesecake Factory, 2133 Green Hills Village Dr, Nashville, TN, 37215, (615) 463-2400, 11 am-11 pm

Chili's, 2322 W End Ave, Nashville, TN, 37203, (615) 327-1588, 11 am-10 pm

CiCi's Pizza, 55 E Thompson Ln, Ste 109, Nashville, TN, 37211, (615) 331-1211, 11 am-9 pm

CiCi's Pizza, 5735 Nolensville Rd, Nashville, TN, 37211, (615) 833-2350, 11 am-9 pm

Cracker Barrel, 2406 Music Valley Dr, Nashville, TN, 37214, (615) 883-5440, 6 am-10 pm

Cracker Barrel, 3454 Percy Priest Dr, Nashville, TN, 37214, (615) 889-4325, 6 am-10 pm

Cracker Barrel, 4323 Sidco Dr, Nashville, TN, 37204, (615) 331-6733, 6 am-10 pm

Cracker Barrel, 6941 Charlotte Pike, Nashville, TN, 37209, (615) 356-5229, 6 am-10 pm

Dave and Buster's, 540 Opry Mills Dr, Nashville, TN, 37214, (615) 514-1200, 11 am-midnight

El Chico Café, 1132 Murfreesboro Rd, Nashville, TN, 37217, (615) 366-6002, 11 am-10 pm

Godfather's Pizza, 701 Dickerson Pike, Nashville, TN, 37207, (615) 254-8328

Hooters, 217 Largo Dr, Nashville, TN, 37211, (615) 331-0842, 11 am-midnight

Hooters, 184 2nd Ave N, Nashville, TN, 37202, (615) 244-4668, 11 am-midnight

J. Alexander's, 73 White Bridge Rd #130, Nashville, TN, 37205, (615) 952-0981, 11 am-10 pm

J. Alexander's, 2609 W End Ave, Nashville, TN, 37203, (615) 340-9901, 11 am-10 pm

Logan's Roadhouse, 2400 Elliston Pl, Nashville, TN, 37202, (615) 320-1161, 11 am-10 pm

Longhorn Steakhouse, 110 Lyle Ave, Nashville, TN, 37203, (615) 329-9195, 11 am-10 pm

Longhorn Steakhouse, 1175 Murfreesboro Rd, Nashville, TN, 37217, (615) 361-0457, 11 am-10 pm

Maggiano's, 3106 W End Ave, Nashville, TN, 37203, (615) 514-0270, 11 am-10 pm

Melting Pot, 166 Second Ave N, Nashville, TN, 37201, (615) 742-4970, 5 pm-10:30 pm

O'Charley's, 1108 Murfreesboro Rd, Nashville, TN, (615) 361-3651, 11 am-10 pm

O'Charley's, 17 White Bridge Rd, Nashville, TN, (615) 356-1344, 11 am-10 pm

O'Charley's, 110 Coley Davis Court (Bellevue), Nashville, TN, (615) 662-4026, 11 am-10 pm

P.F. Changs, 2525 W End, Nashville, TN, 37203, (615) 329-8901, 11 am-10 pm

Romano's Macaroni Grill, 433 Opry Mills Dr # 521, Nashville, TN, 37214, (615) 514-7700, 11 am-10 pm

Newport

Cracker Barrel, 1021 Cosby Hwy , Newport, TN, 37821, (423) 623-0676, 6 am-10 pm

Ryan's Grill Buffet Bakery, 1085 Cosby Hwy, Newport, TN, 37821, (423) 613-8972, 10:45 am-9 pm

Oak Ridge

Ryan's Grill Buffet Bakery, 401 S TuLn Ave, Oak Ridge, TN, 37830, (865) 483-7885, 10:45 am-9 pm

Opry Mills

Tony Roma's, 465 Opry Mills Dr, Opry Mills, TN, 37214, (615) 514-2668, 11 am-10 pm

Pigeon Forge

Cracker Barrel, 2285 Pkwy, Pigeon Forge, TN, 37863, (865) 908-4459, 6 am-10 pm

Cracker Barrel, 3960 Pkwy, Pigeon Forge, TN, 37863, (865) 428-4613, 6 am-10 pm

Godfather's Pizza, 3145 Pkwy, Pigeon Forge, TN, 37863, (865) 774-7120

Golden Corral, 3610 Pkwy, Pigeon Forge, TN, 37863, (865) 453-1827, 11 am-9 pm

O'Charley's, 2167 Pkwy, Pigeon Forge, TN, (865) 429-2201, 11 am-10 pm

Portland

Godfather's Pizza, 5500 Hwy 31 West, Portland, TN, 37148, (615) 325-1159

Sevierville

Cracker Barrel, 690 Winfield Dunn Pkwy, Sevierville, TN, 37876, (865) 908-3202, 6 am-10 pm

Damon's Grill, 1640 Pkwy, Sevierville, TN, 37862, (865) 428-6200

Fuddruckers, 168 Collier Dr, Sevierville, TN, 37862, 11 am-9 pm

Golden Corral, 513 Winfield Dunn Pkwy, Sevierville, TN, 37876, (865) 453-8859, 11 am-9 pm

Ryan's Grill Buffet Bakery, 502 Winfield Dunn Pkwy, Sevierville, TN, 37876, (865) 908-9900, 10:45 am-9 pm

Seymour

Godfather's Pizza, 11510 Chapman Hwy, Seymour, TN, 37865, (865) 577-5553

Smyrna

Chili's, 610 Sam Ridley Pkwy W, Smyrna, TN, 37167, (615) 220-4545, 11 am-10 pm

Cracker Barrel, 2697 Highwood Blvd, Smyrna, TN, 37167, (615) 220-1400, 6 am-10 pm

Logan's Roadhouse, 600 Sam Ridley Pkwy W, Smyrna, TN, 37167, (615) 220-2780, 11 am-10 pm

O'Charley's, 820 Expo Dr, Smyrna, TN, (615) 220-1772, 11 am-10 pm

Spring Hill

Beef O'Brady's, 3011 Longford Dr, Ste 13, Spring Hill, TN, 37174, (615) 302-4017, 11 am-11 pm

Springfield

O'Charley's, 3535 Tom Austin Hwy, Springfield, TN, (615) 382-3321, 11 am-10 pm

Sweetwater

Cracker Barrel, 1391 Murray's Hill Rd, Sweetwater, TN, 37874, (423) 337-3722, 6 am-10 pm

Tiftonia

Cracker Barrel, 50 Birmingham Hwy, Tiftonia, TN, 37419, (423) 825-5885, 6 am-10 pm

Tiptonville

Godfather's Pizza, 1444 Church St, Tiptonville, TN, 38079, (731) 253-8264

Union City

Godfather's Pizza, 1500 Reelfoot Ave, Union City, TN, 38261, (731) 885-1105

Ryan's Grill Buffet Bakery, 1225 E Reelfoot, Union City, TN, 38261, (731) 886-0012, 10:45 am-9 pm

White House

Cracker Barrel, 370 Hester Dr, White House, TN, 37188, (615) 672-1802, 6 am-10 pm

Notes

Notes

Notes

Notes

Notes

Notes

Notes

Notes

Notes

Notes

Notes

Notes